Dictionary of Business Terms

Fourth Edition

Jack P. Friedman, Ph.D., CPA/ABV

CONTRIBUTING AUTHORS

Suzanne S. Barnhill
Jeffrey Clark
Michael Covington
Barry A. Diskin
John Downes
Douglas Downing
Eric S. Friedman
Stephen H. Gifis
Jordan Elliot Goodman
Jack C. Harris
J. Manville Harris, Jr.

Stephen Hartman
Lowell B. Howard
Jane Imber
Theodore C. Jones
Bruce Lindeman
Bob McMahon
Harvey W. Rubin
Jae K. Shim
Joel Siegel
Michael B. Slade
Betsy-Ann Toffler

BARRON'S

W9-BGK-175

Jack P. Friedman is an author and consultant in Dallas, Texas.

All inquiries should be addressed to:
Barron's Educational Series, Inc.
250 Wireless Boulevard
Hauppauge, NY 11788
www.barronseduc.com

Library of Congress Catalog Card No. 2006036882

ISBN-13: 978-0-7641-3534-7
ISBN-10: 0-7641-3534-1

Library of Congress Cataloging-in-Publication Data
Friedman, Jack P.
  Dictionary of business terms / Jack P. Friedman ; contributing
authors, Suzanne S. Barnhill . . . [et al.]. — 4th ed.
    p. cm.
  ISBN-13: 978-0-7641-3534-7
  ISBN-10: 0-7641-3534-1
    1. Business—Dictionaries. 2. Finance—Dictionaries. I. Title.

HF1001.F78   2007
330.03–dc22   2006036882

PRINTED IN CHINA
9 8 7 6 5 4 3 2 1

CONTENTS

PREFACE AND ACKNOWLEDGMENTS

Whether you are majoring in business at a college or graduate school, starting a fresh career in business, venturing into a new enterprise, or just reading a newspaper or writing a business letter, you will find this book to be a valuable reference.

In class, at a meeting, or at home you may read or hear a business term that is unfamiliar to you. Sometimes considerable discussion will revolve around that term, and not understanding it will pose an obstacle to participating in the entire conversation. Indeed, you may feel uneasy or ignorant if there is just one term you don't recognize. At that point this book will be indispensable. Keeping a copy of this handy paperback by your side will provide a useful reference and prevent embarrassing moments in a classroom, conference, meeting with a supervisor, or discussion with an investment advisor or financial planner. Whether the term relates to accounting or economics, management or marketing, business law or business statistics, advertising, transportation, finance, insurance, or real estate, you will probably find it here. A concise definition is provided for more than 7,500 terms, and a further explanation of the term or its use is shown to clarify the definition or use of the term.

Terms defined here are short enough to be read in a few seconds, but complete enough for the reader to fully grasp meanings and usage. Entries have been listed in strict alphabetical order, as if the entry were one uninterrupted word. Terms that help define particular entries that appear elsewhere in this dictionary are shown in SMALL CAPITALS. Terms that are similar to the one being defined are in *italics*. The book is designed to make a user feel comfortable with the style right from the start. Its size and design features are intended to maximize use and convenience.

Many people were involved in this project. Contributors listed by subject areas include:

Accounting and Taxation	Joel Siegel Jae K. Shim Jack P. Friedman
Actuarial	Eric S. Friedman Bob McMahon
Advertising and Direct Mail	Jane Imber Betsy-Ann Toffler
Business Law	Lowell B. Howard
Communications and Transportation	Jack P. Friedman

Computers and Internet	Douglas Downing Michael Covington Suzanne S. Barnhill
Economics	Bruce Lindeman
Finance	John Downes Jordan Elliot Goodman
Insurance	Harvey W. Rubin
International Business	J. Manville Harris, Jr.
Law	Stephen H. Gifis Michael B. Slade
Management	Stephen Hartman
Marketing	Stephen Hartman
Real Estate	Jack C. Harris Jack P. Friedman Barry A. Diskin
Statistics	Theodore C. Jones Jeffrey Clark Douglas Downing

I am also indebted to a number of people for their suggestions and their evaluations of various sections of the word list and the manuscript. They include John Downes, Stephen Hartman, Austin Lynas, Robert Ambrio, Milton Amsel, Harold Baldauf, Donald Homolka, Robert Frick, and Mark Rush.

Suzanne Barnhill, friend and advisor, improved the manuscript in numerous ways. The editorial staff of Barron's Educational Series was essential in producing this book. Darrell Buono and Bob O'Sullivan earned special recognition. Their efficiency and professional ethics in publishing were vital to the successful fruition of this project.

To my wife Anita and to Eric and Renee: I thank them for their love and encouragement.

Jack P. Friedman
General Editor

HOW TO USE THIS BOOK EFFECTIVELY

Alphabetization: All entries are alphabetized by letter rather than by word so that multiple-word terms are treated as single words. For example, **OPENING** precedes **OPEN INTEREST** and **DIRECTOR** follows **DIRECT MATERIAL**. In some cases, abbreviations or acronyms appear as entries in the main text, usually as a cross-reference to the complete term, in addition to appearing in the Abbreviations and Acronyms section of the Appendix.

Where a term has several meanings, alphabetical sequence is used for subheads, except in special instances where clarity dictates a different order. In some entries, the various meanings of the term are presented with simple numerical headings.

Abbreviations and Acronyms: A separate list of abbreviations and acronyms follows the Dictionary. It contains shortened versions of terms defined in the book, plus some related business terms.

Cross-References: In order to gain a fuller understanding of a term, it will sometimes help to refer to the definition of another term. In these cases the additional term is printed in SMALL CAPITALS. Such crossreferences appear in the body of the definition or at the end of the entry (or subentry). Cross-references at the end of an entry (or subentry) may refer to related or contrasting concepts rather than give more information about the concept under discussion. As a rule, a term is printed in small capitals only the first time it appears in an entry. Where an entry is fully defined at another entry, a reference rather than a definition is provided; for example, **PUBLIC CARRIER** *see* COMMON CARRIER.

Italics: Italic type is generally used to indicate the term itself, when used in an example within the definition, or another term that has a meaning identical or very closely related to that of the entry. Occasionally, italic type is also used to highlight the fact that a word used is a business term and not just a descriptive phrase. Italics are also used for the titles of publications.

Parentheses: Parentheses are used in entry titles for three reasons. The first is to indicate that an entry's opposite is such an integral part of the concept that only one discussion is necessary; for example, **CAPITAL GAIN (LOSS)**. The second and more common reason is to indicate that an abbreviation is used with about the same frequency as the term itself; for example, **DOING BUSINESS AS (DBA)**. Finally, information enclosed in parentheses may add to the understanding of the term: **BORROWING POWER (OF SECURITIES)**.

Examples, Illustrations, and Tables: The examples in this Dictionary are designed to help readers gain understanding and to help them relate abstract concepts to the real world of business.

Organizations and Associations: Those that play an active role in the field are included in the Dictionary, along with a brief statement of their mission. They are also listed by initials in Abbreviations and Acronyms.

A

ABANDONMENT voluntary, intentional surrender of property, or of a right to property, without naming a successor as owner or tenant. The property will generally revert to one holding a prior interest or, in cases where no owner is apparent, to the state. Abandonment does not relieve a person from obligations associated with lease or ownership unless the abandonment is accepted by the entity to which the obligation is owed.

ABATEMENT
In general: lessening or reduction.
Law: either a termination or a temporary suspension of a lawsuit. An *abatement of taxes* is a tax rebate or decrease.

ABC METHOD inventory management method that categorizes items in terms of importance. Thus, more emphasis is placed on higher dollar value items ("A"s) than on lesser dollar value items ("B"s), while the least important items ("C"s) receive the least time and attention. Inventory should be analyzed frequently when using the ABC method.

ABILITY TO PAY
Finance: borrower's ability to meet principal and interest payments on long-term obligations.
Industrial relations: ability of an employer, especially a financial organization, to meet a union's financial demands from operating income.
Municipal bonds: issuer's present and future ability to generate enough tax revenue to meet its contractual obligations.
Public policy: charging fees or pricing based on the user's income level.
Taxation: concept that tax rates should vary with levels of wealth or income; for example, the progressive income tax.

ABOVE PAR *see* PAR VALUE.

ABOVE THE LINE in general, amounts on a tax return that are deductible from gross income before arriving at ADJUSTED GROSS INCOME (AGI), such as IRA contributions, half of the self-employment tax, self-employed health insurance deduction, Keogh retirement plan and self-employed SEP deduction, penalty on early withdrawal of savings, and alimony paid. The term is derived from a solid bold line on Form 1040 and 1040A above the line for adjusted gross income. A taxpayer can take deductions *above the line* and still claim the standard deduction.

ABROGATE to annul, repeal, or abolish. This action makes a former rule, order, law, or treaty void or inoperative.

ABSENCE RATE, ABSENTEEISM frequency of employees failing to report to work when they are scheduled to do so. An absence rate above 5 percent is considered high.

ABSENTEE OWNER owner who does not personally manage or reside at the property owned.

ABSOLUTE ADVANTAGE in international economics, capability of one producer to produce a given good using fewer resources than any other producer. Japan produces television sets more efficiently than most other countries and so could be said to have an *absolute advantage* in this area.

ABSOLUTE AUCTION an AUCTION in which the property is sold to the highest bidder regardless of the amount of the winning bid.

ABSOLUTE (CELL) REFERENCE in a spreadsheet program, a cell reference that refers to a fixed location that will not change when a formula is copied to another location. In EXCEL, *absolute references* are indicated by placing dollar signs before the column and row indicators. *Contrast with* RELATIVE (CELL) REFERENCE.

ABSOLUTE LIABILITY liability without fault; also known as *liability without regard to fault* or *strict liability*. Absolute liability is imposed in various states when actions of an individual or business are deemed contrary to public policy, even though an action may not have been intentional or negligent.

ABSOLUTE SALE sale whereby the property passes to the buyer upon completion of an agreement between the parties.

ABSORB
   Business: cost not passed on to a customer; also a firm merged into an acquiring company.
   Cost accounting: indirect manufacturing costs (such as property taxes and insurance), called *absorbed costs*.
   Finance: account that has been combined with related accounts in preparing a financial statement and has lost its separate identity.
   Securities: issue an underwriter has completely sold to the public.

ABSORPTION COSTING in COST ACCOUNTING, applying both fixed and variable costs to derive the cost of the unit produced. *See also* DIRECT COSTING.

ABSORPTION RATE estimate of the expected annual sales or new occupancy of a particular type of land use. For example, the demand for new homes in a market area is estimated to be 500 per year. Developer Abel's new subdivision, when completed, is expected to capture 10% of the market. Therefore Abel's subdivision has an expected *absorption rate* of 50 homes per year (10% of 500 = 50).

ABSTENTION act or instance of deliberately refraining from an action or practice. Abstaining from voting generally means a recorded vote, neither for nor against. Abstention from voting is appropriate when one has a conflict of interest, as when a director owns stock in a competing business or one considered as a target for acquisition.

ABSTRACT OF RECORD condensed history of a case, taken from the trial court records and prepared for use by the APPELLATE COURT.

ABSTRACT OF TITLE short history of TITLE to land, noting all CONVEYANCES, transfers, GRANTS, WILLS and judicial proceedings, and all ENCUMBRANCES and LIENS, together with evidence of satisfaction and any other facts affecting title.

ABUSIVE TAX SHELTER TAX SHELTER claiming illegal tax deductions. For example, a limited partnership inflates the value of acquired property beyond its fair market value in order to claim excessive depreciation deductions. If these writeoffs are denied by the IRS, investors must pay severe penalties, interest, and back taxes.

ABUT or ABUTTING ADJOINING or meeting. *See also* ADJACENT.

ABV Accredited in Business Valuation, a designation awarded by the American Institute of Certified Public Accountants to CPAs who qualify. The resulting designation is CPA/ABV.

ACCELERATED COST RECOVERY SYSTEM (ACRS) a method of tax depreciation introduced in 1981, modified in 1984. ACRS rules are generally applicable to most tangible personal property placed in service between January 1, 1981 and December 31, 1986. ACRS was replaced by the MODIFIED ACCELERATED COST RECOVERY SYSTEM (MACRS) for assets placed in service after 1986.

ACCELERATED DEPRECIATION any one of a number of allowed methods of calculating depreciation that permit greater amounts of deductions in earlier years than are permitted under the straight-line method, which assumes equal depreciation during each year of the asset's life. *See also* ACCELERATED COST RECOVERY SYSTEM; DECLINING-BALANCE METHOD; SUM-OF-THE-YEARS'-DIGITS (SYD) DEPRECIATION.

ACCELERATION in real estate law: (1) hastening of the time for enjoyment of a remainder interest due to the premature termination of a preceding estate; and (2) process by which, under the terms of a MORTGAGE or similar obligation, an entire debt is to be regarded as due upon the borrower's failure to pay a single installment or to fulfill some other duty. *See also* ACCELERATION CLAUSE.

ACCELERATION CLAUSE loan provision giving the lender the right to declare the entire amount immediately due and payable upon the violation of a specific provision of the loan, such as failure to make payments on time.

ACCELERATED DEPRECIATION

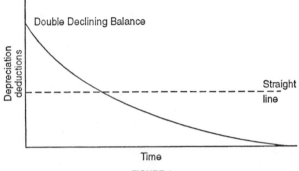

FIGURE 1

ACCELERATOR, ACCELERATOR PRINCIPLE proposition that INVESTMENT responds to growth in output. If the *rate* of growth of output changes, the level of investment will change. The ratio between the change in the rate of growth of output and the change in investment is the accelerator.

ACCEPTABLE USE POLICY a formal set of rules governing how a computer NETWORK may be used. For example, this policy bans the transmission of pornographic material on the Internet. *See also* NETIQUETTE; TERMS OF SERVICE.

ACCEPTANCE
In general: voluntary act of receiving something or of agreeing to certain terms.
Banking: formal procedure whereby the bank on which a check or other NEGOTIABLE INSTRUMENT is drawn promises to honor the DRAFT by paying the payee named on the check.
Contract law: consent to the terms of an OFFER, creating a CONTRACT with all terms binding.
Real property law: essential to completion of a gift INTER VIVOS.

ACCEPTANCE SAMPLING statistical procedure used in quality control. Acceptance sampling involves testing a batch of data to determine if the proportion of units having a particular attribute exceeds a given percentage. The sampling plan involves three determinations: (1) batch size; (2) sample size; and (3) maximum number of defects that can be uncovered before rejection of the entire batch. This technique permits acceptance or rejection of a batch of merchandise or documents under precisely specified circumstances.

ACCESS PROVIDER *see* INTERNET SERVICE PROVIDER.

ACCESS RIGHT right of an owner to get to and from his or her property.

ACCESS TIME
1. time taken by a computer or automated typewriter to locate data or an instruction word in its memory (storage) and transfer it.
2. time taken to transfer information from a computer or automated typewriter to the location in that device where it will be stored.

ACCIDENT AND HEALTH BENEFITS fringe benefits for accidental injury, accidental death, or sickness. Benefits include payment of medical, surgical, and hospital expenses and income payments. An employer is entitled to a deduction for such payments, whereas employees may exclude the benefits from gross income.

ACCIDENT INSURANCE coverage for bodily injury and/or death resulting from accidental means (other than natural causes). For example, an insured is critically injured in an accident. *Accident insurance* can provide income and/or a death benefit if death ensues.

ACCOMMODATION ENDORSER, MAKER, or **PARTY** one who, as a favor to another, signs a NOTE as acceptor, maker, or endorser without receiving compensation or other benefit, and who thus guarantees the debt of the other person. *See also* COSIGN.

ACCOMMODATION PAPER a negotiable instrument signed by a party as maker, drawer, acceptor, or endorser, without receiving value. It has the purpose of enabling another party to obtain money or credit.

ACCORD AND SATISFACTION payment of money or other valuable consideration (usually less than the amount owed) in exchange for extinguishment of a debt. There must be an express or implied agreement that accepting the smaller sum discharges the obligation to pay the larger sum.

ACCOUNT
In general: contractual relationship between a buyer and a seller under which payment is made at a later time. The term *open account* or *charge account* is used, depending on whether the relationship is commercial or personal.
Banking: relationship under a particular name, usually evidenced by a deposit against which withdrawals can be made. Among them are demand, time, custodial, joint, trustee, corporate, special, and regular accounts.
Bookkeeping: assets, liabilities, income, and expenses as represented by individual ledger pages to which debit and credit entries are chronologically posted to record changes in value. Examples are cash, accounts receivable, accrued interest, sales, and officers' salaries.

ACCOUNTABILITY framework for justifying management organizational actions, whether they are financial or employment-related. A junior manager is accountable to a senior manager for the completion of an organizational program by a particular date and within budget guidelines.

ACCOUNTANCY theory and practice of ACCOUNTING.

ACCOUNTANT person who works in the field of accounting; may be an independent accountant, auditor, or one who provides internal accounting services for the employer. *See also* AUDITOR; CERTIFIED PUBLIC ACCOUNTANT (CPA).

ACCOUNTANT'S OPINION statement signed by an independent CERTIFIED PUBLIC ACCOUNTANT describing the scope of the examination of an organization's books and records. Because financial reporting involves considerable discretion, the accountant's opinion is an important assurance to a lender or investor. Major types of opinions are unqualified or clean, qualified, adverse, and disclaimer.

ACCOUNTANTS PROFESSIONAL LIABILITY INSURANCE insurance for accountants covering liability lawsuits arising from their professional activities. For example, an investor bases a buying decision on the balance sheet of a company's annual statement. The figures later prove fallacious and not according to GENERALLY ACCEPTED ACCOUNTING PRINCIPLES (GAAP). The accountant could be found liable for his professional actions, and would be covered by this policy.

ACCOUNT BALANCE *see* BALANCE.

ACCOUNT EXECUTIVE
   Advertising: executive of an ad agency who oversees a particular account and who is the principal coordinator and contact person fo the client within the agency.
   Finance: brokerage firm employee who advises and handles orders for clients and has the legal powers of an AGENT. Every account executive must pass certain tests administered by securities regulatory boards. Also called *registered representative. See also* BROKER.

ACCOUNTING system that provides quantitative information about the finances of a person or business entity. Includes recording, measuring, and describing financial information.

ACCOUNTING CHANGE change in: (1) accounting principles (such as a new depreciation method); (2) accounting estimates (such as a revised projection of doubtful accounts receivable); or (3) the reporting entity (such as a merger of companies). When an accounting change is made, appropriate disclosure is required to explain its justification and financial effect, thereby enabling readers to make appropriate investment and credit judgments.

ACCOUNTING CYCLE accounting procedures beginning with an initial entry, such as recording the first sale of the year, and culminating with the closing entries, which are posted after year-end.

ACCOUNTING EQUATION formula in which ASSETS must equal the sum of LIABILITIES and OWNERS' EQUITY.

ACCOUNTING ERROR inaccurate measurement or representation of an accounting-related item not caused by intentional FRAUD. An error may be due to NEGLIGENCE or may result from the misapplication of GENERALLY ACCEPTED ACCOUNTING PRINCIPLES (GAAP). Errors may take the form of dollar discrepancies or may be compliance errors in employing accounting policies and procedures.

ACCOUNTING METHOD method used by a business in keeping its books and records for purposes of computing INCOME and determining TAXABLE INCOME. The term *accounting method* includes not only the overall method of accounting but also the accounting treatment of any item, such as inventory method or long-term contracts. *See also* CHANGE IN ACCOUNTING METHOD.

ACCOUNTING PERIOD period covered by an income statement, such as January 1 through December 31 of a year; often a quarter, six months, or a year.

ACCOUNTING PRINCIPLES, ACCOUNTING STANDARDS those that govern current accounting practices and are used as references to determine application of the appropriate treatment of complex transactions. *See also* FINANCIAL ACCOUNTING STANDARDS BOARD (FASB).

ACCOUNTING PRINCIPLES BOARD (APB) board of the American Institute of Certified Public Accountants (AICPA) that issued (1959–1973) a series of ACCOUNTANT'S OPINIONS constituting much of what is known as GENERALLY ACCEPTED ACCOUNTING PRINCIPLES (GAAP). *See also* AMERICAN INSTITUTE OF CERTIFIED PUBLIC ACCOUNTANTS (AICPA); FINANCIAL ACCOUNTING STANDARDS BOARD (FASB).

ACCOUNTING PROCEDURE accounting method that a company uses to handle routine accounting matters. These procedures may be written in a manual to assist new employees in learning the system.

ACCOUNTING RATE OF RETURN method of estimating the RATE OF RETURN from an investment using a straight-line approach (not discounted or compounded). The investment inflows are totaled and the investment costs subtracted to derive the profit. The profit is divided by the number of years invested, then by the investment cost, to estimate an annual rate of return. The method is not as sophisticated as a discounted approach, which is used by modern accountants.

ACCOUNTING RECORDS all documents and books used in the preparation of financial statements, including general ledger, subsidiary ledgers, sales slips, invoices, and so on.

ACCOUNTING SOFTWARE programs used to maintain books of account on computers. The software can be used to record transactions, maintain account balances, and prepare financial statements and reports. Many different accounting software packages exist.

ACCOUNTING SYSTEM mechanism within a company that generates its financial information. The system comprises all the people and machines that are involved in accounting information.

ACCOUNT NUMBER number assigned to each customer, supplier, lender, or other entity for ease in referring to that party's activity. Account numbers may be coded alphabetically or chronologically by date opened, and may contain coded information referring to credit terms, salesperson, state or county, and so on.

ACCOUNTS PAYABLE list of debts currently owed by a person or business. These are debts incurred mainly for the purchase of services, inventory, and supplies. The accounts normally do not include accrued salaries payable, accrued interest payable, or rent payable. This list is kept in the ordinary course of the debtor's business. *See also* ACCOUNTS RECEIVABLE.

ACCOUNTS PAYABLE LEDGER listing of detailed accounts, often in the form of a book with pages devoted to each supplier, that shows how much is owed to each supplier. Each credit transaction involving that supplier is listed. The balance in this ledger should agree with that in the GENERAL LEDGER.

ACCOUNTS RECEIVABLE list of money owed on current accounts to a CREDITOR, which is kept in the normal course of the creditor's business and represents unsettled claims and transactions. Accounts receivable normally arise from the sale of a company's products or services to its customers. *See also* ACCOUNTS PAYABLE.

ACCOUNTS RECEIVABLE FINANCING short-term financing whereby accounts receivable serve as collateral for working-capital advances. *See also* FACTORING.

ACCOUNTS RECEIVABLE LEDGER listing of detailed accounts, often in the form of a book with pages devoted to each customer, that shows how much each customer owes. Each transaction that generated a receivable is listed under that customer and a balance by customer is determined. The balance in this ledger should agree with that shown in the GENERAL LEDGER.

ACCOUNTS RECEIVABLE TURNOVER ratio obtained by dividing total credit sales by accounts receivable. The ratio indicates how many times the receivables portfolio has been collected during the accounting period. *See also* ACCOUNTS RECEIVABLE; COLLECTION RATIO.

ACCOUNT STATEMENT
In general: any record of transactions and their effect on charge- or open-account balances during a specified period.
Banking: summary of all checks paid, deposits recorded, and resulting balances during a defined period.
Securities: statement summarizing all transactions and showing the status of an account with a broker-dealer firm, including long and short positions.

ACCREDITED INVESTOR under Rule 501 of Securities and Exchange Commission Regulation D, a wealthy investor who does not count as one of the maximum of 35 people allowed to put money into a PRIVATE LIMITED PARTNERSHIP. Private limited partnerships use accredited investors to raise a larger amount of capital than would be possible if only 35 less wealthy people could contribute. To qualify as an accredited investor, an individual must (1) earn an individual income of more than $200,000 per year, or a joint income of $300,000 in each of the last two years, and expect to reasonably maintain the same level of income; or (2) have a net worth exceeding $1 million, either individually or jointly with his or her spouse; or (3) be a general partner, executive officer, director, or a related combination thereof for the issuer of the security being offered.

ACCRETION
1. asset growth through internal expansion, acquisition, or such causes as aging of whisky or growth of timber.
2. adjustment of the difference between the price of a bond bought at an original discount and the par value of the bond.

ACCRUAL *see* ACCRUED INTEREST.

ACCRUAL BASIS or **ACCRUAL METHOD** accounting method whereby income and expense items are included in taxable income or expense as they are earned or incurred, even though they may not yet have been received or actually paid in cash. Taxpayers having inventories must use the accrual method. Exceptions to the accrual method for tax purposes include the recognition of bad debts and payments received in advance for services or merchandise. *See also* CASH BASIS.

ACCRUE to include an event on the accounting records regardless of whether any cash changed hands. For example, at the end of a fiscal year a company may accrue its income tax expense for that year, even though the money will not be paid for several months. *See also* CASH BASIS.

ACCRUED DEPRECIATION *see* ACCUMULATED DEPRECIATION.

ACCRUED INTEREST or **ACCRUED INCOME** interest or other income that has been earned but not paid.

ACCRUED LIABILITIES amounts owed but not yet paid; does not necessarily indicate a default or delinquency.

ACCRUED TAXES amount of taxes owed, based on income earned or a property value assessment, but not yet paid.

ACCUMULATED BENEFIT OBLIGATION (ABO) similar to the PROJECTED BENEFIT OBLIGATION (PBO), but it is measured using current compensation levels rather than assumptions about future compensation.

ACCUMULATED DEPLETION accumulating CONTRA-ASSET ACCOUNT for a depletable asset, such as a mine. The balance in this account is subtracted from the asset account when shown on the balance sheet, giving rise to the term *contra-asset.*

ACCUMULATED DEPRECIATION in accounting, the amount of DEPRECIATION expense that has been claimed to date. Same as *accrued depreciation. See also* ADJUSTED BASIS.

ACCUMULATED DIVIDEND dividend due, usually to holders of cumulative preferred stock, but not paid. It is carried on the books as a liability until paid. *See also* CUMULATIVE PREFERRED STOCK.

ACCUMULATED EARNINGS (PROFITS) TAX a 15% penalty surcharge on earnings retained in a corporation to avoid the higher personal income taxes to which they would be subject if paid out as dividends to the owners. *See* REASONABLE NEEDS OF BUSINESS.

ACCUMULATED POSTRETIREMENT BENEFIT OBLIGATION (APBO) the actuarial present value of an employer's postretirement benefits other than pensions (often retiree medical or retiree life insurance benefits) attributed to employee service rendered to a particular date.

ACID TEST the most severe test of reliability. Since gold resists acids that corrode other metals, the *acid test* was used for metals purporting to be gold. *See* QUICK RATIO.

ACKNOWLEDGMENT declaration by a person who has signed a document that such signature is a voluntary act, made before a duly authorized person. *See also* NOTARY PUBLIC.

ACQUISITION one company taking over controlling interest in another company. *See also* MERGER; POOLING OF INTERESTS; TAKEOVER.

ACQUISITION COST price and all fees required to obtain a property. For example, XYZ Corp. purchases a property for $90,000 plus $5,000 in CLOSING COSTS (attorney's fees, loan fees, APPRAISAL COSTS, TITLE INSURANCE, and loan DISCOUNT POINTS). XYZ's *acquisition cost* is $95,000.

ACRE measure of land equaling 160 square rods, 10 square chains, 4,840 square yards, 43,560 square feet, or 0.405 hectares.

ACREAGE land measured in acres.

ACROBAT software from ADOBE SYSTEMS, INC., for creating PDF files. The Acrobat Distiller or Adobe PDF Printer functions as a printer driver so that any application can "print" to a PDF file.

ACRONYM word or name that is formed by joining the first letters (or the first few letters) of a series of words. For example, DOS is the *acronym* for *D*isk *O*perating *S*ystem. An acronym is pronounceable, whereas many other abbreviations are not.

ACROSS THE BOARD encompassing everything in a certain class or group; movement in the stock market that affects almost all stocks in the same direction. For example, when the market moves up *across the board*, almost every stock gains in price. An across-the-board pay increase in a company is a raise of a fixed percentage or amount for all employees.

ACRS ACCELERATED COST RECOVERY SYSTEM. *See also* MODIFIED ACCELERATED COST RECOVERY SYSTEM (MACRS).

ACTIVE CORPS OF EXECUTIVES (ACE) association of volunteers, established in 1969 as a supplement to the SERVICE CORPS OF RETIRED EXECUTIVES (SCORE), assisting the small-business community. It is composed of more than 10,500 executives who are still active in the business world but have volunteered their time and talents.

ACTIVE DESKTOP a feature introduced by Microsoft that permits users to put "active content" from the Internet on the desktop. Information from Web sites can thus be constantly updated without having to start and run a BROWSER.

ACTIVE INCOME in taxation, a category of income that includes salaries, wages, and commissions. PORTFOLIO INCOME (interest and dividends) and PASSIVE INCOME (rental real estate and businesses in which the taxpayer does not materially participate) are excluded. Passive losses generally may not be offset against either active or portfolio income.

ACTIVE MARKET heavy volume of trading in a particular market or stock, bond, or commodity. The spread between bid and asked prices is usually narrower in an active market than when trading is quiet.

ACTIVE WINDOW in Microsoft Windows, the WINDOW that currently has the *focus*, that is, the one in which keyboard or mouse actions will be effective. Usually the TITLE BAR of the active window will be a different color from those of other windows.

ACTIVIST POLICY government economic policy that uses monetary and/or fiscal policy activities based on economic conditions.

ACT OF BANKRUPTCY behavior indicating that a person might be judged as bankrupt. Examples of such behavior include transferring property title to another with the intent to delay or defraud creditors, and admitting that one is bankrupt.

ACT OF GOD violent and catastrophic event caused by forces of nature, which could not have been prevented or avoided by foresight or prudence. An act of God that makes performance of a contractual duty impossible may excuse performance of that duty.

ACTUAL CASH VALUE theoretical concept of value, sometimes used as a substitute for MARKET VALUE.

ACTUAL COST amount paid for an asset; not its market value, insurable value, or retail value. It generally includes freight-in and installation costs, but not interest on the debt to acquire it.

ACTUAL DAMAGES losses directly referable to a breach or tortious act; losses that can readily be proven to have been sustained, and for which the injured party should be compensated as a matter of right.

ACTUARIAL SCIENCE branch of knowledge dealing with the mathematics of insurance, including probabilities. It is used in ensuring that risks are carefully evaluated, that adequate premiums are charged for risks underwritten, and that adequate provision is made for future payments of benefits.

ACTUARY one who calculates insurance and property costs, especially the cost of life insurance risks and insurance premiums. To become a fellow of the SOCIETY OF ACTUARIES requires passing a set of highly rigorous examinations. *See* ENROLLED ACTUARY.

ADA *see* AMERICANS WITH DISABILITIES ACT (ADA).

ADDED-VALUE TAX *see* VALUE-ADDED TAX.

ADDENDUM something added, as an attachment to a CONTRACT. Commonly added addenda in real estate purchase agreements describe financing terms and property INSPECTION requirements.

ADDITIONAL FIRST-YEAR DEPRECIATION tax law provision permitting a certain amount of depreciable business personal property purchased each year to be expensed rather than depreciated. The limit of depreciation is $108,000 in 2006, adjusted for inflation in 2007, then falling to $25,000 per year in 2008, without an inflation adjustment. The investment limit to claim this is $430,000 in 2006, adjusted for inflation in 2007, then falling to $200,000 per year in 2008 without an inflation adjustment. The amount is phased out, dollar for dollar, when purchases exceed $200,000 in a year. The expense deduction is limited to the net income the taxpayer earns from the active conduct of all trades or businesses during the year.

ADDITIONAL MARK-ON further increase in a retail merchandise price; often done to take advantage of holiday periods or periods of peak demand.

ADDITIONAL PAID-IN CAPITAL *see* CAPITAL CONTRIBUTED IN EXCESS OF PAR VALUE.

ADD-ON INTEREST interest that is added to the principal of a loan. The amount of interest for all years is computed on the original amount borrowed, so the stated rate is much lower than the ANNUAL PERCENTAGE RATE (APR), which is required to be disclosed by federal law.

ADDRESS (INTERNET) *see* E-MAIL ADDRESS; IP ADDRESS; UNIFORM RESOURCE LOCATOR.

ADEQUACY OF COVERAGE sufficiency of insurance protection to repay the insured in the event of loss. *See also* UNDERINSURED.

ADHESION CONTRACT legally enforceable agreement containing standardized terms, offered by a business to consumers of goods or services. The consumer must accept the standard provisions and does not have the ability to change those terms. Since it is on a take-it-or-leave-it basis, the consumer is unable to bargain with the seller.

AD HOC for this particular purpose, an *ad hoc* committee is one commissioned for a special purpose; an *ad hoc* attorney is one designated for a particular client in a special situation.

AD INFINITUM indefinitely, with no limit on the amount of money or time. An example is a perpetual annuity of payments made by a company to an individual. The individual will receive payments *ad infinitum*.

ADJACENT nearby, but not necessarily touching.

ADJOINING contiguous; attaching; sharing a common border, as in adjoining properties.

ADJUDICATION determination of a controversy and pronouncement of judgment.

ADJUSTABLE MORTGAGE LOAN (AML) mortgage instrument under which interest rates and payments may be adjusted over the maturity of the loan. *See also* ADJUSTABLE-RATE MORTGAGE; HYBRID ADJUSTABLE-RATE MORTGAGE; RENEGOTIATED-RATE MORTGAGE; VARIABLE-RATE MORTGAGE.

ADJUSTABLE-RATE MORTGAGE (ARM) mortgage loan that allows the interest rate to be changed at specific intervals over the maturity of the loan.

ADJUSTED BASIS or **ADJUSTED TAX BASIS** original cost or other basis of property, reduced by DEPRECIATION deductions and increased by CAPITAL EXPENDITURES; base amount from which to measure gains and losses for tax purposes.

ADJUSTED GROSS INCOME (AGI) intermediate step in calculating taxable income, the amount used for computing deductions based on, or limited by, a percentage of income, such as medical expenses, charitable contributions, and miscellaneous itemized deductions. This amount is determined by subtracting from gross income any business expenses and other deductions—for example, KEOGH PAYMENTS, ALIMONY PAYMENTS, and IRA contributions. Itemized deductions for such items as medical expenses, interest payments, and real estate taxes are deductions *from* adjusted gross income; they are *not* subtracted to derive adjusted gross income.

ADJUSTED TAX BASIS *see* ADJUSTED BASIS.

ADJUSTER individual employed by a property and casualty insurance company to settle on its behalf claims brought by insureds. The adjuster evaluates the merits of each claim and makes recommendations to the insurance company. *See also* INDEPENDENT ADJUSTER.

ADJUSTING ENTRY JOURNAL ENTRY posted to the ACCOUNTING RECORDS at the end of an accounting period to record a transaction or event that was not properly posted during the accounting period for some reason.

ADJUSTMENTS (IN APPRAISAL) dollar value or percentage amounts that, when added to or subtracted from the sales price of a COMPARABLE, provide an indication of the value of a subject property. Adjustments are necessary to compensate for variation in the features of the comparable relative to the subject.

ADMINISTER to provide the management actions of planning, directing, budgeting, and implementing necessary to achieve organizational objectives. It is the function of the personnel manager to *administer* the testing and placement of newly hired personnel in an organization.

ADMINISTERED PRICE price of a good that is specified by a governmental or some other nonmarket agency. Wage price controls and rent controls are examples of administered prices.

ADMINISTRATIVE EXPENSE often grouped with GENERAL EXPENSE, expenses that are not as easily associated with a specific function as are direct costs of manufacturing and selling. It typically includes expenses of the headquarters office and accounting expenses.

ADMINISTRATIVE LAW law relating to the powers and the procedures of governmental bodies other than courts and legislatures. This type of law affects the rights of private persons through investigations, hearings, rule making, and adjudication.

ADMINISTRATIVE MANAGEMENT SOCIETY professional management society. It promotes the application of management methods for commerce and industry for the purpose of increasing productivity, lowering costs, and improving quality. It encourages and participates in research while promoting sound employer/employee relations.

ADMINISTRATIVE SKILLS wide range of essential organizational and technical skills. These skills include planning, organizing, staffing, scheduling, and computer SOFTWARE skills comprehending WORD PROCESSING, SPREADSHEETS, DATABASES, and TELECOMMUNICATIONS.

ADMINISTRATOR
1. performer of executive duties; management.
2. court-appointed individual or bank charged with carrying out the court's decisions with respect to a decedent's estate until it is fully distributed to all claimants. Administrators are appointed when a person dies without having made a will or without having named an EXECUTOR, or when the named executor cannot or will not serve.

ADMINISTRATOR'S DEED DEED conveying the property of one who died without a WILL (INTESTATE).

ADOBE SYSTEMS, INC. (San Jose, California) the software company that pioneered the PostScript command language for output devices and introduced the PORTABLE DOCUMENT FORMAT. Adobe is also a leader in producing high-quality font and desktop publishing software. Its recent purchase of Macromedia extends its product range into Web design applications.

ADULT one who has attained the age of MAJORITY.

AD VALOREM Latin for "according to value." An *ad valorem* tax is assessed on the value of goods or property (e.g., real estate and motor vehicles), not on the quantity, weight, extent, etc. An *ad valorem* real estate tax may be a deduction from ADJUSTED GROSS INCOME (AGI) for an individual.
Example: If the *ad valorem* tax rate is 1%, the tax would be $1 per $100 of assessed value.

ADVANCE in general, to proceed, move ahead; amount paid before it is earned or incurred, such as a cash advance for travel expenses.

ADVANCE FUNDED PENSION PLAN retirement plan in which money is currently allocated to fund an employee's pension.

ADVERSARY opponent or litigant, as, for example, in a legal controversy or LITIGATION.

ADVERSE OPINION ACCOUNTANT'S OPINION concerning financial statements, that the statements are not in conformity with GENERALLY ACCEPTED ACCOUNTING PRINCIPLES (GAAP) and/or that they do not present results fairly.

ADVERSE POSSESSION method of acquiring legal TITLE to land through actual, continuous, open occupancy of the property, for a prescribed period of time, under claim of right, and in opposition to the rights of the true owner.

ADVERSE SELECTION the tendency of people with a greater likelihood of filing claims to be more interested in obtaining insurance coverage. For example, those with severe health problems want to buy health insurance, and people going to a dangerous place such as a war zone want to buy more life insurance. To combat the problem of *adverse selection*, insurance companies try to reduce their exposure to large claims by either raising premiums or screening out such applicants.

ADVERTISING paid message communicated through the various media by industry, business firms, nonprofit organizations, or individuals. Advertising is persuasive and informational and is designed to influence the purchasing behavior and/or thought patterns of the audience. Advertising is a marketing tool and may be used in combination with SALES PROMOTIONS, PERSONAL SELLING tactics, or publicity.

ADVOCACY ADVERTISING advertisements placed by companies presenting their own opinion on one or more public issues. The advertisements reflect the opinion of the company and are meant to influence public opinion. Issues include consumer rights, education, the environment, health, and taxation.

AFFECTIVE BEHAVIOR behavior aimed at producing a desired outcome, such as trying to understand the needs of the other party and attempting to satisfy those needs. An example is the personality and salesmanship displayed by a salesperson that leads to a new account.

AFFIANT person who makes and signs a written statement under oath. *See also* AFFIDAVIT.

AFFIDAVIT written statement made under oath before an officer of the court, a NOTARY PUBLIC, or other person legally authorized to certify the statement.

AFFIDAVIT OF DOMICILE notarized form stating the legal residence of a deceased person. It may be executed by an individual familiar with the facts, such as an executor, survivor, or attorney. The form is often required when a shareholder dies and was residing in a state that is different from the address on the account. Also known as an *affidavit of residence.*

AFFILIATED CHAIN group of noncompeting retail stores throughout the United States whose association affords an economic advantage in large-scale purchasing. When a group of small stores get together to form such a chain, they can purchase in bulk and will be entitled to larger discounts. An affiliated chain can purchase advertising time and space as if it were a national advertiser.

AFFILIATED COMPANY
In general: two companies are affiliated when one owns less than a majority of the voting stock of the other, or when both are subsidiaries of a third company.
Banking: organization that a bank owns or controls by stock holdings, or which the bank's shareholders own, or whose officers are also directors of the bank.

AFFILIATED GROUP for purposes of consolidated tax returns, an affiliated group is composed of companies whose common parent or other inclusive corporation owns at least 80% of the voting power and value of the stock of the includable corporations (except preferred stock).

AFFILIATED RETAILER
1. member of an AFFILIATED CHAIN.
2. independent retailer who affiliates with other independent retailers under a common trade name for merchandising purposes. A group of such independent retailers will advertise under this common trade name. *See also* AFFILIATED WHOLESALER.

AFFILIATED WHOLESALER
1. WHOLESALER who sponsors or owns a group of AFFILIATED RETAILERS.
2. wholesaler who affiliates with other wholesalers under a common trade name for merchandising purposes.

AFFIRMATIVE ACTION steps taken to correct conditions resulting from past discrimination or from violations of a law, particularly with respect to employment.

AFFIRMATIVE RELIEF relief, benefit, or compensation that may be granted to the defendant in a judgment or decree in accordance with the facts established in his favor.

AFFREIGHTMENT contract with a carrier for the transportation of goods.

AFL-CIO *see* AMERICAN FEDERATION OF LABOR-CONGRESS OF INDUSTRIAL ORGANIZATIONS.

AFTER-ACQUIRED CLAUSE clause in a mortgage agreement providing that any additional mortgageable property acquired by the borrower after the mortgage is signed will be additional security for the obligation.

AFTER-ACQUIRED PROPERTY
Commercial law: property acquired by a debtor after he has entered into an agreement in which other property is put up as SECURITY for a loan.
Bankruptcy law: property acquired by the bankrupt after he has filed to be declared a bankrupt. This property is generally free of all claims of the bankrupt's creditors.

AFTER MARKET *see* SECONDARY MARKET.

AFTER-TAX BASIS basis for comparing the returns on a corporate taxable bond and a municipal tax-free bond. For example, a corporate bond paying 10% would have an after-tax return of 7.5% for someone in a 33% tax bracket. So any nontaxable municipal bond paying higher than 5% would yield a higher after-tax return.

AFTER-TAX CASH FLOW in REAL ESTATE, CASH FLOW from income-producing property, less income taxes, if any, attributable to the property's income. The tax savings from the possible shelter of income earned outside the property is added to the cash flow that is earned by the property. For example, if a property generates a $1,000 cash flow and $500 tax loss that can be used to offset other income, the *after-tax cash flow* for a 33% tax bracket investor is $1,167 (0.33 × $500 + $1,000).

AFTER-TAX EQUITY YIELD the RATE OF RETURN on an equity interest, taking into account financing costs and income tax implications of the investor.

AFTER-TAX PROCEEDS FROM RESALE the amount of money left for the investor after all obligations of the transaction, and personal income taxes on the transaction. For example:

Resale price	$1,300,000
Less, TRANSACTION COSTS	−100,000
Less, Outstanding mortgage	−900,000
Less, Tax on gain	−180,000
After-tax proceeds from resale	$ 120,000

AFTER-TAX REAL RATE OF RETURN amount of money, adjusted for inflation, that an investor can keep out of the income and capital gains earned from investments.

AGAINST THE BOX *short sale* by the holder of a LONG POSITION in the same stock. *Box* refers to the physical location of securities held in safekeeping by the broker. *See also* SHORT POSITION; SHORTSALE RULE.

AGE DISCRIMINATION denial of privileges as well as other unfair treatment of employees on the basis of age, which is prohibited by federal law under the Age Discrimination Unemployment Act of 1967. This act was amended in 1978 to protect employees up to 70 years of age, and in 1986 to protect mandatory retirement.

AGENCY
In general: relationship between two parties, one a principal and the other an AGENT who represents the principal in transactions with a third party.
Finance: certain types of accounts in trust institutions where individuals, usually trust officers, act on behalf of customers.
Government: securities issued by government-sponsored corporations such as Federal Home Loan Banks or Federal Land Banks.
Investment: act of buying or selling for the account and risk of a client.
Personnel: company that refers potential employees to employers for a fee. *See also* HEADHUNTER.

AGENCY BY NECESSITY agency relationship recognized by the courts that allows a spouse to charge necessities to the other spouse or allows a dependent to charge necessities to a parent.

AGENCY DISCLOSURE a written explanation, to be signed by a prospective buyer or seller of real estate, explaining to the client the role that the broker plays in the transaction. The purpose of disclosure is to explain whether the broker represents the buyer or seller or is a dual agent (representing both) or a subagent (an agent of the seller's broker). This allows the customer to understand to which party the broker owes loyalty.

AGENCY SHOP organization having an employee UNION where nonmembers are required to pay a fee to the union as an offset to the benefits they share with union members. This rule often depends on the terms of collective bargaining agreements and state laws.

AGENT

Law: one who is authorized to act for another, who is the *principal*.
Real estate: a licensed salesperson who typically works under a broker.
Insurance: individual who sells and services insurance policies in either of two classifications:

1. An *independent agent* represents at least two insurance companies and (at least in theory) serves clients by searching the market for the most advantageous price for the most coverage. The agent's commission is a percentage of each premium paid and includes a fee for servicing the insured's policy.

2. A *direct writer* represents only one company and sells only that company's policies. This agent is paid on a commission basis in much the same manner as the independent agent.

AGGLOMERATION
accumulation into a single entity, such as a holding company, of several diverse and unrelated activities. Conglomerate companies are examples of *agglomeration*.

AGGREGATE
referring to the sum total of the whole. Aggregate output, for example, is the total of all output during a given period of time.

AGGREGATE DEMAND *see* AGGREGATE SUPPLY.

AGGREGATE INCOME
sum total of all incomes in an economy, with no adjustment for inflation, taxes, or certain kinds of double-counting. The GROSS DOMESTIC PRODUCT (GDP) is one of many measures of aggregate income.

AGGREGATE INSURANCE LIMIT *see* ANNUAL AGGREGATE LIMIT.

AGGREGATE SUPPLY
in MACROECONOMICS, the total amount of goods and services supplied to the market at alternative price levels in a given period of time; also called *total output*. The central concept in SUPPLY-SIDE ECONOMICS, it corresponds with *aggregate demand*, defined as the total amount of goods and services demanded in the economy at alternative income levels in a given period, including both consumer and producers' goods; aggregate demand is also called *total spending*.

AGGRESSIVE GROWTH (STOCK/MUTUAL) FUND
STOCK or MUTUAL FUND holding stocks of rapidly growing companies. While these companies may be large or small, they all share histories of and prospects for above-average profit growth. *Aggressive growth funds* are designed solely for capital appreciation, since they produce little or no income from dividends.

AGING OF ACCOUNTS RECEIVABLE or AGING SCHEDULE
classification of trade ACCOUNTS RECEIVABLE by date of sale. Usually prepared by a company's auditor, the *aging*, as the schedule is called, is a vital tool in analyzing the quality of a company's receivables investment. The aging schedule reveals patterns of delinquency and shows where collection efforts should be concentrated.

AGREEMENT mutual assent between two or more legally COMPETENT PARTIES, ordinarily leading to a CONTRACT. It includes executed SALES, GIFTS, and other transfers of PROPERTY, as well as promises without legal obligation.

AGREEMENT OF SALE written agreement between seller and purchaser in which the purchaser agrees to buy certain real estate and the seller agrees to sell upon terms of the agreement; also called *contract of sale*; EARNEST MONEY contract.

AGRIBUSINESS large-scale production, processing, and marketing of food and nonfood farm commodities and products. Agribusiness is a major commercial business. California has the largest concentration of agribusiness in the United States.

AI *see* ARTIFICIAL INTELLIGENCE.

AICPA *see* AMERICAN INSTITUTE OF CERTIFIED PUBLIC ACCOUNTANTS.

AIRBILL papers that accompany a package sent through an express mail service. The sender completes a form with multiple copies. It includes origin and destination addresses, services requested, and billing and shipping information. Multiple copies provide a receipt for the sender, another for the carrier's billing records, and at least one copy with the address to accompany the package to its destination.

AIR FREIGHT use of air transportation for sending freight. It is faster and more expensive than truck, rail, or bus service.

AIR RIGHTS right to use, control, or occupy the space above a designated property. Air rights often can be leased, sold, or donated to another party.

AKA also known as. An example is John Jones, who is also called Lucky John by other salespeople in the organization.

ALGOL (*algo*rithmic *l*anguage) name of two computer programming languages that have had a strong impact on programming language design.

ALGORITHM sequence of instructions that tell how to solve a particular problem. An algorithm must be specified exactly, so there can be no doubt about what to do next, and it must have a finite number of steps. A computer program is an *algorithm* written in a language that a computer can understand.

ALIAS otherwise; an indication that a person is known by more than one name. AKA and a/k/a mean "also known as" and are used to introduce the listing of an *alias*.

ALIEN one who is not a citizen of the country in which he lives. *See also* ILLEGAL ALIEN; RESIDENT ALIEN.

ALIENATION in real property law, the voluntary transfer of TITLE and POSSESSION OF REAL PROPERTY to another person. The law recognizes the power to alienate (or transfer) property as an essential ingredient of FEE-SIMPLE ownership of property and generally prohibits unreasonable restraints on alienation.

ALIEN CORPORATION company incorporated under the laws of a foreign country regardless of where it operates. *Alien corporation* can be used as a synonym for the term *foreign corporation.* However, foreign corporation also is used in U.S. state law to mean a corporation formed in a state other than that in which it does business.

ALIMONY payment for the support of one's estranged spouse in the course of divorce or separation. Alimony and separate maintenance payments are taxable to the receiver and deductible by the payor. CHILD SUPPORT and other voluntary payments are not considered *alimony* for tax purposes. Alimony is deductible for ADJUSTED GROSS INCOME (AGI); child support is not tax deductible.

ALLEGATION assertion of fact in a PLEADING. It is a statement of the issue that the contributing party expects to prove.

ALLOCATE
1. to distribute anything for use, including one's time or money.
2. in accounting, to spread a single cost over a number of products, customers, people, or time. For example, DEPRECIATION accounting attempts to allocate the cost of a WASTING ASSET over its estimated useful life.

ALLOCATED BENEFITS payments in a DEFINED-BENEFIT PENSION PLAN. Benefits are allocated to the pension plan participants as premiums are received by the insurance company. Since the benefits purchased are paid up, the employee is guaranteed a pension at retirement, even if the firm goes out of business.

ALLOCATION
Accounting or tax: apportionment or assignment of income or expense for various purposes. For example, income and expense items of a TRUST or ESTATE are allocated between the CORPUS and INCOME components. Also, income, expense, credits, gains, and losses are allocated to the various partners in a PARTNERSHIP and shareholders of an S CORPORATION. *See also* APPORTIONMENT.
Broadcast: range of wavelengths assigned to a broadcast system by the Federal Communications Commission.
Merchandising: quantity of merchandise designated for a particular prospect or MARKET.

ALLOCATION OF RESOURCES central subject of economics: manner in which scarce factors of production are apportioned among producers, and in which scarce goods are apportioned among customers.

ALLODIAL owned freely; not subject to the restriction on ALIENATION that existed in feudal law.

ALLODIAL SYSTEM legal system that allocates full property owner-ship rights to individuals. The allodial system is the basis for property rights in the United States.

ALLOWANCE
In general: reduction in price.
Merchandising: reduction in price offered to a retailer by a manufac-turer or wholesaler that is contingent upon some special arrangement. It usually compensates the retailer for expense incurred in marketing the product. *See also* BROKERAGE ALLOWANCE; RETAIL DISPLAY ALLOWANCE.

ALLOWANCE FOR BAD DEBTS *see* BAD-DEBT RESERVE.

ALLOWANCE FOR DEPRECIATION *see* ACCUMULATED DEPRECIATION.

ALLOWED TIME total time in which a job should be completed at standard performance, inclusive of allowances for fatigue, rest, per-sonal needs, and contingencies; also called STANDARD TIME.

ALL RISK/ALL PERIL insurance that covers each and every loss except for those specifically excluded. If the insurance company does not specifically exclude a particular loss, it is automatically covered. This is the broadest type of property policy that can be purchased. For example, if an insurance policy does not specifically exclude losses from wind damage, or from a meteor falling on the insured's house, the insured is covered for such losses.

ALL THE TRAFFIC WILL BEAR or **AS MUCH AS THE TRAF-FIC WILL BEAR** a policy of charging to the limit that customers will pay. Discussed in connection with products that seem to be overpriced.

ALL WASHED UP a business failure; all the property is cleaned up because there is no more work to be done.

ALPHA measurement of returns from an investment apart from market returns. Represents the amount of return expected from fundamental causes such as the growth rate in earnings per share; *contrast with* BETA, which is a measure of volatility.

ALPHANUMERIC CHARACTER all the characters that are either alphabetic or numeric, that is, all letters from A to Z and all numbers from 0 to 9.

ALTER EGO the other self. Under the doctrine of *alter ego*, the law will disregard the limited personal liability one enjoys when acting in a cor-porate capacity and will regard the act as his or her personal responsi-bility. To invoke the doctrine, it must be shown that the corporation was a mere conduit for the transaction of private business and that no sepa-rate identity of the individual and the corporation really existed.

ALTERNATE VALUATION DATE valuation date six months (*not* 180 days) after the date of a person's death. For estate tax purposes, the executor may place a value on the estate as of the date of death or on the *alternate valuation date.* To use the alternative valuation date, the estate value and tax must be less than on the date of death.

ALTERNATIVE DISPUTE RESOLUTION (ADR) alternatives to the slow and costly process of litigation, including ARBITRATION, CONCILIATION, MEDIATION, and SUMMARY proceedings. Some of these processes, such as mediation and arbitration, are being used by court systems to resolve disputes before trial.

ALTERNATIVE HYPOTHESIS in statistical testing, a HYPOTHESIS is accepted if a sample contains sufficient evidence to reject the NULL HYPOTHESIS. It is usually denoted by H_1. In most cases, the alternative hypothesis is the expected conclusion (why the test was completed in the first place).

ALTERNATIVE INVESTMENTS investments other than stocks and bonds, such as art, coins, precious metals, or stamps. May also include ARBITRAGE, DERIVATIVES, HEDGE FUNDS, LEVERAGED BUYOUTS (LBOs), private equity, real estate, and venture capital investments.

ALTERNATIVE MINIMUM TAX a flat tax to ensure that corporate and high-income noncorporate taxpayers pay at least some tax, regardless of their deductions. A 26% or 28% rate (20% for certain corporations) applies to broadly based income. If the alternative minimum tax exceeds the regular income tax, then the former is to be paid instead of the regular income tax. The rate is applied to alternative minimum taxable income, which is taxable income increased by tax preferences and adjusted by adding back all or a portion of certain items that were deducted in computing regular taxable income.

ALTERNATIVE MORTGAGE INSTRUMENT (AMI) any mortgage other than a fixed-interest-rate, level-payment amortizing loan. *See also* ADJUSTABLE-RATE MORTGAGE; GRADUATED-PAYMENT MORTGAGE; GROWING-EQUITY MORTGAGE; ROLLOVER LOAN; SHARED-APPRECIATION MORTGAGE.

AMASS to accumulate an item such as money, property, or goods. A company may stock up on a commodity now for future sale when it believes that a sharp increase in the price of the commodity will take place at a later date.

AMEND to alter. A statute is amended by changing (but not abolishing) an established law. A pleading is amended by adding to or subtracting from an already existing pleading. *See also* AMENDED (TAX) RETURN.

AMENDED (TAX) RETURN form filed as a correction or supplement to, or replacement for, an original tax return. For example, a corporation may file Form 1120X, or an individual may file Form 1040X, to claim a refund for a prior year's tax return or provide a correction to it. *See also* CLAIM FOR REFUND.

AMENDMENT addition to or change in a legal document. When properly signed, it has the full legal effect of the original document.

AMENITIES in APPRAISAL, the nonmonetary benefits derived from property ownership, such as pride of home ownership.

AMERICAN ARBITRATION ASSOCIATION 75-year-old organization that is available to resolve a wide range of disputes through mediation, arbitration, elections, and other out-of-court settlement procedures. The Association's alternative dispute resolution (ADR) resources—its panels, rules, administration, and education and training services—provide cost-effective value to counsel, businesses, and industry professionals and their employees, customers, and business partners.

AMERICAN ASSOCIATION OF INDIVIDUAL INVESTORS (AAII) organization headquartered in Chicago and committed to the investment education of its more than 150,000 members. Annual membership dues are approximately $29.

AMERICAN AUTOMOBILE ASSOCIATION (AAA) association of motorists who can receive maps, tourist information, and emergency roadside service. Many hotels and motels strive for recommendation by the AAA. Also known as *Triple A*.

AMERICAN BANKERS ASSOCIATION (ABA) a trade organization for officers of commercial banks. Publishes the monthly *ABA Banking Journal* and several other specialized banking periodicals.

AMERICAN BAR ASSOCIATION (ABA) a national organization of lawyers and law students that promotes improvements in the delivery of legal services and the administration of justice.

AMERICAN BUSINESS PRESS, INC. association of specialized business publications, such as industrial, trade, and professional magazines. Abbreviated ABP, it was incorporated in 1965 as a result of the consolidation of Associated Business Publications and National Business Publications. The corporation maintains financial information about advertising agencies that use the business press and reports this information to its members.

AMERICAN DEPOSITARY RECEIPT (ADR) receipt issued by U.S. banks to domestic buyers as a convenient substitute for direct ownership of stock in foreign companies. ADRs are traded on STOCK EXCHANGES and in OVER-THE-COUNTER markets like stocks of domestic companies. Underlying shares are called *American Depositary Shares*.

AMERICAN ECONOMICS ASSOCIATION (AEA) organization of economists, mostly those who are academicians.

AMERICAN FEDERATION OF LABOR-CONGRESS OF INDUSTRIAL ORGANIZATIONS (AFL-CIO) largest national union in the United States. The Congress of Industrial Organizations (CIO) merged with the American Federation of Labor (AFL) in 1955.

AMERICAN INSTITUTE OF CERTIFIED PUBLIC ACCOUNTANTS (AICPA) organization headquartered in New York whose members are

CERTIFIED PUBLIC ACCOUNTANTS. The AICPA prepares the CPA examination and provides educational and newsworthy information to its members. CPAs may prepare tax returns, represent taxpayers during IRS audits, and be called upon for analysis of more complex tax issues.

AMERICAN JOBS CREATION ACT OF 2004 legislation that repeals the Foreign Sales Corporation/Extraterritorial Income regime, creates a new tax deduction for "manufacturers," continues enhanced small business expensing for two more years, reduces the sport utility vehicle (SUV) loophole, accelerates depreciation for leasehold and restaurant improvements, makes significant changes to S CORPORATION rules, simplifies international taxation, gives farmers tax relief, boosts tax shelter penalties, tightens vehicle donation rules, and enacts a host of other changes.

AMERICAN MANAGEMENT ASSOCIATION (AMA) professional management association located in New York, which issues many publications. It conducts nationwide wage surveys on professional and management compensation as well as training seminars and meetings for management personnel.

AMERICAN MARKETING ASSOCIATION (AMA) national professional society of MARKETING and MARKETING RESEARCH executives, sales and promotion managers, advertising specialists, and marketing teachers, headquartered in Chicago. The association publishes *Marketing News,* the *Journal of Marketing,* and the *Journal of Marketing Research* for the benefit of the public. It also offers marketing bibliographies and various books and pamphlets on marketing.

AMERICAN NATIONAL STANDARDS INSTITUTE (ANSI) institution that issues official standards in almost all industries.

AMERICAN PLAN arrangement by a hotel whereby it charges a business person a price that includes room, meals, and services.

AMERICAN SOCIETY OF APPRAISERS an organization of appraisal professionals and others interested in the appraisal profession. International in structure, it is self-supporting and independent. The oldest and only major appraisal organization representing all of the disciplines of appraisal specialists, the society originated in 1936 and incorporated in 1952. ASA is one of the eight founding members of the APPRAISAL FOUNDATION.

AMERICAN STOCK EXCHANGE (AMEX or ASE) stock exchange with the second biggest volume of trading in the United States, located at 86 Trinity Place in downtown Manhattan. Stocks and bonds traded on the Amex are mainly those of small to mediumsize companies, as contrasted with the huge companies whose shares are traded on the New York Stock Exchange. Stock options are also traded on the Amex, which is sometimes referred to as the *Curb.*

AMERICANS WITH DISABILITIES ACT (ADA) federal law that prohibits discrimination against individuals with physical handicaps, including hiring practices and design of buildings intended to serve the public.

AMERICA ONLINE (AOL) a leading commercial ONLINE SERVICE that serves as an entry point to the INTERNET for millions of home and business customers. A part of Time Warner.

AMICUS CURIAE Latin for "friend of the court." A person who is not a party to litigation but provides testimony at the invitation of the court.

AMORTIZE or AMORTIZATION
1. reduction of a DEBT by periodic charges to assets or liabilities, such as payments on mortgages.
2. in accounting statements, the systematic write-off of costs incurred to acquire an intangible asset, such as patents, copyrights, goodwill, organization, and expenses.

AMORTIZATION SCHEDULE table that shows the periodic payment, interest and principal requirements, and unpaid loan balance for each period of the life of a loan.

AMORTIZATION TERM the time it takes to retire a DEBT through periodic payments. Also known as the *full amortization term. See also* FULLY AMORTIZED LOAN.
Example: Many mortgage loans have an *amortization term* of 15, 20, 25, or 30 years. Some have an AMORTIZATION SCHEDULE as a 30-year loan, but require a BALLOON PAYMENT in 5, 10, or 15 years.

AMORTIZED LOAN any loan with at least some payments to PRINCIPAL.

AMOUNT sum, represented by a number; frequently number of dollars.

AMOUNT AT RISK
1. difference between the face value of a permanent life insurance policy and its accrued cash value.
2. in property and liability insurance, the lesser of the policy limit or the maximum possible loss to the insured.

AMOUNT OF ONE same as COMPOUND AMOUNT OF ONE.

AMOUNT OF ONE PER PERIOD same as COMPOUND AMOUNT OF ONE PER PERIOD.

AMPERSAND the character &, which stands for the word *and*.

AMTRAK National Railway Passenger Corporation; federal agency that runs passenger trains throughout the United States.

ANALOG representing data in a form other than binary digits (bits). Analog devices, such as a camera, scanner, or microphone, permit use of unlimited variables to represent a continuous variation of sound or color. Binary digital devices must represent the same information with switches that are either on (1) or off (0).

ANALYSIS examination and division of a business-related situation or problem into major elements in order to understand the item in question and make appropriate recommendations.

ANALYSIS OF VARIANCE (ANOVA) statistical model that tests whether or not groups of data have the same or differing means. The ANOVA model operates by comparing the amounts of dispersion experienced by each of the groups to the total amount of dispersion in the data.

ANALYST person who studies data and makes recommendations on a course of business actions. Analysts may study credit, securities, financial patterns, sales, etc.

ANALYTIC PROCESS procedures and techniques employed to perform an analysis of a situation or event. For example, an investor, in deciding whether to commit funds to a company, would engage in financial statement analysis by looking at trends in the accounts over the years (e.g., sales) and financial ratios.

ANALYTICAL REVIEW auditing process that tests relationships among accounts and identifies material changes. It involves analyzing significant ratios and trends for unusual changes and questionable items. Included in the analytical review process are: (1) reading important documents and analyzing their accounting and financial effects; (2) reviewing the activity in an account between interim and year-end, especially noting entries out of the ordinary; and (3) comparing current period account balances to prior periods as well as to budgeted amounts, noting reasonableness of account balances by evaluating logical relationships among them (i.e., relating payables to expenses, accounts receivable to sales).

ANCHOR TENANT main tenant in a shopping center. It is often essential to have a lease commitment from an anchor tenant before a shopping center can be financed.

ANCILLARY not the most important. For example, *ancillary* income for a hotel may come from vending machines that dispense canned drinks.

ANNEXATION process by which an incorporated city expands its boundaries to include a specified area. The rules of annexation are established by state law and generally require a public ballot within the city and the area to be annexed. Other incorporated areas are generally protected from annexation by an adjacent city.

ANNUAL BASIS statistical technique whereby figures covering a period of less than a year are extended to cover a 12-month period. The procedure, called *annualizing,* must take seasonal variations (if any) into account to be accurate.

ANNUAL DEBT SERVICE required annual principal and interest payments for a loan. In corporate finance, the cash required in a year for payments of interest and current maturities of principal on outstanding debt.

ANNUAL EARNINGS amount of profit realized in one year. Taxable income and the annual income indicated by financial statements may be significantly different. Schedule M is used for corporate tax returns to reconcile the differences.

ANNUAL GIFT TAX EXCLUSION annual amount of up to $12,000 in 2006 per donee per year that a donor may exclude from the gift tax. The amount allowed will be increased with inflation.

ANNUALIZED RATE extrapolation of an occurrence lasting a limited time period to the amount or rate that would be generated in a year. For example, an interest rate of 2½% per quarter would be annualized to 10%, slightly more with compounding. Sales of ice cream in July should be annualized by applying a seasonal adjustment that considers the fact that ice cream sales are higher in July than in a typical month.

ANNUAL MEETING once-a-year meeting when the managers of a company report to stockholders on the year's results and the board of directors stands for election for the next year. The chief executive officer usually comments on the outlook for the coming year and, with other senior officers, answers questions from shareholders.

ANNUAL MORTGAGE CONSTANT amount of ANNUAL DEBT SERVICE compared to the principal; also expressed as a dollar amount. The formula is:

$$\text{Mortgage constant} = \frac{\text{annual debt service}}{\text{mortgage principal}}$$

ANNUAL PERCENTAGE RATE (APR) cost of credit that consumers pay, expressed as a simple annual percentage. According to the federal Truth in Lending Act, every consumer loan agreement must disclose the APR in large bold type. The APR is the annual effective interest rate. *See also* CONSUMER CREDIT PROTECTION ACT OF 1968.

ANNUAL RENEWABLE TERM INSURANCE *see* TERM LIFE INSURANCE.

ANNUAL REPORT formal financial statement issued yearly. The annual report of publicly owned corporations must comply with reporting requirements of the Securities and Exchange Commission, which include BALANCE SHEET, INCOME STATEMENT, and cash-flow reports audited by an independent certified public accountant.

ANNUAL WAGE fixed salary paid out to an employee over the course of a year.

ANNUITANT one who receives the benefits of an annuity.

ANNUITIZE begin a series of payments from the capital that has built up in an ANNUITY. The payments may be a fixed amount, or for a fixed period of time, or for the lifetimes of one or two ANNUITANTS, thus guaranteeing income payments that cannot be outlived.

ANNUITY contract sold by commercial insurance companies that pays a monthly (or quarterly, semiannual, or annual) income benefit for the life of a person (the ANNUITANT), for the lives of two or more persons, or for a specified period of time.

ANNUITY DUE *see* ORDINARY ANNUITY.

ANNUITY FACTOR mathematical figure showing the present value of an income stream that generates one dollar of income each period for a specified number of periods.

ANNUITY IN ADVANCE series of equal or nearly equal payments, each payable at the beginning of the period. For example, a landlord leases property for five years. The rent, payable at the beginning of each period, constitutes an *annuity in advance*. *See also* ORDINARY ANNUITY.

ANNUITY IN ARREARS *see* ORDINARY ANNUITY.

ANNUITY INCOME *see* ANNUITY.

ANSWER defendant's principal PLEADING in response to the plaintiff's complaint. It must contain a denial of all the ALLEGATIONS the defendant wishes to dispute, as well as any affirmative defenses by the defendant and any counterclaim against the plaintiff.

ANTICIPATED HOLDING PERIOD time during which an investment is expected to be held. In the prospectus for a real estate limited partnership, a sponsor will typically say that the anticipated holding period for a particular property is five to seven years.

ANTICIPATORY BREACH breaking a contract before the actual time of required performance. It occurs when one person repudiates his contractual obligation before it is due, by indicating that he will not or cannot perform his contractual duties.

ANTITRUST ACTS federal statutes that regulate trade in order to maintain competition and prevent monopolies. Many common business practices are governed by these statutes. The Sherman Anti-Trust Act of 1890 made price-fixing (the setting of prices in cooperation with competitors) illegal. The Clayton Anti-Trust Act of 1914 outlawed price discrimination (charging different prices to different buyers), as did the Robinson-Patman Act of 1936. Under these Acts, advertising and promotional ALLOWANCES are permitted only if they are offered to all dealers on equal terms.

ANTIVIRUS SOFTWARE software that monitors a computer for VIRUSES by looking for irregularities in a computer system and then comparing its findings to a database of virus information. It is important to update virus *definitions* or *signatures* regularly and upgrade the software periodically to protect against newly created viruses.

AOL *see* AMERICA ONLINE.

APARTMENT dwelling unit within a multifamily structure, generally provided as rental housing.

APARTMENT BUILDING structure with individual apartment units but a common entrance and hallway. An apartment building may have stores in it, for example, on the ground floor. Generally, when 80% or more of the revenue is received from residential rental units, the entire building may be depreciated as residential property over 27½ years rather than 39 years as for commercial property.

APL (*A Programming Language*) interactive computer programming language that is well suited for handling complex operations on arrays. APL uses several Greek letters and some other special symbols and thus requires a specially designed computer terminal.

APPARENT AUTHORITY doctrine that a PRINCIPAL is responsible for the acts of his AGENT where the principal by his words or conduct suggests to a third person that the agent may act in the principal's behalf, and where the third person believes in the authority of the agent.

APPEAL BOND guarantee of payment of the original judgment of a court. When a judgment is appealed, a bond is usually required to guarantee that if the appeal is unsuccessful, funds would be available to pay the original judgment as well as costs of the appeal. This serves to discourage an individual from appealing merely to stall for time or for frivolous reasons.

APPELLANT *see* PETITIONER.

APPELLATE COURT (APPEALS TRIAL COURT) court having authority to review the law applied by a lower court in the same case. In most instances, the trial court first decides a lawsuit, with review of its decision then available in an *appellate court*. Examples of appellate courts are the U.S. Court of Appeals and U.S. Supreme Court.

APPELLEE *see* DEFENDANT.

APPLET a small application or utility that performs one specific task; usually designed to run within a larger program. The Accessories in WINDOWS are *applets*; applets in Microsoft OFFICE include Draw, Graph, and Equation Editor.

APPLICATION (APP) an executable program that performs a specialized function other than system maintenance (which is performed by *utilities*). Commonly used *applications* include WORD PROCESSORS, SPREADSHEETS, DATABASES, communications software, and games.

APPLICATION OF FUNDS uses of the funds section of the statement of changes in financial position. Using the WORKING CAPITAL concept of funds, the four applications are: (1) net loss; (2) increase in noncurrent assets, such as the purchase of land for cash; (3) decrease in noncurrent liabilities such as long-term debt payments; and (4) decrease in stockholders' equity as in the case of the purchase of *treasury stock*. If the CASH concept of funds flow is used, the two additional applications would be: (5) increase in current assets other than cash; and (6) decrease in current liabilities.

APPLICATION SERVICE PROVIDERS (ASPs) companies that replace standalone software, such as e-mail programs and travel reservation systems, with Web-based services that can be billed on a periodic basis.

APPLICATIONS PROGRAMMER person who writes programs that use the computer as a tool to solve particular applied problems. *See also* SYSTEMS PROGRAMMER.

APPLIED ECONOMICS use of principles and results of theoretical economic study in the real world, particularly in the formulation of governmental economic policy. *See also* KEYNESIAN ECONOMICS.

APPLIED OVERHEAD amount of OVERHEAD expenses that are charged in a COST ACCOUNTING system to a production job or a department.

APPLIED RESEARCH research efforts devoted to the development of practical applications from pure research. *Applied research* in the field of electronics developed the microcomputer RAM chip for use in electronic memory storage.

APPOINTMENT, POWERS OF *see* POWERS OF APPOINTMENT.

APPORTION, APPORTIONMENT
1. PRORATING of property expenses, such as taxes and insurance, between buyer and seller.
2. partitioning of property into individual parcels by tenants in common.
3. **Tax (federal):** the IRS can reallocate or reapportion items of income or expense between related taxpayers if the allocation made by the taxpayers was for the purpose of avoiding tax or inaccurately reflects taxable income.
4. **Tax (state):** many states require multistate taxpayers to compute the income taxable to that state by one of two methods:
   (a) direct allocation—income and expense items for a particular state must be specifically reported.
   (b) apportionment—federal income is apportioned between states using any or all of the following factors:
      (i) sales revenue
      (ii) payroll expense
      (iii) property basis

APPRAISAL professional opinion or estimate of the value of a property. For example, a property owner may have an *appraisal* made of a specific property to determine a reasonable offering price in a sale; to determine the value of the property at the time of the gift or death for estate or gift tax purposes; to allocate the purchase price to the land and improvements; or to determine the amount of HAZARD INSURANCE to carry.

APPRAISAL FOUNDATION an organization that came into existence in 1989 in an effort to encourage uniform requirements for APPRAISAL qualifications and reporting standards. Publishes the UNIFORM STANDARDS OF PROFESSIONAL APPRAISAL PRACTICE (USPAP).

APPRAISAL REPORT describes the findings of an appraisal engagement. Reports may be presented in the following formats: restricted, summary, self-contained; *see* UNIFORM STANDARDS OF PROFESSIONAL APPRAISAL PRACTICE.

APPRAISAL RIGHTS statutory remedy available in many states to minority stockholders who object to an extraordinary action taken by the corporation (such as a MERGER). This remedy requires the corporation to repurchase the stock of dissenting stockholders at a price equivalent to its value immediately before the extraordinary corporate action.

APPRAISE to estimate the value of property.

APPRAISER person qualified to estimate the value of real property. The American Society of Appraisers in Washington, D.C. is a leading professional organization for business appraisers and other disciplines; the Appraisal Institute in Chicago is a leading organization for real estate appraisers. *See also* CERTIFIED GENERAL APPRAISER, CERTIFIED RESIDENTIAL APPRAISER, LICENSED APPRAISER.

APPRECIATE
1. increase in value.
2. to understand the significance of something.

APPRECIATED PROPERTY REAL, PERSONAL, or INTANGIBLE ASSETS that have a FAIR MARKET VALUE greater than their original cost, ADJUSTED TAX BASIS, or BOOK VALUE.

APPRECIATION
In general: increase in value over time.
Taxes: excess of the fair market value of property over the taxpayer's cost or basis in such property.

APPRENTICE a person who is learning a skill or trade from more experienced craftsmen while at work.

APPROPRIATE
1. to set apart for, or assign to, a particular purpose or use.
2. to wrongfully use or take the property of another.

APPROPRIATED EXPENDITURE in a BUDGET, amount set aside for a specific acquisition or purpose.

APPROPRIATION money set aside for a specific purpose. Also, in real estate, the setting aside of land for a public use.

APPROVED LIST list of investments that a mutual fund or other financial institution is authorized to make. The approved list may be statutory where a fiduciary responsibility exists. *See also* LEGAL LIST.

APPURTENANT attached to something else. In property law, the term refers to the attachment of a restriction, such as an EASEMENT or COVENANT, to a piece of land, which benefits or restricts the owner of such land in his use and enjoyment.

APR *see* ANNUAL PERCENTAGE RATE.

A PRIORI STATEMENT
  1. conclusion or judgment that is not necessarily true, that is neither proved by nor capable of being disproved by experience, and that is known to be true by a process of reasoning independent of all factual evidence.
  2. assertion introduced presumptively, without analysis or investigation.

APTITUDE intellectual ability of an individual to learn material sufficiently so that he can properly perform the business task required on the job. Some individuals have a natural talent and tendency for specific business areas. An example is a trial lawyer with an intellectual and quick mind for question asking and logic.

ARBITER person (other than a judicial officer) appointed by a court to decide a controversy according to the law. Unlike an ARBITRATOR, the arbiter needs the court's confirmation of his decision for it to be final.

ARBITRAGE financial transaction involving the simultaneous purchase in one market and sale in a different market with a profitable price or yield differential. True *arbitrage* positions are completely HEDGED—that is, the performance of both sides of the transaction is guaranteed at the time the position is assumed—and are thus without risk of loss. A person who engages in arbitrage is called an *arbitrageur* or *arb*.

ARBITRAGE BOND bond issued by a municipality in order to gain an interest rate advantage by refunding higher-rate bonds in advance of their call date. Proceeds from the lower-rate refunding issue are invested in higher-yielding treasuries until the first call date of the higher-rate issue being refunded.

ARBITRAGEUR person or firm engaged in ARBITRAGE. *Arbitrageurs* attempt to profit when the same security or commodity is trading at different prices in two or more markets. Those engaged in *risk arbitrage* attempt to profit from buying stocks of announced or potential TAKEOVER targets.

ARBITRATION submitting a controversy to an impartial person, the ARBITRATOR, chosen by the two parties in the dispute to determine an equitable settlement. Where the parties agree to be bound by the determination of the arbitrator, the process is called *binding arbitration*.

In labor law, arbitration has become an important means of settling disputes, and the majority of labor contracts provide for arbitration of disputes over the meaning of contract clauses. *See also* AMERICAN ARBITRATION ASSOCIATION.

ARBITRATOR impartial person chosen by the parties to solve a dispute between them. An arbitrator is empowered to make a final determination concerning the issue(s) in controversy and is bound only by his own DISCRETION. *See also* ARBITRATION.

ARCHIVE STORAGE area commonly used for storing old documents for safety and security.

AREA
1. two-dimensional space defined by boundaries, such as floor area, area of a lot, and market area.
2. scope or extent, as in area of expertise of a professional.

AREA CODE three-digit telephone number prefix corresponding to a geographical area that allows direct long-distance dialing.

ARGUMENT in a computer spreadsheet program, values that must be specified for a given function. For example, in Excel the PMT function calculates the periodic payment for a loan based on the interest rate charged, the number of payments desired, and the principal amount. The syntax of the function is PMT (rate, nper, pv), where rate, nper, and pv are *arguments*.

ARITHMETIC MEAN average obtained by dividing the sum of two or more items by the number of items.

ARM'S-LENGTH TRANSACTION transaction among parties, each of whom acts in his or her own best interest. Transactions between the following parties would, in most cases, not be considered arm's length: a husband and wife; a father and son; a corporation and one of its subsidiaries.

ARRAY collection of data that is given one name. An array is arranged so that each item in the array can be located when needed. An array is made up of a group of elements, which may be either numbers or character strings. Each element can be identified by a set of numbers known as subscripts, which indicate the row and column in which the element is located.

ARREARAGE
In general: amount of any past due obligation.
Investment: amount by which interest on bonds or dividends on CUMULATIVE PREFERRED STOCK is due and unpaid. In the case of cumulative preferred stock, common dividends cannot be paid by a company as long as preferred dividends are in arrears.

ARREARS, IN
  1. at the end of a term. Interest on mortgage loans is normally paid *in arrears*; that is, interest is paid at the end of a month or other period. Generally, rent and insurance premiums are paid in advance.
  2. in default; overdue in payment.

ARTICLES OF INCORPORATION document that creates a private corporation according to the general corporation laws of the state.

ARTIFICIAL INTELLIGENCE (AI) branch of computer science that deals with using computers to simulate human thinking. Artificial intelligence is concerned with building computer programs that can solve problems creatively, rather than simply working through the steps of a solution designed by the programmer.

ASA a senior professional designation offered by the American Society of Appraisers. The ASA designation is awarded upon meeting rigorous requirements that include extensive experience, education, and approved demonstration reports.

ASCII (*A*merican *S*tandard *C*ode for *I*nformation *I*nterchange) standard code for representing characters as binary numbers, used on most microcomputers, computer terminals, and printers. In addition to printable characters, the ASCII code includes control characters to indicate carriage return, backspace, and the like.

ASIACURRENCY a bank deposit in an Asian country that is denominated in the currency of another country. For example, a U.S. dollar deposited in a bank in Singapore is an Asiadollar.

AS IS commercial term denoting agreement that buyer shall accept delivery of goods in the condition in which they are found on inspection prior to purchase, even if they are damaged or defective.

ASKED selling price a property owner sets for the property. *See also* ASKING PRICE; BID AND ASKED.

ASKING PRICE
  1. price at which an investment is offered for sale; also called *ask price, asked price, ask,* or OFFERING PRICE.
  2. per-share price at which mutual fund shares are offered to the public, usually the NET ASSET VALUE per share plus a sales charge, if any. *See also* BID AND ASKED.

ASSAY test of a metal's purity to verify its content, such as to determine whether gold is 99.5% fine.

ASSEMBLAGE combining of two or more parcels of land. For example, suppose someone buys two ADJOINING properties of land for $10,000 each. The large unified tract is worth $25,000. The process is *assemblage*. *See also* PLOTTAGE VALUE.

ASSEMBLY LANGUAGE computer language in which each statement corresponds to one machine language statement. Assembly languages are more cumbersome to use than regular or high-level programming languages, but they are much easier to use than pure machine languages, which require that all instructions be written in binary code.

ASSEMBLY LINE production method requiring workers to perform a repetitive task on a product as it moves along on a conveyor belt or track. An assembly line has the advantages of part standardization and rationalization of work. *See also* ASSEMBLY PLANT.

ASSEMBLY PLANT physical plant where an assembly line is located, where production-line assembly work occurs. *See also* ASSEMBLY LINE.

ASSESS
1. to determine the value of something.
2. to fix the value of property on the basis of which property taxes will be calculated.

ASSESSED VALUATION dollar value assigned to property by a municipality for purposes of assessing taxes, which are based on the number of mills per dollar of assessed valuation. If a house is assessed at $100,000 and the tax rate is 50 mills, the tax is $5,000.

ASSESSMENT
1. amount of tax or special payment due to a municipality or association. *See also* ASSESSMENT RATIO.
2. proportionate share of a common expense.

ASSESSMENT OF DEFICIENCY amount of tax determined to be due after an appellate review within the Internal Revenue Service and a tax court adjudication (if requested).

ASSESSMENT RATIO ratio of assessed value to MARKET VALUE. For example, a county requires a 40% *assessment ratio* on all property to be taxed. Property with a $10,000 market value is therefore assessed at $4,000 (40% of $10,000), and the TAX RATE is applied to $4,000.

ASSESSMENT ROLL public record of the assessed value of property in a taxing jurisdiction. The assessment roll of a town, for instance, lists each individual tract of land within its taxing jurisdiction and shows the assessed value of each.

ASSESSOR official who determines property values, generally for real estate taxes.

ASSET anything owned that has value; any interest in REAL PROPERTY or PERSONAL PROPERTY that can be used for payment of debts. *See also* CAPITAL ASSETS; CURRENT ASSET; FIXED ASSET; QUICK ASSET.

ASSET ALLOCATION method of targeting investments to appropriate proportions of asset classes to achieve the highest investment return while minimizing risk. Proportions can vary according to market conditions. During a high-interest-rate period, a proportion of the investments will be targeted to interest-bearing securities, while during a period of low interest rates a greater proportion of the investments will be directed into equity investments. *See also* INVESTMENT PORTFOLIO.

ASSET-BACKED SECURITIES BONDS or NOTES backed by loan paper or ACCOUNTS RECEIVABLE originated by banks, credit card companies, or other providers of credit and often enhanced by a bank LETTER OF CREDIT or by insurance coverage provided by an institution other than the issuer.

ASSIGN sign a document transferring ownership from one party to another. Ownership can be in a number of forms, including tangible property, rights (usually arising out of contracts), or the right to transfer ownership at some later time. The party who assigns is the ASSIGNOR and the party who receives the transfer of title—the assignment—is the ASSIGNEE.

ASSIGNED RISK in automobile insurance, a class of persons to whom insurance companies will not issue policies voluntarily, usually because their record of prior accidents has made them a high risk, and who therefore are assigned by state law to insurance companies and must pay higher rates.

ASSIGNEE person to whom an agreement or contract is sold or transferred. *See also* ASSIGNOR.

ASSIGNMENT transfer of rights under an insurance policy to another person or business. For example, to secure a debt, it is not uncommon for the policyowner to transfer to the creditor his rights to borrow on the cash value. Life insurance policies are freely assignable to secure loans and notes (property and casualty insurance policies are not). Creditors such as banks often have printed assignment forms on hand at the time of making loans.

ASSIGNMENT OF INCOME taxpayer's direction that income earned by him be paid to another person so that it will be considered the other person's income for federal tax purposes.

ASSIGNMENT OF LEASE transfer of rights to use leased property. The ASSIGNEE acquires the same rights and privileges as the ASSIGNOR. The assignor remains liable unless released by the landlord.

ASSIGNOR party who assigns or transfers an agreement or contract to another. Suppose Davis has an option to buy certain land. She assigns her rights to Baker, so that Baker now has the same rights. Davis is the *assignor*. Baker is the ASSIGNEE. *See also* ASSIGN.

ASSIMILATION absorption of a new issue of stock by the investing public after all shares have been sold by the issue's underwriters. *See also* ABSORBED.

ASSOCIATION a body of persons united without a charter, but upon the methods and forms used by incorporated bodies, for the prosecution of some common enterprise.

ASSOCIATION OF CERTIFIED FRAUD EXAMINERS (ACFE) a 35,000-member global association dedicated to providing anti-fraud education and training in business. Awards the CFE designation.

ASSUMABLE LOAN a mortgage loan that allows a new home purchaser to undertake the obligation of the existing loan with no change in loan terms. Loans without DUE-ON-SALE CLAUSES, including most FHA and VA mortgages, are generally assumable.

ASSUMPTION FEE a charge levied by a lender on a buyer who assumes the existing loan on the subject property.

ASSUMPTION OF MORTGAGE taking upon oneself the obligations of a mortgagor toward a mortgagee, generally as part of the purchase price of a parcel of real estate. By assuming the mortgage rather than taking SUBJECT TO THE MORTGAGE, the purchaser becomes personally liable on the debt. The seller is not relieved of the obligation unless the lender agrees to do so in a NOVATION. Many lenders refuse to allow mortgage loans to be assumed unless they approve of the transaction; often they require points or increase the face rate of interest.

ASSUMPTION OF RISK technique of risk management (better known as *retention* or SELF-INSURANCE) under which an individual or business firm assumes expected losses that are not catastrophic, but protects against catastrophic losses through the purchase of insurance. For example, a business firm assumes the risk of absenteeism by its employees because of minor illness, but buys disability insurance to cover absences due to extended illness. Also refers to (1) instances where insureds place themselves in situations that they realize pose a danger, and (2) the acceptance of risks by an insurance company.

ASTERISK the * character. It is used as a reference mark for footnotes, to represent multiplication in mathematical expressions, and as a "wildcard" variable in filename and data searches.

ASYNCHRONOUS processes that are not synchronized. For example, most computer terminals use asynchronous data transmission, in which the terminal or the computer is free to transmit any number of characters at any time. (The bits constituting each character are transmitted at a fixed rate, but the pauses between characters can be of any duration.) *Synchronous* terminals, by contrast, transmit an entire screen full of information at once.

AT PAR at a price equal to the face, or nominal, value of a security. *See also* PAR VALUE.

AT RISK exposed to the danger of loss. Investors in a limited partnership can claim tax deductions only if they can prove that there is a chance they can lose money. Deductions will be disallowed if the limited partners are not exposed to economic risk—if, for example, the general partner guarantees to return all capital to limited partners even if the business venture should lose money. It generally applies to tax-sheltered investments, except real estate financed by qualified third-party debt.

AT-RISK RULES tax laws that limit the amount of tax losses an investor (particularly a LIMITED PARTNER) can claim from certain industries, including oil and gas, movie production, farming, and real estate. This means that losses will be deductible only to the extent of money the equity investor stands to lose.

AT SIGN the character @, which stands for the word *at*. Once used in pricing (e.g., three items @ $1 each), it is now more common in E-MAIL ADDRESSES, which usually have the format *jdoe@isp.com*.

ATTACHMENT
Computers: a binary file sent with an E-MAIL message.
Insurance: addition to a basic insurance policy to further explain coverages, add or exclude perils and locations covered, and add or delete positions covered. For example, an *attachment* to the STANDARD FIRE POLICY might add coverage for vandalism and malicious mischief. This form has largely been replaced by an ENDORSEMENT or *rider*.

ATTAINED AGE insured's age at a particular point in time. For example, many term life insurance policies allow an insured to convert to permanent insurance without a physical examination at the insured's then attained age. Upon conversion, the premium usually rises substantially to reflect the insured's increased age and diminished life expectancy. Since later in life rates become prohibitive, many insureds do not make an attained age conversion.

ATTENTION act of noticing an advertisement or commercial; a component of information or perceptual processing. Since consumers will usually take note of things relevant to their needs, attitudes, or beliefs, attention is selective. There have been cases in advertising history where attention was drawn to the advertising but, unhappily, not to the product being advertised.

ATTENTION LINE place on a label or envelope to write the name of the person who should receive the shipment.

ATTEST to affirm as true or bear witness to. One may attest by signing one's name as a witness to the execution of a document.

AT THE CLOSE order to buy or sell a security within the final 30 seconds of trading. Brokers never guarantee that such orders will be executed.

AT THE MARKET *see* MARKET ORDER.

AT THE OPENING customer's order to a broker to buy or sell a security at the price that applies when an exchange opens. If the order is not executed at that time, it is automatically canceled.

ATTITUDES mental position or emotional feelings about products, services, companies, ideas, issues, or institutions. Attitudes are shaped by

DEMOGRAPHICS, social values, and personality. In advertising, the desire is to generate favorable perceptions toward the thing being advertised, and to promote positive consumer attitudes.

ATTORNEY-AT-LAW person admitted to practice law in a jurisdiction, authorized to perform both civil and criminal legal functions for clients. These functions include drafting of legal documents, giving legal advice, and representing clients before courts, administrative agencies, boards, etc.

ATTORNEY-IN-FACT one who is authorized to act for another under a POWER OF ATTORNEY, which may be general or limited in scope. A person need not be an ATTORNEY-AT-LAW to be an *attorney-in-fact*.

ATTORNMENT tenant's formal agreement to be a tenant of a new landlord.

ATTRACTIVE NUISANCE property that is inherently dangerous and particularly enticing to children. For example, a swimming pool has a strong attraction to children and could lead to a liability judgment against the pool's owner. The owner must take all necessary steps to prevent accidents, such as building an adequate fence around the pool.

ATTRIBUTE a characteristic, such as a color, product type, or name, that can be used to group data with similarities. *See* ATTRIBUTE SAMPLING. Also, in WORD PROCESSING programs, a font characteristic such as size, color, bold, italic, all caps, superscript, and the like.

ATTRIBUTE SAMPLING statistical procedure used to study characteristics of a population. An *attribute* is a qualitative characteristic that a unit of a population either possesses or does not possess. For example, an account receivable is either past due or not; proper authorization for a payment either exists or does not. Thus the population under consideration is composed of two mutually exclusive classes—units possessing the attribute and units not possessing it. *See also* VARIABLES SAMPLING.

ATTRITION normal and uncontrollable reduction of a work force because of retirement, death, sickness, and relocation. It is one method of reducing the size of a work force without management taking any overt actions. The drawback to reduction by attrition is that reductions are often unpredictable and can leave gaps in an organization.

AUCTION or **AUCTION SALE** way of marketing property without a set price. BIDS are taken verbally on the spot, by phone, by mail, by telegram, etc., and the property is sold to the highest bidder. Auctioning real estate may require both an auctioneer's license and a real estate license. *See also* DUTCH AUCTION.

AUCTION EXCHANGES centralized securities trading markets where SECURITIES are bought and sold in an orderly manner through security brokers. Securities, including equities, bonds, options, closed-end funds, and futures, are bought and sold through bid and offer prices. The highest bid and the lowest offer have precedence in completing a purchase or sale, respectively. The first bid or offer has priority over later bids and offers. Of the nine major auction exchanges in the United States, the largest is the New York Stock Exchange, where more than 3,000 different securities are traded daily. *See also* DEALER EXCHANGES.

AUCTIONING posting an online request for goods and services, allowing suppliers to bid for the business.

AUDIENCE
In general:
1. group of people assembled in a studio, theater, or auditorium to witness a presentation or performance.
2. personal meeting of a formal nature, as an *audience* with the Pope.
Advertising: total number of people who may receive an advertising message delivered by a medium or a combination of media.
Communications: total number of readers, viewers, or listeners reached by the appropriate medium.

AUDIT inspection of the accounting records and procedures of a business, government unit, or other reporting entity by a trained accountant, for the purpose of verifying the accuracy and completeness of the records. It may be conducted by a member of the organization (internal audit) or by an outsider (independent audit). A CPA audit determines the overall validity of financial statements. A tax (IRS) audit determines whether the appropriate tax was paid. An internal audit generally determines whether the company's procedures are followed and whether embezzlement or other illegal activity occurred.

AUDIT LIMITED AUDIT having a narrow scope, such as being limited to certain accounts, a period shorter than one year, or where the AUDITOR'S access to records was restricted. A tax return audit may be limited to certain deductions.

AUDITING STANDARDS guidelines to which an AUDITOR adheres. *See also* GENERALLY ACCEPTED ACCOUNTING PRINCIPLES (GAAP).

AUDITOR
1. public officer charged by law with the duty of examining and verifying the expenditure of public funds.
2. accountant who performs a similar function for private parties.

AUDITOR'S CERTIFICATE, OPINION, OR REPORT *see* ACCOUNTANT'S OPINION.

AUDIT PROGRAM detailed listing of the steps to be taken by an AUDITOR, such as a CERTIFIED PUBLIC ACCOUNTANT (CPA), when analyzing transactions to determine the acceptability of financial statements. Major accounting firms may prepare an audit program for each client and require the person who does the work to sign or initial each step performed.

AUDIT TRAIL step-by-step record by which accounting data can be traced to their source. Questions as to the validity or accuracy of an accounting figure can be resolved by reviewing the sequence of events from which the figure resulted.

AUTARKY policy of establishing a self-sufficient and independent national economy.

AUTHENTICATION identification of a bond certificate as having been issued under a specific indenture, thus validating the bond. Also, legal verification of the genuineness of a document, as by the certification and seal of an authorized public official.

AUTHORITARIAN dictatorial and domineering. Authoritarian managers value employees' unquestioned obedience. *See also* THEORY X.

AUTHORITARIAN SOCIETY existence of governmental authority over numerous phases of human conduct while approval by the people for governmental action does not exist. An *authoritarian society* is distinguished from a totalitarian society in that the latter covers all phases of human conduct.

AUTHORITY
  1. power over others by sanctioned personnel within an organization. Managers have the *authority* to hire and fire personnel in an organization. With authority comes responsibility for one's actions.
  2. a government corporation or agency that administers a public enterprise.

AUTHORIZED SHARES or **AUTHORIZED STOCK** maximum number of shares a corporation may issue under its charter (as amended). A corporation need not issue all authorized shares.

AUTOGEN (AUTOMATED GENERATION OF FEDERAL TAX DEPOSIT COUPON) form mailed by the IRS to a taxpayer to accompany the employment tax deposit at any Federal Reserve Bank.

AUTOMATED TELLER MACHINE (ATM) computerized terminal providing cash dispensing and deposit acceptance banking transactions. ATM terminals have become very popular in many parts of the United States and provide individuals with 24-hour electronic access to their banking accounts without a bank teller. *See also* DEBIT CARD.

AUTOMATED VALUATION MODEL (AVM) computerized method for estimating the value of a property. Often used for mass APPRAISAL purposes, such as the reassessment of a city's property tax base.

AUTOMATIC CHECKOFF in labor economics, authorization for the employer to deduct union dues and other assessments from an employee's salary automatically and remit them to the labor union; also called *compulsory checkoff*. The deduction is a result of commitments or contractual agreements. An example is a COLLECTIVE BARGAINING agreement that requires union dues to be deducted each payroll period.

AUTOMATIC EXTENSION granting of more time for a taxpayer to file a tax return. By filing an IRS Form 4868 (Form 7004 for corporations) by the original due date of the tax return, a taxpayer can automatically extend his or her filing date by six months, although the tax payment (based on the taxpayer's best estimate) is still due on the original filing date.

AUTOMATIC (FISCAL) STABILIZERS built-in changes in government spending and taxation that tend to dampen the BUSINESS CYCLE. Nonindexed progressive income taxes increase tax collections during inflation, thus reducing demand; unemployment compensation increases during recession, thus increasing demand.

AUTOMATIC REINVESTMENT *see* DIVIDEND REINVESTMENT PLAN.

AUTOMATIC STAY the hold that a bankruptcy petition puts on all actions against a debtor, including sending demands for payment, filing a lawsuit, and repossession or foreclosure actions.

AUTOMATIC WITHDRAWAL mutual fund program that allows shareholders to receive a fixed payment each month or each quarter. The payment comes from dividends, including short-term capital gains, and income on securities held by the fund. Long-term capital gains are distributed annually when realized.

AUTOMATION operating a device by automatic (e.g., mechanical, electronic, or robotic) techniques.

AUTOMOBILE LIABILITY INSURANCE coverage in the event an insured is legally liable for bodily injury or property damage by automobile.

AUTOMOBILE POLICY, PERSONAL replacement for the earlier *Family Automobile Policy (FAP)* with these nine basis coverages:
1. *Coverage A*—Liability.
2. *Coverage B*—Medical Payments.
3. *Coverage C*—Uninsured Motorist Coverage.
4. *Coverage D*—Comprehensive.
5. *Coverage E*—Collision.
6. *Coverage F*—Car Rental Expense (optional).
7. *Coverage G*—Death, Dismemberment, and Loss of Sight (optional).
8. *Coverage H*—Total Disability (optional).
9. *Coverage I*—Loss of Earnings (optional).

AVERAGE
In general: ARITHMETIC MEAN.
Finance: appropriately weighted and adjusted arithmetic mean of selected securities designed to represent market behavior generally or important segments of the market. Among the most familiar averages are the Dow Jones industrial and transportation averages.

AVERAGE COST total of all costs for all units bought (or produced), divided by the number of units acquired (or produced).

AVERAGE (DAILY) BALANCE often used by banks to compute interest charges, for example, on credit card balances, when issuing a monthly statement. It is calculated by summing the amount owed on each day of the month and dividing by the number of days in the month.

AVERAGE DOWN strategy to lower the average price paid for a company's shares. Instead of buying the desired number of shares all at once, the investor would buy some shares initially and then buy additional shares as the price declined, thereby lowering the average cost for all shares bought.

AVERAGE FIXED COST total FIXED COSTS divided by the total output. This may be helpful in determining total costs and per unit costs.

AVERAGE TAX RATE total taxes paid divided by income. It indicates the amount of tax paid per dollar earned. *See also* MARGINAL TAX RATE.

AVOIDANCE OF TAX method by which a taxpayer legally reduces his tax liability, for example, by investing in a TAX SHELTER. *Contrast with* TAX EVASION.

AVOIDING PROBATE using certain techniques to eliminate assets from the legal PROBATE process. Jointly held property, living trusts, and lifetime giving are some ways to avoid probate. *Avoiding probate* does not avoid federal estate or gift tax.

AVOIRDUPOIS measure of weight customarily used for agricultural products and nonprecious metals. An avoirdupois ounce is lighter than a troy ounce; there are 16 ounces in an avoirdupois pound.

AVULSION sudden removal of land from one parcel to another, when a body of water, such as a river, abruptly changes its channel. *See also* ACCRETION.

AWARDS *see* PRIZES AND AWARDS.

AWAY FROM HOME sleeping arrangements are necessary for at least one night before returning home in order to deduct "ordinary and necessary" travel expenses on a business trip.

AXE TO GRIND a personal interest or hidden agenda. Someone with an *axe to grind* gets another person to work for no pay or uses others for his or her personal benefit.

B

BABY BELL one of the regional telephone companies spun off in 1981 by the Justice Department's breakup of American Telephone and Telegraph (derived from the AT&T nickname, "Ma Bell").

BABY BOND bond having a par value of less than $1,000, usually $500 or $25. Baby bonds bring the bond market within reach of small investors and, by the same token, open a source of funds to corporations that lack entree to the large institutional market.

BABY BOOMERS individuals who were born during the years immediately following World War II. This group of people represents a sizable portion of the consuming public, and their spending habits and lifestyle have a powerful influence on the economy. They represent a TARGET AUDIENCE for many advertisers.

BACHELOR OF BUSINESS ADMINISTRATION (BBA) degree from a four-year college where the graduate has concentrated in business subjects. The student takes mostly liberal arts courses for the first two years, an introduction to various business courses in the second and third years, and then specializes in a major subject such as accounting, finance, marketing, management, business statistics, or real estate in the fourth year.

BACKDATING dating any statement, document, check, or other instrument earlier than the date drawn.

BACK-END LOAD redemption charge an investor pays when withdrawing money from an investment. Most common in mutual funds and annuities, the *back-end load* is designed to discourage withdrawals. Back-end loads typically decline for each year that a shareholder remains in a fund. Also called *contingent deferred sales load, deferred sales charge, exit fee, redemption charge*.

BACKGROUND INVESTIGATION process of examining a job applicant's past to determine how well his or her experience and skills match those required for the position.

BACKGROUND PROCESSING investigation by management of an employee's job history and personal references; also called *background check*. A complete BACKGROUND INVESTIGATION is very time-consuming and expensive. However, background checks help to ensure that qualified personnel are placed in an organization.

BACK HAUL shipper's movement when returning over a route previously used.

BACKLIT illuminated from behind. The LIQUID CRYSTAL DISPLAYS of notebook computers are much easier to see with backlighting.

BACKLOG value of unfilled orders placed with a manufacturing company. Whether the firm's backlog is rising or falling is a clue to its future sales and earnings.

BACK OFFICE bank or brokerage house departments not directly involved in selling or trading. The back office sees to accounting records, compliance with government regulations, and communication between branches.

BACK PAY salaries and wages from a prior pay period.

BACKSLASH the character \ as compared to the forward slash / . *Backslashes* are used mainly in DOS, where they separate the names of subdirectories.

BACK-TO-BACK LETTER OF CREDIT (L/C) second LETTER OF CREDIT issued to a different beneficiary on the strength of a primary letter of credit. The second L/C uses the first L/C as collateral for the bank. Used in a three-party transaction.

BACK UP provide a second mechanism, record, or contract to protect against a possible failure of the primary mechanism. It is prudent to *back up* computer files regularly. *See* BACKUP.

BACKUP computer security protection method whereby several duplicate data files are stored on SECONDARY STORAGE DEVICES in the event a catastrophic event damages the computer's main file storage system. It is advisable to store backup data files in different locations to guard against loss in the event of a fire, theft, or other unplanned event.

BACKUP WITHHOLDING procedure used to ensure that federal income tax is paid on earnings even though the recipient cannot be identified by a Social Security number. Banks, brokers, and other entities report nonwage earnings paid out on IRS Form 1099. When the form cannot be filed because it lacks the taxpayer's Social Security number, 28% (in 2006) of the interest, dividends, or fees is withheld by the payer and remitted to the federal government.

BACKWARD-BENDING SUPPLY CURVE graph illustrating the thesis that as wages increase, people will substitute leisure for working. Eventually wages can get so high that if they increase, less labor will be offered in the market.

BACKWARD VERTICAL INTEGRATION process by which a firm takes ownership or increased control of its supply systems. It serves to streamline the organization, to provide better cost controls, and to eliminate the middleman. Because of efficiency and lowered costs of production it is possible for the firm to become more competitive in the marketplace.

BAD CHECK *see* NSF; RUBBER CHECK.

BAD DEBT debt that is not collectible and is therefore worthless to the CREDITOR. A debt may become uncollectible because the debtor is insolvent. A business bad debt may be written off under the SPECIFIC-CHARGE-OFF METHOD. A personal bad debt is normally not deductible and, if allowed deductible by the IRS, would be treated as a short-term capital loss, which is limited to $3,000 per year.

BAD-DEBT RECOVERY receipt of an amount, partially or in full, previously written off as uncollectible.

BAD-DEBT RESERVE offset to ACCOUNTS RECEIVABLE, with amounts that can be expected to be uncollectible. For example, if a business determines that, on the average, 3% of its accounts receivable becomes worthless during the taxable year, the business may deduct 3% and add this amount to its bad-debt reserve. The Tax Reform Act of 1986 repealed this reserve method for all businesses except certain financial and thrift institutions.

BAD TITLE a purported title that is legally insufficient to CONVEY property to the purchaser. A title that is not a MARKETABLE TITLE is not necessarily a *bad title*, but a title that is bad is not marketable and a purchaser ordinarily may not be compelled to accept it.

BAIL BOND monetary guarantee that an individual released from jail will be present in court at the appointed time. If the individual is not present in court at that time (has *jumped bail*), the monetary value of the bond is forfeited to the court.

BAILEE person who has temporary custody of the personal property of another. The degree of liability for such property varies. For example, if furniture is turned over to a moving company for transportation, the moving company is the *bailee* during the time the furniture is in its hands.

BAILEE'S CUSTOMERS INSURANCE coverage for legal liability resulting from damage or destruction of the BAILEE'S property while under the BAILEE'S temporary care, custody, and control. Includes property on or in transit to and from the bailee's premises.

BAILMENT delivery of PERSONAL PROPERTY to be held in TRUST. The term also refers to the relationship that arises where one person, the BAILOR, delivers property to another, the BAILEE, to hold, with control and POSSESSION of the property passing to the bailee.

BAILOR the party who has given custody of property to a BAILEE.

BAIT AND SWITCH ADVERTISING method of consumer deception that involves advertising in such an attractive way as to bring the customer in, followed by disparagement of the advertised product (which the seller in truth does not desire to sell) to cause the customer to switch to a more expensive product. This device is also frequently termed *disparagement*. The Federal Trade Commission and statutes in many states prohibit this sort of advertising.

BAIT AND SWITCH PRICING illegal practice based on a retailer luring customers into a store by advertising items at exceptionally low prices and then telling the customers that the items are out of stock or are of inferior quality. The retailer has no intention of selling the advertised items; instead the consumer is switched to higher price (margin) items.

BAKER'S DOZEN thirteen. Bakers, concerned over possible penalties for short weight in a product, provided an extra for good measure.

BALANCE
1. amount owed on a loan.
2. amount shown in an account; difference between debits and credits in an account. If credits exceed debits, it is called a CREDIT BALANCE.

BALANCED BUDGET *see* BUDGET; GRAMM-RUDMAN-HOLLINGS AMENDMENT. *Contrast with* DEFICIT; SURPLUS.

BALANCED MUTUAL FUND fund that buys common stock, preferred stock, and bonds in an effort to obtain the highest return consistent with a low-risk strategy.

BALANCE OF PAYMENTS system of recording all of a country's economic transactions with the rest of the world during a particular time period. The balance of payments is typically divided into three accounts—current, capital, and official reserves—and these can show a surplus or a deficit. There can be no surplus or deficit on the overall balance of payments. *See also* BALANCE OF TRADE.

BALANCE OF TRADE difference over a period of time between the value of a country's imports and exports of merchandise. When a country exports more than it imports, it is said to have a surplus, or *favorable* balance of trade; when imports predominate, the balance is in deficit and is called *unfavorable*. The balance of trade is made up of transactions in merchandise.

BALANCE SHEET financial statement that gives an accounting picture of property owned by a company and of claims against the property on a specific date. The left (debit) side of a balance sheet states assets; the right (credit) side shows liabilities and owners' equity. The two sides must be equal (balance). The balance sheet is like a snapshot of the position of an individual or business at one point in time.

BALANCE SHEET RESERVES an amount in pension plans expressed as a liability on the insurance company's BALANCE SHEET for benefits owed to policyowners. These reserves must be maintained according to strict actuarial formulas as they serve to guarantee that all benefit payments for which the insurance company has received premiums will be made.

BALLOON, BALLOON NOTE *see* BALLOON PAYMENT.

BALLOON PAYMENT final payment on a loan when that payment is greater than the preceding installment payments and pays the loan in full. For example, a debt requires interest-only payments annually for five years, at the end of which time the principal balance (a *balloon payment*) is due.

BALLOT method whereby members of a work group (BARGAINING UNIT) determine whether they shall be represented by a particular union (bargaining agent). In order for a bargaining agent to be certified, it must receive a majority of the ballots cast in the bargaining unit.

BALLPARK (slang) general range; often an expected or appropriate range of results. A *ballpark figure* is a rough estimate.

BAND-AID TREATMENT treatment of symptoms rather than causes; attempting to cover up a problem rather than get to the root of it.

BAND OF INVESTMENT a weighted average of debt and equity rates. *See* WEIGHTED AVERAGE COST OF CAPITAL (WACC).

Source of Purchase Capital	Percentage Contributed ×	Rate of Interest =	Weighted Rate
Mortgage	60%	10%	6%
Equity	40%	15%	6%
Band of Investment Rate			12%

BANK business entity formed to maintain savings and checking accounts, issue loans and credit, and deal in negotiable securities issued By government agencies and by corporations. Banks are strictly regulated and fall into the following three categories according to the legal limitations upon their activities: COMMERCIAL BANK; SAVINGS AND LOAN ASSOCIATION (S&L); SAVINGS BANK.

BANK DRAFT *same as* BILL OF EXCHANGE.

BANKER'S ACCEPTANCE time draft drawn on and accepted by a bank, the customary means of effecting payment for merchandise sold in import-export transactions, and a source of financing used extensively in international trade. *See also* LETTER OF CREDIT.

BANK FOR INTERNATIONAL SETTLEMENTS an international banking facility located in Switzerland that promotes cooperation among central banks and serves as the lender of last resort to some less-developed countries.

BANK HOLDING COMPANY company that owns or controls two or more banks or other bank holding companies. Such companies must register with the BOARD OF GOVERNORS OF THE FEDERAL RESERVE SYSTEM and hence are called *registered* bank holding companies.

BANK LINE bank's moral commitment, as opposed to its contractual commitment, to make loans to a particular borrower up to a specified maximum during a specified period, usually one year. Because a bank line—also called a *line of credit*—is not a legal commitment, it is not customary to charge a commitment fee.

BANKRUPTCY state of insolvency of an individual or an organization, that is, an inability to pay debts. There are two kinds of legal bankruptcy under U.S. law: Chapter 7 or involuntary, when one or more creditors petition to have a debtor judged insolvent by a court; and Chapter 11, or voluntary, when the debtor brings the petition. In both cases the objective is an orderly and equitable settlement of obligations. *See also* CHAPTER 7 OF THE 1978 BANKRUPTCY ACT; CHAPTER 11 OF THE 1978 BANKRUPTCY ACT.

BANKRUPTCY COURT specialized court established by Congress, pursuant to Article I of the Constitution, to address matters arising in or under a bankruptcy case.

BANKRUPTCY PETITION the document filed with the bankruptcy clerk's office to initiate the bankruptcy. It states which chapter the debtor is filing under, includes information about the debtor, its creditors, and lists assets, liabilities, and asset transfers in the last 12 months.

BANK TRUST DEPARTMENT part of a bank engaged in settling estates, administering trusts and guardianships, and performing agency services. As part of its personal trust and ESTATE PLANNING services, it manages investments for large accounts. Known for their conservative investment philosophy, such departments have custody over billions of dollars. The departments also act as trustees for corporate bonds, administer pension and profit-sharing plans, and function as TRANSFER AGENTS.

BANNER AD rectangular advertisement displayed on a Web page, often appearing at the top. Normally it contains a HYPERLINK to the advertiser's Web site.

BAR
1. in legal procedure, a barrier to relitigating an ISSUE. A *bar* operates to deny a party the right or privilege of rechallenging issues in subsequent litigation. The prevailing party in a lawsuit can use his favorable decision to bar retrial of the action.
2. the legal profession.

BAR CODE pattern of wide and narrow bars, printed on paper or a similar material. A computer reads the bar code by scanning it with a laser beam or with a wand that contains a light source and a photocell. Bar codes have been utilized to encode many kinds of data, including complete programs for some programmable calculators. The most familiar bar code is the Universal Product Code (see illustration) used with cash registers in supermarkets.

BARGAIN AND SALE DEED in the form of a contract that conveys property and transfers title to the buyer but lacks any guarantee from the seller as to the validity of the title. It is commonly used today to convey title to real estate and in effect transfers to the new owner whatever interest the grantor had. *See also* QUITCLAIM DEED; WARRANTY DEED.

BARGAIN BASEMENT retail location of a main store, often in the basement, where discounted merchandise is sold. The original purpose was to move unsold merchandise. The term has been adopted by other retailers that are exclusively bargain basement.

BARGAIN HUNTER
1. consumer very sensitive to price, who will buy the product or service from the cheapest source.
2. investor who buys undervalued stock hoping for price appreciation.

BARGAINING negotiating for a better price, terms, working conditions, etc. *See also* COLLECTIVE BARGAINING; PATTERN BARGAINING.

BARGAINING AGENT union or individual certified through a secret ballot process to be the exclusive representative of all the employees in a BARGAINING UNIT or group; also called *bargaining representative.* In order for a bargaining agent to be certified, it must receive a majority of the BALLOTS cast in the bargaining unit.

BARGAINING UNIT group of employees certified by the NATIONAL LABOR RELATIONS BOARD to be able to be included in a union or BARGAINING AGENT. Legal constraints and guidelines exist for the unit. Professional and nonprofessional groups cannot be included in the same unit, and a craft unit cannot be placed in a larger unit unless both groups agree to it.

BAROMETER selective compilation of economic and market data designed to represent larger trends. Consumer spending, housing starts, and interest rates are *barometers* used in economic forecasting. The Dow Jones Industrial Average and Standard & Poor's 500 Stock Index are prominent stock market barometers.

BARRIERS TO ENTRY conditions making entry into certain businesses extremely difficult. These include high funding requirements, high technological or trade learning curves, unknown or littleknown business practices, tightly controlled markets, stringent licensing procedures, the need for highly skilled or trained employees, long lead times, and specially designed facilities.

BARRISTER in England, a legal practitioner whose function is similar to that of a U.S. trial lawyer, although the barrister does not prepare the case from the start. His *solicitor* assembles the materials necessary for presentation to the court and settles cases out of court.

BARTER trade of goods and services without use of money. Income from a *barter* transaction is taxable income.

BASE PAY RATE employee's hourly wage; regular rate of pay upon which overtime and other wage supplements are computed.

BASE PERIOD particular time in the past used as the yardstick or starting point when measuring economic data. A base period is usually a year or an average of years; it can also be a month or other time period.

BASE RENT minimum rent due under a lease that has a percentage or participation requirement. For example, XYZ Corp. leases retail space in a mall. Under the lease XYZ must pay a base rent of $2,000 per month plus 5% of all sales revenue over $50,000 per month. *See also* PERCENTAGE LEASE.

BASE-YEAR ANALYSIS analysis of trends in economic data using parameters from a specified year. Expressing data such as the GROSS DOMESTIC PRODUCT in CONSTANT DOLLARS uses price levels of a specific base year so as to eliminate the effect of inflation upon the data.

BASIC (*B*eginner's *A*ll-Purpose *S*ymbolic *I*nstruction *C*ode) programming language used in early PCs.

BASIC INDUSTRY MULTIPLIER in economic base analysis, the ratio of total population in a local area to employment in basic industry. *Basic industry* is considered to be any concern that attracts income from outside the local area. The jobs added in basic industry may also contribute to the need for local service jobs (telephone operator, nurse, supermarket clerk, etc.); and, if the workers have families, additional new people may be brought to the area.

BASIS amount usually representing the taxpayer's cost in acquiring an asset. It is used for a variety of tax purposes including computation of gain or loss on the sale or exchange of the asset and depreciation with respect to the asset. *See also* ADJUSTED BASIS; CARRYOVER; RECOVERY OF BASIS; STEPPED-UP BASIS.

BASIS POINT smallest measure used in quoting yields on mortgages, bonds, and notes. One basis point is 0.01% of yield. Thus a yield that changed from 10.67% to 11.57% moved up by 90 *basis points*.

BATCH PROCESSING procedure whereby a user gives a computer a batch of information, referred to as a *job*—for example, a program and its input data on punched cards—and waits for it to be processed as a whole. Batch processing contrasts with *interactive* processing, in which the user communicates with the computer by means of a terminal while the program is running.

BAUD measurement of the speed of a modem, specifically the number of times per second a communications channel changes the carrier signal it sends on the phone line. A 56,000-baud (56K) modem changes the signal 56,000 times a second. *Baud* is often confused with bits per second (BPS); technically, they are different measurements.

BAYESIAN APPROACH TO DECISION MAKING methodology that incorporates new information or data into the decision process. When making a decision for which insufficient empirical estimates are available, certain assumptions are stated. As further information becomes available, the original assumptions are refined and/or corrected.

BBS *b*ulletin *b*oard *s*ervice, offered by on-line computer networks, allowing users to check notices on an electronic bulletin board in various areas of interest.

BEAR person who thinks a market will fall. Bears may sell a stock short or buy a PUT OPTION to take advantage of the anticipated drop. *Contrast with* BULL.

BEARER the person in possession of an instrument, document of title, or security payable to bearer or endorsed in blank. A note payable to "bearer" is payable to any person who successively holds the note BONA FIDE, not by virtue of any assignment of promise, but by an original and direct promise moving from the maker to the "bearer."

BEARER BOND, BEARER FORM, or **BEARER PAPER** security not registered on the books of the issuing corporation and thus payable to the person possessing it. A *bearer bond* has coupons attached, which the bondholder sends in or presents on the interest date for payment, hence the alternative name *coupon bonds*.

BEAR HUG in corporate takeovers, an offer by a suitor at a price well in excess of a target's current market value. If management resists, it risks violating its fiduciary obligation to act in the shareholders' best interest.

BEAR MARKET prolonged period of falling prices. A bear market in stocks is usually brought on by the anticipation of declining economic activity, and a bear market in bonds is caused by rising interest rates. *Contrast with* BULL MARKET.

BEAR RAID attempt by investors to manipulate the price of a stock downward by selling large numbers of shares short. Bear raids are illegal under Securities and Exchange Commission rules. *See* SECURITIES AND EXCHANGE COMMISSION (SEC).

BEDROOM COMMUNITY residential community in the suburbs, often near an employment center, but itself providing few employment opportunities.

BEFORE-AND-AFTER RULE in an EMINENT DOMAIN award, practice followed by many jurisdictions of appraising the property value both before and after the taking, considering enhancement or injury to the property that was the result of CONDEMNATION.

BEFORE-TAX CASH FLOW CASH FLOW prior to deducting income tax payments or adding income tax benefits.

BEHAVIOR MODIFICATION
1. employment of positive or negative reinforcement to alter the actions of an individual or group.
2. change in personality or attitude based on new information and experiences. For example, a salesperson may change the approach of dealing with a customer once the customer's likes and dislikes are known. A change in behavior often occurs with maturity and greater understanding about one's self and others.

BELLS AND WHISTLES innovative and flashy, but often unnecessary and confusing, features of a product such as computer hardware or software. Originally referred to the "toy boxes" on theater organs of the silent-movie era.

BELLWETHER security seen as an indicator of a market's direction. In stocks, IBM has long been considered a *bellwether* because so much of its stock is owned by institutional investors who have much control over supply and demand on the stock market. In bonds, the 30-year U.S. Treasury Bond is considered the bellwether, denoting the direction in which all other bonds are likely to move.

BELOW PAR at a price below the face, or nominal, value of a security, especially a bond. Generally, the difference between the price paid and the amount received upon sale or maturity is taxed as a capital gain.

BELOW-THE-LINE DEDUCTION *see* ITEMIZED DEDUCTION.

BENCHMARK
1. a study to compare actual performance to a standard of typical competence.
2. standard unit for the basis of comparison; universal unit that is identified with sufficient detail so that other similar classifications can be compared as being above, below, or comparable to the benchmark standard. For example, the 3-month federal Treasury Bill rate is a *benchmark* for all U.S. interest rates.

BENEFICIAL INTEREST EQUITABLE interest in a trust held by the BENEFICIARY of the trust, as distinguished from the interest of the TRUSTEE who holds legal title. Any person who under the terms of a trust instrument has the right to the income or principal of the trust fund has a *beneficial interest* in the trust.

BENEFICIAL OWNER person who enjoys the benefits of ownership, even though the title is in another name. When shares of a mutual fund are held by a custodian bank or when securities are held by a broker in STREET NAME, the real owner is the *beneficial owner*, even though, for safety or convenience, the bank or broker holds title.

BENEFICIARY the person who receives or is to receive the benefits resulting from certain acts. In a tax context, a person entitled to the benefits from trust property or from an insurance policy.

BENEFICIARY, CHANGE OF *see* CHANGE OF BENEFICIARY PROVISION.

BENEFIT
1. something that contributes to an organization, such as enhanced profitability, better efficiency, or reduced risk. An example is the technological introduction of a new machine that will enhance the quality and quantity of the production process.
2. payment made by an insurance company to an individual due to the occurrence of an event, such as death or sickness.
3. any fringe benefit, such as subsidized lunches, day care, and health club. *See also* FRINGE BENEFIT.
4. corporation-sponsored performance to raise funds for a needy cause.

BENEFIT-BASED PENSION PLAN corporate-guaranteed payment of insured BENEFITS if covered plans terminate without having sufficient assets to pay such benefits.

BENEFIT PRINCIPLE proposition that those who benefit from government expenditures, which are financed by taxes, also should pay the taxes that finance them.

BEQUEATH make a BEQUEST; transfer PERSONAL PROPERTY by WILL.

BEQUEST gift of PERSONAL PROPERTY by WILL. REAL PROPERTY is usually transferred by a devise. The term *disposition* encompasses both a bequest of personalty and a devise of realty.

BEST EFFORT arrangement whereby investment bankers, acting as agents, agree to do their best to sell an issue to the public. Instead of buying the securities outright, these agents have an option to buy and an authority to sell the securities.

BEST PRACTICES successful standard operating procedures for a given business type. Consultants observe and evaluate various firms and gather information on what works. They then offer their conclusions on the *best practices* for the given industry to another client.

BEST'S RATING rating of financial soundness given to insurance companies by Best's Rating Service. The top rating is A+. A Best's rating is important to buyers of insurance or annuities because it informs them whether a company is financially sound. Best's ratings are also important to investors in insurance stocks.

BETA COEFFICIENT measure of a stock's relative volatility. The beta is the covariance of a stock in relation to the rest of the stock market. The STANDARD & POOR'S INDEX has a *beta coefficient* of 1. Any stock with a higher beta is more volatile than the market, and any with a lower beta can be expected to rise and fall to a lesser extent than the market overall.

BETTERMENT improvement to real estate.

BIANNUAL occurring twice a year; same as SEMIANNUAL. *Contrast with* BIENNIAL—occurring every two years.

BID in negotiations or at an auction, the amount a prospective purchaser is willing to pay. *Contrast with* ASKED or OFFERED.

BID AND ASKED *bid* is the highest price a prospective buyer is prepared to pay at a particular time; *asked* is the lowest price acceptable to a prospective seller of the same item. Together, the two prices constitute a QUOTATION; the difference between the two prices is the *spread*.

BIENNIAL occurring every two years. *Contrast with* BIANNUAL—occurring twice a year.

BIG BLUE nickname for International Business Machines Corporation. The probable origin of the term was the original "blue suit" dress code for employees, but now IBM's corporate color is blue, as seen in its logo.

BIG BOARD popular term for the NEW YORK STOCK EXCHANGE (NYSE).

BIG BUSINESS large corporations in the United States having assets totaling billions of dollars. Today big business in the United States is experiencing intense international competition.

BIG FOUR largest U.S. accounting firms. They do the auditing and much of the tax work for most major corporations, signing the AUDITOR'S CERTIFICATE that appears in every annual report. In 2006 the four, in alphabetical order, were Deloitte & Touche, Ernst & Young, KPMG International, and PricewaterhouseCoopers.

BIGGER FOOL THEORY *see* GREATER FOOL THEORY.

BIG STEEL large U.S. steel producers best exemplified by the USX Corporation (formerly U.S. Steel Corporation). U.S. steel producers are experiencing overwhelming international competition, particularly from the Far East.

BIG THREE AUTOMAKERS General Motors, Ford, and Daimler-Chrysler. At one time these three accounted for more than 90% of cars sold in the United States. Over the past two decades, all have been losing market share, especially to Honda, Toyota, and Nissan.

BIG-TICKET ITEMS retail items of substantial size and price that are often purchased on credit by customers. Examples are appliances and automobiles.

BILATERAL CONTRACT a contract that incorporates a promise by both parties to do, or not to do, something. *See also* UNILATERAL CONTRACT.

BILATERAL MISTAKE error on the part of both parties regarding the same matter. For example, two people sign a contract under a certain understanding, while the contract conveys a different meaning than they expected.

BILL
1. order drawn by one person on another to pay a certain sum of money.
2. in commercial law, an account for goods sold, services rendered, and work done. *See also* COMMERCIAL LAW.
3. in the law of NEGOTIABLE INSTRUMENTS, any form of paper money.
4. in legislation, a draft of a proposed statute submitted to the legislature for enactment.
5. in equity pleadings, the name of the pleading by which the complainant sets out a cause of action.

BILLING CYCLE interval between periodic billings for goods sold or services rendered, normally one month, or a system whereby bills or statements are mailed at periodic intervals in the course of a month in order to distribute the clerical workload evenly (*see* CYCLE BILLING).

BILL OF EXCHANGE papers that require the addressee to pay the bearer or another person on demand.

BILL OF LADING in commercial law, the receipt a COMMON CARRIER gives to a shipper for goods given to the carrier for transportation. The bill evidences the contract between the shipper and the carrier, and can also serve as a document of TITLE, creating in the person possessing the bill ownership of the goods shipped. *See also* ORDER BILL OF LADING; STRAIGHT BILL OF LADING.

BILL OF SALE a document transferring personal property.

BINARY NUMBERS (base-2) numbers written in a positional number system that uses only two digits—0 and 1. Each digit of a binary number represents a power of 2. The rightmost digit is the 1s digit, the next digit to the left is the 2s digit, and so on. The following table shows numbers written in decimal and binary form.

Decimal	Binary
1	1
2	10
3	11
4	100
5	101
6	110
7	111
8	1000
9	1001
10	1010

BINDER a written memorandum of the important terms of a preliminary contract that gives temporary protection to the contract while further investigation is performed. Often used for insurance purposes (when buying a car it is appropriate to call the agent and put an insurance *binder* on it, so the owner is insured before the policy is prepared) and for home purchases until a more formal document is prepared.

BINDING ARBITRATION *see* ARBITRATION.

BIT (*bi*nary digi*t*) digit in base-2 system. There are only two possible binary digits—0 and 1. *See also* BINARY NUMBERS.

BIWEEKLY LOAN a mortgage that requires principal and interest payments at two-week intervals. The payment is exactly half of what a monthly payment would be. Over a year's time, the 26 payments are equivalent to 13 monthly payments on a comparable monthlypayment mortgage. As a result, the loan will be amortized much faster than a loan with monthly payments.

BLACKBERRY electronic device made by Research in Motion (RIM) that adds wireless communication to standard PDA features.

B/L *see* BILL OF LADING.

BLACK BOX in computers, slang for CENTRAL PROCESSING UNIT; also any device that provides answers to complex problems without explaining the solution.

BLACK-BOX ACCOUNTING financial statements based on accounting methodologies so complex that numbers, though accurate and legal, obfuscate rather than clarify. Restatements of revenues, inventory, and earnings and the use of DERIVATIVES and off-the-books partnerships are examples.

BLACK FRIDAY sharp drop in a financial market. The original Black Friday was September 24, 1869, when a group of financiers tried to corner the gold market and precipitated a business panic followed by a depression. The panic of 1873 also began on Friday, and Black Friday has come to apply to any debacle affecting the financial markets.

BLACKLIST originally lists, prepared by merchants, which contained the names of those gone bankrupt. Today it also refers to people who, for any number of reasons, are unacceptable for employment in an organization. An individual can thus be *blacklisted*.

BLACK MARKET extralegal markets in which free-market exchange occurs in commodities and goods whose prices and/or supply are regulated or rationed by government. During World War II a *black market* existed for rationed goods in short supply. Another example is the market for drugs that cannot legally be sold, or sold without a prescription.

BLACK MOLD *see* STACHYBOTRYS CHARTARUM.

BLACK-SCHOLES OPTION PRICING MODEL model developed by Fischer Black and Myron Scholes to gauge whether options contracts are fairly valued. The model incorporates such factors as the volatility of a security's return, the level of interest rates, the relationship of the underlying stock's price to the EXERCISE PRICE of the option, and the time remaining until the option expires.

BLANKET FIDELITY BOND *see* FIDELITY BOND.

BLANKET INSURANCE single policy on the insured's property for: (1) two or more different kinds of property in the same location; (2) same kind of property in two or more locations; (3) two or more different kinds of property in two or more different locations. Blanket coverage is ideal for such businesses as chain stores, all of whose property is covered with no specific limit on each particular property regardless of its location (thereby enabling the business to shift merchandise from store to store).

BLANKET MEDICAL EXPENSE INSURANCE health insurance policy providing coverage for an insured's medical expenses except those that are specifically excluded. This may be the most advantageous medical expense policy for an insured because unless a specific medical expense is excluded it is automatically covered.

BLANKET MORTGAGE single mortgage that covers more than one parcel of real estate. Sometimes a developer subdivides a tract of land into lots and obtains a blanket mortgage on the whole tract. A RELEASE provision in the mortgage allows the developer to sell individual lots over time without RETIRING the entire mortgage.

BLEED to obtain an excessive amount of money or other things of value from a person, usually under a threat of grave harm. It is a form of extortion.

BLEEDING A PROJECT
1. in new construction, overstating expenses and fees so as to divert a larger than normal amount of the project costs to the developer's profit.
2. managing an existing piece of real estate so as to obtain the highest possible current income from it, to the extent that many normal operating expenses are foregone. Usually this results in rapid deterioration and loss of property value.

BLENDED RATE the time- and rate-weighted effective billing rate, interest rate, or tax rate.

BLENDED VALUE average value of tendered stock and residual stock in a self-tender offer.

BLIGHTED AREA section of a city in which a majority of the structures are dilapidated. Urban renewal tries to cure blighted areas of a city. Within these areas, houses that do not meet HOUSING CODES are rehabilitated or demolished and new buildings constructed.

BLIND COPY copy of a letter or e-mail sent to a person without indication on the original that a copy has been sent; symbolized by *bcc*.

The bcc: field of e-mails should be used for sending messages to a mailing list to avoid privacy issues arising from revealing e-mail addresses of recipients to other recipients.

BLIND POOL limited partnership that does not specify the properties the general partner plans to acquire. If, for example, an initial public offering is offered in the form of a *blind pool*, investors can evaluate the project only by looking at the promoter's track record.

BLIND TRUST trust where assets are not disclosed to their owner. This prevents the underlying asset owner, while in an official public capacity, from being charged with favoring companies in which he owns stock.

BLISTER PACKAGING method of packaging items in a clear plastic envelope or window that allows customers to view the contents prior to purchase.

BLOCK large quantity of stock or large dollar amount of bonds held or traded. As a general guide, 10,000 shares or more of stock and $200,000 or more worth of bonds would be described as a block.

BLOCKAGE DISCOUNT discount from fair market value for a decedent's block of inventory for purposes of determining the valuation of an estate.

BLOCKBUSTER
1. broadcast program that far exceeds expected or estimated RATINGS and thus brings in a much larger than expected AUDIENCE to advertisers whose commercials aired during the program.
2. feature movie whose box-office success has been extraordinary. When a *blockbuster* movie is planned for showing on television, the audience estimates are high and thus the estimated ratings are high.
See also BLOCKBUSTING.

BLOCKBUSTING racially discriminatory and illegal practice of coercing a party to sell a home to someone of a minority race or ethnic background, then using scare tactics to cause others in the neighborhood to sell at depressed prices.

BLOCK MOVE in data or word processing, the operation of moving a section of a file from one place to another within the file. Moving a word, sentence, paragraph, or several pages in a document from one place to another can be done through a block move command of a word processor. When the block is identified, it is often highlighted.

BLOCK SAMPLING judgment sample in which accounts or items are chosen in a sequential order. After the initial item in the block is chosen, the balance of the block is automatically selected. *See also* CLUSTER SAMPLING; SYSTEMATIC SAMPLING.

BLOG abbreviation for *Web log,* an online journal or newsletter that is frequently updated and intended for public consumption. Usually presented in reverse chronological order, blogs are published using software (such as that available from www.blogger.com) that can be used by writers with little or no technical background. Also used as a verb: Many companies encourage employees to *blog* about new products. Most *blogging* software includes a way for readers to submit comments on blog entries, which can provide useful feedback on a company's products. Many *bloggers* post links to other blogs they read and recommend; taken together, this rapidly expanding publication medium is often referred to as the *blogosphere.*

BLOOMBERG LP a major business and financial news broadcaster, offering various services including interactive TV, telephone news services, a personal finance magazine, books, and radio and television broadcasts.

BLOWOUT
Merchandising: retail items sold quickly at very low prices.
Securities: quick sale of all shares in a new offering of securities. Corporations like to sell securities in such environments, because they get a high price for their stock. Investors are likely to have a hard time getting the number of shares they want during a blowout.

BLUE-CHIP STOCK common stock or a nationally known company that has a long record of profit growth and dividend payment and a reputation for quality management, products, and services. Named for the color of the most valuable gambling tokens.

BLUE-COLLAR employee performing a type of work that often requires a work uniform, which may be blue in color, hence *blue-collar*. Blue-collar workers range from unskilled to skilled employees. They are not exempt from hour and wage laws and therefore must be paid overtime for working more than 40 hours per week.

BLUE LAWS state or local laws prohibiting business on a given day, usually Sunday. *Blue laws* have been abolished in many places so that people may freely choose activities on any day of the week.

BLUEPRINT
  1. photographic print where lines and solid shapes are developed in white on specially prepared blue paper, also called *blue(s)*. A blueprint of drawings or photographs to be included in a publication serves as a guide for positioning them in a DUMMY copy of the magazine or other publication. It also assists the printer when making plates for the completed work.
  2. plan of action.

BLUE SHIELD independent, nonprofit, membership insurance plan. Benefits cover expenses associated with medical and surgical procedures.

BLUE-SKY LAW state law regulating the sale of corporate securities through investment companies, enacted to prevent the sale of securities of fraudulent enterprises.

BLUETOOTH a technical industry standard for seamless low-power, short-range wireless communication of data and voice between electronic devices such as mobile phones, computers (including handhelds), PDAs, printers, and the like. The specification was designed by the Bluetooth Special Interest Group, a consortium of computer and telecommunications companies founded in 1998 by Ericsson, IBM, Intel, Nokia, and Toshiba.

BOARD OF DIRECTORS group elected by STOCKHOLDERS to set company policy and appoint the chief executives and operating officers. Directors meet several times a year and are paid for their services. They are considered INSIDERS.

BOARD OF EQUALIZATION government entity whose purpose is to assure uniform property tax assessments. A board of equalization at the local level may review tax ASSESSMENTS to be certain that the assessment for each parcel is fair. At the state level, the board will assure that each county is assessing property at the mandated proportion of market value.

BOARD OF GOVERNORS (OF THE FEDERAL RESERVE SYSTEM) seven-member managing body of the FEDERAL RESERVE SYSTEM; commonly called *Federal Reserve Board.* The board sets policy on issues relating to banking regulations as well as to the MONEY SUPPLY. Regulating the money supply is important for regulating inflation, interest rates, and economic growth.

BOARD OF REALTORS® local group of real estate licensees who are members of the state and national associations of REALTORS.

BOARDROOM
1. stockbroker's office where REGISTERED REPRESENTATIVES (that is, securities salespersons registered with the Securities and Exchange Commission) work and where the public is allowed to visit and obtain stock price quotations throughout the market day. Offices are equipped with electronic machines that provide information on trading in LISTED SECURITIES and OVER-THE-COUNTER markets, and that also provide business news.
2. room where a corporation's board of directors holds its meetings.

BODY LANGUAGE nonverbal and often unintended communication on the part of one individual to another. Nonverbal communication takes place by means of facial expressions, head movements, eye contact, hand gestures, body positions and acts, tones of voice, and so on. In general, body language expresses an individual's emotions, feelings, and attitudes.

BOILERPLATE
1. standardized or preprinted form for agreements.
2. standardized language, as on a printed form containing the terms of a lease or sales contract, often phrased to the advantage of the party

furnishing the form, with the expectation that the contract will be signed without being carefully examined.

BOILER ROOM or **BOILER SHOP** place devoted to high-pressure promotion by telephone of stocks, bonds, commodities, contracts, etc., which are of questionable value. Extensive FRAUD is usually involved, but successful prosecution may be difficult since operations often disband before detection and little tangible evidence is obtainable.

BOLSA Spanish term for *stock exchange*. There are Bolsas in Spain, Mexico, Chile, Argentina, and many other Spanish-speaking countries. In French, the term is BOURSE; in Italian, *Borsa*. All mean "purse."

BONA FIDE Latin for "in good faith," that is, without fraud or deceit, genuine.

BONA FIDE PURCHASER (BFP) one who pays a valuable consideration, has no notice of outstanding rights of others, and acts in GOOD FAITH concerning the purchase. In commercial law, the phrase HOLDER IN DUE COURSE signifies the same thing.

BOND obligation to pay. Most federal, municipal, and corporate bonds pay interest twice a year (semiannually). Interest on MUNICIPAL BONDS is generally nontaxable for federal income tax purposes and in the municipality of issue. Interest on federal government bonds is taxable for federal purposes but tax-free for state income tax purposes. CORPORATE BOND interest is generally fully taxable.

BOND BROKER broker who executes bond trades on the floor of an exchange; also, one who trades corporate, U.S. government, or municipal debt issues over the counter, mostly for large institutional accounts.

BOND DISCOUNT difference between a bond's current market price and its higher FACE VALUE or maturity value. Bonds may be issued at a DISCOUNT, or a discount may result from a general interest rate increase or increased risk of default. In either case, a buyer who acquires a bond at a discount realizes the discount as income as the bond matures, in addition to receiving periodic interest payments. The ZERO COUPON BOND offers an extreme example of a bond discount.

BONDED DEBT
1. that part of the entire indebtedness of a corporation or state that is represented by bonds it has issued.
2. debt contracted under the obligation of a bond.

BONDED GOODS goods brought into a country that are placed in a bonded warehouse until all duties are paid.

BOND PREMIUM amount the purchaser pays in buying a bond that exceeds the face or call value of the bond. The PREMIUM can be amortized each year by the bondholder, to reflect that the true interest rate is less than the coupon rate. AMORTIZATION is elective for taxable bonds and not allowed for tax-exempt bonds.

BOND RATING method of evaluating the possibility of default by a bond issuer. Standard & Poor's, Moody's Investors Service, and Fitch Investors Service analyze the financial strength of each bond's issuer, whether a corporation or a government body. Their ratings range from AAA (highly unlikely to default) to D (in default).

BOND YIELD *see* YIELD.

BONUS
1. compensation paid to an employee or employees for achieving a particular sales goal or organizational objective. This is above and beyond either a COMMISSION or a SALARY. A corporation achieving a 10% increase in profits may distribute part of the earnings as a bonus to its employees.
2. an unexpected benefit occurring as the result of making a particular action.

BOOK
1. in an underwriting of securities, (1) preliminary indications of interest on the part of prospective buyers of the issue—What is the *book* on XYZ Company? or (2) record of activity in the syndicate account—Who is managing the *book* on XYZ?
2. record maintained by a specialist of buy and sell orders in a given security. The term derives from the notebook that specialists traditionally used for this purpose.
3. as a verb, to book is to give accounting recognition to something. For example, they booked a profit on the transaction.
4. collectively, books are the journals, ledgers, and other accounting records of a business. *See also* BOOK VALUE.

BOOK DEPRECIATION same as DEPRECIATION (ACCOUNTING).

BOOK-ENTRY *see* BOOK-ENTRY SECURITIES.

BOOK-ENTRY SECURITIES securities that are not represented by a certificate. Purchases and sales of some municipal bonds, for instance, are merely recorded on customers' accounts; no certificates change hands.

BOOK INVENTORY stock in hand according to recorded figures. *See also* PHYSICAL INVENTORY.

BOOKKEEPER person who enters transactions into an ACCOUNTING SYSTEM. In general a *bookkeeper* does not have the advanced education of an ACCOUNTANT.

BOOKMARK
1. a marker within a file that allows a user to easily return to a given position.
2. a remembered address (URL) that allows a user to go directly to a given site on the WORLD WIDE WEB. This terminology is used by

NETSCAPE NAVIGATOR; Microsoft's INTERNET EXPLORER uses the term FAVORITES.

BOOK OF ACCOUNT *see* ACCOUNTING RECORDS.

BOOK PROFIT or **LOSS** *see* UNREALIZED PROFIT (LOSS).

BOOK-TO-BILL RATIO the ratio of orders booked for future delivery to orders being shipped immediately, and therefore billed. The *book-to-bill ratio* is released on a monthly basis for the semiconductor industry because it provides a very sensitive indicator of whether orders for chips are rising or falling and at what pace.

BOOK VALUE value of individual ASSETS, calculated as actual cost less allowances for any DEPRECIATION. Book value may be much more or less than current MARKET VALUE.

BOOMERANG EFFECT use of exported technology to manufacture products that compete with those produced by the original exporter.

BOONDOGGLE a makework project that is useless in function.

BOOT
Computers: to start up a computer. Boot (earlier *bootstrap*) derives from the idea that the computer has to "pull itself up by its bootstraps," that is, load into memory a small program that enables it to load larger programs. The operation of booting a computer that has been completely shut down is known as a *dead start*, or *cold boot*. A *warm start* or *warm boot* is a restarting operation in which some of the needed programs are already in memory.
Tax: unlike property included to balance the values of like properties exchanged under Section 1031 of the Internal Revenue Code.

BOOT DISK *see* STARTUP DISK.

BOOTSTRAP ACQUISITION any of several forms of buyout where a buyer finances an acquisition in part with the target corporation's excess cash or liquid assets.

BORROWED RESERVE funds borrowed by member banks from a FEDERAL RESERVE BANK for the purpose of maintaining the required reserve ratios.

BORROWING POWER OF SECURITIES amount of money that customers can invest in securities on MARGIN.

BOTTOM
In general: support level for market prices of any type. When prices fall below that level and appear to be continuing downward without check, we say that the *bottom dropped out*. When prices begin to trend upward again, we say they have *bottomed out*.
Economics: lowest point in an economic cycle, generally called a TROUGH.

Securities: lowest market price of a security or commodity during a day, a season, a year, a cycle; also, lowest level of prices for the market as a whole, as measured by any of the several indexes.

BOTTOM FISHER investor who is on the lookout for investments that have fallen to their BOTTOM prices before turning up. In extreme cases, bottom fishers invest in bankrupt or near-bankrupt firms.

BOTTOM LINE net profit or loss. It is often used as an expression when seeking the result without asking for the reasons, as in "What is the *bottom line*?"

BOTTOM-UP APPROACH TO INVESTING search for outstanding performance of individual stocks before considering the impact of economic trends. The companies may be identified from research reports, stock screens, or personal knowledge of the products and services. *Contrast with* TOP-DOWN APPROACH TO INVESTING.

BOULEWARISM *take-it-or-leave-it* offer made by management to LABOR in COLLECTIVE BARGAINING. Boulewarism, named for the General Electric vice president who pioneered it, required the take it-or-leave-it offer to be presented directly to union members, thereby circumventing the union. The federal court ruled Boulewarism to be an illegal violation of the WAGNER ACT (NATIONAL LABOR RELATIONS ACT of 1935).

BOUNCE return of a check by a bank because it is not payable, usually due to insufficient funds. In securities, the rejection and subsequent reclamation of a security because of *bad delivery*. Term also refers to a stock price's sudden decline and recovery; *see* DEAD-CAT BOUNCE. *Also* return of a piece of E-MAIL because it could not be delivered to the specified address.

BOUNCE MESSAGE a notification returned to sender indicating that an E-MAIL message could not be delivered. Usually the message is automatically generated by the Postmaster at the recipient's site, sometimes with an indication of what went wrong.

BOUNDARY *see* PROPERTY LINE.

BOURSE French term for *stock exchange*.

BOUTIQUE small, specialized shop that deals with a limited clientele and offers a limited product line. A *boutique* is the opposite of a department store, supermarket, or warehouse club that offers a wide array of products or services. Also, by extension, a small, specialized brokerage firm as contrasted to a *financial supermarket*.

BOY abbreviation for beginning of year.

BOYCOTT to refrain from commercial dealing with a firm by concerted effort. *See also* PRIMARY BOYCOTT; SECONDARY BOYCOTT.

BPS bits per second, a measure of the speed at which computer data is transferred.

BRACKET CREEP edging into higher tax BRACKETS as income rises with inflation. *Bracket creep* increases government revenue without tax increases.

BRAIN DRAIN loss of a nation's best-educated and most intelligent people to other nations.

BRAINSTORMING group session of executives from different business disciplines, where new ideas are expressed to solve a business situation or formulate corporate policy. No criticism of the ideas is allowed. However, the ideas may be modified or combined. The purpose of the session is to come up with originality in thinking based on gut feelings without inhibitions. The *brainstorming* concept was initially developed by Alex Osborn.

BRANCH OFFICE MANAGER person in charge of a branch of a securities brokerage firm or bank.

BRAND identifying mark, symbol, word(s), or combination of same that separate one company's product or services from another firm's. *Brand* is a comprehensive term that includes all BRAND NAMES and TRADEMARKS.

BRAND ASSOCIATION degree to which a particular BRAND is associated with the general product category. Often a consumer will ask for a product by the specific brand name rather than the general name— for example, a person wanting facial tissues may ask for Kleenex. When this happens, the consumer is making a *brand* association.

BRAND DEVELOPMENT measure of the infiltration of a product's sales, usually per thousand population. If 100 people in 1,000 buy a product, the product has a *brand development* of 10%.

BRAND DEVELOPMENT INDEX (BDI) percentage of a brand's sales in an area in relation to the population in that area as compared to the sales throughout the entire United States in relation to the total U.S. population. For example, if Brand X has 15% of its U.S. sales in Area A, in which 20% of the U.S. population lives, the BDI for Area A is 75.

BRAND EQUITY attractiveness and familiarity of a BRAND NAME in the general marketplace. *Brand equity* permits companies to charge premium prices for products and services, contributing to increased profit margins. *Brand equity* is therefore a valuable asset that companies invest huge amounts of money to develop.

BRAND EXTENSION addition of a new product to an already established line of products under the same BRAND NAME. Brand extension allows the new product the benefit of the older product's established reputation.

BRAND IMAGE qualities that consumers associate with a specific BRAND, expressed in terms of human behavior and desires, but that also relate to price, quality, and situational use of the brand. For example: A brand such as Mercedes-Benz will conjure up a strong public image because of its sensory and physical characteristics as well as its price. This image is not inherent in the brand name but is created through advertising.

BRANDING creating a perception in the mind of consumers of the image and quality provided by a company name.

BRAND LOYALTY degree to which a consumer will repeatedly purchase a BRAND. For advertisers to achieve their ultimate goal of *brand loyalty*, the consumer must perceive that the brand offers the right combination of quality and price. Many factors influence brand loyalty, such as consumer attitudes, family or peer pressure, and friendship with the salesperson. The degree of brand loyalty—that is, the brand's MARKET SHARE—is known as the *brand franchise*.

BRAND MANAGER marketing manager for a BRAND; also called *product manager*. This person makes most of the advertising decisions for that brand. Often in a company with many different brand-name products, each product will have a *brand manager*, who competes with the others as if the products were competitive. Each may use a different advertising agency, and each will have a separate advertising budget.

BRAND NAME that part of a BRAND, TRADEMARK, or service mark that can be spoken, as distinguished from an identifying symbol. A brand name may consist of a word, letter, or group of words or letters.

BRAND POTENTIAL INDEX (BPI) relationship between a brand's MARKET DEVELOPMENT INDEX and BRAND DEVELOPMENT INDEX (BDI) in a particular market area. The brand potential index is used to predict future sales and to aid in planning future advertising budget allocations.

BRAND SHARE amount of dollars spent by consumers on a particular brand as compared to the amount in dollars spent by consumers on all competitive brands in the same category, figured in terms of percentages; also called *market share, share of market*. Companies set marketing goals to achieve a specific *brand share*, and plan their strategies to meet those goals.

BRASS top management of an organization; originally term of military origin. It is generally used by those not in top management to indicate a broad area of responsibility without any fixed point of reference.

BRASS TACKS, GET DOWN TO break off preliminaries and proceed to the main business.

BREACH failure to perform some contracted-for or agreed-upon act or to comply with a legal duty owed to another or to society. *See also* BREACH OF CONTRACT; BREACH OF WARRANTY.

BREACH OF CONTRACT
1. wrongful nonperformance of any contractual duty of immediate performance.
2. failing to perform acts promised by hindering or preventing such performance or by repudiating the duty to perform.

BREACH OF WARRANTY infraction of an express or implied agreement as to the TITLE, quality, content, or condition of a thing sold.

BREADWINNER individual capable of furnishing support to others who depend on the income earned. The *breadwinner* is the chief monetary achiever of the family.

BREAK
Finance: in a pricing structure providing purchasing discounts at different levels of volume, a point at which the price changes—for example, a 10% discount for ten cases.
Investment: (1) sudden, marked drop in the price of a security or in market prices generally; (2) discrepancy in the accounts of brokerage firms; (3) stroke of good luck.

BREAK-EVEN ANALYSIS financial analysis that identifies the point at which expenses equal gross revenue for a zero net difference. For example, if a mailing costs $100 and each item generates $5 in revenue, the break-even point is at 20 items sold. A profit will be made on items sold in excess of 20. A loss will result on sales under 20. The break-even point may be analyzed in terms of units, as above, or dollars.

BREAK-EVEN POINT
Finance: point at which revenues equal costs. The point is located by break-even analysis, which determines the volume of sales at which fixed and variable costs will be covered. All sales over the break-even point produce profits; any drop in sales below that point will produce losses.
Real estate: occupancy level needed to pay for operating expenses and debt service, but leaving no cash flow. *See also* CASH FLOW; OPERATING EXPENSES.
Securities: dollar price at which a transaction produces neither a gain nor a loss.

BREAKUP dissolution of any unit, organization, or group of organizations. An antitrust action by the Justice Department may result in the breakup of a large corporation into smaller companies if it is found to be in violation of antitrust laws.

BRETTON WOODS CONFERENCE *see* FIXED EXCHANGE RATE.

BRIBE a voluntary payment offered, usually surreptitiously, in expectation of a special favor. While offering a bribe is not always illegal, accepting one is unethical or frequently illegal.

BRIDGE LOAN short-term loan, also called *swing loan*, made in anticipation of intermediate-term or long-term financing.

BREAK-EVEN POINT

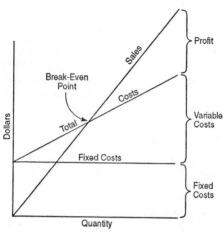

FIGURE 2

BROADBAND high-capacity transmission method that provides multiple channels of data, voice, or video over a single telecommunications medium (wire). Loosely used for high-speed Internet connections such as cable and DSL, which permit simultaneous transmission of voice and data over the same line, especially as contrasted to a DIAL-UP CONNECTION.

BROADBANDING personnel system that collapses numerous pay ranges and classifications into a smaller number of broader pay ranges and classifications. This offers the organization a high degree of salary and job grouping flexibility and responsiveness.

BROCHURE a flyer or small book used to advertise or describe a product for sale or service available.

BROKEN LOT incomplete set of merchandise. Broken lots often are the result of breakage or improper packaging.

BROKER any person who, in the ordinary course of business, stands ready to effect the sales made by others. *See also* AGENT; DEALER; LISTING AGENT; LISTING BROKER.

BROKERAGE
1. business of being a BROKER. One may open a brokerage office, upon receiving a broker's license, for the purpose of engaging in *brokerage*.
2. commission received by a broker for his services. For example, the *brokerage* on the sale of a $100,000 house was $6,000.

BROKERAGE ALLOWANCE commission paid by the seller in a transaction to the broker who arranged the sale, based upon some percentage of the selling price. A brokerage allowance usually refers only to transactions in which the broker does not take possession of the goods sold.

BROKER-DEALER *see* DEALER.

BROKER LOAN RATE interest rate at which stockbrokers borrow from banks to cover the securities positions of their clients. The broker loan rate usually hovers close to the prime rate.

BROKER'S OPINION OF VALUE (BOV) an analysis provided by a real estate broker to assist a buyer or seller in making decisions about the listing price of real estate or a suitable bid for purchase. Also COMPARATIVE MARKET ANALYSIS. A fee may or may not be charged. This analysis may not be represented as an *appraisal*. For mortgage lending purposes, the lender requires an appraisal performed by an appraiser licensed by the state.

BROOKINGS INSTITUTION nonprofit organization in Washington, D.C., which produces scholarly studies of significant economic and political issues and problems.

BROWNFIELD a SITE whose former use involved hazardous materials. Examples are discontinued manufacturing facilities, shut-down military bases, and abandoned gasoline stations. There are federal programs that attempt to make these sites safe for redevelopment to other uses. *See also* SUPERFUND.

BROWSER a computer software application used to view and navigate the WORLD WIDE WEB and other INTERNET resources.

B2B business to business; a transaction that occurs between two companies, as opposed to a transaction involving a consumer. The term may also describe a company that provides goods or services for another company.

B2C Internet marketing between businesses and consumers (as by Amazon.com).

BUCKET SHOP illegal brokerage firm, now almost extinct, which accepts customer orders but does not execute them immediately as Securities and Exchange Commission regulations require. Bucket-shop brokers confirm the price the customer asked for, but in fact make the trade at a time advantageous to the broker. Bucket shops sometimes neglect to fill the customer's order and just pocket the money. *See also* BOILER ROOM; SECURITIES AND EXCHANGE COMMISSION (SEC).

BUDGET estimate of revenue and expenditure for a specified period. Of the many kinds of budgets, a CASH BUDGET shows cash flow, an *expense budget* shows projected expenditures, and a CAPITAL BUDGET shows anticipated capital outlays. The term refers to a preliminary financial plan. In a *balanced* budget, revenues equal expenditures.

BUDGET DEFICIT excess of spending over income for a government, corporation, or individual over a particular period of time. A *budget deficit* accumulated by the federal government of the United States must be financed by the issuance of Treasury BONDS. Corporate deficits must be reduced or eliminated by increasing sales and reducing expenditures, or the company will not survive in the long run. Similarly, individuals who consistently spend more than they earn will accumulate huge debts, which may ultimately force them to declare bankruptcy if the debt cannot be serviced. The opposite of a deficit is a *surplus*.

BUDGET MORTGAGE a MORTGAGE that requires monthly payments for taxes and insurance in addition to interest and principal.

BUFFER device for the temporary storage of electronic data that is located between two other devices of differing speeds. For example, a computer is much faster than a printer output device, so the output from the computer will be sent to the buffer before it is sent to the printer. This allows a computer to continue working instead of waiting for the printer to catch up.

BUFFER STOCK stock used in agriculture to stabilize the price of commodities. The government purchases excess production for storage and sells that storage stock in years of low production. In general the use of buffer stocks stabilizes commodity market price swings.

BUFFER ZONE transitional area between two areas of different predominant land use.

BUG error in a computer program. Bugs can be either *syntax errors*, meaning that the rules of the programming language were not followed, or *logic errors*, meaning that the program does not do what it is supposed to do.

BUILDING AND LOAN ASSOCATION *see* SAVINGS AND LOAN ASSOCIATION.

BUILDING CODE regulations established by a local government describing the minimum structural requirements for buildings. Specifications involve the foundation, roofing, plumbing, electrical, and other matters of safety and sanitation.

BUILDING LINE line fixed at a certain distance from the front and/or sides of a lot, beyond which the building may not project.

BUILDING LOAN AGREEMENT agreement whereby the lender advances money to an owner at specified stages of construction, for example, upon completion of the foundation, framing, etc. Same as CONSTRUCTION LOAN agreement.

BUILDING PERMIT permission granted by a local government to build a specific structure at a particular site. The number of residential building permits will forecast the number of HOUSING STARTS.

BUILD TO SUIT an arrangement whereby a landowner offers to pay for construction on his or her land of a building specified by a potential tenant, and then to lease land and building to the tenant.

BUILT-IN STABILIZER feature of a system that tends to direct the system toward equilibrium or stability in the event of a dislocation of the system. *See also* AUTOMATIC (FISCAL) STABILIZERS.

BULL person who thinks prices will rise. One can be *bullish* on the prospects for an individual stock, bond, or commodity, an industry segment, or the market as a whole. In a more general sense, *bullish* means optimistic, so a person can be bullish on the economy as a whole. When a bull attacks, it throws its opponent upward, whereas a bear grapples its opponent down. The symbol of a bull and bear locked in combat represents the stock market. *See also* BEAR.

BULLET a small graphical element used to set off items in an unnumbered list. Although the name derives from the • character, many other shapes may be used as *bullets*.

BULLETIN
  1. written announcement that arrives with urgency.
  2. description or title of a business or trade periodical that displays merchandise and price information.

BULLET LOAN typically a loan with a 5- to 10-year TERM and no AMORTIZATION. At the end of the term, the full amount is due.

BULLION COINS coins composed of PRECIOUS METALS such as gold, silver, or platinum, which would have value as *bullion* (i.e., if melted down). These coins trade at a slight premium over their metal content, unlike *numismatic coins*, which trade on their rarity and historic and/or artistic value. Popular *bullion coins* minted by major governments around the world include the American Eagle, the Canadian Maple Leaf, the South African Krugerrand, and the Chinese Panda.

BULL MARKET prolonged period of rising prices. *See also* BEAR MARKET.

BUNCHING concentration of gross income in one or more TAXABLE YEARS.

BUNDLED SOFTWARE software that is included with the purchase of hardware or other software. For example, most new computers come with some version of Microsoft WINDOWS already installed. Other *bundled software* may include games, an encyclopedia, and an office suite composed of a WORD PROCESSOR, a SPREADSHEET, and other business applications.

BUNDLE-OF-RIGHTS THEORY in real estate law, theory that ownership of realty implies a group of rights such as occupancy, use and enjoyment, and the right to sell, devise, give, or lease all or part of these rights.

BUNDLING marketing strategy that combines multiple products at a more competitive price.

BURDEN *see* OVERHEAD.

BURDEN OF PROOF
1. duty of a party to substantiate an ALLEGATION or ISSUE, either to avoid dismissal of that issue in the trial or to convince the court of the truth of that claim and hence to prevail in a civil or criminal suit.
2. duty of a PLAINTIFF, at the beginning of a trial, to make a prima facie showing of each fact necessary to establish the existence of a cause of action.
3. obligation to plead each element of a cause of action or affirmative defense or suffer a dismissal.

BUREAU particular department, agency, or office. It is usually accompanied by the name of a particular agency, such as the Federal Bureau of Investigation. *See also* BUREAUCRAT.

BUREAUCRAT government employee who follows a rigid procedure in administering the responsibilities of a position. A classical bureaucrat follows a set of rules and procedures in an impersonal manner. A bureaucrat is a career professional evaluated on the basis of merit and skill.

BURNOUT
Psychology: overexhaustion of a person.
Tax shelter: exhaustion of a tax shelter's benefits, when an investor starts to receive income from the investment. This income must be reported to the Internal Revenue Service, and taxes must be paid on it.

BURN RATE the speed at which a company is spending its cash. Particularly applicable to START-UP enterprises, which may not generate enough new cash flow to offset their rate of spending.

BUS a central set of highly specialized electrical sockets within a computer into which are plugged the CPU, memory, expansion cards, and peripherals. Without a *bus*, a computer would need separate wires between all components to connect them together. Accordingly, a bus allows a computer to operate more efficiently and simply.

BUSINESS commercial enterprise, profession, or trade operated for the purpose of earning a profit by providing a product or service; also called *business enterprise*. Businesses are created by ENTREPRENEURS who put money at risk to promote a particular venture for the purpose of a profit. They vary in size from a one-person SOLE PROPRIETORSHIP to an international CORPORATION having billions of dollars in assets and thousands of employees. *See also* BUSINESS ORGANIZATION.

BUSINESS BAD DEBT a debt resulting from the conduct of a taxpayer's trade or business or a debt that becomes worthless in connection with the taxpayer's trade or business.

BUSINESS COLLEGE school that primarily teaches the clerical parts of business, such as typing, word processing, filing, and bookkeeping.

This is not to be confused with a *business school* or the *college of business* in an accredited college or university.

BUSINESS COMBINATION bringing together a company and one or more incorporated or unincorporated businesses into a single accounting entity that then carries on the activities of the separate entities.

BUSINESS CONDITIONS general climate of the economy and/or the political situation as they relate to the profitability and prosperity of business.

BUSINESS CYCLE recurrent periods during which the nation's economy moves in and out of RECESSION and RECOVERY phases. From historical research, economists have identified short-term (2 to 3 years) to long-term (50- to 60-year KONDRATIEFF CYCLE) business cycles; however, while economic activity in recent years has experienced both booms and lulls, there is little evidence that these periods occur on a regular, predictable basis.

BUSINESS DAY
In general: hours when most businesses are in operation. Although individual working hours may differ, and particular firms may choose staggered schedules, the conventional business day is 9 A.M. to 5 P.M.
Finance: day when financial marketplaces are open for trading. For example, in figuring the settlement date on a REGULAR-WAY securities transaction, Saturday, Sunday, and/or a legal holiday would not be counted.

BUSINESS DAYS

Monday	July 1	trade day
Tuesday	July 2	1
Wednesday	July 3	2
Thursday	July 4	holiday
Friday	July 5	3 settlement day

BUSINESS ENTERPRISE *see* BUSINESS.

BUSINESS ETHICS moral principles concerning acceptable and unacceptable behavior by business people. Executives are supposed to maintain a high sense of values and conduct honest and fair practices with the public.

BUSINESS ETIQUETTE generally accepted behavior, which may be open to dispute. The professional behavior may be based on custom and morality. There are social guidelines and manners to be followed in business situations when dealing with others. An example of a lack of *business etiquette* is when a salesperson is late in visiting a client.

BUSINESS GIFT tax deduction limited to $25 per recipient per year. Advertising items such as pencils, pens, and calendars embossed with a business name and costing $4 or less do not figure into the $25 limitation.

BUSINESS INTERRUPTION INSURANCE indemnification for the loss of profits and continuing fixed expenses when some disaster, such as a fire, prevents business from being carried on.

BUSINESS JUDGMENT RULE deference given by courts to the GOOD-FAITH operations and transactions of a CORPORATION by its executives. Reasonable decisions, even if not the most profitable, will not be disturbed by a court upon application by a disgruntled party such as a STOCKHOLDER. The rationale behind the rule is that stockholders accept the risk that an informed business decision, honestly made and rationally thought to be in the corporation's best interests, may not be second-guessed. Therefore, courts afford business judgments special protection in order to limit litigation and avoid judicial intrusiveness in private-sector business decision making.

BUSINESS LIABILITY INSURANCE coverage for liability exposures of a business to include policies covering individual specific areas of a given business or industry, any of which may be subject to liability.

BUSINESS LIFE AND HEALTH INSURANCE coverage providing funds for maintenance of a business as closely to normal as possible in the event of a loss of a key person, owner, or partner.

BUSINESS MEALS *see* ENTERTAINMENT EXPENSES AND BUSINESS MEALS.

BUSINESS OFFICE location devoted to the conduct of business. A *business office* is dedicated to the purpose of promoting a particular business and is a cost of doing business.

BUSINESS ORGANIZATION structure of a particular business in terms of how it functions. Its purpose is central to its structure. *See also* BUSINESS.

BUSINESS OR PROFESSIONAL ACTIVITY CODE six-digit code numbers for principal business activities, designed to classify enterprises by the type of activity for the administrative purposes of the IRS. They are similar in format to the NORTH AMERICAN INDUSTRY CLASSIFICATION SYSTEM codes.

BUSINESS OR TRADE *see* TRADE OR BUSINESS.

BUSINESSOWNERS POLICY (BOP) combination property and business interruption policy, usually written for small and medium-size businesses, to cover expenses: (1) resulting from damage or destruction of business property or (2) when actions or nonactions of the business's representatives result in bodily injury or property damage to (an)other individual(s).

BUSINESS PLAN document that organizes a business concept, including marketing and management strategies and financial projections.

BUSINESS PROPERTY generally for tax purposes, any property used in a trade or business that is not a CAPITAL ASSET. This would include assets specifically excepted from capital asset status, such as:
1. inventory.
2. property held for sale to customers in the ordinary course of business.
3. trade receivables from the sale of property or services in the normal course of business.
4. depreciable personal property used in a trade or business.
5. real property used in a trade or business.
6. intangible assets such as a copyright or trademark.

BUSINESS PROPERTY AND LIABILITY INSURANCE PACKAGE protection of the property of the business that is damaged or destroyed by perils such as fire, smoke, and vandalism; and/or if the actions (or non-actions) of the business's representatives result in bodily injury or property damage.

BUSINESS PURPOSE a test applied to various transactions. A transaction must serve a BONA FIDE business purpose, other than a tax purpose, to qualify as a valid transaction for tax purposes.

BUSINESS REPLY CARD (BRC) promotion reply postcard preaddressed to the mailer and usually sent as permit mail, requiring no postage payment by the responder. Mailers pay an annual fee for a business reply permit. Business reply cards, which are mailed at first-class postage rates, make it easy for people to respond to a promotion. *See also* BUSINESS REPLY MAIL.

BUSINESS REPLY ENVELOPE (BRE) promotion reply envelope, preaddressed to the seller, for orders, payments, or inquiries. BREs are mailed at first-class rates but usually require no postage payment by the responder. *See* BUSINESS REPLY MAIL.

BUSINESS REPLY MAIL (BRM) preaddressed cards, envelopes, labels, or cartons that can be mailed without prepayment of postage. After delivery of the mailing piece, the U.S. Postal Service collects the postage due, based upon a printed permit number on the envelope that identifies the addressee. The addressee pays an annual fee for the permit. *See also* BUSINESS REPLY CARD; BUSINESS REPLY ENVELOPE.

BUSINESS-TO-BUSINESS ADVERTISING advertising intended to communicate among businesses, as opposed to consumer advertising. Business-to-business advertising is directed at business people or companies who buy (or *specify*—such as architects, engineers, or contractors) products for business use. Businesses advertise in their own trade publications (a practice called *business paper advertising*), of which there are three times as many as consumer magazines. *See also* AMERICAN BUSINESS PRESS, INC.

BUSINESS TRUST *see* MASSACHUSETTS TRUST.

BUSINESS VALUE
   1. the intangible value in a business, above the value of its tangible assets, which include buildings, land, and fixtures.
   2. the entire value of a business; the summation of all its parts, tangible and intangible.

BUST-UP ACQUISITION in corporate acquisitions, a transaction in which a raider sells some of the acquired company's assets to finance the leveraged acquisition.

BUTTON (COMPUTER) a defined area of the screen, usually designed to look like a pushbutton, which, when clicked with a mouse, will perform a given action, usually represented by an ICON on the button face. Fox example, buttons may be used to open files, apply text formatting such as boldface and italic, or print a document.

BUTTON BAR *see* TOOLBAR.

BUY acquire property in return for money. *Buy* can also be used as a synonym for *bargain*.

BUY-AND-SELL AGREEMENT approach used for sole proprietorships, partnerships, and close corporations in which the business interests of a deceased or disabled proprietor, partner, or shareholder are sold according to a predetermined formula to the remaining member(s) of the business. Funds for buying out the deceased partner's interest are usually provided by life insurance policies, with each partner purchasing a policy on the other partners. Each is the owner and beneficiary of the policies purchased on the other partners.

BUY-BACK AGREEMENT provision in a contract under which the seller agrees to repurchase the property at a stated price upon the occurrence of a specified event within a certain period of time. For example, a *buy-back agreement* in a sales contract may require the builder-seller to buy the property back if the buyer-occupant is transferred by his company within six months.

BUY DOWN
   1. paying additional DISCOUNT POINTS to a lender in exchange for a reduced rate of interest on a loan. The reduced rate may apply for all or a portion of the loan term.
   2. home seller arranging a lower interest by making a payment to the lender, thereby *buying down* the loan for the home purchaser.

BUYER one who purchases goods or services; also called *customer*. A consumer makes purchases for his/her own use or purpose. A professional buyer makes bulk purchases on behalf of a retailer or wholesaler. A media buyer purchases media space or time for an advertiser.

BUYER BEHAVIOR field of knowledge on how buyers behave, essential to modern marketing. *Buyer behavior* is also influenced by personality, sociodemographic characteristics, and lifestyle.

BUYER'S BROKER in real estate brokerage, an agent explicitly representing the buyer. The broker may locate appropriate properties and assist in making an offer and negotiating a contract. The buyer may or may not pay a fee for this service.

BUYER'S MARKET
  In general: situation in which supply exceeds demand.
  In real estate: situation where buyers have a wide choice of properties and may negotiate lower prices; often caused by overbuilding, local population decreases, or economic slump. *See also* SELLER'S MARKET.

BUYER'S REMORSE *see* COGNITIVE DISSONANCE.

BUY IN
  Options trading: procedure whereby the responsibility to deliver or accept stock can be terminated.
  Securities: transaction between brokers wherein securities are not delivered on time by the broker on the sell side, forcing the buy-side broker to obtain shares from other sources.

BUYING ON MARGIN buying securities with credit available through a relationship with a broker, called a MARGIN ACCOUNT. Arrangements of this kind are closely regulated by the FEDERAL RESERVE BOARD (FRB). *See also* MARGIN.

BUY ORDER in securities trading, an order to a broker to purchase a specified quantity of a security at the MARKET PRICE or at another stipulated price.

BUYOUT purchase of at least a controlling percentage of a company's stock in order to take over its assets and operations. A buyout can be accomplished through negotiation or through a TENDER OFFER. *See also* LEVERAGED BUYOUT.

BUY-SELL AGREEMENT pact among partners or stockholders under which some agree to buy the interests of others upon some event, such as the death of a partner. *See* BUY-AND-SELL AGREEMENT.

BUZZ WORDS slang words or phrases used by an in-group, sometimes having imprecise meaning but sounding impressive to outsiders. However, if the meaning is clear, and enough people use them, these terms eventually become standard English usage. Examples are *bottom line*, *comes with the territory*, *ripoff*, and *run it up the flagpole*.

BYLAWS rules adopted for the regulation of an association's or a corporation's own actions. In corporation law, bylaws are self-imposed rules that constitute an agreement or contract between a corporation and its members to conduct the corporate business in a particular way.

BYPASS TRUST agreement allowing parents to pass assets on to their children to reduce estate taxes. The trust must be made irrevocable, meaning that the terms can never be changed. Assets put in such a trust usually exceed the amount that children and other heirs can receive tax free at a parent's death. It allows two lifetime exemptions to pass from parents to children while a surviving parent collects income for life. The exemption amount is $2,000,000 in 2006. This amount is expected to change in subsequent years. Parents can arrange to receive income from the assets during their lifetimes and may even be able to touch the principal in case of dire need. One variation of a bypass trust is the QUALIFIED TERMINABLE INTEREST PROPERTY TRUST.

BY-PRODUCT residue arising at various stages in the production of a principal commodity. The by-products of the meat packing industry, for example, are glue and hair. Certain industries produce toxic by-products that can become environmental hazards.

BYTE amount of computer memory space needed to store one character, which is normally 8 bits. A computer with 8-bit bytes can distinguish $2^8 = 256$ different characters. The size of a computer's memory is measured in *kilobytes*, where 1 kilobyte (K) = 1024 bytes.

BY THE BOOK method of acting in a very rigid manner, according to preestablished written guidelines and regulations. Saying an organization is run *by the book* often represents a criticism of how the organization is managed. It implies that the organization lacks flexibility and is unresponsive to changing needs.

C

CABLEGRAM telegram sent overseas by means of a submerged wire.

CABLE TRANSFER arranging for the transfer of something, typically money, overseas. It is an expeditious way of transferring funds overseas, by means of a submerged wire.

CAC-40 a CAPITALIZATION-weighted price index of the 40 most actively traded shares on the Paris BOURSE; the acronym stands for Compagnie des Agents de Change.

CACHE
1. a hiding place where provisions or implements are stored.
2. a place where data can be stored in a computer and retrieved more quickly than from a slower device such as a disk. For example, frequently used disk sectors are copied and stored in a disk *cache* in a computer's RAM so that they are accessed more quickly.

CACHET a mark of quality or distinction, individuality, or authenticity: *A Mercedes-Benz has a certain cachet.*

CADASTRE list of appraised property values in a jurisdiction, used to determine the amount of tax ASSESSED on each parcel.

CAFETERIA BENEFIT PLAN arrangement under which employees may choose their own employee benefit structure. For example, one employee may wish to emphasize healthcare and thus would select a more comprehensive health insurance plan for the allocation of the premiums, while another employee may wish to emphasize retirement and thus allocate more of the premiums to the purchase of pension benefits.

CALENDAR YEAR continuous period beginning January 1 and ending December 31. *Contrast with* FISCAL YEAR.

CALL
Banking: demand to repay a secured loan. When a banker *calls* a loan, the entire principal amount is due immediately.
Bonds: right to redeem outstanding bonds before their scheduled maturity. The first dates when an issuer may *call* bonds are specified in the prospectus of every issue that has a call provision in its INDENTURE. *See also* CALLABLE; CALL FEATURE; CALL PRICE.
Options: right to buy a specific number of shares at a specified price by a fixed date. *See also* CALL OPTION.

CALLABLE security redeemable by the issuer before the scheduled maturity. The issuer must pay the holders a premium price if such a security is retired early. Bonds are usually called when interest rates fall so significantly that the issuer can save money by floating new bonds at lower rates. *See also* CALL PREMIUM; CALL PRICE.

CALL CENTER a center equipped to handle a large volume of telephone calls (especially for taking orders or serving customers). Call centers may be primarily incoming (staffed by ORDER TAKERS or technical support personnel) or outgoing (staffed with TELEMARKETING personnel).

CALL FEATURE or **CALL PROVISION** part of the agreement a bond issuer makes with a buyer, called the INDENTURE, describing the schedule and price of redemptions before maturity. Most corporate and municipal bonds have ten-year *call features* (termed *call protection* by holders); government securities usually have none. *See also* CALL PREMIUM; CALL PRICE.

CALL FORWARDING service offered by the local telephone company at extra cost whereby incoming calls may be automatically transferred to another number.

CALL OPTION the right, purchased by an investor, to buy a certain number of shares of a particular stock or stock index at a predetermined price before a preset deadline. The gain or loss on a call is a short-term or long-term CAPITAL GAIN, depending on the holding period. If the call expires before exercise, it is treated as a short-term gain or loss. *See also* PUT OPTION.

CALL PREMIUM
  1. amount the buyer of a CALL OPTION has to pay to the seller for the right to purchase a stock or stock index at a specified price by a specified date.
  2. in bonds and preferred stock, the amount over par an issuer has to pay to an investor for redeeming the security early.

CALL PRICE price at which a bond or preferred stock with a CALL FEATURE can be redeemed by the issuer; also known as *redemption* price. *See also* CALL PREMIUM.

CALL REPORT report kept by an advertising agency of conferences between agency representatives and current or prospective advertiser clients; also called *conference report, contact report*. The *call report* tells when the meeting took place, who was present, and what was discussed.

CALL WAITING service offered by the local telephone company whereby a tone rings when a person is on the line and another caller has just dialed the person's number. *Call waiting* allows the person called to answer the second call, putting the first caller on hold.

CAMERA-READY COPY (CRC) artwork or printout that is ready to be photographed and made into a printing plate for offset reproduction.

CANCEL
  In general: void a negotiable instrument by annulling or paying it; also, prematurely terminate a bond or other contract.
  Securities: void an order to buy or sell. *See also* GOOD-TILL-CANCELED ORDER (GTC).

CANCELLATION CLAUSE contract provision that gives the right to terminate obligations upon the occurrence of specified conditions or events. A *cancellation clause* in a lease might allow the landlord to break the lease upon the sale of a building.

CANNED APPROACH company-prepared selling presentation. Sales representatives memorize and repeat it verbatim when making a sales presentation. This selling approach can be effective for inexperienced sales personnel, but it is inadequate for complex selling transactions.

CANNED PROGRAM prewritten computer program available for purchase.

CAP *see* CAPS.

CAPACITY
1. mental ability to make a rational decision.
2. ability to produce during a given time period, with an upper limit imposed by the availability of space, machinery, labor, materials, or capital. Capacity may be expressed in units, weights, size, dollars, man hours, labor cost, etc. Typically, there are five different concepts of capacity.
   a. *Ideal capacity:* volume of activity that could be attained under ideal operating conditions, with minimum allowance for inefficiency. It is the largest volume of output possible. Also called *theoretical capacity, engineered capacity,* or *maximum capacity.*
   b. *Practical capacity:* highest activity level at which the factory can operate with an acceptable degree of efficiency, taking into consideration unavoidable losses of productive time (i.e., vacations, holidays, repairs to equipment). Also called *maximum practical capacity.*
   c. *Normal capacity:* average level of operating activity that is sufficient to fill the demand for the company's products or services for a span of several years, taking into consideration seasonal and cyclical demands and increasing or decreasing trends in demand.
   d. *Planned capacity:* similar to *normal capacity* except it is projected against a particular single year. Also called *expected actual capacity.*
   e. *Operating capacity:* similar to *planned capacity* except the time period is within a small slice of a single year (i.e., daily, monthly, quarterly).

CAPACITY PLANNING long-term strategy to effectuate the level of resources required to meet projected consumer demand.

CAPITAL
Finance: money and other property of a corporation or other enterprise used in transacting its business.
Economics: factories, machines, and other human-made inputs into the production process.

CAPITAL ACCOUNT

Finance: group of accounting records that involve transactions in the EQUITY or ownership of a business.

Economics: part of the BALANCE OF PAYMENTS that records a nation's inflow and outflow of financial securities.

CAPITAL ASSET PRICING MODEL (CAPM) sophisticated model of the relationship between *expected risk* and *expected return*. The model is grounded in the theory that investors demand higher returns for higher risks. It says that the return on an asset or a security is equal to the risk-free return—such as the return on a short-term Treasury security—plus a risk premium.

CAPITAL ASSETS

In general: property with a relatively long life; fixed ASSET in a trade or business.

Taxation: property held for investment by the taxpayer that, when sold, has been subject to special tax treatment (as CAPITAL GAINS or CAPITAL LOSSES). A net long-term capital gain is taxed at a maximum of 15% to an individual for sales after May 6, 2003. A 5% rate applies to individuals in the 15% tax bracket. A corporation is taxed at regular tax rates on capital gains. Inventory, property held for resale, real or personal property used in a trade or business, copyrights in certain instances, and certain U.S. government obligations are not capital assets.

The Internal Revenue Code does not define what a capital asset is—only what it is not (IRC §1221). Also the tax code definition of *capital asset* differs significantly from the definition in economics.

CAPITAL BUDGET program for evaluating proposed plant expansion, research and development, and advertising. Among the sophisticated methods used in arriving at a capital budget are NET PRESENT VALUE and INTERNAL RATE OF RETURN.

CAPITAL CALLS requests for additional money required of investors to fund a deficit. A corporate stockholder has no legal obligation to meet a *capital call.*

CAPITAL CONSUMPTION ALLOWANCE amount of depreciation included in the GROSS DOMESTIC PRODUCT (GDP), normally around 11% of GDP. This amount is subtracted from GDP, on the theory that it is "used up" during the year, to arrive at NET NATIONAL PRODUCT.

CAPITAL CONTRIBUTED IN EXCESS OF PAR VALUE amount paid for stock above its stated PAR VALUE, as shown in the OWNER'S EQUITY section of a balance sheet.

CAPITAL CONTRIBUTION cash or property acquired by a corporation from a shareholder without the receipt of additional stock. Such amount is added to the BASIS of the shareholder's existing stock, and the corporation's basis is carried over from the shareholder.

CAPITAL EXPENDITURE an improvement (as distinguished from a REPAIR) that will have a life of more than one year. Capital expenditures are generally depreciated or depleted over their useful life, as distinguished from repairs, which are subtracted from the income of the current year.

CAPITAL EXPENSE *see* capital EXPENDITURE.

CAPITAL FLIGHT movement of large sums of money from one country to another to escape political or economic turmoil or to seek higher rates of return. For example, periods of high inflation or political revolution have brought about an exodus of capital from many Latin American countries to the United States.

CAPITAL FORMATION creation or expansion, through savings, of capital—buildings, machinery, equipment—that produces other goods and services.

CAPITAL GAIN gain on the sale of a CAPITAL ASSET. For sales after May 6, 2003, individuals are taxed at a maximum of 15%. There are limits on the deduction of CAPITAL LOSSES against ordinary income.

CAPITAL GAIN DISTRIBUTION
1. *Mutual funds*—distributions received by mutual funds earned as capital gains retain that character when passed on to the mutual fund's investors.
2. *Corporate liquidation*—the difference between the FAIR MARKET VALUE of property distributed to a shareholder in excess of the shareholder's BASIS in his or her stock is a capital gain or loss.

CAPITAL GAIN DIVIDEND any DISTRIBUTION that is designated as such by a REGULATED INVESTMENT COMPANY in a written notice mailed to its shareholders not later than 60 days after the close of its taxable year. A *capital gain dividend* is treated as a CAPITAL GAIN by the shareholders.

CAPITAL GOODS goods used in the production of other goods such as industrial buildings, machinery, equipment, as well as highways, office buildings, and government installations. In the aggregate, such goods are key determiners of a country's productive capacity.

CAPITAL IMPROVEMENT betterment to a building or equipment, which extends its life or increases its usefulness or productivity. The cost of a capital improvement is added to the basis of the asset improved and then depreciated, in contrast to REPAIRS and MAINTENANCE, which are expensed currently. *See also* ASSET.

CAPITAL INTENSIVE requiring large investments in CAPITAL ASSETS. Motor-vehicle and steel production are capital intensive industries. To provide an acceptable return on investment, such industries must have a high margin of profit or a low cost of borrowing. The term *capital* *intensive* is sometimes used to mean a high proportion of FIXED ASSETS to LABOR.

CAPITAL INVESTMENT money paid out to acquire something for permanent use or value in a business or home. Also, money paid out for an interest in a business, as in a stock purchase.

CAPITALISM economic system in which: (1) private ownership of property exists; (2) the income from property or capital accrues to the individuals or firms that accumulated it and own it; (3) individuals and firms are relatively free to compete with others for their own economic gain; and (4) the profit motive is basic to economic life. *Contrast with* COMMUNISM; SOCIALISM.

CAPITALIZATION *see* CAPITALIZE; MARKET CAPITALIZATION.

CAPITALIZATION RATE rate of interest or discount rate used to convert a series of future payments into a single PRESENT VALUE. In real estate, the rate includes annual capital recovery in addition to interest.

CAPITALIZE, CAPITALIZATION
1. convert a schedule of income into a principal amount, called CAPITALIZED VALUE, by dividing by a rate of interest.
2. issue securities to finance CAPITAL EXPENDITURES (rare).
3. record capital outlays as additions to asset accounts, not as expenses. *See also* CAPITAL EXPENDITURE.
4. convert a lease obligation to an asset/liability form of expression called a CAPITAL LEASE, that is, to record a leased asset as an owned asset and the lease obligation as borrowed funds.
5. turn something to one's advantage economically—for example, sell umbrellas on a rainy day.

CAPITALIZED VALUE current worth of money expected to be earned or received in the future, calculated by using an appropriate discount rate to express current value accurately.

CAPITAL LEASE lease that must be reflected on a company's balance sheet as an asset and corresponding liability. Generally, this applies to leases where the lessee acquires essentially all of the economic benefits and risks of the leased property. *Contrast with* OPERATING LEASE.

CAPITAL LOSS loss from the sale of a CAPITAL ASSET. Individuals are limited to $3,000 of loss that can be used annually to offset ORDINARY INCOME; corporations may offset capital losses against capital gains but not against ordinary income.

CAPITAL MARKET market where capital funds—debt and equity— are traded. Included are private placement sources of debt and equity as well as organized markets and exchanges. The capital market is generally for maturities of greater than one year. *Contrast with* MONEY MARKET.

CAPITAL OUTFLOW exodus of capital from a country. A combination of political and economic factors may encourage domestic and foreign owners of assets to sell their holdings and move their money to other countries that offer more political stability and economic growth potential. If a capital outflow becomes large enough, some countries may try to restrict investors' ability to move money from the country with currency controls or other measures. *See also* CAPITAL FLIGHT.

CAPITAL OUTLAY *see* CAPITAL EXPENDITURE.

CAPITAL PAID IN EXCESS OF PAR VALUE *see* CAPITAL CON-TRIBUTED IN EXCESS OF PAR VALUE.

CAPITAL RATIONING process of selecting the mix of acceptable pro-jects that provides the highest overall NET PRESENT VALUE (NPV) when a company has a limit on the budget for capital spending.

CAPITAL REQUIREMENT
1. permanent financing needed for the normal operation of a business, that is, the long-term and working capital.
2. appraised investment in fixed assets and normal working capital.

CAPITAL RESOURCE any good that is used in the production of other goods. Factories, many buildings, equipment, and the like are *capital resources*. For accounting purposes, economists also include invento-ries in capital.

CAPITAL STOCK amount of money or property contributed by STOCK-HOLDERS to be used as the financial foundation for the corporation. It includes all classes of common and preferred stock.

CAPITAL STRUCTURE corporation's financial framework, including long-term debt, preferred stock, and net worth. It is distinguished from FINANCIAL STRUCTURE, which includes additional sources of capital, such as short-term debt, accounts payable, and other liabilities.

CAPITAL SURPLUS *see* CAPITAL CONTRIBUTED IN EXCESS OF PAR VALUE.

CAPITAL TURNOVER annual sales divided by average stockholder equity (net worth). When compared over a period, it reveals the extent to which a company is able to grow without additional capital investment.

CAP RATE short for CAPITALIZATION RATE.

CAPS limitations, especially those placed on the extent of interest rate or payment adjustments associated with ADJUSTABLE-RATE MORTGAGES. An *annual adjustment* cap places a ceiling on the amount the interest rate can be changed during one year. A *life-of-loan* cap places a ceil-ing on the interest rate over the loan term. A *payment* cap limits the amount of change in the monthly payment amount from year to year.

CAPTIVE FINANCE COMPANY typically a 100-percent-owned subsidiary whose major purpose is to finance consumer purchases from the parent company. General Motors Acceptance Corporation, which provides consumer loans for General Motors' products, is an example.

CAPTURE RATE the portion of total sales in the real estate market that are sold by one entity or one project.

CARGO freight or merchandise on a transportation vehicle (ship or plane), but not passengers.

CARGO INSURANCE shippers' policies covering one cargo exposure or all cargo exposures by sea on ALL RISK/ALL PERIL BASIS. Exclusions include war, nuclear disaster, wear and tear, dampness, mold, losses due to delay of shipment, and loss of market for the cargo. *One Cargo Exposure (Single Risk Cargo Policy)* covers a single shipment of goods and/or a single trip. *All Cargo Exposure (Open Cargo Policy)* covers all shipments of goods and/or all trips.

CARLOAD RATE in transportation, low rate that applies to a certain quantity of freight that is considered to be a (freight) carload.

CARRIER entity in the business of offering transportation of either passengers or cargo. *See also* COMMON CARRIER.

CARRIER'S LIEN right of provider of transportation services to retain cargo shipped as collateral for payment of the transportation services rendered.

CARROT AND STICK strategy often used in negotiations where one side offers the other something it wants while threatening negative sanctions if the other side does not comply with its requests. Thus a union could offer wage concessions in exchange for better workrule provisions while threatening to strike if no accommodation can be reached.

CARRYBACK process by which the DEDUCTIONS or CREDITS of one TAXABLE YEAR that cannot be used to reduce tax liability in that year are applied against tax liability in an earlier year or years. *See also* CARRYOVER.

CARRYFORWARD *see* CARRYOVER.

CARRYING CHARGE
Commodities: charge for carrying the actual commodity, including interest, storage, and insurance costs.
Real estate: carrying cost, primarily interest and taxes, of owning land prior to its development and resale.
Retailing: seller's charge for installment credit, which is added either to the purchase price or to unpaid installments.
Securities: fee that a broker charges for carrying securities on credit (margin).

CARRYOVER a process by which DEDUCTIONS and CREDITS of one taxable year that cannot be used to reduce tax liability in that year are applied against tax liability in subsequent years. Corporations may carry over capital losses for up to 5 years and operating losses for up to 20 years. Amounts are called *carryforwards. See also* CARRYBACK.

CARRYOVER BASIS in a TAX-DEFERRED EXCHANGE, the ADJUSTED TAX BASIS of the property surrendered, used to determine the tax basis of the property acquired. *See also* BASIS (TAX).

CARTAGE charge or service for moving goods by truck, wagon, or other vehicle.

CARTE BLANCHE a blank check, or full authority to act, for example to write one's own job description, carry out a project according to one's own discretion and using one's own creativity, and so on. When one is assigned a job and given *carte blanche*, the methods used to perform the job are guaranteed to be acceptable.

CARTEL group of independent suppliers, which agree to restrict trade to their mutual benefit. Cartels usually do not last indefinitely; when one member breaks the agreement and sells more product than allowed under the cartel's quota, the cartel is weakened or disbands. The Organization of Petroleum Exporting Countries (OPEC) is a very powerful *cartel*.

CARVE OUT separate the present INCOME stream of property from the property itself. For example, if an owner of mineral property sells for a certain number of years a portion of the future mineral production from such property, the sale of such future production is a *carved-out* interest in the mineral property.

CASCADING MENU a secondary MENU that appears next to the original menu when an option with a menu of its own is selected. Often this submenu will also lead to further menus, hence the term. By convention, a menu listing that leads to a submenu is followed by an ellipsis (. . .).

CASE-SENSITIVE distinguishing between upper- and lowercase letters. E-MAIL ADDRESSES at AMERICA ONLINE are *case-sensitive*, although most e-mail addresses are not.

CASE-STUDY METHOD study of information from a hypothetical or actual business situation to formulate a recommended policy based on the facts provided. The Harvard case studies are often used. Relevant data are gathered, organized, evaluated, and generalized. An example of a case study is looking at how a company's management handled an actual occurrence and determining whether or not the policies formulated were correct. If not, recommendations are offered on how things could have been done better.

CASH paper currency and coins, negotiable money orders and checks, and bank balances; also, transactions handled in cash. To *cash* is to convert a negotiable instrument, usually into paper currency and coins.

CASH ACKNOWLEDGMENT notice sent to a CASH BUYER acknowledging receipt of the order. The ACKNOWLEDGMENT may include an offer inviting the buyer to increase the purchase order. Cash acknowledgments are frequently used if delivery of the item ordered is delayed to reinforce the buyer's positive feelings about the purchase and to encourage future orders.

CASH BALANCE PENSION PLAN a type of hybrid pension plan in which each participant's benefit is stated as a hypothetical account balance. The accounts are increased with *pay credits* for additional service and *interest credits* to reflect the passage of time. Although the account balances do not need to be fully funded during the participant's employment, they are usually fully paid out upon termination of employment.

CASH BASIS or **CASH METHOD** accounting method used by most individual taxpayers. The cash method recognizes income and deductions when money is received or paid. See also ACCOUNTING METHOD; ACCRUAL BASIS.

CASHBOOK accounting book that combines cash receipts and disbursements. Its balance ties to the cash account in the general ledger on which the balance sheet is based.

CASH BUDGET estimated cash receipts and disbursements for a future period. A comprehensive cash budget schedules daily, weekly, or monthly expenditures together with the anticipated CASH FLOW from collections and other operating sources.

CASH BUYER customer who pays by sending cash, check, or money order with his order. See also CREDIT ORDER.

CASH COW business that generates a continuing flow of cash. Such a business usually has well-established brand names whose familiarity stimulates repeated buying of the products. Stocks that are *cash cows* have dependable dividends.

CASH DISBURSEMENT amount paid out.

CASH DISCOUNT reduction in a selling price for prompt payment. See also TERMS; TRADE CREDIT.

CASH DIVIDEND cash payment to a corporation's stockholders, distributed from current earnings or accumulated profits and taxable as income. Cash dividends are distinguished from STOCK DIVIDENDS, which are payments in the form of stock. See also YIELD.

CASH EARNINGS cash revenues less cash expenses, specifically excluding noncash expenses such as DEPRECIATION.

CASH EQUIVALENCE market value of an item if sold for cash. In real estate it represents the value of property sold, which can be different from the stated selling price. For example, a seller who accepts a below-market interest rate note should discount the note from its face value to its cash value to derive the *cash equivalence* of the property.

CASH EQUIVALENT a form of payment that is just like cash, such as a *traveler's check* or CASHIER'S CHECK.

CASH FLOW
Finance: analysis of all the changes that affect the cash account during an accounting period. Cash flow from OPERATIONS is one factor in a breakdown, usually shown as *sources of cash* and *uses of cash*.
Investment: net income plus depreciation and other noncash charges. In this sense, it is synonymous with CASH EARNINGS. Investors focus on cash flow from operations because of their concern with a firm's ability to pay dividends. *See also* CASH BUDGET.
Example for a real estate investment:

Potential gross income	$10,000
Less: Vacancy and collection allowance	– 1,000
Add: Miscellaneous income	+ 500
Effective gross income	9,500
Less: Operating expenses	– 3,000
Less: Replacement reserve	– 500
Net operating income	6,000
Less: Interest	– 4,000
Less: Principal payment	– 500
Cash flow	$ 1,500

   Cash flow is not the same as TAXABLE INCOME. Some items subtracted from cash flow to derive TAXABLE INCOME are money received from loans, DEPRECIATION, and AMORTIZATION deductions. Some items that are added to cash flow to derive taxable income are loans retired and purchases of long-term assets. *See also* FREE CASH FLOW, EBIDA.

CASHIER person in a business who accepts payment in money and credit sales, provides change as needed, and records the transaction, generally assisted by a cash register.

CASHIER'S CHECK check issued by an officer of a bank to another person, authorizing the payee to receive upon demand the amount of the check. It is drawn on the bank's own account, not that of a private person, and is therefore accepted for many transactions where a personal check would not be. Cashier's checks are generally considered as good as cash.

CASH MARKET or **SPOT MARKET** market in which transactions are promptly completed, that is, ownership of the commodity is transferred from seller to buyer and payment is given on delivery of the commodity. The cash market contrasts with the FUTURES MARKET, in which contracts are completed at a specified time in the future.

CASH-ON-CASH RETURN method of yield computation used for investments. It simply divides the annual dollar income by the total dollar invested; a $10,000 investment that pays $1,000 annually thus has a 10% *cash-on-cash return*. More sensitive measures are INTERNAL RATE OF RETURN and YIELD TO MATURITY.

CASH ON DELIVERY (COD) transaction requiring that goods be paid for in full by cash or certified check or the equivalent at the point of delivery. The term *collect on delivery* has the same abbreviation and same meaning.

CASH OR DEFERRED ARRANGEMENT (CODA) *see* 401K.

CASH ORDER order accompanied by the required payment. *See also* CASH BUYER.

CASH PAYMENTS JOURNAL book or log where cash disbursements are recorded sequentially.

CASH POSITION amount of cash or equivalent instruments held at any point in time. A commodity or securities trader or an investment company needs to monitor its cash position carefully to maintain adequate LIQUIDITY.

CASH RATIO ratio of cash and marketable securities to current liabilities; refinement of the QUICK RATIO. The *cash ratio* tells the extent to which liabilities could be liquidated immediately. Sometimes called LIQUIDITY RATIO.

CASH RECEIPTS JOURNAL book or log where amounts received are recorded in sequence.

CASH REGISTER machine for recording cash and credit receipts from sales. It generally includes a paper tape that provides a receipt to the customer and prints each transaction. The amount recorded is reconciled daily with the actual amount of cash and credit receipts in the machine, and sales are logged into the appropriate journal.

CASH RESERVE cash kept by a person or business that is beyond their immediate needs.

CASH SURRENDER VALUE money a policyowner is entitled to receive from an insurance company upon surrendering a life insurance policy with cash value. The sum is the cash value stated in the policy minus a surrender charge and any outstanding loans and interest thereon. Increases in *cash surrender value* are not TAXABLE INCOME. Cash value received upon surrender of a policy is also not taxable income.

CASH THROW-OFF *see* CASH FLOW.

CASH VALUE *see* BOOK VALUE; MARKET VALUE.

CASH VALUE LIFE INSURANCE policy that generates a savings element. Cash values are critical to a permanent life insurance policy. The size of a cash value buildup differs substantially from company to company.

CASSETTE easy-to-hold reel of magnetic tape enclosed in a plastic case. Audiocassettes are used for music and voice recordings, while videocassettes can store moving pictures as well as sound. *Microcassettes* are used in some dictation and telephone-answering devices, though they have largely been supplanted by digital recording techniques.

CASUAL LABORER part-time worker whose livelihood is achieved from irregular, often temporary work. Such work is often seasonal and is performed in several successive locations.

CASUALTY INSURANCE coverage primarily for the liability of an individual or organization that results from negligent acts and omissions, thereby causing bodily injury and/or property damage to a third party.

CASUALTY LOSS loss of property due to fire, storm, shipwreck, theft or other casualty, which is allowable, net of insurance reimbursement, as a DEDUCTION in computing TAXABLE INCOME. To qualify as a *casualty loss*, a loss must be due to a sudden, unexpected, or unusual event. A personal casualty loss, to be deductible, must exceed a $100 floor and 10% of adjusted gross income.

CAT *see* COMPUTER-ASSISTED TRANSCRIPTION.

CATASTROPHE HAZARD circumstance under which there is a significant deviation of the actual aggregate losses from the expected aggregate losses. For example, a hurricane is a hazard that is catastrophic in nature, since whole units or blocks of businesses may be threatened. *Catastrophic hazards* often cannot or will not be insured by commercial insurance companies either because the hazard is too great or because the actuarial premium is prohibitive.

CATASTROPHE POLICY major medical expense policy designed to pay all or nearly all expenses above a certain deductible amount, up to the limit of the policy.

CATCH-UP CONTRIBUTIONS supplemental tax-deferred contributions to IRAs and other QUALIFIED PLANS permitted for individuals and employees 50 years or older. Congress added the new catch-up contribution limits out of concern that baby boomers had not been saving enough for retirement. The provisions apply in 401(k), 403(b), and 457 plans and IRAs, but the rules differ among plans. Permitted catch-up contributions in 2006 are $1,000 per person for IRAs and $5,000 for 401(k) plans. Catch-up contributions are made on top of current limits.

CATEGORY KILLERS specialty hard goods retailers that dominate a particular market segment. Well-known examples include Home Depot, Barnes & Noble, Best Buy, Office Depot, PetSmart, and Toys "R" Us.

CATHODE RAY TUBE (CRT) device whereby electrons are sprayed onto a viewing screen, under the direction of magnetic fields, to form patterns. Examples of CRTs include television screens and computer terminals.

CATS *see* CERTIFICATE OF ACCRUAL ON TREASURY SECURITIES.

CATS AND DOGS speculative stocks that have short histories of sales, earnings, and dividend payments. In bull markets, analysts say disparagingly that even the *cats and dogs* are going up.

CATV *see* COMMUNITY ANTENNA TELEVISION.

CAUSE OF ACTION claim in law and fact sufficient to form the basis of a valid lawsuit, as a BREACH OF CONTRACT. A *right of action* is the legal right to sue; a *cause of action* is the composite of facts that gives rise to a right of action.

CAUSE-RELATED MARKETING identifying and targeting specific markets for various social issues.

CAVEAT warning, often written to a potential buyer, to be careful; often offered as a way for the seller or broker to minimize liability for what might otherwise be a deceptive trade practice.

CAVEAT EMPTOR (Latin for "Let the buyer beware.") rule of law that the purchaser buys at his own risk. In recent years this doctrine has eroded to require disclosure by the seller of known defects in the product.

CCH COMMERCE CLEARING HOUSE; publishes extensively on business and tax matters.

C CORPORATION a corporation taxed under Subchapter C of the Internal Revenue Code, a *regular corporation*.

CD *see* CERTIFICATE OF DEPOSIT; COMPACT DISC.

CD-ROM compact *d*isk *r*ead-*o*nly *m*emory, which refers to the use of compact disks similar to audio compact disks as a computer storage medium. A computer CD stores information in digital form, similar to an audio CD, although the computer information may be either text, pictures, or sound. Computer CDs have capacities of several hundred MEGABYTES.

CELL the intersection of a row and a column in a table, especially in a computer SPREADSHEET.

CELLULAR LAYOUT organization of a production facility so that items having similar processing requirements are grouped together.

CENSURE act by a governmental agency or professional organization, indicating condemnation or significant disapproval of an action by an individual or firm. Censure results from a material wrongdoing of an individual or company in the performance of professional duties. An example is when a CPA violates GENERALLY ACCEPTED ACCOUNTING PRINCIPLES (GAAP).

CENSUS OF BUSINESS annual survey by the U.S. Department of Commerce whereby businesses disclose product manufacturing and other activities of the past year.

CENTRAL BANK country's bank that: (1) issues currency; (2) administers monetary policy, including OPEN-MARKET OPERATIONS; (3) holds deposits representing the reserves of other banks; and (4) engages in transactions designed to facilitate the conduct of business and protect the public interest. In the United States, the FEDERAL RESERVE SYSTEM is the central bank.

CENTRAL BUSINESS DISTRICT (CBD) downtown section of a city, generally consisting of retail, office, hotel, entertainment, and governmental land uses with some high-density housing.

CENTRAL BUYING widely used chain store practice whereby all purchasing is done through the central or main office. Shipments of merchandise, however, are usually made to the different branches of the store.

CENTRALIZATION organization along a strictly hierarchical model. No delegation of authority is permitted. Centralization's benefits of clear direction and facilitated planning are offset by its inflexibility as well as poor accountability since no subunit has independent authority to act. *See also* CENTRAL PLANNING.

CENTRALIZED MANAGEMENT a characteristic that indicates that an organization may be taxed as a corporation. Day-to-day business operations are handled by appointed officers rather than the shareholders.

CENTRAL PLANNING organizational strategy development by an agency having these responsibilities. Since no other agency has authority for these responsibilities, this limits communication and spontaneity but has the advantage that all organizational activities are more easily coordinated. *See also* CENTRALIZATION; PLANNED ECONOMY.

CENTRAL PROCESSING UNIT (CPU) part of a computer where arithmetic and logic operations are performed and instructions are decoded and executed. The CPU controls the operation of the computer. A MICROPROCESSOR is an integrated circuit that contains a complete CPU on a single chip.

CENTRAL TENDENCY measure that indicates the typical MEDIAN value of a distribution. The mean and the median are examples of measures of central tendency.

CEO *see* CHIEF EXECUTIVE OFFICER.

CERCLA *see* COMPREHENSIVE ENVIRONMENTAL RESPONSE, COMPENSATION, AND LIABILITY ACT.

CERTIFICATE formal declaration that can be used to document a fact, such as a *birth certificate*.

CERTIFICATE OF ACCRUAL ON TREASURY SECURITIES (CATS) U.S. Treasury issues, sold at a deep discount from face value. A zero coupon security, they pay no interest during their lifetime, but return the full face value at maturity. They are appropriate for retirement or education planning. As Treasury securities, CATS cannot be called.

CERTIFICATE OF DEPOSIT (CD) debt instrument issued by a bank that usually pays interest. Institutional CDs are issued in denominations of $100,000 or more, and individual CDs start as low as $100. Maturities range from a few weeks to several years. Interest rates are set by competitive forces in the marketplace.

CERTIFICATE OF ELIGIBILITY issued by the VETERANS ADMINISTRATION to those who qualify. A person honorably discharged after serving a certain number of days on active duty in the armed forces is entitled to a certificate of eligibility. It indicates eligibility for a VA mortgage loan.

CERTIFICATE OF INCORPORATION document similar to ARTICLES OF INCORPORATION. In some states the certificate is issued by a state agency after the articles of incorporation have been properly filed. The corporation's existence begins upon the issuance of the certificate.

CERTIFICATE OF OCCUPANCY document by a local government agency signifying that a building or dwelling conforms to local building code regulations. Generally, initial occupancy of a building or transfer of title requires valid *certificate of occupancy*.

CERTIFICATE OF REASONABLE VALUE (CRV) document issued by the VETERANS ADMINISTRATION, based on an approved APPRAISAL. It establishes a ceiling on the maximum VA mortgage loan principal. For example, a *certificate of reasonable value* is received for a home that was under a contract of sale. Since the certificate is for $1,000 more than the contracted price, the VA loans the full purchase price.

CERTIFICATE OF TITLE document indicating ownership. It is similar to a BILL OF SALE and is usually associated with the sale of new motor vehicles.

CERTIFICATE OF USE warranty card accompanying new merchandise, which the owner completes certifying his ownership.

CERTIFICATION act of confirming formally as true, accurate, or genuine.

CERTIFICATION MARK
1. license for an activity issued by government or by units authorized by the government.
2. in labor relations, formal recognition by government of a union's status as the recognized collective BARGAINING AGENT.

CERTIFIED ADMINISTRATIVE MANAGER (CAM) certification awarded by the Institute of Certified Professional Managers. It is a professional certificate awarded to an individual who has completed a series of five examinations and a case study. In order to be qualified the individual must have at least three years' management experience.

CERTIFIED CHECK check containing a certification that the drawer of the check has sufficient funds in the bank to cover payment. Although considered absolutely safe by many, there is the possibility of forgery. *See also* CASHIER'S CHECK.

CERTIFIED FINANCIAL PLANNER (CFP) professional license conferred by the International Board of Standards and Practices for Certified Financial Planners. In addition to professional business experience in financial planning, recipients must pass national examinations in insurance, investments, taxation, employee benefit plans, and estate planning.

CERTIFIED FINANCIAL STATEMENT balance sheet, income statement, and perhaps other financial papers that are attested to by a CERTIFIED PUBLIC ACCOUNTANT (CPA) who AUDITED the company.

CERTIFIED GENERAL APPRAISER one qualified to appraise any property, under APPRAISER certification law adopted by most states in the early 1990s.

CERTIFIED HISTORIC STRUCTURE *see* HISTORIC STRUCTURE.

CERTIFIED MAIL service of the U.S. Postal Service, available at extra cost, that provides proof of mailing and delivery for any first-class mail. A sender may request a return receipt or restricted delivery upon paying a supplementary fee. Insurance is not available. *See also* REGISTERED MAIL.

CERTIFIED MANAGEMENT ACCOUNTANT (CMA) certification awarded by the Institute of Management Accountants to an individual who has passed a four-part examination and met certain education and experience requirements.

CERTIFIED PUBLIC ACCOUNTANT (CPA) accountant who has passed certain exams, achieved a certain amount of experience, reached a certain age, and met all other statutory and licensing requirements of the U.S. state where he or she works. In addition to accounting and auditing, CPAs prepare tax returns for corporations and individuals.

CERTIFIED RESIDENTIAL APPRAISER one qualified to APPRAISE residences and up to four units of housing, under appraiser certification law. Standards call for less education, less experience, and a less comprehensive exam than for a CERTIFIED GENERAL APPRAISER.

C&F *cost and freight* charges for a shipment. *See also* COST, INSURANCE, AND FREIGHT.

CFA *see* CHARTERED FINANCIAL ANALYST.

CFE Certified Fraud Examiner, a designation of the ASSOCIATION OF CERTIFIED FRAUD EXAMINERS.

CFO *see* CHIEF FINANCIAL OFFICER.

CHAIN FEEDING
1. successive threading into a machine or device so that each successive piece is held in place by the preceding one.
2. inserting envelopes continuously into a computer printer for rapid addressing.

CHAIN OF COMMAND structure of decision-making responsibilities from the higher levels of authority to the lower levels. It originated in the military and encourages compliance without dissension.

CHAIN OF TITLE a chronological history of all CONVEYANCES and ENCUMBRANCES affecting a land title. *See also* ABSTRACT OF TITLE.

CHAIN STORE individual retail store that is a part of a group of similar retail stores with the same management and ownership.

CHAIRMAN OF THE BOARD member of a corporation's board of directors who presides over its meetings and who is the highest ranking officer in the corporation. The chairman of the board may or may not have the most actual executive authority in a firm. The additional title of CHIEF EXECUTIVE OFFICER is reserved for the principal executive.

CHAMPERTY in common law, an arrangement, once illegal, whereby an attorney or other party underwrites the costs of a lawsuit in return for a portion of the expected damage award. Today the prohibition against *champerty* survives only in a few jurisdictions and only in modified form.

CHANCERY jurisprudence that is exercised in a court of equity. *See also* EQUITY.

CHANGE transaction against a computer file that adds, deletes, or changes information in a record.

CHANGE AGENT a person whose presence or thought processes cause a change from the traditional way of handling or thinking about a problem. Management consultants are often hired as *change agents* for corporate organization development retreats.

CHANGE IN ACCOUNTING METHOD change in the overall method of accounting and any change in a material item used in an overall accounting plan. *See also* ACCOUNTING METHOD. In general, a taxpayer may not change a method of accounting without advance IRS approval.

CHANNEL CAPTAIN dominant company in a vertical marketing system that controls the CHANNEL OF DISTRIBUTION. This company has a major influence on what products or services are developed and distributed throughout the channel.

CHANNEL OF DISTRIBUTION means used to transfer merchandise from the manufacturer to the end user. Intermediaries in the channel are called *middlemen*. Those who actually take title to the merchandise and resell the goods are *merchant middlemen*. Those who act as BROKER but do not take title are *agent middlemen*. Merchant middlemen include wholesalers and retailers. Agent middlemen include MANUFACTURER'S REPRESENTATIVES, brokers, and sales agents.

CHANNEL OF SALES in periodical publishing, SOURCE of subscription orders, such as DIRECT MAIL advertising, agency, or newsstand. Source analysis is the focus of circulation management activity.

CHAPTER 7 OF THE 1978 BANKRUPTCY ACT dealing with LIQUIDATION, provides for a court-appointed interim trustee with broad powers and discretion to make management changes, arrange unsecured financing, and generally operate the debtor business in such a way as to prevent loss.

CHAPTER 11 OF THE 1978 BANKRUPTCY ACT dealing with REORGANIZATION, provides that, unless the court rules otherwise, the debtor remains in possession of the business and in control of its operation. Debtor and creditors are allowed considerable flexibility in working together.

CHARGE
1. cost of goods or services.
2. purchasing goods or services prior to paying for them. The cost will be billed later.
3. in criminal law, description of the underlying offense in an accusation or indictment.
4. in trial practice, address delivered by the court to the jury at the close of the case, telling them the principles of law they are to apply in reaching a decision.

CHARGE BUYER one who makes a purchase on credit to be billed at a later date; also called CREDIT BUYER. *See also* CREDIT ORDER.

CHARGE OFF *see* BAD DEBT.

CHARITABLE CONTRIBUTION DEDUCTION itemized deduction allowed for donations to qualifying charities. A number of limitations apply to this deduction, especially for noncash property donations.

CHARITABLE REMAINDER TRUST IRREVOCABLE TRUST that pays income to one or more individuals until the grantor's death, at which time the balance, which is tax free, passes to a designated charity. It is a popular tax-saving alternative for individuals who have no children or who are wealthy enough to benefit both children and charity.

CHARITABLE TRUST trust originated in an effort to make one or more gifts to a charitable organization.

CHARITY *see* QUALIFIED CHARITY.

CHARTER
Law: document issued by a government establishing a corporate entity. Many kinds of organizations—including cities—are chartered. *See also* ARTICLES OF INCORPORATION; CERTIFICATE OF INCORPORATION.
Transportation: hire a vehicle, usually for exclusive use.

CHARTERED ACCOUNTANT professional designation for British accountant. To be one, a candidate must pass rigorous examinations, as CPAs must do in the United States.

CHARTERED FINANCIAL ANALYST (CFA) a designation conferred by the CFA Institute (formerly the Association for Investment Management and Research), a global nonprofit organization of more than 83,000 investment professionals from 129 countries worldwide. Headquartered in Charlottesville, Virginia, the CFA Institute also has regional offices in Hong Kong, London, and New York. The CFA Program is a globally recognized standard for measuring the competence and integrity of financial analysts. CFA exams at three levels are administered semiannually at 186 test centers in 86 countries (67 in the United States alone).

CHARTERED FINANCIAL CONSULTANT (ChFC) professional designation awarded by The American College in Bryn Mawr, Pennsylvania. In addition to professional business experience in financial planning, recipients are required to pass national examinations in insurance, investments, taxation, employee benefit plans, estate planning, accounting, and management. This program responds to the growing need for help in personal financial planning.

CHARTERED LIFE UNDERWRITER (CLU) professional designation conferred by The American College. In addition to professional business experience in insurance planning and related areas, recipients must pass national examinations in insurance, investments, taxation, employee benefit plans, estate planning, accounting, management and economics. This program responds to a need by individuals for technically proficient help in planning their life insurance.

CHARTERED PROPERTY AND CASUALTY UNDERWRITER (CPCU) professional designation earned after the successful completion of 10 national examinations given by the CPCU Society. Covers such areas of expertise as insurance, risk management, economics, finance, management, accounting, and law. Three years of work experience in the insurance business or a related area are also required.

CHARTIST technical analyst who charts the patterns of stocks, bonds, and commodities to make buy and sell recommendations to clients.

Chartists believe recurring patterns of trading can help them forecast future price movements. *See also* TECHNICAL ANALYSIS.

CHART OF ACCOUNTS organized list of the names and numbers of all ACCOUNTS in the GENERAL LEDGER.

CHAT a form of interactive online communication that permits typed conversations to occur in real time. Messages are instantaneously relayed from one participant in a chat discussion to all other members in the chat room.

CHATTEL any tangible, movable thing; PERSONAL PROPERTY as opposed to REAL PROPERTY; GOODS.

CHATTEL MORTGAGE mortgage on personal property created to secure the payment of money owed or the performance of some other obligation. This security device has for the most part been replaced by the security agreements available under the UNIFORM COMMERCIAL CODE (UCC).

CHATTEL PAPER document that shows both a debt and a SECURITY INTEREST in or a LEASE of specific goods.

CHECK DRAFT upon a bank, payable on DEMAND, and by the *maker* or *drawer*, containing a promise to pay an amount of money to the *payee*. *See also* CASHIER'S CHECK; CERTIFIED CHECK.

CHECK BOX a square in a DIALOG BOX that can be clicked with the mouse to turn an option on (checked) or off (unchecked). *Check boxes* are used for options that are not mutually exclusive; for example, in a font formatting dialog, the user may check boxes for italic, boldface, *and* superscript. *Contrast with* RADIO BUTTON.

CHECK DIGIT digit that is appended to a number so that an accountant can assure the number's correctness following a computation. As the number is utilized in processing, the identical calculation is performed to see if the new check digit is the same as the original one. If so, the number has been read or written accurately. A variation between the check digits indicates an error possibly due to an omission or transposition.

CHECK KITING illegal scheme that establishes a false line of credit by the exchange of worthless checks between two banks. For instance, a check kiter might have empty checking accounts at two different banks, *A* and *B*. The kiter writes a check for $50,000 on the bank *A* account and deposits it in the bank *B* account. If the kiter has good credit at bank *B*, he will be able to draw funds against the deposited check before it CLEARS, that is, is forwarded to bank *A* for payment and paid by bank *A*. Since the clearing process usually takes a few days, the kiter can use the $50,000 for a few days and then deposit it in the bank *A* account before the $50,000 check drawn on that account clears.

CHECK PROTECTOR machine that prints CHECKS in a manner that makes it difficult to alter. Physically, it elevates the written amount to create many small bumps on otherwise smooth paper.

CHECK REGISTER log, book, or journal where each check issued is posted sequentially.

CHECK SIGNER machine that signs checks mechanically, usually creating a FACSIMILE signature.

CHECK STUB stub attached to a check with perforations. The check is detached for payment, while the stub may be retained for convenience, with information concerning the check. Stub and check are both printed with the same number.

CHECK TRUNCATION *see* TRUNCATION.

CHEQUE British term for CHECK.

CHICAGO BOARD OF TRADE *see* SECURITIES AND COMMODITIES EXCHANGE.

CHICAGO BOARD OPTIONS EXCHANGE *see* SECURITIES AND COMMODITIES EXCHANGES.

CHICAGO MERCANTILE EXCHANGE *see* SECURITIES AND COMMODITIES EXCHANGES.

CHIEF EXECUTIVE OFFICER (CEO) officer who has ultimate management responsibility for an organization. The CEO reports directly to a BOARD OF DIRECTORS, which is accountable to the company's owners. The CEO appoints other managers, including a president, to assist in carrying out the responsibilities of the organization. The CEO can also have the title CEO/President if the responsibilities of both positions are combined.

CHIEF FINANCIAL OFFICER (CFO) corporate officer having full financial authority to make appropriations and authorize expenditures for an organization.

CHIEF OPERATING OFFICER (COO) person who has full operational responsibilities for the day-to-day activities of an organization. *See also* PRESIDENT.

CHILD AND DEPENDENT CARE CREDIT nonrefundable TAX CREDIT allowed for a percentage of the expenses incurred for household services or for care of a child or other DEPENDENT where a taxpayer maintains a household that includes one or more dependents who are under 13 years of age or mentally or physically incapacitated. The percentage of credit varies inversely with the taxpayer's ADJUSTED GROSS INCOME (AGI) between $15,000 and $43,000.

CHILD SUPPORT payment specifically designated for the purpose of child support (or treated as such) under a divorce or separation agreement. Such payments are neither deductible by the payer nor taxable to the payee. *Contrast with* ALIMONY.

CHINESE WALL imaginary barrier between departments of a service company (broker, consultant) constructed in an effort to avoid a conflict of interest.

CHIP *see* INTEGRATED CIRCUIT.

CHI-SQUARE TEST statistical method to test whether two (or more) variables are: (1) independent or (2) homogeneous. The chi-square test for independence examines whether knowing the value of one variable helps to estimate the value of another variable. The chi-square test for homogeneity examines whether two populations have the same proportion of observations with a common characteristic. Though the formula is the same for both tests, the underlying logic and sampling procedures vary.

CHOSE IN ACTION CLAIM or DEBT upon which recovery may be made in a lawsuit. It is merely a right to sue, becoming a possessory thing only upon successful completion of a lawsuit.

CHURNING excessive trading in a stock investment account. If the pattern of activity is inappropriate for the customer and if the prime result is excessive brokerage commissions for the REGISTERED REPRESENTATIVE, then the practice is illegal and recovery of damages by the customer is possible.

CHUTZPAH unmitigated gall, generally unacceptable brazen behavior. In some types of business, it is regarded as an asset: a positive quality of heroic audacity or guts.

CIF (COST, INSURANCE, AND FREIGHT) in a contract of sale, the cost of the goods, the insurance, and the freight to the destination are included in the contract price. Unless there is something in a CIF contract to indicate the contrary, the seller completes the contract when the merchandise is delivered to the shipper, the freight to the point of destination is paid, and the buyer has been forwarded the BILL OF LADING, invoice, insurance policy, and receipt showing payment of freight.

CIPHER coded message. A businessperson who is concerned about secret information may use a cipher to prevent others from understanding the secret.

CIRCUIT territory in which a court possesses jurisdiction or travels from place to place to hear and decide cases.

CIRCUIT BREAKERS measures instituted by the major stock and commodities exchanges to halt trading in stocks and stock index futures temporarily when the market has fallen by an amount based on specified percentage declines in a specified period. *Circuit breakers* were originally instituted in 1987. They are subject to change from time to time, but may include trading halts, curtailment of automated trading systems, and/or price movement limits on index futures. Their purpose is to prevent a market free-fall by permitting a rebalancing of buy and sell orders and to give the general public an opportunity to catch up on current news. *See also* PROGRAM TRADING.

CIRCULAR E an IRS publication that provides instructions for employers concerning employment tax withholding amounts and procedures.

CIRCULATION EXPENSES costs of establishing, maintaining, or increasing the circulation of a periodical.

CITIZEN *see* U.S. CITIZEN.

CIVILIAN LABOR FORCE all members of the population aged 16 or over in the United States who are not in the military or institutions such as prisons or mental hospitals and who are either employed or are unemployed and actively seeking and available for work. Every month the U.S. Department of Labor releases the unemployment rate, which is the percentage of the *civilian labor force* that is unemployed. In very bad economic times, the unemployment rate can be deceptive because it does not consider *discouraged workers*, those who are unemployed but have stopped actively seeking employment.

CIVIL LAW
1. Roman law embodied in the Justinian Code. *See also* COMMON LAW.
2. law concerned with noncriminal matters.
3. body of laws established by a state or nation, as distinguished from *natural law*.

CIVIL LIABILITY negligent acts and/or omissions, other than breach of contract, normally independent of moral obligations for which a remedy can be provided in a court of law. For example, a person injured in someone's home can bring suit under *civil liability* law.

CIVIL PENALTY fine or money damages. Civil penalties are imposed as punishment for a certain activity and act as a criminal sanction, while civil remedies redress wrongs between private parties.

CIVIL RIGHTS rights protected by the U.S. Constitution. These rights can be enforced by court action. Among them are the right to own property, to utilize the courts, to marry, to contract, and to obtain other benefits set out by law, including all rights set out in federal statutes.

CIVIL WRONG act, or omission to act, that violates a legal duty; tort. It gives the victim of the wrong the right to bring a civil action for a remedy.

CLAIM request by an insured for indemnification by an insurance company for loss incurred from an insured peril.

CLAIM FOR REFUND claim by a taxpayer to the Internal Revenue Service for a refund of all or part of the taxes paid in earlier years. Such a claim can result from the correction of an error or the availability of a loss or credit that can be carried back and used to reduce the tax liability of a prior year.

CLAIM REPORT report furnished by the ADJUSTER to the INSURANCE COMPANY (INSURER) that documents the amount of payment the insurer is legally obligated to pay to or on behalf of the INSURED under the terms of the policy.

CLASS
1. group of people who meet together for an educational purpose (e.g., elementary school class) or students or alumni who share a certain year of graduation (e.g., ABC College Class of 2005).
2. securities having similar features. Stocks and bonds are the two main classes; they are subdivided into various classes—for example, mortgage bonds and debentures, issues with different rates of interest, common and preferred stock, and Class A and Class B common. The different classes in a company's capitalization are itemized on its balance sheet.
3. group of people who meet certain specified criteria, as in a CLASS ACTION suit.

CLASS A/CLASS B SHARES shares of stock issued by the same company, having some difference, such as voting rights, or a dividend preference or participation.

CLASS ACTION a SUIT brought by one or more members of a large group of persons on behalf of all members of the group. If the court permits the class action, all members must receive notice of the action and must be given an opportunity to exclude themselves. Members who do not exclude themselves are bound by the JUDGMENT, whether favorable or not.

CLASSIFICATION
1. classes or grades by which jobs are evaluated.
2. any method of delineating and categorizing business activities and products.

CLASSIFIED STOCK common STOCK divided into two or more classes. A typical approach is for a company to issue Class A stock to raise the bulk of EQUITY capital, while vesting voting rights in Class B stock, which is retained by management and/or founders.

CLASS LIFE ASSET DEPRECIATION *see* ASSET DEPRECIATION RANGE.

CLASS STRUGGLE antagonism between social classes resulting from different economic and social interests; first identified by Karl Marx. One of Marx's examples is the conflict between the owners of capital (bourgeoisie) and the nonowning employees (proletariat). According to the Communist Manifesto, written during the Industrial Revolution, the workers will rise up and take over the state by force.

CLAUSE in an insurance policy, sentences and paragraphs describing various coverages, exclusions, duties of the insured, locations covered, and conditions that suspend or terminate coverage.

CLAYTON ANTI-TRUST ACT *see* ANTITRUST ACTS.

CLEAN

Accounting: unqualified audit report; called a *clean opinion*. *See also* QUALIFIED OPINION.

Finance: free of debt, as in a *clean* balance sheet.

International trade: without documents, as in *clean* versus documentary drafts.

Securities: block trade that matches corresponding buy or sell orders, thus sparing the block positioner any inventory risk.

CLEAN HANDS
1. honest and professional behavior with nothing done improperly under the table. For example, a salesperson dealing directly and forthrightly with a purchasing agent is acting properly. There are no payoffs of any kind.
2. in law, plaintiff coming to court with no record of misconduct on his part in the same area as that to which he is charging the defendant. An example is where one party charges the other with unfair competition; the suit may be dropped if it can be shown that the complaining party has followed similar practices.

CLEAN OPINION *see* CLEAN; ACCOUNTANT'S OPINION.

CLEANUP FUND informal phrase describing the "needs approach" to determine the amount of life insurance necessary for a family. It is intended to cover last-minute expenses as well as those that surface after the death of an insured, such as burial costs, probate charges, and medical bills.

CLEAR

Banking: COLLECTION of funds on which a check is drawn, and payment of those funds to the holder of the check.

Finance: asset not securing a loan and not otherwise encumbered; to make a profit. For example, after all expenses, they *cleared* $1 million.

Securities: comparison of the details of a transaction between brokers prior to settlement; final exchange of securities for cash on delivery.

CLEARANCE SALE special retail sale, usually held to move out completely a type or brand of product from inventory.

CLEARINGHOUSE
1. association, usually formed voluntarily by banks, to exchange checks, drafts, or other forms of indebtedness held by one member and owed to another. Its object is to settle balances between the banks of a city or region with a minimum of inconvenience and labor.
2. in a stock or commodities exchange, an organization to facilitate settlement of the debits and credits of its members with each other.

CLEAR TITLE TITLE free from any ENCUMBRANCE, obstruction, burden, or limitation that presents a doubtful or even a reasonable question of law or fact as to its validity. *See also* GOOD TITLE; MARKETABLE TITLE.

CLERICAL ERROR mistake made while copying or transmitting legal documents, as distinguished from a *judgment error*, which is an error made in the exercise of judgment or discretion, or a *technical error*, which is an error in interpreting a law, regulation, or principle.

CLERK assistant or subordinate. A *file clerk* maintains papers placed in a file cabinet; *stock clerk* maintains inventory.

CLICK depress one of the buttons on a computer mouse. Different actions are performed by clicking the left (primary) and right (secondary) buttons or the center button (if any) and by DOUBLE-CLICKING. Effects also vary from one application to another.

CLIENT
In general: person, company, or organization that uses the professional services of another.
Advertising: manufacturer, owner, or provider of a product or service who desires to advertise that product or service utilizing the help of a qualified specialist; also called ACCOUNT. The *client* is the customer for whom the advertising agency works.

CLIENT FOCUS company policy, philosophy, or mission intended to be responsive to client needs, attentive to developing client relationships, and committed to client service and innovation.

CLIENT-SERVER MODEL a configuration in which one computer, designated as a server, sends information to a number of other "client" computers.

CLIP ART computer graphics files that can be inserted into a document or other file (the name derives from books of art from which designers literally clipped art to paste into their layouts). Clip art is included in many programs (especially DESKTOP PUBLISHING and drawing applications such as Microsoft Publisher and Corel-DRAW!) and is also sold in separate packages.

CLIPBOARD a computer holding area that temporarily stores information cut or copied from a document. Both MACINTOSH and WINDOWS operating systems support this feature.

CLIPPING COUPONS removing an appropriate portion of a COUPON BOND to submit in order to collect (usually) semiannual interest; before the days of REGISTERED BONDS, BEARER BONDS had such coupons attached. It is because of these coupons that a bond's interest payments are called *coupons*. In recent years, the expression has come to describe clipping newspaper or magazine COUPONS to obtain discounts. Whereas *clipping coupons* used to evoke a vision of a wealthy investor able to live on investment income alone, it now suggests the activity of a penny-pinching homemaker.

CLONE
In general: genetically identical duplicate of an organism.
Business: exact or nearly exact duplicate of some object, such as a typewriter or microcomputer.

CLOSE
1. price of the final trade of a security at the end of a trading day.
2. last half-hour of a trading session on the exchanges.
3. in accounting, transfer of revenue and expense accounts at the end of the period, called *closing the books*.
4. consummating a sale or agreement. *See also* CLOSING.
5. exit a file or program. The term QUIT is often used for the latter, but in WINDOWS the operator exits by closing an application window. In the MACINTOSH environment, *close* is the equivalent of Minimize (reduce to an icon) in Windows, and QUIT is the proper term for exiting.

CLOSE CORPORATION *see* CLOSELY HELD CORPORATION.

CLOSE CORPORATION PLAN prior arrangement for surviving stockholders to purchase shares of a deceased stockholder according to a predetermined formula for setting the value of the corporation. Often, the best source for its funding is a life insurance policy. PREMIUMS on such a policy are not tax deductible as a business expense, but the death benefits are not subject to income tax.

CLOSED ACCOUNT
1. a bank or charge account that has been terminated.
2. in accounting, GENERAL LEDGER account that has been prepared for the next year by closing off the previous year's amount. *See also* CLOSING ENTRY.

CLOSED ECONOMY self-sufficient economic system in which all production and consumption is contained within itself; no commerce (exporting or importing) outside the system itself exists.

CLOSED-END MORTGAGE mortgage-bond issue with an indenture that prohibits repayment before maturity and the repledging of the same collateral without the permission of the bondholders; also called *closed mortgage. See also* OPEN-END MORTGAGE.

CLOSED-END MUTUAL FUND INVESTMENT COMPANY that operates a mutual fund with a limited number of shares outstanding. Unlike a MUTUAL FUND, which creates new shares to meet investor demand, a *closed-end fund* starts with a set number of shares.

CLOSED FUND MUTUAL FUND that has become too large and is no longer issuing shares.

CLOSED PERIOD a period of time, often 10 years, after issuance of a bond when that bond cannot be called. *See also* CALLABLE.

CLOSED SHOP organization where workers are required to be in a UNION before they can be hired. For all practical purposes, closed shops were made illegal by the TAFT-HARTLEY ACT of 1947. *See also* OPEN SHOP.

CLOSED STOCK merchandise sold only in sets. Individual items from a set cannot be purchased and there is no certainty that replacements will be available at a future time. Examples are sets of glassware and china. *Contrast with* OPEN STOCK.

CLOSED UNION *see* CLOSED SHOP.

CLOSELY HELD CORPORATION
1. one that is publicly traded although it has few stockholders. It is distinguished from privately held or closed corporations, which are not publicly traded.
2. in taxation, one in which five or fewer individuals own 50% or more of the outstanding stock during the last half of the year.

CLOSEOUT clearing out merchandise by a sale.

CLOSET INDEXING structuring a MUTUAL FUND or other managed portfolio to nearly replicate an index and avoid the risk of underperforming it, which would reflect negatively on the manager. Closet indexers do not admit they are indexers; they charge the regular fees for active management but deliver results similar to index funds, which are unmanaged and have much lower fees.

CLOSING
1. consummation of a transaction involving the sale of real estate or of an interest in real estate, usually by payment of the purchase price (or some agreed portion), delivery of the DEED or other INSTRUMENT of title, and finalizing of collateral matters.
2. in accounting, the process that occurs at year-end when final accounting entries are made to close the books. *See* CLOSE.

CLOSING AGREEMENT written agreement between a taxpayer and the Internal Revenue Service that conclusively settles a tax liability for the TAXABLE YEAR ending prior to the agreement date or settles one or more issues affecting a tax liability.

CLOSING COST various fees and expenses payable by the seller and buyer at the time of a real estate closing; also termed *transaction cost.* Some closing costs are brokerage commissions; lender discount points and other fees; title insurance premiums; deed recording fees; loan prepayment penalty; inspection and appraisal fees; and attorney's fees.

CLOSING DATE in real estate, date on which the seller delivers the DEED and the buyer pays for the property. For example, the sales contract generally establishes a closing date, at which time the parties will meet and settle all accounts necessary to transfer TITLE to the property.

CLOSING ENTRY in accounting, one of the final entries made at year-end to close accounts and transfer the amounts to financial statements. *See also* CLOSED ACCOUNT.

CLOSING INVENTORY value and quantities of stock in trade at the end of an ACCOUNTING PERIOD.

CLOSING PRICE or **CLOSING QUOTE** price of the last transaction completed during a day's trading session on an organized securities exchange. For purposes of valuation of stock, as in the case of charitable contributions and estates, the *closing quote* is used.

CLOSING STATEMENT accounting of funds from a real estate sale, made to both the seller and the buyer separately. Most states require the broker to furnish accurate closing statements to all parties to the transaction.

CLOUD ON TITLE any matter appearing in the record of a TITLE to real estate that on its face appears to reflect the existence of an outstanding CLAIM or ENCUMBRANCE that, if valid, would defeat or impair title, but that might be proven invalid by evidence outside the title record. *See also* QUITCLAIM DEED.

CLUSTER ANALYSIS method of statistical analysis that groups people or things by common characteristics of interest to the researcher. Can be used to characterize the behavior or interests of various customer clusters such as YUPPIES, so that promotion copy and design can be specifically targeted to them. Cluster analyses are frequently based upon geographic criteria so that mailings can be sent to the best clusters.

CLUSTER HOUSING subdivision technique in which detached dwelling units are grouped relatively close together, leaving open spaces as common areas.

CMO *see* COLLATERALIZED MORTGAGE OBLIGATION.

COACH FARE cost of passenger transportation based on an ordinary class of service that is less luxurious and less expensive than first-class service.

COBOL (*c*ommon *b*usiness-*o*riented *l*anguage) computer language developed in the early 1960s by several computer manufacturers and the U.S. Department of Defense. It was often used to write programs to process business data such as payrolls and accounts payable records.

COBRA acronym for Consolidated Omnibus Budget Reconciliation Act. *See also* CONTINUATION OF BENEFITS.

COD
1. cash on delivery.
2. cancellation of debt.

CODA *see* CASH OR DEFERRED ARRANGEMENT.

CODE
1. the Internal Revenue Code. The latest version, the INTERNAL REVENUE CODE OF 1986 (IRC), comprises the collective statutes govern-

ing the federal taxation of income, estates, gifts, employment, and excise transactions.

2. the instructions within a computer program, known as *source code*.

3. compilation of laws, such as the Motor Vehicle Code.

CODE OF ETHICS statement of principles concerning the behavior of those who subscribe to the code. A code of ethics defines proper professional behavior and practices that are considered unbecoming a person in that profession.

CODE OF PROFESSIONAL RESPONSIBILITY set of rules based on ethical considerations that govern the conduct of lawyers. It was passed by the American Bar Association and adopted by most states and is enforced by state disciplinary boards.

CODICIL supplement to a WILL, whose purpose is to add to, subtract from, or qualify, modify, or revoke the provisions of a prior will.

CODING process of writing an algorithm or other problem-solving procedure in a computer programming language.

CODING OF ACCOUNTS assignment of an identification number to each account in the financial statements. A CHART OF ACCOUNTS lists the account titles and account numbers being used by a business. For example, the numbers 1 to 29 may be used exclusively for asset accounts; numbers from 30 to 49 may be reserved for liabilities; numbers in the 50s may signify OWNER'S EQUITY accounts; numbers in the 60s may represent revenue accounts and numbers from 70 to 99 may designate expense accounts. In large or complex businesses with many more accounts, a more elaborate coding system would be needed.

COEFFICIENT OF DETERMINATION test statistic that shows the amount of variability in a dependent variable explained by the regression model's independent variable(s). It is denoted by R^2 and ranges from 0 to 1. If 0, there is no explanation of the dependent variable at all; if 1, the independent variables explain all the variability of the dependent variable.

COFFEE BREAK brief time period allowed during the working day to permit employees to unwind from the pressures of work so they are refreshed to carry out their chores.

COFFEE, SUGAR, AND COCOA EXCHANGE a division of the New York Board of Trade.

COGNITIVE BEHAVIOR being able to judge and reason effectively and having a perception of surroundings. An example is an advertising executive who, based on awareness and thoughts, derives the content of an ad or promotion for a product line.

COGNITIVE DISSONANCE

In general: psychological theory of human behavior. The theory suggests that human beings justify their behavior by changing their beliefs when these beliefs are inconsistent with behavior. For example, a man who says he does not believe in violence punches a salesperson. This juxtaposition of belief and action creates dissonance (conflict). The theory says that he will change his belief in nonviolence to justify his behavior.

Marketing (buyer's remorse): theory that a consumer may use a particular product because he or she believes the advertising for that product, which claims that the product is the most effective of its kind in the job that it does. The consumer may then see a competitor's advertisement that seems to prove conclusively that this competitive product is better. This creates dissonance. The consumer must now relieve the uncomfortable feeling that the dissonance brings about and will often do so by switching products. Even though advertisers want to create dissonance for nonusers of their product, they do not want to create it for those who do use their product. Cognitive dissonance most often occurs after the purchase of an expensive item such as an automobile. A consumer who is experiencing cognitive dissonance after his or her purchase may attempt to return the product or may seek positive information about it to justify the choice. If the buyer is unable to justify the purchase, he or she will also be less likely to purchase that brand again.

COHESIVENESS measure of organizational work group interpersonal allegiance.

COINCIDENT INDICATORS economic indicators that coincide with the current pace of economic activity. The Index of Coincident Indicators is published monthly by the Conference Board along with the Index of LEADING INDICATORS and the Index of LAGGING INDICATORS to give the public a reading on whether the economy is expanding or contracting and at what pace. The components of the Index of Coincident Indicators are nonfarm payroll workers, personal income less transfer payments, industrial production, manufacturing, and trade sales.

COINSURANCE INSURANCE plan in which the insurer provides indemnity for only a certain percentage of the insured's loss, reflecting the relative division of risk between insurer and insured. A *coinsurance* clause of 80%, for example, requires the property owner to keep property insured to at least that percentage of the property value. If the insured fails to keep that much insurance, he will not be reimbursed for the full loss.

COLA *see* COST-OF-LIVING ADJUSTMENT.

COLD CALLING practice by securities and other salespeople of making unsolicited calls to potential customers. The technique is often effective, even though the process is disliked by both salespeople and customers.

COLD CANVASS process of contacting potential buyers in an area in order to solicit sales of one's products.

COLD TYPE type set by computer, xerographic, or photographic means. Many publications are produced in-house on sophisticated cold-type machines. Formerly much of this work was produced in outside printing plants on HOT-TYPE printing presses.

COLLAPSIBLE CORPORATION a corporation dissolved before realizing a substantial portion of the taxable income to be derived from the property. The Internal Revenue Service treats gain on the sale or LIQUIDATION of a collapsible corporation as ORDINARY INCOME to the stockholder.

COLLAR index level at which a CIRCUIT BREAKER is tripped.

COLLATE arrange in ordered sets. In printing several copies of a multipage document, if the user checks the Collate box, one complete set of pages will be printed, followed by another set. Otherwise, the required number of copies of page 1 will be printed, followed by page 2, and so on.

COLLATERAL
1. secondary; on the side.
2. in commercial transactions, the property offered as security, usually as an inducement to another party, to lend money or extend credit.

COLLATERAL ASSIGNMENT designation of a policy's death benefit or its cash surrender value to a creditor as security for a loan. If the loan is not repaid, the creditor receives the policy proceeds up to the balance of the outstanding loan, and the beneficiary receives the remainder. Because life insurance is freely assignable, it is readily acceptable to lending institutions as security. Also, the lender is certain to receive the money should death strike the borrower before the loan can be repaid.

COLLATERALIZE pledge property as security for a debt. *See also* HYPOTHECATE.

COLLATERALIZED MORTGAGE OBLIGATION (CMO) mortgage-backed security that separates mortgage pools into short-, medium-, and long-term portions. *See also* GINNIE MAE PASS-THROUGH.

COLLEAGUE fellow member of a profession, association, occupation, or organization. Colleagues are important for mutual consultations and discussion as well as for friendship. The basis of being one's colleague is respect for one's position and training.

COLLECTIBLE rare object collected by investors. Examples are stamps, coins, oriental rugs, antiques, baseball cards, and photographs. Collectibles, other than bullion and certain coins typically rise in value during inflationary periods. Other than bullion and certain coins, collectibles are not valid investments for IRAs and self-directed Keogh plans.

COLLECTION
1. presentation of a negotiable instrument such as a draft or check to the place at which it is payable. The term refers to check clearing and payment and to such special banking services as foreign collections, coupon collection, and collection of returned items (bad checks).
2. referral of a past due account to specialists in collecting loans or accounts receivable, either an internal department or a private collection agency.
3. in a general financial sense, conversion of accounts receivable into cash.
4. one's set of COLLECTIBLES.

COLLECTION PERIOD *see* COLLECTION RATIO.

COLLECTION RATIO ratio of a company's accounts receivable to its average daily sales. The *collection ratio* is the average number of days it takes the company to convert receivables into cash. It is also called *average collection period. See also* ACCOUNTS RECEIVABLE TURNOVER.

COLLECTIVE BARGAINING process of settling labor disputes by negotiation between the employer and representatives of employees. *See also* ARBITRATION.

COLLECT ON DELIVERY (COD) *see* CASH ON DELIVERY.

COLLEGE SAVINGS PLAN *see* QUALIFIED TUITION PROGRAM (529 PLAN).

COLLUSION secret agreement among persons to commit FRAUD or engage in another illegal activity or in a legal activity with an illegal end in mind.

COLLUSIVE OLIGOPOLY industry containing few producers (oligopoly), in which producers agree among one another as to pricing of output and allocation of output markets among themselves. CARTELS, such as OPEC, are collusive oligopolies.

COLUMNAR JOURNAL book or ledger with columns to facilitate entering numbers.

COM *see* DOMAIN.

COMBINATIONS
1. see *business combinations.*
2. different subgroups that can be formed by SAMPLING a larger group or population. For example, 12 combinations are available from the toss of a pair of dice. Combinations do not depend on the order in which the elements are drawn. *See also* PERMUTATION.

COMEX *see* SECURITIES AND COMMODITIES EXCHANGES.

COMFORT LETTER
1. independent auditor's letter, required in securities underwriting agreements, to assure that information in the registration statement

and prospectus is correctly prepared and that no material changes have occurred since its preparation.

2. letter from one to another of the parties to a legal agreement stating that certain actions not clearly covered in the agreement will—or will not—be taken.

COMMAND

1. order by a superior to carry out an action. An individual can be commanded to do something. The word has a militaristic connotation in that commands given to those lower in rank must be obeyed. When one is commanded to do something, one is compelled.

2. in computers, instruction to perform a given procedure.

COMMAND ECONOMY economy in which supply and price are regulated or imposed by a central nonmarket authority. Prime examples are genuine communist economies.

COMMENCEMENT OF COVERAGE date at which insurance protection begins.

COMMERCE CLEARING HOUSE (CCH) one of the major publishers of tax services and other business publications.

COMMERCIAL term for an advertising message that is broadcast on television or radio. An advertising message in print is called an *advertisement*. A broadcast message is structured by time rather than by space (as is an advertisement), and so must be creatively designed around words, sound, and music for radio, plus sight and motion for television.

COMMERCIAL BANK most common and most unrestricted type of bank, allowed the most latitude in its services and investments. Insurance for depositors may be provided by the FEDERAL DEPOSIT INSURANCE CORPORATION (FDIC).

COMMERCIAL BLANKET BOND covers the employer for all of the employees on a *blanket* basis, with the maximum limit of coverage applied to any one loss without regard for the number of employees involved. Both *commercial* and *position blanket bonds* work the same way if only one employee causes the loss, or if the guilty employee(s) cannot be identified.

COMMERCIAL BROKER in real estate, one who LISTS and sells COMMERCIAL PROPERTY, which may include shopping, office, industrial, and apartment projects. *See also* RESIDENTIAL BROKER.

COMMERCIAL CREDIT INSURANCE coverage for an insured firm if its business debtors fail to pay their obligations. The insured firm can be a manufacturer or a service organization but it cannot sell its products or services on a retail level to be covered under commercial credit insurance. Under this form of insurance, the insured firm assumes the expected loss up to the retention amount and the insurance company pays the excess losses above that amount, up to the limits of the credit insurance policy.

COMMERCIAL FORGERY POLICY coverage for an insured who unknowingly accepts forged checks.

COMMERCIAL FORMS insurance policies covering various business risks.

COMMERCIAL LAW body of law that concerns the rights and obligations of persons in their commercial dealings with one another, such as the UNIFORM COMMERCIAL CODE (UCC), laws prohibiting unfair trade practices, etc. *See also* MERCANTILE LAW.

COMMERCIAL LOAN short-term (typically 90-day) renewable loan to finance the seasonal working capital needs of a business, such as the purchase of inventory or the production and distribution of goods.

COMMERCIALLY DOMICILED located at the principal place from which a CORPORATION'S trade or business is managed or directed.

COMMERCIAL PAPER short-term obligations with maturities ranging from 2 to 270 days, issued by banks, corporations, and other borrowers to investors with temporarily idle cash. Such instruments are unsecured and usually discounted, although some are interest-bearing. They can be issued directly or through brokers equipped to handle the enormous clerical volume involved. Issuers like commercial paper because the maturities are flexible and because the rates are usually marginally lower than bank rates. Investors— actually lenders, since commercial paper is a form of debt—like the flexibility and safety of an instrument that is issued only by top-rated concerns and is nearly always backed by bank lines of credit.

COMMERCIAL PROPERTY property intended for use by retail, wholesale, office, hotel, or service users, or for manufacturing or other industrial purposes. Examples are shopping centers, office buildings, hotels and motels, and resorts or restaurants. For many years, commercial property has been treated less favorably under the tax laws than residential rental property. *See also* INDUSTRIAL PROPERTY.

COMMERCIAL PROPERTY POLICY coverage for business risks including goods in transit, fire, burglary, and theft. A common example is the SPECIAL MULTIPERIL POLICY (SMP).

COMMERCIAL UNIT a unit considered by trade or usage to be a whole that cannot be divided without materially impairing its value, character, or use, such as a machine or a suite of furniture. Since acceptance of any part of a commercial unit constitutes acceptance of the whole, the term becomes significant when a buyer attempts to reject part of a CONTRACT for nonconformance. If the item rejected is part of a *commercial unit*, the rejection will not be allowed.

COMMINGLING OF FUNDS act of a FIDUCIARY or TRUSTEE, mixing his or her own funds with those belonging to a client or customer. The practice is generally prohibited by law. It is sometimes legal when the fiduciary maintains an exact accounting of the client's funds and how they have been used.

COMMISSARY store selling food and supplies, often at a military outpost. Commissaries are often subsidized, allowing them to charge reduced prices for qualified clientele (e.g., a military PX commissary).

COMMISSION
1. fee paid to an employee or agent for services performed, especially a percentage of a total amount received in a transaction, as distinguished from salary, which is a fixed amount payable periodically.
2. type of governmental regulatory body, such as the Federal Trade Commission.

COMMISSION BROKER broker, usually a floor broker, who executes trades of stocks, bonds, or commodities for a commission.

COMMITMENT
1. promise or pledge made by one individual to another. Example: a sales manager promises a salesperson a certain bonus if the sales quota for the year is met.
2. legal obligation to perform or not perform some act. Example: a purchaser enters into a written purchase *commitment* to buy goods from a supplier at a specified price by a specified date. *See also* MORTGAGE COMMITMENT.

COMMITMENT FEE lender's charge for contracting to hold credit available. Fee may be replaced by interest when money is borrowed, or both fees and interest may be charged, as with a REVOLVING CREDIT.

COMMITMENT LETTER an official notification to a borrower from a lender indicating that the borrower's loan application has been approved and stating the terms of the prospective loan.

COMMITTEE
In general: group that meets regularly for discussion and decision making.
Government: group appointed to investigate some special matter or area of interest and report its findings and recommendations.

COMMITTEE ON UNIFORM SECURITIES IDENTIFICATION PROCEDURES (CUSIP) committee that assigns identifying numbers and codes for all securities. These CUSIP numbers and symbols are used when recording all buy and sell orders.

COMMODITIES FUTURES contracts in which sellers promise to deliver a given commodity by a certain date at a predetermined price. Price is agreed to by open outcry on the floor of the commodity exchange. The contract specifies the item, the price, the expiration date, and a standardized unit to be traded (e.g., 50,000 pounds). Commodity contracts may run up to one year.

COMMODITIES FUTURES TRADING COMMISSION *see* REGULATED COMMODITIES.

COMMODITY any tangible GOOD; product that is the subject of SALE or barter. Bulk goods such as grains, metals, and foods are traded on a commodities exchange or on the SPOT MARKET.

COMMODITY CARTEL organization, usually of producing countries, that tries to control the price and quantity supplied of a particular COMMODITY (usually a raw material). Examples are OPEC (petroleum) and the International Coffee Organization.

COMMON AREA area of a property that is used by all owners or tenants. Examples of *common areas* are the clubhouse and pool of a condominium development; the hallways and stairs of an apartment building; the elevators in an office building; and the mall area of a shopping center.

COMMON CARRIER carrier for hire who transports people or goods as a public utility.

COMMON ELEMENTS in a CONDOMINIUM, those portions of the property not owned individually by unit owners, but in which an indivisible interest is held by all unit owners. Generally includes the grounds, parking areas, recreational facilities, and external structure of the building. *See also* COMMUNITY ASSOCIATION.

COMMON LAW system of jurisprudence that originated in England and was later applied in the United States. It is based on judicial precedent (court decisions) rather than on legislative enactment (statutes) and is therefore derived from principles rather than rules. *See also* CIVIL LAW.

COMMON STOCK security representing an ownership interest in a corporation. Ownership may also be shared with PREFERRED STOCK, which has prior claim on any dividends to be paid and, in the event of liquidation, to the distribution of the corporation's assets. As owners of the corporation, common stockholders assume the primary risk if business is poor, realize the greater return in the event of success, and elect the board of directors that controls the company.

COMMON STOCK EQUIVALENT preferred stock or bond convertible into common stock, or warrant to purchase common stock at a specified price or discount from market price. Common stock equivalents represent potential dilution of existing common shareholder equity.

COMMON STOCK FUND MUTUAL FUND that invests only in common stocks.

COMMON STOCK RATIO percentage of total capitalization represented by common stock. From a creditor's standpoint, a high ratio represents a margin of safety in the event of LIQUIDATION. From an investor's standpoint, a high ratio can mean a lack of LEVERAGE.

COMMUNICATIONS NETWORK well-defined pattern of communications that emerges when a small number of people link themselves together to exchange information, whether to solve a problem or to spread rumors.

COMMUNISM in theory, anticapitalist proposals of Karl Marx and his followers that communal ownership of the means of production is preferable; in practice, economic systems in which production facilities are state-owned and production decisions are made by official policy and not directed by market action.

COMMUNITY ANTENNA TELEVISION (CATV) cable television; using a satellite dish or high master antenna to receive distant television signals and then selling the service to residents of a city or town. Cable subscribers may receive national network television broadcasts, other specialized stations, and the opportunity to subscribe to *premium channels*, such as HBO, at an additional cost.

COMMUNITY ASSOCIATION general name for any organization of property owners to oversee some common interest. In a condominium or planned unit development, the association has the responsibility of managing the COMMON ELEMENTS in the project. A HOMEOWNERS' ASSOCIATION may be established in a subdivision to enforce deed COVENANTS.

COMMUNITY PROPERTY property acquired during marriage and recognized in nine states (Arizona, California, Idaho, Louisiana, Nevada, New Mexico, Texas, Washington, and Wisconsin), whereby the law presumes the property to be the product of joint efforts. Income from community property, salaries, wages, and other compensation is considered to be earned one-half by each spouse. Thus, in a divorce, the couple's total property is divided in half unless a negotiated settlement is reached, even if most of the assets were earned by one member of the couple.

COMMUNITY REINVESTMENT ACT a federal law that requires federal regulators of lending institutions to encourage lending within the local area of the institution, particularly to low- and moderate-income residents and those residing in inner-city neighborhoods. *See also* REDLINING.

COMMUTATION RIGHT privilege of a beneficiary to take unpaid income payments under a settlement option of an annuity or life insurance policy in the form of a lump sum. For example, if a beneficiary has a series of 20 income payments remaining, the present value of these payments can be commuted to a single lump-sum payment.

COMMUTER individual who frequently travels between two places. A person who lives in a residential suburb and works each day in the city is a *commuter*.

COMMUTER TAX tax imposed on those who work in a place other than where they live.

CO-MORTGAGOR one who signs a MORTGAGE contract with another party or parties and is thereby jointly obligated to repay the loan. Generally a co-mortgagor provides some assistance in meeting the requirements of the loan and receives a share of ownership in the encumbered property.

COMPACT DISC (CD) an optical storage device capable of holding up to 650 MB of digital data optically encoded on a 4.75-inch reflective disk and read by a laser beam. Some CDs are read-only (*see* CD-ROM). Others (CD-R) are recordable; that is, they can be written to in one or more sessions. Still others (CD-RW) are rewriteable; that is, they can be erased and written over.

COMPANY group of people organized to perform an activity, business, or industrial enterprise. *See also* CORPORATION; HOLDING COMPANY; JOINT STOCK COMPANY.

COMPANY BENEFITS *see* BENEFITS; FRINGE BENEFITS.

COMPANY CAR car owned by the firm, but available for use by employees.

COMPANY UNION labor union usually considered to be very sympathetic to the management of the company where it is located. It therefore may not represent the true interests of its members since it could be compromised by the company.

COMPARABLES in real estate, properties similar to the one being sold or appraised. Also called COMPS. See *also* ADJUSTMENT; APPRAISAL.

COMPARABLE WORTH employment theory that maintains that jobs should be compensated according to their value to the organization, not according to who holds them; also called *equal pay for equal work.* This is a particular concern in the case of female employees in the United States.

COMPARATIVE ADVANTAGE the economic motive and cause of international trade. Countries increase their economic prosperity by exporting the goods that they are relatively more efficient at producing and importing the goods that other countries are relatively more efficient at producing.

COMPARATIVE FINANCIAL STATEMENTS financial statements covering different dates but prepared consistently and therefore lending themselves to comparative analysis, as accounting convention requires.

COMPARATIVE MARKET ANALYSIS (CMA) an estimate of the value of real property using only a few indicators taken from sales of comparable properties, such as price per square foot. Such value estimates are not APPRAISALS and do not meet the professional standards of appraisal practice.

COMPARATIVE NEGLIGENCE in some states, principle of tort law providing that in the event of an accident each party's negligence is based on that party's contribution to the accident. For example, if in an auto accident both parties fail to obey the yield sign, their negligence would be equal, and neither would collect legal damages from the other.

COMPARISON SHOPPING process whereby a consumer gathers as much information as possible about particular products and services for comparison before purchasing them. Comparison shopping is accomplished by visiting stores having the merchandise, comparing advertisements, and doing related research.

COMPATIBLE
1. term describing two *devices* that can work together. For example, a particular brand of printer is *compatible* with a particular computer to which it can be connected.
2. two computers that can run the same programs. Many microcomputer programs claim to be "IBM-PC *compatible*."

COMPENSATING BALANCE average balance desired by a bank to be kept on deposit in exchange for holding credit available. The more or less standard requirement for a bank line of credit, for example, is 10% of the line plus an additional 10% of the borrowings. Compensating balances increase the effective rate of interest on borrowings.

COMPENSATING ERROR in accounting, mistake to offset a prior mistake and thus reflect appropriate balances.

COMPENSATION direct and indirect monetary and nonmonetary rewards given to employees on the basis of the value of the job, their personal contributions, and their performance. These rewards must meet both the organization's ability to pay and any governing legal regulations.

COMPENSATORY DAMAGES payment to someone who has suffered harm, such as for loss of income, expenses incurred, property destroyed, or personal injury. In general, except for damages for PERSONAL INJURY, receipt of these payments is taxable. Recovery of a person's previously deducted expenses is taxable under the TAX BENEFIT RULE. *Contrast with* DOUBLE DAMAGES.

COMPENSATORY STOCK OPTIONS options offered to employees as partial compensation for their services. Compensation for services is measured by the quoted market price of the stock at the measurement date less the amount the employee is required to pay (option price). The measurement date is the earliest date on which both the number of shares to be issued and the option price are known. *See also* INCENTIVE STOCK OPTION; NONSTATUTORY OPTION; STATUTORY OPTION.

COMPENSATORY TIME time off allowed an employee for overtime, usually on an informal basis and at the discretion of the supervisor. This prevents the company from having to pay overtime for the time worked. Also called *comp time*.

COMPETENT PARTY person legally capable of entering a contract. A person must be of legal age and not insane or a drunkard.

COMPETITION rivalry in the marketplace. Goods and services will be bought from those who, in the view of buyers, provide "the most for the money." Hence competition will tend to reward the more efficient producers and/or suppliers and so lead the economy toward efficient use of resources.

COMPETITIVE ADVANTAGE measure of an organization's product or service distinctiveness in a given market. *See also* CORE COMPETENCE.

COMPETITIVE BID sealed bid, containing price and terms, submitted by a prospective contractor to a purchaser, who awards the contract to the bidder with the best price and terms. Many municipalities and virtually all railroads and public utilities use this bid system.

COMPETITIVE STRATEGY promotional strategy used in an advertising campaign that is designed to compete with rival brands. For example: A *competitive strategy* may try to discredit another brand or undercut another brand in terms of price, or may point out qualities and consumer benefits that are not present in another brand.

COMPETITOR
1. manufacturer or seller of a product or service that is sold in the same market as that of another manufacturer.
2. seller of a product or service whose product or service can be used to fill or satisfy a consumer need (real or imagined) in a market where other sellers offer products that will also fill or satisfy the same need.

COMPILATION presentation of financial statement information by the entity *without* the accountant's assurance as to conformity with GENERALLY ACCEPTED ACCOUNTING PRINCIPLES (GAAP). In performing this accounting service, the accountant must conform to the AMERICAN INSTITUTE OF CERTIFIED PUBLIC ACCOUNTANTS Statements on Standards for Accounting and Review Services (SSARS). The engagement letter should set forth the type of services to be rendered, limitations of the service (such as nonreliance to disclose errors and irregularities), and nature of the compilation report.

COMPILER computer program that translates FORTRAN, PASCAL, or a similar high-level programming language into machine language. It contrasts with an INTERPRETER, which executes high-level-language statements as it reads them.

COMPLAINT
1. in a civil action, the first pleading of the plaintiff setting out the facts on which the claim is based. The purpose is to give notice to the adversary of the nature and basis of the claim asserted.
2. in criminal law, the preliminary charge or accusation made by one person against another to the appropriate court or officer, usually a magistrate. However, court proceedings, such as a trial, cannot be

instituted until an indictment or information has been handed down against the defendant.

COMPLEMENTARY GOODS goods that usually are consumed together; demand for one falls when the other's price rises; demand for one increases when the price of the other decreases. VCRs and videotapes are *complementary goods*; if VCRs become cheaper, people will buy more of them, and, consequently, demand for videotapes will increase.

COMPLETE AUDIT audit examining a company's system of internal control and the details of the books of account, including subsidiary records and supporting documents.

COMPLETED-CONTRACT METHOD an accounting method under which net profit on an entire long-term contract is reported in the year when the contract is completed. Expenses connected with the job are not deducted until the contract is completed. This method may be used for tax purposes only for home construction contracts and certain other small construction contracts. *See also* PERCENTAGE OF COMPLETION METHOD.

COMPLETE LIQUIDATION a series of DISTRIBUTIONS IN REDEMPTION of all the STOCK of a CORPORATION under a plan.

COMPLETION BOND legal instrument used to guarantee the completion of a real-estate development according to specifications. More encompassing than a PERFORMANCE BOND, which ensures that one party will perform under a contract on condition that the other party performs. The completion bond assures production of the development without reference to any contract and without the requirement of payment to the contractor.

COMPLEX CAPITAL STRUCTURE financial structure with stock outstanding that has potential for DILUTION. *Dual presentation* of earnings per share by showing PRIMARY EARNINGS PER COMMON SHARE and FULLY DILUTED EARNINGS PER COMMON SHARE is required.

COMPLEX TRUST trust that under the INSTRUMENT of its creation or under state law may either distribute or retain income or a trust with a charitable BENEFICIARY. A complex trust is allowed only a $100 exemption.

COMPLIANCE AUDIT special auditor's report covering compliance with contractual agreements, such as bond indentures and loan agreements, and regulatory requirements. The lender or agency wishes to obtain the auditor's assurance as to compliance with the terms of the agreement. The data need not be audited for compliance; however, if the financial statements have been audited, the auditor may provide *negative assurance* on compliance.

COMPONENT DEPRECIATION an effort to depreciate a property based on the lives of individual assets within it. For example, a building has electrical components and plumbing components that may be assigned a 20-year life, a roof with 15, and a foundation with a 50-year life. Use has diminished because the 1981 tax act and subsequent acts generally required COMPOSITE DEPRECIATION. *See also* COST SEGREGATION.

COMPONENT PART unit of a system, which performs part of the transformation or processing activity. A carburetor is a *component part* of an automobile's fuel system.

COMPOSITE DEPRECIATION applying one depreciation rate to the entire asset. For example, in real estate the foundation and framing of a building may last over 50 years, whereas the electrical and plumbing systems have much shorter lives, say 20 years. *See also* COMPONENT DEPRECIATION, COST SEGREGATION.

COMPOSITION OF CREDITORS alternative to bankruptcy, in which creditors agree to accept partial payment in full settlement of their claims. Most often seen in failures of small, unincorporated businesses, whose creditors reason that they will benefit more in profits on future sales to a going concern than they would on liquidation.

COMPOUND AMOUNT OF ONE the amount that $1 would grow to if left on deposit with INTEREST allowed to compound. For example: A dollar is deposited in a bank that pays 8% interest with annual compounding. The table below shows the balance each year for 5 years:

Year	Amount
1	1.08
2	1.1664
3	1.2597
4	1.36049
5	1.46933

COMPOUND GROWTH RATE single periodic rate of growth for several periods, generally years. The rate accounts for growth from the base period to the ending period in the same manner as COMPOUND INTEREST.

COMPOUND INTEREST interest earned on principal plus interest that was earned earlier. If $100 is deposited in a bank account at 10%, the depositor will be credited with $110 at the end of the first year and $121 at the end of the second year. That extra $1, which was earned on the $10 interest from the first year, is the *compound interest*. This example involves interest compounded annually; interest can also be compounded on a daily, quarterly, half-yearly, or other basis.

COMPOUND JOURNAL ENTRY more than one debit or credit in a journal entry. For example:

	Debit	Credit
Cash	98	
Sales Discount	2	
Accounts Receivable		100

COMPREHENSIVE ANNUAL FINANCIAL REPORT (CAFR) official annual report of a government. In addition to a combined, combining (assembling of data for all funds within a type), and individual balance sheet, the following are also presented as appropriate on a combined, combining, and individual basis: (1) statement of revenues, expenditures, and changes in fund balance (all funds); (2) statement of revenues, expenditures, and changes in fund balances, budget and actual (for government fund types); (3) statement of revenues, expenses, and changes in retained earnings (for proprietary funds); and (4) statement of changes in financial position (for proprietary funds).

COMPREHENSIVE ENVIRONMENTAL RESPONSE, COMPENSATION, AND LIABILITY ACT (CERCLA) federal law, known as SUPERFUND, passed in 1980 and reauthorized by the Superfund Amendments and Reauthorization Act (SARA) in 1986. The law imposes strict joint and several liability for cleaning up environmentally contaminated land. Potentially responsible parties include any current or previous owner, generator, transporter, disposer, or party who treated hazardous waste at the site. Strict liability means that each and every party is liable for the full cost of remediation, even parties who were not contaminators.

COMPREHENSIVE GENERAL LIABILITY INSURANCE (CGL) coverage against all liability exposures of a business unless specifically excluded. Coverage includes products, completed operations, premises and operations, elevators, and independent contractors. *Products coverage* insures when a liability suit is brought against the manufacturer and/or distributor of a product because of someone incurring bodily injury or property damage through use of the product. *Completed operations coverage* for bodily injury or property damage incurred because of a defect in a completed project of the insured. *Premises and operations coverage* for bodily injury incurred on the premises of the insured, and/or as the result of the insured's business operations. *Elevator coverage* for bodily injury incurred in an elevator or escalator on the insured's premises. *Independent contractors coverage* for bodily injury incurred as the result of negligent acts and omissions of an independent contractor employed by the insured.

COMPREHENSIVE HEALTH INSURANCE complete coverage for hospital and physician charges subject to deductibles and coinsurance. This coverage combines basic medical expense policy and major medical policy. *See also* GROUP HEALTH INSURANCE; HEALTH MAINTENANCE ORGANIZATION (HMO).

COMPREHENSIVE INSURANCE coverage in automobile insurance providing protection in the event of physical damage (other than collision) or theft of the insured car. For example, fire damage to an insured car would be covered under the comprehensive section of the personal automobile policy.

COMPREHENSIVE LIABILITY INSURANCE policy providing businesses with coverage for negligence-based civil liability in: (1) bodily injury and property damage liability, on an occurrence basis, resulting from the ownership, use, and/or maintenance of the premises, completed operations, and products; (2) bodily injury and property damage liability for operation of an elevator; (3) medical expenses resulting from bodily injury incurred by a member of the general public through the use of the premises or involvement in the operations. Medical expense reimbursement of the business is without regard to fault of the business.

COMPREHENSIVE PERSONAL LIABILITY INSURANCE coverage as *Part II—homeowners policy* on an ALL RISK basis for personal acts and omissions by the insured and residents of the insured's household. Included are sports activities, pet activities, and miscellaneous events such as someone tripping in an insured's cemetery plot.

COMPRESSION *see* DATA COMPRESSION.

COMPROMISE trade-off of one factor of comparable value for another in management practice and labor-management relations. In a true compromise each party concedes something the other side finds acceptable.

COMPS appraisal term, short for COMPARABLES.

COMPTROLLER term for a corporate or public official; its meaning and pronunciation are identical to *controller*; *see* CONTROLLER.

COMPTROLLER OF THE CURRENCY federal official, appointed by the President and confirmed by the Senate, who is responsible for chartering, examining, supervising, and liquidating all national banks.

COMPULSORY ARBITRATION forceful submission of a labor dispute to a neutral third party such as a government body or the American Arbitration Association for resolution; also called *binding arbitration*. This method has been strongly resisted by labor unions and employers who prefer to rely on collective bargaining and associated economic pressure, such as strikes and lockouts, to reach a settlement of such disputes.

COMPULSORY CHECKOFF *see* DUES CHECKOFF.

COMPULSORY INSURANCE coverage required by law. For example, more than half the states require operators of automobiles to have a minimum amount of liability insurance.

COMPULSORY RETIREMENT being forced to resign from one's employment at an age specified by union contract or company policy; also called *mandatory retirement*. In most cases in the past, the forced retirement age was 65. However, effective January 1, 1979, federal legislation stipulated that the private sector cannot have compulsory retirement policies. There is no retirement age for federal employees.

COMPUTER machine capable of executing instructions to perform operations on data. The distinguishing feature of a computer is its ability to store its own instructions. This ability makes it possible for a computer to perform many operations without the need for a person to enter new instructions each time. Modern computers are made of high-speed electronic components that enable the computer to perform thousands of operations each second.

COMPUTER-ASSISTED DESIGN (CAD) computer-assisted method of developing three-dimensional designs. This design method is extremely important for the engineering and architectural professions since it permits designs to be subjected to simulated real-time conditions such as temperature changes, wind conditions, or crash impacts without actually building a model. The computer dynamically develops the images, performing all mathematical calculations and reflecting all conditions to which the design is subjected. This encourages design experimentation without large costs or extensive time delays, resulting in high-quality designs and faster product development. *See also* COMPUTER INTEGRATED MANUFACTURING (CIM).

COMPUTER-ASSISTED TRANSCRIPTION (CAT) automatic transcription of machine shorthand notes into a computer from words recorded on magnetic tape.

COMPUTER CONFERENCING bringing participants together at different locations to exchange information and discuss problem situations. Conference members can take part in a discussion whenever they wish by computer or terminal.

COMPUTER INTEGRATED MANUFACTURING (CIM) integrated computerized manufacturing system combining all the elements of COMPUTER-ASSISTED DESIGN (CAD) and computer-aided manufacturing (CAM). This is an interactive computer system usually installed on a LOCAL AREA NETWORK linking several related departmental functions such as design, engineering, production, and marketing. The CIM concept insures rapid high-quality product development and manufacturing through real-time coordination of all related functions. *See also* COMPUTER-ASSISTED DESIGN (CAD).

COMPUTERIZED LOAN ORIGINATION (CLO) origination of a mortgage loan, usually by someone who is not a loan officer, with the assistance of specialized computer software that ties the originator to one or more mortgage lenders. CLO systems allow real estate brokers to provide a wider array of services.

COMPUTER NETWORK *see* LOCAL AREA NETWORK.

COMPUTER SCREEN screen on which a computer or electronic typewriter operator sees what he is doing; similar to, but not the same as, a television screen. *See also* CATHODE RAY TUBE; LIQUID CRYSTAL DISPLAY (LCD).

COMPUTER SECURITY the protection of computers and the information contained in them. Security measures include frequent backups to protect against data loss due to machine failure, encryption, and password protection to prevent unauthorized access to data; FIREWALLS to prevent break-ins through network connections; and physical measures to prevent theft or damage from environmental hazards such as fire or flood.

CON ARTIST, CON MAN a practitioner of FRAUD or *theft by deception* who first wins the *confidence* of a victim. Con artists usually play on the victim's desire to get something for nothing.

CONCEALMENT intention to withhold or secrete information. If an insured withholds information on a material fact, about which the insurance company has no knowledge, the company has grounds to void the contract.

CONCENTRATION BANKING acceleration of cash collections from customers by having funds sent to several geographically situated regional banks and transferred to a main concentration account in another bank. The transfer of funds can be accomplished through the use of depository transfer checks and electronic transfers.

CONCEPTUAL SKILLS ability to understand the interrelationship of ideas or elements in relation to the totality.

CONCEPT TEST research whose primary objective is to test an idea or concept that has been developed. Concept testing is done to assess the effectiveness of the advertising campaign in reaching its objectives.

CONCERN
1. matter of interest to management, requiring attention.
2. in labor relations, a difficulty that could affect the state of labor-management relations if not properly addressed.
3. business organization. For example, he heads a large *concern*.

CONCESSION
1. small shop or vending machine in a hotel or office building lobby, run by a business person.
2. right, usually granted by a government entity, to use property for a specified purpose, such as a service station on a highway.
3. reduced rent for the early portion of a lease, used as an incentive.
4. selling group's per-share or per-bond compensation in a corporate underwriting.

CONCESSION AGREEMENT a contract between a host country's government and a foreign firm that wants to invest in the host country. *Concession agreements* are usually negotiated prior to investment and spell out such things as taxes, remittance of profits, and transfer of ownership.

CONCILIATION in labor disputes, attempt to persuade management and labor to meet and discuss their differences. The purpose of conciliation is to reconcile disputing parties, and its effectiveness results from the likelihood that if the parties can be persuaded to meet, they might find a resolution of their dispute.

CONCILIATOR person who attempts to bring management and labor together. *See also* CONCILIATION.

CONDEMN *see* CONDEMNATION.

CONDEMNATION
1. taking private property for public use with compensation to the owner under EMINENT DOMAIN. Used by governments to acquire land for streets, parks, schools, etc., and by utilities to acquire necessary property. Replacement of the asset with another of equal value within three years of condemnation results in tax deferment of the gain through a BASIS carryover. *See also* INVOLUNTARY CONVERSION.
2. declaring a structure unfit for use.

CONDEMNATION AWARD money or value of other property received for condemned property; also, the amount received from the sale of property under threat of CONDEMNATION.

CONDITION
1. a prerequisite or requirement.
2. a possible future event that will trigger the duty to perform a legal obligation or will cause a REAL PROPERTY interest to arise, vest, or be extinguished.
3. a level of physical quality or wear. For example, an apartment complex may be in good or poor *condition*.

CONDITIONAL CONTRACT contract whose performance depends upon a future event, such as a contract to purchase a car if it passes a motor vehicle inspection.

CONDITIONAL SALE
1. sale in which the vendee receives POSSESSION and right of use of the goods sold, but transfer of title to the vendee is dependent upon PERFORMANCE of some condition, usually full payment of purchase price. The conditional sale becomes *absolute* on fulfillment of the condition.
2. purchase accompanied by an agreement to resell upon particular terms.

CONDITIONAL-USE PERMIT *see* SPECIAL-USE PERMIT.

CONDITION PRECEDENT express or implied provision of a contract calling for the happening of some event or the performance of some act, before the contract will be binding upon the parties.

CONDITIONS, COVENANTS, AND RESTRICTIONS (CCRs) rules, stated in condominium or subdivision deeds or bylaws, that define how property may be used. They prevent property owners from making changes to their individual properties that could result in an unattractive or inharmonious setting that could adversely affect other owners. For example, CCRs may require a certain style for any house in a subdivision, restrict the height of a fence, ban certain types of building materials, or limit or bar satellite dishes.

CONDITION SUBSEQUENT provision in a contract that describes an event or act, upon the happening of which certain obligations under the contract terminate.

CONDOMINIUM form of real estate ownership in which individual residents hold a deed and title to their houses or apartments and pay a maintenance fee to a management company for the upkeep of common property such as grounds, lobbies, and elevators as well as for other amenities. Condominium owners pay real estate taxes on their units and can mortgage, sublet, or sell as they wish. A condominium owner's tax position is equivalent to that of a single-family home owner.

CONDOMINIUM CONVERSION *see* CONVERSION, definition 4.

CONDOMINIUM DECLARATION *see* DECLARATION, definition 2.

CONDOMINIUM OWNERS' ASSOCIATION organization of all unit owners in a CONDOMINIUM to oversee the COMMON ELEMENTS and enforce the bylaws. *See also* COMMUNITY ASSOCIATION.

CONDUIT APPROACH when income or deductions flow through to another entity (for example, partnership income flows through to the partners). Also, a trust beneficiary must include in gross income the amount that the trust is allowed as a deduction for distributions.

CONFERENCE CALL telephone call that allows more than two lines to be connected at the same time so that three or more people can talk together; also called *three-way call*.

CONFIDENCE GAME scheme by which a swindler (CON ARTIST, CON MAN) wins the confidence of his victim and then cheats him of his money by taking advantage of the confidence reposed in him.

CONFIDENCE INTERVAL two possible values, an upper and a lower one, of a parameter being estimated from a sample in which a probability can be assigned representing the likelihood that a population parameter is within the interval. Confidence intervals are typically based on 90, 95, or 99% levels. A 95% *confidence interval* will contain the population parameter 95 out of every 100 samples. As the sample size decreases, the confidence interval widens.

CONFIDENCE LEVEL probability that a CONFIDENCE INTERVAL contains the population parameter being estimated from a SAMPLE; also called *confidence coefficient*.

CONFIDENTIAL private or secret; something treated with trust, resulting in a feeling of security that information will not be disclosed to other parties. An example is the confidentiality of conversations and records between attorney and client.

CONFIGURE set up a computer system or application to be used in a particular way.

CONFIRMATION
  1. formal memorandum from a broker to a client giving details of a securities transaction.
  2. document sent by a company's auditor to its customers and suppliers requesting verification of the book amounts of receivables and payables. *Positive* confirmations request that every balance be confirmed, whereas *negative* confirmations request a reply only if an error exists.

CONFIRMATION POSITIVE written or oral request by the auditor of a party having financial dealings with the client about the accuracy of an item. A response is required whether the particular item is correct or incorrect. For example, *positive confirmation* can be sent to customers to verify account balances.

CONFLICT OF INTEREST inconsistency between the interests of a person, such as a public official, which arises in connection with the performance of his duties. Examples are a judge who decides a zoning case on land he owns and a law firm that represents both plaintiff and defendant.

CONFORMED COPY copy of an original document with the essential legal features, such as signature and seal, being typed or indicated in writing.

CONFORMING LOAN residential mortgage loan that is eligible for purchase by FNMA or FHLMC. Such loans carry lower interest rates and more favorable terms than nonconforming mortgage loans. The dollar limit on principal is revised each year according to the change in average sales price of conventionally financed single-family homes.

CONGLOMERATE corporation composed of companies in a variety of businesses. Conglomerates were popular in the 1970s, when they were thought to provide better management and sounder financial backing, and therefore generate more profit, than small independent companies.

CONGRESS OF INDUSTRIAL ORGANIZATIONS (CIO) labor union formed in 1935 by John L. Lewis as the result of a division with the American Federation of Labor. The two organizations merged in 1955. *See also* AMERICAN FEDERATION OF LABOR-CONGRESS OF INDUSTRIAL ORGANIZATIONS (AFL-CIO).

CONSENT DECREE a judgment whereby the defendant agrees to stop the activity that was asserted to be illegal, without admitting wrongdoing or guilt. *See* CONSENT ORDER.

CONSENT ORDER/DECREE agreement by a defendant to an action to discontinue all activities viewed by the government as being illegal. This agreement occurs with the consent of both parties to the action and has court approval but stops short of a definitive judicial determination. A *consent order* is an unofficial though binding admission of guilt by the concerned parties. Since the facts of the matter have never been proved, however, the government is not bound by a consent order.

CONSERVATISM, CONSERVATIVE

Accounting: understating assets and revenues and overstating liabilities and expenses. Expenses are recognized sooner, revenues later. Hence reported earnings are lower. *Conservatism* holds that in financial reporting it is preferable to be pessimistic rather than optimistic since there is less chance of financial readers being hurt relying on the financial statements. Excessive conservatism may result in misguided decisions.

Business: cautious and careful attitude, such as not taking excessive risk. An example is a portfolio manager who invests in safe securities.

Politics: limited government spending, resulting in lower taxes.

CONSERVATOR court-appointed custodian of assets belonging to someone determined by the courts to be unable to manage his or her own property.

CONSIDERATION

1. under contract law, something of value exchanged for a promise or for performance; needed to make an instrument binding on the contracting parties.
2. adherence to all provisions of an insurance policy by an insured; the insured agrees to make all premium payments when due in order to maintain a policy in full force.
3. payment for an annuity.

CONSIGNEE

1. person to whom goods are shipped for sale under a consignment contract.
2. person named in a BILL OF LADING to whom the bill promises delivery.
3. one to whom a carrier may lawfully make delivery in accordance with his contract of carriage.

CONSIGNMENT BAILMENT for care or sale. It is a delivery of goods, without SALE, to a dealer, who must try to sell the goods and remit the price to the person making delivery. If the goods are not sold, the dealer must return them to the owner.

CONSIGNOR one who sends a CONSIGNMENT. A consignor can be the person calling upon a common carrier for transportation service, though not necessarily the person in whose name a bill of lading is made.

CONSISTENCY using the same accounting procedures by an accounting entity from period to period; using similar measurement concepts and procedures for related items within the company's financial statements for one period. It is easier for financial statement users to make projections when data are measured and classified in the same manner over time.

CONSOLE device, such as a control panel, that allows people to communicate directly with a computer.

CONSOLIDATED FINANCIAL STATEMENT financial statement that brings together all assets, liabilities, and other operating accounts of a parent company and its subsidiaries.

CONSOLIDATED OMNIBUS BUDGET RECONCILATION ACT (COBRA) federal legislation under which group health plans sponsored by employers with 20 or more employees must offer continuation of coverage to employees who leave their jobs, voluntarily or otherwise, and their dependents. The employee must pay the entire premium up to 102% of the cost of coverage extended by COBRA. COBRA was designed to help former employees maintain, at group rates, health insurance coverage that might otherwise be unobtainable or unaffordable.

CONSOLIDATED TAXABLE ITEMS items that are eliminated from separate taxable income, computed on a consolidated basis, and combined with the aggregated separate taxable income (for example, net operating loss, net capital gain or loss, total charitable contributions).

CONSOLIDATED TAX RETURN return combining the reports of the companies in what the tax law defines as an AFFILIATED GROUP. A firm is part of an affiliated group if it is at least 80% owned by a parent or other inclusive corporation.

CONSOLIDATION classified as a "type A" reorganization, in which two or more corporations are combined into a new corporation; also called *statutory merger*. If no BOOT is received, the reorganization is tax-free.

CONSOLIDATION LOAN loan that combines and refinances other loans or debt. It is normally an installment loan designed to reduce the dollar amount of an individual's monthly payments.

CONSOLIDATOR entity that combines *less-than-carload* shipments into full carloads to take advantage of lower shipping rates for full carloads.

CONSORTIUM group of companies formed to promote a common objective or engage in a project of benefit to all members. The relationship normally entails cooperation and a sharing of resources, sometimes even common ownership.

CONSTANT value that remains unchanged, for example, during the execution of a computer program. *Literal expressions*, such as 3.5 and George Washington are *constants* because they always stand for the same value.

CONSTANT DOLLARS dollars of a base year, used as a gauge in adjusting the dollars of other years in order to ascertain actual purchasing power.

CONSTANT-PAYMENT LOAN loan on which equal payments are made periodically so as to pay off the debt when the last payment is made. *See also* BALLOON PAYMENT; CONVENTIONAL MORTGAGE; LEVEL-PAYMENT MORTGAGE.

CONSTITUENT COMPANY company that is one of a group of affiliated, merged, or consolidated corporations. *See also* SUBSIDIARY.

CONSTITUTION fundamental principles of law by which a government is created and a country is administered. In Western democratic theory, a mandate from the people in their sovereign capacity, concerning how they shall be governed. Distinguished from a STATUTE, which is a rule decided by legislative representatives and is subject to limitations of the constitution.

CONSTRAINING (LIMITING) FACTOR item or factor that restricts or limits production or sale of a given product. Virtually all firms suffer from one or more constraining factors. Examples include limited machine-hours and labor-hours and shortage of materials and skilled labor. Other limiting factors may be cubic feet of display or warehouse space, or working capital.

CONSTRUCTION LOAN short-term real estate loan to finance building costs. The funds are disbursed as needed or in accordance with a prearranged plan, and the money is repaid on completion of the project, usually from the proceeds of a mortgage loan. The rate is normally higher than prime, and there is usually an origination fee.

CONSTRUCTIVE DIVIDEND disallowance or reclassification of a transaction between a CLOSELY HELD CORPORATION and a shareholder. Frequently a loan to a stockholder is recharacterized as a dividend.

CONSTRUCTIVE NOTICE notice presumed by law to have been given. It is often accomplished by posting notices or by mailing notification to the defendant if he or she cannot be personally served. In real estate, recording a deed gives *constructive notice* of its existence.

CONSTRUCTIVE OWNERSHIP OF STOCK *see* ATTRIBUTION RULES.

CONSTRUCTIVE RECEIPT OF INCOME doctrine under which a taxpayer is required to include in gross income amounts that, though not actually received, are deemed received during the tax year. Thus there is *constructive receipt* when income is made available to the taxpayer. For example, a lawyer performs services and receives a check for payment in December, but waits until January to deposit it and record it on business records. He is required to report it on his tax return in the year of the December receipt.

CONSULTANT individual or organization providing professional advice to an organization for a fee. A wide variety of consultants exist for many areas of organizational concerns, including management, accounting, finance, and legal and technical matters. A consultant is an INDEPENDENT CONTRACTOR.

CONSUMER ultimate user of a product or service. The consumer is not always the purchaser of a product (CUSTOMER). In the case of pet food, for example, the pet is technically the consumer because it is the ultimate user, although of course the advertising is aimed at the pet owner.

Consumers are considered to be the users of the *final* product. For example, purchasers of building products are *interim users* of these products while constructing the finished product, which may then be purchased by a consumer.

CONSUMER BEHAVIOR in marketing, understanding how and why consumers behave. An appropriate marketing stimulus is formulated based on customer personality and needs to prompt sales. Consumers adjust behavior to the marketplace based on internal needs and interpersonal factors.

CONSUMER CONFIDENCE SURVEY LEADING INDICATOR of consumer spending that gauges public confidence about the health of the U.S. economy. A random sampling of 5,000 people are asked how they feel about business conditions, the labor market, consumer spending, economic growth, and their employment and financial expectations six months into the future.

CONSUMER CREDIT PROTECTION ACT OF 1968 landmark federal legislation establishing rules of disclosure that lenders must observe in dealings with borrowers. The act stipulates that consumers be told annual percentage rates, potential total cost, and any special loan terms. The act, enforced by the FEDERAL RESERVE BOARD (FRB), is also known as the TRUTH IN LENDING ACT. *See also* REGULATION Z.

CONSUMER-DRIVEN HEALTHCARE a broad umbrella of health insurance plan designs that are structured to provide insurance protection for participants while simultaneously encouraging them to be cost-conscious in their healthcare choices.

CONSUMER FINANCE COMPANY *see* FINANCE COMPANY.

CONSUMER GOODS goods bought for personal or household use, as distinguished from CAPITAL GOODS, which are used to produce other goods.

CONSUMER INTEREST interest incurred on personal debt and consumer credit; not deductible after 1990.

CONSUMERISM public concern over the rights of consumers, the quality of consumer goods, and the honesty of advertising. The ideology came into full focus in the 1960s after President John F. Kennedy introduced the Consumer Bill of Rights, which stated that the consuming public has a right to be safe, to be informed, to choose, and to be heard. The primary concern of this force is to fulfill and protect the rights of consumers articulated by President Kennedy more than three decades ago.

CONSUMER PRICE INDEX (CPI) measure of change in consumer prices, as determined by a monthly survey of the U.S Bureau of Labor Statistics. Many pension and employment contracts are tied to changes in consumer prices as protection against inflation and reduced purchasing power. Among the CPI components are the costs of housing, food, transportation, and electricity. Also known as the *cost-of-living index*. Selected values of the index for all items, based on 1982–1984 = 100, are:

1960	29.6	1996	156.9
1970	38.8	1997	160.5
1980	82.4	1998	163.0
1985	107.6	1999	166.6
1990	130.7	2000	172.2
1991	136.2	2001	177.1
1992	140.3	2002	179.9
1993	144.4	2003	184.0
1994	148.2	2004	188.9
1995	152.4	2005	195.3

CONSUMER PRODUCTS any tangible personal property normally used for personal, family, or household purposes.

CONSUMER PROTECTION laws designed to aid retail consumers of goods and services that have been improperly manufactured, delivered, performed, handled, or described. Such laws provide the retail consumer with additional protection and remedies not generally provided to merchants and others who engage in business transactions.

CONSUMER RESEARCH research conducted through the use of various techniques and strategies, such as focus groups, in-depth interviews, inquiry tests, aided recall interviews, consumer surveys, and attitude testing, to obtain information about consumers. One of the major areas in advertising research (along with product research and market analysis), its purpose is to determine what influences consumer buying habits. Consumer research yields information concerning the motivations of consumers, their perceptions about advertising, the reason they buy a particular product, and the things that influence their brand choices.

CONSUMER SURPLUS economic concept describing the excess of the value, to the consumer, of goods consumed over their money value (cost to the consumer). A hungry person pays $2 for a hamburger, but may feel that he/she gets much more than $2 worth of satisfaction from eating it; the excess of the value of the *satisfaction* over the $2 price is consumer surplus.

CONSUMMATE to complete, such as to *consummate* a business arrangement, contract, or other happening. For example, the consummation of a merger of two companies is when it finally takes place.

CONSUMPTION FUNCTION mathematical relationship between level of consumption and level of income. It shows that consumption is greatly influenced by income.

CONTAINER SHIP ship used for carrying cargo that has been packaged in large, standardized containers.

CONTESTABLE CLAUSE *see* INCONTESTABLE CLAUSE.

CONTINGENCY *see* CONTINGENCY FUND; CONTINGENT LIABILITY.

CONTINGENCY FUND amount reserved for a possible loss, such as caused by a business setback. Contingency funds and other reserves set aside are not deductible for tax purposes.

CONTINGENCY LEADERSHIP leadership theory, advanced by Frederick E. Fiedler, that postulates that successful leadership styles are best established by situational determinants. Winning leadership styles conform to varying organizational requirements and events.

CONTINGENCY PLANNING approach seeking to anticipate future events that are not expected to occur but are possible. Should those future events occur, a plan of action to respond effectively would be in place. The concept of *civilian defense* is based on contingency planning.

CONTINGENCY TABLE table presenting sample observations classified by two or more characteristics, such as R and C, into as many classes. The division of homeowners in a condominium project by sex (R = male or female) and by age groups (C = 20 to 30, 31 to 40, and 41 and above) would be representative of a typical contingency table.

CONTINGENT BENEFICIARY one who receives the proceeds or benefits of a TRUST or ESTATE only when a specified event occurs (such as the death of a named beneficiary).

CONTINGENT FEE charge made by a professional for services rendered to a client, recovery of which depends upon a successful outcome of the case. The amount is often agreed to be a percentage of the client's recovery.

CONTINGENT LIABILITY (VICARIOUS LIABILITY) liability incurred by a business for acts other than those of its own employees. This particular situation may arise when an INDEPENDENT CONTRACTOR is hired. The business can be held liable for negligent acts of the contractor to the extent that its representatives give directions or exercise control over the contractor's employees. *See* VICARIOUS LIABILITY.

CONTINUATION OF BENEFITS a right conferred by federal law on employees and their spouses and dependents to continue participation in an employer-sponsored healthcare plan even after their coverage is terminated due to specified events such as death or divorce of the employee. Referred to as COBRA, that acronym does not represent *continuation of benefits*, though it is used popularly for that purpose.

CONTINUING EDUCATION courses offered by colleges or others that are not for degree credit. Many professions require those licensed in the profession to take a certain number of continuing education hours each year.

CONTINUITY existence of a similar theme throughout an advertising or marketing campaign; also length of uninterrupted media schedules.

CONTINUITY OF LIFE one of the unique characteristics of a corporation; present if death, insanity, bankruptcy, retirement, resignation, or expulsion of any member will not cause the dissolution of the organization.

CONTINUOUS AUDIT examination conducted on a recurring basis throughout the accounting period to detect and correct mistakes and improper accounting practices prior to the reporting year-end. A continuous audit also spreads the CPA's work throughout the year.

CONTINUOUS PROCESS industrial process that continuously receives raw materials and processes them through to completed units. Hospital healthcare is a 24-hour-a-day, 7-day-a-week *continuous process*.

CONTINUOUS PRODUCTION production activity yielding a standardized product. Raw materials are continually entered into the production process. For example, oil refining is *continuous production* yielding a standardized petroleum product from raw materials.

CONTINUOUS REINFORCEMENT in motivational theory, reassuring an individual with positive feedback on a continuous basis. It can apply to having an employee receive immediate feedback on the outcome of performance.

CONTRA-ASSET ACCOUNT account that accumulates a balance that is subtracted from another account, as accumulated depreciation is subtracted from the property, plant, and equipment asset account.

CONTRACT agreement between two or more parties whereby each party promises to do, or not to do, something; a transaction involving two or more individuals, whereby each has reciprocal rights to demand performance of what is promised.

CONTRACT CARRIER accepts people who seek transportation for themselves or goods from one or more shippers under an agreement for compensation. This is in contrast to a COMMON CARRIER, which normally accepts for shipment virtually any person or thing, whereas a *contract carrier* narrowly defines acceptable shipments. Consequently, a contract carrier generally carries equipment that is especially helpful in serving its unique customers.

CONTRACTION
1. assets are distributed to corporate shareholders in a partial LIQUIDATION. *Contrast with* a corporate separation in a DIVISIVE REORGANIZATION.

   2. on a national level, a reduction in the level of AGGREGATE INCOME
   or GROSS DOMESTIC PRODUCT; downturn in the business cycle, also
   called *recession.*

CONTRACT OF INDEMNITY property and liability insurance contracts that restore the insured to his/her original financial condition
after suffering a loss. The insured cannot profit by the loss; otherwise
an unscrupulous homeowner, for example, could buy several fire
insurance policies, set fire to the house, and collect on all the policies.

CONTRACT OF SALE *see* AGREEMENT OF SALE.

CONTRACTOR one who contracts to do work for another. An INDE-
PENDENT CONTRACTOR makes an agreement to do a specific piece of
work, retaining control of the means and method of doing the job; neither party has the right to terminate the contract at will. Examples of
independent contractors are physicians, lawyers, construction contractors, and others engaged in a profession in which they offer their services to the public. Federal income taxes and Social Security taxes are
not withheld by employers of independent contractors; independent
contractors are subject to SELF-EMPLOYMENT TAX.

CONTRACT PRICE in an INSTALLMENT SALE, for tax purposes, generally the selling price less existing mortgages assumed by the buyer.

CONTRACT RATE *see* FACE INTEREST RATE.

CONTRACT RENT amount of rent that has been set forth in a contract.
Contrast with ECONOMIC RENT.

CONTRARIAN investor who does the opposite of what most investors
are doing at any particular time. According to contrarian opinion, if
everyone is certain that something is about to happen, it won't. This is
because most people who say the market is going up are fully invested
and have no additional purchasing power, which means the market is
at its peak. When people predict decline, they have already sold out,
so the market can only go up.

CONTRIBUTED CAPITAL, SURPLUS *see* PAID-IN CAPITAL.

CONTRIBUTION PROFIT MARGIN in cost accounting, excess of
sales price over VARIABLE COSTS or expenses. This difference provides an
amount to offset FIXED COSTS and thereby contributes to GROSS PROFIT.

CONTRIBUTIONS
   1. *see* CHARITABLE CONTRIBUTION DEDUCTION.
   2. for UNEMPLOYMENT TAX purposes, payments required by a state to
   be made into an unemployment fund by any business because of
   having individuals employed, to the extent that such payments are
   made without being deducted or deductible from the remuneration
   of employees.

CONTRIBUTION TO CAPITAL *see* CAPITAL CONTRIBUTION.

CONTRIBUTORY NEGLIGENCE principle of law recognizing that injured persons may have contributed to their own injury. For example, by not observing the "Don't Walk" sign at a crosswalk, pedestrians may cause accidents in which they are injured.

CONTRIBUTORY PENSION PLAN pension plan into which the employee pays as well as the employer.

CONTROL measure assuring conformity with an organization's policies, procedures, or standards, as in QUALITY CONTROL.

CONTROL ACCOUNT account that shows totals of amounts entered in a SUBSIDIARY LEDGER, as an accounts payable *control account* would show the total that is detailed in the accounts payable subsidiary ledger.

CONTROL KEY a key on a computer keyboard that has no effect except in combination with other keys. On PC keyboards, these include the Ctrl and Alt keys in addition to Shift. The Apple equivalents are the Command and Option keys.

CONTROLLABLE COSTS costs that can be influenced by the department involved, unlike other FIXED COSTS such as rent, which is contracted by lease in advance.

CONTROLLED CORPORATION corporation whose policies are controlled by another firm owning more than 50% of its voting shares; company not having full management direction of itself. A company that is a SUBSIDIARY of another firm and is controlled by this PARENT COMPANY is a *controlled corporation*.

CONTROLLED ECONOMY economy in which much of the activity is controlled by government policy rather than by the dictates of markets. Examples are socialist and communist economies.

CONTROLLED GROUP two or more corporations whose stock is substantially held by five or fewer persons; includes brother-sister groups, parent-subsidiary groups, combined groups, and certain insurance companies. These corporations are subject to special rules for computing INCOME TAX, the ALTERNATIVE MINIMUM TAX exemption, the accumulated earnings credit, and the environmental tax exemption.

CONTROLLER or **COMPTROLLER** chief accountant of a company. In small companies the controller may also serve as treasurer.

CONTROLLING INTEREST ownership of more than 50% of a corporation's voting shares. A much smaller interest, owned individually or by a group in combination, can be controlling if the other shares are widely dispersed and not actively voted.

CONTROL PREMIUM an amount paid to gain enough ownership to set policies, direct operations, and make decisions for a business. *Contrast with* MINORITY DISCOUNT.

CONUS *con*terminous *U*nited *S*tates, that is, the 48 contiguous states and the District of Columbia. The federal per diem rate for lodging, meals, and incidental expenses for a given locality is a combined maximum rate equal to the sum of the maximum lodging amount and the meals and incidental expenses (M&IE) rate for such locality. *See also* HIGH-LOW METHOD; OCONUS.

CONVENIENCE FOOD processed food products and prepared meals. Convenience foods appeal to those who have neither the desire nor the time to prepare and cook a meal. They are quick and easy.

CONVENIENCE GOODS frequently purchased consumer items providing a convenience in terms of time savings and utilitarianism. Examples include hair spray, shaving cream, and tissues.

CONVENIENCE SAMPLING SAMPLING method where the items that are most conveniently available are selected as part of the sample. It is not appropriate to apply statistical analysis to samples selected in this manner.

CONVENIENCE STORE small centrally located store featuring ease of access, late-night hours, and a limited line of merchandise designed for the convenience shopper. Convenience stores charge above-average prices compared to large supermarkets that generate large-volume sales.

CONVENTIONAL MORTGAGE residential mortgage loan not insured by the FEDERAL HOUSING ADMINISTRATION (FHA) or guaranteed by the VETERANS ADMINISTRATION (VA). Also used to describe a mortgage with a fixed term and fixed rate.

CONVERSION
1. exchange of a convertible security such as a bond into a fixed number of shares of the issuing corporation's common stock.
2. transfer of mutual-fund shares without charge from one fund to another fund in a single family; also known as *fund switching*.
3. in insurance, switch from short-term to permanent life insurance.
4. transfer of rental apartments into cooperatives or condominiums.
5. taking property that belongs to another. *See also* INVOLUNTARY CONVERSION.

CONVERSION COST cost of moving from one kind of equipment or production process to another. Conversion cost is high when converting from a manual system to a computerized system. It includes the cost of new equipment plus training.

CONVERSION PARITY *see* CONVERSION PRICE.

CONVERSION PRICE dollar value at which convertible bonds, debentures, or preferred stock can be converted into common stock; announced when the convertible is issued.

CONVERSION RATIO relationship that determines how many shares of common stock will be received in exchange for each convertible bond or preferred share when the conversion takes place.

CONVERTIBLE CURRENCY a currency for which there are no barriers or restrictions in the foreign exchange market.

CONVERTIBLES corporate securities (usually preferred shares or bonds) that are exchangeable for a set number of another form (usually common shares) at a prestated price.

CONVERTIBLE TERM LIFE INSURANCE coverage that can be converted into permanent insurance regardless of an insured's physical condition and without a medical examination. The individual cannot be denied coverage or charged an additional premium for any health problems.

CONVEY in real property law, to transfer property from one to another by means of a written INSTRUMENT and other formalities. *See also* ALIENATION; GRANT.

CONVEYANCE transfer of the TITLE of real estate from one to another. The term can also refer to the means or medium by which the title of real estate is transferred.

COO *see* CHIEF OPERATING OFFICER.

COOKIE a small file downloaded to your computer when you browse a web page. Cookies hold information that can be retrieved by other pages at the site.

COOLING-OFF PERIOD
   1. interval (usually 20 days) between the filing of a preliminary prospectus with the Securities and Exchange Commission and the offer of the securities to the public. *See also* REGISTRATION.
   2. period during which a union is prohibited from striking, or an employer from locking out employees. The period, typically 30 to 90 days, may be required by law or provided for in a labor agreement.

CO-OP
   1. arrangement between two real estate AGENTS that generally results in splitting the COMMISSION between them.
   2. type of housing in which each tenant is a shareholder in a corporation that owns the building. *See also* COOPERATIVE.

CO-OP ADVERTISING *see* COOPERATIVE ADVERTISING.

COOPERATIVE
   1. type of corporate ownership of real property whereby stockholders of the corporation are entitled to use a certain dwelling unit or other units of space. Special income tax laws allow the tenant stockholders to deduct interest and property taxes paid by the corporation; also known as *co-op*.
   2. organization for the production or marketing of goods owned collectively by members who share the benefits, for example, agricultural *cooperative*.

COOPERATIVE ADVERTISING
1. in retailing, an arrangement between a manufacturer and a retailer whereby the manufacturer will reimburse the retailer in part or in full for advertising expenditures; also called *co-op advertising*. Ads and commercials are usually produced by the manufacturer and placed by the local retailer, using the store's name.
2. individual advertisement sponsored by two or more manufacturers or retailers where the sponsors cooperate in the copy as well as the budget.

COPY-PROTECTED DISK computer disk that cannot be fully copied by the software normally used for such purposes. Disks are copyprotected to prevent unauthorized duplication of copyrighted software. Those who successfully copy such disks are known as *pirates*.

COPYRIGHT protection by statute or by the common law, giving artists and authors exclusive right to publish their works or to determine who may so publish.

CORE-BASED STATISTICAL AREA (CBSA) a statistical geographic entity consisting of the county or counties associated with at least one core (urbanized area or urban cluster) of at least 10,000 people, plus adjacent counties having a high degree of social and economic integration with the core as measured through commuting ties with the counties containing the core. The two categories of CBSAs are METRO-POLITAN STATISTICAL AREAS and MICROPOLITAN STATISTICAL AREAS.

CORE COMPETENCE distinctive employee, product, or service capability leading to a long-term organizational advantage. *See also* COMPETITIVE ADVANTAGE.

CORE INFLATION increases in the PRODUCER PRICE INDEX (PPI) likely to spill over into consumer prices and become the basis of a long-term inflationary trend. Food and energy prices, which tend to be volatile and to cause temporary price shocks, are usually excluded from core inflation calculations. Other measures of core inflation use the CONSUMER PRICE INDEX (CPI) excluding food, energy, and other products with the greatest price fluctuations.

CORE VALUES *see* CREDO.

CORNERING THE MARKET illegal practice of purchasing a security or commodity in such volume that control over its price is achieved.

CORPORATE ACQUISITION *see* CORPORATE REORGANIZATION.

CORPORATE BOND debt instrument issued by a private corporation, as distinct from one issued by a government agency or a municipality. Corporate bonds typically have four distinguishing features: (1) they are taxable; (2) they have a par value of $1,000; (3) they have a fixed maturity; (4) they are traded on major exchanges, with prices published in newspapers.

CORPORATE CAMPAIGN program of coordinated advertisements aimed at improving a business's corporate image rather than selling the company's products or services.

CORPORATE CHARTER *see* ARTICLES OF INCORPORATION.

CORPORATE CULTURE general organizational operating environment including ethical and value structures. It is all-encompassing, affecting employees, management, and customer relations, extending to the types of products and services the organization creates, and including production methods, marketing practices, advertising, and service quality.

CORPORATE INSIDER *see* INSIDER.

CORPORATE REORGANIZATION merger, acquisition, divisive acquisition, or other restructuring of a CORPORATION.

CORPORATE STRATEGIC PLANNING management process involving determination of the basic long-term objectives of the organization and adoption of specific action plans for attaining these objectives. There are five interrelated elements of strategic planning, including: (1) analysis of the environment; (2) establishing objectives; (3) performing a situational analysis; (4) selecting alternative strategies; and (5) implementation and monitoring the strategic plans.

CORPORATE STRUCTURE setup of an organization in terms of departments and agencies; distribution and delegation of functional responsibilities throughout an organization. Reacting to a complex environment of business, the modern organization has become very complex, usually having many departments with a wide array of responsibilities.

CORPORATE VEIL using a corporation to disguise or protect a person's actions. Courts will often pierce the *corporate veil* to try the underlying person.

CORPORATION legal entity, chartered by a state or the federal government, and separate and distinct from the persons who own it, giving rise to a jurist's remark that it has "neither a soul to damn nor a body to kick." Nonetheless, it is regarded by the courts as an artificial person; it may own property, incur debts, sue, or be sued. It has four chief distinguishing features: (1) limited liability (owners can lose only what they invest); (2) easy transfer of ownership through the sale of shares of stock; (3) continuity of existence; and (4) centralized management. Other factors helping to explain the popularity of the corporate form of organization are its ability to obtain capital through expanded ownership, and the shareholders' ability to profit from the growth of the business.

CORPOREAL having material reality; opposite of *incorporeal*, intangible.

CORPUS
1. principal or *res* of an ESTATE, TRUST, DEVISE, or BEQUEST from which income is derived; can consist of funds, real estate, or other tangible or intangible property.
2. in civil law, positive fact, as distinguished from a possibility.

CORRECTION reverse movement, usually downward, in the price of an individual stock, bond, commodity, or index. If prices have been rising on the market as a whole and then fall dramatically, this is known as a *correction within an upward trend.*

CORRELATION an indication of the degree of association between two quantities; its value is always between –1 and 1.

CORRELATION COEFFICIENT statistical measure of the degree to which the movements of two variables are related.

CORRESPONDENCE AUDIT an examination of a tax return that is conducted largely by telephone or mail, usually involving substantiation or explanation of only a few items.

CORRESPONDENT financial organization that regularly performs services for another in a market inaccessible to the other. In banking there is usually a depository relationship that compensates for expenses and facilitates transactions.

COSIGN act of affixing one's signature on a contract, such as a loan, in addition to the principal signature of another. Both signers are liable for the loan or other contract.

COST amount of money that must be paid to acquire something; purchase price or expense.

COST ACCOUNTING branch of accounting concerned with providing detailed information on the cost of producing a product. Necessary for determining INVENTORY valuation.

COST APPLICATION allocation of cost to a product, process, or department using a rational allocation basis. For example, rent expense can be allocated to a department based on square footage.

COST APPROACH method of appraising property based on adding the REPRODUCTION COST of improvements, less depreciation, to the market value of the site.

COST BASIS original price of an asset, used in determining depreciation and capital gains or losses. It usually is the purchase price, but in the case of an inheritance it is the market value of the asset at the time of the donor's death. *See also* BASIS.

COST-BENEFIT ANALYSIS method of measuring the benefits expected from a decision, calculating the cost of the decision, then determining whether the benefits outweigh the costs. Corporations use this method in deciding whether to buy a piece of equipment, and the government uses it in determining whether government programs are achieving their goals or proposed programs are worthwhile.

COST CENTER non-revenue-producing element of an organization, where costs are separately figured and allocated, and for which someone has formal responsibility. The personnel function is a *cost center* in that it does not directly produce revenue.

COST CONTAINMENT process of maintaining organizational costs within a specified budget; restraining expenditures to meet organizational or project financial targets.

COST DEPLETION recovery of the tax BASIS in a mineral deposit by deducting it proportionately over the productive life of the deposit. *Contrast with* PERCENTAGE DEPLETION METHOD.

COST-EFFECTIVENESS ability to generate sufficient value to offset an activity's cost. The value can be interpreted as revenue in the case of a business.

COST ESTIMATING determining the total costs of labor, materials, capital, and professional fees required for a proposed product.

COST, INSURANCE, AND FREIGHT (CIF) *see* CIF.

COST METHOD method of accounting by a parent company for investments in subsidiary companies. The parent maintains the investment in subsidiary account at its cost, not recognizing periodically its share of subsidiary income or loss. This method of accounting is used when one company owns less than 20% of the outstanding voting common stock of another company. It could be used instead of the EQUITY METHOD if 20%–50% of voting common stock is owned but there is a lack of *effective control* (significant influence).

COST OBJECTIVE cost limit of an activity within budget limits. A project cannot exceed the *cost objective* that has been set for it.

COST OF CAPITAL rate of return that a business could earn if it chose another investment with equivalent risk, that is, the OPPORTUNITY COST of the funds employed as the result of an investment decision. Cost of capital is also calculated using a weighted average of a firm's costs of debt and classes of equity. *See also* WACC.

COST OF CARRY out-of-pocket costs incurred while an investor has an investment position, such as interest on long positions in margin accounts, dividends lost on short margin positions, and incidental expenses. *See also* CARRYING CHARGE.

COST OF FUNDS interest cost paid by a financial institution for the use of money. In the banking and savings and loan industry, the *cost of funds* is the amount of interest the bank must pay on money market accounts, passbook savings accounts, CDs, and other liabilities.

COST OF GOODS MANUFACTURED in accounting, total costs during an ACCOUNTING PERIOD of all goods produced, which includes costs of material, labor, and overhead, whether fixed or variable.

COST OF GOODS SOLD figure representing the cost of buying raw materials and producing finished goods. Included are clear-cut factors, such as direct factory labor, as well as others that are less clear-cut, such as overhead.

COST-OF-LIVING ADJUSTMENT (COLA) adjustment of wages designed to offset changes in the cost of living, usually as measured by the CONSUMER PRICE INDEX. COLAs are key bargaining issues in labor contracts and are politically sensitive elements of Social Security payments and federal pensions because they affect millions of people.

COST-OF-LIVING INDEX *see* CONSUMER PRICE INDEX.

COST OF SALES *see* COST OF GOODS SOLD.

COST OR MARKET, LOWER OF *see* LOWER OF COST OR MARKET.

COST OVERRUN excess of a project's cost over budget. A cost overrun necessitates an additional allocation of funds in the budget equaling the size of the overrun. *See also* COST OBJECTIVE.

COST-PLUS CONTRACT contract under which the contractor receives payment for total costs plus a stated percentage or amount of profit. A *cost-plus percentage* contract gives the contractor no incentive to economize; on the contrary he would be better off by spending more. A *cost-plus fixed-fee* contract is a more reasonable contract.

COST-PLUS-PERCENTAGE CONTRACT an agreement on a construction project in which the contractor is provided a specified percentage profit over and above the actual costs of construction. These contracts are considered poor business practice because the contractor has little incentive to hold down costs. A *cost-plus-fixed-fee* contract is a better approach.

COST-PUSH INFLATION inflation caused by rising prices, which follow on the heels of rising costs. When the demand for raw materials exceeds the supply, prices go up. As manufacturers pay more for these raw materials, they raise the prices they charge merchants for the finished products, and the merchants in turn raise the prices they charge consumers. *See also* DEMAND-PULL INFLATION; INFLATION.

COST RECORDS
1. investor records of the prices at which investments were purchased, which provide the basis for computing capital gains.
2. in accounting, anything that can substantiate the costs incurred in producing goods, providing services, or supporting an activity designed to be productive. Ledgers, schedules, vouchers, and invoices are *cost records*.

COST SEGREGATION the process of properly separating property to accurately classify assets for federal tax depreciation. For business, the tax savings from property cost segregation may be very substantial. To fully comply with the multitude and complexity of tax regulations, the engineering/property accounting analysis of faster depreciable assets and costs must be professional and supportable.

CO-TENANCY possession of and holding of rights in a unit of property by two or more persons simultaneously. The term does not describe the estate, but the relationship between persons who share the property. It encompasses JOINT TENANCY, TENANCY BY THE ENTIRETY, and TENANCY IN COMMON. *See also* TENANCY.

COTTAGE INDUSTRY industry in which the production of goods takes place at the home of the producer rather than in a factory or other organized environment. Many kinds of handicrafts are cottage-industry goods.

COUNCIL OF ECONOMIC ADVISERS (CEA) group of economists appointed by the President of the United States to provide counsel on economic policy.

COUNSEL
1. attorney or legal adviser.
2. advice or aid given with respect to a legal matter.

COUNSELOR often used interchangeably with *attorney* for an ATTORNEY-AT-LAW, lawyer. Also, one who provides services required for specific loan programs or who advises on financial matters.

COUNTERCLAIM counterdemand by DEFENDANT against the PLAINTIFF; it is not a mere answer or denial of plaintiff's allegation, but asserts an independent CAUSE OF ACTION in favor of defendant.

COUNTERCYCLICAL POLICY government economic policies designed to dampen the effects of the BUSINESS CYCLE. During the inflation of the early 1980s, the action by the FEDERAL RESERVE BOARD (FRB) to raise interest rates was a *countercyclical policy* designed to reduce demand and thus end inflationary expansion.

COUNTERFEIT forged; fabricated without right; made in imitation of something else with the intent to defraud by passing the false copy for genuine.

COUNTERMAND to revoke; to withdraw an order before it has been carried out by giving a different order. For example, a salesperson who was authorized to sell goods to a particular customer up to a maximum amount of $100,000 is subsequently instructed to disregard the authorization and not to extend credit to the customer.

COUNTEROFFER rejection of an OFFER to buy or sell with a simultaneous substitute offer. For example, a property is put on the market. An investor offers $75,000 in cash. The owner rejects the offer but submits a counteroffer to sell for $80,000. Offers and counteroffers may be negotiated on factors other than price, such as FINANCING arrangements, APPORTIONMENT of CLOSING COSTS, and inclusion of personal property.

COUNTRY SCREENING use of countries as the basic unit of analysis for market evaluation.

COUPON printed ticket, often appearing in a magazine or newspaper, offering a product at a discount. *Coupons* must be presented with the purchase to claim the discount. They generally have an expiration date and frequently have terms and conditions that limit their use.

COUPON BOND bond issued with detachable coupons that must be presented to a paying agent or the issuer for semiannual interest payment. These are BEARER BONDS, so whoever presents the coupon is entitled to the interest. The coupon bond has been rapidly giving way to the REGISTERED BOND.

COUPON COLLECTION *see* COLLECTION.

COUPONING advertising method where vouchers are distributed to consumers allowing discounts on merchandise or service purchased within a stated period of time. *Couponing* provides an incentive for increasing sales.

COURT BOND *see* JUDICIAL BOND.

COURT OF RECORD court that, like most modern courts, is required by law to keep a record of its proceedings, including the orders and judgments it enters. It has the authority to imprison and to levy fines.

COVARIANCE statistical term for the correlation between two variables multiplied by the standard deviation for each of the variables. A positive covariance indicates that the two variables tend to move up and down together; a negative covariance indicates that when one moves higher, the other tends to go lower.

COVENANT
1. to enter a formal agreement; to bind oneself in CONTRACT; to make a stipulation.
2. agreement to do or not to do a particular thing.
3. promise incidental to a DEED or contract, either expressed or implied.

COVENANT NOT TO COMPETE contractual promise to refrain from conducting business or professional activities similar to those of another party. Such a covenant is encountered principally in contracts of employment, partnership, or sale of a business. The protection of TRADE SECRETS, customer lists, business methods specific to a particular employer, and the unique qualifications of the employee have been held to constitute legitimate interests for protection by covenants not to compete. If too restrictive, covenants may be declared invalid.

COVER

1. to buy back contracts previously sold; said of an investor who has sold stock or commodities short.
2. in corporate finance, to meet fixed annual charges on bonds, leases, and other obligations out of earnings.
3. amount of net-asset value underlying a bond or equity security. Coverage is an important aspect of a bond's safety rating. *See also* DEBT COVERAGE RATIO.

COVERDELL EDUCATION SAVINGS ACCOUNT (ESA) form of INDIVIDUAL RETIREMENT ACCOUNT (formerly Education IRA) allowing parents to contribute up to $2,000 per year for each child up to the age of 18. This $2,000 limit is reduced for married couples filing jointly with ADJUSTED GROSS INCOMES between $190,000 and $220,000, or singles reporting incomes between $95,000 and $110,000. Couples with incomes over $220,000 and singles with incomes over $110,000 may not contribute to Coverdell ESAs. Contributions to Coverdell ESAs do not generate tax deductions. However, assets in the Coverdell ESA grow tax free, and principal and earnings can be withdrawn tax free, and principal and earnings can be withdrawn tax free as long as the proceeds are used to pay for education expenses at a postsecondary school, including tuition, fees, books, supplies, and room and board. Money in Coverdell ESAs can be invested in STOCKS, BONDS, MUTUAL FUNDS, and other investments suitable for IRAs.

COVERED OPTION option contract backed by the shares underlying the option. *See also* NAKED OPTION.

CPA *see* CERTIFIED PUBLIC ACCOUNTANT.

CPI *see* CONSUMER PRICE INDEX.

CPU *see* CENTRAL PROCESSING UNIT.

CR abbreviation for CREDIT.

CRAFT UNION union of skilled tradespeople sharing comparable trade skills. Most of these unions are organized on a local basis, but are often affiliated with the AFL-CIO. The opposite of a craft union is an industry-wide union, such as the United Auto Workers or the United Steelworkers.

CRAM DOWN in BANKRUPTCY, the reduction of various classes of debt to a lower amount. For confirming a bankruptcy plan, creditors are divided into *classes* based on the nature of their claims against the debtor. Each class gets the opportunity to vote yes or no on the plan for reorganization, which can be confirmed only if at least one class votes yes—which means a yes vote from more than 50% in the number of creditors (called *numerosity*) and 75% in the total value of claims. If one or more classes vote against the plan, but at least one class votes in favor, the debtor can still get the plan of reorganization approved through the process of cram down. Cram down (under

Section 1129(b) of the Bankruptcy Code), requires a debtor to prove that the plan is fair and equitable to the nonconsenting class and that the plan doesn't unfairly discriminate against them. If the debtor does so, the plan is crammed down the nonconsenting class and approved. For example, the United Airlines plan was crammed down the retired pilots, who voted against it.

CRASH
Finance: precipitate drop in stock prices and economic activity, as in the *crash* of 1929, which initiated the Great Depression. Crashes are usually brought on by a loss in investor confidence.

Data processing: hardware failure or program error causing a computer to become inoperable. A well-designed operating system contains protection against inappropriate input so that a user's program will not be able to cause a system crash.

CREATIVE BLACK BOOK
annual two-volume worldwide directory of creative suppliers such as photographers, illustrators, directors, production facilities, and photofinishers. Sometimes called the *Black Book*, the Creative Black Book sells advertising space on an annual basis.

CREATIVE FINANCING
any FINANCING arrangement other than a traditional MORTGAGE from a third-party lending institution. Creative financing devices include loans from seller; BALLOON-PAYMENT loans; WRAPAROUND MORTGAGES; ASSUMPTION OF MORTGAGE; SALE AND LEASE-BACKS; land contracts and alternative mortgage instruments.

CREDIT
1. loans, bonds, charge-account obligations, and open-account balances with commercial firms.
2. available but unused bank letters of credit and other standby commitments as well as a variety of consumer credit facilities.
3. adjustment in the customer's favor or increase in equity.
4. in accounting, entry that increases liabilities, owners' equity, revenue, and gains and decreases assets and expenses.
5. tax credit, a dollar-for-dollar reduction in a taxpayer's TAX LIABILITY. *See also* specific credits, including CHILD AND DEPENDENT CARE CREDIT, INVESTMENT TAX CREDIT, LOW-INCOME HOUSING CREDIT.

CREDIT ANALYST
1. person who analyzes the financial affairs of an individual or a corporation to ascertain creditworthiness.
2. person who determines the credit ratings of corporate and municipal bonds by studying the financial condition and trends of the issuers.

CREDIT BALANCE
1. account balance in the customer's favor. *See also* CREDIT.
2. overpayment by a DEFINED-BENEFIT PENSION PLAN sponsor that contributes more than the minimum funding requirement in any plan year; serves to offset future contribution requirements.

CREDIT BUREAU private organization that maintains consumer credit data files. A credit bureau provides credit information to authorized users for a fee.

CREDIT BUREAU SCORES *see* CREDIT SCORING; FICO SCORE.

CREDIT CARD indication to sellers that the person who received the card from the issuer has a satisfactory CREDIT rating and that if credit is extended, the issuer of the card will pay (or see to it that the seller receives payment) for the merchandise delivered. Most credit cards are made of plastic with raised letters to facilitate creation of machine-readable sales slips and a magnetically coded strip that is read electronically and verified by telephone.

CREDIT ENHANCEMENT techniques used by debt issuers to raise the credit rating of their offering and thereby lower their interest costs. A municipality may have its bonds insured by one of the large insurance companies such as Municipal Bond Investor's Assurance (MBIA) or American Municipal Bond Assurance Corporation (AMBAC), thereby raising the bond's credit rating.

CREDIT HISTORY an individual's past behavior regarding the taking out and repayment of loans and the use of REVOLVING CREDIT, such as credit cards. Credit histories are recorded by national credit reporting companies (CREDIT BUREAUS) that issue credit reports. These reports are used by lenders to assess an applicants creditworthiness. *See also* CREDIT SCORING; FICO SCORE.

CREDIT LIMIT the maximum balance allowed for a particular customer of a credit card issuer.

CREDIT LINE *see* LINE OF CREDIT.

CREDITOR one to whom money is owed by the debtor; one to whom an obligation exists. In its strict legal sense, a creditor is one who voluntarily gives credit to another for money or other property. In its more general sense it is one who has a right by law to demand and recover of another a sum of money on any account.

CREDIT ORDER order that is received without payment and that requires billing at a later date; also called *bill me* order. *See also* CASH ORDER.

CREDIT RATING formal evaluation of an individual's or a company's credit history and capability of repaying obligations. A number of firms investigate, analyze, and maintain records on the credit responsibility of individuals and businesses, for example TRW (individuals) and Dun & Bradstreet (commercial firms). The bond ratings assigned by Fitch, Standard & Poor's, and Moody's are also a form of credit rating.

CREDIT RATIONING allocation of loans to creditworthy borrowers by other than pure market means. Credit rationing occurs when interest rates are kept below the level at which an unregulated market would set, leading to an excess of demand for loans.

CREDIT REQUIREMENTS standards established by creditors that must be satisfied by potential debtors in order for credit to be given. These requirements typically reflect the applicant's ability to repay the loan or make payments for goods or services acquired. An example is the conditions that a mortgage applicant must meet, such as acceptable salary level, credit history, satisfactory job history, and sufficient down payment.

CREDIT RISK financial and moral risk that an obligation will not be paid and a loss will result.

CREDIT SCORING objective methodology used by credit grantors to determine how much credit to grant to an applicant. Some of the most common factors in scoring are income, assets, length of employment, length of living in one place, and past record of using credit. Any negative events in the past, such as bankruptcies or tax delinquencies, will sharply reduce an applicant's credit score. *See also* FICO SCORE.

CREDIT STANDING reputation one earns for paying debts. CREDIT RATING tends to be more quantitative than *credit standing*.

CREDIT UNION not-for-profit financial institution, typically formed by employees of a company, a labor union, or a religious group and operated as a cooperative. Credit unions may offer a full range of financial services and may pay higher rates on deposits and charge lower rates on loans than commercial banks. Credit unions are regulated by the Federal Credit Union Administration.

CREDIT WATCH used by BOND RATING agencies to indicate that a company's credit is under review and its rating subject to change. The implication is that if the rating is changed, it will be lowered, usually because of some event that adversely affects the income statement or balance sheet.

CREDITWORTHINESS general eligibility of a person or company to borrow money. *See* CREDIT RATING; CREDIT SCORING; CREDIT STANDING.

CREDO a corporate philosophy that guides the way a company does business.

CREEPING INFLATION slow but inexorable continuing INFLATION that, though it seems tolerable in the short run, nonetheless leads to significant long-run price increases. A sustained inflation of 2% per year will cause prices to increase over fivefold in a century.

CRIME a wrong that the government has determined is injurious to the public and that may therefore be prosecuted in a criminal proceeding. Crimes include *felonies* and MISDEMEANORS.

CRISIS MANAGEMENT management system developed for the purpose of diminishing potentially serious outcomes in certain targeted situations. Examples include aircraft and naval disaster management, fire and emergency evacuation procedures, and flood protection.

CRITICAL PATH METHOD (CPM) planning and control technique that optimizes the order of steps in a process given the costs associated with each step. Manufacturing industry uses CPM to plan and control the complete process of material deliveries, paperwork, inspections, and production.

CRITICAL REGION in statistical testing, range of values in which the calculated value of the test statistic falls when the NULL HYPOTHESIS is rejected.

CROSS securities transaction in which the same broker acts as agent in both sides of the trade. The practice, called *crossing*, is legal only if the broker first offers the securities publicly at a price higher than the bid.

CROSS-FOOTING in a SPREADSHEET, totaling rows and columns of numbers and comparing the sums. If the sums are in agreement, then the totals of each row and column are most likely correct.

CROSS-FUNCTIONAL TEAMS employee teams consisting of two or more functional organizational areas.

CROSS MERCHANDISING setting up displays of complementary merchandise, usually in a supermarket, so that they are opposite each other; also called *related item approach* (to merchandising). In this way, a customer may be tempted to "cross over" from one product to another. For example: A manufacturer's display of shampoo may be set opposite a display of hair conditioner made by the same company, to tempt the shampoo buyer to cross over to the hair conditioner as well.

CROSS PURCHASE PLAN *see* PARTNERSHIP LIFE AND HEALTH INSURANCE.

CROSS RATE evaluates the U.S. dollar exchange rate on the basis of two other national currency exchange rates respectively, to compute their direct exchange rate.

CROSS TABULATION statistical technique that establishes an interdependent relationship between two tables of values but does not identify a causal relationship between the values; also called *two-way tabulation*. For example, a *cross tabulation* might show that cars built on Monday have more service problems than cars built on Wednesday. Cross tabulation can be used to analyze the results of a consumer survey that, for example, indicates a preference for certain advertisements based on which part of the country the consumer resides in.

CROWD group of exchange members with a defined area of function, tending to congregate around a trading post pending execution of orders. These are specialists, floor traders, odd-lot dealers, and other brokers, as well as smaller groups with specialized functions.

CROWDING OUT heavy federal borrowing at a time when businesses and consumers also want to borrow money. Because the government can pay any interest rate it has to and individuals and businesses cannot, the latter reduce their demand and are thus *crowded out* of credit markets by high interest rates.

CROWN JEWELS in corporate mergers and acquisitions, target company's most desirable properties, the disposal of which reduces its value and attractiveness as a takeover candidate.

CROWN LOAN demand loan to the children or parents of the lenders. This device was named for Chicago industrialist Harry Crown, who first used it. It puts the money in the lower tax category that applies to the loan recipients. For years, the Crown loan provided a substantial tax benefit for all parties involved, since such loans could be made interest-free. In 1984 the U.S. Supreme Court ruled that such loans had to be made at the market rate of interest or be subject to gift taxes.

CRT *see* CATHODE RAY TUBE.

C-TYPE REORGANIZATION *see* STOCK-FOR-ASSET REORGANIZATION.

CUL-DE-SAC (French for "bottom of the sack") dead-end street; street with an intersection on one end and a closed turning area on the other; often valued in the design of residential SUBDIVISIONS for the privacy provided to homes on the street.

CULPABLE deserving of moral blame or punishment; at fault. One is *culpable* when one has acted with indifference to consequences and to the rights of others.

CUM DIVIDEND, CUM RIGHTS or **CUM WARRANT** stock whose buyer is eligible to receive a declared distribution. *See also* EX-DIVIDEND DATE.

CUMULATIVE BULLETIN (*CB*) a hardbound compilation of the material in the *Internal Revenue Bulletin*, usually issued semiannually.

CUMULATIVE DIVIDEND *see* CUMULATIVE PREFERRED STOCK.

CUMULATIVE LIABILITY
Reinsurance: total of the limits of liability of all reinsurance policies that a reinsurer has outstanding on a single risk. The total of all such limits includes all contracts from all insurers representing all lines of coverage for the single risk.
Liability insurance: total of the limits of liability of all policies that an insurer has outstanding on a single risk. Examples are the *personal automobile policy* (PAP), and *personal umbrella liability policy*.

CUMULATIVE PREFERRED STOCK stock whose dividends, if omitted because of insufficient earnings or any other reason, accumulate until paid out. They have precedence over common dividends, which cannot be paid as long as a cumulative preferred obligation exists. Most preferred stock issued today is cumulative.

CUMULATIVE VOTING system of STOCKHOLDER voting for a board of directors that allows all the votes an individual is eligible to cast to be cast for a single candidate. The system is designed to give minority stockholders representation on the board. For example, the owner of a single share of stock voting in an election for five directors would be able to cast one vote for each position under a straight voting system, but would be able to cast all five votes for a single position or distribute them in any manner desired under a cumulative voting system.

CURABLE DEPRECIATION depreciation or deterioration that can be corrected at a cost less than the value that will be added. *See also* INCURABLE DEPRECIATION.

CURB EXCHANGE *see* AMERICAN STOCK EXCHANGE.

CURRENCY money; coins and bills that are authorized by a government as legal tender for the payment of obligations.

CURRENCY FUTURES contracts in the futures markets that are for delivery in a major currency such as U.S. dollars, Euros, or Japanese yen. Corporations that sell products around the world can hedge the risk of adverse exchange rate movements with these futures.

CURRENCY IN CIRCULATION paper money and coins circulating in the economy, counted as part of the total money in circulation, which includes DEMAND DEPOSITS in banks.

CURRENCY SWAP an exchange of currencies between two firms that is reversed at a specific rate and time in the future.

CURRENT not overdue; occurring this period.

CURRENT ACCOUNT a national balance of payments account that includes international trade in goods and services along with transfer payments and short-term credit.

CURRENT ASSET cash, accounts receivable, inventory, and other assets that are likely to be converted into cash, sold, exchanged, or expensed in the normal course of business, usually within a year.

CURRENT COST present market value of a product or asset, as contrasted with its ACQUISITION COST.

CURRENT DOLLARS cost of an asset in terms of today's price level. For example, if today the CONSUMER PRICE INDEX is 180, an automobile that cost $20,000 when the CPI base was 100 would cost $36,000 in *current dollars*.

CURRENT EARNINGS AND PROFITS arrived at by adding nontaxable or tax-exempt income to taxable income for the tax year. *Current earnings and profits*, if not paid out, become ACCUMULATED EARNINGS AND PROFITS. A distribution comes first from current earnings and profits and then from accumulated earnings and profits and is taxable to the shareholder to the extent of current *and* accumulated earnings and profits. A distribution is taxable to the extent of current earnings and profits even if accumulated earnings and profits are negative.

CURRENT EMPLOYMENT STATISTICS (CES) monthly data on national employment and unemployment, wages and earnings, across all nonagriculture industries, used as indicators of economic trends. Employment data show the well-being of the economy and LABOR FORCE. Wage changes indicate earnings trends and related labor costs. Economists focus on monthly change in total nonfarm payrolls and locations where jobs were gained or lost. Payroll data show the labor market condition.

CURRENT LIABILITY (IES) debt incurred by the reporting entity as part of normal operations and that is expected to be repaid during the following 12 months. Examples are ACCOUNTS PAYABLE, short-term loans, and that portion of long-term loans due in one year.

CURRENT MARKET VALUE worth of property if sold in present-day market.

CURRENT RATIO current assets divided by current liabilities. The ratio shows a company's ability to pay its current obligations from current assets. *See also* QUICK RATIO.

CURRENT VALUE ACCOUNTING attempt to provide an income statement and balance sheet in terms of CURRENT DOLLARS, in an effort to provide better financial information during an inflationary period. *See also* INFLATION ACCOUNTING.

CURRENT YIELD annual interest on an investment divided by the market price. In the case of a bond, it is the actual income rate of return as opposed to the coupon rate or the yield to maturity. For example, a 10% (coupon rate) bond with a face (or par) value of $1,000 is bought at a market price of $800. The annual income from the bond is $100. But since only $800 was paid for the bond, the current yield is $100 divided by $800, or 12½%.

CURRICULUM VITAE biographical résumé of one's career, including educational credentials and professional experience. Its purpose is to give the prospective employer an understanding of the professional abilities of the applicant.

CURSOR symbol on a computer terminal that shows where on the screen the next character to be typed will appear. Cursors often appear as blinking dashes or rectangles.

CURTESY husband's right in common law, upon the death of his wife, to a LIFE ESTATE in all lands that his wife owned in FEE SIMPLE or in fee tail at any time during the marriage, provided that there was ISSUE born of the marriage capable of inheriting the estate. *See also* DOWER.

CURTILAGE IN COMMON LAW, land around the dwelling house.

CUSIP *See* COMMITTEE ON UNIFORM SECURITIES IDENTIFICATION PROCEDURES.

CUSTODIAL ACCOUNT account that parents create for a minor, usually at a bank or brokerage firm. Minors cannot make securities transactions without the approval of the account trustee. *See also* KIDDIE TAX.

CUSTODIAN
1. bank or other financial institution that keeps custody of stock certificates and other assets of a mutual fund, individual, or corporate client.
2. person who has the custody or care of something, such as a facility or building; also called *caretaker* or *janitor*.

CUSTODY
1. as applied to property, condition of holding a thing within one's personal care and control.
2. as applied to persons, such control over a person as will ensure his presence at a HEARING; actual imprisonment of a person.

CUSTOM usual business or individual practice; habitual tendency followed as a matter of course; traditional policy. An example is for the firm to be closed for business on Sunday.

CUSTOM BUILDER one who builds unique houses, often for a specific customer.

CUSTOMER buyer of a product or service.

CUSTOMER PROFILE description of a customer group or type of customer based on various DEMOGRAPHIC, *psychographic*, and/or geographic characteristics. For example, magazine advertising salespeople provide advertisers with customer profiles describing the type of person who will be exposed to advertisements in that magazine. The description may include income, occupation, level of education, age, gender, hobbies, and/or area of residence.

CUSTOMER RELATIONSHIP MANAGEMENT (CRM) the process of storing and analyzing data produced by sales calls, customer service centers, and actual purchases to improve insight into customer behavior.

CUSTOMER SERVICE department or function of an organization that responds to inquiries or complaints from customers of that organization. Customers may communicate in person or via written correspondence, toll telephone, or 800 number. Customer service correspondence may be in letterhead or postcard format. Customer service is an important part of the FULFILLMENT function, ensuring that customers will buy again and/or continue to be good customers.

CUSTOMER SERVICE REPRESENTATIVE employee responsible for maintaining goodwill between a business organization and its customers by answering questions, solving problems, and providing advice or assistance in utilizing the goods or services of the organization. *See also* CUSTOMER SERVICE.

CUSTOMS
1. agency of the federal government responsible for checking all imported goods and assessing and collecting duties.
2. duties, taxes, or tariffs levied on imported goods.

CUSTOMS COURT federal court that reviews decisions of customs collectors.

CUT
1. (*v.*) stop (as in ending the filming of a movie scene).
2. (*n.*) point of pass/fail, as in *making the cut,* or being cut from further consideration.
3. (*v.*) in electronic media, to intentionally remove from a document. In most applications, cut material is placed on the CLIPBOARD and can be pasted multiple times; the Cut command thus differs from Delete, which removes the material entirely.

CUTOFF POINT in capital budgeting, the minimum acceptable rate of return on investments. *See also* DISCOUNTED CASH FLOW.

CYBERSPACE the place where computer networking hardware, NETWORK software, and people using them converge.

CYCLE *see* BUSINESS CYCLE.

CYCLE BILLING sending invoices to customers systematically throughout the month rather than billing all customers on the same day each month, thus spreading work evenly over time.

CYCLICAL DEMAND demand that varies cyclically over time, usually in response to some effect of season or BUSINESS CYCLE. Demand for electricity and Christmas ornaments is seasonally cyclical; demand for housing is affected by the effects of the business cycle upon interest rates.

CYCLICAL INDUSTRY industry in which variation in output occurs frequently. Construction is seasonally cyclical (less work in winter) and also depends on the BUSINESS CYCLE (changes in interest rates and demand).

CYCLICAL STOCK stock that tends to rise quickly when the economy turns up and to fall quickly when the economy turns down. Examples are housing, automobiles, and paper. Stocks of noncyclical industries, such as food, insurance, and drugs, are not as directly affected by economic change.

CYCLICAL UNEMPLOYMENT unemployment caused by a downturn in the BUSINESS CYCLE.

CYCLIC VARIATION any change in economic activity that is due to some regular and/or recurring cause, such as the BUSINESS CYCLE or seasonal influences.

D

DAGGER the † character, used as a footnote reference mark.

DAILY TRADING LIMIT maximum that many commodities and options are allowed to rise or fall in one day. When a market reaches its limit early and stays there all day, it is said to be having an up-limit or down-limit day.

DAISY CHAIN
1. connecting devices in sequence.
2. trading between market manipulators to create the appearance of active volume as a lure for legitimate investors. When the price is driven up, the manipulators unload their holdings, leaving the unwary investors without buyers to trade with in turn.

DAMAGES amount received (other than workers' compensation) through prosecution of a legal suit or action based on tort or tort-type rights, or through a settlement agreement entered into in lieu of such prosecution. Reimbursement for loss of income or recovery of previously deducted expenses is normally taxable. Damage income for personal injuries or sickness is generally not taxable.

DATA factual information. Data is the plural of *datum*, which means a *single fact*. *Data processing* is sorting, recording, and classifying data for making calculations or decisions.

DATABASE collection of DATA stored on a computer storage medium in a common pool for access on an as-needed basis. The same pool of information can serve many applications, even those not anticipated at the time the database was created. This is in contrast to traditional methods of data storage that hold a fixed amount of data retrievable in a predetermined format, often duplicating the storage of information in as many files as there are applications. For example, the name and address of the same customer may be in a marketing file, a billing file, and an addressing file. If any one of these applications changes, and the programs that access and use the customer record change, then the customer file must change.

DATABASE MANAGEMENT methodology of storing, manipulating, and retrieving data in a database. Some aspects of database management are entering, classifying, modifying and updating data and presenting output reports.

DATABASE MARKETING method of using data collected from a wide number of consumer purchasing sources to target individuals for marketing campaigns. This is an accurate, expensive method of reaching a select target audience. The proliferation of computerized databases has created a huge flood of JUNK MAIL and JUNK FAXES. *See also* DIRECT MAIL.

DATA COMMUNICATION exchange of data between two or more connected computers.

DATA COMPRESSION a technology that reduces the size of a computer file. Especially important for files used on Web pages: graphics and sound files are compressed so they can be downloaded faster. Compression methods are described as *lossless* (no data is lost) or *lossy* (some data is sacrificed to achieve greater compression).

DATA ENCRYPTION KEY *see* ENCRYPTION.

DATA ENCRYPTION STANDARD (DES) *see* ENCRYPTION.

DATA INTERCHANGE FORMAT (DIF) FILE system to transfer computer files from one program to another. DIF files created on other systems (e.g., the client's) can be imported into the practitioner's spreadsheet or database. The DIF format is produced as an output or export option by many of the existing spreadsheet programs and by some database programs. Various accounting packages can generate DIF files. An example of an application is extracting a spreadsheet from *Excel* and putting it into another spreadsheet program or a word processing program.

DATA MINING nontrivial extraction of implicit, previously unknown, and potentially useful information from existing data. It uses machine learning, statistical, and visualization techniques to explore and organize existing knowledge in a comprehensible format.

DATA PROCESSING INSURANCE coverage on data processing equipment, data processing media (such as magnetic tapes, disks), and extra expense involved in returning to usual business conditions. Coverage can be obtained on a *specified perils* basis or on an ALL RISK/ALL PERIL basis. The data processing equipment is usually written as all risk/all peril on a specifically scheduled basis. The data processing media is usually written on an all risk/all peril basis.

DATE OF GIFT date on which the donor's dominion and control over the property ceases.

DATE OF ISSUE date when an insurance company issues a policy. This date may be different from the date the insurance becomes effective.

DATE OF RECORD date on which a shareholder must officially own SHARES in order to be entitled to a DIVIDEND. After the date of record, the stock is said to be EX-DIVIDEND. Also called *record date*.

DATING in commercial transactions, extension of CREDIT beyond the supplier's customary TERMS; for example, 90 days instead of 30 days.

DAVIS-BACON ACT (1931) United States federal law requiring the payment of prevailing wages on public works projects. All federal government construction contracts, and most contracts for federally assisted construction over $2,000, must include provisions for paying on-site workers no less than the locally prevailing wages and benefits paid on similar projects.

DAX Deutscher Aktienindex, a stock performance index (dividends added in) composed of the 30 most actively traded German BLUE CHIP stocks on the Frankfurt Stock Exchange.

DAY ORDER order to buy or sell securities that expires unless executed or canceled the day it is placed. All orders are *day orders* unless otherwise specified. The chief exception is a GOOD-TILL-CANCELED ORDER (GTC), though even it can be executed the same day if the price is right.

DAY TRADE purchase and sale of a position during the same day.

DAY TRADER person who buys and sells within a short time, generally minutes or hours, most frequently within the day, though some may hold a position for 2 to 3 days.

DBA *see* DOING BUSINESS AS.

DCF *see* DISCOUNTED CASH FLOW.

DEADBEAT

In general: one who does not pay his bills. In contrast to a *freeloader* or DEADHEAD, who doesn't pay the (train) fare but doesn't necessarily add cost to the service provider, the deadbeat runs up a bill for goods and services that he uses individually, without payment.

Accounting: credit customer who, without just cause, has not paid for his order by the end of the BILLING CYCLE. Names of *deadbeats* are removed from the active customer list and may be used later as a purge file against promotion lists. *See also* BAD DEBT.

DEAD-CAT BOUNCE sharp rise in stock prices after a severe decline. The saying refers to the assumption that a dead cat dropped from a high place will bounce. Often, the bounce is the result of short-sellers covering their positions at a profit.

DEAD-END JOB position that offers no opportunity for promotion, increased pay, or increased responsibility; also called a *blind alley job*.

DEADHEAD act of moving a piece of transportation equipment when it is not carrying a paying load (people or freight). For example, this occurs when a bus is moved to a garage after the route is run for the day. Also, a nonpaid trip or someone who does not pay for a bus ride, movie, or other service.

DEAD KEY nonfunctioning key on a typewriter, computer keyboard, or word processor, by design or disrepair. Also, a key that prints a character for the purpose of placing a grammatical mark or statistical symbol over or under another character, but does not move the cursor or carriage.

DEAD LETTER letter that is undeliverable by the post office and cannot be returned to the sender.

DEADLINE due date, latest time for the completion of a negotiation, project, service, or product. The failure to meet a deadline has negative consequences, such as loss of business, lack of credibility, and penalty charges.

DEAD STOCK goods that cannot be sold.

DEAD TIME period during which a worker is idled because of a machine malfunction or because the flow of materials is interrupted; also called *downtime*. Dead time is a direct cost to the company.

DEALER
1. (SECURITIES) a merchant who regularly engages in the purchase and resale of securities to customers. Stocks, bonds, and other financial instruments are considered INVENTORY and are not subject to capital gain or loss treatment for a dealer.
2. one who buys and sells from his or her own account. The number of sales necessary for dealer status may be low (for example, three or four sales for a real estate dealer). The merchandise is inventory; consequently, any gain on the sale is ORDINARY INCOME.
3. a person who regularly sells or otherwise disposes of personal property on the installment plan, or who disposes of real property that is held by the taxpayer for sale to customers in the ordinary course of the taxpayer's trade or business. A dealer may not use the installment method on certain sales.

DEALER EXCHANGE computerized SECURITIES marketplace where securities are purchased and sold by MARKET MAKERS, stock and bond brokers using DISTRIBUTED PROCESSING to make the market and complete the transaction. This replaces the earlier centralized auction markets where all transactions were completed by floor brokers. *See also* auction exchanges.

DEATHBED GIFT *see* GIFT IN CONTEMPLATION OF DEATH.

DEATH BENEFIT(S) amount of money to be paid to beneficiaries when a life insurance policyholder dies. The *death benefit* is the face value of the policy less any unpaid policy loans or other insurance company claims against the policy. Beneficiaries are not taxed on the death benefit when they receive it.

DEATH TAX often refers to state inheritance taxes; *see* ESTATE TAX; UNIFIED ESTATE AND GIFT TAX.

DEBASEMENT action of deliberately rendering less valuable the currency of a country, not by DEVALUATION but by reducing the precious metal content of the coinage.

DEBENTURE DEBT secured only by the general credit or promise to pay of the issuer. Debentures are the common type of bond issued by large, well-established corporations. Holders of debentures representing corporate indebtedness are creditors of the corporation and entitled to payment before shareholders upon dissolution of the corporation. *See also* CONVERTIBLES; INDENTURE.

DEBIT

    Accounting: entries on the left side of the GENERAL LEDGER. Debits include the acquisition cost of assets and amounts of deductible expenses.

    Real estate: in a CLOSING STATEMENT, item that is charged to a party. For example, the buyer is charged with these typical debits: purchase price, taxes prepaid by the seller, and deed recording fees. Debits charged to the seller include cost to retire the existing mortgage principal, accrued interest on the mortgage being relieved, and a termite inspection fee. *See also* CREDIT.

DEBIT CARD card used for making electronic transfers of cash from a customer's bank account to a store's account. Banking at home is another type of a debit account where transactions are made to a depository institution's account through a computer terminal. These transactions occur simultaneously and replace the need for checks or cash. *See also* AUTOMATED TELLER MACHINE (ATM).

DEBIT MEMORANDUM notice of a charge against an account, such as a deposited check that was returned because of insufficient funds.

DEBT obligation to pay. *See also* ACCOUNTS PAYABLE; LIABILITY; LOAN; MORTGAGE.

DEBT COVERAGE RATIO mathematical relationship of NET OPERATING INCOME divided by ANNUAL DEBT SERVICE; often used as underwriting criterion for INCOME PROPERTY mortgage loans. *See also* DEBT SERVICE COVERAGE.

DEBT/EQUITY RATIO the relationship of these components of PURCHASE CAPITAL. For example, if the outstanding MORTGAGE AMOUNT is $75,000 and the equity is $25,000, the *debt/equity ratio* is 3:1. This is equivalent to a 75% LOAN-TO-VALUE RATIO loan. Similarly, if a corporation's debt is three times the amount of stock, the ratio is 3:1. If the debt/equity ratio of a corporation is too high, the IRS may classify the corporation as a THIN CORPORATION and disallow some of the interest expense, recasting the payment as a dividend to its shareholders.

DEBT FINANCING raising capital through borrowing as with the sale of bonds; *contrast with* EQUITY FINANCING, which is raising capital through the sale of an ownership portion (stock).

DEBT INSTRUMENT written promise to repay a debt, such as a BILL, BOND, BANKER'S ACCEPTANCE, NOTE, CERTIFICATE OF DEPOSIT, or COMMERCIAL PAPER. A formal debt instrument is critical for obtaining a nonbusiness bad-debt deduction.

DEBTOR one who owes another something or is under obligation to pay money or to fulfill some other obligation; in BANKRUPTCY or similar proceedings, the person who is the subject of the proceeding. *See also* CREDITOR.

DEBT RETIREMENT repayment of debt. The most common method of retiring corporate debt is to set aside money each year in a sinking fund. Mortgages are retired through amortization or PREPAYMENT.

DEBT SECURITY SECURITY representing money borrowed that must be repaid and having a fixed amount, a specific MATURITY or maturities, and usually a specific rate of INTEREST or an original purchase DISCOUNT. Examples are BILLS, BONDS, COMMERCIAL PAPER, and NOTES.

DEBT SERVICE cash required in a given period, usually one year, for payments of interest and current maturities of PRINCIPAL on outstanding debt. Debt service in mortgage loans includes interest and principal; in corporate bond issues, the annual interest plus annual SINKING FUND payments; in government bonds, the annual payments into the debt service fund. *See also* ABILITY TO PAY.

DEBT SERVICE COVERAGE
Corporate finance: amount, usually expressed as a ratio, of CASH FLOW available to meet annual interest and principal payments on debt, including SINKING FUND payments. *See also* FIXED-CHARGE COVERAGE.
Government finance: export earnings required to cover annual principal and interest payments on a country's external debts.
Personal finance: ratio of monthly installment debt payments, excluding mortgage loans and rent, to monthly take-home pay.
Real estate: net operating income divided by annual debt service.

DEBT-TO-EQUITY RATIO
1. total LIABILITIES divided by total SHAREHOLDERS' EQUITY. This shows to what extent owners' equity can cushion creditors' claims in the event of LIQUIDATION.
2. total LONG-TERM DEBT divided by total SHAREHOLDERS' EQUITY. This is a measure of LEVERAGE, the use of borrowed money to enhance the return on owners' equity.
3. LONG-TERM DEBT and PREFERRED STOCK divided by COMMON STOCK equity. This relates securities with fixed charges to those without fixed charges. *See also* LOAN-TO-VALUE RATIO.

DEBUGGING process of removing bugs from COMPUTER PROGRAMS, that is, correcting errors. With a complicated program, it may take longer to correct all the errors than it did to write the program in the first place.

DECEDENT a person who has died.

DECENTRALIZATION essential decision making and policy formulation done at several locations throughout an organization. The objective is to give decision-making authority to those most directly responsible for the outcome of those decisions, with first-hand experience and knowledge about the issues involved.

DECEPTIVE ADVERTISING advertising that makes false claims or misleading statements, as well as advertising that creates a false impression. If retailers systematically advertise merchandise at low prices to get customers into their store and then fail to have the merchandise, they are guilty of *deceptive advertising*. Deceptive practices can take many other forms as well, such as false promises, unsubstantiated claims, incomplete descriptions, false testimonials or comparisons, small-print qualifications of advertisements, partial disclosure, or visual distortion of products.

DECEPTIVE PACKAGING packaging that creates an impression that the enclosed material is more than what it really is, in terms of either quantity or quality.

DECISION MODEL formal or informal conceptualization of the relationship of the various factors that are relevant in decision making and planning.

DECISION PACKAGE procedure used in ZERO-BASE BUDGETING when a manager specifies recommended and alternative ways to undertake a proposed project (e.g., product). Dollars and time involved with the recommended and alternative means of accomplishing the project are specified. Thus, upper management has three possible choices: (1) not funding the project at all; (2) accepting the project as recommended; or (3) accepting the project in an alternative form.

DECISION SUPPORT SYSTEM (DSS) branch of the broadly defined MANAGEMENT INFORMATION SYSTEM (MIS). It is an information system that provides answers to problems and that integrates the decision maker into the system as a component.

DECISION TREE diagram that illustrates all possible consequences of different decisions at different stages of decision making.

DECLARATION
1. formal pleadings by a PLAINTIFF as to the facts and circumstances that gave rise to his CAUSE OF ACTION. Also, a statement made out of court.
2. legal document used to create a CONDOMINIUM. It includes a description of the property and the uses to which it is restricted, a description of individual ownership units, COMMON ELEMENTS, and procedures for amending the declaration.
3. statement that an INSURED makes (declares) about loss exposures in an application for a policy. For example, in a personal automobile policy, the applicant states his/her name, address, occupation, type of automobile, expected mileage per year, etc. The insurer uses this information to set a premium rate.

DECLARATION OF ESTIMATED TAX RETURN required of those taxpayers who do not regularly have adequate tax withheld, as in the case of SELF-EMPLOYED taxpayers, who expect that the total amount of their withholdings will not cover their tax liability for the tax year. ESTIMATED TAX is paid on a quarterly basis.

DECLARATION OF TRUST written statement by a TRUSTEE to acknowledge that the PROPERTY is held for the benefit of another.

DECLARATORY JUDGMENT judgment from a district court to establish the right of the parties or express the opinion of the court as to the question of law without ordering anything to be done.

DECLARE
In general: to announce something.
Finance: to authorize the payment of a DIVIDEND on a specified date, an act of the board of directors of a corporation. Once declared, a dividend becomes an obligation of the issuing corporation.
Import: to make a statement to a customs officer of goods imported.
Taxation: to include income on a tax return.

DECLINING-BALANCE METHOD method of accelerated depreciation where a percentage rate of depreciation is applied to the undepreciated balance, not to the original cost. *See also* ACCELERATED DEPRECIATION; DOUBLE-DECLINING-BALANCE; STRAIGHT-LINE (METHOD OF) DEPRECIATION.

DECREASING COSTS the situation in a firm or industry when unit costs of output decrease as volume of output increases.

DECREE an order issued by one in authority; a court order or decision.

DEDICATED used only for a specific purpose, as for example, a *dedicated* phone line for a fax machine or modem. A permanent connection to the INTERNET is also referred to as a *dedicated* line or channel.

DEDICATION CONVEYANCE of land as a GRANT to the public by a private owner and acceptance of that land on behalf of the public. For example, a company buys a large area of land on which it plans to locate its national headquarters. To promote goodwill between the company and the surrounding communities, the company *dedicates* a portion of the land to the county parks committee, which accepts permanent ownership of the land.

DEDUCTIBLE
1. in a tax return, applies to an expense that may be subtracted from income.
2. (noun) the initial amount of an insurable expense that the insured is required to pay before insurance reimbursement is made for a claim. This can take two forms:
   • *Absolute dollar amount*—amount the insured must pay before the company will pay, up to the limits of the policy. The higher the absolute dollar amount, the lower the premium.
   • *Time period amount (elimination period/waiting period)*—length of time the insured must wait before any benefit payments are

made by the insurance company. In disability income policies, it is common to have a waiting period of 30 days during which no income benefits are paid to the insured. The longer this time period, the lower the premium.

DEDUCTION amount allowed to taxpayers under the Internal Revenue Code as an offset against GROSS INCOME or ADJUSTED GROSS INCOME. *See also* ITEMIZED DEDUCTION; STANDARD DEDUCTION; MARITAL DEDUCTION.

DEDUCTIONS FROM GROSS INCOME (DFROM) an individual is allowed to deduct the larger of ITEMIZED DEDUCTIONS or the STANDARD DEDUCTION. *See also* ABOVE THE LINE.

DEDUCTIVE REASONING logical way of reaching a conclusion based on deducing from facts what to do. An example is a manager who considers the competition, customer demand, company financial status, and economic conditions in formulating a business policy. *See also* INDUCTIVE REASONING.

DEED INSTRUMENT in writing that conveys an interest in land (realty) from the grantor to the grantee. Its main function is to pass title to land. *See also* BARGAIN AND SALE; QUITCLAIM DEED; WARRANTY.

DEED IN LIEU OF FORECLOSURE act of giving PROPERTY back to a LENDER without FORECLOSURE.

DEED OF TRUST transfer of legal TITLE to property from its owner to a TRUSTEE, so that the trustee may hold the title as security for the performance of certain obligations, monetary or otherwise, by the owner or a THIRD PARTY. In several states, a deed of trust is virtually equivalent to a mortgage as used in other states.

DEED RESTRICTION clause in a DEED that limits the use of land. For example, a deed might stipulate that alcoholic beverages are not to be sold on the land for 20 years. Restrictions that are against public policy are unenforceable, such as those that prohibit people of certain ethnic groups from using a property. *See also* COVENANT.

DEEP DISCOUNT BOND BOND selling for a DISCOUNT of more than about 25% from its FACE VALUE. Unlike ORIGINAL ISSUE DISCOUNT bonds, deep-discounts were issued at a PAR VALUE of $1,000, but market forces caused a decline.

DEEP POCKETS seemingly inexhaustible financial resources, permitting one to remain in business after a prolonged period of negative cash flow.

DE FACTO in fact; by virtue of the deed of accomplishment; actually. Used to refer to a situation in which a condition or institution is operating as though it were official or pursuant to law, but that is not legally authorized. Such situations may arise where, for example, an authorizing law is declared invalid, or because required legal formalities have not been satisfied.

DE FACTO CORPORATION CORPORATION existing in fact, but without the actual authority of law.

DEFALCATION failure of one entrusted with money to pay over the money when it is due to another. The term is similar to *misappropriation* and EMBEZZLEMENT, but wider in scope because it does not imply criminal FRAUD.

DEFAULT
1. failure of a debtor to make timely payments of INTEREST and PRINCIPAL as they come due or to meet some other provision of a bond, mortgage, lease, or other contract.
2. path a computer follows unless it is given specific instructions to the contrary.

DEFAULTED INTEREST interest that has not been paid on time. The fact that a debtor has failed to make timely payments of interest and principal as they come due does not transform the unpaid interest into principal for determining the tax consequences of later payments.

DEFAULT JUDGMENT
1. a JUDGMENT against defendant who has failed to respond to plaintiff's action or to appear at the trial or hearing.
2. judgment given without the defendant's being heard in his own defense.

DEFEASANCE INSTRUMENT that negates the effectiveness of a deed or a will; COLLATERAL deed that defeats the force of another deed upon the performance of certain conditions. It is a technique used by corporations to avoid retiring low-interest-rate debt. Instead, they purchase U.S. Treasury bonds earning a higher rate and pledge the Treasury bonds as collateral against the debt they owe. The corporation can then disregard certain aspects of the INDENTURE of their bond debt.

DEFECTIVE
1. incomplete, faulty.
2. not reasonably safe for a use that can be reasonably anticipated. *See also* PRODUCT LIABILITY; WARRANTY.

DEFECTIVE TITLE
1. unmarketable right of OWNERSHIP.
2. with reference to land, TITLE that might be subject to partial or complete ownership by someone else.
3. with reference to NEGOTIABLE INSTRUMENTS, title obtained through FRAUD or other illegal means.

DEFENDANT
1. in civil proceedings, party responding to the complaint; one who is sued and called upon to make satisfaction for a wrong complained of by another.
2. in criminal proceedings, the accused. *See also* RESPONDENT.

DEFENSIVE SECURITIES STOCKS and BONDS more stable than average and providing a relatively safe return on an investor's funds. When the stock market is weak, defensive securities tend to decline less than the overall market.

DEFENSIVE SPENDING *see* COMPETITIVE PARITY.

DEFERRAL OF TAXES postponement of tax payments from the current year to a later year. For example, delaying the receipt of income to a subsequent year can postpone payment of taxes, or likekind exchanges may postpone taxes on a gain until the new property is sold. Deferring taxes is worthwhile because interest can be earned on money not yet paid in taxes; moreover, the deferred amount can often be offset by subsequent losses or ended in a year when the taxpayer is in a lower tax bracket.

DEFERRED ACCOUNT account that postpones taxes until a later date. Some examples are INDIVIDUAL RETIREMENT ACCOUNT (IRA); KEOGH PLAN; PROFIT-SHARING PLAN; SALARY REDUCTION PLAN (SEPIRA).

DEFERRED ANNUITY *see* DEFERRED-PAYMENT ANNUITY.

DEFERRED BENEFITS AND PAYMENTS *see* DEFERRED CONTRIBUTION PLAN; DEFERRED RETIREMENT CREDIT.

DEFERRED BILLING delayed invoicing of a CREDIT ORDER buyer at the request of the seller. For example, billing may be deferred on a new subscription order so that the first issue of a magazine is received before the first bill arrives. This is especially important if the subscription promotion promised to send the first issue without obligation to pay.

DEFERRED CHARGE expenditure carried forward as an ASSET and amortized over the life it represents. A fee for arranging a 30-year mortgage on income-producing real estate is a deferred charge.

DEFERRED COMPENSATION plan under whose terms an EMPLOYEE defers payment of a portion of SALARY in return for the EMPLOYER'S promise to pay the employee the salary at some time in the future.

DEFERRED COMPENSATION PLAN means of supplementing an executive's retirement benefits by deferring a portion of his current earnings. Deferring income like this benefits an employer by encouraging the loyalty of his executives. To qualify for a tax advantage, the IRS requires a written agreement between an executive and his employer stating the specified period of deferral of income. An election by an executive to defer income must be irrevocable and must be made prior to performing the service for which income deferral is sought.

DEFERRED CONTRIBUTION PLAN arrangement in which an unused deduction (credit carryover) to a profit-sharing plan can be added to an employer's future contribution on a tax-deductible basis. It occurs when the employer's contribution to a profit-sharing plan is less than the annual 15% of employee compensation allowed by the Federal Tax Code.

DEFERRED CREDIT income items received by a business, but not yet reported as income; also called *deferred revenue* and *deferred income*. An example is a consulting fee received in *advance* before being earned. The term also applies to revenue normally includable in income but deferred until earned and matched with expenses. For example, a magazine publisher might defer a 3-year subscription to match revenue against later publication expenses.

DEFERRED GAIN any gain not subject to tax in the year realized but postponed until a later year.

DEFERRED GROUP ANNUITY retirement income payments for an employee that begin after a stipulated future time period, and continue for life. Each year, contributions are used to buy a paid-up single-premium deferred annuity. These increments, added together, provide income payments at retirement.

DEFERRED INTEREST BOND bond that pays interest at a later date; for example, a ZERO COUPON BOND, which pays interest and repays principal in one lump sum at maturity. Such bonds automatically REINVEST the interest at a fixed rate.

DEFERRED MAINTENANCE in APPRAISAL, a type of PHYSICAL DEPRECIATION owing to lack of normal upkeep. Examples are broken window glass, missing roof shingles, peeling paint, and broken guttering.

DEFERRED-PAYMENT ANNUITY ANNUITY whose CONTRACT provides that payments to the ANNUITANT be postponed until a number of PERIODS have elapsed (e.g., when the annuitant attains a certain age). Also called *deferred annuity*.

DEFERRED PAYMENTS payments extended over a period of time or put off to a future date.

DEFERRED PROFIT SHARING a portion of company profits allocated by an employer, in good years, to an employee's trust. Contributions on behalf of each employee are expressed as a percentage of salary with 5% being common practice. If the profit-sharing plan is a *qualified* plan according to the IRS, employer contributions are tax deductible as a business expense. These contributions are not currently taxable to the employee; benefits are taxed at the time of distribution.

DEFERRED RETIREMENT retirement taken after the normal retirement age. For example, if the normal retirement age is 65 or 70 an employee may continue to work beyond those ages. Normally the election of deferred retirement does not increase the monthly retirement income when the employee actually retires.

DEFERRED WAGE INCREASE delaying the implementation of a wage increase until a later date. In collective bargaining this is a concessionary labor tactic for winning a wage increase from management. It saves management money until the wage increase is actually implemented and allows labor to claim that it won a wage increase for the bargaining unit.

DEFICIENCY (TAX) excess of a taxpayer's correct tax liability for the taxable year over the amount of taxes previously paid for such year. The Internal Revenue Service is authorized to assess deficiencies during an AUDIT of the taxpayer's RETURN, and a deficiency may be used as the basis for penalties for the underpayment of tax, such as for negligence or fraud in filing the return.

DEFICIENCY JUDGMENT court order stating that the borrower still owes money when the SECURITY for a loan does not entirely satisfy a defaulted debt.

DEFICIENCY LETTER written notice from the Securities and Exchange Commission to a prospective issuer of SECURITIES that the preliminary PROSPECTUS needs revision or expansion. Deficiency letters require prompt action; otherwise, the registration period may be prolonged.

DEFICIT
1. insufficiency in an account or number, whether as the result of DEFAULTS and misappropriations or of mistakes or shrinkage in value.
2. excess of the U.S. government's spendings over its revenues. Many economists believe that federal deficits can lead to inflation.

DEFICIT FINANCING borrowing by a government agency to make up for a revenue shortfall. Deficit financing stimulates the economy for a time but eventually can become a drag on the economy by pushing up interest rates. *See also* CROWDING OUT; KEYNESIAN ECONOMICS.

DEFICIT NET WORTH excess of LIABILITIES over ASSETS and CAPITAL STOCK, perhaps as a result of operating losses; also called *negative net worth.*

DEFICIT SPENDING excess of government expenditures over government revenue, creating a shortfall that must be financed through borrowing. *See also* BUDGET; GRAMM-RUDMAN-HOLLINGS AMENDMENT.

DEFINED-BENEFIT PENSION PLAN plan that promises to pay a specified amount (based on a predetermined formula) to each person who retires after a set number of years of service. Such trust plans pay no taxes on their investment income. Employees contribute to them in some cases; in others, all contributions are made by the employer.

DEFINED-CONTRIBUTION PENSION PLAN pension plan in which the amount of contributions is fixed at a certain level, while benefits vary depending on the return from the investments. In some cases, such as 401(k), 403(b), and 457 plans, employees make voluntary contributions into a tax-deferred account, which may or may not be matched by employers. The level of contribution may be selected by the employee within a range set by the employer, such as between

2 and 10% of annual salary. In other cases, contributions are made by an employer into a profit-sharing account based on each employee's salary level, years of service, age, and other factors. Defined-contribution pension plans, unlike DEFINED-BENEFIT PENSION PLANS, give the employee options of where to invest the account, usually among stock, bond, and money market accounts. Definedcontribution plans have become increasingly popular in recent years because they limit a company's pension outlay and shift the liability for investment performance from the company's pension plan to employees.

DEFLATION decline in the prices of GOODS and SERVICES. Deflation is the reverse of INFLATION; it should not be confused with *disinflation*, which is a slowing down in the rate of price increases.

DEFLATIONARY GAP economic term describing the situation when GROSS DOMESTIC PRODUCT is below its full-employment level. In theory, such a situation would lead to the existence of unemployed resources, which should lead to falling prices (deflation) for those resources as the unemployed ones compete in the market.

DEFLATOR statistical factor or device designed to remove the effect inflation has on variables. Inflation-adjusted variables are said to be in real, or constant-value, terms. For example, inflation-adjusted GROSS NATIONAL PRODUCT figures are said to show *real GNP*. *See also* CONSTANT DOLLARS.

DEFUNCT COMPANY company that no longer exists; company that has suspended all operations and is out of business.

DEGRESSION tendency to descend or decrease; progressive decline in an item, such as value, over time. An example is a deterioration in a company's market share for its product line.

DEHIRING laying off, firing, or rejecting a previous hiring decision.

DEINDUSTRIALIZATION collapse or flight of industry previously operating in an area as a result of technological and economic factors. The United States has experienced substantial *deindustrialization* as foreign competition has threatened the U.S. steel, automotive, and electronic industries.

DE JURE by right; lawful; legitimate. Generally used in contrast to DE FACTO; *de jure* connotes "as a matter of law," whereas *de facto* connotes "as a matter of practice not founded upon law."

DELAYED EXCHANGE *see* SECTION 1031; TAX-FREE EXCHANGE, DELAYED.

DELAYED OPENING postponement of the start of trading in a stock until a gross imbalance in buy and sell orders is overcome. Such an imbalance is likely to follow a significant event such as a takeover order.

DELEGATE
1. (verb) appoint, authorize, or commission; transfer authority from one person to another. Efficient management requires delegating authority but not necessarily responsibility.
2. (noun) person commissioned to act instead of another.

DELETE a command used to remove unwanted characters or objects from a document or data from a storage medium. Deleted files are not actually erased, but reference to them is removed from the "table of contents" that tells the computer where they are, and the space they occupy is designated as available for reuse. Until they are actually overwritten by new data, however, they can often be retrieved.

DELINQUENCY
In general: failure to make a payment on an obligation when due.
Finance: amount of past due balances, determined on either a contractual or a recency-of-payment basis.

DELINQUENCY RATE statistically, the number of loans with delinquent payments divided by the number of loans held in a portfolio. Sometimes, the rate is based on the total dollar volume of the loans instead of the number. Generally, delinquency is qualified to include only loans where payments are three or more months past due.

DELINQUENT payable but overdue and unpaid. *See also* DEADBEAT; DEFAULT.

DELINQUENT RETURN tax return not filed within the time prescribed by the Internal Revenue Code (due date). A delinquent return may be subject to a flat penalty or penalties based on any unpaid tax liability. *See also* FAILURE-TO-FILE PENALTY; FAILURE-TO-PAY PENALTY.

DELISTING removal of an issue from trading on an organized STOCK EXCHANGE such as the New York Stock Exchange. If the issuer fails to maintain the minimum listing requirements, trading of its securities on the exchange can be suspended or eliminated.

DELIVERABLES the reports a consultant expects to prepare.

DELIVERY voluntary transfer of TITLE or POSSESSION from one party to another; legally recognized handing over to another of one's possessory rights. Actual delivery of a deed is usually required for a transfer of real estate ownership. Where *actual* delivery is cumbersome or impossible, the courts may find *constructive delivery* sufficient if the intention is clearly to transfer title. Thus, one may deliver the contents of a safety deposit box by handing over the key together with any necessary authorization. *See also* GOOD DELIVERY.

DELIVERY DATE
1. first day on which delivery is to be made under a futures contract.
2. third business day following a REGULAR-WAY transaction on the New York Stock Exchange.

DELPHI TECHNIQUE method of providing members of a group with the ideas of others without a face-to-face meeting. An individual member writes down his thoughts on a problem and submits them to a coordinator. The coordinator then compiles all comments received from the members and sends them to every member for review. Each member then provides feedback on the other members' comments and submits recommendations to the coordinator. Finally, the coordinator attempts to reach a consensus of opinion based on all comments received.

DEMAND economic expression of desire, and ability to pay, for goods and services. Demand is neither need nor desire; the essence of demand is the willingness to exchange value (goods, labor, money) for varying amounts of goods or services, depending upon the price asked.

DEMAND CURVE graphic depiction of DEMAND SCHEDULE. With price on the vertical axis and quantity on the horizontal, the demand curve normally slopes downward from left to right, reflecting higher quantity demanded at lower prices.

DEMAND DEPOSIT account BALANCE that, without prior notice to the bank, can be drawn on by CHECK, by CASH withdrawal from an AUTOMATED TELLER MACHINE (ATM), or by transfer to other accounts using a telephone or home computer. *See also* MONEY SUPPLY.

DEMAND LOAN loan payable on request by the creditor rather than on a specific date.

DEMAND NOTE
   1. INSTRUMENT that by its EXPRESS terms is payable immediately on an agreed-upon date of MATURITY without further demand for payment.
   2. instrument payable at sight or upon presentation, or one in which no time for payment is stated.

DEMAND PRICE price that will be offered in the market by consumers for a given quantity of output. It is derived from the DEMAND SCHEDULE or DEMAND CURVE.

DEMAND-PULL INFLATION price increases occurring when supply is not adequate to meet DEMAND. *See also* COST-PUSH INFLATION.

DEMAND SCHEDULE table expressing the relationship between price and quantity demanded of a good.

DEMING, W. EDWARDS consulting statistician and management expert (1900–1993), best known for his work on statistical quality control in Japan. The Union of Japanese Scientists and Engineers awards its annual Deming Prize to a statistician for contributions to statistical theory. The Deming Application Prize is awarded to a company for improved use of statistical theory in organization, consumer research, design of product, and production. Deming's System of Profound Knowledge is the basis for his 14 Points for Management. *See also* TOTAL QUALITY MANAGEMENT.

DE MINIMIS trifling; of insufficient significance to warrant judicial or tax attention. From the judicial principle *De minimis non curat lex* (i.e., "The law does not concern itself with trifles").

DEMISED PREMISES property subject to LEASE. For example, an apartment is rented under a written lease. In the lease, the apartment is referred to as the *demised premises*.

DEMOGRAPHICS population statistics with regard to socioeconomic factors such as age, income, sex, occupation, education, family size, and the like. Advertisers often define their TARGET MARKET in terms of demographics; thus, demographics are a very important aspect of media planning in matching the media with the market. Each demographic category is broken down (by the various research companies) according to its characteristics.

DEMOLITION destruction and removal of an existing structure from a site; necessary to prepare a site for new construction.

DEMONETIZATION withdrawal from circulation of a specified form of currency. For example, the Jamaica Agreement between major INTERNATIONAL MONETARY FUND (IMF) countries officially *demonetized* gold starting in 1978, ending its role as the major medium of international SETTLEMENT.

DEMORALIZE to decrease the morale. Employee morale can be lowered from many causes such as lack of appreciation by superiors, layoffs, and salary give backs. Where possible, the personnel department should minimize adverse causes on morale since worker productivity and accuracy will typically fall off and the employee turnover rate may rise.

DEMURRAGE charge applied to shipping vehicles when they are held by the CONSIGNOR or the CONSIGNEE for an excessive amount of time.

DEMURRER formal ALLEGATION that facts as stated in the PLEADINGS, even if true, are not legally sufficient for the case to proceed further. It does not admit anything but tests whether the complaint is sufficient to state a cause of action. In modern procedure, a motion to dismiss for failure to state a claim upon which relief may be granted replaces the demurrer.

DEMUTUALIZATION conversion of a member-owned institution or mutually owned company to another form of organization, usually a shareholder-owned company. Demutualization, which is usually done to make access to capital easier, has been a trend in the insurance and savings and loan industries.

DENOMINATION face value of currency units, coins, and SECURITIES. *See also* PAR VALUE.

DE NOVO anew; a second time, as though the first had never taken place. For example, a state statute gives a defendant convicted in a municipal court the right to appeal that conviction *de novo* in a higher court. That right means that the defendant will have a new trial in which the facts and issues will be retried as though the first trial never took place.

DENSITY
   Real estate: intensity of land use. For example, if a 10-acre SUBDIVISION contains 30 single-family houses, the *housing density* is 3 dwelling units per acre. If the population density is 4 people per house, the *population density* per acre is 12.

DENSITY ZONING laws that restrict LAND-USE INTENSITY; for example, a ZONING ORDINANCE stating that all zones designated "R-2" may contain no more than four detached housing units per ACRE.

DENTAL AND VISION INSURANCE employee insurance covering a part of the incurred cost for dental and vision care. The deductible portion and total coverage of the plans vary according to the insurer and the workplace.

DEPARTMENT grouping of jobs in an organization to accomplish particular functions. Once the jobs have been grouped, a manager then can be assigned the responsibility of coordinating each group. When managers make decisions about how to group the individual jobs, they create departments. An example is the payroll department.

DEPARTMENTALIZATION process of forming employees into groups to accomplish specific organizational goals. Departments can be organized according to functions workers perform, as in accounting and human resource departments; by products, as in a department store organized by retail product categories; by type of customer, as in men's wear or women's wear; or by geographic divisions.

DEPARTMENT STORE large retail store having a wide variety of merchandise organized into customer-based departments. A department store usually sells dry goods, household items, wearing apparel, furniture, furnishings, appliances, radios, and televisions, with combined sales exceeding $10 million.

DEPARTURE PERMIT certificate of compliance from the IRS certifying that a departing alien has satisfied U.S. income tax laws; also called *sailing permit*. In order to obtain a departure permit, the departing alien must file Form 1040C, U.S. Departing Alien Income Tax Return, or Form 2063, U.S. Departing Alien Income Tax Statement. The departing alien is still required to file Form 1040NR after the end of the year.

DEPENDENCY EXEMPTION *see* DEPENDENT.

DEPENDENT any person with respect to whom a TAXPAYER can claim a DEPENDENCY EXEMPTION; defined by the Internal Revenue Code as any individual supported by the taxpayer who is related to the taxpayer in specified ways or who makes his principal abode in the taxpayer's household. Six tests must be met:

1. support.
2. relationship *or* household membership the entire year.
3. gross income.
4. joint return.
5. citizenship or residency.
6. legal relationship. The amount of the dependency exemption is indexed for inflation each year (for example, in 2006, the amount was $3,300).

DEPENDENT CARE CREDIT *see* CHILD AND DEPENDENT CARE CREDIT.

DEPENDENT COVERAGE protection under life and health insurance policies for dependents of a named insured, to include a spouse and unmarried children under a specified age. Under some life insurance policies an insured's spouse and dependent children, unmarried and under age 21, can be added at favorable rates. Health insurance policies cover the same dependent individuals at a far cheaper rate than the cost of separate policies for them.

DEPENDENT VARIABLE
Statistics: that element of an equation—usually expressed as "Y"—whose value is determined by the other elements, or *independent variables*, in the equation—usually expressed as "X." The amount of variation of the dependent variable caused by the independent variables can be measured by regression statistical analysis.

DEPLETION process whereby the cost or other BASIS of a natural resource (such as a coal interest) is recovered upon the extraction and sale of the deposit. There are two ways of determining the depletion allowance: (1) cost and (2) percentage.

DEPOSIT
1. cash, checks, or drafts placed with a financial institution for credit to a customer's account.
2. securities placed with a bank or other institution or with a person for a particular purpose.
3. sums lodged with utilities, landlords, and service companies as security.
4. money put down as evidence of an intention to complete a contract and to protect the other party in the event that the contract is not completed.
5. natural resources, such as a *mineral deposit*.

DEPOSITARY RECEIPT *see* AMERICAN DEPOSITARY RECEIPT.

DEPOSIT INSURANCE *see* CREDIT UNION; FEDERAL DEPOSIT INSURANCE CORPORATION (FDIC).

DEPOSIT IN TRANSIT checks or money en route to a bank but not yet posted by the bank to the account or the monthly statement; frequently needed to reconcile a checking account statement.

DEPOSITION method of pretrial DISCOVERY that consists of a steno-graphically transcribed statement of a witness under oath, in response to an attorney's questions, with opportunity for the opposing party or his attorney to be present and to cross-examine. Such a statement is the most common form of discovery and may be taken of any witness (whether or not a party to the action). When taken in the form described, it is called an *oral deposition*. Depositions may also be taken upon written INTERROGATORIES, where the questions are read to the witness by the officer who is taking the deposition.

DEPOSITORY INSTITUTIONS DEREGULATION AND MONE-TARY CONTROL ACT federal legislation of 1980 providing for DEREGULATION of the banking system.

DEPOSITORY TRUST COMPANY (DTC) central SECURITIES reposi-tory where stock and bond certificates are exchanged. Most of these exchanges now take place electronically, and few paper certificates actually change hands. The DTC is owned by most of the major banks, broker-dealers, and exchanges on WALL STREET.

DEPRECIABLE BASIS *see* BASIS (TAX); ADJUSTED TAX BASIS.

DEPRECIABLE LIFE
1. for tax purposes, the number of years over which the cost of an ASSET may be spread.
2. for appraisal purposes, the estimated USEFUL LIFE of an asset.

DEPRECIABLE REAL ESTATE realty that is subject to deductions for DEPRECIATION. It generally includes property used in a trade or business, or an investment subject to an allowance for depreciation under SECTION 167 of the Internal Revenue Code. Land is generally not depreciable, but certain land may be subject to DEPLETION.

DEPRECIATE systematically write off the cost of an asset over a period of time allowed by tax law.

DEPRECIATED COST original cost of a FIXED ASSET less ACCUMU-LATED DEPRECIATION. This is the ADJUSTED BASIS of the asset.

DEPRECIATION
Accounting: DEDUCTION allowed a taxpayer, representing a reasonable allowance for the exhaustion of PROPERTY used in a trade or business, or property held for the production of income. The purpose of charging depreciation against EQUIPMENT is to distinguish the portion of income that is a RETURN OF CAPITAL. This generates a tax-free stream of income equal to the portion of the asset that has been "used up."
Economics: loss in the value of an asset, whether due to physical changes, OBSOLESCENCE, or factors outside the asset.

DEPRECIATION ALLOWANCE total DEPRECIATION deducted against property used in a trade or business or held for the production of income; also called ACCUMULATED DEPRECIATION. Depreciation permits an annual deduction for wear and tear and diminution of the property's value.

DEPRECIATION METHODS accounting techniques for allocating the cost of an asset over its USEFUL LIFE.

Example: $1,000 asset, four-year life:

Annual Depreciation

Year	Straight-Line	Double-Declining-Balance	Sum-of-the-Years'-Digits
1	$250	$500	$400
2	250	250	300
3	250	125	200
4	250	62	100

DEPRECIATION RECAPTURE when personal property is sold at a gain, the gain is ORDINARY INCOME to the extent of DEPRECIATION previously deducted; when real property is sold at a gain and ACCELERATED DEPRECIATION has been claimed, the taxpayer may be required to pay a tax at ordinary rates to the extent of the accelerated part of depreciation or in some cases for all of the depreciation taken.

DEPRECIATION RESERVE total DEPRECIATION charged against all productive ASSETS as stated on the BALANCE SHEET; also called *accumulated depreciation*. The charge is made to allow realistic reduction in the value of productive assets and to allow tax-free RECOVERY of the original investment in assets.

DEPRECIATION SYSTEM *see* GENERAL DEPRECIATION SYSTEM.

DEPRESSED AREA geographic location where economic problems exist. Individuals living in such an area typically have low incomes, the facilities are poor, and there is a greater incidence of crime and other problems.

DEPRESSION economic condition characterized by a massive decrease in business activity, falling prices, reduced PURCHASING POWER, an excess of SUPPLY OVER DEMAND, rising unemployment, accumulating inventories, DEFLATION, plant contraction, public fear, and caution. *See also* GREAT DEPRESSION.

DEPTH INTERVIEW research technique conducted in person in the field (rather than in the researcher's office) by a trained interviewer for the purpose of learning the motivation of consumers in the purchase decision process. *See also* MOTIVATIONAL RESEARCH.

DEREGULATION reducing government REGULATION in order to allow freer MARKETS to create a more efficient marketplace. Industries such as communications, banking, securities, and transportation have been deregulated, with resulting increased competition, heightened innovation, and mergers among weaker competitors. Some government oversight usually remains after deregulation.

DERIVATIVE
  Securities: taking its value from another security, asset, or index. A PUT or a CALL is closely tied to the value of the common stock in the same company. Includes options and futures contracts.

DERIVATIVE ACTION an ACTION based on a primary right of a CORPORATION, but asserted on its behalf by the shareholder because of the corporation's failure, deliberate or otherwise, to assert the right.

DERIVED DEMAND demand for CAPITAL GOODS and/or LABOR (which are used in production). Since production depends upon demand for the finished output, demand for goods and services used in production is derived from demand for finished goods.

DESCENT method of acquiring property, usually real property, through the laws of *descent and distribution* from a decedent without the use of a will.

DESCRIPTION
  In general: statement that describes something, such as a *job description.*
  Real estate: formal depiction of the dimensions and location of a property; generally included in deeds, leases, sales contracts, and mortgage contracts for real property. Specific methods of legal description include GOVERNMENT RECTANGULAR SURVEY, LOT AND BLOCK, and METES AND BOUNDS. *See also* PLAT.

DESCRIPTIVE MEMORANDUM offering circular of property or securities used when a PROSPECTUS is not required.

DESCRIPTIVE STATISTICS quantifying or summarizing data without implying or inferring anything beyond the sample. *See also* INFERENTIAL STATISTICS.

DESK trading desk, or securities department, at the New York FEDERAL RESERVE BANK, which is the operating arm of the FEDERAL OPEN MARKET COMMITTEE. The Desk executes all transactions undertaken by the FEDERAL RESERVE SYSTEM in the MONEY MARKET or the government securities market, serves as the Treasury Department's eyes and ears, and encompasses a foreign desk that conducts transactions in the FOREIGN EXCHANGE market.

DESKTOP the computer screen in a graphical environment such as WINDOWS or the MACINTOSH operating system. Applications and documents are represented by ICONS on the desktop.

DESKTOP COMPUTER a computer designed for desktop use; usually comprises, at a minimum, a central processing unit (CPU), a monitor, and a keyboard as separate units, connected by special cables. Most such computers now also include a POINTING DEVICE. *Contrast with* MAINFRAME; NOTEBOOK COMPUTER.

DESKTOP PUBLISHING (DTP) the use of PERSONAL COMPUTERS to design and print professional-quality typeset documents.

DETAIL PERSON
1. salesperson working as a manufacturer's representative who visits the manufacturer's customers and takes care of details. A detail person's primary responsibility is to promote goodwill by making sure that the manufacturer's customer is happy with the product.
2. salesperson whose primary job is to increase business from current and potential customers by providing them with product information and other personal selling assistance.

DETERMINISTIC a simulation model that offers an outcome with no allowance or consideration for variation. *Deterministic* models are well suited to predict results when the input is predictable. *Contrast with* STOCHASTIC.

DEVALUATION lowering of the value of a country's currency relative to gold and/or the currencies of other nations. The opposite is *revaluation.*

DEVELOPER
Real estate: one who transforms RAW LAND to IMPROVED LAND by use of labor, capital, and entrepreneurial efforts.
Computers: one who writes APPLICATION SOFTWARE, PROGRAMMER.

DEVELOPMENT
1. improving a product or producing new types of products.
2. in real estate, process of placing IMPROVEMENTS on or to a parcel of land; projects where such improvements are being made. Such improvements may include drainage, utilities, subdividing, access, buildings, and any combination of these elements.

DEVELOPMENTAL DRILLING PROGRAM drilling for oil and gas in an area with proven RESERVES to a depth known to have been productive in the past.

DEVELOPMENT STAGE ENTERPRISE enterprise devoting substantially all of its efforts to establishing itself. Either of the following conditions exist: (1) planned principal operations have not started or (2) there has been no significant revenue although principal operations are underway. GENERALLY ACCEPTED ACCOUNTING PRINCIPLES (GAAP) applicable to established companies apply equally to development stage enterprises.

DEVIATION POLICY organizational procedure for dealing with activities or behavior that differs from what is expected. Deviations can be classified according to categories. Management actions will be taken when deviations are detected. An *exception policy* is another method for dealing with deviations from the norm.

DEVICE DRIVER a program that allows a hardware peripheral, such as a printer, to communicate with a computer. DOS applications usually have their own proprietary device drivers; under WINDOWS all applications use the device drivers included with Windows or provided by the hardware manufacturer for installation in Windows.

DEVISE gift of REAL PROPERTY made by will. In modern usage, the term may also embrace testamentary gifts of PERSONAL PROPERTY. *See also* BEQUEST.

DEVISEE one who inherits REAL ESTATE through a will.

DHL company that offers speedy pickup and delivery of letters and packages.

DIAGONAL EXPANSION process whereby a business grows by creating new items that can be produced by using the equipment that is already in use and requiring few additional materials. An example is a company manufacturing chocolate candy that adds a variety of chocolate bunny rabbits for Easter to its normal line of chocolate candy.

DIALOG BOX in graphical user interfaces, a window that collects information from the user. Elements of these windows include *list boxes* (which present a list of options from which to select), *text boxes* (into which the user can type the desired information), *combo boxes* (which combine the features of list and text boxes), CHECK BOXES, RADIO BUTTONS, and (for numerical options) *spin boxes* with up or down arrows to increase or decrease the number selected. When the user has made all the desired choices, he clicks an OK button to accept the choices and close the window.

DIAL-UP CONNECTION a temporary connection between computers established by dialing a telephone number through a MODEM. This contrasts with a DEDICATED channel that provides a continuous connection.

DIARY daily written record of occurrences, experiences, observations, or thoughts. For example, a taxpayer should keep a *diary* of the miles driven for business purposes.

DICKERING petty bargaining.

DIF *see* DATA INTERCHANGE FORMAT.

DIFFERENTIAL ADVANTAGE *see* COMPARATIVE ADVANTAGE.

DIFFERENTIAL ANALYSIS *see* INCREMENTAL ANALYSIS.

DIFFERENTIATION STRATEGY
1. marketing technique used by a manufacturer to establish strong identity in a specific market; also called *segmentation strategy*. Using this strategy, a manufacturer will introduce different varieties of the same basic product under the same name into a particular product category and thus cover the range of products available in that category.
2. positioning a brand in such a way as to differentiate it from the competition and establish an image that is unique; for example, the Wells Fargo Bank positions itself as the bank that opened up the West.

DIGITAL using a limited, predetermined numbering system to measure or represent the flow of data. Digital computers use the binary digits 1 (on) and 0 (off) to represent all data.

DIGITAL COMPUTER type of COMPUTER that represents information in discrete form, as opposed to an *analog computer*, which allows representations to vary along a continuum. All modern general-purpose electronic computers are digital.

DIGITAL COPIER a copier that uses digital scanning techniques for copying. Digital copiers, as contrasted to photocopiers, permit users to scan many pages rapidly, then walk away with the originals while the copies are being produced (or store them in memory for later printing). Some digital copiers offer additional features such as the ability to print multiple copies on a single page, create booklets, digitally edit damaged originals, or fax copied material, and most also function as printers when connected to a computer network.

DIGITIZE reduce to digital form for use by a computer. For example, an optical scanner converts an analog image, such as a photograph, into data represented by binary digits.

DILUTION effect on EARNINGS PER SHARE and BOOK VALUE per share if all convertible securities were converted and/or all *warrants* or STOCK OPTIONS were exercised. *See also* FULLY DILUTED EARNINGS PER (COMMON) SHARE.

DIMINISHING-BALANCE METHOD *see* DECLINING-BALANCE METHOD.

DIMINISHING MARGINAL UTILITY, LAW OF economic proposition that states that successive units of a good or service provide less and less satisfaction to a consumer, given that the previous units already have been consumed. The first helping of food a hungry person receives is very satisfying; subsequent helpings are less and less so.

DIMINISHING RETURNS phenomenon that beyond a certain point, adding additional units of resources to a production process will provide successively smaller increments of additional product. This is due to crowding, adding less experienced or less appropriate resources, and so on.

DINKs acronym for *dual-income, no kids,* referring to a family unit in which there are two incomes and no children. The two incomes may result from both husband and wife working or from one spouse holding two jobs. *DINKs* are the prime targets of marketers selling luxury products and services.

DIP slight drop in securities prices after a sustained uptrend. Analysts often advise investors to buy on *dips,* meaning buy when a price is momentarily weak.

DIPLOMACY
1. process of conducting activities with another with tact in order to bring about a good relationship. An executive who is *diplomatic* in dealings with clients, suppliers, and employees is careful to say the right things at the right time to avoid ill will.
2. carrying out relations between states through official representatives.

DIP SWITCH a tiny switch located on the casing of a *d*ual *i*nline *p*ackage, which encased integrated circuits on older-model computers. Each *DIP switch*, which works like a miniature light switch, turns on or off a certain option on a circuit board.

DIRECT ACCESS method of processing data by which the data can be stored and retrieved without consideration being given to data stored in preceding or subsequent locations; also called RANDOM ACCESS.

DIRECT-ACTION ADVERTISING *see* DIRECT-RESPONSE ADVERTISING.

DIRECT CHARGE-OFF METHOD write-off of a specific BAD DEBT.

DIRECT COST labor and materials that can be identified physically in the product produced. Direct costs for an apartment building, for example, are construction materials and labor; indirect costs include architect's fees, interest during construction, insurance, and builder's overhead and profit allowance.

DIRECT COSTING in COST ACCOUNTING, method that includes only VARIABLE COSTS in the COST OF GOODS SOLD. The direct costing method may be used for internal purposes only.

DIRECT DEPOSIT arrangement whereby a dividend or other receipt can be deposited to the recipient's checking or savings account, often by electronic mail.

DIRECTED VERDICT verdict returned by the jury at the direction of the trial judge, by whose direction the jury is bound. In civil proceedings either party may receive a directed verdict in its favor if the opposing party fails to present a PRIMA FACIE case or a necessary defense.

DIRECT FINANCING LEASE method used by lessors in capital leases when both of the following criteria for the lessor are satisfied: (1) collectibility of minimum lease payments is assured and (2) no important uncertainties surround the amount of unreimbursable costs yet to be incurred. In a direct financing lease, the lessor is *not* a manufacturer or dealer in the item; the lessor purchases the property only for the purpose of leasing it.

DIRECT INVESTMENT buying from the issuer. Contrast the role of a FINANCIAL INTERMEDIARY.

DIRECT LABOR cost of personnel that can be identified in the product, such as the salary of the person who works at the production machine, but not the administrator's or janitor's salary.

DIRECT LIABILITY legal obligation of an individual or business because of negligent acts or omissions resulting in bodily injury and/ or property damage or destruction to another party. There are no intervening circumstances.

DIRECT MAIL form of advertising using the mail as its form of distribution. Mail is the third largest advertising medium after newspapers and television. It can be directed at a specific target audience and used to great effect. Advertisers can obtain a bulk mailing permit providing cheaper rates. *See also* DATABASE MARKETING.

DIRECT MARKETING selling via a promotion delivered individually to the prospective customer. Direct marketing differs from general marketing in that the result of a promotion is measurable in terms of response; also, direct marketing is largely dependent upon the use of customer files and lists. Frequently associated with MAIL ORDER FIRMS, direct marketing also includes a variety of promotion media such as door-to-door selling, VIDEOTEXT services, newspaper inserts, TELE-MARKETING, *take-one* cards, and package inserts. Direct marketing is a more personal type of promotion than advertising. The primary users are magazine publishers, catalog houses, political campaign organizations, and financial institutions.

DIRECT MARKETING ASSOCIATION (DMA) association of DIRECT MARKETING organizations and their suppliers. Its mission is to promote, through responsible self-regulation, the reputation of the industry so as to protect its freedom to operate unencumbered by legal restrictions, and also to provide its members with educational tools and a forum for sharing ideas. The DMA is headquartered in New York City.

DIRECT MATERIAL cost of material that can be specifically identified with the product, such as wood and nails in furniture, but not gasoline that fueled the power saws used to fell the trees.

DIRECTOR
1. member of a BOARD OF DIRECTORS of a company or corporation who shares with other directors the legal responsibility of control over the officers and affairs of the company or corporation.
2. any person who leads or supervises a project or entity.

DIRECTORATE office or group of organizational directors, also called *directorship*. It is a group of people elected by shareholders to establish company policies.

DIRECTORS' AND OFFICERS' LIABILITY INSURANCE coverage when a director or officer of a company commits a negligent act or omission, or misstatement or misleading statement, and a successful libel suit is brought against the company as a result. Usually a large deductible is required. The policy provides coverage for directors' and officers' liability exposure if they are sued as individuals. Coverage is also provided for the costs of defense such as legal fees and other court costs.

DIRECTORY an area on a disk where files are stored; may also contain subdivisions called SUBDIRECTORIES. Later versions of Microsoft Windows have adopted the Macintosh term folder for this concept since, like a file folder, it contains files. *See also* ROOT DIRECTORY.

DIRECT OVERHEAD portion of OVERHEAD costs—rent, lights, insurance—allocated to *manufacturing* by the application of a standard factor termed a *burden rate*. This amount is absorbed as an INVENTORY cost and ultimately reflected as a COST OF GOODS SOLD.

DIRECT PRODUCTION having primary production responsibility for a particular item. A firm that is the primary producer of an item is the *direct producer*.

DIRECT-REDUCTION MORTGAGE LOAN that requires both interest and principal with each payment such that the level payment will be adequate for AMORTIZATION over the loan's term. *See also* LEVEL-PAYMENT MORTGAGE.

DIRECT RESPONSE ADVERTISING advertising whereby the only connection the consumer has to the product is the advertising and the only way a consumer can act on the advertisement or commercial is to return a coupon or make a phone call. Direct response advertising is geared to eliminate an intermediary in the purchase process. It can utilize a wide range of media, from matchbook covers to print or radio and television, although it is typically conducted through the mail.

DIRECT SALES sources of magazine or other periodical subscriptions sold by the publisher without the use of a SUBSCRIPTION AGENT; also called *direct-to-publisher sales*. Direct-sold subscriptions require different renewal promotion copy, and direct-sold subscribers are generally less price sensitive than agency-sold subscribers.

DIRECT SELLER person engaged in the trade or business of selling consumer products either directly or on a buy-sell basis, depositcommission basis, or any similar basis for resale by the buyer in the home.

DISABILITY physical or mental impairment that keeps a person from doing any "substantial" work for at least one year, *or* a condition expected to result in the person's death. The person must qualify to receive payments under Social Security's disability program. Under this definition, Social Security does not cover a disability that is temporary or short-term.

DISABILITY BENEFIT income paid under a disability policy that is not covered under WORKERS' COMPENSATION. It is usually expressed as a percentage of the insured's income prior to the disability, but there may be a limit on the amount and duration of benefits. The most advantageous policy pays a monthly disability income benefit for as long as the insured is unable to perform suitable job functions determined by experience, education, and training.

DISABILITY INCOME INSURANCE health insurance that provides income payments to the insured wage earner when income is interrupted or terminated because of illness, sickness, or accident.

DISABILITY PROGRAM one of five programs in the Social Security System under which monthly payments are made to a disabled worker who has enough Social Security credits. Other family members of a qualifying worker may also receive disability payments under the disability program.

DISABILITY WORK INCENTIVE incentives under the Social Security disability program that encourage disabled workers to return to work. The four specific incentives are trial work period, extended period of eligibility, deductions for impairment-related expenses, and Medicare continuation.

DISAFFIRM to repudiate; to disclaim intention of being obligated. For example, one may *disaffirm* a voidable contract.

DISASTER CLAUSE *see* COMMON DISASTER CLAUSE.

DISASTER LOSS loss from a disaster in an area declared by the president as warranting federal assistance.

DISBURSEMENT paying out of money in the discharge of a DEBT or an EXPENSE, as distinguished from a DISTRIBUTION.

DISC *see* DISK.

DISCHARGE
1. to satisfy or dismiss the obligations of contract or debt.
2. method by which a legal DUTY is extinguished.
3. release from employment. *See also* PERFORMANCE; RESCISSION.

DISCHARGE IN BANKRUPTCY release of a bankrupt debtor from most liabilities pursuant to a confirmed plan of reorganization; some debts are not subject to discharge.

DISCHARGE OF LIEN order removing a LIEN ON PROPERTY after the originating legal claim has been paid or otherwise satisfied. *See also* SATISFACTION PIECE.

DISCIPLINARY LAYOFF suspension or temporary removal of worker as part of a penalty for a violation of work rules on the job. A disciplinary layoff requires a suspension of all salary payments during the layoff period.

DISCLAIMER
1. denial of a person's claim to a thing, though previously that person insisted on such a claim or right.
2. renunciation of the right to POSSESS and of claim to a TITLE.
3. denial of a right of another, for example, where an insurer disclaims an allegation of liability against its insured and thereby refuses to indemnify or defend the insured in a lawsuit.
4. statement whereby a certified public accountant or other professional refuses to express an opinion.

DISCLOSURE release by companies of all information, positive or negative, that might bear on an INVESTMENT decision, as required by the SECURITIES AND EXCHANGE COMMISSION and the stock exchanges. *See also* FULL DISCLOSURE.

DISCLOSURE STATEMENT a statement required by law, in which sellers of particular kinds of property, or under certain circumstances, must reveal specified information to potential buyers. Many sellers of investment interests in real estate are required to disclose their own interest and even the profit potential; home sellers may disclose defects, even though they have been corrected. Failing to provide adequate disclosure may give the buyer grounds for a lawsuit.

DISCONTINUED OPERATION sale, disposal, or planned sale in the near future of a business segment (i.e., product line, class of customer). The results of a discontinued operation are reported separately in the income statement as a separate line item after income from continuing operations and before extraordinary items.

DISCOUNT
1. difference between a bond's current market price and its FACE VALUE.
2. manner of selling securities such as Treasury bills, which are issued at less than face value and are redeemed at face value.
3. relationship between two currencies. The Canadian dollar may sell at a *discount* to the U.S. dollar, for example.
4. to apply all available news about a company in evaluating its current stock price, for instance, taking into account the introduction of an exciting new product.
5. method whereby INTEREST on a bank loan or note is deducted in advance.
6. reduction in the selling price of merchandise.
7. percentage off the INVOICE price in exchange for quick payment.

DISCOUNT BOND BOND offered below FACE VALUE. *See also* BOND DISCOUNT; ZERO COUPON BOND.

DISCOUNT BROKER brokerage house that executes orders to buy and sell securities at COMMISSION rates lower than those charged by a FULL-SERVICE BROKER.

DISCOUNTED CASH FLOW technique to estimate the present value of future expected cash receipts and expenditures, using NET PRESENT VALUE (NPV) or INTERNAL RATE OF RETURN (IRR). It is a factor in analyses of both capital investments and securities investments. The NPV method applies a rate of DISCOUNT (interest rate) based on the MARGINAL COST of capital to future CASH FLOWS to express them in terms of current money. The IRR method finds the average RETURN ON INVESTMENT earned through the life of the investment. It determines the DISCOUNT RATE that equates the present value of future cash flows to the cost of the investment.

DISCOUNTED LOAN one that is offered or traded for less than its face value. *See* DISCOUNT; DISCOUNT POINTS.

DISCOUNTED PRESENT VALUE *see* DISCOUNTED CASH FLOW; NET PRESENT VALUE.

DISCOUNTING the process of estimating the present value of an INCOME STREAM by reducing expected CASH FLOW to reflect the TIME VALUE OF MONEY. *Discounting* is the opposite of compounding. Mathematically they are reciprocals. *See also* DISCOUNTED CASH FLOW.

DISCOUNTING THE NEWS bidding a firm's stock price up or down in anticipation of good or bad news about the company's prospects.

DISCOUNT POINTS amounts paid to the lender (usually by the seller) at the time of origination of a loan, to account for the difference between the market interest rate and the lower FACE INTEREST RATE of the note; often required when VA LOANS are used.

DISCOUNT RATE
1. interest rate that the Federal Reserve charges banks for loans, using government securities or ELIGIBLE PAPER as COLLATERAL.
2. interest rate used in determining the PRESENT VALUE of future cash flows. *See also* DISCOUNTED CASH FLOW.

DISCOUNT STORE retail store having a broad merchandise assortment, resembling that of a department store in variety but featuring lower prices.

DISCOUNT WINDOW place in the Federal Reserve where banks go to borrow money at the DISCOUNT RATE. Borrowing from the Fed is a privilege, not a right, and banks are discouraged from using the privilege except when they are short of RESERVES.

DISCOUNT YIELD YIELD on a security sold at a DISCOUNT; for example, U.S. Treasury bills sold at \$9,750 and maturing at \$10,000 in 90 days. To figure the annual discount yield, divide the discount (\$250) by the face amount (\$10,000) and multiply the number by the approximate number of days in the year (360) divided by the number of days to maturity (90):

$$\frac{\$250}{\$10,000} \times \frac{360}{90} = 0.025 \times 4 = 0.10 = 10\%$$

DISCOVERY modern pretrial procedure by which parties gain information held by the adverse party: Common types of discovery are DEPOSITIONS, INTERROGATORIES, and production of documents.

DISCOVERY SAMPLING in statistics, exploratory sampling to assure that the proportion of units with a particular attribute (i.e., error) is not in excess of a given percentage of the population. Three determinations needed to use discovery sampling are: (1) size of population; (2) minimum unacceptable error rate; and (3) confidence level. Sample size is provided by a sampling table. If none of the random samples has an error, the auditor can conclude that the actual error rate is below the minimum unacceptable error rate.

DISCREPANCY
1. deviation between what is expected and what actually occurs. An example is a variation in a marketing performance report between budgeted sales and actual sales.
2. disagreement between conclusions of two or more people looking at the same thing.

DISCRETION freedom of a person to make choices, within the limits of his authority, among possible courses of action; quality of being careful of what one says or does.

DISCRETIONARY COST cost changed easily by management decision such as advertising, repairs and maintenance, and research and development; also called *managed cost*. The analyst should note whether the current level of discretionary expense is consistent with previous trends and with the company's present and future requirements. Discretionary costs are often reduced when a firm is in difficulty or desires to show a stable earnings trend.

DISCRETIONARY INCOME spendable income remaining after the purchase of physical necessities, such as food, clothing, and shelter, as well as the payment of taxes. Marketers of goods other than necessities must compete for the consumer's discretionary dollars by appealing to various psychological needs, as distinguished from physical needs.

DISCRETIONARY POLICY government economic policy that is not automatic or built into the system. The Federal Reserve Board's implementation of its powers to add to or subtract from the money supply and to set the discount rate are examples of *discretionary policies*.

DISCRETIONARY SPENDING POWER government spending capability that is not mandated by law or required automatically within the system.

DISCRETIONARY TRUST gives the trustee discretion to pay out any trust income deemed desirable to a decedent's surviving spouse during his or her lifetime. The remainder interest is still eligible for the MARITAL DEDUCTION.

DISCRIMINANT FUNCTION SYSTEM an IRS technique with proven mathematical formulas programmed into computers to identify and select tax returns for examination. This secret system permits the IRS to rank the selected returns according to greatest potential tax error by weighing significant return characteristics.

DISCRIMINATION applying special treatment (generally unfavorable) to an individual solely on the basis of the person's ethnicity, age, religion, or sex.

DISECONOMIES costs resulting from an economic process that are not sustained by those directly involved in the process; also called *nega-*

tive externalties. Many types of pollution are *diseconomies* in that those who pollute do not pay the costs resulting from it and, therefore, neither do their customers.

DISHONOR refuse, rightly or wrongly, to make payment on a NEGOTIABLE instrument when such an instrument is duly presented for payment.

DISINFLATION slowing down of the rate at which prices increase— usually during a RECESSION, when sales drop and retailers are not always able to pass on higher prices to consumers. Not to be confused with DEFLATION, when prices actually drop.

DISINTERMEDIATION movement of savings from banks and savings and loan associations directly into MONEY MARKET instruments, such as U.S. Treasury bills and notes. When interest rates are rising, investors can often receive a higher RETURN by investing directly rather than going through a financial INTERMEDIARY.

DISJOINT EVENTS two events that cannot both happen.

DISK computer memory device; a platter with a magnetically encoded surface that is spun past read heads to retrieve data. Disks may be internal (HARD DISKS) or removable. *See also* COMPACT DISC (CD).

DISK DRIVE device that enables a computer to read and write data on disks.

DISK-OPERATING SYSTEM (DOS) one of various computer OPERATING SYSTEMS, including an early operating system for the IBM 360; the disk-operating system for Apple II; MS-DOS, developed by Microsoft originally for 16-bit microcomputers; and PC-DOS, a version of MS-DOS commonly sold with the IBM Personal Computer (PC).

DISMISSAL permanent termination of employment with an organization; being fired from a job. SEVERANCE PAY is sometimes awarded to employees who are dismissed or laid off.

DISPATCHER in transportation, organizer who is responsible for maintaining the route schedule and informing workers of when they are needed.

DISPOSABLE INCOME PERSONAL INCOME remaining after personal taxes and noncommercial government fees have been paid. This money can be spent on essentials or nonessentials, or it can be saved. *See also* DISCRETIONARY INCOME.

DISPOSSESS to oust, eject, or exclude another from the POSSESSION of lands or premises, whether by legal process, as where a LANDLORD lawfully evicts a TENANT, or wrongfully.

DISPOSSESS PROCEEDINGS legal process by a LANDLORD to remove a TENANT and regain POSSESSION of property. *See also* EVICTION.

DISPROPORTIONATE DISTRIBUTION a distribution in which some shareholders receive cash or other property and others receive increased proportionate interests in the assets or earnings and profits of the corporation.

DISSOLUTION in corporation law, the end of the legal existence of a corporation, whether by expiration of charter, decree of court, act of legislature, vote of shareholders, or other means.

DISTRAINT legal right of a LANDLORD to seize a tenant's personal property to satisfy payment of back rent.

DISTRESSED PROPERTY REAL ESTATE that is under FORECLOSURE or impending foreclosure because of insufficient income production. *See also* WORKOUT.

DISTRESS SALE forced sale of property. For example, STOCK, BOND, MUTUAL FUND, or FUTURES positions in a portfolio may have to be sold if there is a MARGIN CALL. Real estate may have to be sold because a bank is in the process of FORECLOSURE on the property. Because distress sellers are being forced to sell, they usually do not receive as favorable a price as if they were able to wait for ideal selling conditions.

DISTRESS TERMINATION *see* TERMINATION OF A PLAN.

DISTRIBUTION
1. in corporate finance, allocation of income and expenses to the appropriate SUBSIDIARY accounts.
2. in economics, (1) movement of goods from manufacturers, or (2) way in which wealth is shared in any particular economic system.
3. in ESTATE law, parceling out of assets to the BENEFICIARIES named in a WILL, as carried out by the EXECUTOR under the guidance of a court.
4. in MUTUAL FUNDS and closed-end investment companies, payout of realized capital gains on securities in the PORTFOLIO of the fund or closed-end investment company.
5. in SECURITIES, sale of a large block of stock in such a manner that the price is not adversely affected. Technical analysts look at a pattern of distribution as a tipoff that the stock will soon fall in price. The opposite of distribution, known as *accumulation*, may signal a rise in price.

DISTRIBUTION ALLOWANCE price reduction offered by a manufacturer to a distributor, retail chain, or wholesaler, which allows for the cost of distributing the merchandise. A distribution allowance is frequently offered in a new product introduction.

DISTRIBUTION CENTER warehouse facility specializing in the collection and shipment of merchandise.

DISTRIBUTION CHANNEL set of institutions that perform all the activities required to move a product and its title from production to consumption.

DISTRIBUTION COST ANALYSIS breaking down direct and indirect costs for marketing a product or service in a specific area.

DISTRIBUTION IN KIND transfer of property other than money. For example, if a corporation distributes an automobile to a shareholder, a *distribution in kind* has occurred.

DISTRIBUTION STRATEGY management's plan for moving products to intermediaries and final customers.

DISTRIBUTIVE SHARE allocation of any item or kind of income, gain, loss, deduction, or credit to a partner. This allocation is, with important exceptions, generally determined by the partnership agreement.

DISTRIBUTOR firm or individual, particularly a wholesaler, who sells or delivers merchandise to customers, such as retail stores. Distributors act as intermediaries between manufacturers and retailers. They maintain a warehouse of merchandise, which is often purchased from many different manufacturers and then is sold (or *distributed*) among various retailers. By buying through a distributor, a retailer can have the advantage of one-stop shopping, rather than having to make individual stock purchases from each of the different manufacturers.

DISTRICT COURT court that hears civil actions against the United States for the recovery of any tax alleged to have been erroneously or illegally assessed or collected by the IRS.

DISTRICT DIRECTOR the chief operating officer of one of the IRS's districts; reports to the appropriate regional commissioner.

DIVERSIFICATION
1. reduction of RISK by putting assets in several categories of INVESTMENTS—stocks, bonds, money market instruments, precious metals, and real estate, for instance—or several industries, or a MUTUAL FUND with a broad range of stocks in one PORTFOLIO.
2. at the corporate level, entering into different business areas, as a CONGLOMERATE does.

DIVERSIFIED COMPANY company that has many products and services serving several markets. A company may attempt to manufacture the products itself, or it may acquire or merge with an ongoing organization. The advantages of diversification include being better able to weather business cycles since some product lines or services may be countercyclical.

DIVERSIFY *see* DIVERSIFICATION.

DIVESTITURE
1. loss or voluntary surrender of a right, TITLE, or interest.
2. REMEDY by which the court orders the offending party to rid itself of assets before the party would normally have done so. This remedy is sometimes used in the enforcement of the ANTITRUST LAWS, whereby a corporation must shed a part of its business to comply with the law.

DIVIDEND payment by a corporation to shareholders, generally taxable as ORDINARY INCOME, for which most corporations receive no deduction.

DIVIDEND ADDITION LIFE INSURANCE in addition to the FACE VALUE of the POLICY, purchased with DIVIDENDS of the policy.

DIVIDEND EXCLUSION the concept that income earned by corporations is taxed at the corporate level, so corporate dividends should not be taxed again at the stockholder level.

DIVIDEND PAYOUT RATIO percentage of earnings paid to shareholders in cash. In general, the higher the payout ratio, the more mature the company. Electric and telephone UTILITIES tend to have the highest payout ratios, whereas fast-growing companies usually reinvest all earnings and pay no dividends.

DIVIDEND REINVESTMENT PLAN (DRP) automatic reinvestment of shareholder DIVIDENDS in more shares of the company's stock. Reinvested dividends are taxable when credited to the taxpayer's account, even though no cash is received. The reinvested dividends also increase the taxpayer's BASIS in the stock, so it is important to retain all records for calculation of gain or loss upon sale.

DIVIDEND REQUIREMENT amount of annual earnings necessary to pay DIVIDENDS on PREFERRED STOCK.

DIVIDEND ROLLOVER PLAN method of buying and selling stocks around their EX-DIVIDEND DATES so as to collect the DIVIDEND and—hopefully—make a small profit on the trade.

DIVIDENDS-PAID DEDUCTION an adjustment from taxable income in computing both the accumulated earnings tax and the personal holding company tax. The amount of the adjustment includes regular dividends, dividends paid during a 2½-month grace period, consent dividends, and deficiency dividends (for the personal holding company tax only).

DIVIDENDS PAYABLE dollar amount of DIVIDENDS that are to be paid, as reported in FINANCIAL STATEMENTS. These dividends become an obligation once declared by the board of directors and are listed as LIABILITIES in annual and quarterly reports.

DIVIDENDS-RECEIVED DEDUCTION tax deduction allowed to a corporation owning shares in another corporation for the dividends it receives. The deduction is often 70%, but in some cases it may be as high as 100% depending on the level of ownership the dividend-receiving company has in the dividend-paying entity.

DIVIDEND YIELD annual percentage of return earned by an investor on a common or preferred stock. The yield is determined by dividing the amount of the annual dividends per share by the current market price per share of the stock. For example, a stock paying a $1 dividend per year that sells for $10 a share has a 10% dividend yield.

DIVISION self-sufficient unit within a company. A division contains all of the departments necessary to operate independently from the parent company. An example is the Chevrolet Division of the General Motors Corporation.

DIVISION OF LABOR separation of the work force into different categories of labor; dividing the work required to produce a product into a number of different tasks that are performed by different workers.

DIVISIVE REORGANIZATION transfer of all or part of a division, a subsidiary, or a corporate segment in a tax-free manner. There are three types of divisive reorganizations in which all or part of the assets are transferred to one or more controlled corporations—SPLIT-UP, SPLIT-OFF, and SPIN-OFF. If a transaction falls within the divisive reorganization provisions, no gain or loss is recognized to a shareholder who receives only stock or securities (that is, receives no BOOT).

DIVORCED TAXPAYER a taxpayer who was divorced under a final decree of divorce or separate maintenance by the last day of the tax year; considered unmarried for the whole year.

DOCKING charging an employee time from his time sheet or card for an infraction of company rules, usually in connection with lateness or absence.

DOCKING STATION a device that acts as a terminal to connect a NOTEBOOK COMPUTER to other equipment, such as a NETWORK or a desktop monitor and keyboard. May also contain a charger for the notebook's battery and possibly additional disk drives.

DOCUMENT
1. any writing, recording, computer file, blueprint, X ray, photograph, or other physical object upon which information is set forth by means of letters, numbers, or other symbols.
2. regarding computers, a word processing file.

DOCUMENTARY DRAFT *see* DRAFT.

DOCUMENTARY EVIDENCE evidence in the form of written or printed papers.

DOCUMENTATION written description of a COMPUTER PROGRAM. It falls into several categories: (1) internal documentation, consisting of comments within the program; (2) on-line documentation, displayed as the program runs or called up with a COMMAND such as HELP; (3) reference cards, containing easily forgotten details for quick reference; (4) reference manuals, setting out complete instructions for the program in a systematic way; and (5) tutorials, serving as introduction for new users.

DOCUMENT LOCATOR NUMBER a number stamped on a tax return, check, or other document that allows the IRS to quickly identify and locate a particular document.

DOING BUSINESS carrying on, conducting, or managing a business. A corporation is *doing business* in a state if it performs some of the ordinary functions for which it was organized or engages in activities that subject it to the laws and jurisdiction of that state.

DOING BUSINESS AS (DBA) assumed name a person uses for a business instead of the actual business name or one's personal name. A certificate should be filed in the courthouse to use an assumed name, and to assure that no one else in that jurisdiction is using the same name.

DOLLAR COST AVERAGING buying a MUTUAL FUND or SECURITIES using a consistent dollar amount of money each month (or other period). More securities will be bought when prices are low, resulting in lowering the average cost per share.

DOLLAR DRAIN amount by which a foreign country's IMPORTS from the United States exceed its EXPORTS to the United States. As the country spends more dollars to finance the imports than it receives in payment for the exports, its dollar RESERVES drain away.

DOLLAR VALUE LIFO inventory method computed in *dollars* (i.e., cost figures) rather than units. After inventory is divided into homogeneous groupings or "pools," each pool is converted to base-year prices by means of appropriate price indices. The difference between beginning and ending balances, as converted, becomes a measure of change in inventory quantity for the year. An increase is recognized as an inventory layer to be added to beginning inventory. It is converted at the current price index and added to the dollars identified with the beginning balance. *See also* LAST IN, FIRST OUT (LIFO).

DOMAIN on TCP/IP NETWORKS, such as the INTERNET, a group of connected computers, which may contain subdomains. On the Internet, domains are denoted by a three-letter suffix. Some of the most common are *edu*—educational institution; *gov*—government site, other than state-funded universities; *com*—commercial site; *mil*— military site; *net*—network site; and *org*—nonprofit or private organization. In addition, most countries, states, provinces, and regions have *domain names*. ISPs that offer domain name hosting may offer "virtual domains." The domain name is actually an alias for the IP address, which is expressed in numbers. The period in a domain name is pronounced "dot," with the result that most large corporations can be found on the Web at some version of "Corporation-Name dot com."

DOMESTIC (CORPORATION, PARTNERSHIP) a corporation or partnership created or organized in the United States or under the laws of the United States or of any state.

DOMICILE permanent home or principal establishment of an individual. RESIDENCE is not the same as *domicile*, since a person can have many transient residences but only one legal domicile, which is the home address to which he always intends to return for prolonged periods. The domicile of a business is the address where the establishment is maintained or where the governing power of the enterprise is exercised. For purposes of taxation, it is often a principal place of business.

DOMINANT TENEMENT land that benefits from an EASEMENT on another property, which is usually ADJACENT.

DONATED STOCK fully paid CAPITAL STOCK of a corporation contributed without CONSIDERATION to the same issuing corporation.

DONATED SURPLUS SHAREHOLDERS' EQUITY account that is credited when CONTRIBUTIONS of cash, property, or the firm's own stock are freely given to the company; also termed *donated capital.*

DONEE recipient of a GIFT or TRUST; one who takes without first giving CONSIDERATION; one who is given a power, right, or interest.

DONOR one who gives a gift; creator of a TRUST; party conferring a power, right, or interest.

DORMANT PARTNER *see* SILENT PARTNER.

DOS *see* DISK-OPERATING SYSTEM.

DOT the period (.) in an Internet DOMAIN name.

DOT-COM (DOT COM, DOTCOM) *see* DOMAIN.

DOUBLE-CLICK click a computer mouse twice in rapid succession. Many actions are achieved by double-clicking on icons or filenames that have been selected with a single click. In some operating systems, users have the option of selecting an item by resting the mouse over it; a single click then replaces the double-click to perform the desired action (this behavior is the default in most Web browsers).

DOUBLE-DECLINING-BALANCE method of DEPRECIATION for tax purposes whereby twice the straight-line rate is applied to the remaining depreciable balance of an asset. For example, the table below is a depreciation schedule for a property with a depreciable BASIS of $10,000 and a DEPRECIABLE life of five years, using the double-declining-balance method.

Year	Remaining Balance	Rate*	Annual Deduction
1	$10,000	0.40	$4,000
2	6,000	0.40	2,400
3	3,600	0.40	1,440
4	2,160	0.40	864
5	1,296	0.40	518

*0.40 is twice the straight-line rate of 20% per year for a five-year-life asset. *See also* DECLINING-BALANCE DEPRECIATION.

DOUBLE-DIGIT INFLATION inflation at a rate of 10% per year or higher.

DOUBLE-DIPPING
   1. practice of retired military personnel of receiving service pensions while also obtaining civilian jobs from the federal government.
   2. practice of local government employees of working full-time but having civilian jobs as well.

DOUBLE-ENTRY ACCOUNTING, DOUBLE-ENTRY BOOK-KEEPING system of financial records used in business whereby equal DEBITS and CREDITS are recorded for each transaction.

DOUBLE PRECISION in calculations performed by a computer, keeping track of twice as many digits as usual. For example, if a computer normally keeps track of six digits for FLOATING-POINT NUMBERS, it will keep track of 12 digits when it is operating in *double-precision* mode.

DOUBLE TAXATION effect of federal tax law whereby earnings are taxed at the corporate level, then taxed again as DIVIDENDS of stockholders.

DOUBLE TIME being paid twice the regular hourly pay rate for overtime, Sunday, or holiday work.

DOUBLE (TREBLE) DAMAGES twice (three times) the amount of DAMAGES that a court or jury would normally award, recoverable for certain kinds of injuries pursuant to a statute authorizing the double (treble) RECOVERY. These damages are intended in certain instances as punishment for improper behavior.

DOWER statutory provision in a common-law state that directs a certain portion of the estate (often one-third) to the surviving spouse. The term CURTESY is used if the surviving spouse is the husband.

DOW JONES highly reputable financial information services company; issuer of *The Wall Street Journal, Barron's National Business and Financial Weekly*, *Smart Money*, and other influential publications as well as computer data bases and additional financial information. The Dow Jones Industrial Average is a closely watched indicator of stock-market performance.

DOW JONES INDUSTRIAL AVERAGE (DJIA) the most widely followed BENCHMARK of stock market performance, containing value changes for stocks of 30 large corporations. In 2006 the index components are: Altria Group, Aluminum Company of America (ALCOA), American International Group, American Express, AT&T, Boeing, Caterpillar, Citigroup, Coca-Cola, Disney, DuPont, Exxon Mobil, General Electric, General Motors, Hewlett-Packard, Home Depot, Honeywell International, IBM, Intel, Johnson & Johnson, JPMorgan Chase, McDonald's, Merck, Microsoft, Pfizer, Procter & Gamble, 3M, United Technologies, Verizon, and Wal-Mart.

DOWN with regard to computers, unavailable for use, out of service, as when a computer malfunctions or is being tested.

DOWNLOAD to transmit a FILE or PROGRAM from a central computer to a smaller computer or vice versa.

DOWNPAYMENT amount one pays for property or goods in CASH in addition to the DEBT incurred.

DOWNSCALE movement of a business activity from a higher to a lower level; pejorative term describing clientele. A retail store deciding to carry lower grade merchandise is moving *downscale*.

DOWNSIDE RISK estimate of an investment's possible decline in value and the extent of the decline, taking into account the total range of factors affecting market price.

DOWNSIZING reducing the layers of management and the work force in order to increase organizational productivity and profits.

DOWNSTREAM flow of corporate activity from parent to subsidiary. In finance it usually refers to loans, since dividends and interest generally flow upstream. In management it usually refers to instructions from headquarters.

DOWN TICK sale of a security at a price below that of the preceding sale; also known as *minus tick*. If a stock has been trading at $15 a share, the next trade is a down tick if it is at or below 14.99.

DOWNTIME *see* DEAD TIME.

DOWNTURN shift of an economic or stock market cycle from rising to falling. The economy is in a *downturn* when it moves from expansion to RECESSION, and the stock market is in a downturn when it changes from a BULL MARKET to a BEAR MARKET.

DOWNZONING act of REZONING a tract of land for a less intensive use than that existing or permitted.

DOWRY money and PERSONAL PROPERTY that a wife brings to her husband in marriage.

DOW THEORY theory that a major trend in the STOCK MARKET must be confirmed by a similar movement in the Dow Jones Industrial Average and the Dow Jones Transportation Average. According to Dow Theory, a significant trend is not confirmed until both Dow Jones indexes reach new highs or lows; if they don't, the market will fall back to its former trading range.

DPI dots per inch, a unit of measurement used to describe the RESOLUTION of inkjet and laser printers.

DR abbreviation for DEBIT.

DRAFT

1. order in writing, directing a person other than the MAKER to pay a specified sum to a named person. Drafts may or may not be NEGOTIABLE INSTRUMENTS, depending on whether the elements of negotiability are satisfied. *Draft* is synonymous with BILL OF EXCHANGE.

2. preliminary form of a legal document; for example, the draft of a contract, often called *rough draft*.
3. process of preparing, or drawing, a legal document, such as a will or a piece of proposed legislation.
4. in a military context, conscription of citizens into the military service.

DRAG AND DROP click with a mouse on a selected object or portion of text and, holding the mouse button down, move the mouse to drag the object. Releasing the mouse button "drops" the object in a new location. On the desktop, actions can be performed by dragging and dropping; for example, the icon for a document can be dragged to a printer icon to print the document.

DRAINING RESERVES actions by the Federal Reserve System to decrease the MONEY SUPPLY by curtailing the funds banks have available to lend. The Fed does this in three ways: (1) by raising RESERVE REQUIREMENTS, forcing banks to keep more funds on deposit with the Federal Reserve Banks; (2) by increasing the DISCOUNT RATE at which banks BORROW reserves from the Fed, thereby making it unattractive to borrow reserves; and (3) by selling bonds in the OPEN MARKET at such attractive rates that dealers reduce their bank balances to buy them.

DRAM SHOP ACT state law stating the liabilities of tavernkeepers serving alcoholic beverages to intoxicated patrons. Serving alcoholic beverages to intoxicated patrons creates unreasonable risk of harm and results in a charge of negligent conduct and legal liability.

DRAW
1. withdraw money from an account in a bank or other depository.
2. receive money in advance, such as a *draw* against commissions or a draw of a loan.
3. execute a check or DRAFT for the withdrawal of money.
4. prepare a draft of a legal document, such as a complaint, a deed, or a will.

DRAWEE one whom a BILL OF EXCHANGE or a check directs to pay to another a specified sum of money. In the typical checking account situation, the bank is the *drawee*, the person writing the check is the MAKER or DRAWER, and the person to whom the check is written is the PAYEE. *See also* BILL; DRAFT.

DRAWER person by whom a check or BILL OF EXCHANGE is drawn. *See also* DRAWEE.

DRAWING ACCOUNT an account used by a proprietorship or partnership to track WITHDRAWALS. It is closed at year-end and the balance transferred to the OWNER'S EQUITY account or profit and loss account.

DRIVE-IN sales or service facility designed to accommodate customers in their automobiles, such as a drive-in bank teller's window or a drive-in dry cleaner.

DROP DEAD DATE an absolute deadline; if not met, it is too late for the report or results to be useful.

DROP-DOWN MENU in a computer application, MENU that appears below a menu item when it is selected. *See also* FLY-OUT MENU; POPUP MENU; PULL-DOWN MENU.

DROP-SHIPPING
Direct marketing: trucking mail to various entry points to avoid U.S. Postal Service zone charges.
Merchandising: arrangement between a retailer and a supplier whereby the retailer can promote and sell merchandise that is stored and shipped by the supplier (jobber) directly to the retailer's customer. Ownership does not transfer until a purchase is made, enabling the seller to avoid tying up funds in inventory.

DRY GOODS fabrics, textiles, and clothing made from cotton, wool, rayon, silk, and related materials, including ready-to-wear clothing and bedding.

DRY HOLE a well with little or no oil or gas, which must be kept properly plugged in most states.

DSL *d*igital *s*ubscriber *l*ine, a BROADBAND technology for bringing high-bandwidth information to homes and small businesses over ordinary copper telephone lines. A DSL line can carry both data and voice signals simultaneously, and the data part of the line is continuously connected to an Internet service provider. The most common type is ADSL (Asymmetric DSL), which offers higher speeds for downstream than for upstream data transmission.

DUAL AGENCY the situation in which a real estate agent represents more than one party to a transaction. It is accepted in most states with full disclosure, though many people do not consider it a good business practice because each party wants representation for his/her position.

DUAL BANKING U.S. system whereby banks are CHARTERED by the state in which they operate or by the federal government. This makes for differences in banking regulations, lending limits, and services available to customers.

DUAL CONTRACT illegal or unethical practice of providing two different CONTRACTS for the same TRANSACTION. The one for the larger amount is used to apply for a loan, while the real contract is for a lower amount.

DUE BILL bill submitted by a COMMON CARRIER for additional charges that were not paid with the freight bill.

DUE CARE the degree of care that a person of ordinary prudence and reason (a REASONABLE MAN) would exercise under given circumstances. The concept is used in TORT law to indicate the standard of care or the legal DUTY one normally owes to others. NEGLIGENCE is the failure to use *due care*.

DUE DATE time fixed for payment of DEBT, TAX, INTEREST, etc.

DUE DILIGENCE
1. making a reasonable effort to perform under a contract.
2. making a reasonable effort to provide accurate, complete information. A study that often precedes the purchase of property or the underwriting of a loan or investment; considers the physical, financial, legal, and social characteristics of the property and expected investment performance.

DUE-ON-SALE CLAUSE provision in a MORTGAGE that states that the loan is due upon the sale of the property. Mortgage lenders sometimes waive this provision provided the INTEREST RATE is raised and the new owner qualifies for ASSUMPTION OF MORTGAGE. Some state-chartered lenders are not allowed to enforce this clause.

DUES AND SUBSCRIPTIONS professional expenses; they are tax deductible as miscellaneous ITEMIZED DEDUCTIONS, subject to the 2% ADJUSTED GROSS INCOME (AGI) floor or MISCELLANEOUS ITEMIZED DEDUCTIONS.

DUES CHECKOFF permission by an employee for the employer to withhold union dues from a paycheck; indicates cooperation between the employer, employee, and union.

DUFF & PHELPS independent financial advisory firm, established in 1932, offering appraisals, credit analysis, and other financial services.

DUMMY individual or ENTITY that stands in the place of the PRINCIPAL to a TRANSACTION; sometimes used to avoid PERSONAL LIABILITY.

DUMP loosely formatted printout of some portion of the contents of a computer file, created for a quick review of the file. Dumps are frequently used by system programmers when working on a revision to a file or to review the contents of a magnetic tape, such as a list rental tape.

DUMPING
1. in international trade, practice of selling goods abroad below cost or at a price below that charged in the domestic market in order to eliminate a surplus or to gain an edge on foreign competition, or when goods are unacceptable for the domestic market.
2. in securities, offering large amounts of stock with little or no concern for price or market effect.

DUN to request payment of past due money. An example is a supplier who asks the customer to remit payment for an account due beyond the original terms of sale.

DUN & BRADSTREET (D&B) information service company that combines CREDIT information obtained directly from commercial firms with data solicited from their CREDITORS. This information is available to subscribers in reports and a ratings directory. D&B also engages in other businesses, including publishing, television audience measurement, and magazine-subscription fulfillment.

DUN'S NUMBER short for Dun's Market Identifier. It is published as part of a list of firms giving information such as an identification number, address code, number of employees, corporate affiliations, and trade styles.

DUPLEX
1. two dwelling units under one roof.
2. apartment having rooms on two floors.

DUPLICATE alike, equivalent.

DUPLICATION OF BENEFITS coverage in health insurance by two or more policies for the same insured loss. In such a circumstance, each policy pays its proportionate share of the loss, or one policy becomes *primary* and the other policy *secondary.*

DURABLE POWER OF ATTORNEY a POWER OF ATTORNEY that survives the subsequent incapacity or disability of the principal. A medical durable power of attorney specifically allows an individual to make health care decisions on behalf of another.

DURATION OF BENEFITS *see* DISABILITY INCOME INSURANCE.

DURESS conduct that has the effect of compelling another person to do what he need not otherwise do. It is a recognized defense to any act, such as a crime, BREACH OF CONTRACT or TORT, all of which must be voluntary to create LIABILITY.

DUTCH AUCTION auction system in which the price of an item is gradually lowered until it meets a responsive bid and is sold. U.S. Treasury bills are sold under this system. Contrasting is the two-sided or *double-auction* system exemplified by the major stock exchanges.

DUTY
1. TAX imposed on the importation, exportation, or consumption of goods.
2. obligation of a FIDUCIARY or other person in a responsible position.

DWELLING place of residence, such as a house or apartment.

DYNAMIC PRICING charging different prices contingent on individual customers and circumstances.

E

EACH WAY commission made by a broker involved on both the purchase and the sale side of a trade. *See also* CROSS.

EAGER BEAVER very hard-working individual, anxious to succeed. The person puts in many hours and is always busy. There is a strong desire for promotion and high compensation.

EARLY RETIREMENT term in pensions; leaving a job before normal retirement age, subject to minimum requirements of age and years of service. There usually is a reduction in the monthly retirement benefit, and an early distribution (before age 59½) from a qualified retirement plan results in an additional 10% tax.

EARLY-RETIREMENT BENEFITS benefits a person is entitled to when retiring before the formal retirement age. Early retirement is increasingly common in the United States. This makes it possible for more senior employees to retire early and for the company to promote younger employees without layoffs. There is an additional 10% tax on early distributions from a qualified retirement plan (before age 59½, for example).

EARLY-WITHDRAWAL PENALTY charge assessed against holders of fixed-term investments, principally CERTIFICATES OF DEPOSIT (CDs), if they WITHDRAW their money before MATURITY. Such a penalty would be assessed if someone who has a four-year certificate of deposit were to withdraw the money after three years.

EARNED INCOME tax term describing "sweat of the brow" income, which requires obvious effort on the part of the recipient. This includes all income generated by providing goods or services, especially wages and salaries but also net profit from a trade or business; it is contrasted with income received as DIVIDENDS, for instance.

EARNED INCOME (TAX) CREDIT TAX CREDIT for qualifying taxpayers with at least one child in residence for more than half the year and incomes below a specified dollar level.

EARNED SURPLUS *see* RETAINED EARNINGS.

EARNEST MONEY DEPOSIT made by a purchaser of real estate to show good faith. *See also* ESCROW.

EARNINGS AND PROFITS tax term that refers to the economic capacity of a corporation to make a distribution to shareholders that is not a return of capital. If distributed, would constitute a taxable dividend to the shareholder to the extent of current and accumulate earnings and profit. Similar to RETAINED EARNINGS, although its calculation starts with taxable income, the amount in the earnings and profits account more closely resembles the economist's approach to income (that is, inflow and outflow of wealth). *See also* CURRENT AND ACCUMULATED EARNINGS AND PROFITS.

EARNINGS BEFORE TAXES sales revenues less cost of sales, operating expenses, and interest, before taxes have been paid.

EARNINGS PER SHARE (EPS) portion of a company's profit allocated to each outstanding share of common stock. For instance, a corporation that earned $10 million last year and has 10 million shares outstanding would report earnings of $1 per share. Current and future earnings per share are key statistics in evaluating a stock's outlook. *See also* PRICE-EARNINGS (P/E) RATIO.

EARNINGS REPORT report likely to be issued monthly or quarterly for a publicly held company; may be internal report, not necessarily the ANNUAL REPORT.

EARN-OUT in mergers and acquisitions, supplementary payments, not part of the original ACQUISITION COST, based on future earnings of the acquired company above a predetermined level.

EASEMENT limited right to use another's land for a special purpose. Such use must not be inconsistent with any other uses already being made of the land. An easement is a privilege connected with the land and is therefore not a possessory interest or fee.

EASY MONEY state of the national MONEY supply when the FEDERAL RESERVE SYSTEM allows ample funds to build in the banking system, thereby lowering interest rates and making loans easier to get. *Easy money* policies tend to encourage economic growth and, eventually, inflation. *See also* TIGHT MONEY.

EATING (A COMPETITOR'S) LUNCH aggressively beating out competition. For example, an analyst might say that one retailer is "eating the lunch" of a competitive retailer in the same town if it is gaining market share through an aggressive pricing strategy. The implication of the expression is that the winning competitor is taking food away from the losing company or individual.

EBITDA Earnings Before Interest, Taxes, Depreciation, and Amortization, calculated by taking OPERATING INCOME and adding back DEPRECIATION and/or AMORTIZATION. Often used for corporate valuation purposes by applying a multiple derived from comparable companies that sold. EBITDA is often appropriate when depreciation or amortization of intangible assets deduced under GAAP overstates the economic decline in value of those assets.

ECHELON
1. level of activity and its personnel in an organization, characterized by a particular responsibility. Usually this refers to the management level.
2. subdivision of a military force.

ECOLOGY subject of environmental science seeking to maintain a systemic natural balance among all living things where they can exist in harmony with each other.

E-COMMERCE the buying and selling of goods over the Internet. E-commerce sites range from a simple Web page highlighting a single item to fully developed online catalogs featuring thousands of products. The common theme in e-commerce sites is instant purchase, instant payment, and rapid delivery.

ECONOMETRICS use of computer analysis and statistical modeling techniques to describe in mathematical terms the numerical relationship between key economic forces such as labor, capital, interest rates, and government policies, then test the effects of changes in economic scenarios.

ECONOMIC pertaining to or having to do with either the economy or the study of economics.

ECONOMIC ANALYSIS study and understanding of trends, phenomena, and information that are economic in nature.

ECONOMIC BASE major industries within a geographic MARKET AREA that provide employment opportunities essential to support the community.

ECONOMIC CYCLE *see* BUSINESS CYCLE.

ECONOMIC DEPRECIATION in real estate, loss of value from all causes outside the property itself. For example, an expensive private home may drop in value when an industrial plant is built nearby. This is a form of *economic depreciation* that must be considered in the APPRAISAL of the property. *See also* DEPRECIATION.

ECONOMIC EFFICIENCY the allocation of resources to their highest valued use and the production and distribution of goods and services at the lowest possible cost. In such a situation, society's resources are allocated so that no change in the allocation can further improve anyone's well-being without making someone else worse off. The unfettered pursuit of self-interest in a perfectly competitive economy leads to *economic efficiency.*

ECONOMIC EXPOSURE variations in the economic or market value of the firm that result from changes in exchange rates. This is due primarily to changes in the firm's competitiveness with importers and exporters.

ECONOMIC FREEDOM freedom from regulation or other dictates from government or other authority in economic (business) matters. In the capitalist system, economic freedom is supposed to lead to efficient ALLOCATION OF RESOURCES.

ECONOMIC GROWTH increase, from period to period, of the REAL value of an economy's production of goods and services, commonly expressed as increase in GROSS NATIONAL PRODUCT (GNP).

ECONOMIC GROWTH RATE rate of change in the GROSS DOMESTIC PRODUCT (GDP), as expressed in an annual percentage. If adjusted for inflation, it is called the *real economic growth rate.*

ECONOMIC INDICATORS key statistics showing the state of the economy. These include the average workweek, weekly claims for unemployment insurance, new orders, vendor performance, stock prices, and changes in the money supply. *See also* COINCIDENT INDICATORS; LAGGING INDICATORS; LEADING INDICATORS.

ECONOMIC INEFFICIENCY the situation in which society's resources are "misallocated"; that is, a different allocation can improve the well-being of some without reducing the well-being of anyone else.

ECONOMIC LIFE remaining period for which a machine or other property is expected to generate more income than operating expenses cost.

ECONOMIC LOSS situation in which a producer does not earn the level of profit that would justify remaining in business in the long run.

ECONOMIC OBSOLESCENCE *see* ECONOMIC DEPRECIATION.

ECONOMIC ORDER QUANTITY (EOQ) inventory decision model to calculate the optimum amount to order based on fixed costs of placing and receiving an order, carrying cost of inventory and the sales. EOQ is used both in manufacturing and retail inventory management.

ECONOMIC RENT
   Appraisal: market rent. *See also* CONTRACT RENT.
   Economics: cost commanded by a factor that is unique or inelastic in supply. An example is the portion of rental income attributable to land, since the land will exist no matter what the rental rate. In this context, *economic rent* carries a connotation of being "unearned" by the owner.

ECONOMICS study of the means by which societies allocate scarce resources. Includes the study of production, distribution, exchange, and consumption of goods and services.

ECONOMIC SANCTIONS internationally, restrictions upon trade and financial dealings that a country imposes upon another for political reasons, usually as punishment for following policies of which the sanctioning country disapproves.

ECONOMIC SYSTEM basic means of achieving economic goals that is inherent in the economic structure of a society. Major economic systems are CAPITALISM, SOCIALISM, and COMMUNISM.

ECONOMIC VALUE value of a good expressed as its exchangeability for other goods, taking into account all relevant costs of the good and social benefits provided by it.

ECONOMIES OF SCALE reduction of the costs of production of goods due to increasing the size of the producing entity and the share of the total market for the good. For example, the largest auto producer may be able to produce a given car for a lower cost than can any of its competitors.

ECONOMIST person who studies economics or who studies and analyzes information pertaining to economic matters.

ECONOMY recognizable and cohesive group of economic performers (producers, labor, consumers) who interact largely together. Economies usually are recognized geographically (countries, states) or, occasionally, as worldwide industries.

EDGAR *E*lectronic *D*ata *G*athering, *A*nalysis, and *R*etrieval system, which performs automated collection, validation, indexing, acceptance, and forwarding of submissions by companies and others who are required by law to file forms with the U.S. Securities and Exchange Commission (SEC). Beginning April 1, 1999, electronic filing of reports was required, and these EDGAR filings are then posted to a searchable ONLINE database on the INTERNET at *http:// www.sec.gov/edgarhp.htm.*

EDGE ACT CORPORATION subsidiary of a U.S. bank that is allowed to offer international banking services across state and national borders.

EDICT official organizational decree that is published; policy statement issued so that all can be aware of an organization's position on a particular matter.

EDU *see* DOMAIN.

EDUCATION EXPENSE DEDUCTION education expenses of individuals are tax deductible as MISCELLANEOUS ITEMIZED DEDUCTIONS only if they are incurred:
1. to maintain or improve skills required in the individual's current occupation, or
2. to meet legal or employer requirements to retain a particular status. Education expenses are not deductible if they are incurred:
1. to meet minimum qualification requirements for the individual's current occupation, or
2. to qualify the individual for a new trade or business.
   Deductible education expenses are subject to the 2% of AGI floor on MISCELLANEOUS ITEMIZED DEDUCTIONS.

EDUCATION IRA *see* COVERDELL EDUCATION SAVINGS ACCOUNT.

EDUCATION SAVINGS BOND exclusion income from certain U.S. government bonds issued after 1989 (including Series EE bonds and Series I Bonds) used by an individual to pay qualified higher education expenses. Interest may be excluded from income, subject to a phase-out for middle- and upper-income taxpayers based on inflation-adjusted ranges.

EEC *see* COMMON MARKET.

EFFECTIVE DATE
   In general: date on which an agreement takes effect.
   Banking, insurance: time when an insurance policy goes into effect.
   Securities: date when an offering registered with the Securities and
   Exchange Commission may commence being sold.

EFFECTIVE DEBT total debt owed by a firm, including capitalized
   value of lease payments.

EFFECTIVE NET WORTH net worth plus SUBORDINATED DEBT, as
   viewed by senior creditors.

EFFECTIVE (INTEREST) RATE YIELD on a DEBT INSTRUMENT as calculated from the purchase price. The effective rate on a bond is determined by the price paid for the security, the *coupon rate*, the time
   between interest payments, and the time until maturity. The effective
   rate is a more meaningful yield figure than the FACE INTEREST RATE or
   the coupon rate. *See also* RATE OF RETURN; YIELD TO MATURITY.

EFFECTIVE TAX RATE rate at which the taxpayer would be taxed if
   his tax liability were taxed at a constant rate rather than progressively.
   This rate is computed by determining what percentage the taxpayer's
   tax liability is of the taxpayer's total taxable income.

EFFICIENCY measure of productivity relative to the input of human
   and other resources; originally a measure of the effectiveness of a
   machine in terms of the ratio of work output to energy input.

EFFICIENCY ENGINEER formerly, management specialist who analyzed and reported on effectiveness in an organization; direct result of
   Frederick W. Taylor's book *The Principles of Scientific Management*,
   which said work can be measured scientifically to determine maximum management effectiveness.

EFFICIENT MARKET theory that market prices reflect the knowledge
   and expectations of all investors. Those who adhere to this controversial
   theory consider it futile to seek undervalued stocks or to forecast market
   movements. According to the theory, any new development is promptly
   reflected in a firm's stock price, making it impossible to beat the market.

EFFICIENT PORTFOLIO PORTFOLIO of investments that has a maximum expected RETURN for a given level of RISK or a minimum level of
   risk for a given expected return.

EGRESS *see* INGRESS AND EGRESS.

EJECTMENT action to regain possession of real property when there is
   no lease.

ELASTIC DEMAND (SUPPLY) *see* ELASTICITY OF SUPPLY AND DEMAND.

ELASTICITY OF SUPPLY AND DEMAND
   Elasticity of supply: responsiveness of output to changes in price;
   computed as the percentage change in the quantity supplied divided by

the percentage change in the price. Supply is said to be elastic (inelastic) if the elasticity exceeds (is less than) 1. The more elastic supply is, the more will a change in price increase production.

Elasticity of demand: responsiveness of buyers to changes in price, defined as the percentage change in the quantity demanded divided by the percentage change in price. Demand for luxury items may slow dramatically if prices are raised, because these purchases are not essential and can be postponed.

ELDERLY OR DISABLED TAX CREDIT a maximum allowable credit of up to $1,125 (15% of $7,500), which varies based on the filing status of an elderly or disabled taxpayer. Social Security benefits and ADJUSTED GROSS INCOME (AGI) in excess of a base amount reduce the available credit.

ELECT choose a course of action. For example, someone who decides to incorporate a certain provision in a will *elects* to do so.

ELECTRONIC BULLETIN BOARD a computer system that allows people to read each other's messages and post new ones. *See also* BBS; NEWSGROUP.

ELECTRONIC BUSINESS (E-BUSINESS) firm that utilizes INTERNET technology at the core of its business operations.

ELECTRONIC COMMERCE *see* E-COMMERCE.

ELECTRONIC COMMUNICATION NETWORK (ECN) network connecting major stock brokerages and individual traders so that they can trade directly among themselves without having to go through a middleman.

ELECTRONIC COMMUNICATIONS PRIVACY ACT (ECPA) U.S. law enacted in 1986 that prohibits unlawful access and certain disclosures in various forms of wire and electronic communications. The law also prevents government entities from requiring disclosure of electronic communications from a provider without proper procedure.

ELECTRONIC COMPUTER-ORGINATED MAIL (E-COM) special service offered by the U.S. Postal System at certain post offices. Computer-generated messages are sent to another post office, printed into letters, inserted in special envelopes, and delivered as first-class mail.

ELECTRONIC DATA INTERCHANGE (EDI) the process of transferring data between and within companies electronically, instead of by paper. It is similar to electronic mail, except that an agreed-upon format is used for a particular type of document, such as an order form, which allows software to automatically process it and generate subsequent documents.

ELECTRONIC FILING system whereby tax returns are transmitted electronically to the IRS by a transmitter, and tapes are created in the receiving station and loaded into the EFS computer system. Especially suitable for taxpayers expecting a tax refund.

ELECTRONIC FUNDS TRANSFER SYSTEM (EFTS) any electronic transmission system that moves funds from one institution to another as opposed to the physical exchange of some other medium such as paper checks.

ELECTRONIC MAIL (E-MAIL) system that allows a person to type a message to one computer or terminal and then send that message to someone at another computer or terminal, usually via INTERNET. The message will be stored until the receiver chooses to read it.

ELECTRONIC RETURN ORIGINATOR (ERO) a preparer or collector who files tax returns electronically.

ELECTRONIC SIGNATURE method for sending identity verification through the Internet, usually in connection with a contract or other type of agreement. The method involves some type of security measure, such as use of a Personal Identification Number (PIN), to indicate the approval of the individual agreeing to the transaction.

ELECTRONIC TRADING purchase or sale of stocks and options via the INTERNET. Customers place orders through brokers ONLINE. Commission rates are much lower than for regular or discount brokers, with some as little as $8 for a trade involving as much as 5,000 shares.

ELECTRONIC TYPEWRITER *see* TYPEWRITER.

ELEVATOR LIABILITY INSURANCE coverage when a liability suit is brought against an insured for bodily injury incurred by a plaintiff as the result of using an elevator on the insured's premises.

ELIGIBILITY REQUIREMENTS conditions required to be covered by employee benefit plans such as pensions, under which minimum requirements, such as a certain number of years of service, must be met by an employee to qualify for benefits.

ELIGIBLE PAPER commercial and agricultural paper, drafts, bills of exchange, banker's acceptances, and other negotiable instruments that were acquired by a bank and that the Federal Reserve Bank will accept for REDISCOUNT.

E-MAIL *see* ELECTRONIC MAIL.

E-MAIL ADDRESS a string, usually of the form *username@host.com* or *username@host.net*, that must be entered into the To: field of an e-mail message to ensure proper delivery.

EMANCIPATION freedom to assume certain legal responsibilities normally associated only with adults; said of a MINOR who is granted this freedom by a court.

EMBARGO government prohibition against the shipment of certain goods to another country. An embargo is most common during wartime, but is sometimes applied for economic reasons as well.

EMBEZZLEMENT fraudulent appropriation, for one's own use, of property lawfully in one's possession; type of larceny. Embezzlement is often associated with bank employees, public officials, or officers of organizations, who may in the course of their lawful activities come into possession of property, such as money, actually owned by others.

EMBLEMENT
1. right of a TENANT of agricultural land to remove crops that he has planted, even if the tenancy has expired before harvest.
2. vegetable CHATTELS, such as corn, produced annually as the result of one's labor and deemed PERSONAL PROPERTY in the event of the death of the farmer before the harvest.

EMERGING ISSUES TASK FORCE group founded in 1984 by the FINANCIAL ACCOUNTING STANDARDS BOARD (FASB) to hold public meetings and identify accounting issues so they can be resolved with standard practices before divergent practices become widespread.

EMINENT DOMAIN inherent right of the state to take private property for PUBLIC USE, without the individual property owner's consent. Just compensation must be paid to the property owner, however. *See also* PUBLIC DOMAIN.

EMOLUMENT income derived from office, rank, employment, or labor, including salary, fees, and other COMPENSATION.

EMPLOYEE person who works for compensation, whether direct or indirect, for another in return for stipulated services. An employee may work on an hourly, daily, or annual wage basis. The EMPLOYER has the right to control the work to be performed as well as the timing and means of accomplishing the work. *Contrast with* INDEPENDENT CONTRACTOR.

EMPLOYEE ACHIEVEMENT AWARD tangible personal property given as award to an employee for length of service, productivity, or safety achievement.

EMPLOYEE ASSISTANCE PROGRAM (EAP) programs implemented by organizations to assist employees being affected by personal problems, including substance abuse. These are comprehensive programs tailored to the needs of the individual and include individual and group counseling, medical and psychological counseling, and individualized fitness programs as well as outside referral when warranted. *See also* WELLNESS PROGRAMS.

EMPLOYEE ASSOCIATION professional organization of employees. These associations are not labor unions per se, and in the past they were generally reluctant to espouse unionlike aims or to endorse union methods. The largest of these associations is the National Education Association (NEA).

EMPLOYEE BENEFITS *see* BENEFIT, definition 3 (fringe).

EMPLOYEE CONTRIBUTIONS workers' premiums toward a contributory employee benefit plan.

EMPLOYEE LEASING COMPANY *see* PROFESSIONAL EMPLOYER ORGANIZATION (PEO).

EMPLOYEE PROFIT SHARING employee benefit plan that entitles employees to a share in the profits of a company. When the company does well, the employees get a bonus; when the company loses money, employees receive only their regularly established pay.

EMPLOYEE RETIREMENT INCOME SECURITY ACT (ERISA) 1974 law governing the operation of most private pension and benefit plans. The law eased pension eligibility rules, set up the Pension Benefit Guaranty Corporation, and established guidelines for the management of pension funds.

EMPLOYEE STOCK OPTION opportunity for employees to purchase stock in the company they work for, often at a discount from market value. The two categories of employee stock options for tax purposes are statutory (incentive stock options) and nonstatutory.

EMPLOYEE STOCK OWNERSHIP PLAN (ESOP) program encouraging employees to purchase stock in their company. Employees may thus participate in the management of the company. Companies with such plans may take tax deductions for ESOP dividends that are passed on to participating employees and for dividends that go to repay stock acquisition loans.

EMPLOYER someone who hires and pays wages, thereby providing a livelihood to individuals who perform work. The employment relationship confers authority on the employer, who has the right to control and direct the work to be performed. An employer also has the right to engage or discharge and furnish the working location and supplies. An employer is responsible for the collection and remission of federal income and Social Security taxes from employees' compensation.

EMPLOYER IDENTIFICATION NUMBER (EIN) a TAXPAYER IDENTIFICATION NUMBER (TIN) for entities other than INDIVIDUALS, such as PARTNERSHIPS, CORPORATIONS, ESTATES, and TRUSTS.

EMPLOYER INTERFERENCE broad category of unfair labor practices by employers against employees. Section 8(a) of the NATIONAL LABOR RELATIONS ACT proscribes interfering with, coercing, or restraining employees in the exercise of their rights to join or assist labor organizations, or not to join or assist.

EMPLOYER RETIREMENT PLAN a retirement plan set up by an employer for the benefit of the employees. For purposes of the INDIVIDUAL RETIREMENT ACCOUNT (IRA) deduction rules, an employer retirement plan is any of the following:

    1. a QUALIFIED PENSION, PROFIT-SHARING, STOCK BONUS, or money purchase plan (including Keogh plan).

2. a SECTION 401(K) PLAN.
3. a union plan.
4. a qualified annuity plan.
5. a plan established for employees of a federal, state, or local government.
6. a tax-sheltered annuity plan for employees of public schools.
7. a SIMPLIFIED EMPLOYEE PENSION (SEP) PLAN.
8. a Section 501(c)(18) trust.

EMPLOYERS CONTINGENT LIEN AGAINST ASSETS LIABILITY claim (lien) of the Pension Benefit Guaranty Corporation (PBGC) against an employer's assets upon termination of a pension plan for the amount of an employee's unfunded benefits.

EMPLOYER'S LIABILITY ACTS statutes specifying the extent to which employers shall be LIABLE to make COMPENSATION for injuries sustained by their employees in the course of employment. Unlike in WORKERS' COMPENSATION laws, which have replaced these acts in many states, the employer is made liable only for injuries resulting from his BREACH of a DUTY owed the employee (i.e., his NEGLIGENCE).

EMPLOYERS LIABILITY COVERAGE *see* WORKERS' COMPENSATION, COVERAGE B.

EMPLOYMENT AGENCY public or private organization providing employment services for those seeking employment as well as for potential employers seeking employees. *Public agencies* provide a wide range of services, most of which are supported by employer contributions to state unemployment funds. *Private agencies* play a major role in recruiting professional and managerial candidates.

EMPLOYMENT AT WILL right of an employer to retain or terminate employees as it so chooses. *See also* RIGHT-TO-WORK LAW.

EMPLOYMENT CONTRACT formal agreement between employer and employee, stating the terms of employment in an organization. Employers are bound by the Federal Affirmation Action laws not to discriminate.

EMPLOYMENT COST INDEX (ECI) report issued quarterly by the U.S. Department of Labor tracking changes in employer payroll costs, including salaries, wages, benefits, and bonuses. Marked increases or upward trends signal INFLATION.

EMPLOYMENT TAX *see* FEDERAL INSURANCE CONTRIBUTIONS ACT (FICA) TAXES; SELF-EMPLOYMENT TAX; SOCIAL SECURITY TAXES.

EMPLOYMENT TEST examination given by a business to prospective employees to aid in the selection process. Examples are a written test of technical abilities, a performance exam where the individual does sample work in a controlled situation, and psychological tests to evaluate an individual's personality.

EMPORIUM originally a marketplace serving more than one merchant; now usually used as a fancy word for "store," generally used to describe a large store containing a wide variety of merchandise.

EMPOWERMENT form of PARTICIPATIVE MANAGEMENT where employees share management responsibilities, including decision making. Self-directed work teams are an outgrowth of empowerment where employee groups establish and implement their own work goals. *See also* PARTICIPATIVE LEADERSHIP; PARTICIPATIVE MANAGEMENT.

EMPOWERMENT ZONE (EZ) designated area within which businesses enjoy very favorable tax credits and other advantages, such as planning exceptions. Empowerment Zones are a joint effort of the U.S. Department of Agriculture (USDA) and Housing and Urban Development (HUD) to revitalize distressed communities. As of 2006, there are 30 urban and 10 rural Empowerment Zones. This designation is generally scheduled to terminate December 31, 2009.

EMPTY NESTERS couple whose children have established separate households. Empty nesters form an important segment of the housing market, since they often seek to reduce the amount of housing space they occupy and are thus one source of demand for smaller housing units.

ENABLING CLAUSE provision in most new laws or statutes that gives appropriate officials the power to implement and enforce the law.

ENCODING putting a message into a certain code, often as a control to assure confidentiality.

ENCROACH to intrude gradually upon the rights or property of another. An *encroachment* is any INFRINGEMENT on the property or authority of another.

ENCROACHMENT building, part of a building, or obstruction that physically intrudes upon, overlaps, or trespasses upon the property of another; verified by a SURVEY.

ENCRYPTION a procedure that renders the contents of a computer message or file unintelligible to anyone not authorized to read it. The message is encoded mathematically with a string of characters called a *data encryption key*. Two widely used encryption methods are DES (Data Encryption Standard), developed by the U.S. National Bureau of Standards and used by the government and many financial institutions, and PGP (Pretty Good Privacy), developed by Philip Zimmerman and adopted by many private users.

ENCUMBRANCE any right to, interest in, or legal LIABILITY upon REAL PROPERTY that does not prohibit passing title to the land but that diminishes its value. Encumbrances include EASEMENTS, licenses, LEASES, timber privileges, homestead privileges, MORTGAGES, and JUDGMENT LIENS. Property is said to be *encumbered* if restricted in such a way.

END OF MONTH transaction period, such as the due date for receivables or the date of a closing inventory.

ENDORSEMENT or **INDORSEMENT**
1. signature of a payee, drawee, or similar party on the back of a check or note to assign or transfer the paper to another; the act of so signing.
2. using celebrities to vouch for (endorse) a product in an advertisement, usually for a fee.
3. written agreement attached to an insurance policy to add or subtract insurance coverage. Once attached, the endorsement takes precedence over the original provisions of the policy. For example, under a homeowner's policy, an inflation guard may be used so that property damage limits are increased automatically to reflect an increase in the cost of construction in the community. Vandalism and malicious mischief can be added to the standard fire policy through an endorsement.

ENDOWMENT permanent fund of PROPERTY or money bestowed upon an institution or a person, the income from which is used to serve the specific purpose for which the gift was intended.

ENDOWMENT CONTRACT a contract with an insurance company that depends in part on the LIFE EXPECTANCY of the insured, but that may be payable in full in a single payment during life.

END USER the person who will ultimately use a product, as opposed to its developers or marketers.

ENERGY MANAGEMENT science of managing energy productivity. As a result of the oil embargo in the 1970s, energy management studies were undertaken in an effort to achieve the most cost-effective energy systems for particular applications.

ENGEL'S LAW observation by 19th-century economist Ernst Engel that as family income rises, the proportion of it devoted to expenditures for food declines.

ENGINEERED CAPACITY *see* CAPACITY.

ENJOIN to command or instruct with authority. *See also* INJUNCTION.

ENROLLED ACTUARY actuary accepted by the Internal Revenue Service. The signature of an enrolled actuary is required for IRS Form 5500 to demonstrate the tax compliance of a pension plan.

ENROLLED AGENT someone other than a CPA or attorney who is qualified to practice before the IRS. *Enrolled agents* have passed a two-day examination or have worked in a technical area at the IRS for at least five years.

ENROLLMENT PERIOD the period immediately following employment during which one may sign up for insurance coverage. If an employee decides later to secure coverage, he or she must wait for a period of time or for an open enrollment period.

ENTERPRISE business firm. The term often is applied to a newly formed venture.

ENTERPRISE APPLICATION INTEGRATION (EAI) making different business software programs work together. EAI advances the compatibility of systems that were originally designed to work independently.

ENTERPRISE RESOURCE PLANNING (ERP) software system designed to assist in the management of an enterprise, including product planning, parts purchasing, maintaining inventories, interacting with suppliers, providing customer service, and tracking orders. It is normally integrated with a DATABASE.

ENTERTAINMENT EXPENSES AND BUSINESS MEALS deductible only if they are "directly related to" or "associated with" the active conduct of a taxpayer's trade or business. Meals and entertainment expenses are not deductible to the extent that they are lavish or extravagant. They include, for example, food, beverages, and entertainment at nightclubs, cocktail lounges, theaters, or sporting events. These are deductible to the extent of 50% of cost.

ENTITLEMENT PROGRAM government program that requires payment to anyone who meets specific qualifications; those who qualify are thus "entitled" to the payments. Social Security, Medicare, food stamps, etc. are entitlement programs.

ENTITY legal form under which property is owned. The benefits and risks of owning a business or property may vary depending on the entity that is formed. Options include a CORPORATION or S CORPORATION, SOLE PROPRIETORSHIP CORPORATION, a JOINT VENTURE, a LIMITED PARTNERSHIP, a PARTNERSHIP, tenancy in common, joint tenancy, LIMITED-LIABILITY CORPORATION, LIMITED-LIABILITY PARTNERSHIP, and a REAL ESTATE INVESTMENT TRUST (REIT).

ENTREPRENEUR individual who initiates business activity. The term is often associated with one who takes business risks.

ENTREPRENEURIAL PROFIT compensation for the expertise and successful effort of a skilled businessperson. In accounting, any and all profit could be attributed to this effort. In economics, this is the portion over and above a normal profit for typically competent management.

ENTRY-LEVEL JOB beginning or first career job; job an individual having little or no experience takes in an organization to begin pursuing a career.

ENVIRONMENTAL *see* SITE ASSESSMENT.

ENVIRONMENTAL ASSESSMENT (EA) a study of land to determine any unique environmental attributes, considering everything from endangered species to existing hazardous waste to historical significance. Depending on the findings of an EA, an ENVIRONMENTAL IMPACT STATEMENT (EIS) may or may not be needed.

ENVIRONMENTAL IMPACT STATEMENT (EIS) analysis of the expected effects of a development or action on the surrounding natural and fabricated environment. Such statements are required for many federally supported developments under the National Environmental Policy Act of 1969.

ENVIRONMENTAL PROTECTION AGENCY (EPA) an agency of the federal government charged with a variety of responsibilities relating to protection of the quality of the natural environment, including research and monitoring, promulgation of standards for air and water quality, and control of the introduction of pesticides and other hazardous materials into the environment.

EOM DATING arrangement whereby all purchases made through the 25th of one month are payable within 30 days of the end of the following month. For example, purchases through the 25th of April would be payable by the end of June. EOM stands for *end of month*.

EOQ *see* ECONOMIC ORDER QUANTITY.

EOY end-of-year.

EPS
1. EARNINGS PER SHARE.
2. *encapsulated PostScript*, a computer graphics file format.

EQUAL CREDIT OPPORTUNITY ACT federal legislation passed in the mid-1970s, prohibiting discrimination in granting credit based on age, race, religion, sex, ethnic background, or whether a person is receiving public assistance or alimony. The Federal Trade Commission enforces the act.

EQUAL EMPLOYMENT OPPORTUNITY COMMISSION (EEOC) federal agency that assures nondiscrimination in hiring and discharging workers.

EQUALIZATION BOARD government agency that determines the fairness of taxes levied against property. It ensures, for example, that all counties within a state assess property at a uniform rate so that the state can redistribute money on a fair basis.

EQUAL OPPORTUNITY EMPLOYER employer who has made a commitment to follow affirmative action legislation in terms of employment opportunities; employer who promotes nondiscrimination in employment opportunities.

EQUAL PROTECTION OF THE LAWS constitutional guarantee embodied in the Fourteenth Amendment to the U.S. Constitution, which states in relevant part that "no State shall . . . deny to any person within its jurisdiction the equal protection of the laws." The essential purpose of this constitutional doctrine is to ensure that the laws and the government treat all persons alike, unless there is some substantial reason why certain persons or classes of persons should be treated differently.

EQUAL RIGHTS AMENDMENT (ERA) proposed constitutional amendment intended to eliminate sex as a basis for any decisions made by a state of the United States. This amendment was not ratified by a sufficient number of states to qualify as a constitutional amendment, but the basic premise underlying the proposal has become an accepted standard in many statutes and court decisions.

EQUILIBRIUM status of a market in which there are no forces operating that would automatically set in motion changes in the quantity demanded or the price that currently prevails.

EQUILIBRIUM PRICE
1. price at which the quantity of goods producers wish to supply matches the quantity demanders want to purchase.
2. for a manufacturer, the price that maximizes a product's profitability.

EQUILIBRIUM QUANTITY quantity of a good that will be produced and sold when the market for the good is in EQUILIBRIUM.

EQUIPMENT machines or major tools necessary to complete a given task. The tools a mechanic needs to repair a machine are an example. Equipment must be capitalized and written off over the appropriate RECOVERY PERIOD. For example, most equipment may be written off over seven years using the 200% declining-balance method.

EQUIPMENT LEASING buying EQUIPMENT such as computers, railroad cars, and airplanes, then leasing it to businesses to receive income from the lease payments and potential tax benefits such as depreciation.

EQUIPMENT TRUST BOND or **EQUIPMENT TRUST CERTIFICATE** bond, usually issued by a transportation company such as a railroad or shipping line, used to pay for new equipment. The bondholder has the first right to the equipment in the event that interest and principal are not paid when due.

EQUITABLE according to natural right or natural justice; marked by due consideration for what is fair and impartial, unhampered by technical rules the law may have devised that limit RECOVERY or defense.

EQUITABLE DISTRIBUTION fair division of property among interested persons.

EQUITABLE OWNER beneficiary of property held in trust.

EQUITABLE TITLE the interest held by one who has agreed to purchase but has not yet closed the transaction.

EQUITY

In general: (1) residual ownership or (2) fairness.

Accounting: paid-in capital plus retained earnings.

Banking: difference between the amount for which a property could be sold and the claims held against it.

Brokerage: excess of securities over debit balance in a margin account. For instance, equity would be $28,000 in a margin account with stocks and bonds worth $50,000 and a debit balance of $22,000.

Investment: ownership interest possessed by shareholders in a corporation—stock as opposed to bonds.

Real estate: property value in excess of debt.

EQUITY BUILDUP the gradual increase in a MORTGAGOR'S EQUITY in a property caused by AMORTIZATION of loan principal.

EQUITY FINANCING raising money by selling part of the ownership, such as stock in a corporation, in contrast with DEBT FINANCING.

EQUITY KICKER *see* KICKER.

EQUITY METHOD means of accounting used by an investor who owns between 20% and 50% of the voting common stock of a company. It can also be used instead of the COST METHOD when the investor owns less than 20% of the company but has *significant influence* over the investee. Further, it is employed instead of CONSOLIDATION, even though more than 50% is owned, when one of the negating factors for consolidation exists (e.g., parent and subsidiary are not economically compatible, parent is not in actual control of subsidiary, parent has sold or contracted to sell subsidiary shortly after year-end).

EQUITY OF REDEMPTION right of mortgagor to redeem his property (save it from FORECLOSURE), after DEFAULT in the payment of the MORTGAGE debt, by subsequent payment of all costs and interest, in addition to the mortgage debt, to the mortgagee.

EQUITY REIT REAL ESTATE INVESTMENT TRUST that takes an ownership position in the real estate in which it invests. Stockholders in equity REITs earn dividends on rental income from the buildings and earn appreciation if properties are sold for a profit. A *mortgage REIT* lends capital to real estate builders and buyers, but does not take an ownership position.

EQUITY YIELD RATE the RATE OF RETURN on the EQUITY portion of an investment, taking into account periodic CASH FLOW and the proceeds from resale. Considers the timing and amounts of cash flow after ANNUAL DEBT SERVICE, but not income taxes.

EQUIVALENT TAXABLE YIELD comparison of the taxable yield on a corporate bond and the tax-free yield on a municipal bond. Depending on the tax bracket, an investor's after-tax return may be greater with a municipal bond than with a corporate bond offering a higher interest rate. For someone in a 33% tax bracket, for instance, a

5% municipal bond would have an equivalent taxable yield of more than 7.5%.

ERGONOMICS the study or science of how people interact with their work areas. Considerable attention has recently been paid to the ergonomic design of computer workstations, including monitor height, keyboard placement, and seating that promotes correct posture and offers the necessary back support.

ERISA *see* EMPLOYEE RETIREMENT INCOME SECURITY ACT.

ERO electronic return originator.

EROSION gradual wearing away of land through processes of nature, as by streams and wind. The term is also used to indicate a gradual decline in such general business phrases as *sales erosion* and *market-share erosion*.

ERROR
1. mistake; act involving a departure from truth or accuracy.
2. in a legal proceeding such as a trial, an *error of law* furnishes grounds for the APPELLATE COURT to reverse a JUDGMENT.
3. type of computer message indicating an inappropriate action.
4. in statistics, a TYPE 1 ERROR or a TYPE 2 ERROR.

ERRORS AND OMISSIONS LIABILITY INSURANCE policies generally available to the various professions that require protection for negligent acts and/or omissions resulting in bodily injury, personal injury, and/or property damage liability to a client.

ESCALATOR CLAUSE provision in a CONTRACT allowing cost increases to be passed on. In an employment contract, an escalator clause might call for wage increases to keep employee earnings in line with inflation. In a lease, an escalator clause could obligate the tenant to pay for increases in fuel or other costs. *See also* COST-OF-LIVING ADJUSTMENT (COLA).

ESCAPE CLAUSE a provision in a contract that allows one or more of the parties to cancel all or part of the contract if certain events or situations do or do not occur.

ESCHEAT the reversion of property to the state in the event that the owner dies without leaving a will and has no legal heirs.

ESCROW
1. written INSTRUMENT, such as a deed, temporarily deposited with a neutral third party, the ESCROW AGENT, by the agreement of two parties to a valid contract. The escrow agent will deliver the document to the benefited party when the conditions of the contract have been met. The depositor has no control over the instrument in escrow. Escrow now applies to all instruments so deposited.
2. money or other property so deposited is also loosely referred to as escrow. Monthly deposits by a homeowner to the mortgage holder to pay for taxes and insurance are called escrows.

ESCROW ACCOUNT same as TRUST ACCOUNT.

ESCROW AGENT person engaged in the business of receiving ESCROWS for deposit or delivery. In real estate, a title company may serve as the escrow agent. It holds the EARNEST MONEY and DEED pending fulfillment of other conditions to the contract.

ESCROW CLOSING term meaning the same as CLOSING, especially in states where deeds of trust are used instead of mortgages.

ESOP *see* EMPLOYEE STOCK OWNERSHIP PLAN.

ESPIONAGE act of spying. An example is spying on the activities of another company by improperly gathering information about the competing company's new products or practices. Usually the spy is paid a fee for the information obtained.

ESQUIRE (ESQ.) title used for lawyers in place of a preceding honorific—that is, "Allen Seegull, Esq." instead of "Mr. Allen Seegull."

ESSENTIAL INDUSTRY industry that, for political or economic reasons, is considered by society to be necessarily located within its own economy, regardless of its comparative advantage or disadvantage with other economies. The society is unwilling to trade for the product of an essential industry with other societies or countries. The defense industry in the United States is an *essential industry*.

ESTATE
1. broadly, all that a person owns, whether REAL PROPERTY or PERSONAL PROPERTY. For instance, the *estate* one leaves at death.
2. nature and extent of a person's interest in or ownership of land.

ESTATE FOR LIFE *see* LIFE ESTATE.

ESTATE IN REVERSION ESTATE left by the grantor for himself or herself, to begin after the termination of some particular estate granted by him or her. For example, a landlord has an *estate in reversion* that becomes his to possess when the lease expires.

ESTATE IN SEVERALTY property owned by a sole person, with no joint ownership. *See also* TENANCY IN SEVERALTY.

ESTATE PLANNING planning for the orderly handling, disposition, and administration of an ESTATE when the owner dies. Estate planning includes drawing up a WILL, setting up TRUSTS, and minimizing estate, income, and trust taxes. In a broad sense, it is the art of designing a program for the effective enjoyment, management, and disposition of property at the minimum possible tax cost.

ESTATE PLANNING DISTRIBUTION plan that involves distribution of property *by living hand* and distribution of property after the death of its owner. Distribution by living hand can take the form of an outright gift, a grant of limited property interest, or a gift in trust. Distribution at death can be accomplished through a will or, if there is no will, as directed by state law; *see*, e.g., BENEFICIARY; LIFE ESTATE; LIVING TRUST; TENANCY; TESTAMENTARY TRUST.

ESTATE TAX amount due to the government, generally based on the FAIR MARKET VALUE of one's property at death, less liabilities. The FEDERAL ESTATE TAX and gift tax have been unified, and one unified credit amount applies to the sum of the property given during one's lifetime and remaining at death. Estate tax exemptions and deductions are numerous, and relevant tax laws can be complex.

ESTATE TAX PAYABLE amount that results from deducting the following from TENTATIVE ESTATE TAX: (1) UNIFIED CREDIT; (2) state death taxes; (3) gift taxes paid on gifts made before 1977; (4) foreign death taxes; and (5) estate taxes on prior transfers to decedent from the estate tax before unified credit.

ESTIMATE
1. to approximate.
2. in statistics, single value (point) or interval (range) of an unknown population parameter based on a sample of the population.

ESTIMATED TAX income taxes that are paid quarterly by a taxpayer on income that is not subject to withholding taxes, in an amount that represents a projection of ultimate tax liability for the taxable period. To avoid a penalty for underestimation, an individual's estimated payments must equal or exceed 90% of the tax due or 100% of the tax paid the previous year.

ESTIMATED TAX, DECLARATION OF *see* DECLARATION OF ESTIMATED TAX.

ESTIMATED USEFUL LIFE period of time over which an ASSET will be used by a taxpayer. In theory, depreciable assets are written off over the *estimated useful life* of the asset for DEPRECIATION purposes. However, more recent tax laws have used artificial RECOVERY PERIODS that are unrelated to the estimated useful life.

ESTIMATOR individual in a large advertising agency whose primary responsibility is to compute the cost of the advertising media schedules.

ESTOPPEL restraint; a bar. Estoppel arises where a person has done some act that the policy of the law will not permit him to deny, or where circumstances are such that the law will not permit a certain argument because it would lead to an unjust result. In the context of contract law, for example, one is *estopped* from denying existence of a binding contract where one has done something intending that another rely on his conduct, and the result of the reliance is detrimental to that other person. *See also* WAIVER.

ESTOPPEL CERTIFICATE document by which the MORTGAGOR (borrower) certifies that the mortgage debt is a LIEN for the amount stated.

The DEBTOR is thereafter prevented from claiming that the balance due differs from the amount stated.

ESTOVERS right of the TENANT, or life tenant, during the period of his lease, to use timber on the leased premises for proper maintenance of the property.

ET AL. abbreviation of *et alii,* Latin for "and others."

ETHERNET a standard method of connecting computers to a LOCAL AREA NETWORK (LAN) using coaxial cable.

ETHICAL, ETHICS (in accordance with) moral and professional principles. In business, work is performed in an honest and diligent way. Rules of conduct in business are formulated by various organizations, for example AICPA's Code of Professional Ethics. The morality displayed by members of a profession is important for public confidence in their work.

ETIN electronic transmitter identification number.

ET NON Latin for "and not."

ET UX. abbreviation of *et uxor,* Latin for "and wife"; used in old legal documents such as wills and deeds.

E-TYPE REORGANIZATION *see* RECAPITALIZATION.

EURO the official currency of the EUROPEAN UNION; recognized as the sole currency in 13 members of the EU (Austria, Belgium, France, Finland, Germany, Greece, Ireland, Italy, Luxembourg, the Netherlands, Portugal, Slovenia, and Spain). In the United Kingdom, Sweden, and Denmark, the euro is accepted in addition to local currency. It is also used in foreign territories of EU member countries and some small nonmember European countries. Nations joining the EU after 2004 are scheduled to adopt the euro between 2007 and 2011. The supply of euros in circulation is controlled by the EUROPEAN CENTRAL BANK.

EUROBANKING banking that involves accepting deposits and making loans that are denominated in many different currencies besides the host country's currency.

EUROBOND BOND denominated in U.S. dollars or other currencies and sold to investors outside the country whose currency is used. The bonds are usually issued by large underwriting groups composed of banks and issuing houses from many countries.

EUROCOMMERCIAL PAPER short-term notes that are issued by firms and denominated in currencies of countries other than the one in which they are sold.

EUROCURRENCY money deposited by corporations and national governments in banks away from their home countries, called *Eurobanks.*

The terms *Eurocurrency* and *Eurobanks* do not necessarily mean the currencies or the banks are European, though more often than not that is the case. The EURODOLLAR is only one of the Eurocurrencies, though it is the most prevalent. Also known as *Euromoney.*

EURODOLLAR U.S. dollar held as a deposit in a European commercial bank (*Eurobank*). Eurodollars were created after World War II by U.S. defense and foreign aid expenditures. When the dollar was backed by gold, it was a popular reserve currency in Europe, and it is still commonly used for settling international transactions. Most Eurodollars are now created by the purchase of European goods by Americans.

EURODOLLAR BOND bond that pays interest and principal in EURODOLLARS.

EURODOLLAR CERTIFICATE OF DEPOSIT CD issued by banks outside the United States, primarily in Europe, with interest and principal paid in dollars. Such CDs usually have minimum denominations of $100,000 and maturities of less than two years. The interest rate on these CDs is usually pegged to the LONDON INTERBANK OFFERED RATE (LIBOR).

EUROPEAN CENTRAL BANK (ECB) bank founded to oversee monetary policy for the 13 countries that converted their local currencies into the EURO as of 2006. The bank's primary mission is to maintain price stability and issue euro currency.

EUROPEAN UNION (EU) union of 25 independent states based on the former European (Economic) Community (EC, EEC) and founded to enhance political, economic, and social cooperation. It seeks to create free trade throughout the continent and a common currency (the EURO). As of 2006, the members are: Austria, Belgium, Cyprus (Greek part), the Czech Republic, Denmark, Estonia, Finland, France, Germany, Greece, Hungary, Ireland, Italy, Latvia, Lithuania, Luxembourg, Malta, the Netherlands, Poland, Portugal, Spain, Slovakia, Slovenia, Sweden, and the United Kingdom.

EVALUATOR independent expert who appraises the value of property for which there is limited trading—antiques in an estate, perhaps, or rarely traded STOCKS or BONDS. The fee for this service is sometimes a flat amount, sometimes a percentage of the appraised value.

EVASION, TAX *see* TAX EVASION.

EVENT RISK the likelihood of a certain occurrence affecting a given business or investment; *contrast with market* or *systematic risk,* which affects all in the same class.

EVICTION physical expulsion of someone from real estate by the assertion of superior title or through legal proceedings. *See* EVICTION, ACTUAL; EVICTION, CONSTRUCTIVE; EVICTION, PARTIAL.

EVICTION, ACTUAL when a person is removed from property, either by force or by process of law.

EVICTION, CONSTRUCTIVE when, through the fault of the landlord, physical conditions of the property render it unfit for the purpose for which it was leased.

EVICTION, PARTIAL when the possessor of a property, such as a tenant, is deprived of a portion thereof. For example, a firm leases a floor of an office building. The landlord wishes to make substantial modifications to one side of the building. Because of the disruption caused by the work, tenant and landlord agree to a partial eviction from the property affected by construction. The tenant's rent is reduced accordingly.

EVIDENCE OF TITLE documents, such as DEEDS, that demonstrate OWNERSHIP. These should be kept in a safe place, such as a bank vault.

EXACT INTEREST interest paid by a bank or other financial institution and calculated on the basis of a 365-day year, as opposed to ORDINARY INTEREST, which is based on a 360-day year.

EXAMINATION OF TITLE research of the title to a piece of real estate; less thorough than a title search, it usually concentrates on recent records.

EXCEL a widely used spreadsheet program produced by Microsoft.

"EXCEPT FOR" OPINION one of the two *qualified opinions* that an auditor can render. The auditor attests that the financial statements present the financial position fairly *except for* repercussions caused by conditions requiring disclosure. There may be a SCOPE LIMITATION in the auditor's work due to factors beyond the auditor's control or due to client restrictions that prevent the CPA from gathering objective and verifiable evidence in support of transactions and events. An example is the inability to confirm accounts receivable. There may exist a lack of conformity of the financial statements to GAAP.

EXCESS (ACCELERATED) DEPRECIATION the accumulated difference between ACCELERATED DEPRECIATION claimed for tax purposes and what STRAIGHT-LINE DEPRECIATION would have been. Generally, *excess accelerated depreciation* is recaptured (taxed) as ORDINARY INCOME upon a sale, instead of receiving more favorable CAPITAL GAINS treatment. *See* DEPRECIATION RECAPTURE.

EXCESS CONTRIBUTIONS contributions to CASH or DEFERRED ARRANGEMENTS for highly compensated employees in excess of the amount allowed under nondiscrimination rules.

EXCESS PROFITS TAX extra federal tax placed on the earnings of a business. Such tax may be levied in times of national emergency, such as wartime, and is designed to increase national revenue. It is distinguishable from a *windfall profits tax*, designed to prevent excessive corporate profit in special circumstances.

EXCESS RESERVES money a bank holds over and above the RESERVE REQUIREMENT. The money may be on deposit with the FEDERAL RESERVE SYSTEM (FED) or with an approved depository bank, or it may be in the bank's possession.

EXCHANGE
   1. to give goods or services and to get goods or services of equal value in return. Generally, a transaction is a SALE when money is received in return for the goods or services and is an *exchange* when specific property is received. *Exchange* is synonymous with BARTER. *See also* TAX-FREE EXCHANGE.
   2. place where securities are traded, such as the New York Stock exchange.
   3. under SECTION 1031 OF THE INTERNAL REVENUE CODE, LIKE-KIND PROPERTY used in a trade or business or held as an investment can be exchanged tax-free. *See also* BOOT; REALIZED GAIN; RECOGNIZED GAIN; DELAYED (TAX-FREE) EXCHANGE.
   4. online locations where companies gather to buy and sell goods and services from one another, often via AUCTION.

EXCHANGE CONTROL government policy limiting the ability of its citizens and/or foreigners to exchange the country's currency for that of other countries and vice versa.

EXCHANGE RATE price at which one country's currency can be converted into another's. The *exchange rate* between the U.S. dollar and the British pound is different from that between the dollar and the German mark, for example. Most exchange rates float freely and change slightly each trading day; some rates are fixed and do not change as a result of market forces.

EXCHANGE RATE DIRTY FLOAT a system in which exchange rates are determined by supply and demand in the foreign exchange market, but where governments buy and sell currencies in order to influence the market.

EXCISE TAX tax imposed on an act, occupation, privilege, manufacture, sale, or consumption. In recent years, this term has been applied to just about every tax except the INCOME TAX and the PROPERTY TAX. In general, federal, state, and local excise taxes (for example, on tobacco, gasoline, and spirits) are not deductible by an individual.

EXCITE an Internet search engine at *http://excite.com.*

EXCLUSION
   Insurance: item not covered by a policy.
   Taxation: amount that otherwise would constitute a part of GROSS INCOME, but is excluded under a specific provision of the Internal Revenue Code.

EXCLUSIONS provision in an insurance policy that indicates what is denied coverage. For example, common *exclusions* are: hazards deemed so catastrophic in nature that they are uninsurable, such as war; wear and tear, since they are expected through the use of a product; property covered by other insurance, in order to eliminate duplication that would profit the insured; liability arising out of contracts; and liability arising out of workers' compensation laws.

EXCLUSIVE AGENCY LISTING contract in real estate giving only one broker, for a specific time, the right to sell a property and also allowing the owner to sell the property without paying a commission. *See also* EXCLUSIVE RIGHT TO SELL LISTING; OPEN LISTING.

EXCLUSIVE DISTRIBUTION marketing strategy that gives intermediaries an exclusive right to sell products in specified geographic areas.

EXCLUSIVE RIGHT TO SELL LISTING contract giving the broker the right to collect a commission if a property is sold by anyone, including the owner, during the term of the agreement. *See also* EXCLUSIVE AGENCY LISTING; OPEN LISTING.

EXCULPATORY
1. evidence or statements that tend to justify or excuse a defendant from alleged fault or guilt.
2. clause in a MORTGAGE that avoids PERSONAL LIABILITY. The property is the sole COLLATERAL for the debt.

EX-DIVIDEND DATE date on which a stock goes *ex-dividend*, typically about three weeks before the dividend is paid to shareholders of record. An investor who buys on or after that date is not entitled to the dividend. The ex-dividend date usually is two business days before the DATE OF RECORD.

EXECUTE
1. to complete, as a legal INSTRUMENT.
2. to perform what is required.
3. to give validity to, as by signing and perhaps sealing and delivering. For example, a contract is *executed* when all acts necessary to complete it and to give it validity as an instrument are carried out, including signing and delivery.
4. to do what an INSTRUCTION in a computer program says to do. The computer alternates between a *fetch* cycle, when it locates the next instruction, and an *execute* cycle, when it carries out the instruction.

EXECUTED fully accomplished or performed. Nothing is left unfulfilled. *See also* EXECUTORY.

EXECUTED CONTRACT contract whose terms have been completely fulfilled. *See also* EXECUTORY.

EXECUTION
Law: signing, sealing, and delivering of a contract or agreement, making it valid.

Securities: carrying out a trade. A broker who buys or sells shares is said to have *executed* an order.

EXECUTIVE employee in a top-level management position; person who has major decision-making authority in an organization. Many executives in the private sector receive INCENTIVE PAY, such as bonuses.

EXECUTIVE COMMITTEE senior-level management committee empowered to make and implement major organizational decisions. An executive committee often acts as an overseer of organizational activities and has the authority to request justification of certain matters as well as to plan activities.

EXECUTIVE INFORMATION SERVICES (EIS) online strategic management system using a central database and designed to fulfill organizational information analysis requirements. It allows querying on a wide range of criteria to assist in the strategic decision-making process. *See also* DECISION SUPPORT SYSTEM (DSS).

EXECUTIVE PAY OVER ONE MILLION DOLLARS tax law introduced in 1993 that prohibits a publicly held corporation from taking a deduction for compensation paid to an executive in excess of $1 million per year. However, the $1 million limitation would not apply to compensation payments that are linked to productivity.

EXECUTIVE PERQUISITES *see* PERQUISITES.

EXECUTIVE SEARCH FIRM *see* HEADHUNTER.

EXECUTIVE SECRETARY individual acting as an administrative and secretarial assistant to top-level management personnel in an organization. Executive secretaries have substantial clerical as well as administrative responsibilities.

EXECUTOR (EXECUTRIX) person designated to carry out the wishes expressed in a WILL as to the administration of the ESTATE and the distribution of the assets in it. An executor may be a bank trust officer, a family member, or a trusted friend. *Executrix* is the term for a woman who fills this role.

EXECUTORY not fully accomplished or completed, but contingent upon the occurrence of some event or the performance of some act in the future; not *vested*; opposite of *executed*. *See also* EXECUTE.

EXEMPTION
1. deduction allowed a taxpayer because of the taxpayer's status or circumstances rather than because of specific economic costs or expenses during the taxable year. For example, a married couple having three children are allowed five personal and dependency exemptions by federal income tax laws, one for each person, on their JOINT TAX RETURN. The exemptions reduce the amount of income upon which the couple are taxed. The amount of the

exemption is indexed for inflation each year. The indexed amount for 2006 was $3,300.

2. the HOMESTEAD EXEMPTION, offered in many jurisdictions, reduces the value of real estate (usually the principal residence or DOMICILE) that would otherwise be subject to an AD VALOREM TAX.

3. the maximum ALTERNATIVE MINIMUM TAX exemptions for 2005 were $58,000 for married filing jointly, $40,250 for single or head of household, and $29,000 for married filing separately. The maximum exemption for corporations was $40,000. The exemptions are phased out for ALTERNATIVE MINIMUM TAXABLE INCOME in excess of $382,000 (joint return), $273,500 (single or head of household return), and $191,000 (married, filing separately).

EXEMPTION PHASE-OUT the amount that can be claimed as a deduction for PERSONAL EXEMPTIONS is phased out as ADJUSTED GROSS INCOME (AGI) rises above a certain level.

EXEMPT ORGANIZATION *see* NOT FOR PROFIT.

EXEMPT SECURITIES stocks and bonds exempt from certain Securities and Exchange Commission and Federal Reserve Board rules. For instance, government and municipal bonds are exempt from SEC registration requirements and from Federal Reserve Board margin rules.

EXEMPT STATUS certain organizations, such as churches, government organizations, and community chests, are exempt from taxation. An organization must submit an application for exempt status and file information returns even though no tax is due.

EXERCISE to make use of a right available in a contract. For example, in options, buying the property; in CONVERTIBLE securities, to make the exchange.

EXERCISE PRICE amount at which a put or call can be used to buy a stock, or a convertible security can be redeemed for shares of stock.

EXIMBANK *see* EXPORT-IMPORT BANK.

EXIT FEE *see* BACK-END LOAD.

EXIT INTERVIEW interview conducted as an employee leaves the employment of an organization. The purpose of the interview is to obtain feedback about the general feelings of the employee in terms of seeking ways to improve the organization. Since the employee is no longer employed at the organization, this may lead to a frank discussion of employment issues.

EX-LEGAL municipal bond that does not have the legal opinion of a bond law firm printed on it, as most municipal bonds do. When such bonds are traded, buyers must be warned that legal opinion is lacking.

EX OFFICIO by right or virtue of the office held; officially. An *ex officio member* is a member of a board, committee, or other body by virtue of his title to a certain office, and does not require further appointment.

EXPANSION any increase of the sales capabilities of a company. Expansion may be necessary to meet new competitive demands as well as to open new markets for a company. Expansion may also result from high profits a company is making, which provide the capital base for increasing the size of the business.

EXPECTANCY THEORY OF MOTIVATION theory of motivation developed by Victor H. Vroom, which maintains that performance will achieve a goal. Motivation is a combination of effort, achievability of goals, and desire. An individual who has a particular goal must practice a certain behavior to achieve it.

EXPECTED ACTUAL CAPACITY *see* CAPACITY.

EXPECTED RETURN *see* MEAN RETURN.

EXPECTED VALUE average value that would appear if a RANDOM VARIABLE were observed many times; also called the *expectation*.

EXPENSE
1. business cost incurred in operating and maintaining property. For purposes of information and in reporting to shareholders of publicly held corporations, expenses are calculated as the cost of goods and services used in the process of profit-directed business activities.
2. costs that are currently deductible, as opposed to CAPITAL EXPENDITURES, which may not be currently deducted but must be depreciated or amortized over the useful life of the property. Certain costs may be expensed for accounting purposes but may not be deductible or may be deductible later for tax purposes (goodwill, for example, and bad debts under the allowance method). Other costs may be tax deductible earlier than for accounting purposes (such as intangible drilling costs).

EXPENSE ACCOUNT
1. in accounting, account used to accumulate expenses such as interest, advertising, and administrative.
2. for salespersons and executives, allowance or account for travel and business entertainment purposes; often subject to close scrutiny by the Internal Revenue Service to determine whether excessive expenditures have been deducted; also called *travel and entertainment account* or *T & E*.

EXPENSE BUDGET limit to the amount anticipated as an expense to be incurred in a future period.

EXPENSE RATIO
1. ratio of OPERATING EXPENSES to GROSS INCOME, especially for a real estate property.
2. amount, expressed as a percentage of total investment, that shareholders pay for MUTUAL-FUND operating expenses and management fees.

EXPENSE REPORT detailed list of expenses incurred by a salesperson or executive, reflecting expenses such as transportation, lodging, meals away from home, and client entertainment, submitted to the employer for reimbursement.

EXPERIENCE CURVE production phenomenon where unit costs decline as volume increases. This results from a wide variety of factors including lower fixed costs per unit, an increase in skills associated with quantity production, and generally lower material costs.

EXPERIENCE RATING insurance company technique to determine the correct price of a policy premium. The company analyzes past loss experience for others in the insured group to project future claims. The premium is then set at a rate high enough to cover those potential claims and still earn a profit for the insurance company.

EXPERIENCE REFUND return of a percentage of premium paid by a business firm if its loss record is better than the amount loaded into the basic premium.

EXPERT POWER ability to influence someone regarding a course of action because of specific knowledge, experience, or expertise. A person may be given the power to make decisions for others because he is an expert on the particular subject.

EXPERT SYSTEM in computer ARTIFICIAL INTELLIGENCE, a reasoning process that allows the computer to draw deductions, producing new information, modifying rules, or writing new rules. The computer is thereby allowed to learn from data it has stored.

EXPERT WITNESS one having special knowledge of the subject about which he or she is testifying. The person must be accepted by the court and must normally testify about facts rather than the law.

EXPIRATION
  In general: date on which a contract, agreement, license, magazine subscription, etc., ceases to be effective.
  Options: last day on which an option can be exercised.

EXPIRATION NOTICE written notice to an insured showing date of termination of an insurance policy.

EXPLOITATION taking advantage of an individual or situation for one's full benefit. It often has a negative connotation to it. An example is paying illegal aliens subminimum wages for services.

EXPONENTIAL SMOOTHING popular technique for short-run forecasting by business forecasters. It uses a weighted average of past data as the basis for a forecast. The procedure gives heaviest weight to more recent information and smaller weights to observations in the more distant past. The reason for this is that the future is more dependent upon the recent past than on the distant past.

EXPORT
1. ship goods produced in one country to be sold in another; also, the goods exported.
2. transfer data from one computer or application to another. This may require the ability to save in some file format other than the native one. For example, you can usually save a word processing or graphics file in a format that can be read by another word processing or graphics application.

EXPORT-IMPORT BANK (EXIMBANK) BANK set up by Congress in 1934 to encourage U.S. trade with foreign countries. Its activities include: (1) financing exports and imports; (2) granting direct credit to non-U.S. borrowers to help finance the purchase of U.S. exports; and (3) providing export guarantees, insurance against commercial and political risk, and discount loans.

EX POST FACTO after the fact, especially a law that makes punishable as a crime an act that was done before the passing of the law and that was innocent when done. Such laws violate the Constitution of the United States.

EXPOSURE
Finance: amount that one can lose; generally cash and notes payable. *See also* AT RISK.

Marketing: advertising, whether free or paid, of goods or services that are for sale. Market *exposure* is provided through such media as radio and television, newspapers, and billboards.

EXPOSURE DRAFT in accounting, preliminary release of a statement by the Financial Accounting Standards Board, which offers the text of the proposed statement for comment. The official statement, which may be modified as a result of constructive criticism of the exposure draft, will be issued after the exposure draft has been circulated for several months.

EXPRESS
1. to set forth an AGREEMENT in words, written or spoken, that unambiguously signify intent.
2. as distinguished from IMPLIED, the term refers to something that is not left to inference from conduct or circumstances.
3. transportation service that makes fewer stops than local service.

EXPRESS AUTHORITY AUTHORITY given explicitly either orally or in writing; authority plainly given to another and not presumed from circumstances.

EXPRESS CONTRACT contract with clear written or spoken terms. *See also* IMPLIED CONTRACT.

EXPRESS MAIL next-day delivery guaranteed for shipments between major U.S. cities, available from the U.S. Postal Service for letters or packages of up to 70 pounds. Postage costs vary by weight, distance, and specific type of Express Mail used.

EXPROPRIATION government seizure of foreign-owned assets. This is legal under international law if JUST COMPENSATION is provided; otherwise it is termed *confiscation.*

EXTENDED COVERAGE ENDORSEMENT extension of coverage available under the STANDARD FIRE POLICY. The standard policy only covers the perils of fire and lightning. The endorsement covers riot, riot attending a strike, civil commotion, smoke, aircraft and vehicle damage, windstorm, hail, and explosion.

EXTENSION
In general: agreement between two parties to extend the time period specified in a contract.
Taxation: additional period of time to file an income tax return.

EXTENSION OF TIME FOR FILING additional period during which a tax return may be filed without penalty. Beginning with tax returns filed in 2006, an automatic six-month extension of time to file an individual tax return (Form 1040) is obtained by filing Form 4868 by April 15. The extension will give the taxpayer extra time to get paperwork to the IRS, but it does not extend the time to pay any tax due. The taxpayer will owe interest on any amounts not paid by the April deadline, plus a late payment penalty if less than 90% of the total tax has been paid by that date. Form 4868 may be obtained by phone (1-800-829-3676) or online at *http://www.irs.gov/formspubs/index.html*; tax software packages also include the form, as well as e-filing options. An extension of more than six months will not be granted if the taxpayer is in the United States. A corporation may obtain an automatic extension of six months for filing a return (Form 1120 or 1120S) by filing Form 7004 by the due date of the tax return.

EXTENUATING CIRCUMSTANCES unusual conditions preventing a policy or project from being carried out correctly on time. The individual has little or no control over the situation. For example, a supplier might be unable to deliver merchandise on time because of a railroad strike.

EXTERNAL AUDIT analysis of the acceptability of a company's financial records provided by an outside firm, generally a CPA firm. *See also* ACCOUNTANT'S OPINION; INTERNAL AUDIT.

EXTERNAL DOCUMENTS documents needed for the company recordkeeping that have somehow been handled by outside individuals. Vendor invoices and canceled checks are examples. The auditor can place much more reliance on external documents than internal documents because of the greater independence and verifiability associated with them.

EXTERNAL FUNDS funds brought in from outside the corporation, perhaps in the form of a bank loan, proceeds from a bond offering, or an infusion of cash from venture capitalists. *See also* INTERNAL FINANCING.

EXTERNAL REPORT organizational report intended for outside circulation. External reports do not contain sensitive organizational information unless it is necessary to achieve a particular purpose.

EXTRACTIVE INDUSTRY industry that involves mining, such as to obtain copper or other valuable minerals found in the ground.

EXTRA DIVIDEND dividend paid to shareholders in addition to the regular dividend. Such a payment is made after a particularly profitable year in order to reward shareholders and engender loyalty.

EXTRA EXPENSE INSURANCE insurance designed to protect businesses in the event of an unforeseen emergency requiring additional expenses, allowing them to continue operations. For example, in the event of a fire, the business may need equipment to continue operations until the main facility and related equipment are restored.

EXTRAORDINARY DIVIDENDS DIVIDENDS of unusual form and amount, paid at unscheduled times from accumulated SURPLUS.

EXTRANET private network utilizing Internet technology to securely share part of a business's information or operations with suppliers, vendors, partners, customers, or other businesses.

EXTRAORDINARY ITEM nonrecurring occurrence that must be explained to shareholders in an annual or quarterly report. Some examples are write-off of a division, acquisition of another company, sale of a large amount of real estate, or uncovering of employee fraud that negatively affects the company's financial condition.

EXTRAPOLATION prediction of values by a statistical model outside of or beyond the range of the data used to estimate the model. A real estate developer predicting office absorption in the year 2010, based on a regression model of actual data from 1995 through 2005, would be *extrapolating*.

F

FAA FEDERAL AVIATION ADMINISTRATION.

FABRICATOR employee who converts materials into units, parts, or items; assembler; manufacturer of goods or materials. A custom fabricator manufactures goods to order.

FACADE outside front wall of a building.

FACE *see* FACE INTEREST RATE; FACE VALUE.

FACE AMOUNT (FACE OF POLICY) sum of insurance provided by a policy at death or maturity.

FACE AMOUNT OF BOND *see* FACE VALUE.

FACE INTEREST RATE percentage interest that is shown on the bond or the loan document. The EFFECTIVE RATE is a more meaningful YIELD figure.

FACE VALUE value indicated in the wording of an INSTRUMENT. For example, the *face value* of a bank check is the amount the check is written for. The interest rate of a bond refers to the face value, not the MARKET VALUE. Face value is also called PAR VALUE or *nominal value*.

FACILITIES MANAGEMENT the process of operating corporate- or government-owned property occupied and used for the corporation's or government's own purposes.

FACILITY unit constructed or work area reserved for a specific function. For example, the cafeteria is a *facility* uniquely designed for the purpose of providing an attractive and sanitary area for serving food to its patrons.

FACSIMILE copy, especially of written business documents or pictures; copy sent by electronic means. *See also* FACSIMILE TRANSMISSION.

FACSIMILE TRANSMISSION (FAX) use of electronics to send printed materials. A picture of the material is coded by an electronic scanning device, sent over phone or electronic wire, and reproduced at its destination.

FACT FINDER neutral party who studies the issues in a dispute and makes a recommendation for a fair settlement.

FACTION informal group of people operating within an organization and often opposing a larger group. Similar to *clique*, a faction is formed through voluntary membership by people who share common goals.

FACTOR agent employed to sell goods or merchandise consigned or delivered to him by or for his principal for a compensation commonly called *factorage,* DISCOUNT, or COMMISSION. A factor may buy and sell in either his own name or the principal's name. *See also* FACTORING; FACTORS.

FACTOR ANALYSIS mathematical procedure used to reduce a large amount of data into a structure that can be more easily studied. Factor analysis summarizes information contained in a large number of variables and condenses it into a smaller number of factors containing variables that are interrelated. For example, in a study about a group of women, their characteristics of height, weight, hobbies, activities, and interests might be summarized, using factor analysis, as *size* (height and weight) and *lifestyles* (the combination of hobbies, activities, and interests). In so doing, five variables have been condensed into two separate *factors*.

FACTORIAL
1. in statistics, design of experiment to investigate a number of VARIABLES or FACTORS. *Factorial* design minimizes the number of observations required to test numerous variables. Every observation yields information on each variable.
2. in mathematics, product of all whole numbers up to the number considered. For example, eight factorial, abbreviated 8!, is $8 \times 7 \times 6 \times 5 \times 4 \times 3 \times 2 \times 1$, or 40,320.

FACTORING type of financial service whereby a firm sells or transfers title to its ACCOUNTS RECEIVABLE to a *factoring* company, which then acts as PRINCIPAL, not as AGENT. The receivables are sold with or without RECOURSE. Factors also accommodate clients with *overadvances,* that is, loans in anticipation of sales, which permit inventory building prior to peak selling periods. Factoring has traditionally been most closely associated with the garment industry but is used in other industries as well.

FACTORS
1. economic resources that go into the production of a good. Economic factors include (a) capital, (b) human resources or labor, and (c) property resources including land. Entrepreneurial ability is considered by some a fourth factor since it organizes the other three factors plus innovation while bearing a capital risk; also called *factors of production*.
2. merchants who work on commission.
3. agents who sell goods entrusted to their possession; *see* FACTORING.
4. business intermediaries.

FACTORY OVERHEAD insurance, electricity, janitorial services, and other expenses of a factory that are allocated to goods manufactured when using an ABSORPTION COSTING system; all manufacturing expenses except DIRECT MATERIALS and DIRECT LABOR.

FAIL, FAILURE not meeting minimal requirements, as to *fail* a test; wear out, as a part in a machine *failed*; to not perform as expected.

FAIL TO DELIVER situation where the broker-dealer on the sell side of a contract has not delivered securities to the broker-dealer on the buy side. A *fail to deliver* is usually the result of a broker not receiving delivery from its selling customer. *See also* FAIL TO RECEIVE.

FAIL TO RECEIVE situation where the broker-dealer on the buy side of a contract has not received delivery of securities from the broker-dealer on the sell side. As long as a *fail to receive* exists, the buyer will not make payment for the securities. *See also* FAIL TO DELIVER.

FAILURE ANALYSIS examination performed on a function, project, or interrelationship that failed to fulfill its objective. Failure analysis is an attempt to determine why a goal was not achieved in order to correct the problem for the future.

FAILURE-TO-FILE PENALTY assessed on a tax return not filed by the due date (including extensions), based on the tax not paid by the original due date. The penalty is usually 5% for each month, or part of a month, that the return is late, up to a maximum of 25%. Fraud and accuracy-related penalties are higher.

FAIR ACCESS TO INSURANCE REQUIREMENTS (FAIR) PLAN type of insurance coverage offered to inner-city business owners or homeowners who cannot purchase property insurance through conventional means. Application is made through an agent who represents an insurance company participating in the FAIR plan. If the property is acceptable to the company, insurance will be provided.

FAIR COMPETITION *see* UNFAIR COMPETITION.

FAIR CREDIT BILLING ACT (FCBA) federal law designed to facilitate the handling of credit complaints and eliminate abusive credit billing practices. It applies to OPEN-END CREDIT accounts, such as credit cards and revolving charge accounts. For example, the law requires that complaints about credit bills be acknowledged within 30 days.

FAIR CREDIT REPORTING ACT federal law giving persons the right to see their credit records at credit reporting bureaus. Individuals may challenge and correct negative aspects of their records if it can be proven that there are mistakes.

FAIR HOUSING LAW a federal law that forbids DISCRIMINATION on the basis of race, color, sex, religion, handicap, familial status, or national origin in the selling or renting of homes and apartments. *See* STEERING.

FAIR LABOR STANDARDS ACT (FLSA) federal law enacted in 1938, setting minimum wages per hour and maximum hours of work. It also provides that employees are paid one and a half times their regular hourly wage (*time and a half*) for work beyond 40 hours in a week.

FAIR MARKET RENT amount a property would command if it were now available for lease.

FAIR MARKET VALUE price at which an asset or service passes from a willing seller to a willing buyer. It is assumed that both buyer and seller are rational and have a reasonable knowledge of relevant facts. *See also* MARKET VALUE.

FAIRNESS OPINION professional judgment offered for a fee by an APPRAISER or INVESTMENT BANKER on the fairness of the price being offered in a MERGER, TAKEOVER, or LEVERAGED BUYOUT. For example, if management is trying to take over a company in a leveraged buyout, it will need a *fairness opinion* from an independent source to verify that the price being offered is adequate and in the best interests of shareholders.

FAIR RATE OF RETURN level of profit that a PUBLIC UTILITY is allowed to earn as determined by federal and/or state regulators. Public utility commissions set the *fair rate of return* based on the utility's needs to maintain service to its customers, pay adequate dividends to shareholders and interest to bondholders, and maintain and expand plant and equipment.

FAIR TRADE term used in retailing that refers to an agreement between a manufacturer and retailers that the manufacturer's product be sold at or above an agreed-upon price. In many states, fair-trade agreements were incorporated into and enforceable by state *fair trade acts* or *fair laws*. However, in 1975, Congress passed the Consumer Goods Pricing Act, which prohibits the use of resale price maintenance laws in interstate commerce. This Act has worked to effectively eliminate fair-trade arrangements.

FAIR USE in copyright law, quotation or reproduction of a small portion of copyrighted material (with proper acknowledgment), which does not require the permission of the copyright holder. The amount varies in proportion to the length of the original, the governing theory being that the use should not decrease the market for the original.

FAIR VALUE *see* FAIR MARKET VALUE. In some definitions, *fair value* applies to a situation where a sale would significantly affect the market; *see* BLOCKAGE DISCOUNT.

FALLBACK OPTION
1. in management, reserve organizational position as a fallback in the event another employment position fails.
2. alternative plan devised by management in the event the primary option falters.

FALL OUT OF BED (of a stock's price) drop sharply, usually in response to negative corporate developments. For example, a stock may *fall out of bed* if a TAKEOVER deal falls apart or if profits in the latest period fall far short of expectations.

FALSE ADVERTISING describing goods, services, or real property in a misleading fashion.

FALSIFY to change something that is true. It may be statements, representations, or acts made to deceive others through distortion, such as an unauthorized altering of the contents of a contract.

FAMILIAL STATUS characteristic determined by a person's household type, such as marriage and existing or prospective children. Referred to in the FAIR HOUSING LAW and FAIR CREDIT REPORTING ACT; prohibits denying rights to people under 18 who live with a parent or legal guardian. Pregnant women are specifically covered.

FAMILY AND MEDICAL LEAVE ACT (FMLA) federal law, administered by the U.S. Department of Labor, that requires employers who have 50 or more employees to provide employees with leave for certain medical and family-related reasons.

FAMILY BRANDING marketing strategy where the same brand name is given to a number of products in order to encourage recognition. It eases the introduction of new products, increases market acceptance, and lowers marketing costs.

FAMILY INCOME POLICY insurance policy that provides extra income during the period when children are growing up. This life insurance contract combines *ordinary life* and *decreasing term insurance*. The BENEFICIARY receives income payments to the end of a specific period if the insured dies prior to the end of the period. If still living at the end of the specified period, the policyholder receives the face amount of the policy.

FAMILY LIFE CYCLE various stages in family life resulting in different buying patterns. It takes into account changes in family structure and behavior accompanying progression from birth to death. Some stages are single, newly married without children, and married with children. At each stage, the person plays a different social role and buys symbols of that particular role at the time. For example, the buying pattern with little children is to buy toys.

FAMILY LIMITED PARTNERSHIP a LIMITED PARTNERSHIP whose interests are owned by members of the same family. By this arrangement, gift and estate taxes may be reduced. However, owners will not enjoy the freedom of complete ownership or free transferability of interest provided by other ownership vehicles. *See* MINORITY DISCOUNT.

FAMILY OF FUNDS group of mutual funds managed by the same investment management company. Each fund typically has a different objective; one may be a growth-oriented stock fund, whereas another may be a bond fund or a money market fund. Shareholders in one of the funds can usually switch their money into any of the family's other funds, sometimes at no charge.

FANNIE MAE *see* FEDERAL NATIONAL MORTGAGE ASSOCIATION.

FAQ frequently asked question(s). A NEWSGROUP user's question may be said to be "a(n) FAQ," and he may be referred to "the FAQ," a newsgroup post, FTP file, or Web site where such questions are answered.

FARE charge for transporting a passenger. *See also* COACH FARE.

FARM
1. agricultural operation.
2. technique whereby a salesperson cultivates a specific geographic area.

The definition for federal tax purposes includes livestock, dairy, fish, poultry, fur-bearing animals, truck farms, orchards, plantations, ranches, nurseries, ranges, and structures such as greenhouses used primarily for the raising of agricultural or horticultural commodities.

FARMER MAC *see* FEDERAL AGRICULTURAL MORTGAGE CORPORATION.

FARMER'S HOME ADMINISTRATION (FmHA) agency within the U.S. Department of Agriculture that administers assistance programs for purchasers of homes and farms in small towns and rural areas.

FARM SERVICE AGENCY an agency of the federal government that makes mortgage loans on rural property to farmers and to individuals who provide services to farmers and ranchers. Loans are made at below-market interest rates. Borrowers are required to purchase stock in their local land bank association, which serves as additional security for the loan.

FARM SURPLUS unsold agricultural goods. The government will often purchase certain farm surplus products in order to maintain a profitable price level for the farmers. The storage and use of farm surplus products is a controversial political problem.

FASB *see* FINANCIAL ACCOUNTING STANDARDS BOARD.

FASCISM doctrine; collection of concepts; and dictatorship by government of a country, often involving hostile nationalistic attitudes, racism, and private economic ownership under rigid government control. A *fascist* regime is often militarily belligerent.

FASHION style of conduct or dress being followed by individuals. The marketing person attempts to develop products that meet the current tastes and inclinations of consumers to enhance sales.

FAST TRACKING choosing certain workers for rapid advancement. Management may identify particular workers as *fast trackers* because of certain outstanding characteristics and put them in midcareer training programs while the remaining workers are essentially bypassed.

FAUX PAS social blunder made by an individual. It may be an improper action or a mistake of speech.

FAVORABLE TRADE BALANCE situation where the value of a nation's exports is in excess of the value of its imports. *See also* BALANCE OF PAYMENTS; BALANCE OF TRADE.

FAVORITES Microsoft's term for documents or URLS that have been marked for easy retrieval.

FAX *see* FACSIMILE TRANSMISSION.

FDA *see* FOOD AND DRUG ADMINISTRATION.

FDIC *see* FEDERAL DEPOSIT INSURANCE CORPORATION.

FEASIBILITY STUDY determination of the likelihood that a proposed product or development will fulfill the objectives of a particular investor. For example, a feasibility study for a proposed housing subdivision should: (1) estimate the demand for housing units in the area; (2) estimate the ABSORPTION RATE for the project; (3) discuss legal and other considerations; (4) forecast CASH FLOWS; and (5) approximate investment returns likely to be produced.

FEATHERBEDDING work rules requiring payment to employees for work not done or not needed. One variation is for a union to preserve existing jobs by prohibiting the use of new technology.

FEATHER ONE'S NEST make a comfortable place, as by making provision for retirement. Nowadays, often has the connotation of misappropriating funds entrusted to one's care.

FED, THE *see* FEDERAL RESERVE BOARD.

FEDERAL AGENCY ISSUE or **FEDERAL AGENCY SECURITY** debt instrument issued by an agency of the federal government, such as the Federal National Mortgage Association, the Federal Farm Credit Bank, or the Tennessee Valley Authority (TVA). Though not general obligations of the U.S. Treasury, such securities are sponsored by the government and therefore have high credit ratings.

FEDERAL AGRICULTURAL MORTGAGE CORPORATION federal agency established in 1988 to provide a secondary market for farm mortgage loans. Informally called *Farmer Mac*.

FEDERAL AVIATION ADMINISTRATION (FAA) agency of the U.S. Department of Transportation, charged with regulating air commerce, promoting aviation safety, and overseeing the operation of airports, including air traffic control.

FEDERAL DEFICIT (SURPLUS) shortfall that results when the federal government spends more in a FISCAL YEAR than it receives in revenue. To cover the shortfall, the government borrows from the public by floating long and short-term debt. *See also* GRAMM-RUDMAN-HOLLINGS AMENDMENT.

FEDERAL DEPOSIT INSURANCE CORPORATION (FDIC) independent federal agency, established in 1933, that insures deposits up to $100,000 in member commercial banks. It has its own reserves and can borrow from the U.S. Treasury, and sometimes acts to prevent bank failures, for instance by facilitating bank mergers.

FEDERAL DEFICIT

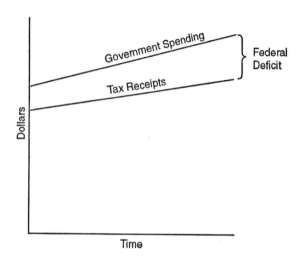

FIGURE 3

FEDERAL ENERGY REGULATORY COMMISSION (FERC) an independent agency that regulates the interstate transmission of electricity, natural gas, and oil. FERC also reviews proposals to build liquefied natural gas (LNG) terminals and interstate natural gas pipelines and also licenses hydropower projects.

FEDERAL ESTATE TAX federal government tax imposed on the ESTATE of a DECEDENT according to the value of that estate. The first step in the computation of the federal estate tax owed is to determine the value of the decedent's GROSS ESTATE. The determination can be made by adding the values of the following assets owned by the decedent at the time of death:

1. property owned outright.
2. gratuitous lifetime transfers but with the stipulation that the decedent retained the income or control over the income.
3. gratuitous lifetime transfers subject to the recipient's surviving the decedent.
4. gratuitous lifetime transfers subject to the decedent's retaining the right to revoke, amend, or alter the gift.
5. ANNUITIES purchased by the decedent that are payable for the lifetime of the named survivor as well as the ANNUITANT.

6. property jointly held in such a manner that another party receives the decedent's interest in that property at the decedent's death because of that party's survivorship.
7. life insurance in which the decedent retained incidents of ownership.
8. life insurance that was payable to the decedent's estate.

The second step in the computation of the federal estate tax owed is to subtract allowable deductions (including bequests to charities, bequests to the surviving spouse, funeral expenses, and other administrative expenses) from the gross estate. This results in the TAXABLE ESTATE. Adjustable taxable gifts are then added to the taxable estate, resulting in the *computational tax base*. The appropriate tax rate is then applied to the computational tax base, resulting in the tentative federal estate tax (certain credits may still be subtracted).

FEDERAL EXPRESS *see* FEDEX.

FEDERAL FARM CREDIT BANK, FEDERAL FARM CREDIT SYSTEM *see* FARM SERVICE AGENCY.

FEDERAL FLOOD INSURANCE coverage made available to residents of a community on a subsidized and nonsubsidized premium rate basis once the governing body of the community qualifies that community for coverage under the National Flood Insurance Act. Residents include business and nonbusiness operations with coverage written on structures and their contents.

FEDERAL FUNDS
1. funds deposited by commercial banks at Federal Reserve Banks, including funds in excess of bank RESERVE REQUIREMENTS. Banks may lend federal funds to each other on an overnight basis at the FEDERAL FUNDS rate to help the borrowing bank satisfy its reserve requirements.
2. money used by the Federal Reserve to pay for purchases of government securities.
3. funds used to settle transactions where there is no FLOAT.

FEDERAL FUNDS RATE interest rate charged by banks with excess reserves at a Federal Reserve district bank to banks needing overnight loans to meet RESERVE REQUIREMENTS. The federal funds rate is the most sensitive indicator of the direction of interest rates, since it is set daily by the market.

FEDERAL HOME LOAN BANK SYSTEM former system that supplied credit reserves for SAVINGS AND LOAN ASSOCIATIONS, cooperative banks, and other mortgage lenders in a manner similar to the Federal Reserve Bank's role with commercial banks.

FEDERAL HOME LOAN MORTGAGE CORPORATION (FHLMC) publicly chartered agency, nicknamed *Freddie Mac*, which buys qualifying residential mortgages from lenders, packages them into new securities backed by those pooled mortgages, provides certain guarantees, and then resells the securities on the open market.

FEDERAL HOUSING ADMINISTRATION (FHA) agency (founded in 1934) within the U.S. Department of Housing and Urban Development that administers many loan, loan guarantee, and loan insurance programs designed to increase the availability of housing.

FEDERAL HOUSING FINANCE BOARD a federal agency created under the FINANCIAL INSTITUTIONS REFORM, RECOVERY AND ENFORCEMENT ACT (FIRREA) to regulate and supervise the 12 district Federal Home Loan Banks. The functions of the Board were the responsibility of the Federal Home Loan Bank Board prior to passage of the Act.

FEDERAL INSURANCE CONTRIBUTIONS ACT (FICA) the federal law that provides for the imposition of the Social Security tax.

FEDERAL INTERMEDIATE CREDIT BANK one of 12 banks that make funds available to production credit associations, commercial banks, agricultural credit corporations, livestock loan companies, and other institutions extending credit to crop farmers and cattle raisers. Each bank's stock is owned by farmers and ranchers.

FEDERAL LAND BANK an agency that makes mortgage loans on rural property to farmers and individuals who provide services to farmers and ranchers. Borrowers are required to purchase stock in their local land bank association that serves as additional security for the loan.

FEDERAL NATIONAL MORTGAGE ASSOCIATION (FNMA) publicly owned, government-sponsored corporation chartered in 1938 to purchase mortgages from lenders and resell them to investors. The agency, known by the nickname *Fannie Mae*, mostly packages mortgages backed by the Federal Housing Administration, but also sells some nongovernmentally backed mortgages. Shares of FNMA itself, known as Fannie Maes, are traded on the New York Stock Exchange.

FEDERAL OPEN MARKET COMMITTEE (FOMC) key committee in the Federal Reserve System, which sets short-term monetary policy for the Fed. The committee comprises the seven governors of the Federal Reserve System, the president of the New York Federal Reserve Bank, and the presidents of four other Federal Reserve Banks. To tighten the money supply, which decreases the amount of money available in the banking system, the Fed sells government securities.

FEDERAL POWER COMMISSION (FPC) *see* FEDERAL ENERGY REGULATORY COMMISSION (FERC).

FEDERAL REGISTER daily publication by the U.S. government that prints the regulations of the various governmental agencies (for example, the Treasury Department, Housing and Urban Development, and Environmental Protection Agency regulations will be published in the *Federal Register*).

FEDERAL RESERVE BANK one of the 12 banks that, with their branches, make up the FEDERAL RESERVE SYSTEM. These banks are located in Boston, New York, Philadelphia, Cleveland, Richmond, Atlanta, Chicago, St. Louis, Minneapolis, Kansas City, Dallas, and San Francisco. The role of each Federal Reserve Bank is to monitor the commercial and savings banks in its region to ensure that they follow FEDERAL RESERVE BOARD regulations and to provide those banks with access to emergency funds from the DISCOUNT WINDOW.

FEDERAL RESERVE BOARD (FRB) governing board of the FEDERAL RESERVE SYSTEM. Its seven members are appointed by the President of the United States, subject to Senate confirmation, and serve 14-year terms. The Board establishes Federal Reserve System policies on such key matters as RESERVE REQUIREMENTS and other bank regulations, sets the DISCOUNT RATE, tightens or loosens the availability of credit in the economy, and regulates the purchase of securities on margin.

FEDERAL RESERVE DISTRICT *see* FEDERAL RESERVE BANK.

FEDERAL RESERVE OPEN MARKET COMMITTEE *see* FEDERAL OPEN MARKET COMMITTEE.

FEDERAL RESERVE SYSTEM (FED) system established by the Federal Reserve Act of 1913 to regulate the U.S. monetary and banking system. The Federal Reserve System comprises 12 regional Federal Reserve Banks, their 25 branches, and all national and state banks that are part of the system. National banks are stockholders of the FEDERAL RESERVE BANK in their region. The Federal Reserve System's main functions are to regulate the national money supply, set RESERVE REQUIREMENTS for member banks, supervise the printing of currency at the mint, act as CLEARINGHOUSE for the transfer of funds throughout the banking system, and examine member banks to make sure they meet various Federal Reserve System regulations.

FEDERAL SAVINGS AND LOAN ASSOCIATIONS federally chartered institutions with a primary responsibility to accept people's savings deposits and provide mortgage loans for residential housing. Their role and scope was broadened by the Depository Institutions Deregulation and Monetary Control Act of 1980. Accounts are insured up to $100,000 by the FDIC.

FEDERAL SAVINGS AND LOAN INSURANCE CORPORATION (FSLIC) agency of the federal government, founded in 1934 and disbanded in 1989, that insured depositors in SAVINGS AND LOAN ASSOCIATIONS against loss of PRINCIPAL. Since 1989 this function has been performed by the FEDERAL DEPOSIT INSURANCE CORPORATION (FDIC).

FEDERAL TAX LIEN lien of the United States on all property and rights to property of a taxpayer who fails to pay a tax for which he is liable to the federal government.

FEDERAL TRADE COMMISSION (FTC) government agency created in 1915, under the Federal Trade Commission Act of 1914, whose purpose is to protect the system of free enterprise and competition in the interests of a strong economy. In the words of the Federal Trade Commission Act, Section 5, the FTC is responsible to "promote free and fair competition in interstate commerce in the interest of the public through prevention of price-fixing agreements, boycotts, combinations in restraint of trade, unfair methods of competition, and unfair and deceptive acts and practices."

FEDERAL UNEMPLOYMENT TAX ACT (FUTA) provides for federal unemployment insurance and is paid by employers. The maximum tax rate is 6.2% on the first $7,000 of wages for 2006. The maximum tax rate can be reduced to a minimum of 0.8% by credits for state unemployment taxes.

FEDEX company (formerly Federal Express) that offers speedy pickup and delivery of letters and parcels.

FED FUNDS *see* FEDERAL FUNDS; FEDERAL FUNDS RATE.

FED WIRE high-speed, computerized communications network that connects all 12 Federal Reserve Banks, their 25 branches, the Federal Reserve Board office in Washington, D.C., U.S. Treasury offices in Washington, D.C., and Chicago, and the Washington, D.C., office of the Commodity Credit Corporation; also spelled *FedWire* and *Fedwire*. The Fed wire has been called the central nervous system of money transfer in the United States. It enables banks to transfer reserve balances from one to another for immediate available credit and to transfer balances for business customers.

FEE
1. in real property, ESTATE of complete ownership that can be sold by the owner or devised to his heirs. *Fee*, FEE SIMPLE, and FEE SIMPLE ABSOLUTE are often used synonymously.
2. cost of professional services, such as *legal fee* or *recording fee*.

FEEDER LINES local and regional airlines or railroads that bring traffic to national carriers.

FEE SIMPLE or **FEE ABSOLUTE** or **FEE SIMPLE ABSOLUTE** absolute ownership of REAL PROPERTY; owner is entitled to the entire property with unconditional power of disposition during his life, and upon his death the property descends to his designated heirs. The only power that can override *fee simple* ownership is that of *eminent domain* (*see* CONDEMNATION).

FENG SHUI (pronounced *fung shway*) ancient Asian art of creating harmony and balance within an environment.

FF&E *see* FURNITURE, FIXTURES, and EQUIPMENT.

FFO *see* FUNDS FROM OPERATIONS.

FHA MORTGAGE LOAN mortgage loan insured by the FEDERAL HOUSING ADMINISTRATION (FHA). Section 203(b) is the most popular program.

FIAT MONEY currency that is made legal tender by government law or regulation. In the United States, Federal Reserve Notes are *fiat money*. Fiat money always has a legal value that exceeds its intrinsic value.

FIBER OPTICS tiny cylindrical strands of glass that carry light rather than electrical energy. Fiber-optic cable is increasingly used for long-distance phone lines because it can carry large amounts of data, is not subject to crosstalk or electromagnetic noise, and cannot be tapped into without producing a noticeable drop in signal level.

FICA *see* SOCIAL SECURITY ACT OF 1935.

FICO SCORE a measure of borrower credit risk commonly used by creditors, including mortgage loan originators. The score, developed by Fair Isaac Corporation, is based on applicants' credit history and how much they use credit. Expressed as a number between 300 and 850, the score determines not only whether the loan is approved, but also what types of terms are offered by the lender. All three national CREDIT BUREAUS (Equifax, Experían, and TransUnion) now report FICO scores.

FIDELITY BOND coverage that guarantees that the insurance company will pay the insured business or individual for money or other property lost because of dishonest acts of its bonded employees, either named or by positions; also called *blanket fidelity bond*. The bond covers all dishonest acts, such as larceny, theft, embezzlement, forgery, misappropriation, wrongful abstraction, or willful misapplication, whether employees act alone or as a team.

FIDUCIARY person, company, or association holding assets in TRUST for a BENEFICIARY. The fiduciary is charged with the responsibility of investing the money wisely for the beneficiary's benefit. Some examples of fiduciaries are EXECUTORS of wills and estates, RECEIVERS in bankruptcy, TRUSTEES, and those who administer the assets of underage or incompetent beneficiaries.

FIDUCIARY BOND *see* JUDICIAL BOND.

FIELD group of adjacent characters in a computer word- or data-processing system. For example, in a company payroll system the information about a single individual can be stored as one record. Each record will be divided into several fields. One field will contain the employee's name, another field the Social Security number, a third field the pay rate, and so on.

FIELD STAFF company employees whose work is in the marketplace outside of the company office and who are thus said to work *in the Field*. In retailing, the field staff are the manufacturer's representatives, also known as DETAIL PERSONS.

FIFO *see* FIRST IN, FIRST OUT.

FIFTEEN-YEAR MORTGAGE a fixed-rate, level-payment mortgage loan with a maturity of fifteen years. Beginning in the 1980s, *fifteen-year mortgages* became popular as a way to reduce the amount of interest paid over the life of the mortgage loan. Although the monthly payment is somewhat higher than that of a comparable thirty-year loan, the interest savings are substantial.

FILE
1. to place material in a given order for accessible retrieval. Items may be arranged alphabetically, numerically, chronologically, geographically, or by subject.
2. collection of stored information. The data in a computer file is stored in such a way that the computer can read information from the file or write information to the file. Personal computers can store files on magnetic tape, floppy disks, or hard disk.
3. to formally submit a document, especially to an office, an agency, or a unit of the legal system. For example, one files an expense account.

FILE SERVER a computer on a LOCAL AREA NETWORK that provides network users access to shared data and program files. Often a larger, faster computer than the users' WORKSTATIONS.

FILE TRANSFER the process of moving or transmitting a computer file from one location to another, as between two programs or from one computer to another.

FILE TRANSFER PROTOCOL (FTP) an Internet protocol that permits transferring files between computers via the Internet.

FILING STATUS for tax purposes, governs the form of return used, which may be one of the following:
1. Single Individual.
2. Married Individuals Filing Jointly and Surviving Spouse.
3. Separate Returns, Married Persons.
4. Heads of Households.

FILL OR KILL (FOK) order to buy or sell a particular security that, if not executed immediately, is canceled.

FILTERING DOWN process whereby, over time, a housing unit or neighborhood is occupied by progressively lower-income residents. For example, many older residences near the downtown of big cities were once occupied by the upper classes, but have filtered down to the relatively poor. At some point in the filtering process, many large houses may be converted into rented MULTIFAMILY HOUSING.

FINAL ASSEMBLY assembling all components into a finished product. In an automobile *final assembly* plant the power train is installed in the chassis together with the automobile body components to make a completed automobile.

FINAL GOODS goods, such as consumer goods, that are not currently used up in the production of other goods.

FINANCE CHARGE any charge for an extension of credit. INTEREST and DISCOUNT POINTS are two major types of finance charge.

FINANCE COMPANY company engaged in making loans to individuals or businesses. Unlike a bank, it does not receive deposits but rather obtains its financing from banks, institutions, and other MONEY MARKET sources. Generally, finance companies fall into three categories: (1) consumer finance companies; (2) sales finance companies; and (3) commercial finance companies. *See also* CAPTIVE FINANCE COMPANY.

FINANCIAL ACCOUNTING accounting system that provides BALANCE SHEET and INCOME STATEMENT results. *See also* MANAGERIAL ACCOUNTING.

FINANCIAL ACCOUNTING STANDARDS BOARD (FASB) independent board responsible for establishing and interpreting GENERALLY ACCEPTED ACCOUNTING PRINCIPLES (GAAP). It was formed in 1973 to succeed and continue the activities of the Accounting Principles Board (APB).

FINANCIAL ADVERTISING ADVERTISING geared to the world of finance, such as Wall Street brokerage firms, banks, or insurance companies. Typical products in financial advertising are publicly offered financial products such as mutual fund shares or limited partnership shares. The Securities and Exchange Commission (SEC) enforces strict legal regulations in regard to promotional advertising of public offerings of securities and requires some amount of MANDATORY COPY on most other products.

FINANCIAL ADVISER professional adviser offering financial counsel. Some financial advisers charge a fee and earn commissions on the products they recommend to implement their advice. Other advisers only charge fees and do not sell any products or accept commissions. Some financial advisers are generalists, while others specialize in specific areas, such as investing, insurance, estate planning, or taxes.

FINANCIAL ANALYSIS analysis of the FINANCIAL STATEMENT of a company.

FINANCIAL ASSETS assets in the form of STOCKS, BONDS, rights, certificates, bank balances, etc., as distinguished from tangible, physical assets. For example, REAL PROPERTY is a physical asset, but shares in a REAL ESTATE INVESTMENT TRUST (REIT) or the stock or bonds of a company that held property as an investment would be *financial assets*.

FINANCIAL FEASIBILITY the ability of a proposed land use or change of land use to justify itself from an economic point of view. *Financial feasibility* is one test of the HIGHEST AND BEST USE of land, but not the only test. Nor does the financial feasibility of a project make it the most rewarding use of the land.

FINANCIAL FUTURE FUTURES CONTRACT based on a *financial instrument*. Such contracts usually move under the influence of interest rates. As rates rise, contracts fall in value; as rates fall, contracts gain in value. Examples of instruments underlying financial futures contracts are U.S. Treasury bills and notes, foreign currencies, and certificates of deposit.

FINANCIAL INSTITUTION institution that collects funds from the public to place in financial assets such as stocks, bonds, money market instruments, bank deposits, or loans. Depository institutions (banks, savings and loan associations, savings banks, and credit unions) pay interest on deposits and invest the deposit money mostly in loans. Nondepository institutions (insurance companies and pension plans) collect money by selling insurance policies or receiving employer contributions, invest the money, and pay it out for insurance claims or for retirement benefits.

FINANCIAL INSTITUTIONS REFORM, RECOVERY AND ENFORCEMENT ACT (FIRREA) federal law passed in 1989 that restructured the regulatory and deposit insurance apparatus dealing with savings and loan associations and changed the rules under which federally regulated S&Ls operate. *See also* FEDERAL HOUSING FINANCE BOARD; RESOLUTION TRUST CORPORATION (RTC).

FIRREA was intended to address the major problem of failing S&Ls due to mounting nonperforming loans held in portfolio, as well as to make reforms that would prevent the problem from recurring. Often referred to as the "S&L bailout," the law represents a large expenditure of federal funds to pay off depositors at failed associations. The law also created the RESOLUTION TRUST CORPORATION, which is charged with managing and liquidating the assets of associations seized by the government. The FSLIC was abolished by the law, and its insurance and regulatory responsibilities were brought under the FDIC, which also insures commercial banks.

FINANCIAL INTERMEDIARY commercial bank, savings and loan association, mutual savings bank, credit union, or other INTERMEDIARY that smooths the flow of funds between *savings surplus* units, which are individuals and businesses that save, and *savings deficit* units, which are individuals and businesses that need credit.

FINANCIAL LEASE lease in which the service provided by the LESSOR to the LESSEE is limited to financing the property. All other responsibilities related to the possession of property, such as maintenance, insurance, and taxes, are borne by the lessee. A financial lease is likely to be treated by the IRS as though it were a loan.

FINANCIAL LEVERAGE *see* LEVERAGE.

FINANCIAL MANAGEMENT RATE OF RETURN (FMRR) method of measuring the performance of real estate investments that is a variation of the INTERNAL-RATE-OF-RETURN (IRR) method.

FINANCIAL MARKET market for the exchange of CAPITAL and CREDIT in the economy. Examples of financial markets are stock markets, bond markets, commodities markets, and foreign exchange markets. *See also* CAPITAL MARKET; MONEY MARKET.

FINANCIAL PLAN strategy to meet short- or long-term financial objectives. Financial planning is essential for businesses and individuals.

FINANCIAL PLANNER professional who analyzes personal financial circumstances and prepares a program to meet financial needs and objectives. Financial planners, who may be accountants, bankers, lawyers, insurance agents, real estate or securities brokers, or independent practitioners, should have knowledge in the areas of wills and estate planning, retirement planning, taxes, insurance, family budgeting, debt management, and investments.

Leading financial planning designations include the following:

1. **CFP** (Certified Financial Planner) has passed various courses in such areas as investments and estate planning and passed a comprehensive examination on these topics. Required to have three years of work experience and to participate in continuing education courses.

2. **CPA/PFS** (Certified Public Accountant/Personal Financial Specialist). The CPA must pass a rigorous exam in taxes and accounting and be licensed in the state where he or she practices. The PFS is a designation given to accountants whose annual practice has included 750 hours of financial planning over three years, who pass a test covering topics such as retirement planning, and who participate in continuing education courses.

3. **ChFC** (Chartered Financial Consultant) has passed a financial services curriculum, with emphasis on life insurance. Must have three years of work experience and participate in continuing education courses.

FINANCIAL POSITION status of a firm's assets, liabilities, and equity accounts as of a certain time, as shown on its FINANCIAL STATEMENT; also called *financial condition*.

FINANCIAL PYRAMID

1. risk structure many investors aim for in spreading their investments among low-, medium-, and high-risk vehicles. In a financial pyramid, the largest part of the investor's assets is in safe, liquid investments that provide a decent return. At the top of the financial pyramid, where only a small amount of money is committed, are high-risk ventures that have a slight chance of success, but that will provide substantial rewards if they succeed.

2. acquisition of holding company assets through financial leverage. *Financial pyramid* is not to be confused with fraudulent selling schemes, sometimes called *pyramiding* or *pyramid distribution*.

FINANCIAL STATEMENT written record of the financial status of an individual, association, or business organization. The financial statement includes a BALANCE SHEET and an INCOME STATEMENT (or *operating statement* or *profit and loss statement*) and may also include a statement of changes in WORKING CAPITAL and net worth.

FINANCIAL STRUCTURE makeup of the right-hand side of a company's BALANCE SHEET, which includes all the ways its assets are financed, such as trade accounts payable and short-term borrowings as well as long-term debt and ownership equity. *Financial structure* is distinguished from CAPITAL STRUCTURE, which includes only long-term debt and equity.

FINANCIAL SUPERMARKET company that offers a wide range of financial services under one roof. For example, some large retail organizations offer stock insurance and real estate brokerage as well as banking services.

FINANCING borrowing money. *See also* CREATIVE FINANCING.

FINDER'S FEE
In general: fee paid to an individual or company whose function is to bring together the parties involved in a business deal. The *finder* will often serve as an intermediary until the deal is consummated. The fee is usually a percentage of either the profit created by the deal or the value of the deal, but it may also be a flat rate paid by one or all of the parties involved.
Advertising: fee paid by an advertising agency to the individual or firm responsible for bringing a large account into the agency.

FINISHED GOODS products or goods that have been completely assembled or built; also called *finished products*. The goods are now ready for the marketplace.

FINISH OUT *see* TENANT FINISH-OUT ALLOWANCE.

FIRE discharge or terminate (an employee). *See also* SACK.

FIRE INSURANCE—STANDARD FIRE POLICY policy known as the *165-line policy* because of the standard form used in most states. The policy has four sections:
1. DECLARATIONS—description and location of property, insured amount, name of insured.
2. *insuring agreements*—premium amount, obligations of the insured, actions the insured must take in the event of loss and resultant claim.
3. *conditions*—describe what suspends or restricts the coverage, such as an increase in the hazard with the knowledge of the insured.
4. EXCLUSIONS—perils not covered under the policy, such as enemy attack, including action taken by military force in resisting actual or impending enemy attack.

FIREPROOF having all exposed surfaces constructed of noncombustible materials or protected by such materials. *See also* FIRE-RESISTIVE.

FIRE-RESISTIVE capable of withstanding exposure to flame of a specified intensity or for a specified time. *See also* FIREPROOF.

FIRE-RESISTIVE CONSTRUCTION use of engineering-approved masonry or fire-resistive materials for exterior walls, floors, and roofs to reduce the severity of a potential fire and lower premium rates.

FIREWALL software or hardware that limits certain kinds of access to a computer from a NETWORK or other outside source. Commonly used to thwart HACKERS and limit VIRUS infection.

FIRM
1. general term for a business, corporation, partnership, or proprietorship. Legally, however, *firm* refers only to a nonincorporated business.
2. solidity with which an agreement is made. For example, a FIRM ORDER with a manufacturer or a *firm bid* for a stock at a particular price means that the order or bid is assured.

FIRM COMMITMENT in securities underwriting, arrangement whereby INVESTMENT BANKERS make outright purchases from the issuer of securities to be offered to the public; also called *firm commitment underwriting*. *See also* BEST EFFORT.

FIRM OFFER offer stating in writing that it is irrevocable for a set time. As long as it is stipulated in a signed writing that the offer is to be held open, it need not be supported by CONSIDERATION to be binding.

FIRM ORDER
Commerce: written or verbal order that has been confirmed and is not subject to cancellation.
Securities: (1) order to buy or sell for the proprietary account of the broker-dealer firm; (2) buy or sell order not conditional upon the customer's confirmation.

FIRM QUOTE securities industry term referring to any ROUND-LOT bid or offer price of a security stated by a market maker and not identified as a *nominal*, or *subject*, *quote* (which requires further negotiation or review).

FIRREA *see* FINANCIAL INSTITUTIONS REFORM, RECOVERY and ENFORCEMENT ACT.

FIRST CALL Boston-based global investment research service providing research opinion and data on over 7,000 companies from more than 400 brokers; owned by Thomson Financial.

FIRST-CLASS MAIL class of mail service that receives quick handling and delivery, free forwarding, and is not subject to opening for postal inspection. Letters, postcards, bills, and personal correspondence must be sent by first-class mail. *See also* PRIORITY MAIL.

FIRST IN, FIRST OUT (FIFO) method of inventory valuation in which cost of goods sold is charged with the cost of raw materials, semi-finished goods, and finished goods purchased "first" and in which inventory contains the most recently purchased materials. In times of rapid inflation, FIFO inflates profits, since the least expensive inventory is charged against cost of current sales, resulting in *inventory profits*.

FIRST LIEN debt recorded first against a property. *See also* FIRST MORTGAGE.

FIRST-LINE MANAGEMENT supervisors on an organizational level immediately above nonmanagerial workers. First-line managers primarily oversee performance on line tasks. Some typical titles associated with supervisory positions are *foreman, shift boss, sergeant, section head*, and *ward nurse*.

FIRST MORTGAGE MORTGAGE that has priority as a lien over all other mortgages. In cases of foreclosure, the first mortgage will be satisfied before other mortgages. *See also* JUNIOR MORTGAGE; SECOND MORTGAGE.

FIRST REFUSAL RIGHT *see* RIGHT OF FIRST REFUSAL.

FISCAL pertaining to public finance and financial transactions; belonging to the public treasury.

FISCAL AGENT usually a bank or a trust company that handles such matters as disbursing funds for dividend payments, redeeming bonds and coupons, handling taxes related to the issue of bonds, and paying rents.

FISCALIST economist who prefers that government affect the economy by raising and lowering taxation and/or government spending; *contrast with* MONETARIST.

FISCAL POLICY use of government spending and taxation policies to achieve desired goals. *See also* KEYNESIAN ECONOMICS; MONETARY POLICY.

FISCAL TAX YEAR
1. A regular fiscal tax year is a 12-month period that ends on the last day of any month except December.
2. A *52/53-week fiscal tax year* varies from 52 to 53 weeks and ends on a particular day of the week (for example, the last Friday in September).

FISCAL YEAR any continuous 12-month period used by a business or government as its accounting period. *See also* CALENDAR YEAR.

FISHER EFFECT an economic relation between interest rates and inflation rates. Interest rates reflect expected inflation rates.

FIT situation where the features of a particular product, such as an investment, match the requirements of a buyer.

FIT INVESTMENT *see* FIT.

FIXATION setting of a present or future price of a commodity. For example, twice each business day the price of gold is *fixed* in London at a price arrived at after assessing market forces of supply and demand.

FIXED AND VARIABLE RATE ALLOWANCES (FAVR) allowable method for computing a business automobile mileage allowance that is not reported as wages on Form W-2. An employer may give an employee a cents-per-mile rate to cover gasoline and other operating costs, plus a flat amount to cover depreciation and insurance. *See also* STANDARD MILEAGE METHOD.

FIXED ANNUITY investment contract sold by an insurance company that guarantees fixed payments, either for life or for a specified period, to an annuitant. *See also* VARIABLE ANNUITY.

FIXED ASSET in accounting, property used for production of goods and services, such as plant and machinery, buildings, land, and mineral resources. *See also* CURRENT ASSET; INTANGIBLE ASSET.

FIXED BENEFITS payment to a beneficiary that does not vary. An example is a fixed monthly retirement income benefit of $800 paid to a retired employee.

FIXED CHARGE charge that remains the same regardless of the extent of use. For example, rent and property insurance are often fixed charges that are unaffected by the production level of a factory. *See also* FIXED COST.

FIXED-CHARGE COVERAGE ratio of PROFITS before payment of interest and income taxes to INTEREST on bonds and other contractual long-term debt. It indicates how many times interest charges have been earned by the corporation on a pretax basis.

FIXED COST cost that remains constant regardless of sales volume. Fixed costs include salaries of executives, interest expense, rent, depreciation, and insurance expenses. They contrast with *variable costs* (direct labor, materials costs) and *semivariable costs*, which vary, but not necessarily in direct relation to sales.

FIXED DISK *see* HARD DISK.

FIXED EXCHANGE RATE set rate of exchange between the currencies of countries. At the Bretton Woods International Monetary Conference in 1944, a system of fixed exchange rates was set up, which existed until the early 1970s, when a FLOATING EXCHANGE RATE system was adopted.

FIXED EXPENSES in the operation of a business, those that remain the same regardless of production or sales. *Contrast with* VARIABLE EXPENSES.

FIXED FEE set price for the completion of a project. For a contractor, setting a fixed fee entails the risk of absorbing higher than anticipated costs before a project is completed, whereas for the customer a fixed fee is more easily budgeted.

FIXED-INCOME income that is not adjusted to reflect changes in prices. Interest on most bonds and income from most ANNUITIES and some pensions are *fixed incomes*.

FIXED-INCOME INVESTMENT security that pays a fixed rate of return. This usually refers to government, corporate, or municipal bonds, which pay a fixed rate of interest until the bonds mature, and to preferred stock, which pays a fixed dividend.

FIXED-POINT NUMBER number in which the decimal point is fixed. For example, the population of a city can be represented by a fixed-point number (e.g., 25,000) with no digits to the right of the decimal point. An amount of money in U.S. currency can be represented by a fixed-point number (e.g., $10.50) with two digits to the right of the decimal point. *See also* FLOATING-POINT NUMBER.

FIXED PREMIUM payment for coverage that remains throughout the same premium-paying period.

FIXED-PRICE CONTRACT type of CONTRACT where the price is pre-set and invariable, regardless of the actual costs of production. *See also* COST-PLUS CONTRACT.

FIXED-RATE LOAN type of LOAN in which the interest rate does not fluctuate with general market conditions. Examples include fixed-rate mortgage loans, also known as *conventional mortgages*, and consumer installment loans. *See also* ADJUSTABLE-RATE MORTGAGE (ARM).

FIXTURE something that was once PERSONAL PROPERTY, but is attached to REAL PROPERTY in such a way that its removal would damage the property, and hence is considered part of the realty. Fixtures may be written off over a MACRS 7-year recovery class, using the 200% declining-balance method.

FLAME
1. (noun) a public post or E-MAIL message expressing a strong opinion or criticism of another post or e-mail.
2. (verb tr.) send or post such a message to someone.

FLAT
1. apartment, generally on one level.
2. LEVEL-PAYMENT MORTGAGE or flat lease requirement.
3. without spark or motivation, bubble, or sizzle.
4. in bond trading, without ACCRUED INTEREST. Issues in DEFAULT and INCOME BONDS are normally quoted and traded *flat*.
5. inventory of a market maker with a net zero position, that is, neither LONG nor SHORT.

6. position of an UNDERWRITER whose account is completely sold.
7. unchanged, as in a flat line on a graph. Thus, earnings the same as last year's may be called "flat."

FLAT RATE
In general: per unit price that remains the same regardless of the quantity purchased or other considerations. Many products are sold at variable rates that decline as the number of units purchased increases. Paper is usually sold at a variable rate. *See also* VARIABLE PRICING.
Advertising: fixed price of nondiscounted advertising space or time.
Direct marketing: fixed cost for a *list rental* regardless of the number of names remaining after a *merge/purge* is performed. A flat rate is usually used only for small lists typically of fewer than 10,000 names.

FLAT SCALE in industry, labor term denoting a uniform rate of pay that makes no allowance for volume, frequency, or other factors.

FLAT TAX tax applied at the same rate to all levels of income. It is often discussed as an alternative to the PROGRESSIVE TAX. Proponents of a flat tax argue that people able to retain larger portions of higher income would have added incentive to earn, thus stimulating the economy.

FLEA MARKET an open-air display of goods, usually secondhand.

FLEET FACTORS landmark 1990 court decision regarding a lender's potential exposure to liability for environmental cleanup if the lender acquires the property by foreclosure.

FLEXIBLE BUDGET statement of projected revenue and expenditure based on various levels of production. It shows how costs vary with different rates of output or at different levels of sales volume.

FLEXIBLE MANUFACTURING computer-controlled manufacturing process providing flexibility in adapting machinery to various products. In this process a computer can easily adapt equipment for a process permitting flexibility in manufacturing numerous products. This permits rapid production customization to customer needs at very competitive costs.

FLEXIBLE SPENDING ACCOUNT plan under which employees may make tax-free salary-reduction contributions to a medical or dependent care reimbursement plan, or to purchase group health insurance or life insurance coverage on a pretax basis. *See also* CAFETERIA BENEFIT PLAN.

FLEXTIME, FLEXITIME daily work system where the employee can decide when to report for work and when to leave, as long as the minimum number of hours are worked. For example, a worker could work 7 A.M. to 3 P.M. or 9 A.M. to 5 P.M.

FLIGHT TO QUALITY moving capital to the safest possible investment to protect oneself from loss during an unsettling period in the market.

FLIPPING buying and selling real estate or securities, especially IPOs, within a very short period.

FLOAT
   Banking: checks in transit between banks and not yet paid; checks in the process of COLLECTION that remain conditional credits in a depositor's checking account until the checks are paid to the bank.
   Securities: to sell a new issue of securities. *See also* FLOTATION COST.
   Insurance: the accumulation of insurance premiums collected prior to losses incurred.

FLOATER coverage for property that moves from location to location either on a scheduled or unscheduled basis. If the floater covers scheduled property, coverage is listed for each item. If a floater covers unscheduled property, all property is covered for the same limits of insurance.

FLOATING AN ISSUE *see* NEW ISSUE; UNDERWRITE.

FLOATING CURRENCY EXCHANGE RATE movement of a foreign currency exchange rate in response to changes in the market forces of supply and demand; also known as *flexible exchange rate.* Currencies strengthen or weaken based on a nation's reserves of hard currency and gold, its international trade balance, its rate of inflation and interest rates, and the general strength of its economy. The country itself does not engage in policies that would affect this value. *See also* FIXED EXCHANGE RATE.

FLOATING DEBT short-term obligation of a business that is continuously refinanced, such as bank loans due in one year and COMMERCIAL PAPER. Government floating debt consists of Treasury bills and short-term Treasury notes. Long-term debt, such as Treasury bonds, is referred to as FUNDED DEBT.

FLOATING-POINT NUMBER number in which the decimal point is allowed to float. A floating-point number is represented by a base and an exponent. For example, in the floating-point number 4.65 E 4, 4.65 is the base and 4 is the exponent. The expression 4.65 E 4 means 4.65×10^4, or 46,500. A floating-point number is like a number written in scientific notation. *See also* FIXED-POINT NUMBER.

FLOATING-RATE NOTE DEBT INSTRUMENT with a variable interest rate. Interest adjustments are made periodically, often every six months, and are tied to a MONEY-MARKET index such as Treasury bill rates. Floating-rate notes usually have a MATURITY of about five years.

FLOATING SECURITIES
   1. securities bought for the purpose of making a quick profit on resale and held in a broker's name.
   2. outstanding stock of a corporation that is traded on an exchange.
   3. unsold units of a newly issued security.

FLOATING SUPPLY
  Bonds: total dollar amount of municipal bonds in the hands of speculators and dealers that is for sale at any particular time.
  Stocks: number of shares of a stock available for purchase.

FLOOD INSURANCE insurance policy that covers property damage due to natural flooding. Flood insurance is offered by private insurers, but is encouraged and subsidized by the federal government.

FLOODPLAIN level land area subject to periodic flooding from a contiguous body of water. Floodplains are delineated by the expected frequency of flooding. For example, an *annual floodplain* is expected to flood once each year. The Army Corps of Engineers has floodplain maps for most metropolitan areas.

FLOOR-AREA RATIO arithmetic relationship of the total square feet of a building to the square footage of the land area:

$$\text{Floor-area ratio} = \frac{\text{building area}}{\text{land area}}$$

FLOOR DUTY in sales, especially in a real estate brokerage firm, a period of time that a salesperson is required, by office policy, to be in the office to accept phone calls and visits from potential clients who have no previous relationship. Rotated among salespersons.

FLOOR LOAN minimum that a lender is willing to advance. *See also* GAP LOAN.

FLOOR PLAN arrangement of rooms in a building. Also, one-plane diagram of that arrangement.

FLOOR PLAN INSURANCE coverage for a lender who has accepted property on the floor of a merchant as security for a loan. If the merchandise is damaged or destroyed the lender is indemnified. The policy is on an ALL RISK basis.

FLOPPY DISK a thin, flexible plastic disk with a magnetic coating, now usually encased in rigid plastic. Once one of the most popular devices for storage and transfer of computer data, it has now been generally supplanted by COMPACT DISCS and USB DRIVES, both of which have much greater capacity and provide faster access. Data is also increasingly transferred over networks, including the Internet.

FLOTATION (FLOATATION) COST cost of issuing new stocks or bonds.

FLOWCHART diagram consisting of symbols and words that completely describe an algorithm, that is, how to solve a problem. Each step in the flowchart is followed by an arrow that indicates which step to do next. A flowchart can also track a procedure, such as the steps involved in manufacturing a product.

FLOWCHART

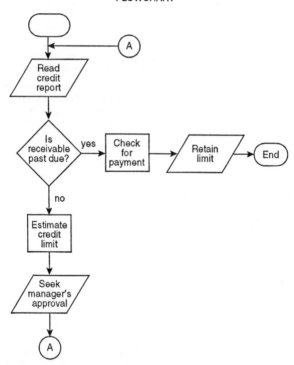

FIGURE 4

FLOW OF FUNDS

Economics: the way funds in the national economy are transferred from savings surplus units to savings deficit units through FINANCIAL INTERMEDIARIES.

Municipal bonds: statement found in the bond resolutions of MUNICIPAL REVENUE BONDS showing the priorities by which municipal revenue will be applied.

FLUCTUATION

1. change in prices or interest rates, either up or down. *Fluctuation* may refer to either slight or dramatic changes in the prices of stocks, bonds, or commodities.
2. ups and downs in the economy.

FLUCTUATION LIMIT limit placed by the commodity exchanges on the daily ups and downs of futures prices. If a commodity reaches its limit, it may not trade any further that day. *See also* LIMIT UP, LIMIT DOWN.

FLY-BY-NIGHT originally referred to a swindler who fled hurriedly from a business situation after his modus operandi had been discovered by the locals; now refers to a shady business, often operating out of a post office box or accommodation address, that cannot be located when its merchandise or product proves unsatisfactory.

FLY-OUT MENU a secondary MENU that appears to the side when you click a menu item.

FNMA *see* FEDERAL NATIONAL MORTGAGE ASSOCIATION.

FOB *see* FREE ON BOARD.

FOCUSED FACTORY form of production limited to a very small number of products for a particular target market. This requires a smaller investment and allows a greater degree of expertise to be developed than a more diversified manufacturing operation.

FOCUS GROUP a form of market research in which a group of people (typically 5–10) are asked about their attitude toward a product, concept, advertisement, idea, or packaging. Can provide feedback about new or proposed products. A recent innovation is to conduct an online focus group.

FOIA *see* FREEDOM OF INFORMATION ACT.

FOLDER the term used by Apple for what in DOS was called a DIRECTORY. Windows 95 and later versions adopted this terminology. Programs or files are stored in folders just as one would store documents in folders in a file cabinet.

FOLLOW-UP LETTER sales letter sent to someone who has made an inquiry inviting the inquirer to make a purchase; part of the *inquiry conversion* process. This process is generally used for expensive items requiring a lot of information and thought before a purchase decision is made, such as an automobile or an insurance policy.

FONT the set of characters in one size and style of a TYPEFACE. For example, Garamond is a typeface, while 14-point Garamond Italic is a *font*.

FOOD AND DRUG ADMINISTRATION (FDA) administrative agency of the U.S. Department of Health and Human Services that regulates the safety and quality of foodstuffs, pharmaceuticals, cosmetics, and medical devices.

FOOTER bottom margin of printed document, which repeats on every page and, according to a specific computer program, can include text, pictures, automatic consecutive page numbers, date, and time. *See also* HEADER.

FOOTING totaling a column of numbers. *See also* CROSS-FOOTING.

FOOTSIE popular name for the *Financial Times'* FT-SE 100 Index, a MARKET CAPITALIZATION-weighted index of 100 blue-chip stocks traded on the London Stock Exchange.

FORBEARANCE a policy of restraint in taking legal action to remedy a DEFAULT or other breach of contract, generally in the hope that the default will be cured, given additional time.

FORCED SALE sale that the seller must make immediately, without opportunity to find a buyer who will pay the reasonable worth of the item. Examples include property sold by FORECLOSURE, in BANK-RUPTCY, or under DURESS.

FORCED SAVING when consumers are not allowed to spend all of their incomes upon current consumption. It can be self-imposed (savings plan), imposed by CONTRACT (whole-life insurance), or by government (rationing).

FORCE MAJEURE an unavoidable cause of delay or of failure to perform a CONTRACT obligation on time.

FORECAST, FORECASTING estimating future trends. Stock market forecasters try to predict the direction of the stock market by relying on technical data of trading activity and fundamental statistics on the direction of the economy. Economic forecasters try to foretell the strength of the economy, often by utilizing complex ECONOMETRIC models as tools to make specific predictions of future levels of inflation, interest rates, and employment. *See also* PREDICTION; PROJECTION.

FORECLOSURE termination of all rights of a MORTGAGOR or the GRANTEE in the property covered by a mortgage. *Statutory foreclosure* is effected without recourse to courts but must conform to laws (statutes). *Strict foreclosure* forever bars equity of redemption. The foreclosed property may be sold to satisfy a debt. If a foreclosure sale fails to repay the debt, the creditor may obtain a DEFICIENCY JUDGMENT. *See also* DEFAULT.

FOREIGN CORPORATION
1. corporation chartered under the laws of a state other than the one in which it conducts business. Because of inevitable confusion with the term *alien corporation*, *out-of-state* corporation is preferred.
2. corporation organized under the laws of a foreign country, i.e., ALIEN CORPORATION.

FOREIGN CURRENCY TRANSLATION process of expressing amounts denominated in one currency in terms of a second currency, by using the exchange rate between the currencies. Assets and liabilities are translated at the current exchange rate at the balance sheet date. Income statement items are typically translated at the weighted-average exchange rate for the period.

FOREIGN DIRECT INVESTMENT
1. investment in the United States by foreign citizens; often involves majority stock ownership of an enterprise.
2. joint ventures between foreign and U.S. companies.

FOREIGN EXCHANGE instruments employed in making payments between countries—paper currency, notes, checks, bills of exchange, and electronic notifications of international debits and credits.

FOREIGN INCOME income from sources outside the United States. *See also* BLOCKED INCOME; FOREIGN EARNED INCOME EXCLUSION; FOREIGN INVESTMENT COMPANY; PASSIVE FOREIGN INVESTMENT COMPANY.

FOREIGN INVESTMENT investment by citizens and government of one country in industries of another; also investment within a country by foreigners. The income tax treatment of foreign investment income is often governed by TAX TREATIES between the country of the investment owner and the country where the investment is located. *See also* FOREIGN INVESTMENT COMPANY.

FOREIGN TAX CREDIT credit allowed against U.S. income taxes for foreign taxes paid. The credit can be used only to lower U.S. taxes on *income earned overseas*. A foreign tax credit limitation is computed by multiplying the U.S. tax liability prior to the credit by the ratio of foreign taxable income to total taxable income (U.S. and foreign).

FOREIGN TAX DEDUCTION individuals may deduct foreign income taxes paid or accrued, or may apply the taxes as a credit against U.S. income tax (*see* FOREIGN TAX CREDIT).

FOREIGN TRADE ZONE separate, enclosed place near a port where goods may be brought for storage, inspection, packaging, or other processes; also called *free trade zone*. No duties are assessed while the goods are in the foreign trade zone.

FORENSIC ACCOUNTANT person who applies accounting principles, theories, and discipline to facts and hypotheses at issue in a legal dispute. The forensic accountant melds the skills of an investigator and accountant to look behind the numbers and the financial statements. For example, a forensic accountant may be used to detect the ploys used by people to hide their earnings and assets during a divorce.

FORFEITABLE with reference to a PENSION or a PROFIT-SHARING PLAN, benefits in which a participant has no ownership rights until length-of-service or performance requirements for VESTING have been met.

FORFEIT PENALTY *see* INVESTMENT PENALTY.

FORFEITURE permanent loss of PROPERTY for failure to comply with the law; the DIVESTITURE of the title of property, without compensation, for a DEFAULT or an offense.

FORGERY preparing or altering writings or paintings with the intention of prejudicing the rights of others.

FORM model of a legal document containing the phrases and *words of art* needed to make the document technically correct for procedural purposes.

FORM 8-K form a public company files with the Securities and Exchange Commission when an event deemed material requires public disclosure. For example, a sudden and drastic lawsuit contingency or a change in auditors.

FORM 10-K detailed annual filing required by the Securities and Exchange Commission of every issuer of a registered security, every exchange-listed company, and any company with 500 or more shareholders or $1 million or more in gross assets. The 10-K is more detailed, but otherwise similar, to a firm's ANNUAL REPORT.

FORM 10-Q quarterly report required by the Securities and Exchange Commission of companies with listed securities. It is less comprehensive than the FORM 10-K annual report and does not require that figures be audited.

FORM 1040, 1040A, 1040EZ individual U.S. income tax return; generally required to be filed by April 15 to report income for the previous year. *Form 1040* is the long form, which must be used by taxpayers who itemize deductions or have high incomes. *Form 1040A* is limited to those who have less than $100,000 of taxable income and limited income sources and do not itemize deductions. *Form 1040EZ* is the easiest to complete, but may be used only by single people claiming only themselves as a personal exemption, with income only from wages, salaries, and tips, and no more than $1,500 of interest income.

FORM 1065 U.S. tax form used by PARTNERSHIPS and JOINT VENTURES.

FORM 1099 U.S. tax form used by payer to report interest, dividends, royalties, capital gains, miscellaneous income, and other distributions.

FORM 1120 U.S. corporate income tax return, generally required to be filed by March 15 of each year.

FORMAT
In general: arrangement of data; method of presentation of data.
Computers: method of arranging information that is to be stored or displayed. Format can refer to: (1) how information is stored on a computer disk and (2) making the computer record a pattern of reference marks on a disk. A brand-new disk must always be *formatted* before it can be used. Formatting a used disk erases any information previously recorded on it. In FORTRAN, the *format statement* specifies the form in which data items, especially numbers, are to be read or written.

FORMER BUYER customer who has not made any additional purchases within a specified period of time, usually a year. Former buyers are generally better prospects for additional sales than nonbuyers because they have already shown a willingness and ability to buy. However, lists of former direct-mail buyers decline in value over time because many of the customers will have moved to a new address.

FORMULA INVESTING investment technique based on a predetermined timing or asset allocation model that eliminates emotional decisions.

FORM UTILITY enhancing the marketability of a product by changing its physical characteristics. For example, boxed detergent can be produced in liquid form, which may be more advantageous for certain consumer requirements. *See also* PLACE UTILITY; POSSESSION UTILITY; TIME UTILITY.

FOR-PROFIT CORPORATION corporation expressly developed for the purpose of earning a profit. *Contrast with* NONPROFIT; NOT FOR PROFIT.

FORTRAN (*for*mula *tran*slation) computer programming language developed by IBM in the late 1950s. It was the first language allowing programmers to describe calculations by means of mathematical formulas.

FORTUITOUS LOSS loss occurring by accident or chance, not by anyone's intention. Insurance policies provide coverage against losses that occur only on a chance basis, where the insured cannot control the loss; thus the insured should not be able to burn down his or her own home and collect. Insurance is not provided against a certainty such as wear and tear. Life insurance will not pay a death benefit if the insured commits suicide within the first two years that the policy is in force. Even though death is a certainty, the insured cannot buy a policy with the intention of suicide within the first two years.

FORTUNE 500 annual listing by *Fortune* magazine of the 500 largest U.S. industrial (manufacturing) corporations. *Fortune* in addition publishes the Fortune Service 500, which ranks the 500 largest U.S. nonmanufacturing companies. *Forbes* magazine also publishes annual rankings of the 500 biggest U.S. publicly owned corporations.

FORUM An ONLINE discussion group on a particular subject that is hosted by a BBS, a NEWSGROUP, a mailing list, or another ONLINE SERVICE. The term Trusted Forum has been registered by CompuServe as a trademark for its discussion groups.

FORWARD in shipping, to send to another destination. A package addressed to a former address is forwarded or returned. *See also* FORWARDING COMPANY.

FORWARD BUYING retail practice of purchasing more materials than immediately needed in order to take advantage of special discounts or a TRADE ALLOWANCE, or to increase profits.

FORWARD CONTRACT actual purchase or sale of a specific quantity of a commodity, government security, foreign currency, or other financial instrument at a price specified now, with delivery and settlement at a specified future date. *See also* FUTURES CONTRACT; OPTION.

FORWARDING COMPANY business that accepts freight from businesses or the general public and finds an appropriate transportation carrier; also called *freight forwarder*.

FORWARD INTEGRATION *see* INTEGRATION, FORWARD.

FORWARD-LOOKING STATEMENTS statements in annual reports and other financial communications that are based on management's expectations, estimates, projections, and assumptions, and are made pursuant to safe harbor provisions of the PRIVATE SECURITIES LITIGATION REFORM ACT OF 1995, as amended. Such statements are accompanied by caveats saying that actual future results and trends may differ materially from what is forecast.

FORWARD PRICING method of pricing used by open-end investment companies. The share price is always determined by the NET ASSET VALUE of the outstanding shares, and all incoming buy and sell orders are based on the next net asset valuation of fund shares. For example, when a mutual fund receives money from an investor, it calculates the number of shares the investor acquires based on their next computation of net asset value.

FORWARD STOCK merchandise carried in the selling areas of a retail store, but not accessible to the patrons. Examples are perfume, jewelry, and cameras, which are kept in protected showcases.

FOR YOUR INFORMATION (FYI)
In general: prefix to a memorandum that indicates that no action is required on the contents.
Finance: prefix to a security price quote by a market maker that indicates the quote is not a firm offer to trade at that price.

FOUL BILL OF LADING BILL OF LADING stating that goods were damaged or shipped short.

401(K) PLAN plan that allows an employee to contribute pretax earnings to a company pool, which is invested in stocks, bonds, or money market instruments; also known as a SALARY REDUCTION PLAN. The contributions as well as earnings on them are only taxed when withdrawn. Annual contributions are limited to $15,000 in 2006, indexed for inflation, plus up to $5,000 CATCH-UP CONTRIBUTIONS for qualified persons.

FOUR Ps four marketing ingredients: *product, price, place,* and *promotion*. A businessperson must decide what product or service to produce, the price to charge, how products are to be distributed to the marketplace, and methods to use for promoting the product or service. *See also* MARKETING MIX.

FOURTH-CLASS MAIL *see* PARCEL POST; SPECIAL FOURTH-CLASS MAIL.

FOURTH MARKET direct trading of large blocks of securities between institutional investors to save brokerage commissions.

FRACTIONAL INTEREST ownership of some but not all of the rights in REAL ESTATE. Examples are EASEMENT, hunting rights, and LEASEHOLD.

FRACTIONAL SHARE unit of stock less than one full share. For example, if a shareholder owns 50 shares and the company declares a 5% STOCK DIVIDEND, the owner gets 2.5 shares as a dividend. The stockholder may round the fraction up by purchasing the necessary part of a share or receive cash for the fractional share.

FRAGMENTATION a situation where many files are broken up into small fragments scattered over the surface of a hard disk. A computer can keep track of where the pieces are, but finding and linking them slows its operations. Most operating systems have utilities to *defragment* drives when they become too fragmented. Fragmentation occurs over time as files are erased and portions of new files are tucked into the resulting empty spots. Also refers to the effect of the multiplicity of securities market makers due to electronic trading systems.

FRANCHISE
1. license granted by a company (the *franchisor*) to an individual or firm (the *franchisee*) to operate a retail, food, or drug outlet where the franchisee agrees to use the franchisor's name; products; services; promotions; selling, distribution, and display methods; and other company support. McDonald's, Midas, and Holiday Inn are all examples of franchise operations.
2. right to market a company's goods or services in a specific territory, which right has been granted by the company to an individual, group of individuals, marketing group, retailer, or wholesaler.
3. specific territory or outlet involved in such a right.
4. right of an advertiser to exercise an option to sponsor a television or radio show, as well as the granting of such a right by the broadcast medium (as "to exercise a franchise" or "to grant a franchise").
5. right granted by a local or state government to a cable television operator to offer cable television service in a community.

FRANCHISE TAX state tax, usually regressive, that is, the rate decreases as the tax base increases, imposed on a state-chartered corporation for the right to do business under its corporate name.

FRANK exemption of certain mail from postage charges, often provided for members of Congress.

FRAUD intentional deception resulting in injury to another. Fraud usually consists of a misrepresentation, concealment, or nondisclosure of a material fact, or at least misleading conduct, devices, or contrivance.

FRAUDULENT MISREPRESENTATION dishonest statement to induce an insurance company to write coverage on an applicant. If the company knew the truth it would not accept the applicant. Fraudulent misrepresentation gives a property and casualty company grounds to terminate a policy at any time.

FREDDIE MAC *see* FEDERAL HOME LOAN MORTGAGE CORPORATION.

FREE ALONGSIDE SHIP (FAS) seller accepts responsibility for the shipment; for example, from factory to pier. The buyer assumes risk and expenses from there.

FREE AND CLEAR unencumbered. In property law, TITLE is *free and clear* if it is not encumbered by any LIENS or restrictions. One conveys land free and clear if he transfers a GOOD TITLE or MARKETABLE TITLE.

FREE AND OPEN MARKET market in which price is determined by the free, unregulated interchange of supply and demand. The opposite is a *controlled market*, where supply, demand, and price are artificially set.

FREE CASH FLOW the amount of cash a company has after expenses, debt service, capital expenditures, and dividends. Free cash flow, which is measured at least annually, suggests the financial comfort level of the company as a going concern. The higher the free cash flow, the stronger the company's value. *See* EBITDA.

FREEDOM OF INFORMATION ACT (FOIA) federal law requiring that, with specified exemptions, documents and materials generated or held by federal agencies be made available to the public and establishing guidelines for their disclosure. Exemptions include issues relating to national security.

FREE ENTERPRISE conduct of business without direct government interference; conducting business primarily according to the laws of supply and demand; risking capital for the purpose of making a profit.

FREEHOLD (ESTATE) estate in FEE or a LIFE ESTATE; an estate or interest in real property for life or of uncertain duration.

FREE LUNCH expression meaning something good available at no cost. The full expression is "there's no such thing as a free lunch."

FREE MARKET market in which there is little or no control or interference by government or by any other powerful economic force or entity, such as a MONOPOLY, CARTEL, or COLLUSIVE OLIGOPOLY.

FREE ON BOARD (FOB) transportation term meaning that the INVOICE price includes delivery at the seller's expense to a specified point and no further. For example, "FOB our Newark warehouse" means that the buyer must pay all shipping and other charges associated with transporting the merchandise from the seller's warehouse in Newark to the buyer's receiving point. Title normally passes from seller to buyer at the FOB point by way of a BILL OF LADING. *See also* FREE ALONGSIDE SHIP.

FREE PORT port where no duties are imposed on ships that load or unload.

FREE-REIN LEADERSHIP indirect supervision of subordinates, form of management supervision that allows others to function on their own without extensive direct supervision. People are allowed to prove themselves based upon accomplishments rather than meeting specific supervisory criteria.

FREE RIDERS team members in an organization who benefit from but do not contribute adequately to the group's efforts because there are no individual responsibility controls.

FREE TRANSFERABILITY OF INTEREST the right to sell an ownership interest to another party who acquires all of the seller's rights, without permission from others. This is a characteristic of corporate stock (though not of RESTRICTED STOCK) as contrasted with a PARTNERSHIP interest.

FREEWARE computer software, usually in the early stages of development, that is freely distributed at no charge, usually via the Internet. The author often hopes to benefit from improvements added by other developers and eventually market the program commercially or as SHAREWARE.

FREEWAY multiple-lane divided highway with fully controlled access, as by cloverleafs, for intersecting roads; highway without toll charges.

FREIGHT FORWARDER *see* FORWARDING COMPANY.

FREIGHT INSURANCE coverage for goods during shipment on a common carrier. *See also* CARGO INSURANCE.

FREQUENCY
1. in general, number of times something occurs within a specified period of time. *Frequency* may refer to the issues of a periodical, the purchases made by a customer over time, or the number of times a commercial or an advertisement is aired or printed or reaches its audience.
2. number of times an advertising message is presented within a given time period.
3. average number of times a commercial or advertisement has been viewed per person (or per household) during a specific time period. The idea of frequency is the same throughout all of the possible advertising media choices.
4. wavelength allocations made by the Federal Communications Commission for broadcasting, including radio stations, television channels, amateur radio (ham) operators, citizens' band radios, police radios, and the like.

FREQUENCY DIAGRAM a bar diagram that illustrates how many observations fall within each category.

FRICTIONAL UNEMPLOYMENT normal and unavoidable UNEM-
PLOYMENT caused by people changing jobs, moving, rearranging their
economic activity, and so on.

FRIENDLY FIRE a fire kindled intentionally to serve a useful purpose
and contained in a receptacle such as a fireplace or stove; any damage
it may do is not covered by fire insurance. A military use of the term
means being shot at by your own troops.

FRIENDLY SUIT action authorized by law, brought by agreement
between the parties, to secure a JUDGMENT that will have a binding
effect in circumstances where a mere agreement or settlement will not.
For example, a claim in favor of an infant or another lacking legal
capacity to enter into a binding contract can for that reason be settled
only through the entry of a judgment.

FRIENDLY TAKEOVER MERGER supported by the management and
board of directors of the target company. The board will recommend
to shareholders that they approve the takeover offer because it represents fair value for the company's shares. In many cases, the acquiring
company will retain many of the existing managers of the acquired
company to continue to run the business. *Contrast with* HOSTILE
TAKEOVER.

FRINGE BENEFITS *see* BENEFITS, FRINGE; TAXABLE FRINGE BENEFIT.

FRIVOLOUS LAWSUIT an insufficient claim, not supported by the
facts. Courts frown upon these as a waste of time and money and may
make the party who brings the suit responsible to the defendant for litigation costs.

FRIVOLOUS POSITION a tax position that is knowingly advanced in
bad faith and is patently improper.

FRONTAGE linear distance of a piece of land along a lake, river, street,
or highway. Land along such property is often priced at a rate per
FRONT FOOT.

FRONT-END LOAD sales charge applied to an investment at the time
of purchase. A back-end load is a redemption charge paid when withdrawing funds from an investment.

FRONT FOOT standard measurement of land, applied at the FRONTAGE
of its street line. It is used for lots of generally uniform depth in downtown areas.

FRONT MONEY cash necessary to start a project. Front money is generally required for purchasing a SITE, preparing plans and studies,
obtaining PERMITS, and obtaining loan COMMITMENTS.

FRONT OFFICE offices of the major executives within a company;
nucleus of the operational management center. Often found near the
entrance to the organization.

FROZEN ACCOUNT bank account from which funds may not be withdrawn until a LIEN is satisfied and a court order is received freeing the balance. A bank account may also be frozen by court order in a dispute over the ownership of property.

FSA Fellow, SOCIETY OF ACTUARIES.

F STATISTIC value calculated by the ratio of two sample variances. The *F* statistic can test the null hypothesis: (1) that the two sample variances are from normal populations with a common variance; (2) that two population means are equal; (3) that no connection exists between the dependent variable and all or some of the independent variables.

FTC *see* FEDERAL TRADE COMMISSION.

FULFILLMENT processes necessary to receive, service, and track orders sold via DIRECT MARKETING. There are different types of fulfillment systems depending on the product or service sold, including SUBSCRIPTIONS, book club memberships, CONTINUITIES, catalog merchandise, and FUND RAISING.

FULL COSTING *see* ABSORPTION COSTING.

FULL COVERAGE all insured losses paid in full.

FULL DISCLOSURE
In general: requirement to disclose all material facts relevant to a transaction.
Securities: public information requirements established by the Securities Act of 1933, the Securities Exchange Act of 1934, and the major stock exchanges.

FULL DUPLEX in computer usage, transmission of data in two directions simultaneously. *See also* HALF-DUPLEX; MODEM.

FULL EMPLOYMENT a rate of employment defined by government economists to take into account the percentage of unemployed who would not be employed regardless of the nation's economy (*see* STRUCTURAL UNEMPLOYMENT).

FULL FAITH AND CREDIT phrase meaning that the full taxing and borrowing power, *plus* revenue other than taxes, is pledged in payment of interest and repayment of principal of a bond issued by a government entity. U.S. government securities and general obligation bonds of states and local governments are backed by this pledge.

FULL RETIREMENT AGE for Social Security purposes, the retirement age at which full retirement benefits will be received. *Full retirement age* is 65 for those who were born in 1937 or earlier. It rises in steps, reaching 66 for those born between 1943 and 1954, and 67 for those born in 1960 or later. For earlier retirement, the Social Security benefit will be reduced. If retirement occurs later than full retirement age, the benefit may be increased in some instances.

FULL-SERVICE BROKER BROKER who provides a wide range of services to clients. Unlike a DISCOUNT BROKER, who usually just executes trades, a full-service broker offers advice on which stocks, bonds, commodities, and mutual funds to buy or sell.

FULLY AMORTIZED LOAN one having payments of INTEREST and PRINCIPAL that are sufficient to LIQUIDATE the loan over its term; self-liquidating.

FULLY DEPRECIATED said of a fixed asset to which all the DEPRECIATION the accounting or tax law allows has been charged. The asset is carried on the books at its RESIDUAL VALUE, although its LIQUIDATING VALUE may be higher or lower.

FULLY DILUTED EARNINGS PER (COMMON) SHARE figure showing earnings per common share after assuming the exercise of all outstanding warrants and stock options, and the conversion of convertible bonds and preferred stock, all potentially dilutive securities. *See also* DILUTION.

FULLY PAID POLICY limited pay whole life policy under which all premium payments have been made. For example, a 20-pay policy is completely paid for after 20 payments; no future premiums have to be made and the policy remains in full force for the life of the insured.

FUNCTIONAL AUTHORITY staff ability to initiate as well as to veto action in a given area of expertise. Functional authority allows decisions to be implemented directly by the staff in question. Areas where functional authority is found are accounting, labor relations, and employment testing.

FUNCTIONAL OBSOLESCENCE decline in value due to changing tastes or technical innovation.

FUNCTIONAL ORGANIZATION structure of an organization based on functional performance; organizational departments created to fulfill organizational functions such as marketing, finance, and personnel. This type of organization has characteristics of both line and staff functions.

FUND an amount of money that may be available either for general uses or purposes or that may be dedicated to a specific use or purpose; to pay such an amount. *See* FAMILY OF FUNDS; FUNDING; GENERAL FUND; HEDGE FUND; INDEX FUND; MUTUAL FUND.

FUND ACCOUNTING system used by nonprofit organizations, particularly governments. Since there is no profit motive, *accountability* is measured instead of profitability. The main purpose is stewardship of financial resources received and expended in compliance with legal requirements. Financial reporting is directed at the public rather than investors.

FUNDAMENTAL ANALYSIS analysis of the BALANCE SHEET, INCOME STATEMENT, and other basic economic and managerial data of companies in order to forecast their future stock price movements. In contrast, TECHNICAL ANALYSIS concentrates on market factors like price and volume movements of stocks.

FUNDED DEBT
1. debt that is due after one year and is formalized by the issuing of bonds or long-term notes.
2. bond issue whose retirement is provided for by a SINKING FUND.

FUNDED PENSION PLAN plan in which funds are currently allocated to purchase retirement benefits. An employee is thus assured of receiving retirement payments even if the employer is no longer in business at the time the employee retires.

FUNDED RETIREMENT PLAN *see* FUNDED PENSION PLAN.

FUND FAMILY *see* FAMILY OF FUNDS.

FUNDING
1. refinancing a debt on or before its maturity.
2. putting money into investments or another type of RESERVE FUND to provide for future pension or welfare plans.
3. in corporate finance, the word *funding* is preferred to *financing* when referring to bonds in contrast to stock.
4. providing funds to finance a project, such as a research study.

FUND OF FUNDS MUTUAL FUND that invests in other mutual funds. The concept behind such funds is that they are able to move money between the best funds in the industry and thereby increase shareholders' returns with more diversification than is offered by a single fund.

FUND RAISING effort to solicit contributions from individuals or organizations for nonprofit organizations having educational, medical, religious, political, charitable, or other stated purposes. The most common techniques of fund raising are DIRECT MAIL advertising and TELEMARKETING.

FUNDS FROM OPERATIONS (FFO) a measure of the profitability of a REAL ESTATE INVESTMENT TRUST (REIT). *FFO* begins with net income as derived using GENERALLY ACCEPTED ACCOUNTING PRINCIPLES (GAAP). To that it adds depreciation deductions and deductions for amortization of deferred charges, which are noncash deductions. FFO does not consider extraordinary items and gains (losses) on the sale of real estate.

FUND SWITCHING moving money from one MUTUAL FUND to another within the same fund family. Purchases and sales of funds may be made to time the ups and downs of the stock and bond markets or because investors' financial needs have changed.

FUNGIBLES bearer instruments, securities, or goods that are equivalent, substitutable, and interchangeable. Commodities such as soybeans or wheat, common shares of the same company, and dollar bills are examples of *fungibles*.

FURLOUGH permission to take a leave of absence from an organization for a specified period of time. A training *furlough* is an example in which an employee is granted permission.

FURNITURE, FIXTURES, AND EQUIPMENT (FF&E) a term frequently found in the ownership of a hotel or motel. This type of property wears out much more rapidly than other components of a hotel or motel, so an owner or prospective buyer needs to establish the condition, cost, and frequency of replacement of *FF&E*.

FUTA *see* FEDERAL UNEMPLOYMENT TAX ACT.

FUTURE INTEREST interest in presently existing real property or personal property, or in a gift or trust, that will commence in use, possession, or enjoyment in the future. A legatee to receive an annual income upon reaching the age of 21 has a future interest that, when that age is reached, will ripen into a present interest.

FUTURES CONTRACT agreement to buy or sell a specific amount of a COMMODITY or *financial instrument* at a particular price on a stipulated future date. A futures contract obligates the buyer to purchase the underlying commodity and the seller to sell it, unless the contract is sold to another before settlement date. This contrasts with OPTIONS trading, in which the option buyer may choose whether or not to exercise the option by the exercise date. *See also* FORWARD CONTRACT.

FUTURES MARKET commodity exchange where FUTURES CONTRACTS are traded.

FUTURES OPTION OPTION on a FUTURES CONTRACT.

FUTURES TRANSACTION *see* HEDGE.

FUTURE WORTH (OR VALUE) OF ONE same as COMPOUND AMOUNT OF ONE.

FUTURE WORTH (OR VALUE) OF ONE PER PERIOD same as COMPOUND AMOUNT OF ONE PER PERIOD.

FUZZY LOGIC in computer ARTIFICIAL INTELLIGENCE, a system of computer instructions enabling the computer to deal with ambiguities. The instructions are not restricted to "either/or" choices. *Fuzzy logic* emulates the way humans think, so its decisions appear to be more natural.

FYI *see* FOR YOUR INFORMATION.

G

GAAP *see* GENERALLY ACCEPTED ACCOUNTING PRINCIPLES.

GAIN increase in value, measured by the difference between the ADJUSTED TAX BASIS and the selling price. *See also* CAPITAL GAIN; REALIZED GAIN; RECOGNIZED GAIN.

GAIN CONTINGENCY potential or pending development that may result in a future gain to the company, such as a successful lawsuit against another company. Conservative accounting practice dictates that gain contingencies should *not* be booked although footnote disclosure of the particulars may be made. *See also* LOSS CONTINGENCY.

GAINFUL EMPLOYMENT/OCCUPATION employment suited to the ability of the one employed. For purposes of disability covered by insurance, it may mean the ordinary employment of the insured, or other employment approximating the same livelihood as the insured might be expected to follow in view of his or her circumstances and physical and mental capabilities.

GAIN SHARING employee motivational technique where compensation is given for measurable performance gains in such areas as sales, customer satisfaction, and cost reductions. The compensation is often given to employee teams for achieving specified goals.

GALLOPING INFLATION episode in which the rate of INFLATION is viewed as being extraordinarily high.

GALLUP POLL a public opinion poll. Although originated by Dr. George Gallup, the term has taken on a more generic meaning.

GAMING process of two or more participants attempting to reach conflicting objectives or goals. The process of bidding for contracts is a game. Logically, each participant would bid estimated costs plus some amount for profit. Since only one contract would be awarded, the outcome depends jointly on the actions of all bidders.

GANTT CHART graphical production scheduling method showing the various production stages and how long each stage should take. By charting the production steps through a *Gantt chart*, the manager is easily able to visualize and schedule production stages.

GAO *see* GENERAL ACCOUNTING OFFICE.

GAP amount of a financing need for which provision has yet to be made. *See also* GAP LOAN.

GAP LOAN loan filling the difference between the FLOOR LOAN and the full amount of the permanent loan. For example, a developer arranges a permanent mortgage that will fund $1 million when the apartments he is building are 80% occupied. From completion of construction until 80% occupancy is reached, the mortgage is only $700,000. The developer arranges a *gap loan* of $300,000 for the RENT-UP PERIOD.

GARDEN APARTMENTS housing complex where some or all TENANTS have access to a lawn area.

GARNISH to bring a GARNISHMENT proceeding; to attach wages or other property pursuant to such a proceeding.

GARNISHEE person, often an employer, who receives notice to retain *custody of assets* in his control that are owed to or belong to another person. The garnishee merely holds the assets until legal proceedings determine who is entitled to the property.

GARNISHMENT court order to an employer to withhold all or part of an employee's wages and send the money to the court or to a person who has won a lawsuit against the employee. An employee's wages will be *garnished* until the court-ordered debt is paid. Garnishing may be used in a divorce settlement or for repayment of creditors.

GAS GUZZLER TAX tax imposed on the sale, use, or lease by the manufacturer or importer of an automobile of a model type that does not meet certain standards for fuel economy. Automobiles imported for business or personal use are subject to the tax. An *automobile* is defined as any four-wheeled vehicle rated at 6,000 pounds or less unloaded gross weight that is propelled by an engine powered by gasoline or diesel fuel and is intended for use mainly on public streets, roads, and highways.

GATT (GENERAL AGREEMENT ON TARIFFS AND TRADE) *see* WORLD TRADE ORGANIZATION.

GB *see* GIGABYTE.

GDP *see* GROSS DOMESTIC PRODUCT.

G-8 FINANCE MINISTERS the major economic powers: Canada, France, Germany, Italy, Japan, Russia, United Kingdom, and the United States. They meet periodically to coordinate global monetary policy.

GENDER ANALYSIS analyzing names on a mailing list to determine which represent male or female individuals according to a list of typically male or female names. Mailing list selections may then be made on the basis of gender to promote products suitable to only one gender.

GENERAL ACCOUNTING OFFICE (GAO) independent Congressional agency established in 1921, which reviews federal financial transactions. It examines the expenditures of appropriations of federal agencies and reports directly to Congress.

GENERAL CONTRACTOR CONTRACTOR who constructs a building or other improvement for the OWNER or DEVELOPER. The contractor may retain a construction labor force or use SUBCONTRACTORS.

GENERAL DEPRECIATION SYSTEM (GDS) the main system for tax DEPRECIATION under the MODIFIED ACCELERATED COST RECOVERY SYSTEM (MACRS). GDS permits the use of the DECLINING-BALANCE METHOD over a shorter recovery period than the ALTERNATIVE DEPRECIATION SYSTEM (ADS).

GENERAL EQUILIBRIUM ANALYSIS in economics, complex and systematic theoretical model that includes all markets simultaneously; used to examine relationships among markets.

GENERAL EXPENSE expense incurred for operations other than selling, administrative, or cost of goods sold.

GENERAL FUND main operating accounts of a nonprofit entity, such as a government or government agency.

GENERALIST person with many abilities and interests or whose job description contains many varied duties. *Contrasts with* SPECIALIST.

GENERAL JOURNAL books of original entry where all transactions are first posted, except those recorded in specialized journals; also where JOURNAL ENTRIES are recorded.

GENERAL LEDGER formal ledger containing all the financial statement accounts of a business. It contains offsetting debit and credit accounts. Certain accounts in the general ledger, termed *control accounts*, summarize the details booked on separate subsidiary ledgers.

GENERAL LIABILITY INSURANCE coverage for an insured when negligent acts and/or omissions result in bodily injury and/or property damage on the premises of a business, when someone is injured as the result of using the product manufactured or distributed by a business, or when someone is injured in the general operation of a business.

GENERAL LIEN LIEN that includes *all* the property owned by the debtor, rather than a specific property.

GENERALLY ACCEPTED ACCOUNTING PRINCIPLES (GAAP) conventions, rules, and procedures that define accepted accounting practice, including broad guidelines as well as detailed procedures. *See also* FINANCIAL ACCOUNTING STANDARDS BOARD (FASB).

GENERAL OBLIGATION BOND or **G-O BOND** municipal bond backed by the FULL FAITH AND CREDIT (which includes the taxing and further borrowing power) of a municipality. A G-O bond is repaid with general revenue and borrowings. *See also* REVENUE BOND.

GENERAL PARTNER in a PARTNERSHIP, a partner whose liability is not limited. All partners in an ordinary partnership are *general partners*. As a general rule, partners include on their personal tax returns their share of partnership income, loss, and deductions.

GENERAL PARTNERSHIP an organization with only GENERAL PARTNERS. Each partner is liable beyond the amount invested, and each may bind the entire partnership. Typically, a general partnership is not a taxable entity because its income and losses are passed through to the partners. *Contrast* LIMITED PARTNERSHIP.

GENERAL POWER OF APPOINTMENT one under which holders have the right to dispose of the property in favor of: (1) themselves; (2) their estate; (3) their creditors; or (4) the creditors of their estate. A trust GRANTOR is treated as the owner and is therefore taxed on trust income if he or she has the power to control the beneficial enjoyment of the trust corpus or income, without the approval of an adverse party.

GENERAL POWER OF ATTORNEY means whereby a person (the PRINCIPAL) nominates another person to act on his behalf. This power will include the right to act for the principal in all matters.

GENERAL PROPERTY TAX *see* PROPERTY TAX.

GENERAL RETIREMENT SYSTEM any PENSION, ANNUITY, retirement, or similar fund or system established by a state or by a political subdivision thereof for employees of the state, political subdivision, or both. Does not include a fund or system that covers only service performed in positions connected with the operation of its public transportation system.

GENERAL REVENUE in state and local governments, total revenue less revenue from utilities, sales of alcoholic beverages, and insurance trusts.

GENERAL SCHEME delivery plan for a state or section of a state describing the flow of mail to various local post offices. The general scheme could be consulted by your U.S. Postal Service CUSTOMER SERVICE REPRESENTATIVE to help identify the source of a delivery problem.

GENERAL STRIKE coordinated national, regional, or municipal work stoppage designed to pressure management or the government into agreeing to contract terms, correct an unsettled grievance, or recognize a union. A general strike is an action by most organized workers and occurs rarely in the United States.

GENERAL TAX LIEN a TAX LIEN attached to all property belonging to a person liable for a tax and continued for six years.

GENERAL WARRANTY DEED DEED in which the grantor agrees to protect the grantee against any other claim to title of the property and provides other promises. *See also* WARRANTY DEED.

GENERATION-SKIPPING TRANSFER transfer of financial assets or property to a recipient more than a single generation removed from the transferor, such as from a grandfather to a grandchild. May be subject to the generation-skipping tax.

GENERIC
1. relating to or describing an entire class.
2. in marketing, pertaining to a whole product or service category.

GENERIC APPEAL advertising appeal on behalf of a product category in which no mention is made of a specific BRAND NAME—for example, the advertising that encourages the drinking of milk, sponsored by the American Dairy Association.

GENERIC BRAND plainly labeled, unadvertised product. At present generic brands are mostly limited to prescription drugs and grocery items and may cost up to 40% less than advertised brands.

GENERIC MARKET broad group of buyers with approximately the same general needs; different sellers who offer varying ways of satisfying those needs.

GENETIC ENGINEERING techniques by which genetic material can be altered by recombinant DNA so as to change or improve the hereditary properties of microorganisms, plants, and animals.

GENTRIFICATION displacement of lower-income residents in a neighborhood by higher-income residents, generally occurring when an older neighborhood is revitalized.

GEODEMOGRAPHY attribution of DEMOGRAPHIC characteristics to a group of individuals residing in the same geographic area based on an *overlay* of demographic survey data against a geographically segmented list. For example, *geodemography* might determine that Stamford, Connecticut, comprises a high proportion of affluent married people with young children. It would thus be appropriate to target Stamford for children's furniture promotions and so forth.

GEOGRAPHIC DIVISION divisional unit within an organization structured on the basis of its operational location.

GEOGRAPHIC INFORMATION SYSTEM (GIS) a computer mapping program whereby land characteristics and/or DEMOGRAPHIC information are color-coded and often overlaid. The purpose is to determine locations of various business activities and demographics.

GEOGRAPHIC SEGMENTATION customer market classification based on geographic location.

GIC *see* GUARANTEED INCOME CONTRACT.

GIF (pronounced *jif*) a file formatted in *G*raphics *I*nterchange *F*ormat, a data compression format used initially by CompuServe to compress and transfer graphic images for screen display. The format is commonly used for transferring graphics files on the Internet. Bitmapped files compressed in this format are known by the three-digit .gif extension at the end of the filename.

GIFT voluntary transfer of property made without CONSIDERATION, that is, for which no value is received in return. *See also* TAXABLE GIFT; GIFT TAX.

GIFT CARD a type of gift certificate in the form of a card into which value can be encoded. Used much like a CREDIT CARD for the purchase of consumer goods and services, up to the limit of stored value.

GIFT CAUSA MORTIS transfer of property by a person who faces impending death. The donee therefore shall become the owner of the property, but on condition that the donor's failure to die shall revoke the gift.

GIFT DEED DEED for which CONSIDERATION is love and affection, and no material consideration is involved.

GIFT INTER VIVOS transfer of property to a donee during the life of the donor, for no consideration. The donor thus divests himself of control or dominion over the subject of the gift.

GIFT SPLITTING a husband and wife may *combine* their annual gift tax exclusions and UNIFIED ESTATE AND GIFT TAX CREDITS. For example, a husband and wife may consent to jointly give a child $24,000 annually by combining their individual annual exclusions of $12,000 per DONOR per DONEE in 2006. Gift splitting is accomplished even when only one spouse has assets sufficient to make the combined gift.

GIFT TAX graduated excise tax levied on the donor of a gift by the federal government and most state governments when assets are passed from one person to another. Generally, in 2006 each person may give up to $12,000 per year to each DONEE without imposition of a federal gift tax. On higher gifts in the same year, there may be a gift tax, or the gift may affect the donor's ESTATE TAX by reducing the lifetime gift and estate tax exclusion.

GIFT TAX EXCLUSION an annual exclusion of $12,000 per DONEE in 2006, indexed for inflation, allowed for present-interest gifts to arrive at taxable gifts. Also called *annual exclusion.*

GIGA- metric prefix denoting multiplication by 10^9 or 1,000,000,000. In measuring the capacity of computer disks and RAM, equivalent to $\times 2^{30}$ or 1,073,741,824.

GIGABYTE (GB) in computers, 2^{30}, or approximately one billion, BYTES of storage. *See also* KILOBYTE; MEGABYTE.

GIGO garbage in, garbage out: if poor data are used as input into an equation or model, the result will be erroneous.

GI LOAN *see* VETERANS ADMINISTRATION.

GILT a fixed-interest British government debt security.

GILT-EDGED SECURITY stock or bond of a company that has demonstrated over a number of years that it is capable of earning sufficient profits to cover dividends on stocks and interest on bonds with great dependability. The term is used with corporate bonds more often than with stocks, where the term *blue chip* is more common.

GINNIE MAE nickname for GOVERNMENT NATIONAL MORTGAGE ASSOCIATION; generally refers to mortgage-based securities guaranteed by the association. *See also* GINNIE MAE PASS-THROUGH.

GINNIE MAE PASS-THROUGH security backed by a pool of mortgages and guaranteed by the GOVERNMENT NATIONAL MORTGAGE ASSOCIATION, which passes through to investors the interest and principal payments of homeowners. Homeowners make their mortgage payments to the bank or savings and loan that originated their mortgage. After deducting a ⅜ to ½% service charge, the bank forwards the mortgage payments to the pass-through buyers, who may be institutional investors or individuals.

GLAMOR STOCK stock with a wide public and institutional following. Glamor stocks achieve this following by producing steadily rising sales and earnings over a long period of time. In BULL MARKETS, glamor stocks tend to rise faster than market averages.

GLASS CEILING term describing discrimination that women and minorities often experience when trying to advance into an organization's senior management levels.

GLASS INSURANCE *see* COMPREHENSIVE GLASS INSURANCE.

GLASS-STEAGALL ACT OF 1933 legislation passed by Congress authorizing deposit insurance and prohibiting commercial banks from owning brokerage firms. Largely repealed by the Financial Services Modernization Act of 1999.

GLITCH *see* BUG.

GLOBAL FISHER EFFECT an economic equilibrium that exhibits an equality of expected real interest rates among countries when there are no restrictions on international trade, credit, and currency exchanges.

GLOBAL HEDGING a risk management strategy to balance positions of different business units or with unrelated third parties.

GLOBALIZATION worldwide economic interaction resulting in a dynamic global market.

GLOBAL SEARCH computer search throughout an entire document for words, characters, or other data that might need to be located or changed.

GLUT OVERPRODUCTION of a good or service; specifically, situation in which the available supply will not all be bought at the current price.

GNP *see* GROSS NATIONAL PRODUCT.

GOAL individual or organizational objective target to be achieved within a particular time period. An organizational goal, for example, may be to become number one in market share of a particular product within the following year.

GOAL CONGRUENCE consistency or agreement of actions with organizational goals. It identifies the managerial principle that all of a firm's subgoals must be congruent to achieve one central set of objectives.

GOAL PROGRAMMING form of *linear programming* allowing for consideration of multiple goals that are often in conflict with each other. With multiple goals, all goals usually cannot be realized. For example, the goals of an investor who desires investments that will have maximum return and minimum risk are generally incompatible and therefore unachievable. Other examples of multiple conflicting objectives can be found in organizations that want to: (1) maximize profits and increase wages; (2) upgrade product quality and reduce product cost; (3) pay larger dividends to stockholders and retain earnings for growth; and (4) reduce credit losses and increase sales.

GOAL SETTING establishing steps to meet the objectives of an individual or a firm. For example, in order to meet the organization's objective of a 10% increase in sales, the sales quota of each salesperson is increased by $10,000.

GO-BETWEEN intermediary between two people or groups who handles needed particulars with regard to the relationship. The intermediary typically has a vested interest that everything runs smoothly. The intermediary may arrange a compromise between the groups or just keep the lines of communication open. An example is when a supplier is introduced to a new customer by a *go-between* who receives a referral fee.

GOING-CONCERN VALUE value of a company as an operating business to another company or individual. The excess of the *going-concern value* over the asset value, or LIQUIDATING VALUE, is the value of the operating organization as distinct from the value of its assets, called GOODWILL.

GOING LONG purchasing a stock, bond, or commodity for investment or speculation. Such a security purchase is known as a LONG POSITION. Conversely, when an investor sells a security he does not own, he creates a SHORT POSITION.

GOING PRIVATE movement of a company from public to private ownership, either by the company's repurchase of its shares or through purchases by an outside private investor.

GOING PUBLIC securities industry phrase used when a private company first offers its shares to the public. The firm's ownership shifts from the hands of a few private stockowners to a base that includes public shareholders and becomes subject to some new legal requirements.

GOING SHORT selling a stock or commodity that the seller does not have. *See also* GOING LONG; SHORT SALE.

GOLDBRICK to shirk one's responsibilities. A person who is goldbricking is not doing what is expected. When goldbricking, one is wasting time.

GOLDBUG analyst enamored of gold as an investment. Goldbugs usually are worried about possible disasters in the world economy, such as a depression or hyperinflation, and therefore recommend gold as a safe haven for anxious investors.

GOLDEN HANDCUFFS method of retaining key employees in a firm through the use of stock options. Golden handcuffs have been found to be particularly useful in rapidly growing startup companies requiring highly trained engineers and technical personnel. They literally cannot afford to leave.

GOLDEN HANDSHAKE early retirement incentives given to an employee by a firm. The nature of the incentives varies from an acceleration of retirement benefits to a direct cash award.

GOLDEN PARACHUTE lucrative contract given to top executives of a company. It provides lavish benefits in case the company is taken over by another firm, resulting in the loss of the job. A golden parachute might include generous severance pay, stock options, or a bonus payable when the executive's employment at the company ends.

GOLD FIXING daily determination of the price of gold by selected gold specialists and bank officials in London, Paris, and Zurich. The price is fixed at 10:30 A.M. and 3:30 P.M. London time every business day according to the prevailing market forces of supply and demand.

GOLDILOCKS ECONOMY term coined in the mid-1990s to describe an economy that was "not too hot, not too cold, just right," like the porridge in the fairy tale. Adroit MONETARY POLICY was credited for an economy that enjoyed steady growth with a nominal rate of inflation.

GOLD STANDARD monetary system under which units of currency are convertible into fixed amounts of gold. Such a system is said to be anti-inflationary. The United States has been on the gold standard in the past but was taken off in 1933. *See also* HARD CURRENCY.

GOOD DELIVERY securities industry designation meaning that a certificate has the necessary endorsements and meets all other requirements (signature guarantee, proper denomination, and other qualifications) so that title can be transferred by delivery to the buying broker, who is then obligated to accept it.

GOOD FAITH total absence of intention to seek unfair advantage or to defraud another party; honest intention to fulfill one's obligations; observance of reasonable standards of fair dealing.

GOOD-FAITH DEPOSIT
In general: money advanced to indicate intent to pursue a contract to completion; *see* EARNEST MONEY.
Commodities: initial margin deposit required when buying or selling a futures contract. Such deposits generally range from 2 to 10% of the contract value.

Securities:
1. deposit, usually 25% of a transaction, required by securities firms of individuals who are not known to them but wish to enter orders with them.
2. deposit left with a municipal bond issuer by a firm competing for the underwriting business. The deposit typically equals 1 to 5% of the principal amount of the issue and is refundable to the unsuccessful bidders.

GOOD HOUSEKEEPING SEAL seal of approval of a product that meets standards established by the Good Housekeeping Institute as directed by *Good Housekeeping* magazine in a policy designed for consumer protection.

GOOD MONEY
Banking: federal funds, which are good the same day, in contrast to CLEARINGHOUSE funds. Clearinghouse funds are understood in two ways: (1) funds requiring three days to clear and (2) funds used to settle transactions on which there is a one-day FLOAT.
Gresham's law: theory that money of superior intrinsic value, *good money*, will eventually be driven out of circulation by money of lesser intrinsic value. *See also* GRESHAM'S LAW.

GOODNESS-OF-FIT TEST statistical procedure to test the hypothesis that a particular probability distribution fits an observed set of data. The Chi-square statistic provides a goodness-of-fit test.

GOODS species of PROPERTY that is not real estate, CHOSE IN ACTION, investment securities, or the like.

GOODS AND SERVICES products of any economy. Services are tasks done by people and goods are material items.

GOOD-TILL-CANCELED ORDER (GTC) brokerage customer's order to buy or sell a security, usually at a particular price, that remains in effect until executed or canceled. *See also* FILL OR KILL ORDER.

GOOD TITLE CLEAR title, free from present litigation, obvious defects, and grave doubts concerning its validity or merchantability. Such title is marketable to a reasonable purchaser or mortgaged as security for a loan of money to a person of reasonable prudence.

GOODWILL intangible but recognized business asset that is the result of such features as the production or sale of reputable brand-name products, a good relationship with customers and suppliers, and the standing of the business in its community. *See also* GOING-CONCERN VALUE.

GOOGLE a search engine owned by Google Inc., currently the largest and most popular on the Web. As of July 2006, *google* (lowercase) entered Merriam-Webster dictionaries as a verb defined as "to use the Google search engine to obtain information about (as a person) on the World Wide Web."

GOV *see* DOMAIN.

GOVERNMENT ACCOUNTING principles and procedures in accounting for federal, state, and local governmental units. The National Council on Governmental Accounting establishes rules. There is also a governmental group in the FASB. Unlike commercial accounting for corporations, encumbrances and budgets are recorded in the accounts. Assets of a governmental unit are restricted for designated purposes. *See also* MODIFIED ACCRUAL.

GOVERNMENT AGENCY SECURITIES securities issued by U.S. government agencies, such as the former Federal Home Loan Bank, the Federal Farm Credit Bank, or the Federal National Mortgage Association. Although these securities have high credit ratings, they are not backed by the FULL FAITH AND CREDIT of the U.S. government.

GOVERNMENT ENTERPRISE governmentally sponsored business activity. A utility plant may be a *government enterprise*, even though it raises revenue by charging for its services rather than by levying taxes.

GOVERNMENT NATIONAL MORTGAGE ASSOCIATION (GNMA) government organization to assist in housing finance. There are two main programs: (1) to GUARANTEE payments of principal and interest to investors in mortgage-backed securities and (2) to absorb the WRITE-DOWN of low-interest-rate loans that are used to finance low-income housing. *See also* SECONDARY MORTGAGE MARKET.

GOVERNMENT OBLIGATIONS *see* GOVERNMENTS.

GOVERNMENT RECTANGULAR SURVEY rectangular system of land SURVEY that divides a district into 24-square-mile *quadrangles* from the *meridian* (north-south line) and the *base line* (east-west line). The tracts are divided into *townships*, each 6 square miles and containing 36 square miles, which are in turn divided into 36 tracts, each 1 mile square, called *sections*. The system is used in most western states.

GOVERNMENTS securities issued by the U.S. government, such as Treasury bills, bonds, notes, and savings bonds. Governments are the most creditworthy of all debt instruments since they are backed by the FULL FAITH AND CREDIT of the U.S. government.

GRACE PERIOD period of time provided in most loan contracts and insurance policies during which default or cancellation will not occur even though payment is past due.

GRADUATED LEASE lease that provides for changes, at stated intervals, in the amount of rent.

GRADUATED PAYMENT MORTGAGE (GPM) mortgage requiring lower payments in early years than in later years. Payments increase in steps each year until the installments are sufficient to amortize the loan. Most GPMs have been written under FHA Section 245.

GRADUATED WAGE salary structure of incremental wage levels in an organization. Wages are graduated by job grade, seniority, experience, or performance.

GRAFT fraudulent obtaining of public money by the corruption of public officials; money used fraudulently as a payoff; dishonest advantage that one person by reason of his position, influence, or trust acquires from another.

GRAHAM AND DODD METHOD OF INVESTING investment approach outlined in Benjamin Graham and David Dodd's landmark book *Security Analysis*, initially published in the 1930s. They believed that investors should buy stocks with undervalued assets and that eventually those assets would appreciate to their true value in the marketplace.

GRAMM-RUDMAN-HOLLINGS AMENDMENT federal legislation passed in 1986 that sets budget deficit reduction goals and mandates reductions in federal expenditures if Congress does not meet the annual goals.

GRANDFATHER CLAUSE provision included in a new rule that exempts from the rule a person or business already engaged in the activity coming under regulation.

GRANT
1. term used in deeds of CONVEYANCE of property to indicate a transfer.
2. transfer of funds from a government body or private foundation to another unit of government or private individual for a project deemed in the public interest.

GRANTEE party to whom the TITLE to REAL PROPERTY is conveyed; the buyer. *See also* GRANTOR.

GRANTOR
Investments: OPTIONS trader who sells a CALL OPTION or a PUT OPTION and collects PREMIUM INCOME for doing so. The grantor sells the right to buy a security at a certain price in the case of a call, and the right to sell at a certain price in the case of a put.
Law: one who executes a deed to real estate conveying title to property or who creates a trust. Also called *settlor*. *Grantors* include: (1) an individual (former) owner, (2) a bankruptcy TRUSTEE, (3) a GUARDIAN for an INCOMPETENT, (4) an individual who places assets in a trust.

GRANTOR TRUST trust that has beneficiaries other than the grantor but, because of the retention of certain interests or certain powers over the trust, all income of the trust is taxed to the grantor.

GRAPEVINE unofficial path of verbal communication. Rumors or scuttlebutt are spread from person to person through an informal network.

GRAPHICAL USER INTERFACE (GUI) a way of communicating with a computer that uses visual feedback to the user as much as possible. Features of a GUI include the use of icons to represent commands and options, pull-down menus that appear when called for and then disappear when no longer needed, and the use of a mouse to move a pointer around the screen. By pointing to the appropriate icons or menu items and clicking a mouse button, various commands can be activated. It is also possible to use the mouse in drawing programs. *See* MACINTOSH; WINDOWS.

GRAPHICS INTERCHANGE FORMAT *see* GIF.

GRAPHIC SOFTWARE program for depicting information in graphic form, including charts, diagrams, and signs. This enhances understanding of financial statement accounts, trends, and relationships. Graphs may be turned into photographic slides, overhead transparencies, and images on paper.

GRATIS free; given or performed without reward or CONSIDERATION.

GRATUITOUS uncalled for; item or service given free of charge. Examples are a sample given to a potential customer to promote a product or service performed by an employee working voluntarily on his personal time.

GRATUITY *see* TIP.

GRAVEYARD MARKET bear market wherein investors who sell are faced with substantial losses, while potential investors prefer to stay liquid until market conditions improve. Like a graveyard, those who are in cannot get out, and those who are out have no desire to get in.

GRAVEYARD SHIFT work shift in the middle of the night; third shift in a manufacturing operation. The graveyard shift usually begins at midnight and ends at 8 A.M., although there are variations.

GRAY MARKET sale of products by unauthorized dealers, frequently at discounted prices. Consumers who buy *gray market* goods may find that the manufacturer refuses to honor the product warranty. In some cases, gray market goods may be sold in a country they were not intended for, so the instructions may be in a foreign language.

GREAT DEPRESSION period from the end of 1929 until the onset of World War II, during which economic activity slowed tremendously and unemployment was very high.

GREATER FOOL THEORY theory that even though a stock or the market as a whole is OVERVALUED, speculation is justified because there are enough fools to push prices further upward.

GREENBACK specifically, U.S. paper currency. so named because much of the printing on the reverse is green. Generally it also refers to any paper money that may not be exchangeable for precious metals.

GREEN CARD a registration card (once green in color) carried by immigrants with permanent residence status. This is an intermediate step toward becoming a naturalized U.S. citizen.

GREEN INVESTING owning the stock of environmentally friendly companies.

GREENMAIL in corporate takeovers, a target company's acquisition of its stock from a hostile suitor at a premium to its market value; a variant of *blackmail*, descriptive of the color of money. The suitor profits at the expense of the target corporation's remaining stockholders.

GREGG a system of shorthand developed in England in 1885 by John Robert Gregg (1867–1948).

GRESHAM'S LAW theory in economics that bad money drives out good money. Specifically, people faced with a choice of two currencies of the same nominal value, one of which is preferable to the other because of metal content, will hoard the good money and spend the bad money, thereby driving the good money out of circulation.

GRID a pattern of intersecting horizontal and vertical lines. In word processing tables, the *grid*, which represents cell borders, can be displayed or hidden. In graphics programs, users can choose to enable or disable the "snap to grid" feature. When it is turned on, objects are automatically aligned with the nearest horizontal and/or vertical line of the grid. Grid intervals can usually be set by the user.

GRIEVANCE one's allegation that something imposes an illegal burden, denies some equitable or legal right, or causes injustice. An employee may be entitled by a COLLECTIVE BARGAINING agreement to seek relief through a *grievance procedure*.

GROSS
1. highest amount, as when referring to sales or income.
2. in quantity of merchandise, 12 dozen, or 144.

GROSS AMOUNT total amount of something without accounting for costs, taxes, or loss. For example, *gross revenues* do not account for taxes, depreciation, and other costs.

GROSS BILLING
1. cost of advertising with a communications medium, including the advertising agency commission.
2. cost of a one-time insertion in a communications medium.

GROSS DOMESTIC PRODUCT (GDP) total final value of goods and services produced in a national economy over a particular period of time, usually one year. The GDP growth rate is the primary indicator of the status of the economy. The U.S. GDP includes the private and governmental sectors and foreign business operations within the confines of the United States; it does not include overseas operations of domestic corporations. Formerly called *Gross National Product (GNP)*.

GROSS EARNINGS employee's salary prior to deductions for taxes, Social Security, and employee benefit contributions.

GROSS EARNINGS FORM insurance coverage for loss in the gross earnings of the business (minus expenses that cease while the business is inoperative) as the result of the interruption of normal business activities caused by damage to the premises by an insured peril. Noncontinuing expenses include light, gas, and advertising for which there is no contractual obligation.

GROSSED-UP GIFT result of adding the GIFT TAX paid by the decedent of the estate back to the gift when it is included in the GROSS ESTATE.

GROSS ESTATE total value of a person's assets before liabilities such as debts and taxes are deducted. After someone dies, the EXECUTOR of the WILL makes an assessment of the stocks, bonds, real estate, and personal possessions that comprise the *gross estate*. Debts and taxes are paid, as are funeral expenses and estate administration costs. *See also* UNIFIED ESTATE AND GIFT TAX; FEDERAL ESTATE TAX.

GROSS FEDERAL DEBT total amount of debt in existence within the economy, public and private.

GROSS INCOME total of a taxpayer's income from any source, except items specifically excluded by the Internal Revenue Code and other items not subject to tax.

GROSS INCOME MULTIPLIER (GIM) *see* GROSS RENT MULTIPLIER.

GROSS LEASABLE AREA total floor area of a building, usually measured from its outside walls. *See also* NET LEASABLE AREA.

GROSS LEASE lease of property whereby the landlord (LESSOR) is responsible for paying all property expense, such as taxes, insurance, utilities, and repairs. Under a gross lease the landlord receives rent as a gross figure and must pay operating expenses. *See also* NET LEASE.

GROSS MARGIN *see* GROSS PROFIT; GROSS PROFIT RATIO.

GROSS NATIONAL EXPENDITURE total of all expenditure of all kinds within the economy, public and private. It is usually different from GROSS DOMESTIC PRODUCT (GDP) because expenditures on imports are included, but exports (goods produced within the economy but sold outside of it) are not.

GROSS NATIONAL PRODUCT (GNP) *see* GROSS DOMESTIC PRODUCT (GDP).

GROSS PROFIT difference between revenue (*sales*) and the cost of goods sold. For example, XYZ Company sold through a newspaper advertisement 120 belts that cost XYZ $10 each. XYZ sold each belt for $18. The gross profit is calculated as follows:

(sales)	$120 \times \$18 =$	$2,160
(cost of sales)	$120 \times \$10 =$	$1,200
Gross profit		$ 960

The gross profit as a percentage of revenue is termed the *gross profit margin*. Gross profit is different from NET PROFIT, which is gross profit net of other income or expenses, interest expense, and taxes.

GROSS PROFIT METHOD system used to estimate inventory at the end of an interim period (e.g., quarter) when preparing INTERIM STATEMENTS. However, estimating inventory for annual reporting is not acceptable. The method can be used to estimate what the inventory was at the date of a loss (e.g., fire, theft, other type of casualty loss) for insurance reimbursement.

GROSS PROFIT RATIO in an INSTALLMENT SALE, the relationship between the gross profit (gain) and the CONTRACT PRICE. The resulting fraction is applied to periodic receipts from the buyer to determine the taxable gain from each receipt.

GROSS RATING POINT (GRP)
1. sum of all rating points over a specific time period or over the course of a MEDIA PLAN; sometimes called *homes per rating point*.
2. in outdoor advertising, percentage of the population that passes an outdoor advertising structure daily.

GROSS RECEIPTS
1. total sales of a business in a year, before deductions for returns and allowances or trade discounts.
2. for purposes of the BUILT-IN GAIN TAX, gross receipts of an S CORPORATION include revenue from inventory sales, sales of fixed assets, and various other items. Also, a foreign tax must satisfy the gross receipts test in order to qualify for a FOREIGN TAX CREDIT.

GROSS RENT MULTIPLIER (GRM) in real estate, sales price divided by the CONTRACT RENTAL rate; a method of estimating the value of income-producing real estate that is somewhat crude since it fails to consider operating expenses, debt service, and income taxes. For example, if the sales price is \$400,000 and the gross monthly contract rent is \$4,000, then the GRM = \$400,000 ÷ \$4,000 = 100. GRM may also be expressed as the number of years of rent equaling the purchase price (GRM = \$400,000 ÷ \$48,000 annual rent = 8.333).

GROSS REVENUE or **GROSS SALES** total sales at invoice values, not reduced by customer discounts, returns, or allowances or other adjustments. *See also* NET SALES.

GROSS TON 2,240 pounds AVOIRDUPOIS weight.

GROSS WEIGHT combined weight of contents and shipping container. *See also* TARE WEIGHT.

GROUND LEASE lease that rents the land only. One who plans to develop a structure on land that is ground leased will usually insist on a long-term-lease, such as for 30 or more years.

GROUND RENT the rent earned by leased land. Ground rent received is taxable as ORDINARY INCOME when received. If the lease is considered a financing device, portions of the rent may be treated as interest, gain, and nontaxable recovery of investment. If ground rent is a financing device, it is treated as a MORTGAGE payment.

GROUND ZERO actual point of impact; point where the full impact of an action will be experienced. In the military it applies to the point of the blast of a bomb. The center of Hiroshima was *ground zero* for the atomic bomb in 1945.

GROUP CREDIT INSURANCE coverage issued to a creditor on the lives of debtors for outstanding loans. If a debtor dies before repayment, the policy pays the remainder of the loan to the creditor. The contract covers an entire group of debtors, rather than each debtor separately.

GROUP DISABILITY INSURANCE coverage of an employee group whose members receive a monthly disability income benefit, subject to a maximum amount, if illness or accident prevents a member from performing the normal functions of his job. Benefits are usually limited to a stated length of time, and the maximum monthly income benefit is usually no more than 50–60% of earnings prior to the disability, or a flat dollar amount, whichever is less.

GROUP DYNAMICS social interaction of the participants in a group; dynamics of the group interaction process whereby creative contributions occur.

GROUP HEALTH INSURANCE coverage underwritten on members of a natural group, such as employees of a particular business, union, association, or employer group. Each employee is entitled to benefits for hospital room and board, surgeon and physician fees, and miscellaneous medical expenses.

GROUP INTERVIEW process whereby individuals are interviewed as a group. The process can be used to solicit opinions or as a form of employment interview.

GROUP LEGAL SERVICES PLAN legal services provided under such a plan or amounts paid for them are tax free.

GROUP LIFE INSURANCE basic employee benefit under which an employer buys a master policy and issues certificates to employees denoting participation in the plan. Group life is also available through unions and associations. It is usually issued as yearly renewable term insurance although some provide permanent insurance. Employers may pay all the cost, or share it with employees.

GROUP NORMS behavior norms applied to group members. Group norms are extremely important in determining group behaviors and how they will conform to management goals.

GROUP OF ELEVEN eleven major industrialized countries that try to coordinate monetary and fiscal policies to create a more stable world economic system. The eleven are Belgium, Canada, France, Germany, Italy, Japan, the Netherlands, Sweden, Switzerland, the United Kingdom, and the United States.

GROWING-EQUITY MORTGAGE (GEM) MORTGAGE loan in which the payment is increased by a specific amount each year, with the additional payment amount applied to PRINCIPAL retirement. As a result of the added principal retirement, the maturity of the loan is significantly shorter than for a comparable LEVEL-PAYMENT MORTGAGE.

GROWTH FUND mutual fund that invests in growth stocks. The goal is to provide capital appreciation for the fund's shareholders over the long term. Growth funds are more volatile than more conservative income or money market funds. *See also* GROWTH STOCK.

GROWTH RATE amount of change in some financial characteristic of a company:
1. percentage change in earnings per share, dividends per share, revenue, market price of stock, or total assets compared to a base year amount.
2. percentage change in an item such as net income considering the time value of money.
3. change in retained earnings divided by beginning stockholders' equity.
4. net income less dividends divided by common stockholders' equity. A high ratio reflects a company's ability to generate internal funds and thus it does not have to rely on external sources.

GROWTH STOCK stock of a corporation that has exhibited faster than average gains in earnings over the last few years and is expected to continue to show high levels of profit growth. Growth stocks are riskier investments than average stocks, however, since they usually sport higher price-earnings ratios and make little or no dividend payments to shareholders.

G-TYPE REORGANIZATION a transfer by a corporation in BANK-RUPTCY of all or part of its assets to another corporation, but only if stocks or securities of the transferee corporation are distributed to the shareholders tax free or partially tax free.

GUARANTEE
1. take responsibility for payment of a debt or performance of some obligation if the person primarily liable fails to perform.
2. promise to repair or replace a defective product. *See also* WARRANTY.

GUARANTEED ANNUAL WAGE (GAW) plan provided by an employer to assure eligible employees a minimum amount of work or pay during the year. Employees must meet certain requirements such as willingness to change jobs or to work overtime when needed.

GUARANTEED BOND bond on which the principal and interest are guaranteed by a firm other than the issuer. Such bonds are nearly always railroad bonds, where one road has leased the road of another and the security holders of the leased road require assurance of income in exchange for giving up control of the property. *See* CREDIT ENHANCEMENT.

GUARANTEED INCOME CONTRACT (GIC) contract between an insurance company and a corporate profit-sharing or pension plan that guarantees a specific rate of return on the invested capital over the life of the contract. *See also* YIELD TO CALL.

GUARANTEED INSURABILITY additional life insurance that may be purchased without physical examination (1) at stated times; (2) upon the birth of each child; and (3) upon specified policy anniversaries such as every fifth year. Usually there is a maximum age at which guaranteed insurability ends.

GUARANTEED MORTGAGE *see* PRIVATE MORTGAGE INSURANCE; VETERANS ADMINISTRATION (VA).

GUARANTEED PAYMENTS FOR CAPITAL payment to a partner by a partnership that is determined without regard to partnership income and is for the use of that partner's capital.

GUARANTEE LETTER letter by a commercial bank that guarantees payment of the exercise price of a client's PUT OPTION if or when a notice indicating its exercise, called an *assignment notice*, is presented to the option seller (writer).

GUARANTEE OF SIGNATURE certificate issued by a bank or brokerage firm vouching for the authenticity of a person's signature; may be necessary when stocks, bonds, or other registered securities are transferred from a seller to a buyer.

GUARANTOR one who guarantees, endorses, or provides indemnity agreements with respect to debts owed to others. Any losses are deductible when sustained.

GUARANTY
1. promise to be responsible for the DEBT, DEFAULT, or miscarriage of another.
2. WARRANTY or promise to undertake an original obligation.
3. something given as security for the performance of an act or the continued quality of a thing. *See also* SURETY BOND.

GUARDIAN
In general: anyone who protects another person or property.
Law: one appointed by a court to administer the personal affairs or property of an individual who is not capable of such duties.

GUARDIAN DEED deed given for the sale of real estate by one appointed by a court to administer the personal affairs or property of an individual who is not capable of such duties.

GUARDIANSHIP EXPENSES tax-deductible expense for the services of a guardian of a minor.

GUEST WORKER foreign worker legally brought into a nation to satisfy its labor shortage.

GUI *see* GRAPHICAL USER INTERFACE.

GUIDE manual or other model outlining policies or procedures used to instruct a sequence of actions. A company policy guide is an example of a policy model to be followed when making day-to-day operational decisions.

GUILD medieval organization, predecessor to unions; usually association of artisans or merchants; any association where the interests and needs of a particular professional or business group are represented. An example would be the Author's Guild.

H

HABEAS CORPUS procedure for obtaining a judicial determination of the legality of an individual's custody. Technically, it is used in the criminal law context to bring the petitioner before the court to inquire into the legality of his confinement. The writ of federal habeas corpus is used to test the constitutionality of a state criminal conviction. The writ is used in the civil context to challenge the validity of child custody and deportations.

HABENDUM clause of the DEED that names the GRANTEE and defines the estate to be granted. It begins with the words "to have and to hold. . ."

HACKER an expert computer programmer who enjoys figuring out the inner workings of computer systems or NETWORKS. Some have a reputation for using their expertise to illegally break into secure programs in computers hooked up to the Internet or other networks. This sense, however, has now been taken over by the term *cracker*, and *hacker* is again a title to be proudly claimed.

HALF DUPLEX in telecommunications, transmission of data in only one direction at a time.

HALF-LIFE point in time at which half the principal has been repaid in a mortgage-backed security. Normally, it is assumed that such a security has a half-life of 12 years, but specific mortgage pools can have vastly longer or shorter half-lives, depending on interest rate trends.

HALFTONE a method of representing continuous tone images with dots of solid color. The more closely spaced the dots, the darker the color. The resolution, or number of dots per inch (DPI), determines how many shades of gray can be produced.

HALO EFFECT positive or negative opinion about a person based on an impression formed from performance in one area. For example, an interviewer might judge an applicant's entire potential for job performance on the basis of a single characteristic such as how well the applicant dresses or talks.

HALSEY PREMIUM PLAN first successful incentive wage system in U.S. industry, devised by Frederick A. Halsey (1856–1935). The purpose was to improve upon the straight piece-rate system. Halsey's premium plan was an original contribution with an avowed aim of eliminating management rate cutting commonly experienced with the piece-rate system.

HAMMERING THE MARKET intense selling of stocks by those who think prices are inflated. Speculators who think the market is about to drop, and therefore sell short, are said to be *hammering the market*. *See also* SELLING SHORT.

HANDICAPPED PERSON one who has a physical or mental disability (including, but not limited to, blindness or deafness) that constitutes or results in a functional limitation to employment; or who has any physical or mental impairment that substantially limits one or more major life activities.

HANDLING ALLOWANCE discount or special price offered by a manufacturer to a wholesaler, distributor, or retailer when the manufacturer's product requires special handling. For example, grocery stores may be eligible for a handling allowance from a manufacturer if they redeem the manufacturer's discount coupons, since the coupons require extra work on the part of the store staff.

HANDSHAKE exchange of signals between computers or between a computer and a peripheral to establish communication. During the *handshake*, the two devices greet and identify each other and then determine which protocols will be used to transfer data.

HANDYMAN SPECIAL in real estate brokerage jargon, a property that is in need of repair, a *fixer-upper*. The implication is that the property is a bargain for someone who can accomplish the repairs economically.

HANGOUT remaining balance of a loan when the term of a loan is beyond the term of the LEASE. For example a lender offers a 30-year loan on property that is leased to Big Buy Foods for the next 25 years. In 25 years the loan balance will be $100,000, which is the *hangout*. The lender estimates that the land value in 25 years will greatly exceed $100,000, so concern for the hangout is minimized.

HANG SENG INDEX the major indicator of stock market performance in Hong Kong. The index comprises 33 companies and is computed on an arithmetic basis, weighted by MARKET CAPITALIZATION.

HARD
1. not easily dented, crushed, or pierced.
2. difficult, demanding great physical or mental effort; hard work, hard problem.
3. firm; settled; definite; hard data, hard facts, hard answers.
4. physical, tangible, concrete: HARD COPY.

HARD CASH historically, coin made of precious metal. Nowadays it may refer to any readily available money, whether paper or metal.

HARD COPY printout on paper of computer output, as contrasted with the information shown on a CRT screen.

HARD-CORE UNEMPLOYED people who either have never had a full-time job or have been unable to find work over an extended period of time. The hard-core unemployed are usually disadvantaged people who lack education and job skills.

HARD CURRENCY currency recognized internationally to be relatively stable in value and readily acceptable in most international transactions. Examples of *hard currency* are the U.S. dollar, the Swiss franc, and the German mark.

HARD DISK or **DRIVE** computer storage medium using rigid aluminum disks coated with iron oxide. Hard disks have much greater storage capacity than removable media such as FLOPPY DISKS and CDs.

HARD DOLLARS actual payments made by customer or investor; *contrast with* SOFT MONEY that may be tax deductible or money that otherwise need not be paid in full. *See also* HARD MONEY.

HARD GOODS durable merchandise such as televisions, appliances, hardware, furniture, or recording equipment. *See also* SOFT GOODS.

HARD HAT rigid helmet usually worn by workers on a job site; also, such a worker. The hard hat provides a degree of protection from job-related hazards to the head region.

HARD MANUFACTURING fixed production equipment used to manufacture large production runs of similar items. *Hard manufacturing* equipment usually represents a large FIXED COST and cannot be easily adapted to new products. It is not designed to be moved from one location to another.

HARD MONEY
1. currency in which there is widespread confidence; the currency of an economically and politically stable country, such as the United States or Switzerland; also called HARD CURRENCY.
2. gold or coins, as contrasted with paper currency, which is considered soft money; *see also* HARD CASH.

HARD SELL aggressive sales practices aimed at pressuring a customer into completing a transaction quickly.

HARDSHIP DISTRIBUTION DISTRIBUTION from a SECTION 401(K) PLAN that is made because of the distributee's immediate and heavy financial needs and does not exceed the amount necessary to satisfy such need (e.g., medical problems, post-secondary tuition, to stave off eviction from or foreclosure of a principal residence).

HARDWARE mechanical and electronic parts that constitute a computer system, as distinguished from the computer programs (SOFTWARE) that drive the system. The main hardware elements are the CENTRAL PROCESSING UNIT, DISK or *magnetic tape* data storage devices, CATHODE-RAY TUBE display terminals, keyboards, and PRINTERS.

HASH TOTAL summation of numbers having no practical meaning as a control precaution; used by auditors primarily in a computer application. The purpose is to identify whether a record has been lost or omitted from processing. For example, check numbers may be summed to get a hash total. If the total of the check numbers processed does not agree with the hash total, a discrepancy exists and investigation is required to uncover the error.

HATCHET MAN company employee responsible for reducing personnel or telling them of their dismissal and the terms of severance.

HAWTHORN EFFECT effect of the interrelationship between management supervision and employee NORMS. In the Hawthorn study the employees reacted favorably to the supervision of the researchers who took great interest in their activities. This one finding was far more significant than any other outcome of the study.

HAZARD INSURANCE form of insurance that protects against certain risks, such as fires or storms.

HD *see* HARD DISK.

HDD HARD DISK drive.

HEAD AND SHOULDERS in a chart of market prices, patterns resembling the head and shoulders outline of a person. The pattern signals the reversal of a trend. As prices move down to the right shoulder, a head and shoulders top is formed, meaning that prices should be falling.

HEADER top margin of a printed document, which repeats on every page and, according to a specific computer program, can include text, pictures, automatic consecutive page numbers, date, and time. *See also* FOOTER.

HEADHUNTER private employment agency specializing in the recruiting of professional and managerial personnel; also called *executive search firm*. The fees charged by these agencies range up to one-third of the first year's total salary and bonus package for the job to be filled.

HEAD OF HOUSEHOLD for tax filings, unmarried TAXPAYER who maintains as his home a household that is the principal residence of a designated DEPENDENT. A qualified head of household is subject to a lower TAX RATE than that applied to a single person not a head of household. Other tax-filing statuses are single; married filing a joint return; and married filing separate returns. *See also* FILING STATUS; QUALIFYING PERSON.

HEALTH CARE POWER OF ATTORNEY gives a person the right to make medical treatment decisions for the PRINCIPAL when the principal is unable to do so. The agent may decide on the use of extraordinary life support measures, such as artificial breathing machines.

HEALTH INSURANCE CREDIT a part of the EARNED INCOME CREDIT that is based on health insurance premiums that provide coverage for one or more qualifying children.

HEALTH MAINTENANCE ORGANIZATION (HMO) prepaid group health insurance plan that entitles members to services of participating physicians, hospitals, and clinics. Emphasis is on preventive medicine. Members of the HMO pay a flat periodic fee (usually deducted from each paycheck) for a number of medical services.

HEALTH SAVINGS ACCOUNT (HSA) type of account created by the MEDICARE bill signed by President George Bush on December 8, 2003, that allows tax-free contributions, earnings, and withdrawals if used for medical care. HSAs must be used in conjunction with a high-deductible health insurance plan. Allowable contributions cannot exceed the deductible; in 2006 the maximum allowable contribution was $2,700 for an individual ($5,450 for a family), plus an additional $700 CATCH-UP CONTRIBUTION for people 55 or over. These amounts will be increased for inflation in future years. Within limits, accounts can be drawn down without penalty at any time for medical bills.

HEARING
1. formal procedure, with issues of fact or law to be tried, in which parties have a right to be heard. It is similar to a trial and may result in a final order.
2. generally, a proceeding to determine an issue of fact on the basis of evidence available.
3. the second level of appeal by one who disagrees with a Social Security Administration decision on a disability claim. Under the *hearing* level of appeal, a worker is entitled to apply to be heard by a judge.

HEARSAY
1. statement made by an individual within the organization that is based on rumor rather than substantiated facts; gossip.
2. in law, testimony of one person as to the statement of another. It does not prove what the other said but proves the truth of the fact asserted by the other.

HEAVY INDUSTRY traditional production industries in the auto, steel, rubber, petroleum, and raw material areas, requiring high capitalization and producing large quantities of output. Heavy industry employs many people, and is often beset by environmental impacts.

HECTARE metric area measurement equal to about 2.471 ACRES or 107,637 square feet.

HEDGE or **HEDGING** strategy used to offset business or investment risk. A perfect hedge is one that eliminates the possibility of future gain or loss. Futures hedging income is taxable ORDINARY INCOME, but futures hedging losses are capital losses and are deductible only to the extent of CAPITAL GAIN income (or $3,000 for individuals).

HEDGE FUND private investment partnership in which the general partner has made a substantial personal investment, and whose offering memorandum allows for the fund to take both LONG and SHORT POSITIONS, use LEVERAGE and DERIVATIVES, and invest in many markets. *Hedge funds* often take large risks on speculative strategies.

HEIRS strictly, those whom statutory law would appoint to inherit an estate should the ancestor die without a WILL (INTESTATE). The term is often applied indiscriminately to those who inherit by will or DEED, as well as by operation of law.

HEIRS AND ASSIGNS term often found in DEEDS and WILLS to grant a FEE SIMPLE estate.

HELP WANTED ADVERTISING classified newspaper advertisements by job category, placed by management seeking potential employees. Help wanted advertising is a *leading economic indicator* in that a greater number of advertisements indicates increasing job opportunities and economic growth.

HEMLINE THEORY whimsical idea that stock prices move in the same general direction as the hemlines of women's dresses. Short skirts in the 1920s and 1960s were considered bullish signs that stock prices would rise, whereas longer dresses in the 1930s and 1940s were considered bearish (falling) indicators.

HETEROGENEOUS consisting of dissimilar parts. The term describes an organization selling many different products.

HEURISTIC method of solving problems that involves intelligent trial and error, such as playing chess. By contrast, an algorithmic solution method is a clearly specified procedure that is guaranteed to give the correct answer. *See also* ALGORITHM.

HIDDEN AGENDA unannounced objectives, needs, expectations, or strategies of a person or group when participating in an activity. Since individuals keep their agendas secret, one has to rely on minimal clues to determine what others are thinking.

HIDDEN ASSET or RESERVE property value that is understated on the BALANCE SHEET of a company because of accounting convention or deliberate action of management.

HIDDEN INFLATION price increase implemented by offering a smaller quantity or poorer quality for the old price.

HIDDEN TAX indirect tax paid unwittingly by the consumer in the form of higher prices. Such taxes are levied on goods at some point in their production or transport prior to retail sale. For example, the federal tax on an airline ticket is included in the quoted price of the ticket.

HIERARCHY ordering by importance of roles, responsibilities, or objectives in an organization. The chief executive officer is at the pinnacle of the management *hierarchy*.

HIERARCHY OF NEEDS *see* MASLOW'S HIERARCHY OF NEEDS.

HIGH CREDIT
Banking: maximum amount of loans outstanding recorded for a particular customer.
Finance: highest amount of TRADE CREDIT a particular company has received from a supplier at one time.

HIGHER EDUCATION EXPENSES, QUALIFIED *see* COVERDELL EDUCATION SAVINGS ACCOUNT.

HIGHEST AND BEST USE real estate APPRAISAL term meaning the legally and physically possible use that, at the time of appraisal, is most likely to produce the greatest net return to the land or buildings over a given period.

HIGH FLYER high-priced and highly speculative stock that moves up and down sharply over a short period. The stock of unproven high-technology companies might be high flyers.

HIGH-GRADE BOND bond rated AAA or AA by Standard & Poor's or Moody's rating services.

HIGH-GROWTH VENTURES small businesses designed for the purpose of achieving high growth and rapid profit increases. Often, to achieve profit and growth objectives, these businesses develop products and promotion strategies with a pool of investors providing working capital.

HIGHLY LEVERAGED (a business or investment) financed to a large degree using borrowed money. High leveraging increases financial risk and the potential for gains and losses.

HIGH RISE generally a building that exceeds six stories in height and is equipped with elevators.

HIGHS stocks that have hit higher prices in daily trading compared to prices of the past 52-week period. They are listed as highs in daily newspapers. Technical analysts consider the ratio between new highs and new lows in the stock market to be significant for pointing out stock market trends.

HIGH TECHNOLOGY advanced developments in an area of technology. The term is often associated with computer-related developments, being on the technological *cutting edge* of a field.

HIGH-TECH STOCK stock of companies involved in high-technology fields such as computers, semiconductors, biotechnology, robotics, or electronics. Successful high-tech stocks have above-average earnings growth and therefore typically very volatile stock prices.

HISTOGRAM a bar graph in which the frequency of occurrence for each class of data is represented by the relative height of the bars.

HISTORICAL COST accounting principle requiring assets to be based on original cost or a substituted BASIS; a STEPPED-UP BASIS to MARKET VALUE is provided to the heirs upon death of the former owner.

HISTORICAL YIELD YIELD provided by a mutual fund, typically a money market fund, over a particular period of time. For instance, a money market fund may advertise that its historical yield averaged 10% over the last year.

HISTORIC DISTRICT a designated area where the buildings are considered to have some significant historic character. Such designation makes the area eligible for certain federal assistance programs and protects the area from clearance in conjunction with federally sponsored programs. Older areas, such as the French Quarter in New Orleans, enjoy protection by being designated as *historic districts*.

HISTORIC STRUCTURE building that is officially recognized for its historic significance. A special tax law allows a 20% TAX CREDIT for rehabilitation of certified historic structures. A nonresidential building, other than a certified historic structure, placed in service before 1936 may qualify for a 10% rehabilitation tax credit.

HIT
1. something successful. A product may be a *hit* with customers; an employee may make a *hit* with the boss.
2. a visit to a WEB PAGE. Many WEB SITES have *hit counters* to keep track of the number of times a page is accessed.

HIT LIST group of people or organizations that are to be approached for a sales presentation or request for money.

HIT THE BRICKS employees going on strike against the employer.

HOARDING excess accumulation of commodities or currency in anticipation of scarcity and/or higher prices.

HOBBY LOSS loss incurred by a taxpayer in an activity not pursued for profit. In general, hobby losses are deductible only to the extent of income generated by the hobby. An activity that generates a profit in three of five years is presumed to be operated for profit.

HOCKEY STICK PROJECTION the expectation of sharply increasing earnings following a period of modest growth. From the shape of the graph produced by plotting the dollar amount of earnings over time.

HOLDBACK in real estate, money not paid until certain events have occurred, such as a FLOOR LOAN of a LOAN COMMITMENT or RETAINAGE on a construction contract.

HOLDBACK PAY wages or salary withheld from an employee by the employer until a particular condition is satisfied. It may occur: (1) because of the time gap needed to compute pay and prepare payroll or (2) to provide security against cash advances made or tools lent to the employee in the event of his sudden departure.

HOLDER IN DUE COURSE *good-faith holder* who has taken a negotiable instrument for value, without NOTICE that it was overdue or had been DISHONORED or that there was any defense against or CLAIM to it. In property law, the innocent buyer or holder in due course is referred to as a *bona fide purchaser*.

HOLDER OF RECORD owner of a company's securities as recorded on the books of the issuing company or its TRANSFER AGENT as of a particular date. Dividend declarations always specify payability to *holders of record* as of a specific date. *See also* DATE OF RECORD.

HOLD HARMLESS AGREEMENTS assumption of liability through contractual agreement by one party, thereby eliminating liability on the part of another party. An example is a railroad sidetrack agreement with a manufacturing company under which the manufacturer is held harmless for damage to railroad equipment and tracks.

HOLD HARMLESS CLAUSE in a CONTRACT, a clause whereby one party agrees to protect another party from claims.

HOLDING in commercial and property law, PROPERTY to which one has legal TITLE and of which one is in POSSESSION. The term may be used to refer specifically to ownership of stocks or shares of corporations.

HOLDING COMPANY corporation organized for the purpose of owning stock in and managing one or more corporations. Holding companies traditionally own many corporations in widely different business areas.

HOLDING PERIOD length of time an investment is owned or expected to be owned. The holding period is important in determining whether a gain or loss from the sale or exchange of a capital asset is long-term or short-term. For tax purposes, the holding period generally begins and ends on the settlement date of the purchase and sale transactions. *See* CAPITAL GAIN; CAPITAL LOSS.

HOLDOUT one who attempts to realize the highest possible price by refusing to sell in the early stages of negotiation.

HOLDOVER TENANT TENANT who remains in possession of leased property after expiration of the lease TERM. *See also* TENANCY AT SUFFERANCE.

HOME EQUITY CONVERSION the process of liquidating all or a portion of the equity in one's home. *See* HOME EQUITY LOAN; REVERSE ANNUITY MORTGAGE.

HOME EQUITY LINE OF CREDIT a type of HOME EQUITY LOAN that establishes an account that the borrower can draw upon as desired. There is generally a maximum amount placed on the outstanding debt, similar to a credit card spending limit. Interest accrues based on the amount of money actually borrowed, not the full amount of the credit line. The product is intended for people who may need to access cash in the future but have no immediate need for a loan.

HOME EQUITY LOAN a loan secured by a second mortgage on one's principal residence, generally to be used for some nonhousing expenditure. *Home equity loans* became popular in the latter 1980s as a way to finance purchases or consolidate existing debts while retaining tax-deductible status for the interest paid on the loan. Home equity loans up to $100,000 above the cost of purchase and improvement generate tax-deductible interest.

HOME LOAN *see* MORTGAGE.

HOME MORTGAGE INTEREST any interest paid on a loan secured by the taxpayer's personal residence (principal residence or second home). *See* INTEREST DEDUCTIONS.

HOME OFFICE
1. the headquarters location of a company; an employee may also refer to the office to which he or she reports as the *home office*.
2. an office in a personal residence used exclusively for business on a regular and continuing basis. To be tax deductible, the home office must be the taxpayer's principal place of business (that is, where the majority of his or her work is performed) or used as a place to meet customers or clients and, if the taxpayer is not self-employed, must be used for the convenience of his or her employer.

Beginning in 1999, the "principal place of business includes a place of business used by the taxpayer for the administrative or management activities of any trade or business of the taxpayer if there is no other fixed location of such trade or business where the taxpayer conducts substantial administrative or management activities of such trade or business. For a qualifying home office, the taxpayer may claim a portion of utilities and a depreciation deduction for the office and any furniture and equipment. Upon sale of the home, however, gain attributable to the business portion cannot be deferred."

HOMEOWNERS' ASSOCIATION organization of the homeowners in a particular SUBDIVISION, planned unit development, or CONDOMINIUM. It is generally formed for the purpose of enforcing deed restrictions or managing the COMMON ELEMENTS of the development. *See also* COMMUNITY ASSOCIATION.

HOMEOWNER'S EQUITY ACCOUNT credit line offered by banks and brokerage firms allowing a homeowner to tap the built-up equity in his or her home. Such an account is, in effect, a REVOLVING-CREDIT second mortgage.

HOMEOWNERSHIP state of living in a structure that one owns; *contrast with* being a renter or TENANT in one's home.

HOMEOWNERSHIP RATE the percentage ratio of owner-occupied dwelling units to total occupied dwelling units in an area. In 2005, the *homeownership rate* for the United States was 69.1%, indicating the proportion of all households owning the home in which they lived. Within the population, the rate varies greatly by age and type of household, with higher incidence for married and older households than for young singles.

HOMEOWNER'S POLICY insurance policy designed especially for homeowners; usually protects the owner from losses caused by most common disasters, theft, and LIABILITY. Coverage and costs vary widely.

HOMEOWNER WARRANTY PROGRAM (HOW) private insurance program, in which the builder participates, protecting purchasers of newly constructed homes against structural and mechanical faults.

HOME PAGE
1. a WEB PAGE that is the first page that appears when you access a WEB SITE. It may be a simple portal or a complex table of contents; in the latter case the URL usually has the suffix *INDEX*.
2. sometimes used as a synonym for *start page*, the initial page displayed by a WEB BROWSER, which can usually be selected by the user.

HOMESTEAD house and surrounding land owned and used as a dwelling. Under modern HOMESTEAD EXEMPTION laws, enacted in most states, any property designated as a *homestead* is exempt from EXECUTION and SALE by creditors in case of bankruptcy.

HOMESTEAD EXEMPTION in some jurisdictions, a reduction in the assessed value allowed for one's principal residence. For example, the *homestead exemption* in one state permits a homeowner, upon application, to have the assessor's appraisal of the home reduced by $5,000, thereby reducing the property tax burden.

HOMEWORK
1. self-study assignment that a student in a business course must complete to reinforce material covered in the lecture.
2. work employees are assigned to do at home, usually on a piecework basis.

HOMOGENEOUS having the same composition or form; organization that produces or sells products having great similarities, often using the same components. Homogeneous products reduce organizational development and manufacturing costs.

HOMOGENEOUS OLIGOPOLY OLIGOPOLY in which there is very little product differentiation among producers. Examples are the petroleum industry and network television.

HONOR
1. to accept and pay an obligation when due.
2. significant reward or accolade for an accomplishment, enhancing the individual's reputation. An example is the presentation of an award to the salesperson with the highest sales for the year.

HONORARIUM fee paid by an organization to a professional to perform a service. For example, a guest lecturer may receive an *honorarium* for a presentation at a seminar.

HOPE TAX CREDIT an allowance for students in their first or second year of post-secondary education. A parent is allowed a credit for each dependent. Students must attend at least half-time and must be in a program that leads to a certificate or degree. The Hope credit allows a reduction in taxes of up to $1,500 per student to offset the cost of tuition and fees (but not room, board, or books) and applies to the tax-payer, spouse, and children. Married couples filing jointly in 2006 get the full credit on AGI up to $90,000, phasing out at $110,000. Singles get full credit in 2006 on incomes up to $45,000, phasing out at $55,000. Credits are claimed on IRS Form 8863. *See also* LIFETIME LEARNING CREDIT.

HORATIO ALGER author whose novels often depicted poor but honest characters who, by persistent, spirited efforts, succeeded against all odds.

HORIZONTAL ANALYSIS time series analysis of financial statements covering more than one accounting period. It looks at the percentage change in an account over time. The percentage change equals the change over the prior year. By examining the magnitude of direction of a financial statement item over time, the analyst can evaluate its reasonableness. *See also* VERTICAL ANALYSIS.

HORIZONTAL CHANNEL INTEGRATION strategy in which a company seeks ownership or increased control of some of its competitors.

HORIZONTAL COMBINATION business combination of companies with similar functions in the production or sale of comparable products. *See also* HORIZONTAL MERGER.

HORIZONTAL CONFLICT conflict between competitors of the same marketing channel, resulting in oversaturation of the target population area and extreme competition. For example, if two or more large home product retailers operate in the same marketing area, smaller competitors will be at an extreme disadvantage. *Contrast with* VERTICAL CONFLICT.

HORIZONTAL EXPANSION expansion of business capacity through the absorption of facilities or buildings as well as through the acquisition of new equipment to handle an increased volume in sales in which the business is already engaged.

HORIZONTAL INTEGRATION a company's domination of a market at one stage of the production process by monopolizing resources at that stage. *Contrast with* VERTICAL INTEGRATION.

HORIZONTAL MERGER merging of companies with similar functions in the production or sale of comparable products. Depending upon the total market share, a horizontal merger is considered by the FEDERAL TRADE COMMISSION (FTC) to be the most blatantly anti-competitive merger strategy. *See also* HORIZONTAL COMBINATION.

HORIZONTAL SPECIALIZATION organizational process whereby a single management function, such as recruiting, is divided among one or more subordinates; also known as *functional management*. Horizontal specialization usually occurs because growth in an organization requires additional management coordination and control.

HORIZONTAL UNION craft union whose organization includes all workers in a particular craft or skill throughout an industry, region, or country.

HOSPITALIZATION INSURANCE form of health insurance covering hospital stays and related medical costs, including medicine and physicians' services. Many organizations provide at least a part of the cost of hospitalization insurance for their employees. The hospitalization insurance coverage varies depending on the specific policy. *See also* GROUP HEALTH INSURANCE.

HOST
1. a computer that allows users to communicate with other host computers on a network.
2. a chat term for someone who is managing a chat room on the Internet.

HOSTILE FIRE unfriendly fire not confined to its normal habitat. For example, fire in the fireplace leaps onto the sofa. Property contracts protect against damage from a hostile fire, not from damage from fire in the fireplace, its normal habitat. The insurance is designed to cover FORTUITOUS LOSS, which the hostile fire is.

HOSTILE TAKEOVER TAKEOVER of a company against the wishes of current management and the board of directors. This takeover may be attempted by another company or by a well-financed RAIDER. If the price offered is high enough, shareholders may vote to accept the offer even if management resists and claims the company is actually worth even more. If the takeover is successful, the existing management is usually terminated. The target company's management therefore uses a wide variety of strategies to foil the merger attempt. Also called *unfriendly takeover. Contrast with* FRIENDLY TAKEOVER. *See also* GREENMAIL; POISON PILL; SCORCHED-EARTH DEFENSE.

HOT ISSUE newly issued stock that is in great public demand. Hot issue stocks usually shoot up in price at their initial offering since there is more demand than there are shares available. Also called *hot new issue.*

HOTLINK a connection between programs that lets the user change information in one program while the computer changes the same information in the programs linked to it. Objects may be linked by OLE or the older DDE (dynamic data exchange) method.

HOT STOCK
1. stock that has been stolen.
2. newly issued stock that rises quickly in price. *See also* HOT ISSUE.

HOUDINI named after the escape magician, a computer chip in certain computers that allows the machine to run both IBM-compatible computers and Apple computers. The Houdini chip transfers information between the two computer processors.

HOUSE
1. free-standing dwelling.
2. business establishment that is occupied heavily by customers, such as a bar, theater, or casino.
3. firm or individual engaged in business as a broker-dealer in securities or investment banking and related services.
4. nickname for the London Stock Exchange.
5. synonym for company or firms, such as in the term *publishing house*.

HOUSE ACCOUNT account handled at the main office or managed by an executive of the firm, distinguished from one that is normally handled by a salesperson in the territory.

HOUSEHOLD WORKERS federal income tax withholding is not required on payments made to household workers, but Social Security taxes must be paid on household workers whether or not the employer withholds any such amount from the employee's compensation.

HOUSE TO HOUSE transportation from door of shipper to door of receiver.

HOUSE-TO-HOUSE SAMPLING distribution of a product sample to individual homes in a market area to induce trial and subsequent purchase. Many manufacturers use house-to-house sampling as a promotional tactic to stimulate word-of-mouth advertising.

HOUSE-TO-HOUSE SELLING direct sale made by calling upon prospective customers at their homes with or without an appointment; also called *door-to-door*.

HOUSING AFFORDABILITY INDEX an indicator of the proportion of the population that can afford to buy the average home sold during the current period. There are many types of affordability indexes in use. One of the best-known is the index compiled by the NATIONAL ASSOCIATION OF REALTORS. The index is formed by the ratio of a percentage of the average income of all families in the area to the monthly loan payment needed to purchase the average priced home sold in that area. An index value of 1.00 indicates that half of the families in the area could afford to buy the average home. The higher the index, the more affordable is the housing in the area at the time.

HOUSING AND URBAN DEVELOPMENT (HUD) DEPART-MENT cabinet-level U.S. government agency established (in 1965) to implement certain federal housing and community development programs. The Federal Housing Administration is part of HUD.

HOUSING BOND short- or long-term bond issued by a local housing authority to finance short-term construction of (typically) low- or middle-income housing or long-term commitments for housing, plants, pollution control facilities, or similar projects.

HOUSING CODE local government ORDINANCE that sets minimum standards of safety and sanitation for existing residential buildings, as opposed to BUILDING CODES, which pertain to new construction.

HOUSING COMPLETIONS statistic compiled and reported by the U.S. Census Bureau (Census) that represents the number of new housing units completed during the reporting period. The Census defines a completion as a unit that has a roof and is ready for occupancy.

HOUSING FINANCE AGENCY governmental (state or local) organization established to provide housing assistance. In most cases, the agency can issue bonds that pay tax-free interest and therefore sell at below taxable yields. The low-cost money is then used to fund low-interest mortgage loans for eligible borrowers. The amount of bond financing available to each state is limited by the U.S. Treasury.

HOUSING STARTS important economic indicator that offers an estimate of the number of dwelling units on which construction has begun during a stated period. The number of housing starts is closely related to interest rates and other basic economic factors.

HTML *see* HYPERTEXT MARKUP LANGUAGE.

http *see* HYPERTEXT TRANSFER PROTOCOL.

HUCKSTER seller of a good or service who will try to sell anything by making misleading promises and assurances. An example is a peddler who will make any kind of guarantee to a tourist to make the sale.

HUD *see* HOUSING AND URBAN DEVELOPMENT DEPARTMENT.

HUMAN CAPITAL the accumulated investment that has improved the productive capacity of the population. Examples are education, health care, training.

HUMAN FACTORS part of INDUSTRIAL PSYCHOLOGY concerned with designing machines so that humans can use them effectively; also called *human factors engineering, human engineering,* and *engineering psychology.* A human factors engineer may design an easy-to-read dial or study how to design control knobs so each can be easily distinguished.

HUMAN RELATIONS school of management theory stressing the importance of understanding human motivation in the workplace. The human relations school believes that employee motivation is a result of recognition, encouragement, and rewarding of individual contributions.

HUMAN RELATIONS SKILLS management skills facilitating effective interaction with personnel. These skills include leadership, communication, decision making, negotiation, counseling, and conceptual skills.

HUMAN RESOURCE ACCOUNTING reporting and emphasizing the value of the contributions of skilled and loyal employees to a firm's earning potential; matching an organization's job requirements with the skills and abilities of its WORK FORCE in terms of measuring employee productivity contributions.

HUMAN RESOURCES personnel pool available to an organization. The most important resources in any organization are its human resources. Appropriate human resources assure an organization that the right number and kind of people are available at the right time and place so that organizational needs can be met.

HUMAN RESOURCES MANAGEMENT (HRM) term that is replacing *personnel management* and implying that personnel managers should not merely handle recruitment, pay, and discharging, but should maximize the use of an organization's human resources.

HUNDRED-PERCENT LOCATION *see* ONE-HUNDRED-PERCENT LOCATION.

HUNKERING DOWN (*slang*) taking a defensive position, waiting for business conditions to improve.

HURDLE RATE budgeting capital expenditures, the REQUIRED RATE OF RETURN in a DISCOUNTED CASH FLOW analysis. If the *expected* rate of return on an investment is below the *hurdle rate*, the project is not undertaken. The hurdle rate should be equal to the MARGINAL COST OF CAPITAL.

HUSH MONEY cash given to assure the silence of the receiver, as in a bribe. An example is a payoff to an employee who uncovers theft in the organization.

HYBRID ACCOUNTING METHODS those methods that are neither strictly cash nor strictly accrual but combine elements of both. A taxpayer may use a hybrid accounting method authorized by the TREASURY REGULATIONS if it clearly reflects income and is consistently used. A taxpayer may use a different accounting method for separate businesses.

HYBRID ADJUSTABLE-RATE MORTGAGE an ADJUSTABLE-RATE MORTGAGE (ARM) that has a fixed interest rate for 3, 5, 7, or 10 years. After the fixed period ends, the rate is adjusted annually.

HYBRID ANNUITY contract offered by an insurance company that allows an investor to mix the benefits of both fixed and variable annuities. A FIXED ANNUITY promises a certain rate of return and a stock or bond fund VARIABLE ANNUITY offers a chance for higher return but takes more risk.

HYBRID INVESTMENT/SECURITY investment vehicle that combines two different kinds of underlying investments. For example, a structured NOTE, in the form of a BOND, may have the interest rate it pays tied to the rise and fall of a commodity's price. *Hybrid investments* are also called DERIVATIVES.

HYBRID PENSION PLAN a general term that encompasses pension plans with elements of both DEFINED-CONTRIBUTION and DEFINED-BENEFIT plans. Often, hybrid plans are DEFINED-BENEFIT PLANS that express the participant's benefit as a lump sum instead of an annuity. Hybrid plans often appear to participants to be similar to DEFINED-CONTRIBUTION PENSION PLANS, but they are regulated as defined-benefit plans. *Cash balance* and *pension equity* plans are examples of hybrid pension plans.

HYBRID VEHICLE a vehicle that uses two or more propulsion systems. The most common are gas/electric hybrids, which use gasoline to power internal combustion engines and electric batteries to power electric motors. Modern hybrids, such as the Toyota Prius and Honda Civic, recharge their batteries with kinetic energy produced while decelerating.

HYDROELECTRIC electric energy produced from water power. The Niagara Falls are the source of tremendous hydroelectric power.

HYGIENE FACTORS in the concept developed by Frederick Herzberg, factors that do not motivate employees, but are essential to maintain satisfaction. These include a satisfactory salary and related employee benefits, considerate HUMAN RELATIONS SKILLS, and satisfactory working conditions. The absence of any of these hygiene factors will cause employee dissatisfaction. Also called *maintenance factors*.

HYPE in broadcast, special promotional activities in programming presented by a station or network in order to attract a large audience and therefore generate higher audience ratings for a particular time period; also called *hypo*. For example: Traditionally, broadcast rating measurements are made for local stations in February, May, and November (*sweeps months*). Accordingly, local stations have been known to hype their audiences during these time periods.

HYPERINFLATION inflationary episode in which the currency becomes virtually worthless. The classic example is Germany in the mid 1920s, when it eventually cost billions of marks to mail a letter or buy bread.

HYPERLINK an icon, graphic, or word in a file that, when clicked with the mouse, opens another file for viewing or takes the user to another location in the file. WEB PAGES often include *hyperlinks* (often called simply LINKS) to other pages at the same or another WEB SITE.

HYPERTEXT MARKUP LANGUAGE (HTML) the tag-based ASCII language used to create pages on the WORLD WIDE WEB.

HYPERTEXT TRANSFER PROTOCOL (http) the protocol used by the WORLD WIDE WEB to transfer HTML files.

HYPOTHECATE to pledge something as security without turning over possession of it. Hypothecation creates a right in the CREDITOR to have the pledge sold to satisfy the claim out of the sale proceeds.

HYPOTHESIS in empirical research, assertion made about some property of elements being studied. Such an assumption is made early in the investigation, guiding the investigator in searching for supporting data. The hypothesis is found to be true or false at the conclusion of the research study, depending on whether or not the proposed property actually characterizes the elements.

HYPOTHESIS TESTING statistical procedure that involves stating something to be tested, collecting evidence, and then making a decision as to whether the statement should be accepted as true or rejected.

I

IBBOTSON & ASSOCIATES provider of historical data for various financial investments. Well known for certain publications, particularly *Stocks, Bonds, Bills & Inflation,* published annually.

ICC *see* INTERSTATE COMMERCE COMMISSION.

ICON a small graphic used to represent a computer program, file, or function in a GRAPHICAL USER INTERFACE (GUI).

IDB *see* INDUSTRIAL DEVELOPMENT BOARD.

IDEAL CAPACITY largest volume of output possible if a facility maintained continuous operation at optimum efficiency, allowing for no losses of any kind, even those deemed normal or unavoidable; also called *maximum capacity.* Since it is impossible to obtain ideal capacity, unfavorable variances will result if it is used to apply fixed cost.

IDLE CAPACITY
1. presence of unused capacity together with insufficient raw materials or skilled labor. When idle capacity exists, a firm can take on an incremental order without increasing the fixed costs.
2. economic situation wherein the market will not absorb all of the maximum possible output at a price exceeding the variable cost of production.

IDLE TIME
Administration: time when an employee is unable to work because of machine malfunction or other factors beyond the employee's control. Usually the worker receives compensation during idle time. *See also* DEAD TIME; DOWNTIME.
Computers: available time during which the computer is not in use.

ILLEGAL ALIEN non-citizen who has not been given permission by immigration authorities to reside in the country in which he is living.

ILLEGAL DIVIDEND dividend declared by a corporation's board of directors in violation of its charter or of state laws. Most states stipulate that dividends be paid out of current income or retained earnings. They prohibit dividend payments that come out of capital surplus, that would make the corporation insolvent, or that are prohibited by a bond indenture.

ILLEGAL INCOME proceeds of theft, for example, or embezzled funds, which are taxable income. Such income is taxable irrespective of the legitimacy of its source.

ILLEGAL STRIKE strike in violation of the law. Most public-sector strikes are illegal. Strikes that violate an existing labor contract, are not properly authorized by the union membership, or violate a court order are also illegal.

ILLIQUID
   Finance: firm that lacks sufficient CASH FLOW to meet current and maturing obligations.
   Investments: not readily convertible into cash, such as real estate, collectibles (rare stamps, coins, antique furniture, etc.), or inactive securities.

IMAGE ADVERTISING advertising directed at the creation of a specific image for an entity (such as a company, product, or brand), as distinguished from advertising directed at the specific attributes of the entity. The image may be one of sophistication, reliability, elegance, or luxury.

IMF *see* INTERNATIONAL MONETARY FUND.

IMMEDIATE RUN a period of time so short that firms in an industry cannot make any adjustments in response to changes in market conditions.

IMPAIRED CAPITAL total capital that is less than the stated or par value of the company's CAPITAL STOCK. *See also* DEFICIT NET WORTH.

IMPASSE deadlock. An example is no movement in negotiations between an employer and a labor union because of a lack of compromise by either party.

IMPERFECT MARKET market in which some of the producers and/or consumers are significant enough to affect the price and quantity of goods by their actions alone.

IMPERIALISM policy of systematic domination and exploitation of a country by another country or an empire. Marxists assert that the United States engages in imperialism because powerful U.S. businesses need to protect their foreign markets.

IMPLIED not explicitly written or stated; determined by deduction from known facts.

IMPLIED AGENCY occurs when the words and actions of the parties indicate that there is an agency relationship.

IMPLIED CONTRACT contract created by actions but not necessarily written or spoken. *See also* STATUTE OF FRAUDS.

IMPLIED EASEMENT EASEMENT established by use and acceptance, rather than through a legal document. Evidence of an implied easement may consist of the grantee's continual use of the easement with no effort of the grantor to constrain that use.

IMPLIED IN FACT CONTRACT contract deduced from the conduct of the parties or from the facts, as distinguished from an express oral or written contract.

IMPLIED WARRANTY warranty that is not written but exists under the law; contrast with *expressed* warranty.

IMPORT
1. bring into an economy goods produced outside that economy; also, the goods so introduced.
2. bring into one computer application a file created by another application. Most word processing, spreadsheet, and graphics applications have *import filters* for files created in competing programs.

IMPORT DUTY *see* TARIFF.

IMPORT QUOTA imposed limit upon the quantity of a good that may be brought into a country or economy over a period of time. Quotas may be imposed by government, foreign governments, or producers themselves.

IMPOSITION
1. excessive and unwarranted request. For example, it is an *imposition* for an employer to ask an employee to work 16 hours a day to meet an unreasonable deadline.
2. levying a tax or a fine on a specific item.

IMPOUND to seize and retain merchandise, funds, or records in the CUSTODY of an officer of the law.

IMPOUND ACCOUNT fund set aside for future needs. *See also* RESERVE FUND.

IMPREST FUND, IMPREST SYSTEM PETTY CASH FUND used to pay small amounts. The balance is always kept at a certain amount, such as $100, and replenished to that amount.

IMPROVED LAND land that has been partially or fully developed for use. Any of the following activities on a piece of RAW LAND will result in improved land: landscaping and grading; installation of utilities; construction of roads, curbs, or gutters; and construction of buildings. *See also* IMPROVEMENT.

IMPROVEMENT any permanent, fixed development of land or buildings through expenditure of money or labor that more than merely replaces, repairs, or restores to original condition and tends to increase the value of the property. Improvements are not deductible for tax purposes, but are capitalized and, if made to depreciable property, are depreciable over the same life as the asset that was improved.

IMPROVEMENTS AND BETTERMENTS INSURANCE tenant's modifications of leased space to fit his particular needs. Up to 10% of contents coverage inside the structure may be applied to insure against damage or destruction of improvements or betterments made by a tenant who does not carry coverage on the structure itself.

IMPUTED COST expense not incurred directly, but actually borne. For example, a person who owns a home debt-free has an imputed rent expense equal to the amount of interest that could be earned on the proceeds from the sale of the home if the home were sold.

IMPUTED INCOME economic benefit a taxpayer obtains through performance of his own services or through the use of his own property. In general, imputed income is not subject to income taxes. For example, if a taxpayer is a plumber and repairs his own toilet, such repair service is not subject to tax. *See also* IMPUTED INTEREST.

IMPUTED INTEREST implied interest. In a MORTGAGE that states an insufficient interest rate, tax law will impute a higher rate and a lower PRINCIPAL, which will increase taxes on the receipt of payments. The *imputed interest* is based on the difference between the rate the federal government pays on new borrowings and the interest charged on the loan. *See also* ORIGINAL ISSUE DISCOUNT (OID).

IMPUTED VALUE or **IMPUTED INCOME** logical or implicit value that is not recorded in any account. For example, in projecting annual figures, values are imputed for months for which actual figures are not yet available. Cash invested unproductively has an imputed value consisting of what it would have earned in a productive investment. *See also* OPPORTUNITY COST.

INACTIVE STOCK or **INACTIVE BOND** security traded relatively infrequently, either on an exchange or over the counter. The low volume makes the security ILLIQUID, and small investors tend to shy away from it.

INADVERTENTLY done unintentionally, accidentally, often with no one accepting blame.

INCAPACITY lack of legal, physical, or intellectual power. *See also* INCOMPETENT; MINOR.

INCENDIARISM act of starting a fire; arson. Arson is a covered peril under a PROPERTY INSURANCE contract, provided that the owner of the property is not responsible for the arson.

INCENTIVE FEE payment or fee given as an incentive to become part of a test-marketing audience group.

INCENTIVE PAY wage system that rewards a worker for productivity above an established standard. A variation of the piece-rate system developed by Frederick W. Taylor, incentive pay is based on a bonus given to the worker or workers who exceed a given standard production rate within a defined period of time. *See also* INCENTIVE WAGE PLAN.

INCENTIVE STOCK OPTION (ISO) equity-type of compensation plan under which qualifying stock options are free of tax at the date of grant and the date of exercise but are taxed when sold.

INCENTIVE WAGE PLAN wage program where wages rise with productivity increases above an established standard. Individual incentive wage plans are based on the performance of the individual employee, while group incentive plans are based on the performance of the work group, with individual members receiving a respective proportion of the pay allocated. *See also* INCENTIVE PAY.

INCHOATE not yet completed. In *inchoate* offenses, something remains to be done before the crime can be accomplished as contemplated.

INCIDENCE OF TAX the distribution of the "burden" of paying a tax. Smokers bear the *incidence* of tobacco taxes.

INCIDENTAL DAMAGES in law, losses reasonably incident to conduct, giving rise to a claim for actual damages.

INCIDENT OF OWNERSHIP an element of ownership or degree of control. For example, if a GRANTOR retains control of property transferred to an individual or trust, the property will be included in the grantor's GROSS ESTATE for ESTATE TAX purposes.

INCOME economic benefit; money or value received. *See also* GROSS INCOME; NET INCOME; TAXABLE INCOME.

INCOME ACCOUNTS in accounting, revenue and expense accounts, as opposed to BALANCE SHEET accounts. Income accounts reflect what has occurred during the ACCOUNTING PERIOD that offers profit or loss as the bottom line.

INCOME APPROACH method of appraising real estate based on the property's anticipated future income. The formula for appraisal by the income approach is:

$$\frac{\text{Expected annual income}}{\text{Capitalization rate}} = \text{Market value}$$

See also CAPITALIZATION RATE; GROSS RENT MULTIPLIER (GRM).

INCOME BENEFICIARY BENEFICIARY of a TRUST or ESTATE who is entitled to income from property rather than the CORPUS or principal.

INCOME BOND obligation on which the payment of interest is contingent on sufficient earnings from year to year. Such bonds are traded FLAT—that is, with no accrued interest—and are often an alternative to bankruptcy.

INCOME EFFECT in economics, effect upon the PURCHASING POWER of a consumer because of a change in the price of a good that he consumes. If the price of beef falls, the consumer has money left over to buy more of other goods, as well as more beef.

INCOME FUND MUTUAL FUND designed to produce current income for shareholders. Some examples of *income funds* are government, mortgage-backed security, municipal, international, and junk bond funds. Several kinds of equity-oriented funds also can have income as their primary investment objective, such as *utilities income funds* and *equity income funds*.

INCOME GROUP collection of consumers or other entities with similar INCOMES, demonstrated by categorization of the entities according to their incomes.

INCOME PROPERTY real estate bought for the income it produces. The property may be placed in a LIMITED PARTNERSHIP, or it may be owned by one individual or company. Buyers also hope to achieve long-term capital gains when they sell the property.

INCOME REDISTRIBUTION way of spending personal income among various classes in society. An *income redistribution* program, for example, could take from the rich and give to the poor (as do the PROGRESSIVE TAX structure and the federal ESTATE TAX).

INCOME REPLACEMENT benefit in disability income insurance whereby an injured or ill wage earner receives a monthly income payment to replace a percentage of his lost earnings. *See also* DISABILITY INCOME INSURANCE.

INCOME SHIFTING transfer of GROSS INCOME to another taxpayer in a lower tax bracket, thereby reducing the overall tax liability of the group or family. *See also* INCOME SPLITTING.

INCOME SPLITTING generally refers to a married couple filing a JOINT RETURN. May also refer to giving income property to children, or using multiple trusts or multiple business entities in an effort (not necessarily successful) to use lower tax rates or threshold amounts.

INCOME STATEMENT financial statement that gives operating results, such as net income and loss and depreciation, for a specific period; also referred to as *earnings report, operating statement,* and *profit-and-loss statement.*

INCOME STREAM regular flow of money generated by a business or investment. Its value can be estimated by discounting the CASH FLOW to a PRESENT VALUE.

INCOME TAX tax based on income earned by a person or business. The income tax is the main source of revenue for the federal government and one of the main sources for many states. *See also* AD VALOREM; PROGRESSIVE TAX; SALES TAX; VALUE-ADDED TAX (VAT).

INCOME TAX LIEN *see* TAX LIEN.

INCOME TAX PREPARER a person who prepares for compensation, or who employs or engages one or more persons to prepare for compensation, all or a substantial portion of any income tax return under the tax laws or any claim for refund of income tax.

INCOME TAX RETURN *see* FORM 1040; FORM 1120.

INCOMPETENT
   Law: one not legally capable of completing a CONTRACT; includes the mentally ill, MINORS, and others considered incapable.
   Personal: one poorly suited to perform the work required.

INCONTESTABLE CLAUSE section in a life insurance policy stating that after the policy is in force two years, the company cannot void it because of misrepresentation or concealment by the insured in obtaining the policy. For example, when asked on the application if there is a history of diabetes in the family, the applicant writes no, knowing that both her father and mother have diabetes. This does not void the policy after two years.

INCONVERTIBLE MONEY money that cannot be converted to precious metal or other commodities generally accepted as backing up money. Federal reserve notes (the U.S. currency) are *inconvertible*.

INCORPORATE
1. to organize and be granted status as a CORPORATION by following prescribed legal procedures.
2. to include, as to *incorporate* additional materials in a report.
3. to provide a geographic area a legal status. Cities generally are *incorporated* entities.

INCORPORATION process by which a company receives a state charter allowing it to operate as a corporation. The fact of incorporation must be acknowledged in the company's legal name, using the word *incorporated*, the abbreviation *inc.*, or acceptable variations.

INCORPOREAL PROPERTY legal interests in REAL PROPERTY that do not entail the *right of possession. See also* EASEMENT; LICENSE.

INCOTERMS International Commercial Terms, first published in 1936 by the International Chamber of Commerce to promote standardized major international trade terminology; *see also http://www.export.gov/ incoterms.html.*

INCREASING COSTS the circumstance in an industry or firm in which unit costs increase as quantity of output increases.

INCREMENTAL ANALYSIS decision-making method that utilizes the concept of *relevant cost* also known as the *relevant cost approach* or *differential analysis.* Under this method, the decision involves the following steps: (1) gather all costs associated with each alternative: (2) drop the *sunk costs*; (3) drop those costs that do not differ between alternatives; (4) select the best alternative based on the remaining cost data.

INCREMENTAL CASH FLOW net of cash outflows and inflows attributable to a corporate investment project.

INCREMENTAL COST OF CAPITAL *see* MARGINAL COST.

INCREMENTAL SPENDING budget allocation that allows for increased or decreased spending on media for advertising in direct proportion to sales. The problem with allocating funds in this manner is that rarely is budget size tied in with the advertising objectives and, therefore, it is difficult to evaluate the success or failure of the advertising in terms of expenditure. *See also* COMPETITIVE PARITY.

INCUBATOR facility that provides small entrepreneurial businesses with affordable space, shared support, and business development services such as financing, marketing, and management. Incubators play an important role in helping young businesses survive and grow during the startup period, when they are most financially vulnerable.

INCURABLE DEPRECIATION real estate appraisal, when the cost to correct a defect would exceed the benefit gained. Thus spending money for the repair is uneconomical.

INDEMNIFY
1. to insure; to secure against loss or damage that may occur in the future.
2. to compensate for loss or damage already suffered.
3. investing through an index security or fund.

INDEMNITY
1. obligation to make good any loss or damage another person has incurred or may incur.
2. right that the person suffering loss or damage is entitled to claim. *See also* CONTRIBUTION.

INDENTURE formal agreement, also called *deed of trust*, between an issuer of bonds and the bondholder, covering such considerations as: (1) form of bond; (2) amount of issue; (3) property pledged (if not a debenture issue); (4) protective COVENANTS, including any provision for a sinking fund; (5) WORKING CAPITAL and *ratio*; and (6) redemption rights or call privileges.

INDEPENDENCE condition of accountant having no bias and being neutral regarding the client or another party in performing the audit function. Some independence guidelines for an auditor engaged in the attest function include: (1) no family relationship with the client's executives; (2) no financial interest in the company; and (3) no contingent fee based on the type of audit opinion rendered.

INDEPENDENT ADJUSTER independent contractor who adjusts claims for different insurance companies. Such services are used by insurance companies whose financial resources or volume of claims do not warrant employing their own in-house adjusters. *See* PUBLIC ADJUSTER.

INDEPENDENT CONTRACTOR contractor who is self-employed. The contracting party need not pay Social Security taxes and the like; the independent contractor must instead pay a self-employment tax.

INDEPENDENT DIRECTOR member of a company's board of directors who has not been an officer or employee for one year preceding any action on an offer.

INDEPENDENT EVENTS two or more events that do not affect each other.

INDEPENDENT PRODUCER taxpayer who produces oil for the market without a pipeline system or refinery. A 15% percentage depletion rate applies to independent producers and royalty owners.

INDEPENDENT STORE
1. classification used by A.C. NIELSEN COMPANY in their retail indexes to indicate an individual store or a small chain store with no more than three branches.
2. individually owned and operated retail shop.
3. casual reference to an independent station.

INDEPENDENT UNION union that is not affiliated with the AFL-CIO. The United Mine Workers and the Teamsters are two of the largest *independent unions. See also* UNAFFILIATED UNION.

INDEPENDENT VARIABLES two or more variables that are in no way associated with or dependent on each other.

INDEX statistical compilation that puts in context a current economic or financial condition, especially by relating it to a base year, the previous year, the previous month, etc. Indexes are often used to make adjustments in wage rates, rental rates, loan interest rates, and pension benefits set by long-term contracts. A widely used index is the CONSUMER PRICE INDEX (CPI).

INDEXATION process of relating an economic variable to an indicator of some kind, usually INFLATION. Federal income taxes are indexed to inflation to prevent BRACKET CREEP.

INDEX BASIS comparative calculation that defines the relationship between two or more values by calling one value the standard with a value of 100 and all other values some percent over or under the base standard of 100. For example, if the standard is 20, a value of 30 would be expressed as 150.

INDEXED LIFE INSURANCE policy with a face value that varies according to a prescribed index of prices; otherwise benefits provided are similar to ordinary whole life. The death benefit is based on the particular INDEX used, such as the Consumer Price Index (CPI). The policyowner has the choice of having the index applied either automatically or on an elective basis.

INDEXED LOAN long-term loan in which the term, payment, interest rate, or principal amount may be adjusted periodically according to a specific index. The index and the manner of adjustment are generally stated in the loan contract.

INDEX FUND MUTUAL FUND whose portfolio matches that of a broad-based index such as Standard & Poor's and whose performance therefore mirrors the market as a whole.

INDEXING
1. weighting one's portfolio to match a broad-based index such as Standard & Poor's 500 Index so as to match its performance.
2. tying wages, taxes, or other rates to an index. For example, a labor contract may call for indexing wages to the CONSUMER PRICE INDEX (CPI).

INDEX LEASE rental agreement that requires changes in rent based on a published record of cost changes. *See also* CONSUMER PRICE INDEX (CPI); GROUND LEASE.

INDEX OF LEADING INDICATORS *see* LEADING INDICATORS.

INDEX OPTIONS calls and puts on indexes of stocks. These options are traded on the New York, American, and Chicago Board Options exchanges, among others. They allow investors to trade in a particular market or industry group without having to buy all the stocks individually.

INDIRECT COST manufacturing cost that cannot be easily seen in the product. Electricity, hazard insurance on the factory building, and real estate taxes are indirect costs. *See also* DIRECT LABOR; DIRECT MATERIAL; FACTORY OVERHEAD.

INDIRECT LABOR wages and related costs of factory employees, such as inspectors and maintenance crews, whose time is not charged to specific finished products; sometimes combined with indirect materials costs, such as supplies, to derive INDIRECT COSTS.

INDIRECT OVERHEAD narrower term than INDIRECT COSTS, referring to OVERHEAD items only. Thus, in making furniture, rent on the manufacturing plant is *indirect overhead* whereas glue is not indirect overhead but may be classified as a direct or indirect cost, depending on whether it is used in the product or in the environment that is used to make the product.

INDIRECT PRODUCTION production of an item needed for the manufacture of major goods or services; for example, machine produced for the purpose of manufacturing automobile hubcaps.

INDIVIDUAL *see* SINGLE TAXPAYER.

INDIVIDUAL BARGAINING negotiations between a single employee and his employer. Individual bargaining gives the employer much greater strength than COLLECTIVE BARGAINING where the employer must deal with the employees as a group. *See also* COLLECTIVE BARGAINING.

INDIVIDUALISM philosophy or quality that characterizes a manager or employee who makes decisions and performs tasks in his own way or style. The advantage of encouraging individualism is that creativity and naturalism may result in greater motivation and accomplishment. However, the company must be careful that the employee does not ignore corporate goals and policies.

INDIVIDUAL LIFE INSURANCE coverage of a single life, in contrast to GROUP LIFE INSURANCE, which covers many lives.

INDIVIDUAL RETIREMENT ACCOUNT (IRA) trust fund to which any individual employee can contribute up to $4,000 per year in 2005–2007, $5,000 in 2008, indexed for inflation beginning in 2009.

The maximum annual CATCH-UP CONTRIBUTION is $1,000 after 2005. Income level and eligibility for an employee's pension plan determine whether or not the employee's contribution is tax-deductible. The employee may not take a deduction for an IRA contribution if he or she is an active participant in any QUALIFIED PLAN and his or her MODIFIED ADJUSTED GROSS INCOME is $60,000 or more for a single individual or $80,000 or more for married couples filing jointly. *See also* SPOUSAL IRA.

INDIVIDUAL RETIREMENT ACCOUNT (IRA) ROLLOVER provision of the IRA law that enables persons receiving lump-sum payments from their company's pension or profit-sharing plan due to retirement or other termination of employment to roll the amount over, tax free, into an IRA investment plan within 60 days. For distributions, unless the IRA funds are transferred directly to an eligible plan, the payor must withhold 20% of the distribution. If the participant then transfers only the remaining 80% to a new IRA, he or she will pay income tax and a penalty tax on the 20% withheld.

INDUCTIVE REASONING adjusting a course of action based upon a limited amount of information gathered. It is a process where one starts from a specific experience and draws inferences (generalizations) from it. For example, a salesperson, by observing a potential customer's reaction to the sales presentation, may *induce* what the customer's needs and personality are and what should be said to obtain the sale. *See also* DEDUCTIVE REASONING.

INDUSTRIAL classification by stock market analysts of company that produces and distributes goods and services. Excluded from the industrials are utilities, transportation companies, and financial service companies.

INDUSTRIAL ADVERTISING field of advertising directed at commercial business customers. The advertised products are raw materials, components, or equipment needed in the production or distribution of other goods and services. *See also* BUSINESS-TO-BUSINESS ADVERTISING.

INDUSTRIAL CONSUMER user of industrial products. (The use of the word CONSUMER here is actually incorrect, since a consumer is an individual purchasing or using a product or service for personal use. The actual term should be *industrial customer*. However, the term *industrial consumer* is used informally throughout the industry to distinguish one type of user of a product from another.) *See also* INDUSTRIAL ADVERTISING.

INDUSTRIAL DEVELOPMENT BOND (IDB) obligation issued where the proceeds are used in the trade or business of a nonexempt person and the payment of the principal or interest is secured by an interest in, or derived from payment with respect to, property or borrowed money used in a trade or business. State and local government bond interest is exempt from federal income tax; however, interest from IDBs is taxable unless certain requirements are met to qualify the bonds for tax exemption.

INDUSTRIAL DISTRIBUTOR wholesaler who sells products to industrial customers rather than to retailers.

INDUSTRIAL ENGINEER person who studies industrial productivity and makes and implements recommended changes. Industrial engineers seek an integrated system of workers, materials, and equipment utilizing the mathematical, physical, and social sciences. These areas are combined with the principles and methods of engineering.

INDUSTRIAL FATIGUE employee burnout characterized by physical or emotional exhaustion, resulting in lowered job productivity and performance. The employee becomes tired of doing the job, which results in poor motivation. The fatigue may be caused by such factors as understaffing, unpleasant surroundings, and high pressure.

INDUSTRIAL GOODS products or services purchased for use in the production of other goods or services, in the operation of a business, or for resale to other consumers. Industrial products include heavy machinery, raw materials, typewriters, tools, and cash registers.

INDUSTRIALIST individual involved in the business of industry. The term evolved from the early industrial period, where large trusts and monopolies were formed by a group of business people referred to as industrialists.

INDUSTRIAL PARK area designed and zoned for manufacturing and associated activities. *See also* ZONING.

INDUSTRIAL PRODUCTION monthly statistic released by the FEDERAL RESERVE BOARD (FRB) on the total output of all U.S. factories and mines. These numbers are a KEY ECONOMIC INDICATOR.

INDUSTRIAL PROPERTY property used for industrial purposes. Types of industrial property include factory-office multiuse property; factory-warehouse multiuse property; heavy manufacturing buildings; industrial parks; light manufacturing buildings; and research and development parks.

INDUSTRIAL PSYCHOLOGY area of psychology dealing with job analysis, defining and measuring job performance, performance appraisal, tests, employment interviews, employee selection and training, and HUMAN FACTORS; also called *personnel* psychology.

INDUSTRIAL RELATIONS dealings of a company with others, particularly employees. The Japanese are noted for good industrial relations due to the teamwork among workers, government, and employers.

INDUSTRIAL REVENUE BOND *see* INDUSTRIAL DEVELOPMENT BOND (IDB).

INDUSTRIAL REVOLUTION period marking the introduction of mass production, improved transportation, technological progress, and the industrial factory system. In the United States this period is generally agreed to have begun at the time of the Civil War (1861–1865).

INDUSTRIAL UNION organization of all crafts within an industry under one union. The CIO under the leadership of John L. Lewis used the industrial union concept to organize General Motors, United States Steel, and Ford Motor Company. Industrial unionism was the basis of the original break from the AFL, which organized by craft.

INDUSTRY
1. privately owned profit-seeking manufacturing establishment.
2. segment of the business world, such as steel industry or automobile industry.

INDUSTRY STANDARD orderly and systematic formulation, adoption, or application of standards used in the industrial sector of the economy. An industrial standard is a generally accepted requirement to be met for the attainment of a recurrent industrial objective. In the automotive industry, standardized tire sizes are an example.

INEFFICIENCIES IN THE MARKET failure of investors to recognize that a particular stock or bond has good prospects or may be headed for trouble. According to the EFFICIENT MARKET theory, current prices reflect all knowledge about securities. But theory and practice are not always in agreement. For example, *arbitrageurs* profit from market inefficiencies.

INELASTICITY *see* ELASTICITY OF SUPPLY AND DEMAND.

INELASTIC SUPPLY AND DEMAND *see* ELASTICITY OF SUPPLY AND DEMAND.

INFANT INDUSTRY ARGUMENT case made by developing sectors of the economy that their industries need protection against international competition while they establish themselves. In response to such pleas, the government may enact a TARIFF or import duty to stifle foreign competition.

INFERENTIAL STATISTICS process of drawing information from sampled observations of a population and making conclusions about the population. Inferential statistics have a two-prong approach. First, sampling must be conducted to be representative of the underlying population. Second, the procedures must be capable of drawing correct conclusions about the population. *See also* DESCRIPTIVE STATISTICS.

INFERIOR GOOD good of which less is consumed (rather than more) when the consumer's income increases. For some consumers hamburger is an *inferior good* because when income increases, they can afford to consume more steak and, so, less hamburger.

INFERRED AUTHORITY authority assumed when the next higher person leaves his post; authority exercised as a result of inferred ability.

INFLATION rise in the prices of goods and services, as happens when spending increases relative to the supply of goods on the market; in other words, too much money chasing too few goods. *See also* CONSUMER PRICE INDEX (CPI); COST-PUSH INFLATION; DEMAND-PULL INFLATION.

INFLATION ACCOUNTING showing the effects of inflation in financial statements. The Financial Accounting Standards Board (FASB) requires major companies to supplement their traditional financial reporting with information showing the effects of inflation.

INFLATIONARY GAP when aggregate demand exceeds aggregate supply, thus causing prices to increase if the economy is at full employment, or bringing about increases in production if it is not. It is usually attributed to government operating on deficit, thereby spending more than it receives in taxes and, so, creating excess demand.

INFLATIONARY SPIRAL episode of inflation in which price increases occur at an increasing rate, and currency rapidly loses value.

INFLATION ENDORSEMENT attachment to a property insurance policy that automatically adjusts its coverage according to the construction cost index in a community. This endorsement is necessary in a property contract to maintain adequate coverage. Otherwise, it is advisable for a policyowner, at time of renewal, to adjust the limits of coverage to reflect the increased cost of construction and the market value of the property.

INFLATION HEDGE INVESTMENT designed to protect against the loss of purchasing power from INFLATION. Traditionally, gold and REAL ESTATE have a reputation as good *inflation hedges*, though growth in STOCKS also can offset inflation in the long run.

INFLATION-INDEXED SECURITIES BONDS or NOTES that guarantee a return that beats INFLATION if held to maturity. Also applied to shares in MUTUAL FUNDS that hold such securities. TREASURY INFLATION-PROTECTED SECURITIES (TIPS) were introduced in 1997 in 10-year maturities and were subsequently issued as 5-year notes. *See also* SERIES I BONDS.

INFLATION RATE rate of change in prices. Two primary U.S. indicators of the inflation rate are the CONSUMER PRICE INDEX and the PRODUCER PRICE INDEX, which track changes in prices paid by consumers and by producers.

INFORMAL LEADER leader whose power and authority over a group are derived from his acceptance by the group rather than from his office, position, status, or rank in the formal chain of command in the formal organization. An informal leader has earned a group leadership role by the group's acceptance.

INFORMAL ORGANIZATION aspects of an organization that are undefined in the formal structure. These aspects include human relationships, actual power versus formal power, communication and social networks. Informal organizations can be both beneficial as well as negative for an organization depending on whether it is consistent with organizational goals or opposed to it. *See also* GRAPEVINE.

INFORMATION RETURN one of a number of returns that only communicate to the Internal Revenue Service information relevant to tax liability and do not compute the actual liability of any taxpayer or accompany the actual payment of tax; used for dividends, sale of property, and others. Examples are Forms 1099 and W-2.

INFORMATION SUPERHIGHWAY a description used in the 1990s of the electronic transfer of information including access to databases, banking, television and movie programs, libraries, and so on.

INFORMATION SYSTEMS any written, electronic, or graphical method of communicating information. The basis of an information system is the sharing and processing of information and ideas. Computers and telecommunication technologies have become essential information system components.

INFRASTRUCTURE nation's basic system of water supply, sewerage, transportation, communications, and other aspects of its physical plant. The efficiency of the national economy usually is closely related to the quality of the infrastructure.

INFRINGEMENT overstepping another's protected right. *See also* COPYRIGHT; PATENT INFRINGEMENT; TRADEMARK.

INGOT bar of metal, such as iron.

INGRESS AND EGRESS entrance and departure; the means of entering and leaving and the right to do so.

INHERENT EXPLOSION CLAUSE provision of a property insurance policy that covers conditions inherent in an explosion. For example, carbon monoxide fumes are inherent in operating a garage.

INHERIT to acquire a property from one who died, either by devise (WILL) or by descent (from one's ancestor by operation of law).

INHERITANCE REAL PROPERTY or PERSONAL PROPERTY that is received by heirs. A nontechnical meaning of *inheritance* includes property passed by WILL. Although federal estate tax may have to be paid on the estate itself, the recipient is not subject to federal income tax on the inheritance.

INHERITANCE TAX state tax based on the value of property passing to each particular heir. It differs from the federal estate tax in that the degree of kinship of the heir to the decedent generally determines the exempt amounts and tax rates. An ESTATE TAX is based on the value of all property left by the decedent, whereas an *inheritance tax* is based on the amount that an heir receives. *See also* UNIFIED ESTATE AND GIFT TAX.

IN-HOUSE performed within an organization as opposed to by an outside contractor. A continuing controversy exists in organizations concerning the costs of providing in-house capabilities as opposed to the cost of having outside contractors.

INITIAL
1. starting at the beginning. The *initial* product is the first one.
2. first letter of a name. Memos, for example, are often *initialed* (signed with initials).

INITIALIZE prepare for use. For a computer or printer, this may involve a sequence of error checking and other self-diagnostics.

INITIAL PUBLIC OFFERING (IPO) corporation's first offering of stock to the public. *See also* HOT ISSUE.

INITIATIVE action of creating or starting. A manager with *initiative* possesses the aptitude to bring forth new ideas or techniques; he will take action on his own without having to wait for instructions. People with initiative are self-starters and self-motivators. In the business world, initiative is associated with entrepreneurial activities.

INJUNCTION judicial REMEDY awarded to restrain a particular activity; first used by courts of EQUITY to prevent conduct contrary to equity and good conscience. The injunction is a preventive measure to guard against future injuries, rather than one that affords a remedy for past injuries.

INJURY INDEPENDENT OF ALL OTHER MEANS injury covered in a health insurance policy that is isolated from any previous injury.

IN KIND
1. of the same or similar type or quality.
2. in the same or similar manner.

IN-KIND DISTRIBUTION distribution of property instead of selling the property and then distributing the proceeds.

IN-KIND INCOME benefits that one receives for which one is not required to pay directly. Examples are public schools, non-toll roads, food stamps.

INKJET PRINTER printer that forms characters by firing tiny dots of ink at the paper. For many applications, it is an acceptable alternative to the much more expensive LASER PRINTER.

INLAND CARRIER in transportation, company in the business of meeting goods at a port of entry and shipping them to a point inside the continent.

INLAND MARINE transit over land.

INLAND MARINE INSURANCE *see* MARINE INSURANCE, INLAND.

INNER CITY generally the older and more urbanized area of a large city surrounding the CENTRAL BUSINESS DISTRICT. The term often refers to densely populated blighted areas characterized by low-income residents and a high proportion of minority racial and ethnic groups.

INNOCENT PURCHASER one who buys an asset without knowing of a flaw in the title or property. *See* BONA FIDE PURCHASER.

INNOVATION use of a new product, service, or method in business practice immediately subsequent to its discovery.

IN PARI DELICTO Latin for "equally at fault"; exception to the general rule that illegal transactions or contracts are not legally enforceable. Where the parties to an illegal agreement are not *in pari delicto*, the agreement may nevertheless be enforceable at EQUITY by the innocent or less guilty party. *See also* DURESS; FRAUD.

IN PERPETUITY existing forever.

IN PERSONAM into or against the person. In PLEADING, an action against a person or persons, founded on personal LIABILITY and requiring JURISDICTION by the court over the person sought to be held liable, i.e., the defendant.

INPUT data fed into a computer for processing. (Note that the terms *input* and *output* are always used from the computer's point of view.) The computer receives input through an input device, such as a keyboard, or from a storage device, such as a disk drive.

IN REM actions against the *res*, or thing, rather than against the person. The goal of a proceeding in rem is the disposition of property without reference to the TITLE of individual claimants. *See also* IN PERSONAM.

INSERTION POINT the location, usually represented by a blinking vertical line (the *cursor*), where input from the keyboard or mouse will be placed. If you start typing in a word processing program, the text is inserted at the *insertion point*.

INSIDE INFORMATION corporate affairs that have not yet been made public. The officers of a firm would know in advance, for instance, if the company was about to be taken over, or if the latest earnings report was going to differ significantly from information released earlier. Under Securities and Exchange Commission rules, an INSIDER is not allowed to trade on the basis of such information.

INSIDE LOT in a SUBDIVISION, lot surrounded on each side by other lots, as opposed to a corner lot, which has road FRONTAGE on at least two sides.

INSIDER person whose opportunity to profit from his position of power in a business is limited by law to safeguard the public good. Both federal securities acts and state BLUE-SKY LAWS regulate stock transactions of individuals with access to INSIDE INFORMATION about a corporation.

INSIDER TRADING security trading performed by those having first-hand knowledge of relevant proprietary information. Those having this knowledge have an unfair advantage. Insider trading is an illegal activity.

INSOLVENCY
1. inability to meet financial obligations as they mature in the ordinary course of business.
2. excess of liabilities over assets at any given time. *See also* BANKRUPTCY.

INSOLVENCY CLAUSE provision of a reinsurance contract that states that the reinsurance company remains liable for its predetermined share of a claim submitted by an insured, even though the primary insurance company is no longer in business.

INSPECTION physical scrutinizing review of goods, property, or documents. Inspections of real estate may be required for the following purposes: compliance with BUILDING CODES; sale requirements as to property conditions, such as wood-destroying insects or structural soundness; and legal review of documents such as LEASES OR MORTGAGES to determine whether they are as purported. There are also customs inspections for imports and quality control inspections.

INSTALL load and configure a piece of software on a computer.

INSTALLMENT
In general: anything given or received as part of a series of steps. *See also* REVOLVING CREDIT.
Finance: part of the same DEBT, payable in one of successive periods as agreed; payment made to reduce a MORTGAGE or other debt.

INSTALLMENT CONTRACT contract in which the obligation of one or more of the parties, such as an obligation to pay money, deliver goods, or render services, is divided into a series of successive performances.

INSTALLMENT LAND SALES CONTRACT *see* LAND CONTRACT.

INSTALLMENT SALE
In general: sale made with the agreement that the purchased goods or services will be paid for in fractional amounts over a specified period of time.
Real estate: when a seller accepts a MORTGAGE for part of a sale, the tax on the gain from the sale is paid as the mortgage PRINCIPAL is collected. *See also* CONTRACT PRICE; GROSS PROFIT RATIO; IMPUTED INTEREST.

INSTALLMENT TO AMORTIZE ONE DOLLAR a mathematically computed factor derived from COMPOUND INTEREST functions that offers the level periodic payment required to retire a $1 loan within a certain time frame. The periodic installment must exceed the periodic interest rate. *See also* AMORTIZATION; AMORTIZATION SCHEDULE.

INSTITUTIONAL ADVERTISING form of IMAGE ADVERTISING intended to change the public perception of a company in relationship to an issue such as the environment, health, product safety, or some public issue. It is an attempt to create a positive public awareness of a company and distinguish it from competitors.

INSTITUTIONAL INVESTOR organization that trades large volumes of securities. Some examples are mutual funds, banks, insurance companies, pension funds, labor union funds, corporate profit-sharing plans, and college endowment funds.

INSTITUTIONAL LENDER financial intermediary who invests in loans and other securities on behalf of depositors or customers. Lending and investment activities are regulated by laws to limit risk. Institutional lenders are a prime source of bond purchases and real estate loans. Many organizations, such as SAVINGS AND LOAN ASSOCIATIONS and COMMERCIAL BANKS, originate loans directly; others, such as insurance companies, are active in the secondary market.

INSTRUMENT
In general: tool to perform a task or a measurement.
Law: legal document that records an act or agreement and provides the evidence of that act or agreement. Instruments include contracts, notes, and leases.

INSTRUMENTALITY federal agency whose obligations, while not direct obligations of the U.S. government, are sponsored or guaranteed by the government and backed by the FULL FAITH AND CREDIT of the government. Well over 100 series of notes, certificates, and bonds have been issued by such instrumentalities as Federal Intermediate Credit Banks, Federal Land Banks, Federal Home Loan Bank Board, and Student Loan Marketing Association.

INSURABILITY circumstance in which an insurance company can issue life or health insurance to an applicant based on standards set by the company.

INSURABLE INTEREST relationship with a person or thing that supports issuance of an INSURANCE policy. A person having an *insurable* interest can derive financial advantage from preservation of the subject matter insured or suffer loss from its destruction. An insurable interest in the life of another requires that the continued life of the insured be of real interest to the insuring party. The connection may be financial (as when a CREDITOR insures the life of his DEBTOR), or it may consist of familial or other ties of affection.

INSURABLE RISK risk situation meeting an insurance company's standards in that it: (1) is measurable; (2) is accidental; (3) meets a standard classification; and (4) has a premium proportional to a possible loss.

INSURABLE TITLE TITLE that can be insured by a TITLE INSURANCE company. In some contracts for the sale of real estate the buyer must receive insurable title or he is not obligated to purchase the property. *See also* MARKETABLE TITLE.

INSURABLE VALUE the cost of total replacement of destructible improvements to a property; may be based on replacement cost rather than market value.

INSURANCE system whereby individuals and companies concerned about potential hazards pay premiums to an insurance company, which reimburses (in whole or part) them in the event of loss. The insurer profits by investing the premiums it receives. Some common forms of insurance cover business risks, automobiles, homes, boats, worker's compensation, and health. Life insurance guarantees payment to the beneficiaries when the insured person dies. In a broad economic sense, insurance transfers risk from individuals to a larger group, which is better able to pay for losses.

INSURANCE AGENT representative of an insurance company who sells the firm's policies. INDEPENDENT agents sell the policies of many companies. Agents must be licensed to sell insurance in the states where they solicit customers.

INSURANCE, AUTOMOBILE *see* PERSONAL AUTOMOBILE POLICY.

INSURANCE BROKER independent broker who searches for the best insurance coverage at the lowest cost for the client. *Insurance brokers* do not work for insurance companies but for the buyers of insurance products. They are constantly comparing the merits of competing insurance policies to find the best deal for their customers.

INSURANCE, BUSINESS *see* BUSINESSOWNERS POLICY (BOP); OPEN FORM; OWNERS AND CONTRACTORS PROTECTIVE LIABILITY.

INSURANCE CLAIM request for payment from an INSURANCE COMPANY by the INSURED. For example, a homeowner files a claim after suffering damage from a fire, theft, or other loss. Survivors submit a life insurance claim when the insured dies.

INSURANCE COMPANY (INSURER) organization that underwrites insurance policies. There are two principal types of insurance companies: MUTUAL and STOCK. A mutual company is owned by its policy-owners, who elect a board of directors that is responsible for its operation. A stock company is owned by its stockholders. In a mutual company, profits take the form of *policy dividends*, or refunds of part of premiums paid, which are distributed to policyowners. Profits in a stock company take the form of stockholders' dividends, which are distributed to stockholders.

INSURANCE CONTRACT legally binding unilateral agreement between an insured and an insurance company. In exchange for premium payment(s) the company covers stipulated perils.

INSURANCE COVERAGE total amount and type of insurance carried. *See also* BUSINESS INTERRUPTION INSURANCE; FIRE INSURANCE; HAZARD INSURANCE; LIABILITY INSURANCE.

INSURANCE DIVIDEND money paid, usually once a year, to CASH VALUE LIFE INSURANCE policyholders with participating policies. Dividend rates are based on the insurance company's mortality experience, administrative expenses, and investment returns. Policyholders may choose to take these dividends in cash or may purchase additional life insurance.

INSURANCE LIMIT *see* ANNUAL AGGREGATE LIMIT.

INSURANCE POLICY insurance contract specifying what risks are insured and what PREMIUMS must be paid to keep the policy in force. The *policy* is the written document that both INSURED and INSURANCE COMPANY refer to in determining whether or not a claim is covered.

INSURANCE PREMIUMS amounts paid to an insurance company to cover potential hazards. Most insurance premiums are tax deductible to a business, except life insurance premiums when the company is the beneficiary. Most insurance premiums are not deductible by an individual, except that medical insurance premiums may be considered an itemized medical expense.

INSURANCE, PROPERTY COVERAGE coverage for direct or indirect property loss, which can be analyzed under the following headings:
1. *Peril*—a particular peril may be included or excluded.
2. *Property*—a policy may cover only specified or *scheduled* property such as an automobile.
3. *Person*—the person covered must be specifically identified as the *named insured* in a policy.
4. *Duration*—policies are usually written for one year; a personal automobile policy is usually for six months.
5. *Limits*—limits are stated as a face amount in a policy.
6. *Location*—a policy may cover perils that strike only the premises of the insured, or it may provide off-premises coverage subject to a geographic restriction.
7. *Hazard*—the exclusions and suspension section states that if the insured increases a covered hazard (for example, if the insured starts processing explosives at home), the company can suspend or exclude the coverage.
8. *Loss*—insurance contracts cover either direct or indirect (*consequential*) loss.

INSURANCE SETTLEMENT receiving proceeds of an INSURANCE policy. Settlement terms are stated in the policy and are sometimes optional. When optional, beneficiaries may claim an immediate lump sum payment or choose periodic payments.

INSURED person whose interests are protected by an INSURANCE policy; person who contracts for a policy of insurance that INDEMNIFIES him against loss of property, life, health, etc.

INSURED ACCOUNT account at a bank, SAVINGS AND LOAN ASSOCIATION (S&L), CREDIT UNION, or BROKERAGE firm that belongs to a federal, state, or private insurance organization. Most bank and S&L accounts are insured up to $100,000 by the FEDERAL DEPOSIT INSURANCE CORPORATION (FDIC); credit union accounts are insured by the National Credit Union Administration; and brokerage accounts are insured by the SECURITIES INVESTOR PROTECTION CORPORATION (SIPC).

INSURED MAIL parcels sent via U.S. Postal Service that are insured for loss or possible damage by paying an insurance fee. A claim is then filed if the package fails to arrive at its destination. *See also* REGISTERED MAIL.

INSURGENT person who challenges the current state of affairs. An insurgent group is one that seeks to overthrow the present leadership or regime and install a new order.

INSURING AGREEMENT, LIABILITY *see* INSURING AGREEMENT, PROPERTY AND CASUALTY POLICY.

INSURING AGREEMENT, PROPERTY AND CASUALTY POLICY section of a policy specifying: (1) *parties to the contract* (the insurance company and the person or business to be insured); (2) terms of the policy—when it goes into force, and when it ends; (3) premiums and their due date; (4) limits of insurance; (5) types and location of property to be insured; (6) CONSIDERATION; (7) perils; and (8) ASSIGNMENT (and under what conditions the policy can be assigned).

INTANGIBLE ASSET right or nonphysical resource, including copyrights, patents, trademarks, goodwill, computer programs, capitalized advertising costs, organization costs, licenses, leases, franchises, exploration permits, and import and export permits.

INTANGIBLE DRILLING AND DEVELOPMENT COST cost incurred in drilling, testing, completing, and reworking oil and gas wells, such as labor, core analysis, fracturing, drill stem testing, engineering, fuel, geologists' expenses; also abandonment losses, management fees, delay rentals, and similar expenses.

INTANGIBLE PROPERTY possessions that only represent real value, such as STOCK CERTIFICATES, BONDS, PROMISSORY NOTES, FRANCHISES. *See also* TANGIBLE ASSET; TANGIBLE PERSONAL PROPERTY.

INTANGIBLE REWARD nonmonetary reward for performance; not always requiring recognition of others. An example is when the sales manager gives the salesperson recognition by a "pat on the back" to show appreciation for a job well done. *See also* PSYCHIC INCOME.

INTANGIBLE VALUE value that cannot be seen or touched, such as the GOODWILL of an established business or the value of a TRADEMARK.

INTEGRATE
1. bring together the races of people.
2. any bringing together of different parts; for example, integrating R&D with product development to get new products faster.

INTEGRATED CIRCUIT electronic device consisting of many miniature transistors and other circuit elements on a single silicon chip. The number of components that can be placed on a single chip has been steadily rising. The ultimate integrated circuit is the MICROPROCESSOR, which is a single chip that contains the complete arithmetic and logic unit of a computer.

INTEGRATION, BACKWARD process whereby a firm purchases or creates production facilities needed to produce its goods, such as an automobile manufacturer that buys a steel mill.

INTEGRATION, FORWARD expanding the area of operation of a business to include activity near the ultimate user; for example, a manufacturer building a retail outlet.

INTEGRATION, HORIZONTAL absorption by one firm of other firms on the same level of production stage and sharing resources at that stage.

INTEGRATION, VERTICAL absorption by one firm of other firms involved in all stages of the firm's activities, from raw materials to the sale of finished goods.

INTEGRATION WITH SOCIAL SECURITY method of reducing an employee pension according to IRS procedures.

INTEGRITY quality characterized by honesty, reliability, and fairness, developed in a relationship over time. Customers and clients have much more confidence when dealing with a business when they can rely on the representations made.

INTELLECTUAL PROPERTY any concept, idea, literary creation, computer program, or other artistic or creative work that is definable, measurable, and proprietary in nature.

INTENSIVE DISTRIBUTION method of distribution where products are given maximum exposure through positioning in as many outlets as possible.

INTERACTIVE SYSTEM computer system in which the user and the computer communicate by using a keyboard and a CRT. The computer responds almost immediately after an instruction has been entered, and the user can enter new instructions after seeing the results of the previous instructions. *See also* BATCH PROCESSING.

INTER ALIA (Latin) among other things.

INTERBANK RATE *see* LONDON INTERBANK OFFERED RATE (LIBOR).

INTERCOMPANY TRANSACTIONS transactions between members of an affiliated group filing a consolidated financial statement or tax return; gain or loss is deferred until the property is disposed of outside the group.

INTEREST

1. cost of using credit or another's money, expressed as a rate per period of time, usually one year, in which case it is called an *annual rate of interest.*
2. share, right, or title in property.

INTEREST DEDUCTIONS treated as follows:

Investment interest: Investment interest deductions are limited to net investment income.

Construction interest: Interest incurred during the construction and development of most real estate (but not a personal residence) must be capitalized and deducted over its depreciable life, beginning when the property is ready to be placed in service or sold.

Business interest: Interest incurred in an active trade or business in which the investor materially participates is fully deductible.

Housing interest: Interest on up to $1 million of acquisition debt (used to purchase or improve a home) plus $100,000 of home equity debt is tax deductible. This may be claimed for a principal residence plus one vacation home.

Consumer interest: Interest on credit cards and auto loans is not deductible.

INTEREST, ECONOMIC ACCRUAL OF the cost of an indebtedness

for a given period. The amount of interest payable for the use of money for a given period is determined by multiplying the interest rate for that period by the unpaid balance of the loan, which includes any prior accrued but unpaid interest. An ACCRUAL BASIS taxpayer is required to use the *economic accrual of interest* for calculating the INTEREST DEDUCTION.

INTEREST EXPENSE, PERSONAL *see* PERSONAL INTEREST EXPENSE.

INTEREST INCOME

1. income derived from an investment on which the payments reflect the time value of money, or
2. income derived from transactions in which the payments are for the use or forbearance of money.

INTEREST GROUP group that forms because of some special topic of

concern. Usually when the interest declines or the goals have been reached, the group disbands.

INTEREST-ONLY LOAN loan in which interest is payable at regular

intervals until loan MATURITY, when the full loan principal is due. Does not require AMORTIZATION. *See also* BALLOON PAYMENT; SELF-AMORTIZING MORTGAGE.

INTEREST RATE cost of using money, expressed as a rate per period

of time, usually one year, in which case it is called *annual rate of interest. See also* ORIGINAL ISSUE DISCOUNT (OID).

INTEREST-RATE RISK RISK that changes in interest rates will adversely affect the value of an investor's securities portfolio. For example, an investor with large holdings in long-term BONDS and PUBLIC UTILITY stocks has assumed a significant *interest-rate risk* because the value of those bonds and utilities will fall if interest rates rise.

INTEREST RATE SWAP contractual agreement entered into between two counterparties under which each agrees to make periodic payments to the other for an agreed period of time based upon an amount of PRINCIPAL. A common form occurs when a series of payments calculated by applying a fixed rate of interest to a notional principal amount is exchanged for a stream of payments similarly calculated but using a floating rate of interest. A swap may also be used to effectively change the maturity term of a debt. The two parties are often a corporation and a bank; the bank in turn likely hedges the transaction with a derivative product tied to U.S. Treasury bonds.

INTEREST SENSITIVE POLICIES a newer generation of life insurance policies that are credited with interest currently being earned by insurance companies on these policies.

INTERFACE
1. interaction between two different data processing devices or systems that handle data differently, such as different formats or codes.
2. device converting signals from one device into signals that the other device understands. For example, a *serial interface* is employed with a modem when data are transmitted to distant locations, usually over telephone lines.

INTERIM AUDIT examination of a company's financial records conducted as of a certain period that is not the end of a FISCAL YEAR or ACCOUNTING PERIOD.

INTERIM FINANCING loan, including a real estate CONSTRUCTION LOAN, used when the borrower is unable or unwilling to arrange long-term or permanent financing; generally arranged for less than three years. It is used to gain time for financial or market conditions to improve.

INTERIM STATEMENT financial report covering only a portion of a fiscal year. Public corporations supplement the ANNUAL REPORT with quarterly statements informing shareholders of changes in the balance sheet and income statement, as well as other newsworthy developments. Interim statements usually are not as detailed or as exact as annual statements.

INTERINDUSTRY COMPETITION competition that develops between companies in different industries. For example, an automobile company may compete with an aerospace company for a government manufacturing contract for a military subsystem.

INTERLOCKING DIRECTORATE membership on more than one company's board of directors. This is legal so long as the companies are not competitors. Interlocking directorates of competing companies were outlawed by the Clayton Anti-Trust Act of 1914.

INTERLOCUTORY DECREE intermediate court decree issued before a final court decree. An interlocutory decree deals with one or more parts of an issue until the final decree is issued resolving the matter.

INTERMEDIARY

In general: anyone who serves as a go-between, including an executive recruiter or broker.

Finance: person or institution empowered to make investment decisions for others. Some examples are banks, savings and loan institutions, insurance companies, brokerage firms, mutual funds, and credit unions.

INTERMEDIATE GOODS materials transformed by production into another form. Steel is considered intermediate goods that may be transformed into automobiles or ships.

INTERMEDIATE TERM period between the short and long term, the length of time depending on the context. Stock analysts, for instance, mean 6 to 12 months, whereas bond analysts most often mean 3 to 10 years.

INTERMEDIATION placement of money with a financial INTERMEDIARY like a broker or bank, which invests it in bonds, stocks, mortgages, or other loans, money market securities, or government obligations. The opposite is DISINTERMEDIATION, withdrawal of money from an intermediary.

INTERMITTENT PRODUCTION producing several different products on the same production line. After an initial production run has been made with one product, a second product will be produced, and so on. It allows maximizing productivity on the production line.

INTERNAL AUDIT audit where the auditor is an employee of the company. It is generally used to ensure that employees are following the company's accounting policies, but not to determine the fairness of financial presentation, as would an EXTERNAL AUDIT.

INTERNAL CHECK company policy to safeguard property from theft and damage; for example, the use of locked fences to secure property kept outdoors.

INTERNAL CONTROL accounting method, procedure, or system designed to promote efficiency, assure the implementation of policy, safeguard assets, discover and avoid fraud or error, etc.

INTERNAL DATA information, facts and data available from within a company's INFORMATION SYSTEM. Internal data is normally not accessible by outside parties without the company's express permission.

INTERNAL EXPANSION asset growth financed out of internally generated cash, usually termed INTERNAL FINANCING, or through ACCRETION or APPRECIATION.

INTERNAL FINANCING funds produced by the normal operations of a firm, as distinguished from external financing, which includes borrowings and new equity.

INTERNAL RATE OF RETURN (IRR) true annual rate of earnings on an investment. It equates the value of cash returns with cash invested; considers the application of compound interest factors; and requires a trial-and-error method for solution. The formula is:

$$\sum_{t=1}^{n} \frac{\text{periodic } cash\ flow}{(1+i)^t} = \text{Investment amount}$$

where i is the internal rate of return, t is each time interval, n the total number of time intervals, and $\sum$ is summation.

INTERNAL REVENUE BULLETIN (IRB) a weekly publication summarizing various IRS administrative rulings.

INTERNAL REVENUE CODE OF 1986 (IRC) law passed by Congress that specifies what income is to be taxed and how, and what may be deducted from taxable income. Court cases, regulations, revenue rules, and revenue procedures attempt to properly interpret the Internal Revenue Code. The Code has been significantly amended by tax reform acts.

INTERNAL REVENUE SERVICE (IRS) agency of the federal government that is responsible for the administration and collection of federal income taxes. The IRS prints and distributes tax forms and audits tax returns. It is part of the Department of the Treasury.

INTERNAL STORAGE memory that is built into a computer.

INTERNATIONAL BANK FOR RECONSTRUCTION AND DEVELOPMENT (IBRD) international bank that finances projects, mostly in developing nations; known as the *World Bank*. It does not compete with commercial banks, but may participate in a loan set up by a commercial bank. World Bank loans must be backed by the government in the borrowing country. The World Bank, founded in 1944, is headquartered in Washington, D.C.; it works in close conjunction with the INTERNATIONAL MONETARY FUND (IMF).

INTERNATIONAL BANKING FACILITY special departments of U.S. banks that are free to accept dollar deposits and make loans to foreign residents without reserve requirements or interest rate regulations. They are permitted so that U.S. banks can pursue business in the EURODOLLAR market.

INTERNATIONAL BOYCOTT COUNTRY a country that might require participation in, or cooperation with, an international boycott.

INTERNATIONAL LAW law governing relations of nations with one another. It arises principally from international agreements or from customs that nations adopt. In a broader sense, international law includes both public law and private law. The public law regulates political relations between nations. The private law is the comity nations grant to each other's laws in enforcing rights arising under foreign law.

INTERNATIONAL MONETARY FUND (IMF) an international organization of 184 member countries, established to promote international monetary cooperation, exchange stability, and orderly exchange arrangements; to foster economic growth and high levels of employment; and to provide temporary financial assistance to countries to help ease balance-of-payments adjustment. The IMF, founded in 1945, is headquartered in Washington, D.C.

INTERNATIONAL MONETARY MARKET (IMM) division of the Chicago Mercantile Exchange that trades futures in U.S. Treasury bills, foreign currency, certificates of deposit, and Eurodollar deposits.

INTERNATIONAL UNION union having affiliated LOCALS in more than one country. Examples include International Ladies Garment Workers Union (ILGWU), International Longshoremen's and Warehousemen's Union, and International Typographical Union.

INTERNET a global TCP/IP NETWORK linking millions of computers for communication purposes. Internet users can exchange E-MAIL, participate in NEWSGROUPS, send files from any computer to another using FTP, retrieve information via HYPERTEXT TRANSFER PROTOCOL (http), and even, with appropriate passwords, use each other's computers through Telnet. The most popular aspect of the Internet is the WORLD WIDE WEB. Inexpensive and easy-to-use software now allows anyone to set up a WEB SITE, and many commercial companies use such sites to advertise and/or sell products online.

INTERNET EXPLORER a popular WEB BROWSER from Microsoft. May be downloaded free from *http://www.microsoft.com*.

INTERNET SERVICE PROVIDER (ISP) a business that provides access to the Internet, usually for a monthly or hourly fee. Although distinctions are blurring, ISPs do not ordinarily provide the type of custom interface or member-only forums and other services provided by ONLINE SERVICES.

INTERPERIOD INCOME TAX ALLOCATION timing difference between years in which a transaction affects taxable income and accounting (book) income. Temporary differences originate in one period and subsequently reverse in another.

INTERPLEADER equitable action in which a DEBTOR, not knowing to whom among his creditors a certain debt is owed, and having no CLAIM on the property in dispute, will petition a court to require the creditors to litigate the claim among themselves.

INTERPOLATION estimation of an unknown number intermediate between known numbers. For instance, interpolation is a way of approximating price or yield using tables that do not give every possible answer.

INTERPRETER
In general: person who translates orally foreign languages for people using different languages.
Computers: program that executes a source program by reading it one line at a time and doing the specified operations immediately. Most BASIC systems are interpreters. *See also* COMPILER.

INTERROGATORIES written questions about facts in a civil suit, which are submitted by one party to the other party or witnesses. These questions are asked under oath, with the questions and sworn answers being used as evidence in the trial. The court may submit questions and answers to the jury as part of the evidence. Court time is saved by the use of interrogatories.

INTERSTATE COMMERCE business activity among inhabitants of different states, including transportation of persons and property and navigation of public waters for that purpose, as well as purchase, sale, and exchange of commodities.

INTERSTATE COMMERCE COMMISSION (ICC) independent federal agency founded in 1887 for the purpose of ensuring that the public receives fair and reasonable rates and services from carriers and transportation service firms involved in interstate commerce.

INTERSTATE LAND SALES ACT federal law, administered by the U.S. Department of HOUSING AND URBAN DEVELOPMENT (HUD), which requires certain disclosures and advertising procedures when selling land to purchasers in other states. *See also* OFFICE OF INTERSTATE LAND SALES REGISTRATION (OILSR).

INTERVAL SCALE level of measurement in which the difference between observations provides information, such as the quality rating of bonds, AAA, AA, A, BBB. *See also* NOMINAL SCALE; ORDINAL SCALE; RATIO SCALE.

INTERVIEW conversation between two or more people for the purpose of yielding information for guidance, counseling, treatment, or employment.

INTERVIEWER BIAS influences resulting from the personal prejudice of the individual conducting the interview. Interviewer bias is important in determining the initial impression formed with regard to a job.

INTERVIEW EXPENSES travel expenses paid to a prospective employee that are typically reimbursed by the employer.

INTERVIEW, STRUCTURED INTERVIEW where the interviewer carefully controls the subjects discussed and the nature of the question and response format.

INTERVIEW, UNSTRUCTURED INTERVIEW where the interviewer does not determine the format or subject to be discussed. It leaves the interviewee with major control of the conversation.

INTER VIVOS TRANSFER transfer of property or interest during a person's lifetime.

INTER VIVOS TRUST trust established between living persons, for instance, between father and child; also called *living trust*. In contrast, a TESTAMENTARY TRUST goes into effect when the person who establishes the trust dies.

INTESTATE
1. (adj.) having made no valid will.
2. (noun) a person who dies leaving no will or leaving one that is defective. Property goes to the legal heirs of the intestate.

If a person dies *intestate,* his or her heirs under state law will inherit the property. If there are no heirs, the property will *escheat* (pass to the state).

IN THE MONEY option contract on a stock whose current market price is above the striking price of a call option or below the striking price of a put option.

IN THE TANK lack of objectivity; tendency of individuals to analyze events in terms of their own personal experiences, whether they are positive or negative.

INTRANET a NETWORK confined to a single organization (but not necessarily a single site); often set up as a WEB SITE, but accessible only to organization members.

INTRINSIC VALUE
1. value of tangible material, regardless of its use; for instance, the value of silver used in a coin.
2. valuation determined by applying data inputs to a valuation theory or model. The resulting value is then compared to the prevailing market price.

INURE to take effect; to serve to the benefit of someone; in property, to VEST.

INVENTORY
Corporate finance: value of a firm's raw materials, work in process, supplies used in operations, and finished goods. There are a number of inventory valuation methods; the most widely used are FIRST IN, FIRST OUT (FIFO) and LAST IN, FIRST OUT (LIFO). Financial statements normally indicate the basis of inventory valuation, generally the lower figure of either cost or current market price.
Personal finance: list of all assets owned by an individual and the value of each, based on cost, market value, or both. Such inventories are usually required for property insurance purposes.

INVENTORY CERTIFICATE management representation to an independent auditor regarding inventory balance on hand. It typically details the method used in computing inventory quantity, pricing basis, and condition.

INVENTORY CONTROL accounting system of maintaining inventories to prevent stockouts, reduce holding costs, and permit detecting theft.

INVENTORY FINANCING
1. synonym for overadvances in FACTORING, where loans in excess of accounts receivable are made against inventory in anticipation of future sales.
2. financing by a bank or sales finance company of the inventory of a dealer in consumer or capital goods. Such loans, also called *wholesale financing or floor planning*, are secured by the inventory.

INVENTORY LOAN *see* INVENTORY FINANCING.

INVENTORY PLANNING planning the quantity of inventory and its timing; coordinating inventory with production or sales needs. Effective inventory planning is instrumental in reducing costs and increasing productivity.

INVENTORY SHORTAGE (SHRINKAGE) unexplained difference in inventory between a physical count and the amount recorded. Causes may range from normal evaporation of a liquid to theft.

INVENTORY TURNOVER ratio of annual sales to inventory, which shows how many times the inventory of a firm is sold and replaced during an accounting period.

INVERSE CONDEMNATION legal procedure to obtain compensation when a property interest has been taken or diminished in value by a government activity. For example, Abel owns a home near a public airport. The city constructs a new runway that sends air traffic directly over Abel's house, seriously diminishing Abel's enjoyment of his property. Abel may sue for *inverse condemnation* and, if successful, may force the airport authority to take Abel's house in exchange for just compensation.

INVERTED YIELD CURVE unusual situation where short-term interest rates are higher than long-term rates; also called *negative yield curve*.

INVEST transfer CAPITAL to an enterprise in order to secure income or profit for the investor.

INVESTMENT purchase of stocks, bonds, mutual fund shares, real property, collectible annuities, etc., with the expectation of obtaining INCOME or CAPITAL GAIN—or both—in the future. Investment tends to be longer term and less risky than SPECULATION.

INVESTMENT ADVISERS ACT legislation passed by Congress in 1940 that requires all investment advisers to register with the Securities and Exchange Commission. The Act is designed to protect the public from fraud or misrepresentation by investment advisers.

INVESTMENT ADVISORY SERVICE service providing investment advice for a fee. Investment advisers must register with the Securities and Exchange Commission and abide by the rules of the INVESTMENT ADVISERS ACT.

INVESTMENT ANALYSIS a study of the likely return from a proposed investment with the objective of evaluating the amount an investor may pay for it, the investment's suitability to that investor, or the feasibility of a proposed real estate development.

There are various methods of investment analysis, including cash on cash return, payback period, internal rate of return, and net present value. Each provides some measure of the estimated return on an investment based on various assumptions and investment horizons.

INVESTMENT BANKER firm, acting as underwriter or agent, that serves as intermediary between an issuer of securities and the investing public. *See also* BEST EFFORT; FIRM COMMITMENT.

INVESTMENT CLUB group of people who pool their assets in order to make joint investment decisions. Each member of the club contributes a certain amount of capital, with additional money to be invested every month or quarter. Decisions on which stocks or bonds to buy are made by a vote of members.

INVESTMENT COMPANY a real estate investment trust, a regulated investment company, or a corporation, more than 80% of the value of whose assets are held for investment and are readily marketable stock or securities or interests in regulated investment companies or real estate investment trusts. Generally, these must pay at least 90% of their income to shareholders, and they are not taxed on the amounts distributed. The shareholders are taxed on the income received, so the corporate double tax is avoided.

INVESTMENT COMPANY ACT OF 1940 legislation passed by Congress requiring registration and regulation of investment companies by the Securities and Exchange Commission. The Act sets the standards by which mutual funds and other investment companies operate.

INVESTMENT COUNSEL person with the responsibility for providing investment advice to clients and executing investment decisions. Financial planners, stockbrokers, and others perform similar functions.

INVESTMENT CREDIT *see* INVESTMENT TAX CREDIT.

INVESTMENT-GRADE term used to describe bonds suitable for purchase by prudent investors. Standard & Poor's rating service designates the bonds in its four top categories (AAA down to BBB) as investment-grade. In their FIDUCIARY roles, institutional investors, such as pension funds, insurance companies, and banks, must maintain a certain level of credit quality in the bond portfolios they purchase, so they tend to buy mostly investment-grade bonds. *Contrast with* JUNK BOND.

INVESTMENT INCOME PORTFOLIO INCOME such as dividends, interest, and gains from the sale of INVESTMENT PROPERTY. *See also* INVESTMENT INTEREST EXPENSE; KIDDIE TAX.

INVESTMENT INTEREST EXPENSE interest paid to carry portfolio investments such as bonds, stocks, and undeveloped land. Tax deductions for interest expense are limited to the income received from the investment such as dividends and interest.

INVESTMENT LIFE CYCLE time span from acquisition of an investment to final disposition. The best way to measure the RATE OF RETURN from an investment is over its life cycle. All relevant investment contributions, CASH FLOWS, and resale proceeds are known.

INVESTMENT MANAGEMENT decisions of ASSET selection, as contrasted with PROPERTY MANAGEMENT of REAL ESTATE or custodial care of INVESTMENTS.

INVESTMENT OBJECTIVE financial objective that an INVESTOR uses to determine which kind of INVESTMENT is appropriate. For example, if the investor's objective is growth of capital, he may opt for growth-oriented MUTUAL FUNDS or individual STOCKS. If he is more interested in income, he might purchase income-oriented mutual funds or individual stocks instead.

INVESTMENT PORTFOLIO DIVERSIFICATION of investments in various securities and other investment instruments to maximize opportunities while minimizing risk exposure. *See also* ASSET ALLOCATION.

INVESTMENT SOFTWARE computer program that tracks investments in shares, cost, and revenue. Some investment software includes price and dividend histories of securities. Comparisons can be made with major market indicators. Automatic valuation of securities, including current value, unrealized gain or loss, and daily price change, can be made. Tax ramifications of investment decisions can be analyzed by some packages.

INVESTMENT STRATEGY plan to allocate assets among such choices as stocks, bonds, cash equivalents, commodities, and real estate. An investment strategy should be formulated based on an investor's outlook on interest rates, inflation, and economic growth, among other factors, and also taking into account the investor's age, tolerance for risk, amount of capital available to invest, and future needs for capital.

INVESTMENT TAX CREDIT includes the REHABILITATION TAX CREDIT, the BUSINESS ENERGY INVESTMENT CREDIT, gasification, advance coal, and the REFORESTATION CREDIT.

INVESTMENT TRUST *see* INVESTMENT COMPANY.

INVESTMENT VALUE the estimated value of an investment to a particular individual or institutional investor. It may be greater or less than MARKET VALUE depending on the investor's particular situation.

INVESTOR party who purchases an ASSET with the expectation of financial rewards. Typically, an *investor* exercises greater DUE DILIGENCE or conservatism than does a SPECULATOR.

INVESTOR RELATIONS DEPARTMENT in major public companies, a staff position responsible for investor relations, reporting either to the chief financial officer or to the director of public relations. The duties vary, and may include: (1) making sure the company is understood properly in the investment community; (2) ensuring there is full and timely public disclosure; and (3) responding to requests for information from shareholders and others.

INVISIBLE HAND description of business motivation in a free economy. Reference to the doctrine of Adam Smith that the pursuit of self-interest promotes the public good. Because "the annual revenue of every society is always precisely equal to the exchangeable value of the whole annual produce of its industry," then each person, in "directing [his] industry in such a manner as its produce may be of the greatest value," is "led by an invisible hand to promote an end which was no part of his intention. . . . By pursuing his own interest he frequently promotes that of the society more effectually than when he really intends to promote it." The *invisible hand* doctrine is one of the cornerstones of the free enterprise system.

INVOICE bill prepared by a seller of goods or services and submitted to the purchaser. The invoice lists all items bought, together with amounts owed.

INVOLUNTARY unwilling, forced, opposed. *See* DURESS.

INVOLUNTARY BANKRUPTCY *see* BANKRUPTCY.

INVOLUNTARY CONVERSION
1. CONDEMNATION, that is, the taking by government of private property for public use, with compensation being paid.
2. sudden destruction of an asset by nature, as by fire, storm, or sudden insect damage.

INVOLUNTARY EXCHANGE the destruction, THEFT, CONDEMNATION, or disposal under the threat of condemnation of property if the owner receives money or other property in payment.

INVOLUNTARY LIEN LIEN imposed against property without consent of the owner to cover unpaid taxes, special assessments, etc. *See also* MORTGAGE LIEN.

INVOLUNTARY TRUST TRUST relationship that courts recognize because of the legal association between parties, although no formal written trust document was ever prepared.

INVOLUNTARY UNEMPLOYMENT condition of being unemployed against one's wishes. Despite concerted search efforts, those who are involuntarily unemployed are unable to find employment for their skills and background.

INWOOD ANNUITY FACTOR number that when multiplied by the periodic payment from a *level-payment income stream*, indicates the present value of the income stream, based on a specific interest rate. Same formula and use as ORDINARY ANNUITY factor. For example, an investment is expected to provide income of $100 per month for 10 years. At the end of 10 years the investment has no value. At an interest rate of 10%, the present value (PV) of the investment is

$$PV = \$100 \times 75.67 = \$7,567$$

where 75.67 is the Inwood annuity factor.

IOTA very small or insignificant quantity.

IOU a signed document that recognizes a debt and agrees on payment, often in the form "IOU (phonetic abbreviation of 'I owe you') $x."

IPO *see* INITIAL PUBLIC OFFERING.

IRA *see* INDIVIDUAL RETIREMENT ACCOUNT.

IRD *see* INCOME IN RESPECT OF A DECEDENT.

IRR *see* INTERNAL RATE OF RETURN.

IRRATIONAL EXUBERANCE characterization of the market mood in a 1996 speech by then Federal Reserve Chairman Alan Greenspan. In context, the typically cautious Greenspan posed the question, "How do we know when irrational exuberance has unduly escalated asset values, which then become subject to unexpected and prolonged contraction?"

IRREGULARS goods failing to meet manufacturing specifications that may affect appearance, but not usability.

IRREPARABLE HARM, IRREPARABLE DAMAGE in law, something that cannot be compensated for in a court of law by way of injunction or by SPECIFIC PERFORMANCE; something that is almost impossible to be assigned a value. Reasonable redress for the injury inflicted cannot be received.

IRREVOCABLE incapable of being recalled or revoked, unchangeable. For example, a bank issues an *irrevocable* LETTER OF CREDIT, stating that if the terms of the CONTRACT are met, the bank will lend the money requested.

IRREVOCABLE TRUST trust that cannot be changed or terminated by the one who created it without the agreement of the BENEFICIARY.

IRS *see* INTERNAL REVENUE SERVICE.

ISDN *i*ntegrated *s*ervices *d*igital *n*etwork, a telecommunications technology offered by telephone companies that provides transmission speeds up to 128Kbps. Because the network is all-digital, in contrast to the analog telephone system, it can easily send voice, data, and video over the same line simultaneously. Although ISDN uses existing phone lines, it does require specialized equipment: a network terminator and an ISDN adapter, sometimes referred to as a *digital modem.*

ISLAND DISPLAY merchandise displayed in the aisle of a store. The merchandise can be displayed either on racks or on a fixture.

ISP *see* INTERNET SERVICE PROVIDER.

ISSUE
1. stock or bonds sold by a corporation or a government entity at a particular time.
2. selling of new securities by a corporation or government entity, either through an underwriter or by a private placement.
3. descendants, such as children and grandchildren. For example, a person's estate may be passed, at his death, to his *issue.*
4. in legal practice, point of fact or law disputed between parties to the litigation, generally an assertion by one side and a denial by the other.

ISSUED AND OUTSTANDING shares of a corporation, authorized in the corporate charter, which have been issued and are outstanding. These shares represent capital invested by the firm's shareholders and owners, and may be all or only a portion of the number of shares authorized.

ISSUER legal entity that has the power to issue and distribute a security. Issuers include corporations, municipalities, foreign and domestic governments and their agencies, and investment trusts. Issuers of stock are responsible for reporting on corporate developments to shareholders and for paying dividends once declared. Issuers of bonds are committed to making timely payments of interest and principal to bondholders.

ITEMIZED DEDUCTION LIMITATION taxpayers with ADJUSTED GROSS INCOME (AGI) in excess of a prescribed threshold are required to reduce their otherwise allowable itemized deductions. The required reduction equals 3% of the amount by which the taxpayer's AGI exceeds the prescribed threshold. For 2006, the prescribed threshold is $150,500. The threshold for subsequent years will be indexed for inflation. Otherwise allowable deductions, however, cannot be reduced by more than 80%. Further, the reduction does not apply to medical expenses, casualty and theft losses, investment interest, and gambling losses. This limit will be phased out and entirely repealed after 2009.

ITEMIZED DEDUCTIONS specific individualized tax deductions, allowed under provisions of the Internal Revenue Code and state and municipal tax codes for specific expenses incurred by the TAXPAYER during the TAXABLE YEAR (e.g., unreimbursed medical expenses, qualified residence interest expense, casualty loss, charitable contributions). These deductions are allowed in computing TAXABLE INCOME. There is an overall limitation on certain itemized deductions. An alternative is to claim the STANDARD DEDUCTION.

ITERATION process of repeating a particular action. A *definite iteration* occurs when the specified action will be repeated a fixed number of times. An *independent iteration* occurs if the repetitions stop when a particular condition is met, but the number of repetitions is not known in advance.

ITINERANT WORKER worker who continually moves from job to job. Itinerant workers are often used for harvesting agricultural crops, and they move from harvest to harvest. *See also* MIGRATORY WORKER.

J

JAVA an object-oriented programming language created by Sun Microsystems. Java is a device-independent language, meaning that programs compiled in Java can be run on any computer.

JAWBONING attempt to persuade others to act in a certain way by using the influence or pressure of a high office. An example is public criticism by the federal administration of increases in wages or prices deemed unreasonable or expanding inflation.

J-CURVE in economics, description of an expected turnaround in an activity such as foreign trade. The former trend continues for a while, then bottoms out and turns up the right side of the J.

JOB
1. nature of one's employment activities; all activities performed while working on a job. *See also* JOB DESCRIPTION.
2. specific project, often given a *job identification number*.

JOB ANALYSIS organizational analysis of a job to determine the responsibilities inherent in the position as well as the qualifications needed to fulfill its responsibilities. Job analysis is essential when recruiting in order to locate an individual having the requisite capabilities and education.

JOB BANK data bank of job listings by category, usually contained on a computer. Job banks are used by employment agencies as well as by larger organizations for the purpose of providing job applicants with greater access to job openings and managers with a larger pool of workers from which to choose.

JOBBER middleman in the sale of goods; one who buys from a wholesaler and sells to a retailer. A jobber, who actually purchases goods himself and then resells them, is distinguished from a BROKER or AGENT, who sells goods on another's behalf. *See also* RACK JOBBERS.

JOB CLASSIFICATION method of categorizing jobs into ranks or classes for the purposes of work comparison and wage comparability.

JOB COST SHEET list of budgeted or actual costs of materials and labor that are required to produce a product.

JOB DEPTH ability and power an employee has to influence his or her work environment. It refers to the amount of discretion an employee has in a job. A highly specialized position, such as a high-level manager, provides many decision opportunities characteristic of a job with great depth.

JOB DESCRIPTION detailed analysis and definition of a job; all the duties, responsibilities, and conditions required in the performance of a particular job.

JOB ENRICHMENT motivating employees through expanding job responsibilities and giving increased control over the total production process. Employees normally receive training and additional support as well as increased input, or "say," into the total manufacturing procedure.

JOB EVALUATION systematic method of determining the relative worth of jobs in an organization. Job evaluation is important when an organization seeks to establish relative pay levels for job classifications based upon an equitable ranking of job importance and responsibilities.

JOB HUNTING EXPENSES expenses incurred while looking for a new job in the same line of work, whether or not a new job is found. These miscellaneous ITEMIZED DEDUCTIONS for tax purposes are subject to the 2% AGI floor. Expenses of search for one's first job after completing school are not deductible.

JOB JUMPER or **JOB HOPPER** individual who changes jobs frequently. Being categorized as a *job jumper* is detrimental to one's career since it indicates an inability either to make a commitment to an organization or to maintain employment.

JOB LOT form of contract authorizing the completion of a particular order size; production run size that a job order calls for. *See also* JOB ORDER.

JOB ORDER internal management authorization order for the production of a specified number of goods or services. *See also* JOB LOT.

JOB PLACEMENT placement of individuals in jobs matching their abilities. Personnel offices interview and test applicants for the purpose of achieving suitable job placements where there is a good match between management needs and employee qualifications.

JOB RELATED INJURIES *See* WORKERS' COMPENSATION ACTS.

JOB ROTATION moving an employee from job to job. The purposes of job rotation are (1) to give employees experience with all organizational activities as a training process and (2) to offset boredom, which can occur when performing the same job over an extended period of time.

JOB SATISFACTION sense of inner fulfillment and pride achieved when performing a particular job. Job satisfaction occurs when an employee feels he has accomplished something having importance and value worthy of recognition; sense of joy.

JOBS CREDIT *see* TARGETED JOBS CREDIT.

JOB SECURITY freedom from the fear of dismissal or job loss. Some professions and employment activities have greater job security than others. The government civil service has more job security than many occupations in the private sector.

JOB SHARING dividing responsibilities and hours of one job between two people. Job sharing is an alternative to LAYOFFS in that both employees can at least have part-time work until economic conditions improve.

JOB SHOP business that makes products to order (that is, responds to jobs), instead of to anticipated demand.

JOB SPECIFICATION personnel requirements of a particular job. A job specification sets forth the skills, education, and experience required for a particular position.

JOB TICKET instruction card that accompanies a particular job assignment through all phases of production.

JOINT ACCOUNT bank or brokerage account owned jointly by two or more people. A *joint account* may be set up in either of two ways: (1) all parties to the account must sign checks and approve all withdrawals or brokerage transactions or (2) any one party may take such actions on his or her own.

JOINT AND SEVERAL LIABILITY liability under which a CREDITOR can demand full repayment from any and all of those who have borrowed. Each borrower is liable for the full debt, not just the PRORATED share.

JOINT AND SURVIVOR ANNUITY annuity that makes payments to two or more beneficiaries, often a husband and wife. When one of the annuitants dies, the survivor continues to receive annuity payments. However, the payments that had been made to the deceased party are not paid to the survivor.

JOINT COST *see* JOINT PRODUCT COST.

JOINT ECONOMIC COMMITTEE OF CONGRESS (JEC) joint House and Senate committee that concerns itself with significant economic matters. It also is charged with keeping abreast of significant economic developments in order to keep Congress informed about them.

JOINT FARE, JOINT RATE in transportation, published fare or shipping rate that includes the cost of two or more carriers (airlines, railroads) that must be used to reach the destination sought.

JOINT LIABILITY
  1. sued person being allowed the right to insist that others be sued jointly with him.
  2. more than one party obligated to repay a loan.

JOINTLY AND SEVERALLY legal phrase used in definitions of liability, meaning that an obligation may be enforced against all obligators jointly or against any one of them separately.

JOINT PRODUCT COST in accounting, cost of two or more products that arise from the same manufacturing process, as when silver and gold are taken from the same mine. It is impossible to distinguish the cost of mining each, so costs are generally allocated based on the relative selling price of each product. *See also* BY-PRODUCT.

JOINT STOCK COMPANY form of business organization that combines features of a corporation and a partnership. Under U.S. law, joint stock companies are recognized as corporations, but with unlimited liability for their stockholders.

JOINT (TAX) RETURN tax return filed by a husband and wife, setting forth tax information concerning each of them, and computing a combined tax liability. Taxable income is calculated with progressive rates based on the assumption that the couple's income is earned equally by the two spouses. A husband and wife can also file separate returns, and the total tax liability may differ from that of a joint return for the same two people. Typically, the joint return provides a lower total tax than do separate returns.

JOINT TENANCY ownership of an asset by two or more persons, each of whom has an UNDIVIDED INTEREST with the RIGHT OF SURVIVORSHIP. Thus, if one of the tenants should die, the entire value becomes the property of the surviving tenant(s). Typically used by related persons. Also referred to in bank and brokerage accounts as *joint tenancy with the right of survivorship.*

JOINT VENTURE agreement by two or more parties to work on a project together. A joint venture, which is usually limited to one project, differs from a PARTNERSHIP, which forms the basis for cooperation on many projects.

JOURNAL
In general: academic or professional periodical.
Accounting: book, typically to record accounting transactions as they occur. *See also* GENERAL JOURNAL; SALES JOURNAL; LEDGER.

JOURNAL ENTRY recording of a transaction in an accounting journal, such as the GENERAL JOURNAL. The journal entry has equal debit and credit amounts, and it usually includes a one-sentence explanation of the purpose of the transaction.

JOURNALIZE in accounting, to enter into a journal, such as the GENERAL JOURNAL.

JOURNAL VOUCHER piece of paper explaining the need for and leading to a JOURNAL ENTRY.

JOURNEYMAN skilled tradesperson who has completed a prescribed apprenticeship in a particular craft. The status of journeyman indicates that an individual has mastered all the specific skills of the craft.

JOYSTICK computer input device, especially helpful when playing computer games. It consists of a handle that can be pointed in different directions. Because the computer can sense which direction the joystick is pointed, it can be used to control the movements of objects displayed on the computer screen.

JPEG (pronounced, *Jay-peg*) a file formatted in the color graphics compression format devised by the Joint Photographic Experts Group and having the filename extension jpg. The JPEG standard uses a "lossy" DATA COMPRESSION method in which some data is sacrificed (lost) to achieve greater compression. JPEGs are widely used on the Internet and are especially suited for photographs and other graphics with continuous tones, as compared to GIFs, which are better suited to rendering line art and graphics with large masses of solid color.

JUDGMENT
1. determination of a court of competent jurisdiction upon matters submitted to it.
2. payment for private property taken for public use.
3. use of one's understanding and intuition to resolve a problem.

JUDGMENT CREDITOR creditor who has obtained against a debtor a JUDGMENT through which the creditor can obtain the sum due him. The effect of becoming a judgment creditor is to create against other creditors a certain priority right to have the debt satisfied out of the debtor's assets, and to extend the life of the claim under the STATUTE OF LIMITATIONS.

JUDGMENT DEBTOR person against whom there is a legal JUDGMENT for repayment of a DEBT. The effect of becoming a judgment debtor is that the debtor's property may be subject to creditors' claims.

JUDGMENT LIEN claim upon the property of a debtor resulting from a JUDGMENT. For example, Abel won't pay his debt to Baker. After establishing the debt in court, Baker may be allowed by the court to put a *judgment lien* on Abel's real estate. Baker becomes the JUDGMENT CREDITOR, while Abel is the JUDGMENT DEBTOR.

JUDGMENT PROOF people from whom a creditor cannot collect money, even when there is a court order stating there is a debt. Such people may be insolvent or their wages or assets protected by state law.

JUDGMENT SAMPLE determination by an auditor, based on personal experience and familiarity with the client, of the number of items, as well as the particular items, to be examined in a population. This function allows the accountant to maintain objectivity and thoroughness in testing the sampled items for accuracy.

JUDICIAL FORECLOSURE or **JUDICIAL SALE** having a defaulted debtor's property sold where the court ratifies the price paid. For example, XYZ Mortgage Company is owed $50,000 on a first mortgage by Mr. Baker. At *judicial foreclosure*, XYZ Mortgage Company bids $30,000 for the property, which is more than anyone else bids. They then claim the property and are awarded a $20,000 DEFICIENCY JUDGMENT against Mr. Baker.

JUMBO CERTIFICATE OF DEPOSIT certificate with a minimum denomination of $100,000. Jumbo CDs are usually bought and sold by large institutions such as banks, pension funds, money market funds, and insurance companies and generally carry a higher interest rate than smaller-denomination CDs.

JUMBO MORTGAGE a loan for an amount exceeding the statutory limit placed on the size of loans that FREDDIE MAC and FANNIE MAE can purchase. Such loans must be maintained in the lender's portfolio or sold to private investors rather than Fannie or Freddie. These loans are often sought for purchase of luxury homes. *See also* NONCONFORMING LOAN.

JUNIOR ISSUE issue of debt or equity that is subordinate in claim to another issue in terms of dividends, interest, principal, or security in the event of liquidation. *See also* JUNIOR SECURITY.

JUNIOR LIEN LIEN that will be paid after earlier liens have been paid. *See also* JUNIOR MORTGAGE; SUBORDINATION.

JUNIOR MORTGAGE MORTGAGE whose claim against the property will be satisfied only after prior mortgages have been repaid. *See also* SECOND MORTGAGE; WRAPAROUND MORTGAGE.

JUNIOR PARTNER partner in a firm who is limited as to both profits and management participation.

JUNIOR SECURITY security with lower priority claim on assets and income than a senior security. For example, a PREFERRED STOCK is junior to a DEBENTURE, but a debenture, being an unsecured bond, is junior to a MORTGAGE BOND; COMMON STOCK is junior to all corporate securities.

JUNK BOND bond with a speculative credit rating of BB or lower by Standard & Poor's and Moody's rating systems. Junk bonds are issued in LEVERAGED BUYOUTS and other TAKEOVERS, by companies without long track records of sales and earnings, or by those with questionable credit strength.

JUNK FAX unsolicited FAX messages often distributed by mass marketers. Junk fax messages can be a nuisance since they occupy the machine when other messages may be pending, use fax paper, and can be confused with other fax messages. *See also* FACSIMILE TRANSMISSION.

JUNK MAIL unsolicited mail often distributed by mass marketers. This mail usually is sent third class mail to reduce mailing cost. Junk mail can be a nuisance in that it creates waste, can be confused with higher-priority mail, and is time-consuming to sort through.

JURISDICTION power, right, or authority to interpret and apply tax laws or decisions. For example, the U.S. Court of Appeals has exclusive jurisdiction to review decisions of the U.S. TAX COURT and the U.S. District Courts, and the U.S. Court of Appeals of the Federal

Circuit has jurisdiction over decisions from the U.S. Court of Federal Claims.

JURISPRUDENCE
1. science of law. It includes the study of the structure of legal systems, such as EQUITY, and of the principles underlying those systems.
2. collective term denoting the course of judicial decision.
3. sometimes a synonym for law.

JURY group composed of the peers of the parties or a cross section of the community, summoned and sworn to decide on the facts in issue at a trial.

JUST COMPENSATION full indemnity for the loss or damage sustained by the owner of property taken under the power of EMINENT DOMAIN. The measure generally used is the FAIR MARKET VALUE of the property at the time of taking.

JUSTIFIABLE
1. facts that will excuse the doing of something or another party's acts. If the seller of a car fails to make delivery of it, the buyer's failure to pay will be *justifiable*.
2. some act that is otherwise criminal. For example, the courts would probably regard it justifiable should a shopkeeper kill an attacker armed with a deadly weapon, and the shopkeeper may be excused from criminal responsibility.

JUSTIFICATION text alignment in which both left and right edges are smooth, achieved by varying the space between words (and sometimes between characters) to make the lines of equal length.

JUSTIFIED PRICE fair market price an informed buyer will pay for an asset, whether it be a stock, a bond, a commodity, or real estate. *See also* FAIR MARKET VALUE.

JUST-IN-TIME INVENTORY CONTROL (JIT) method of close coordination with suppliers maximizing the relationship between production and sales levels with inventory, reducing carrying costs. Often JIT is linked with a computerized POINT-OF-SALE SYSTEM and inventory levels are maintained through an automated reordering system connected to suppliers, so that stockouts are minimized.

K

KANGAROO BONDS bonds denominated in Australian dollars and sold in Australia by foreign firms.

KB *see* KILOBYTE.

KEOGH PLAN also known as H.R. 10 Plan for self-employed individuals. *See also* 401(K) PLAN; SIMPLE IRA; SIMPLIFIED EMPLOYEE PENSION PLAN.

KEY-AREA EVALUATION evaluation of management in eight key areas. Management theorist Peter Drucker suggests that an organization needs to have result-oriented objectives in at least eight key areas: market standing, productivity, profitability, physical and financial resources, innovation, manager performance and development, worker performance and attitudes, and public and social responsibility.

KEY CURRENCIES major currencies in the global economy. Key currencies include the U.S. dollar, the euro, the British pound sterling, the Swiss franc, the Japanese yen, and the Canadian dollar.

KEYNESIAN ECONOMICS body of economic thought originated by the British economist and government adviser, John Maynard Keynes (1883–1946). He held essentially that insufficient demand causes unemployment and that excessive demand results in inflation; government should therefore manipulate the level of aggregate demand by adjusting levels of government expenditure and taxation. For example, to avoid depression Keynes advocated increased government spending and EASY MONEY, resulting in more investment, higher employment, and increased consumer spending.

KEY PERSON LIFE AND HEALTH INSURANCE *see* BUSINESS LIFE AND HEALTH INSURANCE; LIFE AND HEALTH INSURANCE, BUSINESS EXPOSURES.

KEYPUNCH type of data entry that involves punching holes into 80-column computer cards in a code (Hollerith) that can be machine read by a computer. Keypunch has been replaced by electronic keyboard technology. *See* PUNCHED CARD.

KICKBACK
Finance: practice whereby sales finance companies reward dealers who discount installment purchase paper through them with cash payments.
Government and private contracts: payment made secretly by a seller to someone instrumental in awarding a contract or making a sale—an illegal payoff.
Labor relations: illegal practice whereby employers require the return of a portion of wages established by law or union contract, in exchange for employment.

KICKER added feature of a debt obligation, usually designed to enhance marketability by offering the prospect of equity participation. For instance, a bond may be convertible to stock. Other examples are rights and warrants. Some mortgage loans also include kickers in the form of ownership participation or in the form of a percentage of gross rental receipts. Kickers are also called *sweeteners*.

KIDDIE TAX tax liability for children under age 14 on net unearned income (for example, interest and dividend income) over $1,400 in 1998 (subject to indexing) at their custodial parents' highest marginal tax rate.

KILLING significant reward for an effort of investment; for example, to make a *killing* in the stock market. Also to stop an undertaking, such as *killing* a project.

KILOBYTE (K or KB) in computers, approximately 1,000 (2^{10}, or 1,024) BYTES of information.

KIOSK an independent stand from which merchandise is sold, often placed in the common area of a regional SHOPPING CENTER.

KITING
Banking: (1) depositing and drawing checks between accounts at two or more banks and thereby taking advantage of the FLOAT; (2) fraudulently altering the figures on a check to increase its face value. *See* CHECK KITING.
Securities: driving stock prices to high levels through manipulative trading methods, such as the creation of artificial trading activity by the buyer and the seller working together and using the same funds.

KNEE-JERK automatic, involuntary; a reference to the involuntary contraction of the leg when the knee is tapped with a doctor's mallet. A *knee-jerk* reaction is a response without thought, conditioned by one's prevailing philosophy, such as "knee-jerk liberalism."

KNIGHTS OF LABOR originally a fraternal order of tailors, established in Philadelphia in approximately 1869 by Uriah Smith Stevens. The Noble Order of the Knights of Labor quickly grew to a national union having, in the mid-1880s, more than 700,000 members from every occupation. The Knights of Labor collapsed in 1893 after a national public reaction against labor agitators.

KNOCK-OFF a low-priced imitation of a name-brand product.

KNOW-HOW ability to perform a particular function; knowing how to do something. For example, one has the know-how to fly an airplane.

KNOWLEDGE-BASED PAY compensation predicated upon an employee's level of skill and educational attainment. Knowledge-based pay can be an incentive for employees to acquire additional training and education, thus upgrading overall work force skills.

KNOWLEDGE MANAGEMENT orderly retention and analysis of data for trends and other useful insights.

KNOW-YOUR-CUSTOMER RULE ethical concept in the securities industry holding that when recommending a financial transaction a broker should have reasonable grounds for believing the recommendation suits the customer's financial situation and needs. Customers opening accounts at brokerage firms must supply financial information that satisfies the know-your-customer requirement for routine purposes.

KONDRATIEFF CYCLE or **KONDRATIEFF WAVE** theory of the Soviet economist Nikolai Kondratieff, in the 1920s, that the economies of the Western capitalist world are prone to major up-and-down "supercycles" lasting 50 to 60 years.

K-1 *see* SCHEDULE K-1.

KRUGERRAND gold bullion coin minted by the Republic of South Africa and containing one troy ounce of gold. The *Krugerrand* is a frequently traded gold coin.

KUDOS recognition given by an entity for achievements. Credit can be given in various forms, such as a bonus, medal, or trophy.

L

LABELING LAWS federal and state statutes that require safe packaging and warning labels on hazardous materials, such as poisons and other dangerous substances; also called *packaging laws.*

LABOR
1. to exert the effort necessary to accomplish a particular work-related function.
2. physical or mental work performed for remuneration.
3. group or class of people who work for others performing particular jobs in organizations.

LABOR AGREEMENT accommodation reached between management and labor over the terms of employment. In labor relations, labor agreements result in a labor contract establishing the terms and conditions of the work environment.

LABOR DISPUTE controversy between management and labor over the terms and conditions of the workplace. Labor disputes can include any aspect of the work environment, including working conditions, wages, job descriptions, and fringe benefits.

LABOR FEDERATION overall umbrella labor organization having many affiliated local labor unions and providing extensive support services. The national AFL-CIO is a central trade union federation in the United States having numerous affiliates.

LABOR FORCE number of people over 16 years of age who are employed or seeking employment, as calculated by the U.S. Bureau of Labor Statistics. By the end of 2005, there were approximately 150 million men and women in the U.S. civilian labor force, of whom approximately 5% were unemployed.

LABOR-INTENSIVE activity in which labor costs are more important than capital costs. Deep-shaft coal mining and computer programming are labor-intensive.

LABOR-MANAGEMENT RELATIONS ACT the TAFT-HARTLEY ACT of 1947, which amended the WAGNER ACT of 1935. The law's provisions: (1) outlawed the CLOSED SHOP; (2) instituted an 80-day cooling-off period for strikes threatening the national health or safety; (3) prohibited unions from using union monies for national elections; (4) allowed suits for BREACH OF CONTRACT against unions; and (5) defined UNFAIR LABOR PRACTICES of unions.

LABOR-MANAGEMENT REPORTING AND DISCLOSURE ACT (LMRDA) OF 1959 *see* LANDRUM-GRIFFIN ACT.

LABOR MOBILITY ability of workers to change employment easily. Highly mobile workers are found in occupations that are in great demand.

LABOR PIRACY act of attracting workers away from a firm through inducements. Labor piracy often occurs as another firm makes extremely attractive employment offers to employees who are in great demand.

LABOR POOL source of trained personnel from which prospective workers are recruited. For example, college graduates from business schools represent an attractive labor pool for recruiting management trainees.

LABOR UNION association of workers for the purpose, in whole or in part, of bargaining, on behalf of workers, with employers about the terms and conditions of employment.

LACHES doctrine providing a party a defense when long-neglected rights are sought to be enforced against him. Laches signifies an undue lapse of time in enforcing a right of action, and negligence in failing to act more promptly.

LADDERING purchasing bonds that mature at various intervals. This provides the investor with greater regularity of income and provides some protection from interest rate fluctuations. *See also* STAGGERING MATURITIES.

LADING in transportation, cargo that is shipped.

LAFFER CURVE curve, named for U.S. economist Arthur Laffer, that relates marginal tax rates to total tax revenue. At first, increases in the marginal tax rate raise total tax revenue, but eventually, a tax rate is reached beyond which total tax revenues decrease.

LAFFER CURVE

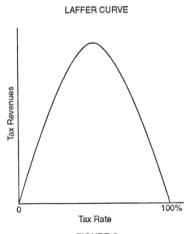

FIGURE 5

LAGGING INDICATORS ECONOMIC INDICATORS that change *after* a change in the economy has occurred. *Lagging indicators* are observed as a means of confirming trends. *See also* COINCIDENT INDICATORS; LEADING INDICATORS.

LAISSEZ-FAIRE doctrine that interference of government in business and economic affairs should be minimal. Adam Smith's *The Wealth of Nations* (1776) described laissez-faire economics in terms of an INVISIBLE HAND that would provide for the maximum good for all, if businessmen were free to pursue profitable opportunities as they saw them.

LAISSEZ-FAIRE LEADERSHIP unstructured leadership where a manager gives subordinates direct decision-making responsibilities. While this is the weakest form of management style, it is consistent with employee EMPOWERMENT.

LAN *see* LOCAL AREA NETWORK.

LAND
1. REAL ESTATE or REAL PROPERTY, or any tract that may be conveyed by deed.
2. ESTATE or INTEREST in real property; often refers not only to the earth itself but also to things of a permanent nature found or affixed there.

LAND BANKING purchasing land not presently needed for use, but expected to be needed in five to ten years.

LAND CONTRACT real estate INSTALLMENT selling arrangement whereby the buyer may use, occupy, and enjoy land, but no DEED is given by the seller (so no title passes) until all or a specified part of the sale price has been paid. Also called *contract for deed* and *installment land contract*.

LAND DEVELOPMENT process of improving raw land to support construction. The process may include planning, acquisition of government permits, subdivision, construction of access roads, installation of utilities, landscaping, and drainage. *See also* DEVELOPMENT.

LAND LEASE *see* GROUND LEASE.

LANDLOCKED
1. condition of a lot that has no access to a public thoroughfare except through an adjacent lot. *See also* INGRESS and EGRESS.
2. country with no access to the sea.

LANDLORD one who rents property to another, a *lessor.* A property owner who surrenders the right to use property for a specific time in exchange for the receipt of RENT. The landlord retains title to the property, but the rights of the tenant, or *lessee,* are spelled out in a LEASE.

LANDMARK
Real estate: fixed object serving as a BOUNDARY mark for a tract of land. *See also* MONUMENT.

LANDMARK DECISION case that sets an important precedent.

LAND OFFICE BUSINESS booming trade; perhaps derived from the activity of U.S. government land offices established to give away land to Western settlers.

LANDRUM-GRIFFIN ACT Labor-Management Reporting and Disclosure Act passed in 1959 to eliminate union corruption. The Landrum-Griffin Act contains a "bill of rights" for union members, including procedures to be followed in union elections, ability to sue unions, and right to have a copy of the COLLECTIVE BARGAINING agreement. It also forbids HOT CARGO clauses and specific types of picketing.

LAND SALE LEASEBACK *see* SALE AND LEASEBACK.

LANDSCAPE paper or screen orientation (for viewing or printing) in which the horizontal dimension is greater than the vertical. *Compare with* PORTRAIT.

LAND, TENEMENTS, AND HEREDITAMENTS phrase used in early English law to express all sorts of REAL ESTATE.

LAND TRUST TRUST agreement pertaining to REAL PROPERTY. Under the agreement, the property is managed by a TRUSTOR on behalf of the BENEFICIARY.

LAND-USE INTENSITY measure of the extent to which a land parcel is developed in conformity with ZONING ordinances. *See also* DENSITY.

LAND-USE PLANNING activity, generally conducted by a local government, that provides public and private land-use recommendations consistent with community policies. It is generally used to guide decisions on ZONING.

LAND-USE REGULATION government ORDINANCES, codes, and permit requirements intended to make the private use of land and natural resources conform to policy standards. Common regulations include building codes; curb-cut permit systems; historic preservation laws; housing codes; subdivision regulations; tree-cutting laws; and ZONING.

LAND-USE SUCCESSION change in the predominant use of a NEIGHBORHOOD or area over time.

LANHAM ACT popular name for the Federal Trade-Mark Act of 1946, which became effective in 1947; properly called the Lanham Trade-Mark Act. The Lanham Act governs the registration of TRADEMARKS, trade names, and other identifying marks used in interstate commerce and protects registered trademarks from interference or infringement.

LAPPING concealing a shortage by delaying the recording of cash receipts. For example, cash received from customer X is withheld by the cashier, and a subsequent cash receipt from customer Y is entered as a credit to X's account. Customer Y's account will not be credited until a collection is received from customer Z. If the money taken by the cashier is not replaced, there is an overstatement in total accounts receivable. However, by carefully shifting the overstatement from one customer to another the bookkeeper averts customer complaints when the monthly statements are received.

LAPSE

1. in property and casualty insurance, termination of a policy because of failure to pay a renewal premium.
2. in life insurance, termination of a policy because of failure to pay a premium and lack of sufficient cash value to make a premium loan.

LAPTOP (COMPUTER) *see* NOTEBOOK COMPUTER.

LARGE-CAP STOCK with a LARGE MARKET CAPITALIZATION. Largecap stocks typically have at least $5 billion in outstanding MARKET VALUE. Numerous MUTUAL FUNDS specialize in *large-cap* stocks, and many have the words "Large Cap" in their names.

LASER PRINTER computer printer using a laser beam that generates an image, then transfers it to paper electrostatically. Laser-printer output may be produced very fast, with quality that approaches that of typesetting.

LASH (Lighter Aboard SHip) system in which fully laden barges (lighters) may be loaded aboard a larger vessel for transport. The host vessel or *mothership* is specially designed or modified with a door at the waterline to facilitate loading and unloading the barges. Since the LASH vessels have onboard cranes and the barges are floated away from the ship, they do not require special docks or terminals.

LAST IN, FIRST OUT (LIFO) a method of INVENTORY whereby the most recent items acquired are considered the first ones sold. Items in inventory at the end of the year are treated as though they had been in the opening inventory, plus or minus acquisitions during the year as needed to make up the correct total. LIFO offers a lower amount of income during a period of rising inventory prices. *Contrast with* FIFO.

LAST SALE most recent trade in a particular security. Not to be confused with the final transaction in a trading session, called the *closing sale*.

LATE CHARGE fee charged by a lender when the borrower fails to make timely payment.

LATENT DEFECT defect that is hidden from knowledge as well as from sight and one that would not be discovered even by the exercise of ordinary and reasonable care. One who sells a house with knowledge of a latent defect must disclose the defect to the buyer or the buyer may later claim misrepresentation.

LATITUDE ability to exercise judgment within a range of authority without outside interference. For example, a supervisor has the *latitude* to recommend employees for promotions based upon his judgment.

LAUNCH
1. start or load a computer operating system or program.
2. advertise and release a new product.

LAUNDER make illegally acquired cash look as if it were acquired legally. The usual practice is to transfer the money through foreign banks, thereby concealing its source.

LAVISH OR EXTRAVAGANT EXPENSE expense that is not reasonable based on the facts and circumstances. These are not tax deductible.

LAW
1. legislative pronouncement of rules to guide one's actions in society.
2. total of those rules of conduct put in force by legislative authority or court decisions, or established by local custom.

LAWFUL MONEY *see* LEGAL TENDER.

LAW OF DIMINISHING RETURNS "rule" of economics that states that beyond a certain production level, productivity increases at a decreasing rate. *See also* DIMINISHING RETURNS.

LAW OF INCREASING COSTS corollary of the LAW OF DIMINISHING RETURNS. As the productivity of a factor of production decreases due to increasing production, the cost of successive units produced must increase.

LAW OF LARGE NUMBERS mathematical premise stating that the greater the number of exposures: (1) the more accurate the prediction; (2) the less the deviation of the actual losses from the expected losses ($X - \bar{x}$ approaches zero); and (3) the greater the credibility of the prediction (credibility approaches one). This law forms the basis for the statistical expectation of loss upon which premium rates for insurance policies are calculated.

LAW OF SUPPLY AND DEMAND economic proposition that, in any free market, the relationship between supply and demand determines price and the quantity produced. A change in either will lead to changes in price and/or amount produced in order to achieve EQUILIBRIUM in the market.

LAY OFF remove, temporarily or permanently, an employee from a payroll because of an economic slowdown or a production cutback, not because of poor performance or an infraction of company rules.

L/C *see* LETTER OF CREDIT.

LCD *l*iquid *c*rystal *d*isplay, a thin, flat, low-power display used in notebook computers, PDAS, calculators, watches, cameras, and similar devices. Liquid crystals are chemicals whose response to polarized light can be controlled by an electric field. A polarizing filter is built into the LCD; through this filter, the liquid crystal compound looks light or dark depending on its electrical state. LCD screens may be either color or monochrome; color screens are usually backlit.

LDC (LESS-DEVELOPED COUNTRY) a term used to describe countries in a poor and primitive economic condition.

LEAD-BASED PAINT considered a hazardous material. It is potentially poisonous, and its existence in property is to be disclosed. Its presence is often difficult to determine because applications of lead-based paint may have been covered over by more recent applications of paint that is free of lead.

LEADER
1. stock or group of stocks at the forefront of an upsurge or a downturn in a market.
2. product that has a large market share.
See also LOSS LEADER.

LEADER PRICING reduction in the price of a high-demand item to get people to come into a retail store or to encourage a direct-mail purchase that may inspire additional purchases; also called LOSS LEADER pricing. It is believed that once a decision to purchase an item is made, the customer's resistance to purchasing additional items at full price will be lower.

LEADERSHIP upper level of management that provides vision and direction for the company.

LEADING INDICATORS components of an index released monthly by the U.S. Commerce Department's Bureau of Economic Analysis. These often forecast business conditions, as contrasted with coincident or LAGGING INDICATORS.

LEAD TIME lag time between the placement of an order and its actual receipt. Lead time can be reduced by implementing JUST-IN-TIME INVENTORY CONTROL (JIT).

LEAKAGE loss of business that was expected, as, for example, when guests of a hotel eat breakfast at a restaurant across the street instead of in the hotel dining room or coffee shop.

LEARNING CURVE a figurative graph of mastery of a skill plotted against the time spent learning it. Software that is difficult to master is illogically said to have a *steep learning curve*.

LEASE contract granting use of real estate, equipment, or other fixed assets for a specified time in exchange for payment, usually in the form of rent. The owner of the leased property is called the LESSOR, the user the LESSEE. *See also* CAPITAL LEASE; FINANCIAL LEASE; OPERATING LEASE; SALE AND LEASEBACK.

LEASE BONUS amount paid to induce a lessor to execute a mineral lease.

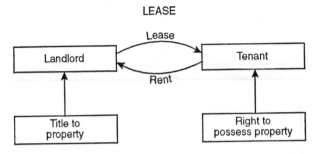

FIGURE 6

LEASED FEE the landlord's ownership interest of a PROPERTY that is under LEASE. Its value is based on the anticipated income from RENT, and the reversionary property value upon lease expiration.

LEASEHOLD estate in real property of a LESSEE, created by a LEASE; generally an estate of fixed duration, but may also describe TENANCY AT WILL, a month-to-month tenancy, etc. The value of a leasehold depends on whether the rent is below market and on the length of the remaining lease term.

LEASEHOLD COSTS costs of purchasing and maintaining a lease. These costs are capitalized as part of the basis of the property.

LEASEHOLD IMPROVEMENTS fixtures, attached to real estate that are generally acquired or installed by the TENANT. Upon expiration of the LEASE the tenant can generally remove them, provided such action does not damage the property or conflict with the lease. For example, the cabinets, light fixtures, and window treatments of a retail store in a leased building are *leasehold improvements. See also* TENANT FIXTURES.

LEASEHOLD INSURANCE coverage for a tenant (the LESSEE) with a favorable lease (enabling the lessee to rent premises for less than the rental market value). If the lease is canceled by the LESSOR because an insured peril (such as fire) strikes, the lessee is indemnified for the loss incurred. The premise is that the lessee will have to forgo earnings derived from having an advantageous lease, and should be indemnified for this incurred loss.

LEASEHOLD MORTGAGE LIEN on the tenant's INTEREST in real estate; generally subordinate to other liens on the property.

LEASEHOLD VALUE value of a tenant's interest in real estate, especially under a long-term lease at below-market rental rates.

LEASE WITH OPTION TO PURCHASE LEASE that gives the lessee (tenant) the right to purchase the property at an agreed-upon price under certain conditions. If a lease bears characteristics similar to a financing device, the arrangement will be treated as financing, not a lease. An option to purchase at FAIR MARKET VALUE would appear to be a lease; by contrast, an option at a bargain price would indicate EQUITY build-up through the "rent" and would be an indication of a purchase with a financing lease.

LEAVE OF ABSENCE approved absence period from work without loss of seniority or other job-related perquisites. A leave of absence is often granted to employees for particular purposes, such as attending an educational program or performing a special research project.

LED (*l*ight-*e*mitting *d*iode) electronic display that lights up when the proper current is passed through it.

LEDGER book; in accounting transactions, book of accounts. *Contrast with* JOURNAL, in which the transactions are initially recorded.

LEFT-CLICK click the left or primary button on a computer mouse.

LEGACY disposition by will of PERSONAL PROPERTY. *See also* BEQUEST.

LEGACY COST the cost of retiree pension, health insurance, and other benefits to an employer; employment costs that continue after an employee retires.

LEGAL AGE age at which a person can enter into binding contracts or agree to other legal acts without the consent of another adult. In most states the *legal age*, also called the *age of majority*, is 18 years. *See* MINOR.

LEGAL DESCRIPTION legally acceptable identification of REAL ESTATE by one of the following: the government rectangular survey; metes and bounds; recorded PLAT (lot and block number).

LEGAL ENTITY person or organization that has the legal standing to enter into a contract and may be sued for failure to perform as agreed in the contract. A child under legal age is not a legal entity. A corporation is a legal entity since it is a person in the eyes of the law.

LEGALESE the jargon of attorneys, which often seems redundant or unclear to the layperson.

LEGAL EXCHANGE INFORMATION SERVICE (LEXIS) online database for legal research; its resources include the Federal Tax library, which contains the full text of the Internal Revenue Code, as well as regulations, revenue rulings, and court decisions of interest to tax practitioners.

LEGAL EXPENSE INSURANCE prepaid legal insurance coverage plan sold on a group basis. It entitles a group member to a schedule of benefits, at a stipulated premium, for adoptions, probates, divorces and other legal services. This emerging employee benefit has had wide acceptance in some localities but limited acceptance elsewhere. After scheduled benefits have been exhausted, subsequent legal fees are usually based on the attorney's customary rate. For example, a prepaid legal insurance plan may provide only three legal consultations a year.

LEGAL INVESTMENT investment permissible for investors with FIDUCIARY responsibilities. INVESTMENT-GRADE BONDS, as rated by Standard & Poor's or Moody's, usually qualify as legal investments. Guidelines designed to protect investors are set by the state in which the fiduciary operates. *See also* LEGAL LIST; PRUDENT-MAN RULE.

LEGAL LIST high-quality securities selected by a state agency, usually a banking department, as permissible holdings of mutual savings banks, pension funds, insurance companies, and other FIDUCIARY institutions. *See also* PRUDENT-MAN RULE.

LEGAL MONOPOLY exclusive right to offer a particular service within a particular territory. In exchange, the company agrees to have its policies and rates regulated. Electric and water utilities are legal monopolies. *See also* NATURAL MONOPOLY.

LEGAL NAME name one has for official purposes; not a nickname.

LEGAL NOTICE notification of others using the method required by law. *See also* CONSTRUCTIVE NOTICE; NOTICE.

LEGAL OPINION
1. statement as to legality, written by an authorized official such as a city attorney or an attorney general.
2. statement as to the legality of a MUNICIPAL BOND ISSUE, usually written by a law firm specializing in public borrowings.
3. statement from a lawyer describing what is legal or lawful.

LEGAL REPRESENTATIVE one who oversees the legal affairs of another person or taxpayer (e.g., EXECUTOR or ADMINISTRATOR of an estate).

LEGAL RIGHT interest that the law will protect.

LEGAL-SIZE a U.S. paper size standard, 8½ by 14 inches.

LEGAL TENDER kind of money lawfully acceptable for payment of a debt. All coins and paper money of the United States as well as Federal Reserve notes and circulating notes of Federal Reserve Banks and national banking associations are *legal tender.*

LEGAL TITLE a collection of rights of ownership that are defined or recognized by law or that could be successfully defended in a court of law.

LEGAL WRONG invasion of a LEGAL RIGHT.

LEGATEE one who receives property by WILL. *See also* DEVISEE.

LEGGING-IN entering into a HEDGING contract after becoming the debtor or creditor under a DEBT INSTRUMENT. Any gain or loss from *legging-in* is deferred until the qualifying debt instrument matures or is disposed of in the future.

LEGGING-OUT disposing of one or more unmatured elements of a qualified HEDGING transaction. Any gain or loss from *legging-out* is deferred until the qualifying DEBT INSTRUMENT matures or is disposed of in the future.

LEGISLATION action with respect to acts, bills, and resolutions or similar items by Congress, a state legislature, local governing body, public referendum, or constitutional amendment. *Legislation* does not include acts or rulings of executive, judicial, or administrative bodies.

LEMON product or investment producing poor performance. A car that continually needs repairs is a *lemon*, and consumers are guaranteed a full refund in several states under so-called *lemon laws*. A promising stock that fails to live up to expectations is also called a lemon.

LENDER individual or firm that extends money to a borrower with the expectation of being repaid, usually with interest. Lenders create debt in the form of loans, and in the event of corporate LIQUIDATION, they are paid off before stockholders receive distributions.

LENDER LIABILITY the responsibility of a bank, S&L, or credit union to a potential borrower to whom it has made a loan commitment. Should the lender fail to provide the loan as promised, it may be responsible for damages suffered by the potential borrower. These can be substantial amounts, especially if the borrower's business failed because of a cash shortage.

LESSEE one who holds an ESTATE by virtue of a LEASE; TENANT of a LANDLORD.

LESSOR one who grants a lease to another, thereby transferring to him exclusive temporary right of POSSESSION of certain property, subject only to rights expressly retained by the owner; same as LANDLORD.

LESS THAN CARLOAD (LCL) amount of freight that is insufficient to command the lower shipping rates that apply to full carloads.

LET LEASE, i.e., grant the use of REALTY for a compensation. Note, however, that the term does not always connote the act of leasing but may refer to the granting of a LICENSE.

LETTERFOOT part of letterhead information printed at the bottom of a sheet of letter paper.

LETTER OF CREDIT (L/C) instrument or document issued by a bank, guaranteeing the payment of a customer's drafts up to a stated amount for a specified period. It substitutes the bank's credit for the buyer's and eliminates the seller's risk. It is used extensively in international trade.

LETTER OF INTENT
1. any letter expressing an intention to take (or not to take) an action, sometimes subject to other action being taken.
2. preliminary agreement between two companies that intend to merge.
3. promise by a MUTUAL FUND shareholder to invest a specified sum of money monthly for about a year.

LETTER RULING *see* ADVANCE RULING.

LETTER-SIZE a U.S. paper size standard, 8½ by 11 inches.

LETTER STOCK category of stock that derives its name from an inscription on the face of the STOCK CERTIFICATE, indicating that the shares have not been registered with the Securities and Exchange Commission and, therefore, cannot be sold to the general public.

LEVEL DEBT SERVICE provision in a municipal charter stipulating that payments on municipal debt be approximately equal every year. This makes it easier to project the amount of tax revenue needed to meet obligations.

LEVEL OUT standard unit of measure achieved after considerable experience; highly predictable sequence of actions. In a factory it is important to have a *leveled-out* production run so that there are few crises caused by either inventory or personnel shortages.

LEVEL-PAYMENT INCOME STREAM *see* ANNUITY.

LEVEL-PAYMENT MORTGAGE mortgage that requires the same payment each month or other period, for FULL AMORTIZATION. *See also* DIRECT-REDUCTION MORTGAGE; FLAT.

LEVEL PLAYING FIELD government policy of reducing the differences between the least and most favored industries or between the United States and foreign competitors.

LEVEL PREMIUM premium that remains unchanged over time, regardless of any change in the nature of the risk.

LEVERAGE
In general: use of borrowed funds to increase purchasing power and, ideally, to increase profitability of an investment business.
Operations: extent to which a company's costs of operating are fixed (rent, insurance, executive salaries) as opposed to variable (materials, direct labor).
Finance: debt in relation to equity in a firm's capital structure. The more long-term debt there is, the greater the financial leverage. Shareholders benefit from financial leverage to the extent that return on the borrowed money exceeds the interest costs so that the market value of their shares rises.

Personnel: use of additional employees or contractors to complete a task sooner than one person could.

LEVERAGED BUYOUT (LBO) TAKEOVER of a company, using borrowed funds. Most often, the target company's assets serve as security for the loans taken out by the acquiring firm or investors, who repay the loans out of cash flow of the acquired company.

LEVERAGED COMPANY company with debt in addition to equity in its CAPITAL STRUCTURE. In its popular connotation, the term is applied to companies that are highly leveraged. Although the judgment is relative, industrial companies with more than one-third of their capitalization in the form of debt are considered highly leveraged.

LEVERAGED ESOP an employee stock ownership plan that borrows money and purchases employer stock directly from the company.

LEVERAGED LEASE LEASE that involves a lender in addition to the lessor and lessee. The lender, usually a bank or insurance company, puts up a percentage of the cash required to purchase the asset, generally more than half. The balance is put up by the lessor, who is both the equity participant and the borrower.

LEVY
1. to raise or collect.
2. to seize.
3. to assess, as to levy a tax.
4. seizure or levying, as of land or other property or rights, through lawful process or by force.

LEXIS *see* LEGAL EXCHANGE INFORMATION SERVICE.

LIABILITY
1. money owed.
2. obligation to do or refrain from doing something.
3. duty that eventually must be performed. *See also* CURRENT LIABILITIES; LONG-TERM LIABILITIES; PERSONAL LIABILITY.

LIABILITY, CIVIL alleged torts or breaches of contract, but not crimes. Action is brought by one individual against another at the litigant's own expense, within the statute of limitations. The losing party must pay any judgment plus court expenses. CASUALTY INSURANCE provides coverage for an insured in a civil liability suit for alleged negligent acts or omissions, even if the suit is without foundation.

LIABILITY, CRIMINAL wrong against the government or society as a whole. An individual representing the State (usually the district attorney) brings an action on behalf of the State against an individual(s) or entity who has broken a criminal (noncivil) law. Insurance is not designed to cover criminal liability; to so do would encourage criminal behavior.

LIABILITY, CURRENT *see* CURRENT LIABILITY.

LIABILITY INSURANCE protection from claims arising from injuries or damage to other people or property. Liability protection is very important for motor vehicle, home, and business owners. Business liability insurance premiums are deductible.

LIABILITY INSURANCE, PREMISES AND OPERATIONS part of a business liability policy that covers an INSURED for bodily injury or property damage liability to members of the public while they are on business premises.

LIABILITY, LEGAL obligations and responsibilities subject to evaluation, interpretation, and enforcement in a court of law. Casualty insurance provides coverage for an insured against a civil legal liability suit, not criminal legal liability, intentional torts, or liability for breach of contract.

LIABILITY, MARKET SHARE legal extension of the product liability concept where a company is mandated to assume legal liability for a product despite the fact that it did not produce the actual product that caused the action. For example, all the pharmaceutical companies that produce a certain drug may be found to have legal liability for the side effects of the drug since affected consumers are not aware of who the actual manufacturer was. Legal liability is therefore divided among the companies proportional to their respective market shares.

LIABILITY, PROFESSIONAL liability created when an individual holds himself out to the general public as having expertise greater than the ordinary layman in a particular area. Today, suits are frequently brought alleging that a professional, such as a physician, attorney, or CPA, has committed negligent acts or omissions in performing the purchased service. For some professions, such as medical specialties, it has become impossible to purchase professional liability insurance at a reasonable price. Premiums have become prohibitive because of the frequency and severity of both reasonable and unreasonable professional liability suits. *See also* MALPRACTICE.

LIABLE responsible or obligated. *See also* EXCULPATORY; NONRECOURSE.

LIBEL tort consisting of a false, malicious, unprivileged publication aiming to defame a living person or to mar the memory of one dead. Printed or written material, signs or pictures that tend to expose a person to public scorn, hatred, contempt or ridicule may be considered libelous. *See also* SLANDER.

LIBOR *see* LONDON INTERBANK OFFERED RATE.

LIBRARY RATE special postage rate for mailing books and other educational materials between libraries and colleges. Packages must be marked *library rate*.

LIBSON SHOPS DOCTRINE Supreme Court limitation on the survival of net operating loss CARRYOVER after a statutory merger, which is based on the continuity of enterprise theory.

LICENSE grant of permission needed to legalize doing a particular thing, exercising a certain privilege, or pursuing a particular business or occupation. Licenses may be granted by private persons or by governmental authority. In property law, a license is a personal privilege or permission with respect to some use of LAND, and is revocable at the will of the landowner. The privilege attaches only to the party holding it and not to the land itself, since, unlike an EASEMENT, a license does not represent an ESTATE or INTEREST in the land.

LICENSE BOND instrument that guarantees compliance with various city, county, and state laws that govern the issuance of a particular license to conduct business.

LICENSED APPRAISER generally an APPRAISER who meets certain state requirements, but lacks the experience or expertise of a certified appraiser. *See also* CERTIFIED RESIDENTIAL APPRAISER; CERTIFIED GENERAL APPRAISER.

LICENSEE one to whom a LICENSE has been granted; in property, one whose presence on the premises is not invited, but tolerated. Thus, a licensee is neither a customer, nor a servant, nor a trespasser, and does not stand in any contractual relation with the owner of the premises, but is permitted to go upon the property of another merely for his own interest, convenience, or gratification.

LICENSE LAWS laws that govern the activities of occupations that require licensing, such as accountants, lawyers, physicians, nurses, barbers, and insurance and real estate brokers.

LICENSING EXAMINATION test given to a prospective LICENSEE to determine his ability to represent the public.

LIEN charge against property making it SECURITY for the payment of a debt, judgment, mortgage, or taxes. It is a type of ENCUMBRANCE. A SPECIFIC LIEN is against certain property only. A GENERAL LIEN is against all the property owned by the debtor.

LIENHOLDER one who holds, or benefits from, a LIEN.

LIEN-THEORY STATES states whose laws give a lien on property to secure debt; contrasted with TITLE-THEORY STATES in which the lender becomes the title owner. In either case the borrower has the right to use and enjoy the property in the absence of default. In the event of default, lenders may foreclose.

LIFE AND HEALTH INSURANCE, BUSINESS EXPOSURES loss of a key person due to death, disability, sickness, resignation, incarceration, or retirement. Because of the expertise of such an individual, there could be a loss of income, market share, research and development advantage, and line of credit by the firm. Also, there are extra expenses associated with training a replacement for a key person. Coverage for many of these exposures is available under *key person life and health insurance*. *See also* BUY-AND-SELL AGREEMENT.

LIFE ANNUITY annuity that makes a guaranteed fixed payment for the rest of the life of the annuitant. After the annuitant dies, the beneficiaries receive no further payments.

LIFE BENEFICIARY party entitled to the use of or income from property during his or her lifetime; *see* REMAINDER PERSON.

LIFE CYCLE movement of a firm or its product through stages of development, growth, expansion, maturity, saturation, and decline. Not all products go through such a life cycle. For example, paper clips, nails, knives, drinking glasses, and wooden pencils do not seem to exhibit such a life cycle. Most new products do. Some current examples include high-tech items such as computers, VCRs, and black-and-white TVs. *See also* PRODUCT LIFE CYCLE.

LIFE ESTATE ESTATE whose duration is limited by the life of the person holding it or by that of some other person. It is a freehold interest in land.

LIFE EXPECTANCY age to which an average person can be expected to live, as calculated by an ACTUARY. Insurance companies base their projections of benefit payouts on actuarial studies of such factors as sex, heredity, and health habits and base their rates on actuarial analysis.

LIFE INSURANCE insurance policy that pays a DEATH BENEFIT to beneficiaries if the INSURED dies. In return for this protection, the insured pays a PREMIUM, usually annually. *Term insurance* pays off upon the insured's death but provides no buildup of cash value in the policy. Term premiums are cheaper than premiums for *cash-value policies* such as WHOLE LIFE, VARIABLE LIFE, and UNIVERSAL LIFE, which pay death benefits and also provide for buildup of cash value in the policy.

LIFE INSURANCE, RENEWABLE TERM coverage that is renewable at the option of the INSURED, who is not required to take a medical examination. Regardless of physical condition, the insured must be allowed to renew the policy, and the premium cannot be increased to reflect any adverse physical condition. However, the premium of each renewal increases to reflect the LIFE EXPECTANCY of the individual at that particular age.

LIFE INSURANCE SETTLEMENT *see* INSURANCE SETTLEMENT.

LIFESTYLE BUSINESS small business that reflects the general lifestyle of the individual entrepreneur. Lifestyle businesses are not high-growth enterprises. The principal objective is to earn a sufficient income. For example, an artist may have a sign-painting business, or a writer may have a résumé-writing business.

LIFE TENANT one who is allowed to use property for life or the lifetime of another designated person.

LIFETIME EXEMPTION *see* UNIFIED ESTATE AND GIFT TAX.

LIFETIME GIFTS effective vehicle of transfer in estate planning. Gifts eliminate all probate and administration expenses on the property transferred.

LIFETIME LEARNING CREDIT a tax credit usable in any year by any student of any age. The credit is worth up to $2,000 (20% of the first $10,000 paid in tuition and fees). Only one Lifetime Learning credit may be claimed, regardless of the number of students in the family, and it may not be combined with the HOPE TAX CREDIT for a single student, but it can be taken for one student in addition to the Hope credit for one or more additional students. Unlike the Hope credit, the Lifetime Learning credit is applicable to any kind of study, including adult-education courses or a single course to improve job skills. Married couples filing jointly get the full credit on AGI up to $90,000, phasing out at $110,000. Singles get the full credit with incomes up to $45,000, phasing out at $55,000. IRS Form 8863 is used to claim the Lifetime Learning credit; the IRS will cross-check claims with data it gets from schools.

LIFETIME SECURITY form of employee job security guaranteeing protection against layoffs during economic slowdowns or plant closings.

LIFO *see* LAST IN, FIRST OUT.

LIGHTERAGE charge for unloading a ship, using barges to assist in the unloading process.

LIKE-KIND EXCHANGE *see* TAX-FREE EXCHANGE.

LIKE-KIND PROPERTY tax term defining property having the same nature or character, without reference to grade or quality. One kind or class of property may not be exchanged tax free for property of a different kind or class (for example, real estate may be exchanged for real estate, an automobile for another automobile, but not real estate for an automobile). *See also* TAX-FREE EXCHANGE.

LIMITATIONS, STATUTE OF *see* STATUTE OF LIMITATIONS.

LIMITATION YEAR *see* STATUTE OF LIMITATIONS.

LIMITED COMPANY form of business most common in Great Britain, where registration under the Companies Act is comparable to incorporation under state law in the United States. It is abbreviated Ltd. or PLC.

LIMITED DISTRIBUTION distribution of a product only to specific geographic locations or to specific stores or a specific area within a geographic location.

LIMITED LIABILITY the restriction of one's potential losses to the amount invested; absence of personal liability. *Limited liability* is provided to stockholders of a CORPORATION and limited partners of a LIMITED PARTNERSHIP. Those parties cannot lose more than they contribute to the corporation or partnership unless they agree to become personally liable. For example, if a person buys $1,000 worth of stock in a corporation, he or she cannot lose more than that amount. However, many lenders require personal guarantees from major stockholders before lending to small or closely held corporations.

LIMITED LIABILITY COMPANY (LLC) organization form in some states that may be treated as a partnership for federal tax purposes and has limited liability protection for the owners at the state level.The entity may be subject to the state franchise tax as a CORPORATION. The two forms available in most states are *Limited Liability Corporations (LLCs)* and *Limited Liability Partnerships (LLPs),* in which the individual partners are protected from the liabilities of the other partners. These entities are considered PARTNERSHIPS for both federal and state tax purposes.

LIMITED OCCUPANCY AGREEMENT in real estate, agreement allowing a prospective buyer to obtain POSSESSION under a temporary arrangement, usually prior to CLOSING.

LIMITED PARTNERSHIP entity in which one or more persons, with unlimited liability, called GENERAL PARTNERS, manage the partnership, while one or more other persons contribute only CAPITAL. This latter group of partners, called LIMITED PARTNERS, have no right to participate in the management and operation of the business and assume no liability beyond the capital contributed. A limited partnership is often used for real estate ownership because of favorable tax treatment allowing pass-through of losses and avoiding double taxation of income. However, if a limited partnership has more characteristics of a CORPORATION than of a partnership, it will be construed as an association taxable as a corporation.

LIMITED (SPECIAL) PARTNER within a LIMITED PARTNERSHIP, a part owner whose liability is limited to the amount invested and whose role in business management is restricted.

LIMITED WARRANTY WARRANTY that imposes certain limitations and is therefore not a full warranty. For example, an automaker may issue a warranty that covers parts, but not labor, for a particular period.

LIMIT ORDER order to buy or sell a security at a specific price or better. The broker will execute the trade only within the price restriction.

LIMIT UP, LIMIT DOWN maximum price movement allowed for a commodity FUTURES CONTRACT during one trading day. In the face of a particularly dramatic development, a futures price may move limit up or limit down for several consecutive days.

LINE

1. persons concerned with actual production or, depending on the organization, distribution. A foreman and a plant manager are line personnel. *See also* LINE MANAGEMENT; STAFF.
2. type of goods produced or carried; product line.

LINEAL FOOT a measure of one foot, in a straight line, along the ground.

LINE AND STAFF ORGANIZATION delineation of organizational authority between management personnel (staff) having overall planning and direction responsibilities and operational personnel (line) having direct job performance responsibilities. Staff is advisory to the line function.

LINEAR PROGRAMMING (LP) a mathematical model for decisions with a large number of alternatives. LP is typically used to either maximize profit or minimize costs in a manufacturing process with varying levels of inputs.

LINE AUTHORITY authority exercised over line personnel in an organization.

LINE CONTROL
1. organizational control exercised over line functions in an organization. *See also* LINE FUNCTION.
2. operating procedures and control signals by which a telecommunications system is controlled.

LINE EXTENSION adding of another variety of a product to an already established brand line of products. For example, when a coffee manufacturer adds decaffeinated coffee to the same brand line of coffee products already on the market (such as regular coffee and instant coffee), a line extension has been made. *See also* BRAND EXTENSION; DIFFERENTIATION STRATEGY; FLANKER BRAND.

LINE FUNCTION activity contributing directly to the output of an organization. In a service organization the line functions may be operations and sales.

LINE MANAGEMENT administration of the line functions of an organization; administration of all activities that contribute directly to an organization's output.

LINE OF CREDIT agreement whereby a financial institution promises to lend up to a certain amount without the need to file another application. The borrower is expected to reduce the debt after having reached the full amount of credit. *See also* BANK LINE.

LINE ORGANIZATION organizational structure of activities contributing directly to the organization's output; arrangement of line functions in an organization.

LINE PRINTER high-speed printer for computer output. A line printer can print an entire line of output at one time. Fast *line printers* are capable of printing at rates of up to 1,400 lines per minute.

LINK a highlighted word, phrase, or graphic within a hypertext document (on a computer or on the INTERNET) that, when clicked, will take the user to another location within the document or to another document altogether. WEB SITES contain many *links* to other pages at the site as well as to other, related sites.

LIQUID ASSET cash or easily convertible into cash. Some examples are money market fund shares, U.S. Treasury bills, and bank deposits. In a corporation's financial statements, liquid assets are cash, marketable securities, and accounts receivable.

LIQUIDATE to settle; to determine the amount due and extinguish the indebtedness. Although the term more properly signifies the adjustment or settlement of DEBTS, to liquidate often means to pay. *See also* LIQUIDATION.

LIQUIDATED DAMAGES stipulated contractual amount that the parties agree is a reasonable estimation of the DAMAGES owed to one in the event of a BREACH by the other.

LIQUIDATED DEBT debt undisputed as to its existence or amount.

LIQUIDATING (or LIQUIDATION) VALUE projected price for an asset of a company that is going out of business, for instance, a real estate holding or office equipment. Liquidating value is distinguished from GOING-CONCERN VALUE, which may be higher because of what accountants term *organization value* or GOODWILL.

LIQUIDATION procedure in which shareholders surrender all of their shares in a corporation and receive, after all creditors are paid, their pro rata share of any remaining assets and accumulated earnings and profits. Liquidation is deemed to occur when a corporation ceases to be a going concern and its activities are merely for the purpose of winding up its affairs, paying its debts, and distributing any remaining balance to its shareholders.

LIQUIDATION DIVIDEND dividend resulting from winding up affairs of a business, settling with its DEBTORS and CREDITORS, and appropriating and distributing to its shareholders a residue proportionate to the profit and loss.

LIQUIDITY
1. ability of an individual or company to convert assets into cash or cash equivalents without significant loss. Investments in money market funds and listed stocks are much more liquid than investments in real estate, for instance.
2. characteristic of a security or commodity with enough units outstanding to allow large transactions without a substantial drop in price. A stock, bond, or commodity that has a great many shares outstanding therefore has *liquidity*.

LIQUIDITY PREFERENCE element of KEYNESIAN ECONOMIC theory. The relative preference of investors to hold money (liquidity) rather than bonds or other investments is a key determinant of the level of economic activity. It is related to the level of INTEREST RATES and RETURN ON INVESTMENT (ROI) within the economy.

LIQUIDITY RATIO ratio of balance sheet items, which measures a firm's ability to meet maturing short-term obligations. *See also* CASH RATIO; CURRENT RATIO; NET QUICK ASSETS; QUICK RATIO.

LIS PENDENS pending lawsuit; refers to the maxim that pending the SUIT, nothing should be changed. For example, one who acquired an interest in property from a party to LITIGATION with respect to such property takes that interest subject to the decree or judgment in such litigation and is bound by it.

LIST

Real estate: place for sale in the hands of a real estate BROKER. *See also* LISTING.

Securities: enter a stock to be traded on a stock exchange. *See also* LISTED SECURITY; OVER THE COUNTER.

LISTED OPTION put or call OPTION that an exchange has authorized for trading; properly called an *exchange-traded option.*

LISTED PROPERTY in taxation, automobiles, computers, and cellular phones that are subject to the 50% business use test. If *listed property* is used predominantly for business, the statutory percentage depreciation method is available. If used less than 50% of the time for business, the cost is depreciated by the STRAIGHT-LINE METHOD. Passenger automobiles have additional recovery limitations imposed upon depreciation deductions.

LISTED SECURITY stock or bond traded on an exchange, the two largest of which are the New York Stock Exchange and the American Stock Exchange. More than 6,000 issues of some 3,500 corporations are listed. *Contrast with* UNLISTED SECURITIES, which are traded OVER THE COUNTER, through a network of dealers.

LISTING

1. written engagement contract between a principal and an agent, authorizing the agent to perform services for the principal involving the latter's property.
2. record of property for sale by a broker who has been authorized by the owner to sell.
3. property so listed. *See also* EXCLUSIVE AGENCY LISTING; EXCLUSIVE RIGHT TO SELL LISTING; MULTIPLE LISTING; OPEN LISTING.

LISTING AGENT or **LISTING BROKER** licensed real estate AGENT or BROKER who secures a listing of the property. *Contrast with* SELLING AGENT/SELLING BROKER.

LISTING REQUIREMENTS minimal tests a company must meet for its stock to be listed on a STOCK EXCHANGE. The New York Stock Exchange has the most rigorous requirements of any exchange.

LIST OWNER refers to mailing lists used for solicitation. Mailing lists are generally sold on a price per name basis.

LIST PRICE in retail, price regularly quoted to customers before applying discounts. List prices are usually the prices printed on dealer lists, invoices, price tags, catalogs, or dealer purchase orders. *See* MSRP.

LIST SERVER an automated E-MAIL list distribution system. List servers maintain a list of E-MAIL ADDRESSES to be used for mass e-mailing.

LITIGANT party actively involved in a lawsuit; PLAINTIFF or DEFENDANT involved in LITIGATION.

LITIGATION judicial contest through which legal rights are sought to be determined and enforced.

LITIGATION SUPPORT any professional assistance nonlawyers provide to lawyers in the litigation process. Those involved in *litigation support* (such as FORENSIC ACCOUNTANTS) perform investigative accounting, auditing, and tax determinations, provide expert testimony, or produce financial valuations in dispute situations.

LIVING BENEFITS OF LIFE INSURANCE benefits provided to and obtained by those insured, while still alive.

LIVING TRUST trust established and in operation during the settler's life; INTER VIVOS TRUST. *See also* TESTAMENTARY TRUST.

LIVING WILL legal document that permits an individual to declare his/her desires concerning the use of life-sustaining treatment to be made when death is imminent and the individual no longer has control of his/her faculties. This type of will has the advantages of ensuring that the individual's wishes are followed to the conclusion. It is the requirement of most state statutes that such a will be signed, dated, and witnessed (excluding anyone who has an interest in the estate of the individual affirming the will).

LLOYD'S OF LONDON insurance facility composed of many different syndicates, each specializing in a particular risk, such as, for example, hulls of ships. Lloyd's provides coverage for primary jumbo risks in addition to offering REINSURANCE and retrocessions. Insuring exotic risks such an actress's legs represents only a very small portion of its total business, most of which involves reinsurance and retrocessions.

LOAD
Computers: moving a program from a disk to a computer's memory.
Finance: sales charge paid by an investor who buys shares in a load MUTUAL FUND, typically 8½% of invested funds. Loads are usually charged when fund shares are purchased; a charge for withdrawing shares from a fund is called a *back-end load*. A fund that does not charge this fee is a NO-LOAD FUND.

LOAD FUND MUTUAL FUND that is sold for a sales charge by a brokerage firm or other sales representative. *See also* NO-LOAD FUND.

LOAN transaction wherein an owner of property, called the lender, allows another party, the borrower, to use the property. The borrower customarily promises to return the property after a specified period with payment for its use, called INTEREST. The documentation of the promise is called a PROMISSORY NOTE when the property is cash.

LOAN AMORTIZATION reduction of debt by scheduled, regular payments of principal and interest sufficient to repay the loan at maturity.

LOAN APPLICATION document required by a lender prior to issuing a loan commitment. The application generally includes the following information: (1) name of the borrower; (2) amount and terms of the loan; (3) description of the collateral; and (4) the borrower's financial and employment data.

LOAN CLOSING *see* CLOSING.

LOAN COMMITMENT agreement to lend money, generally of a specified amount, at specified terms at some time in the future.

LOAN ORIGINATION FEE *see* POINTS.

LOAN PACKAGE *see* LOAN APPLICATION.

LOAN-TO-VALUE RATIO (LTV) portion of the amount borrowed compared to the cost or value of the property purchased. Home mortgages at more than an 80% LTV ratio generally require MORTGAGE INSURANCE.

LOAN VALUE
1. amount a lender is willing to loan against collateral. For example, at 50% of appraised value, a piece of property worth $800,000 has a *loan value* of $400,000.
2. amount that a policyholder can borrow from the cash value of a permanent life insurance policy.

LOBBYING EXPENDITURES amounts paid or incurred in connection with influencing federal or state legislation, or any communication with certain federal executive branch officials in an attempt to influence the official actions or positions of such officials. Not tax deductible after 1993.

LOBBYIST a person retained by another with compensation for the specific purpose of influencing the formation of legislation or the administration of rules, regulations, and policies.

LOCAL local union representing the BARGAINING UNIT in an organization. Locals have significantly greater authority over the work environment than does the national union.

LOCAL AREA NETWORK (LAN) connecting individual computer terminals, or NODES, with coaxial cables, optical fibers, or standard telephone lines. Networks that are set up for individual businesses and schools, and that are usually contained within a single building, are called local area networks, or LANs. Wider networks, WIDE AREA NET-WORKS (WANS), are possible using telecommunications to span states, countries, or the entire globe. The advantages of computer networks are many: they speed up word processing and database analysis in busy systems, reduce costs, increase worker productivity, and offer tremendous convenience. *See also* distributed processing.

LOCATION, LOCATION, LOCATION the "three most important things about real estate"—a popular statement that emphasizes the importance of location with respect to the value of urban real estate. The value of real estate depends largely on where it is. However many other elements besides location also affect value, and those who believe that location is the only important factor lack ideas.

LOCK BOX
1. cash management system whereby a company's customers mail payments to a post office box near the company's bank. The bank collects checks from the lock box (sometimes several times a day), deposits them to the account of the firm, and informs the company's cash manager by telephone of the deposit.
2. In residential real estate sales, a small locked box placed near the front door in which the key to enter the house is inserted. Only real estate agents possess the key or combination to unlock the box; thus the key to the house is reasonably secure, while allowing agents to enter the property offered for sale.

LOCKED IN
1. said of a rate of return that has been assured for a length of time through an investment such as a certificate of deposit or a fixedrate bond; also said of profits or yields on securities or commodities that have been protected through hedging techniques. *See also* HEDGE.
2. commodities position in which the market has an up or down limit day, and investors cannot get in or out of the market.
3. situation in which an investor would ordinarily sell a security but doesn't because of taxes to be paid on the sale.

LOCKED-IN INTEREST RATE the rate promised by a lender at the time of loan application. The promise is a legal commitment of the lender, though there may be qualifications or contingencies that allow the lender to charge a higher rate. On home loans, the lock-in is customarily provided for 1% of the amount borrowed, though often it is free of charge. However, many prospective lenders find ways to renege on commitments when interest rates rise.

LOCKOUT management action preventing employees from performing work in the organization until a labor settlement is reached. Employees are physically barred from entering the workplace.

LOCK, STOCK, AND BARREL describes all the components of a rifle; used to mean an entire business.

LOCK-UP OPTION in corporate takeovers, option granted by a target to a friendly suitor to acquire the target's CROWN JEWELS when there is a hostile suitor on the scene.

LOGISTICS comprehensive plan for scheduling the delivery of required supplies and materials at destinations as needed.

LOGO logotype; unique design, symbol, or other special representation of a company name, publishing house, broadcast network, or other organization, used as a TRADEMARK.

LOG ON (LOG IN) establish a connection from a terminal to a computer and identify oneself as an authorized user.

LOGOTYPE *see* LOGO.

LONDON GOLD FIXING *see* GOLD FIXING.

LONDON INTERBANK OFFERED RATE (LIBOR) rate that the most creditworthy international banks dealing in EURODOLLARS charge each other for large loans; Eurodollar equivalent of the federal funds rate. The LIBOR rate is usually the base for other large Eurodollar loans to less creditworthy corporate and government borrowers.

LONG *see* GOING LONG; LONG POSITION.

LONG BOND bond that matures in more than 10 years. Since these bonds commit investors' money for a long time, they are riskier than shorter-term bonds of the same quality and therefore normally pay investors a higher yield.

LONG COUPON
1. first interest payment of bond issue, covering a longer period than the remaining payments.
2. interest-bearing bond maturing in more than 10 years.

LONGEVITY PAY salary or wages based on seniority or length of service with an organization. The greater the length of service, the greater the longevity pay. It may also be used as a bonus for remaining on a job beyond a certain period.

LONG POSITION
1. ownership of an asset, such as a security, giving the investor the right to transfer ownership to someone else by sale or by gift; right to receive any income paid by the security; right to any profits or losses as the security's value changes.
2. investor's ownership of securities held by a brokerage firm.

LONG-RANGE PLANNING planning beyond five years. Longrange planning takes into account the future as a consequence of present, short-range, and intermediate-range events.

LONG RUN a period of time long enough for an industry to make *all* necessary adjustments to changing economic conditions, to increase or decrease capacity, or for firms to enter or leave the industry.

LONG-TERM CAPITAL GAIN (LOSS) profit (loss) on securities or capital assets and §1231 assets when the interval between purchase and sale is longer than 12 months. Net long-term capital gains (LTCG) are taxed at a maximum of 15% for individuals. Individuals in the 10% or 15% bracket pay 5% on capital gain. A 0% rate will replace the 5% rate beginning in 2008. Only up to $3,000 of a net long-term capital loss (LTCL) is deductible per year by an individual. For a corporation, a net LTCG is taxed as ORDINARY INCOME, and a net LTCL is not deductible; though it may be carried back three years or forward five years, it may not cause a NET OPERATING LOSS.

LONG-TERM CARE (LTC) day-to-day care that a patient (generally older than 65) receives in a nursing facility or in his/her residence following an illness or injury, or in old age, when the patient can no longer perform at least two of the five basic activities of daily living: walking, eating, dressing, using the bathroom, and mobility from one place to another.

LONG-TERM CONTRACT any contract for the manufacture, building, installation, or construction of property if the contract is not completed within the year into which it is entered.

LONG-TERM DEBT or LONG-TERM LIABILITY
Accounting: LIABILITY due in a year or more. Normally, interest is paid periodically over the term of the loan, and the principal amount is payable as notes or bonds mature.
Finance: generally, debts due in more than 10 years. *See also* LONG BOND.

LONG-TERM LEASE generally, a commercial lease of five years or longer, or a residential lease longer than one year.

LONG-TERM LIABILITIES any monies that are not payable on demand or within one year. The *current portion of long-term debt* is a CURRENT LIABILITY, as distinguished from a long-term liability.

LONG-TERM TREND TREND whose effects are observed to exist over a lengthy period of time. The generally continuous rise in the Dow-Jones industrial average from 1980 to 1999 was a long-term trend. Most trends eventually end; however, long-term trends can mislead people into thinking that they will continue indefinitely.

LONG-WAVE CYCLE *see* KONDRATIEFF CYCLE/KONDRATIEFF WAVE.

LOOP set of statements in a computer program that is to be executed repeatedly. For example, the BASIC program below is a loop. Statement 20 will be executed five times, first with *I* equal to 1, then with *I* equal to 2, and so on.

```
10    FOR      I = 1 TO 5
20    PRINT    I
30    NEXT     I
```

LOOPHOLE technicality making it possible to circumvent a law's intent without violating its letter. For instance, a TAX SHELTER may exploit a *loophole* in the tax law.

LOOSE REIN management method that stresses a generally relaxed supervisory style where individual creativity and contributions are encouraged. *See also* LAISSEZ-FAIRE.

LOSS
1. expenses exceeding sales or revenues; an item is sold for less than its cost or ADJUSTED BASIS. *See also* PROFIT.
2. damage through an insured's negligent acts and/or omissions resulting in bodily injury and/or property damage to a third party; damage to an insured's property; or amount an insurance company has a legal obligation to pay.

LOSS CARRYBACK offsetting the current year's net loss against net income of the previous years (currently three years) for tax purposes, frequently obtaining a refund for taxes paid in previous years.

LOSS CARRYFORWARD offsetting the current year's net operating loss against future years' net incomes for tax purposes, assuming that a LOSS CARRYBACK is not possible in whole or in part. For financial reporting purposes, the tax effects of a loss carryforward should not be recognized until the year in which the tax liability is reduced unless earlier realization is assured beyond any reasonable doubt. This assurance is indicated when the entity has been profitable, future earnings are assured, and the loss results from a nonrecurring event.

LOSS CARRYOVER see CARRYOVER.

LOSS DENIAL RULE *see* HOBBY LOSS.

LOSS EXPOSURE in insurance, areas in which the risk of loss exists. Four loss risk areas are: (1) property; (2) income; (3) legal vulnerability; and (4) key personnel in an organization.

LOSS LEADER retail merchandise that is advertised and sold at a price representing a loss of profit for the retailer, but is used to draw (*lead*) customers into the store in the hope that they will make additional purchases.

LOSS OF INCOME INSURANCE coverage in property insurance for an employee's lost income if a peril such as fire damages or destroys the place of employment, causing the worker to become unemployed. For example, a fire destroys a manufacturing plant and as a result employees are placed on indefinite leave without pay. This coverage would then go into effect. In health insurance, loss of income benefits are paid when an insured becomes disabled and cannot work.

LOSS RATIO
Finance: loan losses of a bank or receivables losses of a corporation compared to all debt of that class.

Insurance: ratio of losses paid or accrued by an insurer to premiums earned, usually for a one-year period.

LOSS REDUCTION management methods used to limit the extent of losses when they do happen. Practicing strict legal compliance with all environmental laws and safety procedures as well as maintaining good public relations is extremely important in managing *loss reduction* when unfortunate situations develop.

LOT AND BLOCK method of locating a parcel of land based on its lot and block on a PLAT of a subdivision. *See also* LEGAL DESCRIPTION.

LOT LINE line bounding a lot as described in a SURVEY of property.

LOTTERY contest that requires a purchase be made in order to qualify for a random drawing. Lotteries—as opposed to SWEEPSTAKES, which do not require that entrants make a purchase—are not legal according to U.S. Postal Service regulations governing direct mail promotions, because they are considered a form of gambling.

LOTUS 1-2-3 integrated computer software package produced by Lotus Development Corporation, which once was one of the best selling business decision-making tools. *Lotus 1-2-3* combines the functions of a spreadsheet program with data management capabilities and graphics.

LOW bottom price paid for a security over the past year or since trading in the security began; in the latter sense also called *historic low*.

LOW-BALL OFFER an offer from a prospective property buyer that is much lower than the listing price. Such an offer may indicate the buyer's belief that the property will not attract many good offers and that the asking price is unrealistic. Also, it probably means the buyer is interested in the property only if it can be purchased at a bargain price.

LOWER OF COST OR MARKET accounting inventory method. An asset is recorded at its historical cost, but the amount is written down to market if this becomes lower than the original cost. *Market*, for this purpose, is replacement cost, but not greater than net realizable value (NRV) nor less than NRV minus a normal profit.

LOW-GRADE lower level of quality. For example, low-grade paper is extremely porous and thin.

LOW-TECH products using earlier or less developed technology. An example is a chocolate candy bar, which is very much the same as its earliest varieties and is primarily a simple recipe of ingredients.

LTD. *see* LIMITED COMPANY.

LTV abbreviation for LOAN-TO-VALUE RATIO.

LUMP SUM in life insurance, single payment instead of a series of installments.

LUMP-SUM DISTRIBUTION payment of the entire amount of retirement benefits due at one time rather than in installments. *See also* FIVE-YEAR AVERAGING; TEN-YEAR AVERAGING; IRA ROLLOVER.

LUMP-SUM PURCHASE acquisition of two or more assets for one price. The acquisition price is allocated to the assets based on their relative fair market values. For example, land and a building having separate fair market values of $30,000 and $70,000 are purchased for the lump-sum price of $90,000.

LUXURY AUTOMOBILE for tax purposes of LISTED PROPERTY depreciation limitations, *any* four-wheeled vehicle manufactured for use on public streets and highways, with an unloaded gross weight of 6,000 pounds or less. Depreciation deductions are severely limited on such vehicles.

M

MACHINE LANGUAGE instructions that a computer can execute directly. Machine language statements are written in a binary code, and each statement corresponds to one machine action. Programs are efficient to run, but the absence of words in commands makes for difficult programming.

MACHINE READABLE printed pattern that can be read or scanned by a specific device, usually an electronic device. Most grocery products now have a BAR CODE label that can be read by a machine at the register; most checks have machine readable preprinted account numbers.

MACHINE SCANNING optical scanning device that facilitates data input by reading printed data and converting them into computerreadable electronic signals. Machine scanners can be used to read text, graphics, or special marks.

MACINTOSH the Apple Macintosh computer, introduced in 1984, which was the first widely used computer with a GRAPHICAL USER INTERFACE (GUI).

MACRO a series of computer keyboard or mouse actions recorded to be replayed. The sequence can be assigned to a key combination, a menu item, or a toolbar button for convenience. Macros can also be written using the programming language of a given application, such as VBA (Visual Basic for Applications) in Word and Excel.

MACROECONOMICS study of the aggregate forces of a nation's economy as a whole, using such data as price levels, unemployment, inflation, and industrial production. *See also* MICROECONOMICS.

MACROENVIRONMENT totality of national and international institutional forces acting upon societies and organizations; dynamics of environmental interaction on a global scale.

MACRS *see* MODIFIED ACCELERATED COST RECOVERY SYSTEM.

MADISON AVENUE avenue in New York City that was once the address of many of the major advertising agencies. Some of these agencies are still located in New York City but have expanded to include offices in Chicago, Los Angeles, and other national and international locations.

MAIL FRAUD illegal promotion that is designed to deceive consumers and is delivered through the mail. For example, it would be fraudulent to advertise a "miracle weight-loss pill guaranteed to make an individual lose 10 pounds overnight."

MAILING LIST compilation of possible customers prepared as a list for use in direct-mail solicitation.

MAIL ORDER FIRMS companies using catalog marketing with direct merchandise shipments to customers. Many mail order firms market only one particular type of merchandise. For example, there are many computer mail order firms that specialize in either computer SOFTWARE or hardware. Many mail order firms now sell on the Internet.

MAINFRAME COMPUTER large computer supporting typically 100 to 500 users at a time. The IBM 370 and IBM 3081 are examples of mainframe computers. *Contrast with* MINICOMPUTER, MICROCOMPUTER, and PERSONAL COMPUTER (PC), all of which are much smaller than a mainframe.

MAINTENANCE necessary care and management of equipment and operations. All mechanical equipment and organizations need continual maintenance to forestall the total breakdown of the system.

MAINTENANCE BOND legal instrument posted by a contractor or craftsman to guarantee that completed work is free of flaws and will perform its intended function for a specified period of time.

MAINTENANCE FEE
1. assessment by a homeowners' association, cooperative association, or condominium owners' association to pay costs of operating the COMMON ELEMENTS.
2. charge by a bank or broker for keeping an account.

MAINTENANCE OF MEMBERSHIP requirement for UNION members to keep their membership for the life of a LABOR AGREEMENT. Workers are not required to join unions under a maintenance of membership arrangement.

MAJORITY
1. more than half, as when a vote is taken. *See also* MAJORITY SHAREHOLDER.
2. age at which one is no longer a MINOR and is fully able to conduct one's own affairs. Majority (full legal age) is 18 to 21 years, depending on the state.

MAJORITY SHAREHOLDER one of the shareholders who together control more than half the outstanding shares of a corporation.

MAJOR MEDICAL INSURANCE form of supplemental medical insurance indemnifying all medical costs not covered under health and hospitalization insurance. Normally, there is a deductible the insured must pay before the major medical insurance plan becomes effective.

MAKER
In general: producer of a product, such as a car.
Commercial law: person who EXECUTES a NOTE or ENDORSES it before its delivery to the payee, and who thereby assumes an obligation to make payment on the note.

MAKE-WORK uneconomic utilization of work force for the purpose of creating employment; job having no value.

MALE CHAUVINISM attitude of superiority or dominance by men over women, regardless of all factors being constant. A male chauvinist discriminates against women by applying stereotyped ideas. The term was first used in the United States in the 1960s by the feminist movement.

MALICIOUS MISCHIEF intentional damage or destruction of another person's or business's property. Insurance can be purchased by the owner of the property to protect against this exposure. *See also* SPECIAL MULTIPERIL POLICY (SMP); VANDALISM AND MALICIOUS MISCHIEF INSURANCE.

MALINGERER employee who pretends to be ill so as to be relieved of work assignments or job responsibilities.

MALL public area connecting individual stores in a SHOPPING CENTER, generally enclosed; an enclosed shopping center.

MALPRACTICE improper or immoral conduct of a professional in the performance of his duties, done either intentionally or through carelessness or ignorance; commonly applied to physicians, surgeons, dentists, lawyers, and public officers to denote negligent or unskillful performance of duties where professional skills are obligatory.

MALPRACTICE INSURANCE form of insurance for professional legal liability in the accounting, architectural, educational, legal, medical, and other areas. Depending on the profession, malpractice insurance can be prohibitively expensive.

MALTHUSIAN LAW OF POPULATION proposition by the early 19th-century philosopher Thomas Malthus that economic growth occurs more slowly than population growth and that, therefore, general prosperity is impossible. Malthus did not reckon with the very rapid increases in productivity brought on by industrialization.

MALWARE *mal*icious soft*ware,* a generic term for programs designed to attack, degrade, or prevent the intended use of a single computer, server, or network; includes VIRUSES, WORMS, TROJANS, and SPYWARE.

MANAGE administer an organization's activities to achieve particular objectives.

MANAGED ACCOUNT investment account consisting of money that one or more clients entrust to a manager, who decides when and where to invest it. Such an account may be handled by a bank trust department or by an investment advisory firm.

MANAGED CARE health care program established by employers with a group of medical professionals and hospitals agreeing to discount rates in return for exclusive treatment rights for their employees. Properly managed, these networks can be extremely cost-effective.

MANAGED CURRENCY CURRENCY whose international value and exchangeability is heavily regulated by its issuing country.

MANAGED ECONOMY economy in which considerable government intervention takes place in order to direct economic activity. Socialist and communist economies are managed much more than capitalist economies, which rely more upon market forces to direct economic activity.

MANAGEMENT
1. combined fields of policy and administration and the people who provide the decisions and supervision necessary to implement the owners' business objectives and achieve stability and growth.
2. key people in an organization. Those who make the most important decisions are called *top management*.

MANAGEMENT ACCOUNTING *see* MANAGERIAL ACCOUNTING.

MANAGEMENT AGREEMENT administrative understanding allowing individual managers to control specified organizational activities for a particular period of time. Management agreements can also exist between companies where an intercompany agreement is developed to manage certain activities cooperatively.

MANAGEMENT AUDIT method of reviewing the quality of managers by evaluating them on an individual basis. A management audit can also be used to evaluate the entire management system of an organization based upon individual contributions.

MANAGEMENT BY CRISIS reactive method of administration whereby strategies are formulated as events occur; basically short-sighted policy often leading to organizational confusion.

MANAGEMENT BY EXCEPTION administrative policy of focusing on those events deviating from an established standard. Management by exception practices are established where it has been determined that only those events that deviate from a standard are significant. For example, only those creditors having outstanding accounts for more than 45 days will receive a second billing notice.

MANAGEMENT BY OBJECTIVE (MBO) planning and control method of management that seeks congruence between management and employee goals. Performance goals are jointly agreed upon by management and the employee and subsequently evaluated.

MANAGEMENT BY WALKING AROUND (MBWA) management method emphasizing the importance of interpersonal contact. The objective of MBWA is to achieve harmony in an organization between management and employees through face-to-face contact as well as to keep abreast of current operational developments.

MANAGEMENT COMPANY *see* INVESTMENT COMPANY.

MANAGEMENT CONSULTANT individual or organization acting in a professional management advisory capacity for the purpose of assisting managers in analyzing management problems. Working on a fee basis, consultants make practical management recommendations and provide actual services for the employing organization.

MANAGEMENT CYCLE
1. established time in which a particular management operation will occur, such as a maintenance schedule.
2. fad or style of management methods.

MANAGEMENT DISCUSSION AND ANALYSIS a section of a corporate ANNUAL REPORT where the company's management provides insights as to expected future developments, analysis of results of operations, and its financial position, including cash flows, liquidity, and capital resources.

MANAGEMENT FEE
Finance: charge against assets for managing the PORTFOLIO of a mutual fund or other investment entity, as well as for such services as shareholder relations or administration.
Real estate: charge to manage real estate, including rent collection, assuring proper maintenance, and bookkeeping.

MANAGEMENT GAME simulation exercise designed for management applications and used for training purposes. Management games can be group or individual exercises. Increasing numbers of management exercises are computer applications.

MANAGEMENT GUIDE manual or other collection of organizational policies intended for the use of a manager. Management guides outline organizational policies that should be implemented in resolving particular situations.

MANAGEMENT INFORMATION SYSTEM (MIS) system providing uniform organizational information to management in the areas of control, operations, and planning. MIS usually relies on a well-developed data management system, including a data base for helping management reach accurate and rapid organizational decisions.

MANAGEMENT PREROGATIVE rights believed by management to be exclusively theirs and not subject to bargaining in a collective bargaining contract; also called *management rights*. Management prerogatives can be summarized in a management rights clause that is often inserted into a contract, usually covering specific rights to hire and fire.

MANAGEMENT RATIO ratio of management personnel to 1,000 employees; further broken down into the ratio of top management and middle management personnel per 1,000 employees.

MANAGEMENT SCIENCE study of management; school of management emphasizing the use of mathematics and statistics as an aid in resolving production and operations problems. A major objective is to provide management with a quantitative basis for decisions.

MANAGEMENT STYLE the leadership method a manager uses in administering an organization. For example, it may be said a manager has a very informal style, which signifies that the manager does not practice close supervision and believes in open communication.

MANAGEMENT SYSTEM
1. four basic leadership styles developed by Dr. Renesis Likert: exploitative-authoritative, benevolent-authoritative, consultativedemocratic, and participative-democratic.
2. comprehensive organizational management method.

MANAGER person charged with the responsibility of administering and directing an organization's activities.

MANAGERIAL ACCOUNTING system using financial accounting records as basic data to enable better business planning decisions. It is designed to aid decision making, planning, and control. *See also* FINANCIAL ACCOUNTING.

MANAGERIAL INTEGRATOR staff manager who manages one or more functional departments without having direct operational responsibilities. The principal role of a *managerial integrator* is coordinating the functions and activities of the various departments to achieve maximum cooperation and productivity. Managerial integrators may have such titles as *branch manager* or *project manager*.

MANDATE
1. court order to an authorized agency or officer to enforce a decree, judgment, or sentence to the court's satisfaction.
2. directive to do something, as in "I've been given a *mandate* by management to get to the bottom of this problem."

MANDATORY RETIREMENT *see* COMPULSORY RETIREMENT.

MANDATORY SUBJECT topic that must be discussed in collective bargaining. *Mandatory subjects* include hours, medical benefits, pensions, and wages. If one party to the negotiations refuses to discuss a particular topic, the NLRB can be asked to rule on whether or not it is a mandatory subject.

MAN-HOUR unit of labor or productivity that one person produces in one hour's time. It is used as a method of determining the labor content of a particular project. For example, if a particular project takes 3 man-hours to complete, then the total cost can be accurately projected.

M&IE abbreviation for *meals and incidental expense.*

MANIFEST detailed statement of the contents put on a ship or other vehicle. A copy of the manifest is put in a safe place so that the exact cargo is known, even in the event the vessel is destroyed. A copy of a ship's manifest is kept on board for cargo identification purposes in the event of a search.

MANIPULATION
Finance: buying or selling a security to create a false appearance of active trading and thus influence other investors to buy or sell shares. Those found guilty of manipulation are subject to criminal and civil penalties.
Psychology: controlling by shrewdness or influence.

MANUAL
1. small book generally used for the purposes of reference, containing a listing of information, instructions, or other related data.
2. physical labor performed by hand.

MANUAL SKILL ability to use one's hands efficiently in the performance of a specific task or operation. An individual with a high degree of manual skill is said to have a great deal of *dexterity*. For example, a juggler has a great deal of manual skill.

MANUFACTURE making or fashioning by hand or machinery, especially in large quantities.

MANUFACTURED HOUSING *see* MOBILE HOME; MOBILE (MANUFACTURED) HOME PARK.

MANUFACTURERS AND CONTRACTORS LIABILITY INSURANCE coverage for liability exposures that result from manufacturing and/or contracting operations in process on a manufacturer's premises or, in the case of the contractor, offpremises operation at a construction site. Excluded are activities of independent contractors, damage to property by explosion, collapse, and underground property damage.

MANUFACTURER'S REPRESENTATIVE a salesman for the company that produces the product.

MANUFACTURER'S SUGGESTED RETAIL PRICE (MSRP) as the name implies, merely a suggestion: the manufacturer cannot require retailers to charge that price. Prices for some products, such as computers and other consumer electronics, are so volatile that reviews often quote a STREET PRICE instead. *See* FAIR TRADE.

MANUFACTURING AND TRADE INVENTORIES AND SALES combined values of trade sales and shipments by manufacturers and values of inventories and business sales. Inventory rates of change give signs about the growth or contraction of the economy.

MANUFACTURING COST cost to a manufacturing company of making a product consisting of direct materials, direct labor, and factory overhead; also called *manufacturing expense*. For example, in the production of a car, if direct materials are $2,000, direct labor $3,000, and factory overhead $1,500, the total manufacturing cost is $6,500.

MANUFACTURING EXPENSE *see* MANUFACTURING COST.

MANUFACTURING INVENTORY parts or materials on hand, needed for the manufacturing process. Adjusting manufacturing inventory to current production needs is a critical management responsibility.

MANUFACTURING OVERHEAD *see* FACTORY OVERHEAD.

MAP management simulation technique used for management development training. The MAP technique allows group members to define their task groups by choosing those people most appropriate for working in them.

MAQUILADORA a manufacturing operation at the U.S.-Mexican border, mostly in Texas and California, that usually includes two plants, one on each side of the border, to take advantage of free trade allowed between the two, low Mexican wages, and U.S. distribution facilities.

MARGIN
In general: amount a customer deposits with a broker when borrowing from the broker to buy securities.
Accounting: difference between gross and net amounts of income. *See also* MARGIN OF PROFIT.
Banking: difference between the current market value of collateral backing a loan and the face value of the loan.
Communication: white space along borders of a printed page. *See also* FOOTER; HEADER.
Corporate finance: difference between the price received by a company for its products and services and the cost of producing them. Also known as GROSS PROFIT margin.
Economics: usefulness or cost of the next item.
Futures: good-faith deposit an investor must put up when buying or selling a contract. If the futures price moves adversely, the investor must put up more money to meet margin requirements.

MARGIN ACCOUNT brokerage account allowing customers to buy securities with money borrowed from the broker. Margin accounts are governed by REGULATION T of the Federal Reserve Board, by the National Association of Securities Dealers (NASD), by the New York Stock Exchange, and by individual brokerage house rules.

MARGINAL COST increase or decrease in costs as the result of one more or one less unit of output; also called *incremental cost* or *differential cost*. Determining marginal cost is important in deciding whether or not to vary a rate of production.

MARGINAL COST CURVE graphic depiction of the MARGINAL COST experienced by a producer at different levels of production.

MARGINAL COST OF CAPITAL the cost of financing for the next dollar of capital raised. Some sources of capital are more expensive than others; for example, low-grade subordinated debt would be more expensive to raise (require a higher interest rate) than unsubordinated debt. Because capital must be raised to finance a new project, the marginal cost of capital should be the HURDLE RATE used in discounted cash flow present value analysis, not the average cost of capital.

MARGINAL EFFICIENCY OF CAPITAL annual percentage yield earned by the last additional unit of capital; also known as *marginal productivity of capital, natural interest rate, net capital productivity,* and *rate of return over cost.* The significance of the concept to a business firm is that projects whose marginal efficiency of capital exceeds the market rate of interest are profitable to undertake.

MARGINAL PRODUCER in an industry, individual producer who is just barely able to remain profitable at current levels of price and production.

MARGINAL PROPENSITY TO CONSUME (MPC) proportion of additional income (expressed as a decimal) that will be consumed, rather than saved, by a consumer or by an entire economy. If 90 cents of an additional dollar of income will be consumed, then MPC = 0.90. *See also* MARGINAL PROPENSITY TO SAVE (MPS).

MARGINAL PROPENSITY TO INVEST proportion of additional NATIONAL INCOME that will be invested, rather than consumed or spent.

MARGINAL PROPENSITY TO SAVE (MPS) proportion of additional income that will be saved rather than consumed. Since consumers can only consume or save additional income, MPS = 1 – MPC (MARGINAL PROPENSITY TO CONSUME). If 90 cents of an additional dollar are consumed, then the rest must be saved, and MPS = 1 – 0.90 = 0.10. Since saving provides funds for investment, MPS can be an indicator of the economy's potential for investment and growth.

MARGINAL PROPERTY property that is barely profitable to use. For example, if cotton that has been efficiently raised can sell for $100.00, yet cost $99.99 to raise, the land on which the cotton was raised is considered marginal property.

MARGINAL REVENUE change in total revenue caused by one additional unit of output. It is calculated by determining the difference between the total revenues produced before and after a one-unit increase in the rate of production. *See also* MARGINAL COST.

MARGINAL TAX RATE, BRACKET tax rate on an additional dollar of income. Due to the progressive rate structure of income taxes, an additional dollar of income could be taxed at a higher rate than all previous income. The highest MARGINAL TAX BRACKET for single individuals with taxable income above $336,550 is 35% in 2006.

MARGINAL UTILITY additional usefulness or satisfaction a consumer receives from the consumption of one more unit of a good.

MARGIN CALL demand, usually resulting from the price decline of a security bought on margin, that a customer deposit enough money or securities to bring a margin account up to the initial margin or minimum maintenance requirements. If a customer fails to respond, securities in the account may be liquidated.

MARGIN OF PROFIT relationship of gross profits to net sales. Returns and allowances are subtracted from gross sales to arrive at net sales. Cost of goods sold is subtracted from net sales to arrive at gross profit. Gross profit is divided by net sales to get the profit margin, which is sometimes called the *gross margin*. The result is a ratio, and the term is also written as *margin of profit ratio. See also* MARGIN.

MARGIN OF SAFETY measure of the financial position of a company; amount at which present sales exceed the break-even sales. For example, if actual sales are $10,000 and the BREAK-EVEN POINT is $8,000, the *margin of safety* is $2,000.

MARINE INSURANCE coverage for goods in transit and the vehicles of transportation on waterways, land, and air. *See also* MARINE INSURANCE, INLAND; INSTRUMENTALITIES OF TRANSPORTATION.

MARINE INSURANCE, INLAND INSURANCE protecting against loss on inland waterways and loss by one to whom property is entrusted for any means of shipment. Policies vary as to the coverage provided.

MARITAL DEDUCTION federal ESTATE TAX deduction permitting a spouse to take, tax free, the decedent spouse's total ESTATE. The marital deduction thus permits property to pass to the surviving spouse without being depleted by the federal estate tax. The same is true with the gift tax marital deduction, which allows property to be given to a spouse without being taxed by the federal gift tax. In this way, estate taxes are levied as property passes to the next generation, but not within a generation.

MARITAL STATUS refers to the type of return filed: single, joint, married filing separately, or head of household. Different tax rates apply to the different marital statuses. *See also* FILING STATUS.

MARKDOWN reduction in the original retail selling price, which was determined by adding a percentage factor, called a *markup*, to the cost of the merchandise. The term markdown does not apply unless the price is dropped below the original selling price. *See* DISCOUNT.

MARKET
1. public place where products or services are bought and sold, directly or through intermediaries; also called *marketplace*.
2. aggregate of people with the present or potential ability and desire to purchase a product or service; equivalent to DEMAND.
3. securities markets in the aggregate; the New York Stock Exchange in particular.
4. to sell. *See also* MARKETING.

MARKETABILITY speed and ease with which a particular product or investment may be bought and sold. In common use, *marketability* is interchangeable with *liquidity*, but *liquidity* implies the preservation of value when a security is bought or sold.

MARKETABILITY STUDY an analysis, for a specific client, of the likely sales of a specific type of product. A *market analysis* or *study* is an effort to glean information from the market on prices, quantities, and type of product that is selling. A *marketability study* presumes a particular product and seeks to determine its MARKET PRICE and rate of sales.

MARKETABLE SECURITIES securities that are easily sold. On a corporation's balance sheet, they are assets that can be readily converted into cash—for example, government securities, banker's acceptances, and commercial paper.

MARKETABLE TITLE TITLE a reasonably well-informed purchaser would, in the exercise of ordinary business prudence, be willing to accept. A title, to be marketable, need not be free from every technical criticism, but it must be demonstrated to be reasonably free of ENCUMBRANCES.

MARKET ANALYSIS
1. bond, or commodity markets, based on technical data about the movement of market prices or on fundamental data such as corporate earnings prospects or supply and demand.
2. study designed to define a company's current or potential markets, forecast their directions, and decide how to expand the company's share and exploit any new trends.

MARKET APPROACH *see* MARKET COMPARISON APPROACH.

MARKET AREA geographic region from which one can expect the primary demand for a specific product or service.

MARKET BASKET combination of goods, in statistically derived proportions, used to track price changes. It is used in such indicators as the CONSUMER PRICE INDEX (CPI), and the PRODUCER PRICE INDEX (PPI).

MARKET CAPITALIZATION value of a corporation as determined by the market price of its issued and outstanding common stock. It is calculated by multiplying the number of outstanding shares by the current market price of a share.

MARKET COMPARISON APPROACH in real estate, one of three APPRAISAL approaches. The value is estimated by analyzing sales prices of similar properties (COMPARABLES) sold recently. *See also* COST APPROACH; INCOME APPROACH.

MARKET DEMAND total demand of all consumers in a market. The sums of the quantities demanded by each consumer at every price are used to determine the level of demand experienced by the entire market at each price.

MARKET DEVELOPMENT INDEX relationship between potential and actual customers of a brand in a particular market (geographical area) compared to the relationship nationally; rate of sales throughout the United States.

MARKET ECONOMY economy that relies largely upon market forces to allocate resources and goods, and to determine prices and quantities of each good that will be produced. Capitalist economies are market economies, while MANAGED ECONOMIES are less so. *See also* CAPITALISM.

MARKET EQUILIBRIUM situation in a market where the prevailing price causes producers to produce exactly the quantity demanded by consumers at that same price. A market in EQUILIBRIUM will not experience changes in price or quantity produced.

MARKET INDEX numbers representing weighted values of the components that make up the index. A stock market index, for example, may be weighted according to the prices and number of outstanding shares of the various stocks.

MARKETING process associated with promoting for sale goods or services. The classic components of marketing are the FOUR PS: product, price, place, and promotion—the selection and development of the *product*, determination of *price*, selection and design of distribution channels (*place*), and all aspects of generating or enhancing demand for the product, including advertising (*promotion*). *See also* DIRECT MARKETING; MARKET; MARKET PROFILE; TARGET MARKET.

MARKETING CONCEPT
1. idea or strategy for marketing a product or service.
2. philosophy of marketing a product or service that is benefit oriented rather than product oriented. For example, a successful marketing concept in the perfume industry is that the industry is in the business of selling dreams, sex, and romance—that is, the *benefits* to be derived from perfume, but not the perfume itself.

MARKETING DIRECTOR head of all marketing functions within the structure of an advertiser's company, including advertising, sales promotion, research, and all other marketing elements.

Marketing Director

Advertising Director

Advertising Agency

Advertising Brand Management

Sales Promotion

Research

MARKETING INFORMATION SYSTEM processes associated with collecting, analyzing, and reporting MARKETING RESEARCH information.

MARKETING MIX combination of the four controllable variables of Product, Price, Place, and Promotion that are essential to define and fulfill a target market. *See also* FOUR PS.

MARKETING PLAN plan that details a company's marketing effort; also called *action program*, *marketing strategy*. The marketing plan may be laid out for an individual product or for the entire company and all its products.

MARKETING RESEARCH gathering and analysis of information about the moving of goods or services from producer to consumer. Marketing research covers three wide areas: *market analysis*, which yields information about the marketplace; *product research*, which yields information about the characteristics and desires for the product; and *consumer research*, which yields information about the needs and motivations of the consumer.

MARKETING STRATEGY plan for promoting products and services.

MARKET LETTER newsletter provided to brokerage firm customers or written by an independent market analyst, registered as an investment adviser with the Securities and Exchange Commission, who sells the letter to subscribers.

MARKET MAKERS dealers in the securities exchange who buy and sell securities for their own account to maintain an orderly market in the specific securities they manage. The basic role of the *market maker* is to maintain liquidity in the securities industry for buyers and sellers. *See also* SPECIALIST.

MARKET ORDER order to buy or sell a security at the best available price at that moment.

MARKET PENETRATION
1. marketing strategy used by a manufacturer to increase the sales of a product within an existing market through the employment of more aggressive marketing tactics.
2. degree to which a particular product is purchased in a particular market.

MARKET PRICE
In general: recent price agreed upon by buyers and sellers of a product or service, as determined by supply and demand.
Finance: last reported price at which a security was sold.

MARKET PROFILE the demographic characteristics of potential buyers for a product or product line.

MARKET RENT RENT a comparable unit would command if offered in the competitive market. *See also* CONTRACT RENT; ECONOMIC RENT.

MARKET RESEARCH exploration of the size, characteristics, and potential of a market to find out, usually before developing a new product or service, what people want and need. Market research is an important step in marketing; it stretches from the original conception of a product to its ultimate delivery to the consumer.

MARKET RISK *see* SYSTEMATIC RISK.

MARKET SCREENING method of scanning desirable markets based on environmental factors that preclude undesirable markets.

MARKET SEGMENT one of two or more subgroups within a target market. Different MARKETING MIX strategies can be developed to reach each of the target market segments.

MARKET SEGMENTATION process of dividing the market according to similarities that exist among the various subgroups within the market. The similarities may be common characteristics, or common needs and desires.

MARKET SHARE percentage of industry sales of a particular company or product.

MARKET SYSTEM economic system that relies upon markets to allocate resources and determine prices. *See also* MARKET ECONOMY.

MARKET TEST EXPOSURE of goods or services to a small sample of the entire market to test various marketing strategies. Some areas of the country are considered better barometers of demand than others, because the tastes of a particular area for certain products seem to resemble those of the whole country.

MARKET TIMING decisions on when to buy or sell securities, in light of economic factors such as the strength of the economy and the direction of interest rates, or technical indications such as the direction of stock prices and the volume of trading.

MARKET VALUE *see* FAIR MARKET VALUE.

MARKET VALUE CLAUSE provision of property insurance that establishes the amount for which an insured must be reimbursed for damaged or destroyed property according to the price a willing buyer would pay for the property purchased from a willing seller, as opposed to the actual cash value of the damaged or destroyed property. *See also* MARKET VALUE VS. ACTUAL CASH VALUE.

MARKET VALUE VS. ACTUAL CASH VALUE value of property as established by the price a willing buyer would pay for property purchased from a willing seller, compared with the replacement cost of damaged or destroyed property minus depreciation and obsolescence.

MARK TO (THE) MARKET
1. assess the value of a securities portfolio to ensure that a MARGIN ACCOUNT is in compliance with maintenance requirements.
2. MUTUAL FUND valuation of current portfolio to current market prices to obtain the daily net asset value reported to shareholders.

MARKUP

Marketing:

1. *see* GROSS PROFIT.

2. determination of a retail selling price, based on some percentage increase in the wholesale cost; also called *margin*. For example, a 20% markup on an item wholesaling at $100 would be $20, resulting in a retail selling price of $120.

Printing: written instructions for the typesetter on copy—for instance, underlining words to indicate they should be set in italics.

MARRIAGE PENALTY various provisions of the tax law that require married people to pay more taxes in some situations than if they were single. The penalty is most pronounced for higher-taxbracket couples earning equal amounts of income. Although married taxpayers may file separate returns, the total tax result will not be the same as if they were unmarried and may even be more than the result from the joint return.

MARRIED FILING JOINTLY filing status option for taxpayers who are married to each other and agree to report their combined income and deductions. For a given level of income, filing jointly typically results in a lower tax than filing separately. However, *see* MARRIAGE PENALTY.

MARRIED FILING SEPARATELY filing status option for taxpayers who are married to each other but wish to be responsible for only their individual tax returns. In noncommunity property states, each taxpayer would report only his or her own income and deductions. In community property states, each taxpayer would report his or her own income and deductions from separate property and half of the income and deductions from COMMUNITY PROPERTY.

MARRIED TAXPAYER taxpayer who was married on the last day of the tax year. Taxpayers who marry before the end of the tax year can file a joint tax return and be taxed as though they had been married for the entire year. Legally married taxpayers who have not obtained a final decree of divorce or separate maintenance by the last day of the tax year are considered to have been married for the entire tax year.

MARXISM political, social, and economic theories of Karl Marx. Applied Marxism, in an economy, results in either a communist economy or a heavily socialist economy.

MASLOW'S HIERARCHY OF NEEDS hierarchy of five human motivational needs arranged by ascending order of importance, developed by Abraham Maslow. The five ascending needs are (1) physiological, (2) safety, (3) social, (4) esteem, and (5) self-actualization. Only unsatisfied needs are motivators. Once a need is satisfied, the next level emerges as a motivator.

MASSACHUSETTS TRUST business TRUST that confers limited liability on the holders of trust certificates; also called *common law trust*. It is a voluntary association of investors who transfer contributed cash or other property to trustees with legal authority to manage the business.

MASS APPEAL nondirected marketing approach designed to appeal to all possible users of a product.

MASS COMMUNICATION using widely circulating media such as newspapers, magazines, television, and radio to inform the general public.

MASS CUSTOMIZATION MASS PRODUCTION methods used to produce customized goods and services.

MASS MEDIA broad spectrum of radio and television broadcast stations and networks, newspapers, magazines, and outdoor displays designed to appeal to the general public. *See also* MEDIA.

MASS PRODUCTION manufacturing or processing of uniform products in large quantities using interchangeable parts and machinery. Mass production is either a wholly automated process or a series of short, repetitive procedures.

MASTER LEASE controlling LEASE; *contrast with* SUBLEASE. One cannot grant a greater interest in real estate than one has; so if a master lease is for a five-year term, a sublease cannot legally exceed five years. *See also* PROPRIETARY LEASE.

MASTER LIMITED PARTNERSHIP agreement certified in a public office, creating an unincorporated business and specifying one master partner to be in control of the partnership for the benefit of himself and other limited partners for a particular purpose.

MASTER OF BUSINESS ADMINISTRATION (MBA) graduate degree offered by many universities in which the student generally spends two years learning the common body of knowledge in business and a specialty such as accounting, business analysis, finance, management, marketing, or real estate.

MASTER PLAN
General: overall strategy.
Real estate: document that describes, in narrative and with maps, an overall development concept of a city or planned-use development.
Tax: IRS-approved model form of QUALIFIED RETIREMENT PLAN in which the funding medium's identity is specified.

MASTER POLICY single contract coverage on a group basis issued to an employer. Group members receive certificates as evidence of membership summarizing benefits provided. *See also* GROUP HEALTH INSURANCE; GROUP LIFE INSURANCE.

MASTER-SERVANT RULE assumption that an employer is liable for negligent acts or omissions of employees that result in bodily injury and/or property damage to third parties if those acts are in the course of employment.

MASTHEAD
1. name of a newspaper displayed at the top of the first page.
2. in a newspaper or magazine, printed section, usually located on the editorial page, that details the title and address of the publication, the owner and/or publisher, the staff, and the advertising and subscription rates.

MATCHING PRINCIPLE (COSTS WITH REVENUES) accounting concept of pairing REVENUES with the costs that were incurred to generate the revenues. For example, wages and materials bought to construct a rental property are depreciated over the period the building generates income, not during the construction period.

MATERIAL
1. goods used in the manufacturing process. *See also* DIRECT MATERIAL.
2. important, as a material fact in a trial, a material amount of money.

MATERIAL FACT fact that is germane to a particular situation; one that participants in the situation, such as a trial, may reasonably be expected to consider.

MATERIALITY in accounting reports, concept that only important disclosures are required. A CPA performing an AUDIT for a phone company does not need to count the last dime deposited in a pay phone just before the fiscal year ends, because of lack of materiality.

MATERIAL MAN person who supplies materials used in the construction or repair of a building or other property. If unpaid, a material man may file a MECHANIC'S LIEN.

MATERIAL PARTICIPATION
Tax: year-round active involvement in the operations of a business activity on a regular, continuous, and substantial basis. Three main factors to consider in determining the presence of *material participation* are: (1) Is the activity the taxpayer's principal trade or business? (2) How close is the taxpayer to the business? (3) Does the taxpayer have knowledge and experience in the enterprise?
Limited partners: limited partnership interests are considered inherently passive.

MATERIAL REQUIREMENTS PLANNING (MRP) *see* JUST-INTIME INVENTORY CONTROL (JIT).

MATERIALS HANDLING moving, packaging, and storing of materials in every form, ranging from raw materials to finished goods. It includes the shipping, receiving, and processing of incoming items and outgoing products, returns to suppliers, and disposal of scrap.

MATERIALS MANAGEMENT administration of all activities concerned with the ordering, storage, and movement of materials. This includes the storage of raw materials and parts and the manning of production operation centers.

MATRIX mathematical term describing a rectangular array of elements (numerical data, parameters or variables). Each element within a matrix has a unique position, defined by the row and column.

MATRIX ORGANIZATION superimposing a group or interdisciplinary team of project specialists, such as scientific and engineering personnel, on a functional organizational design. In a matrix organization members have dual allegiance, to a particular assignment or project and to their organizational department.

MATURE ECONOMY economy of a nation whose population has stabilized or is declining, and whose economic growth is no longer robust. Such an economy is characterized by a decrease in spending on roads or factories and a relative increase in consumer spending.

MATURITY
In general: date at which legal rights in something ripen. In the context of COMMERCIAL PAPER (negotiable instruments), it is the time when the paper becomes due and demandable, that is, the date when an action can enforce payment.
Personnel: character and emotional development of an employee.

MATURITY DATE time at which life insurance death proceeds or endowments are paid, either at the death of an insured or at the end of the endowment period.

MAXIMUM CAPACITY *see* CAPACITY.

MB *see* MEGABYTE.

M-CATS municipal CERTIFICATE OF ACCRUAL ON TREASURY SECURITIES, that is, a ZERO COUPON bond issued by a municipality.

MEALS AND ENTERTAINMENT EXPENSE expense for meals and entertainment that qualifies for a tax deduction. Under current tax law, employers may deduct 50% of meals and entertainment expenses that have a BONA FIDE business purpose. For example, a business meal must include a discussion producing a direct business benefit.

MEAN, ARITHMETIC statistic calculated as the sum of all values in the sample divided by the number of observations. *See also* MEAN, GEOMETRIC.

MEAN, GEOMETRIC statistic calculated by taking the nth root of all values in a sample multiplied together. The geometric mean is used most often in change and index calculations, such as the change in rural land values from one year to the next. *See also* MEAN, ARITHMETIC.

MEAN RETURN in security analysis, expected value, or average, of all the likely returns of investments comprising a portfolio; in capital budgeting, mean value of the probability distribution of possible returns.

MECHANIC'S LIEN LIEN against buildings or other structures, allowed by some states to contractors, laborers, and suppliers of materials used in their construction or repair. The lien remains in effect until these people have been paid in full and may, in the event of a liquidation before they have been paid, give them priority over other creditors.

MECHANIZATION accomplishment of tasks with machines, mechanical equipment, or aids. Mechanization does not provide for self-correcting feedback, whereas automation does.

MEDALLION STAMP PROGRAM a program approved by the Securities Transfer Association that enables participating financial institutions to guarantee signatures. The Medallion programs ensure that the individual signing the certificate or stock power is in fact the registered owner as it appears on the stock certificate or stock power. Any U.S. financial institution that belongs to a Medallion Stamp Program can provide Medallion guarantees. Such institutions include banks, savings and loans, credit unions, and U.S. stock brokerage firms.

MEDIA
1. plural of medium.
2. channels of communication that serve many diverse functions, such as offering a variety of entertainment with either mass or specialized appeal, communicating news and information, or displaying advertising messages.

MEDIA BUYER individual responsible for the purchase of time and space for the delivery of advertising messages in the media. A media buyer may be an employee of an advertising agency who specializes in such purchases.

MEDIAN middle value, midpoint, in a range of values; half the numbers in the list are above it and half below it. The median value is used to obtain a representation of a data set without distortion due to large deviations.

MEDIA PLAN specification of the MEDIA to be used in an advertising plan. A media plan will state the media objectives and explain the media strategy to be followed within a specific time frame and budget.

MEDIATION process of bringing conflicting parties together using a third party. The third party has no authority to force a settlement, unlike ARBITRATION.

MEDIA WEIGHT volume of audience delivered by an advertising campaign in terms of the number of commercials and advertisements, number of insertions, time parameters, and budget; the total audience delivery.

MEDICAID jointly administered federal and state government health insurance provided under Title XIX of the 1965 amendment of the Social Security Act. *Medicaid* provides health insurance assistance for people who have low income and limited assets. It is usually run by state welfare or human service agencies. A person may qualify for both MEDICARE and *Medicaid* or for only one of the programs.

MEDICAL CARE amounts paid for the diagnosis, cure, mitigation, treatment, or prevention of disease, or for the purpose of affecting any structure or function of the body, for transportation for and essential to such medical care, and medical insurance premiums.

MEDICAL EXAMINATION physical checkup required of applicants for life and/or health insurance to ascertain if they meet a company's underwriting standards or should be classified as substandard or uninsurable.

MEDICAL EXPENSE DEDUCTION allowable ITEMIZED DEDUCTION by individuals for unreimbursed payments for medical care, prescription drugs, and medical insurance premiums. Limited to the amount that exceeds 7.5% of the taxpayer's ADJUSTED GROSS INCOME (AGI).

MEDICARE federal health insurance provided under Title XVIII of the Social Security Act. Medicare is a basic health insurance program that covers people who are 65 or older, people of any age with permanent kidney failure, and those under 65 who have been receiving Social Security disability benefits for the past 24 months. One of five programs under the Social Security System in which hospital and medical insurance coverage is provided to those who are covered, Medicare is run by the Health Care Financing Administration. The Social Security Administration takes applications for Medicare, assists beneficiaries in claiming Medicare payments, and provides information about the program.

MEDICARE HOSPITAL INSURANCE also referred to as Medicare Part A. A monthly premium is not required in order to receive this coverage if the worker or spouse is entitled to benefits under either the Social Security or Railroad Retirement System, or has worked a sufficient time in federal, state, or local government employment to be insured. Medicare hospital insurance helps pay for medically necessary services furnished by Medicare-certified hospitals, skilled nursing facilities, home health agencies, and hospices.

MEDICARE MEDICAL INSURANCE also referred to as Medicare Part B. Part B is optional, but a monthly premium is required in order to receive this coverage. It is offered to all beneficiaries when they enroll in Part A. Medicare medical insurance helps to pay for physician services and many other medical services and supplies that are not covered by Medicare Part A.

MEDICARE TAX the hospital insurance portion of the tax assessed on compensation and self-employment earnings under the FEDERAL INSURANCE CONTRIBUTIONS ACT. The Medicare tax is 2.9% of all earnings. An employer is required to withhold half of the tax (1.45%) from employees' wages and also to make a matching contribution of the other half of the tax. Self-employed individuals include the 2.9% tax with their quarterly ESTIMATED INCOME TAX PAYMENTS.

MEDIGAP type of health insurance policy designed to cover the areas of noncoverage under Medicare. Examples of noncoverage areas targeted by Medigap policies are the deductibles under the Medicare insurance policy, coinsurance amounts specified in the Medicare insurance policy, medical charges that exceed Medicare's approved amounts, and various medical services and supplies not paid for by Medicare.

MEDIUM
1. *see* MEDIA.
2. method, instrument, or material used by an artist in the creation of a work, such as pen and ink, oil, watercolor, or photography.

MEDIUM OF EXCHANGE COMMODITY or product that is generally accepted in a market as a standard of value and as a measure of value and wealth. The most common medium of exchange is money; however, in some primitive markets other commodities (cattle, precious metals, etc.) may be used.

MEDIUM-TERM BOND bond with a maturity of 2 to 10 years. *See also* INTERMEDIATE TERM; LONG BOND; SHORT TERM.

MEETING OF THE MINDS mutual assent to terms by parties to a CONTRACT. A traditional rule of contract law is that the agreement, to be legally enforceable, must be accurately expressed within the terms of the contract the parties create, for therein lies the required meeting of the minds.

MEGA- metric prefix denoting multiplication by 10^6 or 1,000,000. In measuring the capacity of computer disks and RAM, equivalent to $\times 2^{20}$ or 1,048,576.

MEGABYTE (MB) in computers, 2^{20}, or approximately one million, BYTES of information. The capacity of microcomputer HARD DISKS is usually measured in *megabytes*, as are HIGH DENSITY FLOPPY DISKS.

MELTDOWN a state of complete computer NETWORK overload that grinds all traffic to a halt.

MEMBER BANK member of the FEDERAL RESERVE SYSTEM including all nationally chartered banks and the state-chartered banks that are accepted for membership.

MEMBER FIRM or MEMBER CORPORATION brokerage firm that has at least one membership on a major stock exchange, even though, by exchange rules, the membership is in the name of an employee and not of the firm itself.

MEMORANDUM
1. informal record.
2. brief note, in writing, of some transaction.
3. outline of an intended instrument.
4. instrument written in concise summary.

MEMORY electronic device within a computer, where information is stored while being actively worked on; formerly called *core*. The memory requirements of a computer are dictated by the software that is to be run on it. Microcomputer memory is usually 16 to 128 MEGABYTES. *See also* RAM.

MEMORY TYPEWRITER *see* TYPEWRITER.

MENIAL work pertaining to servants; work that is demeaning or insulting to the person performing it.

MENTAL HEALTH INSURANCE health insurance policy providing for psychiatric and psychological care and counseling. Many policies also cover treatment for substance abuse counseling and treatment. Most mental health insurance policies have a deductible payment clause.

MENTOR experienced manager or employee who guides and advises new employees and managers about the dynamics of an organization and its procedures.

MENU in a computer application, a list of available commands or choices. The area below the TITLE BAR in an application window is usually the *menu bar*. Menu items vary from one application to another but (in Windows) generally include File, Edit, View, Tools, and Help. Each of these items has a PULL-DOWN or DROP-DOWN MENU listing choices in that category. For example, the File menu generally lists New, Open, Close, Save, Save As, Print, and so on. *See also* FLY-OUT MENU; POP-UP MENU.

MERC nickname for the CHICAGO MERCANTILE EXCHANGE (CME). The exchange trades many types of FUTURES, FUTURES OPTIONS, and foreign currency futures contracts. *See also* SECURITIES AND COMMODITIES EXCHANGES.

MERCANTILE system of commerce operated by merchants.

MERCANTILE AGENCY organization that supplies businesses with credit ratings and reports on other firms that are or might become customers. The largest of the agencies, Dun & Bradstreet, provides credit information on companies of all descriptions, along with a wide range of other credit and financial reporting services.

MERCANTILE LAW branch of law, often called COMMERCIAL LAW, that deals with rules and institutions of commercial transactions; derived from *law merchant*.

MERCANTILE ROBBERY INSURANCE coverage for actual or attempted robbery of money, securities, or other property.

MERCANTILE SAFE BURGLARY INSURANCE coverage in the event a safe of a business is forceably entered, either on or off the premises, and property is stolen from the safe. Also covered is damage to the premises during actual or attempted burglary.

MERCANTILISM
 1. seventeenth and eighteenth century economic policy under which trading nations generated wealth and power by exporting manufactured goods in exchange for gold.
 2. in modern times, second-rate status of nations having a heavy dependence on imported manufactured goods.

MERCHANDISE goods and commodities sold at the retail level. Merchandising is the buying, presenting, and selling of merchandise. This includes all the related activities of advertising, displaying, and promoting merchandise to the retail customer.

MERCHANDISE ALLOWANCE sum of money given or allowed for merchandise that has been returned because of either poor quality or overstocking.

MERCHANDISE BROKER agent acting for merchandise buyers and sellers who is paid a commission or fee for negotiating sales of specific lots of goods. A merchandise broker puts the merchandise buyer and seller together for the purposes of a sale without taking possession of the actual merchandise.

MERCHANDISE CONTROL process of collecting and evaluating data on all aspects of each retail merchandise category, including sales, costs, shrinkage, profits, and turnover. Control is achieved through the maintenance of an inventory book where all data are evaluated.

MERCHANDISE INVENTORY (TURNOVER) *see* INVENTORY; INVENTORY TURNOVER.

MERCHANDISING
 1. "The planning involved in marketing the right merchandise or service at the right place, at the right time, in the right quantities, and at the right price." (American Marketing Association)
 2. promotional sales activities of an advertiser's sales force, retailers, wholesalers, or dealers, including advertising, point-of-purchase displays, guarantee seals, special sales, and in-store promotions.

MERCHANDISING ALLOWANCE *see* PROMOTIONAL ALLOWANCE.

MERCHANDISING DIRECTOR individual responsible for directing the merchandise sales effort for a manufacturer, retailer, wholesaler, distributor, dealer, or advertising agency. *See also* MERCHANDISING.

MERCHANT one in the business of purchasing and selling goods with the expectation of earning a profit. Commonly refers to a person who buys goods at a wholesale price level for sale at retail; a retailer or a trader. Under the UNIFORM COMMERCIAL CODE (UCC), the definition of *merchant* may include some businesses not engaged in retail trade, such as car dealers, producers of remanufactured engines, manufacturers of mobile homes, and, with respect to the leasing of an apartment, landlords. A merchant is considered knowledgeable of the goods he trades in.

MERCHANTABLE
1. salable.
2. reasonably fit for the purpose for which an article is manufactured and sold.
3. having at least average quality, compared to similar products.

MERCHANTABLE TITLE *see* MARKETABLE TITLE.

MERCHANT BANK
1. financial institution that engages in investment banking, counseling, negotiating in mergers and acquisitions, and a variety of other services.
2. bank that has entered into an agreement with a merchant to accept deposits generated by bank credit/charge card transactions.

MERCOSUR/MERCOSUL Southern Common Market (Spanish: *Mercado Común del Sur,* Portuguese: *Mercado Comum do Sul*), established by a free trade agreement among Argentina, Brazil, Paraguay, and Uruguay.

MERGE
1. combine two or more lists or files by combining duplicate records into single records. Merging is normally done in conjunction with a purging process that eliminates undesirable names.
2. financially combine two companies so that only one of the companies survives as a legal entity.

MERGENT, INC. part of Xinhua Finance, which acquired Moody's publications group in 1998; provides global business and financial information on publicly traded companies and fixed-income securities. Products include Mergent Online, Mergent BondSource, the Dividend Achiever Index series, Mergent Manuals and Handbooks, and other products. Four exchange-traded funds are based on Dividend Achiever Index methodologies.

MERGER classified as a type A reorganization, in which one corporation absorbs the corporate structure of another, resulting in liquidation of the acquired enterprise. If no BOOT is received, the reorganization may be tax free.

MERIT INCREASE increase in wages achieved through superior performance on the job; also called *merit pay; merit raise.* Merit increases are commonly specified as being negotiable in a contract between a union and management.

MERIT RATING
1. employee rating achieved through a periodic employee evaluation system, often used as the basis for pay increases and/or promotion.
2. rating achieved on a standard civil-service type merit examination, signifying the level of achievement on the exam.

METADATA *data about data.* In the context of computer files, it includes information such as the dates the file was created, modified, or accessed, the author's name and company, the computer it was created on, and so on. Hidden data, such as file properties, comments, or revision markings in a word processing document, can cause considerable embarrassment (and even legal repercussions) if not removed before the file is shared. File security settings and application add-ins such as Microsoft's Remove Hidden Data tool can be used to sanitize documents before making them available electronically via e-mail or on the Web.

METERED MAIL letters and packages stamped by a POSTAGE METER rather than a stamp.

METER RATE, METERAGE charge assessed according to the amount shown on a meter, as contrasted with a specified price. The user pays for the amount or consumption shown on the meter. Utility usage is commonly metered, although the price is not determined by the meter itself.

METES AND BOUNDS territorial limits of property expressed by measuring distances and angles from designated landmarks and in relation to adjoining properties.

METHODS-TIME MEASUREMENT (MTM) standardizing the time needed to complete a task by determining the average production time interval. This is a part of the scientific management school or the efficiency management approach to work standardization.

METRICATION process of convening an existing system of weights and measures to the metric system of weights and measures. *See also* METRIC SYSTEM.

METRIC SYSTEM decimal system of weights and measures in which the gram, meter, and liter are the basic units of weight, length, and capacity, respectively. *See also* METRICATION.

METROPOLITAN AREA generally the developed region economically attached to a large central city. *See also* CONSOLIDATED METROPOLITAN STATISTICAL AREA; METROPOLITAN STATISTICAL AREA; PRIMARY METROPOLITAN STATISTICAL AREA.

METROPOLITAN STATISTICAL AREA a CORE-BASED STATISTICAL AREA associated with at least one urbanized area that has a population of at least 50,000. The Metropolitan Statistical Area comprises the central county or counties containing the core, plus adjacent outlying counties having a high degree of social and economic integration with the central county as measured through commuting.

MEZZANINE FINANCING debt that is subordinate in priority to a company's SENIOR DEBT, yet ahead of JUNIOR DEBT.

MFD *see* MULTIFUNCTION DEVICE.

MICROCAP stocks in very small companies with market capitalizations of $250 million or less.

MICROCOMPUTER computer whose CENTRAL PROCESSING UNIT (CPU) consists of a single integrated circuit known as the MICROPROCESSOR. Ordinarily a microcomputer is used by only one person at a time. All home or personal computers (PCs) are microcomputers.

MICROECONOMICS study of the behavior of basic economic units such as companies, industries, or households. Research on the companies in the airline industry would be a microeconomic concern, for instance. *See also* MACROECONOMICS.

MICROMOTION STUDY analysis of a series of very short motions succeeding each other so rapidly that the eye confuses them. Micromotion study can be used for the reconstruction of an action through an analysis of its micromotions.

MICROPOLITAN STATISTICAL AREA a CORE-BASED STATISTICAL AREA associated with at least one urban cluster that has a population of at least 10,000 but less than 50,000. The Micropolitan Statistical Area comprises the central county or counties containing the core, plus adjacent outlying counties having a high degree of social and economic integration with the central county as measured through commuting.

MICROPROCESSOR integrated circuit containing the entire CENTRAL PROCESSING UNIT (CPU) of a computer, all on one chip, so that only the memory and input-output devices need to be added.

MICROSOFT the world's leading software-producing company, headquartered in Redmond, Washington, and founded by William Gates and Paul Allen in 1975. Among its early products were BASIC and MS-DOS (marketed to IBM for use in its computers as PC-DOS). For further information see http://www.microsoft.com.

MICROSOFT WORD *see* WORD.

MID-CAP stock with a middle-level MARKET CAPITALIZATION. Midcap stocks typically have between $1 billion and $5 billion in outstanding market value. Many mutual funds specializing in mid-cap stocks will use the word "Mid-cap" in their names.

MIDCAREER PLATEAU point in a middle manager's career when advancement opportunities appear to be blocked by severe obstacles and little challenge is left in the current position. A midcareer plateau is best alleviated by midcareer advancement programs of education and training.

MIDDLE MANAGEMENT managers with full management responsibilities reporting to higher level managers. In many organizations middle managers are called departmental managers, plant managers, assistant managers, and so on.

MID-MONTH CONVENTION in taxation, with respect to depreciating residential and nonresidential real property, convention whereby property is deemed placed in service or disposed of at the midpoint of the calendar month in which it was placed in service or disposed of.

MIDNIGHT DEADLINE completion requirement ending at midnight, which marks the end of a calendar day (such as April 15 for personal tax returns).

MIDWEST STOCK EXCHANGE *see* REGIONAL STOCK EXCHANGE.

MIGRANT WORKER worker moving from one region of the country to another to find employment. *Migrant* workers are used extensively for crop harvesting, mandating that they follow the harvest seasons.

MIL or MILL one tenth of a cent. The term is used in expressing tax rates on a per-dollar basis. For example, a tax rate of 60 mills means that taxes are 6 cents per dollar of ASSESSED VALUATION.

MILEAGE (TAX) *see* STANDARD MILEAGE METHOD.

MILITARY-INDUSTRIAL COMPLEX relationship between the military and industry. It was first described by President Eisenhower in his farewell address, where he warned of the irresponsible power of the military-industrial complex.

MILKING taking full advantage of a situation for a company's or one's own personal gain. An example is a business person who is *milking* a customer for all he is worth.

MILKING STRATEGY short-range marketing strategy planned to take the largest possible profit from an item in the shortest amount of time without regard to the item's long-range possibilities for sales.

MILLAGE RATE tax rate applied to property. Each MILL represents $1 of tax assessment per $1,000 of assessed property value. For example, the millage rate for property taxes in the Bumpton school district is 20 mills. A home with assessed value of $100,000 pays $2,000 a year in property taxes to the district.

MILLENNIUM BUG *see* YEAR 2000 PROBLEM.

MILLIONAIRE individual whose net worth exceeds $1 million.

MILLIONAIRE ON PAPER individual whose assets exceed $1 million but are not in the form of cash. For example, the assets could be in the form of securities or real estate.

MIME *see* MULTIPURPOSE INTERNET MAIL EXTENSIONS.

MINERAL LEASE an agreement that provides the lessee the right to excavate and sell minerals on the property of the lessor or to remove and sell petroleum and natural gas from the pool underlying the property of the lessor. In return, the lessor receives a royalty payment based on the value of the minerals removed.

MINERAL RIGHTS privilege of gaining INCOME from the sale of oil, gas, and other valuable resources found on or below land. Mineral rights can be sold or leased separately from the land ownership.

MINIMAX PRINCIPLE decision criterion based on reducing to the lowest level the difference between the possible outcomes and the best possible outcome resulting from the decision. The minimax principle is used to select result(s) with the least amount of regret in case of failure.

MINIMUM LEASE PAYMENTS regular rental payments excluding EXECUTORY costs to be made by the lessee to the lessor in a CAPITAL LEASE. The lessee reports an asset and liability at the discounted value of the future minimum lease payments.

MINIMUM LOT AREA smallest building lot area allowed in a SUBDIVISION, generally specified by a ZONING ORDINANCE.

MINIMUM PAYMENT minimum amount that a consumer is required to pay on a revolving charge account in order to keep the account in good standing. If the minimum payment is not made, late payment penalties are due. If the minimum is still not paid within a few months, credit privileges will be revoked. If a consumer pays just the minimum due, interest charges continue to accrue on all outstanding balances, including new purchases.

MINIMUM PENSION LIABILITY condition that is recognized when the accumulated benefit obligation is greater than the fair value of plan assets. However, *no* recognition is given in the opposite case. When an accrued pension liability exists, only an additional liability for the difference between the minimum liability and the accrued pension liability can be recorded.

MINIMUM WAGE lowest allowable hourly wage permitted by the government or a union contract for an employee performing a particular job.

MINI-WAREHOUSE a building separated into relatively small, lockable individual units, typically with a garage door–style opening, that provides storage. Units are typically rented month to month and are sized from $5' \times 5'$ to $25' \times 25'$. A typical $10' \times 20'$ *mini-warehouse* can be rented for $100 per month to be used for the storage of excess business or household goods.

MINOR person under the age of MAJORITY specified by law (18 to 21 years, depending on the state). Certain contracts, entered into by a minor, are voidable by the minor. Note that the other party is bound; only the minor may void them. For purposes of the kiddie tax, a minor is anyone under age 14.

MINORITY BUSINESS increasing number of businesses owned by females or African Americans. Their success is hampered by a lack of financing and management experience. The federal government has responded to their particular needs by earmarking a percentage of government contracts for minority businesses.

MINORITY DISCOUNT a reduction from the MARKET VALUE of an asset because the MINORITY INTEREST owner(s) cannot direct the business operations. *See* FAMILY LIMITED PARTNERSHIP. *Contrast with* CONTROL PREMIUM.

MINORITY INTEREST or **MINORITY INVESTMENT** interest of shareholders who, in the aggregate, own less than half the shares in a corporation. *See also* MAJORITY SHAREHOLDER.

MINT, MINTAGE, MINTING OF MONEY production, usually by government, of money. *Mintage* usually refers to the production of coins rather than paper money.

MINUS TICK *see* DOWNTICK.

MINUTES transcription or other written record of a meeting. Corporations keep *minutes* of important meetings in their permanent records.

MISCELLANEOUS ITEMIZED DEDUCTIONS job expenses and other miscellaneous expenses that are deductible by individual taxpayers but are not categorizable as medical expenses, taxes, interest, charitable contributions, casualty and theft losses, or moving expenses. Most miscellaneous itemized deductions are subject to a 2% floor (a reduction of the total deduction by 2% of ADJUSTED GROSS INCOME (AGI)).

MISDEMEANOR class of criminal offenses less serious than felonies and sanctioned by less severe penalties.

MISMANAGEMENT poorly managed activities in an organization. A mismanaged operation fails to achieve its goals, is extremely wasteful, and is generally indicative of administrative procedures that are not well thought out and directed.

MISREPRESENTATION untrue statement, whether unintentional or deliberate. It may be a form of nondisclosure where there is a duty to disclose, or the planned creation of a false appearance. Where there is misrepresentation of MATERIAL FACT, the person injured may sue for damages or rescind the contract. *See also* FALSE ADVERTISING; FRAUD.

MISSIONARY SALESPERSON *see* DETAIL PERSON.

MISSION STATEMENT definition of a corporation's vision and values, often printed on plaques and wallet cards, posted on its WEB SITE, and otherwise publicized. The *mission statement* typically emerges as part of the STRATEGIC PLANNING process. *See also* CREDO.

MISSTATEMENT OF AGE falsification of birth date by an applicant for a life or health insurance policy. If the company discovers that the wrong age was given, the coverage will be adjusted to reflect the correct age according to the premiums paid in.

MISTAKE in law, act or omission arising from ignorance or misconception, which may, depending upon its character or the circumstances surrounding it, justify rescission of a contract, or exoneration of a defendant from TORT or criminal liability.

MISTAKE OF LAW ignorance of the legal consequences of one's conduct, though one may be cognizant of the facts and substance of that conduct.

MITIGATION OF DAMAGES
1. requirement that one injured by another's BREACH of an agreement or TORT employ reasonable diligence and care to avoid aggravating the injury or increasing the DAMAGES.
2. defendant's request to the court for a reduction in damages owed to the PLAINTIFF, a request that the DEFENDANT justifies by evidence demonstrating that the plaintiff is not entitled to the full amount that might otherwise be awarded.

MIX
1. in recording or broadcast, combination of different sound elements, such as music, direct voice, sound effects, announcer voice, or singing voice, into a sound track for radio and television commercials or programs or audio recordings.
2. in television broadcast, combination of programs in a television contract for a series.
3. in retailing, combination of merchandise in a retail package or the entire variety of inventory of a retailer, wholesaler, or distributor.
4. combination of products, including various sizes of the same product for a particular brand in a given store.
5. *see* MARKETING MIX; PRODUCT MIX.

MIXED ECONOMIC SYSTEM, MIXED ECONOMY economy in which both market forces and government intervention and direction are used to determine resource allocation and prices. The U.S. economy is a mixed economy; while it relies to a great extent upon markets, government also regulates some of the private economy.

MIXED SIGNALS unclear message; usually two contradicting messages.

MLM *see* MULTILEVEL MARKETING; *see also* PYRAMIDING.

MLP *see* MASTER LIMITED PARTNERSHIP.

MO
1. *see* MONEY ORDER.
2. *see* MODUS OPERANDI, or operating method.

MOBILE COMMERCE (M-COMMERCE) electronic commerce transactions using wireless devices and Internet access instead of PC-based technology.

MOBILE HOME dwelling unit manufactured in a factory and designed to be transported to a site and semipermanently attached. The preferred industry term is *manufactured housing*.

MOBILE (MANUFACTURED) HOME PARK SUBDIVISION of plots designed for siting of mobile homes. Plots are generally leased to mobile home owners and include utilities, parking space, and access to utility roads. Many parks also include such amenities as swimming pools and clubhouses.

MODE
1. manner of existing or acting; way, method, or form. An example is a company that has a particular *mode* of operation that employees are expected to follow.
2. **Statistics:** the most commonly occurring value in a data set. Normally the mode is presented in a graphical format illustrating the common occurrence. It is extremely useful when making graphical presentations regarding data occurrences.

MODELING designing and manipulating a mathematical representation that simulates an economic system or corporate financial application so that the effect of changes can be studied and forecast. *See also* MODEL UNIT.

MODEL UNIT representative product, such as a home, apartment, or office space, used as part of a sales campaign to demonstrate the design, structure, and appearance of units in a development.

MODEM device that links computer systems via telephone lines enabling computers in different locations to exchange information; short for modulator-demodulator. Modems convert telephone impulses to computer-interpretable impulses. There must be a modem at each end of the communications link to either send or receive converted impulses.

MODERNIZE alter a property by installing up-to-date equipment, making contemporary cosmetic improvements, and deleting obsolete facilities.

MODERN PORTFOLIO THEORY (MPT) investment portfolio decision approach that applies a systematic method of elevating rates of return while minimizing risk. The portfolio must include both risky and risk-free securities that run counter, in some degree, to each other.

MODIFIED ACCELERATED COST RECOVERY SYSTEM (MACRS) a method of DEPRECIATION introduced in 1986. Assets are depreciated over longer lives than provided by the ACCELERATED COST RECOVERY SYSTEM (ACRS). Personal property can be depreciated using DECLINING-BALANCE METHODS. Real property can be depreciated only under the STRAIGHT-LINE METHOD. MACRS also provided different conventions for calculating depreciation, determined by when assets were placed in service. *See also* GENERAL DEPRECIATION SYSTEM (GSU).

MODIFIED ACCRUAL governmental accounting method. Revenue is recognized when it becomes available and measurable.

MODIFIED ADJUSTED GROSS INCOME (MAGI) the amount of a taxpayer's ADJUSTED GROSS INCOME (AGI) from federal Form 1040, without certain income/deductions that are normally included/deducted. All tax-exempt interest income is included. *Modified* *adjusted gross income* is used to determine whether a Social Security recipient who has other income is required to pay tax on Social Security income.

MODULAR HOUSING DWELLING units constructed from components prefabricated in a factory and erected on the site. *See also* MOBILE HOME.

MODUS OPERANDI (MO) manner of operation; the means of accomplishing an act; especially, the characteristic method employed by a person in certain acts; the way one (who often is sly in business dealings) operates.

MOLD, BLACK *see* STACHYBOTRYS CHARTORUM.

MOM AND POP STORE small retail store having limited capital, principally employing family members.

MOMENTUM rate of acceleration of an economic, price, or volume movement. An economy with strong growth that is likely to continue is said to have a lot of *momentum.*

MOMENTUM PLAYER trader in the stock or commodities market who identifies a trend in the price movement of a security and rides the trend as long as it is profitable.

MONETARIST economist who believes that the MONEY SUPPLY is the key to the ups and down in the economy. Monetarists such as Milton Friedman think that the money supply has far more impact on the economy's future course than, say, the level of federal spending. Monetarists advocate slow but steady growth in the money supply. *Contrast with* KEYNESIAN ECONOMICS.

MONETARY pertaining to, or having to do with, money, money creation, money supply, and government management of money.

MONETARY ITEM asset or liability whose amounts are fixed or determinable in dollars without reference to future prices of specific goods or services. Their economic significance depends heavily upon the general purchasing power of money. The two types of monetary items are *monetary assets* and *monetary liabilities.*

MONETARY POLICY the efforts of a nation's central bank aimed at influencing inflation rates, economic growth, and interest rates by varying the supply of money. *Contrast with* FISCAL POLICY.

MONETARY RESERVE
1. government's stockpile of foreign currency and precious metals, used to back up its currency, also called *international* reserves.
2. Federal Reserve Board's requirements that banks keep on hand certain proportions of their deposits in cash or near-cash equivalents.

MONETARY STANDARD manner in which a government creates faith in the value and reliability of its currency.

MONEY coinage, currency, and other commodities recognized by members of an economy as being reliable stores of value and MEDIA OF EXCHANGE.

MONEY CENTER BANK one of the largest banks in one of the major financial centers of the world, among them New York, Chicago, San Francisco, Los Angeles, London, Paris, and Tokyo. These banks have major national and international influence.

MONEY FUND REPORT AVERAGE average of all major MONEY MARKET FUND yields, published weekly for 7- and 30-day yields. The average is compiled by iMoneyNet, a subsidiary of Informa Financial Information, which publishes the *Money Fund Report,* an industry-leading weekly newsletter since 1975.

MONEY ILLUSION when increase in money income is thought to increase the overall purchasing power when, in fact, price increases of similar proportion result in the purchasing power actually remaining the same.

MONEY INCOME income measured only in money. It contrasts with REAL INCOME, which takes into account changes in the PURCHASING POWER of money due to inflation or deflation.

MONEY MARKET market for short-term debt instruments, such as negotiable certificates of deposit, Eurodollar certificates of deposit, commercial paper, banker's acceptances, U.S. Treasury bills, and discount notes of the Federal National Mortgage Association and Federal Farm Credit System.

MONEY MARKET FUND open-ended MUTUAL FUND that invests in commercial paper, bankers' acceptances, repurchase agreements, government securities, certificates of deposit, and other highly liquid and safe securities and pays money market rates of interest. The fund's net asset value remains a constant $1 a share—only the interest rate goes up or down.

MONEY ORDER financial instrument that can be easily converted into cash by the payee named on the money order. The money order lists both the PAYEE and the person who bought the instrument, known as the *payor*. Money orders are issued by banks, telephone companies, post offices, and travelers' check issuers to people presenting cash or other forms of acceptable payment.

MONEY SUPPLY the total stock of money in the economy. Economists identify several types of "money supply," based on liquidity:
M1: the sum of currency, demand deposits (checking, NOW accounts), travelers' checks, etc.
M2: M1 plus savings and other highly liquid time deposits.
M3: M2 plus other very liquid instruments.

MONITOR
   In general: anything that keeps track of something else.
   Computers:
   1. program that supervises the activity of other programs.
   2. device similar to a television set that accepts video signals from a
     computer and displays information on its screen.

MONOPOLIST firm or individual entrepreneur that is the sole producer
of a good and so represents the entire market supply of that good.

MONOPOLY control of the production and distribution of a product or
service by one firm or a group of firms acting in concert. In its pure
form, monopoly, which is characterized by an absence of competition,
leads to high prices and a general lack of responsiveness to the needs
and desires of consumers. The most flagrant monopolistic practices in
the United States were outlawed by antitrust laws. *See also* CARTEL;
MONOPSONY; NATURAL MONOPOLY; OLIGOPOLY; PERFECT COMPETITION.

MONOPOLY PRICE EQUILIBRIUM price arrived at in a market in which
the supply is a MONOPOLY. According to economic theory, the *monopoly
price* is higher than the price that would prevail if competition existed.

MONOPSONY market situation in which there is only a single consumer of the good produced.

MONTE CARLO simulation method that uses random numbers to determine events. Suppose that you know the probability that a particular
event will happen, but it is too difficult to calculate the probability that
a complicated combination of events will occur. In the Monte Carlo
method you use a random number generator to calculate a random number and then compare that number with the probability of the event.

MONTHLY INVESTMENT PLAN plan whereby an investor puts a
fixed dollar amount into a particular investment every month, thus
building a position at advantageous prices by means of DOLLAR COST
AVERAGING.

MONTH-TO-MONTH TENANCY LEASE agreement extendable or
cancelable each month.

MONTREAL EXCHANGE/BOURSE DE MONTRÉAL Canada's
oldest stock exchange and second-largest (after Toronto) in dollar
value of trading. STOCKS, BONDS, FUTURES, and OPTIONS are traded
through a specialist system combined with automated systems.

MONUMENT fixed object and point established by SURVEYORS to determine land locations. *See also* LANDMARK.

MOODY'S INVESTMENT GRADE rating assigned by MOODY'S
INVESTORS SERVICE to certain municipal short-term debt securities,
classified as MIG-1, 2, 3, and 4 to signify best, high, favorable, and
adequate quality, respectively. All four are INVESTMENT GRADE or bank
quality.

MOODY'S INVESTORS SERVICE financial services company head-quartered with its parent, Dun & Bradstreet, in downtown Manhattan. Moody's is one of the four best known bond rating agencies in the country, the others being Fitch's, Standard & Poor's, and Duff & Phelps.

MOONLIGHTING employees who work a second job for additional income. The term derives from the fact that many of these jobs are night jobs.

MOOT POINT a matter that is still open to discussion or debatable, but usually with the connotation that it is an academic question because it is no longer significant or because agreement is unlikely to be reached.

M1, M2, M3 *see* MONEY SUPPLY.

MORALE collective feeling or attitude in a work group. A good manager tries to keep the morale high in an organization. High morale tends to motivate workers in a group toward the achievement of a goal.

MORAL HAZARD circumstance that increases the probability of loss because of an applicant's personal habits or morals; for example, an applicant is a known criminal.

MORAL LAW law of behavior underpinning the morality of a civilization. Moses' Ten Commandments are moral laws setting forth the moral and religious principles of Western civilization.

MORAL OBLIGATION BOND tax-exempt bond issued by a municipality or a state financial intermediary and backed by the moral obligation pledge of a state government. The state's obligation to honor the pledge is moral rather than legal because future legislatures cannot be legally obligated to appropriate the funds required.

MORAL SUASION persuasion through influence rather than coercion; said of the efforts of the FEDERAL RESERVE BOARD to achieve member bank compliance with its general policy.

MORATORIUM
   1. time period during which a certain activity is not allowed.
   2. delay granted in the repayment of a debt or in the fulfillment of another legal obligation.

MORE OR LESS approximation, whereby a contract will be valid although the amount is not exact. For example, land is described as 100 acres, more or less. The contract is valid if the actual size of the parcel varies slightly from 100 acres.

MORNINGSTAR Chicago-based company best known for evaluating MUTUAL FUNDS. Morningstar rates funds from one to five stars, using a risk-adjusted performance rating in which performance equals total return of the fund.

MORTALITY TABLE chart showing rate of death at each age in terms of number of deaths per thousand.

MORTGAGE debt instrument by which the borrower (mortgagor) gives the lender (mortgagee) a LIEN on property as security for the repayment of a loan. The borrower has use of the property, and the lien is removed when the obligation is fully paid. A mortgage normally involves real estate. For personal property, such as machines, equipment, or tools, the lien is called a CHATTEL MORTGAGE. *See also* ADJUSTABLE-RATE MORTGAGE (ARM); CLOSED-END MORTGAGE; MORTGAGE BOND; OPEN-END MORTGAGE.

MORTGAGE ASSUMPTION *see* ASSUMPTION OF MORTGAGE.

MORTGAGE-BACKED CERTIFICATE security backed by mortgages. Investors receive payments out of the interest and principal on the underlying mortgages. Mortgage-backed certificates and the SECONDARY MORTGAGE MARKET in which they are traded have helped keep mortgage money available for home financing.

MORTGAGE-BACKED SECURITY type of security backed by a mortgage on real estate. *See also* COLLATERALIZED MORTGAGE OBLIGATION (CMO); MORTGAGE-BACKED CERTIFICATE.

MORTGAGE BANKER one who originates, sells, and services MORTGAGE loans, funding new loans from the proceeds of loan sales rather than from deposit accounts as in the case of a commercial bank or thrift association.

MORTGAGE BOND tax-exempt security sold by municipal and state authorities for the purpose of providing low-interest-rate MORTGAGE loans to qualified individuals For most programs, mortgage borrowers must be first-time home buyers with moderate income. The amount of these bonds that may be issued by each state each year is restricted by federal tax law.

MORTGAGE BROKER one who, for a fee, places loans with investors, but does not service such loans. *See also* MORTGAGE BANKER.

MORTGAGE COMMITMENT agreement between a lender and a borrower to lend money at a future date, subject to the conditions described in the agreement. *See also* LOAN COMMITMENT.

MORTGAGE CONSTANT percentage ratio between the annual DEBT SERVICE and the loan PRINCIPAL.

MORTGAGE CORRESPONDENT one who services loans for a fee. *See also* MORTGAGE BANKER; MORTGAGE BROKER.

MORTGAGE DEBT amount of money owed under a MORTGAGE.

MORTGAGE DISCOUNT amount of PRINCIPAL that lenders deduct at the beginning of the loan. *See also* DISCOUNT POINTS.

MORTGAGEE one who holds a LIEN on property or TITLE to property as SECURITY for a debt; lender with collateral.

MORTGAGE INSURANCE insurance generally required by lenders of those who borrow more than 80%, generally up to 95% of a home's price. It will indemnify the lender in case of foreclosure of the loan. Indemnification is typically limited to losses suffered by the lender in the foreclosure process, up to 20% of the mortgage. *See also* FHA MORTGAGE LOAN; MORTGAGE LIFE INSURANCE; PRIVATE MORTGAGE INSURANCE.

MORTGAGE INSURANCE POLICY *see* MORTGAGE LIFE INSURANCE; PRIVATE MORTGAGE INSURANCE.

MORTGAGE INSURANCE PREMIUM (MIP) the fee paid by a mortgagor to obtain MORTGAGE INSURANCE on a mortgage loan. The fee may be collected as a lump sum at loan closing or as a periodic amount included in the monthly payment, or both.

MORTGAGE INTEREST DEDUCTION *see* INTEREST DEDUCTIONS.

MORTGAGE LIEN ENCUMBRANCE on property used to secure a loan. The holder of the LIEN has a claim to the property in case of loan default. The priority of the claim depends on the order of recording and any subordination agreements. Thus a FIRST MORTGAGE generally has prior claim to all other mortgage lien holders.

MORTGAGE LIFE INSURANCE generally TERM LIFE INSURANCE to the extent of a MORTGAGE DEBT, on the life of the household money earners.

MORTGAGE NOTE the document that states the names of the borrower and lender, amount borrowed, interest rate, repayment terms, and other loan provisions. The MORTGAGE pledges property as collateral; the NOTE provides the amount of debt and repayment requirements.

MORTGAGE OUT obtain financing in excess of the cost to construct a project. Developers *mortgage out* by obtaining a permanent LOAN COMMITMENT based on a high percentage of the completed project's value. Opportunities to mortgage out have been virtually eliminated by stricter underwriting criteria.

MORTGAGE REIT REAL ESTATE INVESTMENT TRUST that lends stockholder capital to real estate builders and buyers. Mortgage REITs also borrow from banks and relend that money at higher interest rates.

MORTGAGE RELIEF acquired freedom from mortgage debt, generally through ASSUMPTION OF MORTGAGE by another party or debt retirement. In a TAX-FREE EXCHANGE, mortgage relief is considered BOOT received, causing a taxable gain to the extent of the lesser of the realized gain or the fair market value of the boot. Mortgage relief in excess of the TAX BASIS of property will result in taxable gain in the case of abandonment, which can be reduced if there are continuing obligations on the debt.

MORTGAGE SERVICING administration of a mortgage loan, including collecting monthly payments and penalties on late payments, keeping track of the amount of principal and interest that has been paid at any particular time, acting as escrow agent for funds to cover taxes and insurance, and, if necessary, curing defaults and foreclosing when a homeowner is seriously delinquent.

MORTGAGOR one who pledges property as SECURITY for a loan. *See also* MORTGAGE; MORTGAGEE.

MOST FAVORED NATION a designation by the U.S. government that lowers tariffs and other restrictions on imports from that nation. It also permits assistance from the Export-Import Bank.

MOTION STUDY process of analyzing work in order to determine the cost-efficient motions for performing tasks. Motion study, a major contribution of *scientific management*, was developed principally through the efforts of Frederick W. Taylor and Frank and Lillian Gilbreth.

MOTIVATION inner strivings of individuals that direct behavior. Unsatisfied desires create the motivation to act with purposeful behavior to achieve gratification.

MOTIVATIONAL RESEARCH studies conducted in order to determine the motivations behind consumer purchases. The research is psychologically oriented and attempts to learn why people behave as they do, why they make certain purchases, and why they respond to specific types of advertising appeals.

MOTOR FREIGHT use of trucks (as contrasted with railroad trains) to ship freight. Motor freight is frequently faster, on a door-to-door basis, than rail.

MOTOR TRUCK CARGO INSURANCE protection required under the Motor Carrier Act of 1935. The policy covers the motor truck carrier if it is legally liable for the damage, destruction, or other loss of the customer's property being shipped. This includes lost packages, broken contents, and stolen articles.

MOUSE computer input device, connected to a computer. The mouse has a roller on its bottom designed to roll along the desktop beside the computer. When the mouse is moved, the CURSOR will move along the screen in the same direction in which the mouse is being moved.

MOVEMENT
1. price changes or fluctuations in a market. For example, the stock market is described as having a strong upward or downward movement in a particular trading day or period.
2. political action. *See also* MUCKRAKER.

MOVER AND SHAKER individual who has a dramatic impact on an organization or a series of events. For example, an individual may be known as a *mover and shaker* in a particular business activity because of his ability to get things done quickly and successfully.

MOVING AVERAGE average price of a security or inventory, constructed on a fixed period and showing trends for the latest interval. For example, a 30-day *moving average* includes prices for the past 30 days. Each day the oldest price is dropped from the average and the current day's price is included.

MOVING EXPENSE DEDUCTION any amount paid to or on behalf of an individual to move to a new residence that is included in the individual's gross income as compensation for services. If the taxpayer's new job is at least 50 miles farther from his former residence than was his former job, the taxpayer is permitted a deduction for certain moving expenses incurred in connection with starting work at the new location.

MS-DOS (*M*icrosoft *d*isk *o*perating *s*ystem) OPERATING SYSTEM for most microcomputers. *See also* DISK-OPERATING SYSTEM; WINDOWS.

MTC *see* MULTISTATE TAX COMMISSION.

MUCKRAKER individual who consciously searches for corruption on the part of public officials or business and exposes it to the public. *Muckraker* described members of the American Progressive movement of political activists during the years 1890–1912 who sought to expose graft and corruption.

MUD municipal utility district, a political subdivision that provides utility-related services and may issue SPECIAL ASSESSMENT BONDS.

MULTIBUYER duplicate record on two or more customer lists, indicating that the person has made purchases from each list owner; also called *multiple buyer.* Multibuyers may be moved to a special promotion list because they have demonstrated an exceptional propensity to buy.

MULTICOLLINEARITY the presence of independent variables in regression analysis that are associated to each other (having some degree of correlation). The presence of multicollinearity implies that there are fewer data to explain the dependent variable.

MULTIEMPLOYER BARGAINING association of employers in the same industry who bargain with labor as a collectivity; also called *association bargaining.* This pattern of bargaining is characteristic of the maritime trades, printing, longshoring, trucking, clothing manufacture, construction, and coal mining.

MULTIFAMILY HOUSING residential structure with more than one DWELLING unit in the same building.

MULTIFUNCTION DEVICE (MFD), MULTIFUNCTION PRODUCT (MFP), ALL-IN-ONE an electronic device that performs more than one function. The most common MFD is a desktop printer (usually color) in combination with a SCANNER (flatbed or sheetfed); together the two operate as a digital copier. Some MFDs also incorporate fax modems or software to permit scanned documents to be faxed using a computer modem.

MULTILEVEL MARKETING (MLM) a system of retailing in which consumer products are sold by independent businessmen and women (distributors) usually in customers' homes. Distributors are also encouraged to build and manage a sales force by recruiting, motivating, supplying, and training others to sell the products or services. Distributors' compensation is then based on the sales of the entire sales force in addition to personal sales. What distinguishes *multilevel marketing* from illegal PYRAMIDING is the possibility (however small) of making money at a single level, without sponsoring representatives at lower levels.

MULTIMEDIA
1. advertising promotion that utilizes two or more MEDIA. In many cases, a primary medium is supported by a secondary medium, such as a radio or television commercial that supports a Sunday newspaper insert.
2. describes computer applications that combine text and highresolution graphics (often animated) with sound, usually using CD-ROM drives and generally requiring a sound card and speakers.

MULTINATIONAL CORPORATION (MNC) corporation that has production facilities or other fixed assets in at least one foreign country and makes its major management decisions in a global context; sometimes called *transnational corporation.*

MULTIPLE *see* PRICE-EARNINGS (P/E) RATIO.

MULTIPLE LISTING arrangement among a group of real estate BROKERS who agree in advance to provide information about some or all of their LISTINGS to the others and also to split COMMISSIONS on sales of such listings between listing and selling brokers. *See also* MULTIPLE LISTING SERVICE (MLS).

MULTIPLE LISTING SERVICE (MLS) association of real estate BROKERS who agree to share LISTINGS with one another. The listing broker and the selling broker share the COMMISSION. The MLS usually distributes a book with all listings to its members, updating it frequently. Prospective buyers benefit from the ability to select from among many homes from any member broker.

MULTIPLE LOCATIONS FORMS type of coverage of property owned by one person at several locations, including merchandise, materials, futures, furniture, specified machinery, betterments, and improvements made by tenants.

MULTIPLE-MANAGEMENT PLAN top management integrating lower and middle level managers in the planning and administration of corporate affairs. Multiple-management plans provide an enhanced opportunity for an on-the-job training and assessment process whereby future top level managers are chosen and trained.

MULTIPLE REGRESSION statistical method for analyzing the relation between several independent variables and one dependent variable.

MULTIPLE RETIREMENT AGES arrangement by which an employee can retire and receive benefits without reduction, or reduced benefits subject to a penalty. These ages can be classified in the following manner:

1. *Normal retirement*—earliest time at which an employee can retire and receive full benefits, having reached a minimum age with a minimum number of years of service.

2. *Early retirement*—earliest time that an employee can retire, having reached a minimum age and a minimum number of years of service, but there is a penalty in the form of a reduction in benefits. The reduction is usually a percentage of benefits subtracted for each month of retirement earlier than the normal retirement age.

3. *Deferred retirement*—work beyond the normal retirement age, usually an increase of benefits.

MULTIPLE SHOP having professional and nonprofessional employees represented in the same BARGAINING UNIT. All the members of the bargaining unit must agree to this type of representation under the law before the NATIONAL LABOR RELATIONS BOARD (NLRB) will certify it.

MULTIPLIER a factor, used as a guide, applied by multiplication to derive or estimate an important value. For example:

1. A GROSS RENT MULTIPLIER of 6 means that property renting for $12,000 per year can be sold for six times that amount, or $72,000.

2. A *population multiplier* of 2 means that for each job added, two people will be added to a city's population.

3. The *investment multiplier* or *Keynesian multiplier* calculates the effects of investment spending in terms of total income.

4. The *deposit multiplier* or *credit multiplier* calculates how small changes in bank reserves are converted into changes in the amount of outstanding credit and the money supply. *See also* PRICE-EARNINGS (P/E) RATIO.

MULTIPURPOSE INTERNET MAIL EXTENSIONS (MIME) an extension to Internet E-MAIL that provides the ability to transfer nontextual data, such as graphics, audio, and fax.

MULTITASKING running more than one computer application at the same time. An operating system that permits *multitasking* allows the user to be printing a document from one program while working in another, as well as downloading content from the Internet in the background.

MUNICIPAL BOND bond issued by a state or local government body such as a county, city, town, or municipal authority. Interest earned on municipal bonds is generally not taxable by the U.S. government, nor in the jurisdiction that issued it. Any gain realized from the sale of these bonds is taxable as a CAPITAL GAIN, and any loss is a capital loss, subject to the capital loss deduction.

MUNICIPAL REVENUE BOND bond issued to finance public works such as bridges or tunnels or sewer systems and supported directly by the revenues of the project. *See also* GENERAL OBLIGATION BOND.

MUNIMENTS OF TITLE documents, such as DEEDS or CONTRACTS, one uses to indicate ownership.

MURPHY'S LAW administrative aphorism stating that whatever can go wrong, will. The law originated with developmental engineer Ed Murphy in 1949, who was allegedly frustrated by a laboratory technician's error.

MUTUAL ASSOCIATION SAVINGS AND LOAN ASSOCIATION (S&L) organized as a cooperative owned by its members. Members' deposits represent shares. Shareholders vote on association affairs and receive income in the form of dividends.

MUTUAL COMPANY corporation whose ownership and profits are distributed among members in proportion to the amount of business they do with the company. The most familiar examples are: (1) mutual insurance companies, whose members are policyholders; (2) state-chartered MUTUAL SAVINGS BANKS, whose members are depositors sharing in net earnings; (3) federal savings and loan associations, MUTUAL ASSOCIATIONS whose members are depositors entitled to vote and receive dividends.

MUTUAL FUND a type of regulated INVESTMENT COMPANY that raises money from shareholders and invests it in stocks, bonds, options, commodities, or money market securities. At least 90% of its income must come from dividends, interest, and gains from the sale of securities; not more than 30% can come from stock held less than three months, options, and futures transactions. It must distribute at least 90% of its income; a corporate tax is paid on undistributed income.

MUTUAL INSURANCE COMPANY company owned by its *policy-owners;* no stock is available for purchase on the stock exchange. *See also* PARTICIPATING INSURANCE; STOCK INSURANCE COMPANY.

MUTUALITY OF CONTRACT reciprocal understanding or agreement between parties that is a requirement in the creation of a legally enforceable CONTRACT.

MUTUAL SAVINGS BANK state-chartered banks owned by depositors and operated for their benefit. Most of these banks hold a large portion of their assets in home mortgage loans. They are mostly located in the northeast United States. *See also* SAVINGS AND LOAN ASSOCIATION (S&L).

N

NAFTA *see* NORTH AMERICAN FREE TRADE AGREEMENT.

NAKED OPTION OPTION for which the buyer or seller has no underlying security position. The writer of the naked option could be subject to huge losses or gains. *See also* COVERED OPTION.

NAKED POSITION securities position that is not hedged from market risk; for example, the position of someone who writes a CALL or PUT option without having the corresponding long or short position on the underlying security.

NAME POSITION BOND FIDELITY BOND that covers an employer if employees in listed positions commit dishonest acts, such as stealing money. *See also* NAME SCHEDULE BOND.

NASD *see* NATIONAL ASSOCIATION OF SECURITIES DEALERS.

NASDAQ *see* NATIONAL ASSOCIATION OF SECURITIES DEALERS AUTOMATED QUOTATIONS.

NATIONAL ADVERTISING advertising for companies that have a nationwide market. *National advertising* refers to the fact that a company has a national target market and does not imply that the advertisement *per se* is nationwide.

NATIONAL ASSOCIATION OF CERTIFIED VALUATION ANALYSTS (NACVA) a global professional association that supports the business valuation, litigation consulting, and fraud deterrence disciplines within the CPA and professional business advisory communities. Along with its training and certification programs, NACVA offers research support, marketing tools, software, journals, reference materials, and proprietary databases to its members.

NATIONAL ASSOCIATION OF HOME BUILDERS (NAHB) organization of home builders, providing educational, political, information, and research services.

NATIONAL ASSOCIATION OF MANUFACTURERS (NAM) association of manufacturers founded in 1895 and based in Washington, D.C. It brings the manufacturing industry's views on national and international problems to government, and reviews current and proposed legislation, administrative rulings, judicial decisions, and legal matters affecting industry.

NATIONAL ASSOCIATION OF REALTORS (NAR) organization of REALTORS, devoted to encouraging professionalism in real estate activities. There are over 1 million members of NAR, 50 state associations, and several affiliates. Members are required to abide by the CODE OF ETHICS of the NAR.

NATIONAL ASSOCIATION OF SECURITIES DEALERS (NASD) organization of stock brokerage firms dealing in the OVER-THE-COUNTER (OTC) market. Operating under the supervision of the SEC, the NASD's basic purposes are to: (1) standardize practices in the field; (2) establish high moral and ethical standards in securities trading; (3) provide a representative body to consult with the government and investors on matters of common interest; (4) establish and enforce fair and equitable rules of securities trading; and (5) establish a disciplinary body capable of enforcing the above provisions.

NATIONAL ASSOCIATION OF SECURITIES DEALERS AUTOMATED QUOTATIONS (NASDAQ) computerized system that provides brokers and dealers with price quotations for securities traded OVER THE COUNTER (OTC) as well as for many New York Stock Exchange-listed securities. NASDAQ quotes are published in the financial pages of most newspapers.

NATIONAL BANK commercial bank whose charter is approved by the U.S. Comptroller of the Currency rather than by a state banking department. National banks are required to be members of the FEDERAL RESERVE SYSTEM and to belong to the FEDERAL DEPOSIT INSURANCE CORPORATION (FDIC).

NATIONAL BRAND a product distributed, sold, and known nationally, as contrasted with a STORE BRAND or generic product. Levi's is a national brand for jeans, whereas Gap does not manufacture jeans, but its stores sell jeans under their own private label.

NATIONAL BUREAU OF STANDARDS established by an Act of Congress in 1901, it conducts research providing groundwork for the nation's physical measurement system as well as scientific and technological services for industry and government.

NATIONAL BUSINESS PUBLICATIONS *see* AMERICAN BUSINESS PRESS, INC.

NATIONAL DEBT debt owed by the federal government. The national debt is made up of such debt obligations as Treasury bills, Treasury notes, and Treasury bonds. The interest due on the national debt is one of the major annual expenses of the federal government.

NATIONAL FLOOD INSURANCE PROGRAM *see* FLOOD INSURANCE.

NATIONAL INCOME NET NATIONAL PRODUCT minus indirect business taxes. This also equals the sum of all payments made to sum FACTORS of production.

NATIONALIZATION takeover of a private company's assets or operations by a government. The company may or may not be compensated for the loss of assets.

NATIONAL LABOR RELATIONS ACT (NLRA) Wagner Act (1935). Federal statute establishing COLLECTIVE BARGAINING by: (1) creating the NATIONAL LABOR RELATIONS BOARD (NLRB); (2) providing NLRB-supervised elections; (3) outlawing UNFAIR LABOR PRACTICES by employers; and (4) authorizing the NLRB to conduct unfair labor practice hearings.

NATIONAL LABOR RELATIONS BOARD (NLRB) independent agency created by Congress that oversees relationships between unions and employees. The board has the power to settle labor disputes and to enforce its judgments in the federal courts.

NATIONAL MEDIATION BOARD three-member board established by the Railway Labor Act in 1926. The National Mediation Board designates the bargaining representative for any BARGAINING UNIT included in the railway or air transport industries.

NATIONAL QUOTATION BUREAU former name of the publisher of PINK SHEETS, now Pink Sheets, LLC.

NATIONAL UNION *see* INTERNATIONAL UNION.

NATIONAL WEALTH sum total of the value of all of the capital and goods held within a nation.

NATURAL BUSINESS YEAR fiscal year based on the cycle of the given business rather than a calendar year. The year ends with inventories and activities at a low level, such as after winter shipments for a ski manufacturer.

NATURAL MONOPOLY industry in which the most efficient producer is a MONOPOLY. Most natural monopolies are UTILITIES or similar entities.

NATURAL RESOURCES actual and potential forms of wealth supplied by nature, such as coal, oil, wood, water power, and arable land. Many natural resources may be subject to DEPLETION and thus eligible for a depletion deduction.

NAVIGATION finding one's way around a complex system of menus, files, or the WORLD WIDE WEB.

NAVIGATOR a popular WEB BROWSER produced by Netscape Communications Corporation (see *http://www.netscape.com*), which is now a wholly owned subsidiary of AMERICA ONLINE.

NDA *see* NONDISCLOSURE AGREEMENT.

NEAR MONEY assets that are easily convertible into cash. Some examples are government securities, bank TIME DEPOSITS, and MONEY MARKET FUND shares. Bonds close to REDEMPTION date are also called *near money*.

NEED SATISFACTION fulfillment of a motivational desire. After need satisfaction has occurred, there is no further motivation for gratifying that need.

NEGATIVE AMORTIZATION increase in the OUTSTANDING BALANCE of a loan resulting from the failure of periodic DEBT SERVICE payments to cover required interest charged on the loan. It generally occurs under INDEXED LOANS for which the applicable interest rate may be changed without affecting the monthly payments. Negative amortization will occur if the indexed interest rate is increased and the payment is less than the interest required.

NEGATIVE CARRY situation when the cost of money borrowed to finance securities is higher than the yield on the securities. If an investor borrowed at 12% to finance, or "carry," a bond yielding 10%, the bond would have a negative carry.

NEGATIVE CASH FLOW situation in which a business spends more cash than it receives through earnings or other transactions in an accounting period.

NEGATIVE CORRELATION inverse association between two variables. As one variable becomes large, the other becomes small. Negative correlation is represented by correlation coefficients less than 0. *See also* POSITIVE CORRELATION.

NEGATIVE INCOME TAX proposed system of providing financial aid to poverty-level individuals and families, using the mechanisms already in place to collect income taxes. After filing a tax return showing income below subsistence levels, low-income people would receive a direct subsidy, called a negative income tax.

NEGATIVE LEVERAGE *see* REVERSE LEVERAGE.

NEGATIVE NET WORTH *see* DEFICIT NET WORTH.

NEGATIVE WORKING CAPITAL situation in which the current liabilities of a firm exceed its current assets. Unless the condition is corrected, the firm may not be able to pay debts when due, threatening its ability to keep operating and possibly resulting in bankruptcy.

NEGATIVE YIELD CURVE *see* INVERTED YIELD CURVE.

NEGLIGENCE lack of due care or failure to do what is reasonable and prudent under the circumstances. Omission of something that a reasonable person, guided by those considerations that ordinarily regulate the conduct of human beings, would do, or doing something that a prudent, reasonable person would not do.

NEGOTIABLE
1. something that can be sold or transferred to another party in exchange for money or as settlement of an obligation.
2. matter of mutual concern to one or more parties that involves conditions to be worked out to the satisfaction of the parties.
3. type of security the title to which is transferable by delivery.

NEGOTIABLE CERTIFICATE OF DEPOSIT above $100,000. These certificates are payable either to the bearer or to the order of the depositor and, being NEGOTIABLE, enjoy an active SECONDARY MARKET, where they trade in round lots of $5 million.

NEGOTIABLE INSTRUMENT unconditional order or promise to pay an amount of money; easily transferable from one person to another. Examples are a check, promissory note, and draft (bill of exchange).

NEGOTIABLE ORDER OF WITHDRAWAL (NOW) bank or savings and loan withdrawal ticket that is a NEGOTIABLE INSTRUMENT. The accounts from which such withdrawals can be made, called NOW accounts, are thus, in effect, interest-bearing checking accounts.

NEGOTIATED MARKET PRICE price that is set by negotiation between producers and government, usually due to wartime restrictions, unexpected shortages, or natural monopoly situations.

NEGOTIATION process of bargaining that precedes an agreement. Successful negotiation generally results in a CONTRACT between the parties. *See also* ARBITRATION; MEDIATION.

NEIGHBORHOOD district or locality characterized by similar or compatible land uses. Neighborhoods are often identified by a place name and have boundaries composed of major streets, barriers, or abrupt changes in land use.

NEIGHBORHOOD STORE retail store designed to blend in with the surrounding neighborhood and specializing in local tastes and needs.

NELLIE MAE CORPORATION division of SLM CORPORATION providing education financing for undergraduate and graduate students and families; originated in 1982 as New England Education Loan Marketing Corporation, it was acquired by SLM in 1999.

NEOCLASSICAL ECONOMICS school of economic theory that flourished from about 1890 until the advent of KEYNESIAN ECONOMICS. Neoclassical economics asserted that market forces always would lead to efficient allocation of resources and full employment.

NEPOTISM employment and economic policies practicing favoritism toward one's family. Firms give favored employment positions to family members as well as encouraging business transactions with other family members. Many U.S. businesses discourage nepotism in personnel practices.

NEST EGG assets put aside for a large purchase or a person's retirement. Such assets are usually invested conservatively.

NET
1. figure remaining after all relevant deductions have been made from the gross amount. For example, *net sales* are equal to gross sales minus discounts, returns, and allowances; *net profit* is gross profit less operating (sales, general, and administrative) expenses; *net worth* is assets (worth) less liabilities.
2. to arrive at the difference between additions and subtractions or plus amounts and minus amounts. For example, in filing tax returns, long-term capital losses are *netted* against long-term capital gains.

3. to realize a net profit, as in "last year we *netted* a million dollars after taxes."

4. short for NETWORK.

NET ASSETS difference between a company's total assets and liabilities; OWNER'S EQUITY or NET WORTH.

NET ASSET VALUE (NAV) accounting term similar in meaning to BOOK VALUE and NET WORTH; most often used in reference to the value of MUTUAL FUND and similar investment shares.

NET BOOK VALUE on FINANCIAL STATEMENTS, amount of ASSETS less LIABILITIES. *See also* BOOK VALUE.

NET CASH FLOW *see* AFTER-TAX CASH FLOW; CASH FLOW.

NET CHANGE difference between the last trading price on a stock, bond, commodity, or mutual fund from one day to the next. The net change in individual stock prices is listed in newspaper financial pages.

NET CONTRIBUTION excess of selling price over variable costs per unit; residual positive effect from an action taken. For example, an increase in sales costs of $100 generating revenue of $120 will result in a *net contribution* to the company of $20.

NET COST gross costs of purchasing an asset less income received. For example, to find the *net cost* of the insurance in a whole life policy, subtract income received or cash surrender value from the premiums paid.

NET CURRENT ASSETS difference between current assets and current liabilities; another name for WORKING CAPITAL.

NET DOMESTIC PRODUCT measure of economic activity derived by subtracting the capital consumption allowance from GROSS DOMESTIC PRODUCT (GDP).

NET EARNINGS *see* NET INCOME.

NET ESTATE ESTATE that under federal and state statutes is subject to an ESTATE TAX; generally that estate remaining after all debts of the decedent, funeral and administrative expenses, and other deductions prescribed by law have been subtracted from the GROSS ESTATE (total valuation of the estate's assets at decedent's death).

NET INCOME
In general: sum remaining after all expenses have been met or deducted; synonymous with *net earnings* and with *net profit* or *net loss* (depending on whether the figure is positive or negative).
Business: difference between total sales and total costs and expenses. Total *costs* comprise cost of goods sold including depreciation; total *expenses* comprise selling, general, and administrative expenses plus income deductions. Net income after taxes is the *bottom line*. It is out of this figure that dividends are normally paid.
Tax: *See* GROSS INCOME; TAXABLE INCOME.

NET INCOME PER SHARE OF COMMON STOCK amount of all profit or earnings allocated to each share of common stock after all costs, taxes, allowance for depreciation, and possible losses have been deducted; often referred to as EARNINGS PER SHARE (EPS). *See also* FULLY DILUTED EARNINGS PER (COMMON) SHARE.

NET INVESTMENT INCOME excess of investment income over investment expenses. Individuals are allowed to deduct for tax purposes INVESTMENT INTEREST EXPENSE to the extent of net investment income.

NETIQUETTE NETWORK etiquette, or the set of informal rules of behavior that have evolved in cyberspace, including the INTERNET and ONLINE SERVICES.

NET LEASABLE AREA in a building or project, floor space that may be rented to tenants; area upon which rental payments are based. It generally excludes common areas and space devoted to the heating, cooling, and other equipment of a building. *See also* GROSS LEASABLE AREA.

NET LEASE lease whereby, in addition to the rent stipulated, the lessee (tenant) pays such expenses as taxes, insurance, and MAINTENANCE. The landlord's rent receipt is thereby net of those expenses. *See also* GROSS LEASE.

NET LISTING listing in which the broker's commission is the excess of the sale price over an agreed-upon (net) price to the seller; illegal in some states because it may place the broker in an unethical situation.

NET LOSS when expenses for the period exceed income for the same period.

NET OPERATING INCOME (NOI) income from property or business after OPERATING EXPENSES have been deducted, but before deducting income taxes and financing expenses (INTEREST and PRINCIPAL payments).

NET OPERATING LOSS (NOL) excess of allowable DEDUCTIONS over gross income with certain specific adjustments set forth in the Internal Revenue Code, which are generally designed to limit the net operating loss deductions of individual taxpayers to business losses. Corporations that incur a net operating loss pay no tax in the current year and can claim a refund for 2 prior years' taxes paid, then carry over the NOL to as many as 20 future years.

NET OPERATING LOSS DEDUCTION deduction in one tax year of a NET OPERATING LOSS generated in another year. A net operating loss from a prior year may be shown as a deduction on the current year's tax return. An anticipated net operating loss may be deducted in a year prior to its occurrence by filing an amended return (Form 1040X or 1120X) or an application for tentative refund (Form 1045 or 1139).

NET PRESENT VALUE (NPV) method of determining whether the expected financial performance of a proposed investment promises to be adequate. *See also* DISCOUNTED CASH FLOW; INTERNAL RATE OF RETURN (IRR); PRESENT VALUE OF 1.

NET PROCEEDS amount (usually cash) received from the sale or disposition of property, from a loan or the sale or issuance of securities after deduction of all costs incurred in the transaction.

NET PROFIT amount of money earned after all expenses, including overhead, employee salaries, manufacturing costs, and advertising costs, have been deducted from the total revenue. *See also* NET INCOME.

NET PROFIT MARGIN generally, percentage of after-tax profit as a fraction of sales. *See also* GROSS PROFIT.

NET PURCHASES equals gross purchases less purchases returned and allowances, and less purchase discounts. For example, if a purchase is made for $1,000 on terms of 2/10, net/30 and there is a return of $200, assuming payment is made within the discount period, net purchases equals:

Gross Purchases	$1,000
less purchase returns	– 200
less purchase discounts	– 20
Net Purchases	$ 780

NET QUICK ASSETS cash, marketable securities, and accounts receivable minus current liabilities. Inventory is excluded in order to determine whether, if sales evaporate, a business could meet its current liabilities with the readily convertible (to cash) assets on hand. *See also* QUICK RATIO.

NET RATE effective interest rate on a loan equal to the interest divided by the proceeds received. For example, on a $1,000 discounted loan having an interest rate of 10%, the net interest would be $100/$900 = 11.1%.

NET REALIZABLE VALUE selling price of an asset, less expenses to bring it to a salable condition and less expenses of sale.

NET SALES gross sales less returns and allowances, freight out, and cash discounts allowed.

NET SURFING *see* SURFING.

NET TRANSACTION securities transaction in which the buyer and seller do not pay fees or commissions. For instance, when an investor buys a new issue, no commission is due. If the stock is initially offered at $15 a share, the buyer's total cost is $15 per share.

NETWORK a system where different computers are linked together. A LOCAL AREA NETWORK (LAN) links computers in the same or adjacent buildings together. A WIDE AREA NETWORK (WAN) links computers over a wide area—in some cases worldwide. Networks are valuable because they allow the users to share data, send electronic mail to each other, and share access to hardware devices such as printers.

NETWORKING

In general: making use of professional contacts.

Broadcast: television or radio stations and programs banded together for network broadcasting. Stations agree in affiliation contracts to broadcast the programs furnished by the network. Stations are provided with a varied program schedule, and advertisers are given the chance to tie their commercials to network programming.

Computers: connecting computers in a network.

NET WORKING CAPITAL current ASSETS less current LIABILITIES. *See also* WORKING CAPITAL.

NET WORTH the amount by which the FAIR MARKET VALUE of all assets exceeds liabilities. *See also* EQUITY.

NET YIELD return on an investment after subtracting all expenses. *See also* CURRENT YIELD; YIELD TO MATURITY.

NEW DEAL collection of political and economic policies and programs promulgated by the first two administrations of the presidency of Franklin D. Roosevelt. The New Deal policies were aimed at combating the economic miseries of the GREAT DEPRESSION.

NEW ECONOMICS revisions of KEYNESIAN ECONOMICS that appeared in the 1970s and attempted to deal with modern economic problems that did not seem to be effectively handled through Keynesian approaches.

NEW HIGH/NEW LOW stock prices that have hit the highest or lowest prices in the last year. Next to each stock's listing in a newspaper will be an indication of a new high with the letter *u* or a new low with the letter *d*. Newspapers publish the total number of new highs and new lows each day on various exchanges.

NEW ISSUE stock or bond being offered to the public for the first time, the distribution of which is covered by Securities and Exchange Commission rules. *New issue* usually refers to INITIAL PUBLIC OFFERINGS (IPOs) by previously private companies, but can include additional stock or bond issues by companies already public and often listed on the exchanges. *See also* HOT ISSUE; UNDERWRITE.

NEW LISTING SECURITY that has just begun to trade on a stock or bond exchange. A *new listing* on the New York or American Stock Exchange must meet all LISTING REQUIREMENTS and may be either an INITIAL PUBLIC OFFERING (IPO) or a company whose shares have previously traded on the NASDAQ.

NEW LONDON, CONNECTICUT, DECISION U.S. Supreme Court decision (*Kelo et al. v. City of New London et al.*) that expanded the concept of a constitutionally allowable taking of private property for public use under EMINENT DOMAIN to include takings for commercial developments that benefit the community (if only through increases in property tax revenue).

NEW MONEY amount of additional long-term financing provided to a company or government by a NEW ISSUE or issues in excess of the amount of a maturing issue or by issues that are being refunded.

NEWSGROUP a public forum or discussion area on the INTERNET where messages are posted for public consumption and response. The most famous *newsgroups* are those distributed worldwide by the *Usenet* system, covering thousands of topics.

NEWS RELEASE brief written statement or video released to the mass media announcing new products, changes in management, sales and earnings information, and other items of interest; also called *press release; see* PRESS KIT.

NEW TOWN large mixed-use development designed to provide residences, general shopping, services, and employment. The basic concept of a *new town* is to construct a community in a previously undeveloped area under a central plan to avoid unplanned development. Some European and South American countries use new towns to attract population into less developed regions. Well-known new towns in the United States include Columbia, Md., and Reston, Va.

NEW YORK COTTON EXCHANGE *see* SECURITIES AND COMMODITIES EXCHANGES.

NEW YORK CURB EXCHANGE *see* AMERICAN STOCK EXCHANGE.

NEW YORK FUTURES EXCHANGE *see* SECURITIES AND COMMODITIES EXCHANGES.

NEW YORK MERCANTILE EXCHANGE *see* SECURITIES AND COMMODITIES EXCHANGES.

NEW YORK STOCK EXCHANGE (NYSE) *see* NYSE GROUP, INC.

NEW YORK STOCK EXCHANGE COMPOSITE INDEX market-value-weighted price index for all stocks listed on the New York Stock Exchange.

NEXUS a sufficient presence within the jurisdiction of a taxing authority. The taxable income of a multistate corporation may be apportioned to a specific state only if the corporation has a sufficient *nexus* in the state. The nexus for state sales tax purposes requires a physical presence in the taxing state, and the nexus for state income tax purposes requires more than mere solicitation.

NICHE particular specialty in which a firm or person finds they prosper. Niche strategy in marketing is to market to a small but lucrative portion of the market. The small size of the niche generally ensures efficient marketing efforts and few if any direct competitors.

NIFTY FIFTY 50 STOCKS most favored by institutions. The membership of this group is constantly changing, although companies that continue to produce consistent earnings growth over a long time tend to remain institutional favorites. Nifty Fifty stocks also tend to have higher than market average price/earnings ratios since their growth prospects are well recognized by institutional investors. The Nifty Fifty stocks were particularly famous in the bull markets of the 1960s and early 1970s.

NIKKEI STOCK AVERAGE index of 225 leading STOCKS traded on the Tokyo Stock Exchange. Called the Nikkei Dow Jones Stock Average until renamed in May 1985, it is similar to the DOW JONES INDUSTRIAL AVERAGE because it is composed of representative BLUE CHIP companies (termed *first-section* companies in Japan) and is a price-weighted index.

90-DAY LETTER a formal notice after an audit indicating that a proposed deficiency will be assessed unless the taxpayer files a petition with the U.S. Tax Court.

NLA abbreviation for *net leasable area.*

NLRA *see* NATIONAL LABOR RELATIONS ASSOCIATION.

NO-BRAINER (*slang*) a decision-making situation where the correct choice is so obvious that it requires no thought.

NODES individual workstations in LOCAL AREA or WIDE AREA NETWORKS, interconnected through coaxial cables, telephone wires, or telecommunications.

NO FAULT a system of INSURANCE where all persons who are insured in an automobile accident may be compensated for any injuries resulting therefrom, without regard to who was at fault.

NO-FAULT AUTOMOBILE INSURANCE LIABILITY type of coverage in which an insured's own policy indemnifies him for bodily injury and/or property damage without regard to fault. In many instances it is difficult if not impossible to determine the original cause, such as who is at fault, in a chain car collision. In states with no-fault liability insurance, an insured cannot sue for general damage until special damages, including medical expenses, exceed a minimum amount. This is an effort to eliminate groundless suits for general damages.

NO-GROWTH description of little or no economic growth as measured by changes in the GROSS DOMESTIC PRODUCT (GDP). The U.S. economy during much of the 1970s and 1980s was characterized as *no-growth* since the gross domestic product showed only a negligible increase during much of the period.

NOI *see* NET OPERATING INCOME.

NO-LOAD FUND MUTUAL FUND offered by an open-end investment company that imposes no sales charge (load) on its shareholders. Investors buy shares in no-load funds directly from the fund companies, rather than through a broker, as is done in load funds.

NOLO CONTENDERE "I do not wish to contend, fight, or maintain [a defense]"; statement that the DEFENDANT will not contest a CHARGE made by the government. The defendant will lose the case, but this cannot be used as an admission of guilt in any other legal proceedings.

NOMINAL ACCOUNT income statement account (revenue and expense) that is closed out at the end of the year. *See also* CLOSING ENTRY; REAL ACCOUNT.

NOMINAL DAMAGES trivial sum awarded as recognition that a legal injury was sustained, though slight. Nominal damages will be awarded for a BREACH OF CONTRACT or for an intentional TORT to vindicate the PLAINTIFF'S claim where no recoverable loss can be established.

NOMINAL DOLLARS amounts that have not been adjusted to the present for inflation.

NOMINAL INTEREST RATE interest rate in terms of dollars, without adjusting for inflation. *See also* NOMINAL YIELD.

NOMINAL LOAN RATE *see* FACE INTEREST RATE.

NOMINAL RATE the rate of return on an investment that is unadjusted for the effect of inflation. It is distinguished from the real rate, which is the nominal rate less the rate of inflation.

NOMINAL SCALE observations distinguished by name alone. Types of housing would be distinguished on a *nominal scale*: single-family, patio home, condominium, or townhouse. The nominal scale is the weakest of measurements. *See also* INTERVAL SCALE; ORDINAL SCALE; RATIO SCALE.

NOMINAL WAGE evaluation of wage without considering its current purchasing value.

NOMINAL YIELD annual dollar amount of income received from a fixed-income security divided by the PAR VALUE of the security and stated as a percentage. Thus a bond that pays $90 a year and has a par value of $1,000 has a *nominal yield* of 9%, called its *coupon rate*. *See also* YIELD TO MATURITY.

NOMINEE
1. someone nominated for an elective position.
2. person or firm, such as a bank official or brokerage house, into whose name securities or other properties are transferred by agreement. Securities held in STREET NAME, for example, are registered in the name of a broker (nominee) to facilitate transactions, although the customer remains the true owner.
3. any payee who is not the actual owner of a DIVIDEND or INTEREST payment, but who would be required to furnish his/her identifying number to the payor.

NONACQUIESCENCE announcement that a court or agency will not follow a regular court decision.

NONBANK BANK an institution that provides most of the services of a bank but is not a member of the FEDERAL RESERVE SYSTEM and does not have a charter from a state banking agency. A *nonbank bank* may offer credit cards, consumer and commercial loans, savings accounts, and accounts with services similar to bank checking accounts. By avoiding government regulation, such businesses may be able to be more innovative and profitable than traditional government-regulated banks.

NONBUSINESS INCOME
1. in taxation, income from passive sources such as interest and dividends, along with nonbusiness capital gains in excess of nonbusiness capital losses. This concept is used to calculate the net operating loss deduction.
2. income from investment assets in a multistate corporation that is removed from the apportionment process and allocated to the state in which the nonbusiness asset is located.

NONCALLABLE preferred stock or bond that cannot be redeemed at the option of the issuer. A bond may offer *call protection* for a particular length of time, such as 10 years. After that, the issuer may redeem the bond if it chooses and can justify doing so.

NONCOMPETITIVE BID bids to buy U.S. Treasury bills, submitted by smaller investors through a Federal Reserve Bank, the Bureau of Federal Debt, or certain commercial banks. These bids will be executed at the average of the prices paid in all the competitive bids accepted by the Treasury. The minimum noncompetitive bid for a Treasury bill is $10,000.

NONCONFORMING LOAN home mortgage loan that does not meet the standards of, or is too large to be purchased by, FNMA or FHLMC. The INTEREST RATE is at least half a percentage point higher than for a conforming loan.

NONCONFORMING USE use of land that lawfully existed before enactment of a ZONING ORDINANCE and that may be maintained after the effective date of the ordinance, although it no longer complies with use restrictions newly applicable to the area. *See also* GRANDFATHER CLAUSE; VARIANCE.

NONCONTESTABILITY CLAUSE provision in an INSURANCE policy that precludes the insurer from disputing the validity of the policy on the basis of FRAUD or mistake after a specified period, two years in many states. If the insurer wishes to contest the policy, it must do so within the prescribed period, either by suing to cancel the policy or by asserting fraud or MISREPRESENTATION.

NONCONTRIBUTORY QUALIFIED PENSION OR PROFIT-SHARING PLAN plan funded entirely by the employer, with no employee contributions.

NONCURRENT ASSET asset not expected to be converted into cash, sold, or exchanged within the normal operating cycle of the firm, usually one year. Examples of noncurrent assets include FIXED ASSETS, such as real estate, machinery, and other equipment.

NONDISCLOSURE AGREEMENT (NDA) a contract commonly used by computer and other companies to protect the confidentiality of unreleased products and other sensitive information. In the computer world, software developers, reporters, and sometimes beta testers are often required to sign these before they are given access to information about products.

NONDISCRETIONARY TRUST investment trust that may buy only the securities on a list set forth when the trust is organized. The percentage of total assets that may be invested in a specific security or type of securities is usually predetermined. Also called *fixed investment trust.*

NONDISTURBANCE CLAUSE
1. agreement in mortgage contracts on income-producing property that provides for the continuation of LEASES in the event of loan FORECLOSURE.
2. agreement in a sales contract, when the seller retains MINERAL RIGHTS, that provides that exploration of minerals will not interfere with surface development.

NONDIVISIVE REORGANIZATION *see* SPIN-OFF.

NONDURABLE GOODS goods that do not last a long time, are quickly consumed, and so must continually be replaced by consumers. Food is the most prevalent example of nondurable goods.

NONEXCLUSIVE LISTING *see* OPEN LISTING.

NONFEASANCE nonperformance of a duty or responsibility to which one is legally bound; for example, an unfulfilled contractual duty.

NONFORFEITABLE with reference to a PENSION or a PROFITSHARING PLAN, benefits that are not conditioned upon length of service or performance requirements.

NONFORFEITURE PROVISION value in life insurance policies that entitle the insured to these choices:
1. to relinquish the policy for its CASH SURRENDER VALUE.
2. to take *reduced paid-up term insurance* instead of the cash surrender value.
3. to take *extended term insurance* for the full face amount instead of the cash surrender value.
4. to borrow from the company, using the cash value as collateral.

NONMEMBER BANK bank that is not a member of the FEDERAL RESERVE SYSTEM and is regulated by the banking laws in the state in which it is chartered.

NONMEMBER FIRM brokerage firm that is not a member of an organized exchange. Such firms execute their trades either through MEMBER FIRMS, on regional exchanges, or in the THIRD MARKET.

NONMERCHANTABLE TITLE *see* MARKETABLE TITLE.

NONMONETARY ITEM item stated in *older* dollars and therefore requiring direct adjustment in the price-level financial statements. It is any financial statement item that is not classified as a monetary item.

NONNEGOTIABLE INSTRUMENT *see* NEGOTIABLE INSTRUMENT.

NONOPERATING EXPENSE (REVENUE) expenses (income) of the business that are incidental to its main purpose. For example, the sale of land by a mattress maker provides nonoperating revenue because the land has nothing to do with the main business.

NONPARAMETRIC STATISTICS procedures not concerned with population PARAMETERS; based on distribution-free procedures.

NONPERFORMANCE failure to do something that one was legally bound to do. The nonperforming party is liable for damages or action requiring a SPECIFIC PERFORMANCE.

NONPERFORMING ASSET ASSET not effectual in the production of income. In banking, commercial loans 90 days past due and consumer loans 180 days past due are classified as *nonperforming*.

NONPRODUCTIVE not contributing to the production of the goods sought or the realization of the effects expected. Something that is nonproductive results in wasted effort and money.

NONPROFIT ACCOUNTING accounting policies, procedures, and techniques employed by nonprofit organizations. Nonprofit accounting is somewhat different for governmental units than for nongovernmental units (i.e., colleges, hospitals, voluntary health and welfare organizations, and charities).

NONPROFIT CORPORATION *see* NOT FOR PROFIT.

NONPROFIT ORGANIZATION association that is allowed to exist without paying income taxes. Most nonprofit organizations are in a socially desirable business (hospital, educational institution, charity) and those qualified by the Internal Revenue Service may receive contributions that are tax deductible to the donor. *See also* NOT FOR PROFIT.

NONPUBLIC INFORMATION information about a company, either positive or negative, that will have a material effect on the stock price when it is released to the public. Insiders, such as corporate officers and members of the board of directors, are not allowed to trade on material nonpublic information until it has been released to the public. *See also* DISCLOSURE; INSIDER.

NONRECOGNITION TRANSACTION any disposition of property in a transaction in which gain or loss is not recognized in whole or in part (e.g., a LIKE-KIND EXCHANGE).

NONRECOURSE DEBT debt for which a person has no personal liability. For example, a lender may take the property pledged as collateral to satisfy a debt, but it has no RECOURSE to other assets of the borrower. The AT-RISK RULE bars claiming tax losses beyond equity contributions where there is nonrecourse financing, except for third-party debt on real estate used in a trade or business.

NONRECURRING CHARGE one-time expense or write-off appearing in a company's financial statement; also called *extraordinary charge*. Nonrecurring charges would include, for example, a major fire or theft, the write-off of a division, and the effect of a change in accounting procedure.

NONREFUNDABLE provision in a bond INDENTURE that either prohibits or sets limits on the issuer's retiring the bonds with the proceeds of a subsequent issue, called REFUNDING. Such a provision often does not rule out refunding altogether but protects bondholders from REDEMPTION until a specified date.

NONREFUNDABLE FEE or NONREFUNDABLE DEPOSIT any charge for a product or service that will not be refunded if the product is returned or service declined; often used like a penalty charge in situations where people frequently back out of commitments.

NONRENEWABLE NATURAL RESOURCES resources that cannot be replenished. These are resources that are not capable of being restored to a former state. Once the world's oil supply is exhausted, for example, it cannot be replenished. It is therefore *nonrenewable*.

NONRESIDENT ALIEN an alien who is not a lawful permanent resident of the United States during the calendar year and who does not meet the requirements of the SUBSTANTIAL PRESENCE TEST and does not elect to be treated as a RESIDENT ALIEN.

NONSTANDARD MAIL first-class or single-piece third-class mail weighing less than one ounce and exceeding certain dimensions, namely, length of 11½ inches, height of 6⅛ inches, or thickness of 1/4 inch. *Nonstandard mail* is subject to an additional charge.

NONSTOCK CORPORATION corporation owned by its members under the membership charter or agreement, rather than through the issue of shares.

NONSTORE RETAILING retailing done without conventional store-based locations. Nonstore retailing includes such services as vending machines, direct-to-home selling, telemarketing, catalog sales, mail order, and television marketing programs.

NONTAXABLE DIVIDENDS dividends from a REGULATED INVESTMENT COMPANY (MUTUAL FUND) that were earned by the fund as interest from tax-exempt state and municipal debt obligations and other exempt obligations. At least 50% of the regulated investment company's assets must be invested in tax-exempt obligations for dividends to be tax-free.

NONTAXABLE INTEREST interest on state and municipal debt obligations (MUNICIPAL BONDS), which is generally excludable from federal TAXABLE INCOME, though interest from certain municipal bonds is subject to the ALTERNATIVE MINIMUM TAX. Qualified scholarship funding bonds and qualified fire department bonds may also be treated as state or municipal debt obligations. Interest on certain PRIVATE ACTIVITY BONDS that qualify for tax exemption is also nontaxable.

NONVERBAL COMMUNICATION *see* BODY LANGUAGE.

NONVOTING STOCK corporate securities that do not empower a holder to vote on corporate resolutions or the election of directors. Such stock is sometimes issued in connection with a takeover attempt, when management creates nonvoting shares to dilute the target firm's equity and discourage the merger attempt. PREFERRED STOCK is normally nonvoting stock.

NO-PAR STOCK stock issued with NO PAR VALUE stated in the corporate charter or on the stock certificate; also called *no-par-value stock.*

NO PAY *see* DEADBEAT.

NORM
1. rule or standard considered to be acceptable behavior in a group or society.
2. in psychology, average standard of achievement on a test for a selected group.

NORMAL COST for a DEFINED-BENEFIT PENSION PLAN, generally represents the portion of the economic cost of the participant's anticipated pension benefits allocated to the current plan year. It is often different from accounting accrual cost or the cash outlay required in that year.

NORMAL DISTRIBUTION in STATISTICS, completely defined by two parameters, the MEAN (measure of central location) and the STANDARD DEVIATION (measuring the dispersion or variability). It is most often used in statistical procedures to detect variability away from the norm.

NORMAL GOOD a good for which demand increases when income increases, all other things being equal.

NORMAL OPERATING CYCLE the period of time required to convert cash into raw materials, raw materials into inventory finished goods, finished good inventory into sales and accounts receivable, and accounts receivable into cash.

NORMAL PRICE price that one would expect to prevail in a market over the long term. Unexpected shortages or gluts can cause prices to deviate from the normal price.

NORMAL PROFIT profit that is sufficient to keep a producer in business in a certain industry over the long run. Any profit over the normal profit, according to economic theory, will induce additional producers to enter a market and thus drive profit down to the normal level over time.

NORMAL RETIREMENT AGE earliest age at which an employee can retire without a penalty reduction in pension benefits after having (1) reached a minimum age and (2) served a minimum number of years with an employer. Historically, this has been 65 years, but many private pension plans now envision earlier or later normal retirement ages. *See also* MULTIPLE RETIREMENT AGES.

NORMAL WEAR AND TEAR physical DEPRECIATION arising from age and ordinary use of a property. *See also* USEFUL LIFE.

NORMATIVE ECONOMICS label attributed to the economist Milton Friedman concerning economic policy that attempts to have direct effects in markets and in the economic process; contrasts with *positive economics*.

NORTH AMERICAN FREE TRADE AGREEMENT (NAFTA) law passed in 1993. Affects trade, investment, and social conscience (environment, labor abuses, retraining). NAFTA is to completely end U.S. and Mexican tariffs and quotas on imports and agricultural products mostly over the mid-1990s, with some requiring 15 years from 1993 to phase out. Applies only to goods made from labor and materials originated within the countries; other imports are acceptable only if they are substantially transformed within the United States, Mexico, or Canada. Major commodities affected are automobiles, textiles and apparel, and agriculture.

NORTH AMERICAN INDUSTRY CLASSIFICATION (NAICS) SYSTEM system for classifying business activities developed jointly by the United States, Canada, and Mexico. Uses six-digit codes and will replace the U.S. STANDARD INDUSTRIAL CLASSIFICATION (SIC) SYSTEM. Its data can be used to measure productivity, construct input-output relationships, and estimate employment-output relationships and other statistics.

NO-STRIKE CLAUSE no-strike pledge by a union, usually in return for management agreement to accept binding ARBITRATION of grievances. A no-strike clause requires the union not to strike over grievances while the union and management accept neutral binding arbitration of unresolved grievances.

NOTARIZE attest, in one's capacity as a NOTARY PUBLIC, to the genuineness of a signature.

NOTARY PUBLIC public officer authorized to administer oaths, to attest to and certify certain types of documents, to take DEPOSITIONS, and to perform certain acts in commercial matters. The seal of a notary public authenticates a document.

NOTE written paper that acknowledges a DEBT and promises payment to a specified party of a specific sum, and that describes a time of MATURITY that is either definite or will become definite. *See also* PROMISSORY NOTE.

NOTEBOOK COMPUTER a small, lightweight portable computer, also called a *laptop*. The LCD screen is back-hinged and folds open for viewing. Though designed to be powered by rechargeable batteries, usually also has an adapter for AC current. Most notebook computers also have connections for external monitors, keyboards, and pointing devices, and some come with *docks* that facilitate attachment to these peripherals.

NOTE PAYABLE written promise to pay a certain amount of money at a certain time.

NOTE RECEIVABLE one's right in a PROMISSORY NOTE in which the MAKER agrees to pay a certain amount of money at a certain time. *See also* NOTE PAYABLE.

NOT FOR PROFIT organization in which no stockholder or trustee shares in profits or losses; usually exists to accomplish some charitable, humanitarian, or educational purpose; also called *nonprofit*. Such groups are exempt from corporate income taxes (except for UNRELATED BUSINESS INCOME), and donations to these groups may be tax deductible for the donor. Some examples are hospitals, colleges and universities, and foundations.

NOTICE information concerning a fact actually communicated to a person by an authorized person, or actually derived by him from a proper source. Notice to a DEFENDANT of a lawsuit that has been instituted against him or of an ACTION in which he may have an interest to defend is accomplished by service of process on him.

NOTICE OF DEFAULT letter sent to a defaulting party as a reminder of the DEFAULT. It may state a GRACE PERIOD and the PENALTIES for failing to cure the default.

NOTICE OF DEFICIENCY a notice sent by the IRS to a taxpayer determining the tax due from the taxpayer and a summary showing how the deficiency was computed. To be valid, a notice of deficiency must be sent to a taxpayer's last known address.

NOTICE TO QUIT
  1. notice to a tenant to VACATE rented property.
  2. notice sometimes used by a tenant who intends to vacate on a certain date.

NOT RATED (NR) indication used by securities rating services (such as Standard & Poor's or Moody's) and mercantile agencies (such as Dun & Bradstreet) to show that a security or a company has not been rated. It has neither negative nor positive implications.

NOVATION substitution of another PARTY for one of the original parties to a CONTRACT, with the consent of the remaining party. The old contract is then extinguished, and a new contract, with the same content but with at least one different party, is created. A novation often involves a transaction whereby the original debtor is discharged from liability to his creditor by substitution of a second debtor.

NOW *see* NEGOTIABLE ORDER OF WITHDRAWAL.

NOW ACCOUNT *see* NEGOTIABLE ORDER OF WITHDRAWAL.

NSF nonsufficient funds CHECK. If the drawee (bank) discovers that the drawer lacks funds to cover the presented check, the drawee can dishonor the check, and the presenter is powerless to make the drawee pay.

NUISANCE
  1. anything that disturbs the free use of one's property, or that renders its ordinary use uncomfortable.
  2. in tort law, a wrong arising from unreasonable or unlawful use of property to the annoyance or damage of another or of the public. *See also* ATTRACTIVE NUISANCE.

NUKE (*slang*) to intentionally delete the entire contents of a given directory, hard drive, or other storage device of a computer.

NULL AND VOID that which cannot be legally enforced, as with a CONTRACT provision that is not in conformance with the law.

NULL HYPOTHESIS the tested statement in a statistical procedure, designated as H0. The tested statement is called the *null hypothesis* because it is often in the form, "No relationship exists between x and y." When the statistical test cannot disprove the null hypothesis, it is termed "failure to reject the null hypothesis," rather than acceptance. Statistical testing does not prove hypotheses; rather it disproves them via rejection. *See also* ALTERNATIVE HYPOTHESIS; HYPOTHESIS.

NUNCUPATIVE WILL oral will, which is seldom valid.

NUMBER CRUNCHER person who spends much time calculating and manipulating numbers; also, computer that performs calculations involving very many numbers.

NUMERIC KEYPAD on a computer keyboard, separate set of keys beside the main alphabetic keypad that contains the digits 0 to 9 and a decimal point key. The digits are arranged in the same way as they are on an adding machine. A numeric keypad is quicker to use than the number keys on the regular keyboard row.

NYSE GROUP, INC. a HOLDING COMPANY that, through its subsidiaries, is a leading global multi-asset financial marketplace that operates multiple securities market centers, including the New York Stock Exchange (the NYSE) and NYSE Arca (formerly known as the Archipelago Exchange, or Arca Ex, and the Pacific Exchange).

Through these market centers, the NYSE Group is a leader in securities listings and market information products and services and offers a range of investment vehicles and order execution services.

NYSE is the world's largest and most liquid equities market where customers can choose between the floor-based auction market and sub-second electronic trading. The NYSE provides a reliable, orderly, and efficient marketplace where investors meet directly to buy and sell listed companies' common stock and other securities. On an average day, over 1.8 billion shares valued at more than $69 billion trade on the NYSE, where the total global MARKET CAPITALIZATION for its listed companies is $22.5 trillion.

NYSE Arca is the first open, all-electronic stock market in the United States enabling customers to trade equity securities, including those listed on NYSE Arca, the NYSE, and other U.S. equities markets, and options products. NYSE Arca's trading platform links traders to multiple U.S. market centers where buyers and sellers meet directly in a highly liquid electronic environment without intermediaries for fast order execution and open, direct, and anonymous market access.

O

OAG *see* OFFICIAL AIRLINE GUIDE.

OBJECTIVE
1. free of personal bias and opinion, as in an *objective* evaluation.
2. ultimate goal or target of an individual's or a group's efforts and strategy, as in final *objective*.

OBJECTIVE VALUE value set by the market. *See also* MARKET VALUE.

OBJECT LINKING AND EMBEDDING (OLE) a method of inserting information from one computer application into another. For example, a drawing created in CorelDRAW! can be inserted into a Microsoft Word document. The OLE object may be *embedded*, in which case it is merely a static copy of the original drawing, or *linked*, in which case it will reflect any changes made to the original drawing. In either case, double-clicking on the drawing in Word calls up a CorelDRAW! window, with all its menus and toolbars, for editing the drawing within Word. OLE superseded an older feature of Windows called *dynamic data exchange* (DDE).

OBJECT-ORIENTED PROGRAMMING a style of computer programming that entails building independent pieces of code that interact with each other. JAVA and C++ are object-oriented programming languages.

OBLIGATION BOND type of mortgage bond in which the face value is greater than the value of the underlying property. The difference compensates the lender for costs exceeding the mortgage value.

OBLIGEE person in whose favor an obligation is entered into.

OBLIGOR person who binds himself to another; one who has engaged to perform some obligation; one who makes a BOND.

OBRA *see* OMNIBUS BUDGET RECONCILIATION ACT OF 1993.

OBSERVATION TEST physical and visual verification by inspection of financial statement items or activities. The external auditor observes and evaluates how company employees conduct a variety of accounting-related tasks such as documenting the existence and valuation of assets, safeguarding assets, approving expense accounts, and counting inventory.

OBSOLESCENCE process by which property becomes useless, not because of physical deterioration, but because of changes outside the property, notably scientific or technological advances. *See also* ECONOMIC DEPRECIATION.

OCCUPANCY LEVEL percentage of currently rented units in a building, city, neighborhood, or complex. Generally hotels need a 60% occupancy rate to break even, whereas office buildings, shopping centers, and apartments break even at 80% to 90%. *See also* VACANCY RATE.

OCCUPANCY, OCCUPANT use of real estate; one living in or using real estate.

OCCUPATION trade, job, business, or vocation of an individual. An *occupation* is the principal means by which one earns a livelihood.

OCCUPATIONAL ANALYSIS process of describing an occupation in terms of several characteristics, including the purposes, task characteristics, task duties, necessary skills, and abilities. Upon completion of an occupational analysis it is possible to create a JOB DESCRIPTION and a JOB SPECIFICATION.

OCCUPATIONAL GROUP grouping of classes of responsibilities within the same broad occupational category, such as marketing, accounting, and management.

OCCUPATIONAL HAZARD condition surrounding a work environment that increases the probability of death, disability, or illness to a worker. This class of hazard is considered when writing WORKERS' COMPENSATION insurance or determining which underwriting classification to select for life or health insurance.

OCCUPATIONAL SAFETY AND HEALTH ADMINISTRATION (OSHA) office that administers and enforces the federal Occupational Safety and Health Act, regulating safety and health in the workplace.

OCCUPATIONAL TAXES state or local taxes applied to various trades or businesses (e.g., taxicab permits and liquor store licenses), or a fee to practice a profession (e.g., accounting, law, medicine).

OCEAN MARINE PROTECTION AND INDEMNITY INSURANCE coverage for bodily injury and property damage liability excluded under standard ocean marine INSURANCE policy. Coverage includes protection of wharfs, docks, and harbors; bodily injury; cost of removing the wreck if ship is sunk; and the cost of disinfecting and quarantining a ship.

OCONUS *o*utside *con*terminous *U*nited *S*tates. Federal per diem rates for lodging, meals, and incidental expenses for travel *OCONUS* are published under the Federal Travel Regulations and updated periodically. *See also* CONUS.

OCR optical character recognition, used to convert scanned text documents to editable text files.

ODD LOT in the SECURITIES trade, stocks or bonds in a block of fewer than 100 shares.

ODD-VALUE PRICING setting retail prices below even dollar amounts, such as $5.99, $0.39, and $98.99. Odd-value pricing is based on a psychologically unproven assumption that consumers will feel they are not paying full value for an item and are thus getting a better value for their dollar.

OEM original equipment manufacturer. A company that assembles complete pieces of equipment from parts. *OEM* is also used as an adjective to describe software bundled with a computer or supplies provided initially with computer peripherals or sold by the manufacturer for use in its product. The term is also often used to avoid responsibility; for example, software publishers usually do not provide support for OEM (bundled) software.

OEX pronounced as three letters, Wall Street shorthand for the Standard & Poor's 100 stock index, which is composed of stocks for which options are traded on the CHICAGO BOARD OPTIONS EXCHANGE (CBOE). OEX index options are traded on the CHICAGO BOARD OF TRADE (CBOT), and futures are traded on the CHICAGO MERCANTILE EXCHANGE (CME).

OFF-BALANCE-SHEET FINANCING financing that does not add debt on a balance sheet and hence does not affect borrowing capacity as it would be determined by financial ratios. The most common example would be a lease structured as an OPERATING LEASE rather than a CAPITAL LEASE. GENERALLY ACCEPTED ACCOUNTING PRINCIPLES (GAAP) require that information be provided in financial statements about *off-balance-sheet financing* involving credit, market, and liquidity risk. *See also* SPECIAL-PURPOSE ENTITY.

OFFER
1. manifestation of willingness to enter into an AGREEMENT.
2. promise, commitment to do or refrain from doing some specified thing in the future.
3. in the securities trade, indication of price and volume available from open market sellers of stocks and bonds.
4. UNDERWRITING in which a broker offers a large quantity of a specific issue at a fixed price, called an *offering.*

OFFER AND ACCEPTANCE *see* AGREEMENT OF SALE; CONTRACT.

OFFEREE person who receives an offer from another. The offeree may accept or reject the offer.

OFFERER party who presents an offer. The offer may be rescinded by the offerer anytime before it is accepted.

OFFERING *see* PUBLIC OFFERING.

OFFERING CIRCULAR *see* PROSPECTUS.

OFFERING DATE date on which a distribution of stocks or bonds will first be available for sale to the public.

OFFERING PRICE price per share at which a new or secondary distribution of securities is offered for sale to the public; also called PUBLIC OFFERING price.

OFFEROR *see* OFFERER.

OFFICE the name of software suites by both Microsoft and Corel. The "premium" or "professional" versions usually include a word processor, a spreadsheet program, a database manager, presentation graphics software, a personal information manager, an Internet browser, and other utilities.

OFFICE BUILDING a structure used primarily for the conduct of business, such as administration, clerical services, and consultation with clients and associates. Such buildings can be large or small, and may house one or more business concerns.

OFFICE MANAGEMENT organizing and administering the activities that normally occur in any day-to-day business office environment. An *office manager* is one who has the administrative responsibilities of office management.

OFFICE OF INTERSTATE LAND SALES a division of the Department of Housing and Urban Development that oversees the sale of building lots or recreational lots across state borders.

OFFICE OF MANAGEMENT AND BUDGET (OMB) at the federal level, agency within the Office of the President responsible for: (1) preparing and presenting to Congress the President's budget; (2) working with the Council of Economic Advisers and the Treasury Department in developing a fiscal program; (3) reviewing the administrative policies and performance of government agencies; (4) advising the President on legislative matters.

OFFICE PARK a planned development specially designed for OFFICE BUILDINGS and supportive facilities, such as restaurants. Some office parks are designed to attract specific tenants, such as a research park or a medical services park.

OFFICIAL AIRLINE GUIDE (OAG) detailed listing of the origin and destination of commercial flights and other information, published by Dun & Bradstreet and revised monthly.

OFFICIAL EXCHANGE RATE EXCHANGE RATE of a country's currency as set by the government of that country. Many countries, including the United States, do not have official exchange rates for their currencies.

OFFICIAL RESERVES deposits of gold, currency, and SDRs held at the IMF by member countries.

OFFLINE not connected. A printer is *offline* when it does not have an active connection to the computer; Internet users can download mail and NEWSGROUP messages and work *offline*, that is, not connected to their ISP.

OFF PEAK period of minimum usage, often used as a basis for usage charges. The telephone company has off-peak rates during the latenight and holiday periods.

OFF-PRICE STORES retail stores offering merchandise at prices less than other retail stores. They acquire out-of-season products and distressed merchandise from other retailers, including bankruptcies, and from manufacturers having production overruns. Off-price stores can threaten retailers carrying name-brand merchandise at full retail prices.

OFF-SALE DATE date that newsstand returns are tabulated and reported back to the wholesaler or distribution. *See also* ON-SALE DATE.

OFFSET
Accounting: amount equaling or counterbalancing another amount on the opposite side of the same ledger or the ledger of another account.
Banking: legal right of a bank to seize deposit funds to cover a loan in default, called *right of offset.*
Printing: common printing method, in which an intermediate blanket cylinder is used to transfer an image from the image carrier to the target material (such as a piece of paper). Also called *offset lithography.*
Securities, commodities, options: (1) closing transaction involving the purchase or sale of an option having the same features as one already held. (2) HEDGE, such as the short sale of a stock to protect a capital gain.

OFFSHORE
1. term used in the United States for any financial organization with headquarters outside the country. Many banks have *offshore* subsidiaries that engage in activities that are either heavily regulated or taxed or are not allowed under U.S. law.
2. oil and gas drilling ventures in the sea.

OFFSHORE EXCHANGE RATE the market price of a regulated currency outside the legal jurisdiction of the regulating government. It could be described as a legal black market rate.

OFF-SITE COST expenditure related to construction that is spent away from the place of construction. In creating a subdivision, offsite costs include the costs of extending roads, sewers, and water lines to the SITE. Site costs include landscaping and other site improvements.

OFF THE BALANCE SHEET financial transaction where the property involved does not appear on the BALANCE SHEET. For example, a company may lease rather than buy real estate or transportation equipment. Depending on the lease terms, a CPA may not require the asset and obligation for future lease payments to be on the balance sheet.

OFF THE BOOKS payments or BARTER of which no formal record is kept so that both parties can hide the transaction from taxation and/or other government regulation.

OFF TIME period of time when not in service. Off time for a computer or machine is when it is not scheduled for use or needs maintenance, alterations, or repairs.

OF RECORD refers to the recording of DOCUMENTS such as DEEDS or MORTGAGES with the appropriate entity as well as to the testimony recorded as the official transcript of a legal case. The *attorney of record* is the official designate of a party upon whom service of papers may be made.

OIL AND GAS LEASE agreement that gives the right to explore for oil, gas, and sometimes other minerals and to extract them from the ground.

OIL AND GAS LIMITED PARTNERSHIP partnership consisting of one or more limited partners and one or more general partners that is structured to find, extract, and market commercial quantities of oil and natural gas.

OIL PATCH states in the United States that produce and refine oil and gas, including Texas, Oklahoma, Louisiana, California, and Alaska. Economists refer to *oil patch* states when assessing the strength or weakness of a region of the country tied to movements in oil prices.

OLE (pronounced *olé) see* OBJECT LINKING AND EMBEDDING.

OLIGOPOLY
1. industry in which a few large sellers of similar products, such as automobiles, dominate the market.
2. condition of a specific products market so dominated. An oligopolistic industry is more concentrated than a competitive one but less so than a MONOPOLY. *See also* OLIGOPSONY.

OLIGOPSONY market in which a few large buyers control the purchase of a product; in the tobacco industry there are about five major companies that purchase from numerous growers.

OMBUDSMAN
1. originally government official appointed to act as a representative for citizen complaints and queries concerning governmental activities.
2. any organizational official who serves to channel any outside or inside complaints or questions concerning an organization.
3. a member of the IRS Commissioner's immediate staff who directs the IRS's PROBLEM RESOLUTION PROGRAM.

OMITTED DIVIDEND dividend that was scheduled to be declared by a corporation, but instead was not voted for the time being by the board of directors. Dividends are sometimes omitted when a company has run into financial difficulty and its board decides it is more important to conserve cash than to pay a dividend to shareholders. *See also* CUMULATIVE PREFERRED STOCK.

OMNIBUS BUDGET RECONCILIATION ACT OF 1993 legislation signed into law by President Clinton after passing both House and Senate by the narrowest of margins. Some highlights effective at that time were tax rate increases for high-income earners (new 36 and 39.6%

tax brackets) and higher ALTERNATIVE MINIMUM TAX rates. Social Security recipients with incomes above $44,000 ($34,000 if single) might have to pay tax up to 85% of their benefits. The Act also increased the gasoline tax by 4.3 cents and raised the corporate tax to 35% for income above $1 million. Many provisions have since been altered.

ON ACCOUNT
In general: in partial payment of an obligation.

Finance: on credit terms. It applies to a relationship between a seller and a buyer wherein payment is expected sometime after delivery and the obligation is not documented by a NOTE; synonymous with *open account.*

ON CONSIGNMENT *see* CONSIGNMENT.

ON DEMAND when asked for. For example, a note payable *on demand* is payable when the sum is requested. It is called a DEMAND NOTE if no due date is included.

ONE-HUNDRED-PERCENT LOCATION location where a retail establishment would achieve maximum sales volume compared to other locations in the local market area.

O*NE MINUTE MANAGER* title of book by Kenneth Blanchard and Spencer Johnson; simplification of management issues into superficial one-minute praise or reprimand; oversimplification of complex management situations.

ONE-TIME BUYER customer on a LIST who has made only one purchase from the list owner since his or her initial order. *See also* MULTI-BUYER.

ONE-TIME RATE rate paid by an advertiser who uses less space than is necessary to qualify for a discount. The one-time rate, therefore, is a full-cost advertising rate without any discounts.

ONLINE connected to a computer, NETWORK, or host, especially to the Internet; *contrast with* OFFLINE. A user may consult *online* Help (application documentation in searchable form stored in the computer) or "go online" to check E-MAIL.

ONLINE DATA BASE information transmitted by telephone, microwaves, etc. that may be accessed with a decoding device (called a MODEM) and displayed on a monitor or as a printout. A database for accountants may consist of information such as tax laws and regulations, accounting practices and footnote references, industry data, financial information on companies, investment information, or economic and political statistics.

ONLINE SERVICE a commercial service that provides access to electronic mail, news services, specialized forums and chat rooms, and the Internet for a monthly fee. Examples include AMERICA ONLINE, COMPUSERVE, and PRODIGY. *Contrast with* INTERNET SERVICE PROVIDER.

ONLINE SYSTEM in computer applications, system where data are entered into a device, such as a terminal, that is connected directly to a computer. The user can interact with the computer through a terminal.

ON MARGIN *see* MARGIN.

ON ORDER goods ordered but are not yet paid for or received.

ON-SALE DATE date new issues of a periodical are scheduled to be delivered by the WHOLESALER or DISTRIBUTOR to newsstands for sale to the public. The on-sale date drives the publication and printing process.

ON-THE-JOB TRAINING (OJT) job-related training that occurs on the actual job site while engaged in the occupation; hands-on instruction.

OPEC *O*rganization of the *P*etroleum *E*xporting *C*ountries, 11-nation oil-producing organization made up of Algeria, Indonesia, Iran, Iraq, Kuwait, Libya, Nigeria, Qatar, Saudi Arabia, the United Arab Emirates, and Venezuela. Since 1965 its international headquarters have been in Vienna, Austria.

OPEN
Banking: to establish an account or a LETTER OF CREDIT.
Finance: unpaid balance of an account.
Securities: status of an order to buy or sell securities that has still not been executed; GOOD-TILL-CANCELED ORDER. *See also* OPEN ORDER.
Computers: call a file up from disk in order to work on it. You *create* a new file and *open* a saved one.

OPEN ACCOUNT
1. unpaid CREDIT ORDER; also called *open credit.*
2. credit relationship between a buyer and a seller.

OPEN BID offer to perform a contract by quoting the price for the materials or work, but with the right to reduce that price to meet the quotes made by others for the same job. In a governmental contract bid, a bidder using an *open bid* may agree to lower the quoted price if competitors outbid him.

OPEN DATING expiration date understandably stated up front on a retail-packaged food item subject to deterioration to aid consumers in determining the product's useful life. Open dating is a relatively recent consumer marketing practice.

OPEN DISTRIBUTION distribution of the same merchandise within a specified region or area by different dealers. In this type of distribution, dealers can carry competitive lines and there are no restrictions regarding the number of products a dealer can sell, offer for sale, or deliver to retailers.

OPEN-DOOR POLICY
1. management policy of encouraging a relaxed environment with employees by leaving the manager's door open to encourage informal employee interaction.

2. national trading policy where citizens and products of foreign countries receive equal treatment with domestic citizens and products.

OPEN ECONOMY economy in which foreign investment, imports, and exports are easy to accomplish and play a substantial role in economic life.

OPEN-END
Broadcast:
1. ending to a network program or commercial that is left blank for local advertising.
2. radio or television program with no specific scheduled completion time. For example, a radio talk show is sometimes scheduled to go on until its subject matter is exhausted, rather than rigidly adhere to the usual time schedule.
3. unscheduled termination of a television or radio program. A sudden cessation of programming may be due to a special news alert or may be caused by technical difficulties.

Production: envelope that opens at the end rather than at the side.

OPEN-END CREDIT revolving LINE OF CREDIT offered to consumers by banks, savings and loans, and other lenders. After the line of credit has been set up with a particular limit, consumers can borrow up to that limit using a credit card, check, or cash advance.

OPEN-END INVESTMENT COMPANY a MUTUAL FUND that accepts new investments at all times.

OPEN-END LEASE lease agreement that provides for an additional payment after the property is returned to the lessor, to adjust for any change in the value of the property.

OPEN-END MANAGEMENT COMPANY INVESTMENT COMPANY that sells mutual funds to the public. The term arises from the fact that the firm continually creates new shares on demand. Mutual fund shareholders buy the shares at NET ASSET VALUE and can redeem them at any time at the prevailing market price. *See also* CLOSED-END MUTUAL FUND.

OPEN-END MORTGAGE MORTGAGE under which the mortgagor (borrower) may secure additional funds from the mortgagee (lender), usually stipulating a ceiling amount that can be borrowed.

OPEN ENROLLMENT PERIOD a brief period, 10 to 30 days, when employees who have not previously signed up for a certain type of insurance may do so. There may be exclusions, however, such as for preexisting conditions.

OPEN FORM (REPORTING FORM) single policy covering all insurable property of specified type(s) at all locations of an insured business. The form is appropriate for the business that has several locations. *See also* BLANKET INSURANCE.

OPEN HOUSE method of showing a home for sale whereby the home is left open for inspection by interested parties. It frequently occurs on weekends, with banners placed on the lot to attract attention.

OPEN HOUSING condition under which housing units may be purchased or leased without regard for such matters as the ethnic or religious characteristics of the buyers or tenants.

OPENING
1. price at which a security or commodity starts a trading day.
2. short time frame of market opportunity, also called an *opening in the market* or a *window of opportunity.*

OPEN INTEREST total number of contracts in a commodity or options market that are still outstanding, that is, they have not been exercised, closed out, or allowed to expire.

OPEN LISTING in real estate, LISTING given to any number of brokers without liability to compensate any except the one who first secures a buyer who is ready, willing, and able to meet the terms of the listing or secures the seller's acceptance of another offer. The sale of the property automatically terminates all open listings. *See also* EXCLUSIVE AGENCY LISTING.

OPEN MARKET COMMITTEE *see* FEDERAL OPEN MARKET COMMITTEE (FOMC).

OPEN-MARKET OPERATIONS activities by which the securities department of the Federal Reserve Bank of New York—popularly called the DESK—carries out instructions of the FEDERAL OPEN MARKET COMMITTEE (FOMC) designed to regulate the money supply. Such operations involve the purchase and sale of government securities, which effectively expands or contracts funds in the banking system.

OPEN-MARKET RATES interest rates on various debt instruments bought and sold in the open market that are directly responsive to supply and demand. Such open-market rates are distinguished from the DISCOUNT RATE, set by the Federal Reserve Board as a deliberate measure to influence other rates, and from bank commercial loan rates, which are directly influenced by Federal Reserve policy.

OPEN MORTGAGE MORTGAGE that has matured or is overdue, and the property is therefore open to FORECLOSURE at any time.

OPEN OPERATING SYSTEM computer operating system that will operate with many different computer processors, affording portability to APPLICATION SOFTWARE and computer data. *See also* UNIX.

OPEN ORDER buy or sell order for securities that has not yet been executed or canceled; GOOD-TILL-CANCELED ORDER.

OPEN OUTCRY method of trading on a commodity exchange. Traders must shout out their buy or sell offers. When a trader shouts he wants to sell at a particular price and someone else shouts he wants to buy at that price; the two traders have made a contract that will be recorded.

OPEN SHOP enterprise that employs workers without regard to whether they are members of a labor union. *See also* CLOSED SHOP.

OPEN SPACE land, within a developed area, that is left undeveloped and serves as an amenity to surrounding occupants.

OPEN STOCK retail items that can be purchased singly or in a particular pattern. The retailer having open stock makes no promise to have the item always in stock, but will usually order it from the manufacturer unless it has been discontinued.

OPEN-TO-BUY method for a retailer to adjust merchandise purchases to reflect changes in sales, markdowns, and so on. The open-to-buy method provides flexibility for the retailer in purchasing new inventory as the old items sell out and to take advantage of special product deals.

OPEN UNION union that admits any qualified worker to its membership without requiring the payment of an initiation fee, high dues, examinations, or any other practice designed to discourage membership.

OPERATING CYCLE average time period between buying inventory and receiving cash proceeds from its eventual sale. It is determined by adding the number of days inventory is held and the collection period for accounts receivable.

OPERATING ENVIRONMENT shell surrounding the DISK OPERATING SYSTEM (DOS) of a personal computer. It turns the display into a desktop that is basically a menu from which one selects and runs PC applications.

OPERATING EXPENSE amount paid to maintain property, such as property taxes, utilities, hazard insurance. It excludes financing expenses, depreciation, and income taxes.

OPERATING INCOME *see* NET OPERATING INCOME; OPERATING PROFIT (LOSS).

OPERATING INTEREST form of ownership in mineral property in which the owner is responsible for operating costs. Royalties, production payments, and net profit interests are not operating interests.

OPERATING LEASE type of LEASE, normally involving equipment, whereby the contract is written for considerably less than the life of the equipment and the lessor handles all maintenance and servicing; also called *service lease*. Operating leases are the opposite of CAPITAL LEASES, where the lessee acquires essentially all the economic benefits and risks of ownership.

OPERATING LEVERAGE *see* LEVERAGE.

OPERATING PROFIT (LOSS) difference between the revenues of a business and the related costs and expenses, excluding income or expenses from sources other than its regular activities and before income deductions; synonymous with *net operating profit (loss)* and *operating income (loss)*.

OPERATING RATIO any of a group of ratios that relate various income and expense figures from the profit and loss statement to each other and to balance sheet figures. Among the ratios used are sales to cost of goods sold, operating expenses to operating income, net profits to gross income, and net income to net worth.

OPERATING STATEMENTS financial reports on the cash flow of a business or property. *See* CASH FLOW; RENT ROLL.

OPERATING SYSTEM program that controls a computer and makes it possible for users to enter and run other programs. Most computers are set up so that, when first turned on, they automatically begin running a small program supplied in read-only memory or occasionally in another form (*see* BOOT). This program in turn enables the computer to load its operating system from disk or tape. *See also* DISK-OPERATING SYSTEM; MS-DOS.

OPERATIONAL AUDIT process to determine ways to improve production. *Contrast with* EXTERNAL AUDIT, which relates to financial statements.

OPERATIONAL CONTROL power of management over the daily activities of a business.

OPERATIONAL OBJECTIVES short-term organizational objectives necessary to achieve longer-term tactical and strategic goals. They are usually managed by supervisory personnel concerned with immediate results.

OPERATIONS RESEARCH (OR) research concerned with the development of mathematical models of repetitive activities, using numerous variables, such as traffic flow, assembly lines, military campaigns, and optional production scheduling. Operations research makes extensive use of computer simulation.

OPINION reason given for a court's judgment, finding, or conclusion. *See also* ACCOUNTANT'S OPINION.

OPINION LEADER individual whose ideas and behavior serve as a model to others. Opinion leaders communicate messages to a primary group, influencing the attitudes and behavior change of their followers. Therefore, in certain marketing instances, it may be advantageous to direct the communications to the opinion leader alone to speed the acceptance of an advertising message.

OPINION OF TITLE certificate, generally from an attorney, as to the validity of TITLE to property being sold. Based upon an attorney's opinion of title, a TITLE INSURANCE company insures title to the property.

OPM

1. other people's money; on Wall Street, use of borrowed funds by individuals or companies to increase the return on invested capital. *See also* LEVERAGE.
2. options pricing model. *See also* BLACK-SCHOLES OPTION PRICING MODEL.

OPPORTUNITY COST

In general: price or rate of return that the best alternative course of action would provide.

Corporate finance: in evaluating a CAPITAL INVESTMENT project, return that capital would earn on the highest yielding alternative investment involving similar risk, as compared to the projected return on the proposed project.

OPT decide or make a choice. For example, an individual may opt to lease rather than purchase facilities.

OPTIMUM CAPACITY level of output of manufacturing operations that produces the lowest cost per unit.

OPTION

1. things one purchases to add to a basic product, such as air conditioning for a motor vehicle.
2. alternative courses of action that face a decision maker.
3. the right, but not obligation, to buy or sell property that is granted in exchange for an agreed-upon sum. If the right is not exercised after a specified period, the option expires and the option buyer forfeits the money. *See also* CALL OPTION; NAKED OPTION; PUT OPTION.

OPTIONEE one who receives or purchases an option.

OPTION HOLDER someone who has bought a CALL or PUT OPTION but has not yet exercised or sold it. A call option holder wants the price of the underlying security to rise; a put option holder wants it to fall.

OPTIONOR one who gives or sells an option.

OPTION TO PURCHASE a contract that gives one the right (but *not* the obligation) to buy a property within a certain time, for a specified amount, and subject to specified conditions.

ORAL CONTRACT one that is not in writing or that is not signed by the parties. Oral contracts for most purposes are enforceable, but contracts for the sale of real estate must be in writing.

OR BETTER indication, abbreviated OB on the order ticket of a LIMIT ORDER to buy or sell securities, that the broker should transact the order at a price better than the specified limit price if a better price can be obtained.

ORDER

Commercial law: payee's request to the maker, as on a check, stating, "pay to the order of (when presented by) John Doe."

Investments: instruction to a broker or dealer to buy or sell securities or commodities. Securities orders fall into four basic categories: market order, limit order, time order, and stop order.

Law: direction from a court of jurisdiction; regulation.

Trade: request to buy, sell, deliver, or receive goods or services that commits the issuer of the order to the terms specified.

ORDER BILL OF LADING negotiable bill of lading that can be negotiated like any other NEGOTIABLE INSTRUMENT, so that the shipper can sell it to anyone, not just the intended recipient of the goods. The bill requires the carrier to release the goods only when the bill of lading is given him by the recipient.

ORDER CARD ORDER FORM printed on a BUSINESS REPLY CARD.

ORDER FORM
1. form used to request merchandise, usually from a wholesaler, manufacturer, or direct-mail retailer.
2. document provided by a DIRECT MARKETING FIRM to a customer so that order information can be communicated back to the marketer. It is essential that order forms capture all the information required by the seller without being difficult, time-consuming, or confusing for the buyer.

ORDER NUMBER reference number used by a wholesaler, manufacturer, or retailer to identify a particular order.

ORDER PAPER NEGOTIABLE INSTRUMENT that by its term is payable to a specified person or his ASSIGNEE, rather than, for instance, to cash or to bearer. The PAYEE must be named or otherwise indicated with reasonable certainty. *See also* BEARER PAPER.

ORDER-POINT SYSTEM predetermined point at which inventory is automatically reordered. When inventory drops to the order point, the reordering process is triggered. Presumably the order point is the amount needed until stocks can be replenished, including a margin for safety.

ORDER PROCESSING activities involved in managing the details of preparing and receiving a customer order.

ORDER TAKER sales representative who takes customer orders without giving sales presentations.

ORDINAL SCALE observations distinguished by relative amounts, such as ranks. For example, one can evaluate competitive products on an ordinal scale from best to worst by using a letter-grade system. *See also* INTERVAL SCALE; NOMINAL SCALE; RATIO SCALE.

ORDINANCE local law that applies to persons and things subject to the local JURISDICTION. Usually it is an act of a city council or similar body and has the same force as a statute when it is duly enacted.

ORDINARY AND NECESSARY BUSINESS EXPENSES tax term that allows a current deduction for business expenses; contrasted with CAPITAL EXPENDITURE and *unreasonable expense*. An ordinary and necessary business expense of a sole proprietor would appear on Schedule C of Form 1040.

ORDINARY ANNUITY series of equal or nearly equal payments, each payment occurring at the end of each equally spaced period. *See also* ANNUITY IN ADVANCE.

ORDINARY COURSE OF BUSINESS common practices of commercial transactions; refers to a necessary activity that is normal and incidental to the business.

ORDINARY INCOME income that is fully subject to ordinary income tax rates (for example, interest income, salary income), as distinguished from income that is subject to the benefit of special tax rates for CAPITAL GAINS. The tax rate for capital gains is less than the ordinary income rate.

ORDINARY INCOME PROPERTY for charitable contribution purposes, property whose sale at FAIR MARKET VALUE on the date of the contribution would have resulted in ORDINARY INCOME or in short-term CAPITAL GAIN. It includes INVENTORY, works of art or manuscripts created by the donor, and CAPITAL ASSETS held one year or less.

ORDINARY INTEREST simple interest based on a 360-day year rather than a 365-day year; the latter is called *exact interest.* The difference between the two bases when calculating daily interest on large sums of money can be substantial. The ratio of ordinary interest to exact interest is 1.0139.

ORDINARY LOSS for income tax purposes, loss that is deductible against *ordinary income*; usually more beneficial to a taxpayer than a CAPITAL LOSS, which has limitations on deductibility.

ORE, OREO abbreviations for *other real estate; other real estate owned.* Generally, FORECLOSED PROPERTY held by lending institutions. Shown in an account of a bank or savings and loan association that includes property other than real estate used for bank operations.

ORG *see* DOMAIN.

ORGANIZATION structure of roles and responsibilities functioning to accomplish predetermined objectives. Organizations have grown tremendously in size in the twentieth century and are found in all parts of the private and public sectors.

ORGANIZATIONAL BEHAVIOR academic field of study concerned with human behavior in organizations; also called organizational *psychology.* It covers topics such as MOTIVATION, GROUP DYNAMICS, leadership, organization structure, decision making, careers, conflict resolution, and ORGANIZATIONAL DEVELOPMENT. When this subject is taught in business schools, it is called *organizational behavior;* when it is taught in psychology departments, it is called *organizational psychology.*

ORGANIZATIONAL CHART chart showing the interrelationships of positions within an organization in terms of authority and responsibility. There are basically three patterns of organization: *line organization, functional organization,* and *line and staff organization.*

ORGANIZATIONAL PLANNING process of transforming organizational objectives into specific management strategies and tactics designed to achieve the objectives. Organizational planning is one of the most important management responsibilities.

ORGANIZATIONAL PSYCHOLOGY *see* ORGANIZATIONAL BEHAVIOR.

ORGANIZATIONAL STRUCTURE apportionment of responsibility and AUTHORITY among the members of an organization. FUNCTIONAL ORGANIZATION, MATRIX ORGANIZATION, and LINE ORGANIZATION are three common types of organizational structure.

ORGANIZATION COST amounts spent to begin a business enterprise, such as legal fees, business filing fees, and franchise acquisition.

ORGANIZATION DEVELOPMENT planned, systematic process in which behavioral science principles and practices are used to improve organizational functioning; also called *organizational development* or *OD.*

ORGANIZATION FOR ECONOMIC COOPERATION AND DEVELOPMENT (OECD) a group of the major Western economic powers that cooperate to improve international economic development.

ORGANIZATION MAN, ORGANIZATION WOMAN individual whose behavior and lifestyle slavishly conform to the social mores of an organization; derived from William F. Whyte's book *The Organization Man.*

ORGANIZATION, QUALIFIED *see* QUALIFIED ORGANIZATION.

ORGANIZED LABOR unionized labor. The AFL-CIO is the largest union representing organized labor in the United States.

ORIENTATION
1. position of a structure on a site relative to sunlight angles and prevailing winds.
2. program or lecture to a newcomer in a school or company.
3. describing the nature of a person's strength, such as having a technical *orientation.*

ORIGINAL COST
1. in accounting, all costs associated with the acquisition of an asset.
2. in public utilities accounting, the acquisition cost incurred by the entity that first devotes a property to public use; normally the utility company's cost for the property.

ORIGINAL ENTRY entry in a JOURNAL, such as the first entry to record a sale or purchase.

ORIGINAL EQUIPMENT MANUFACTURER (OEM) a manufacturer of parts that are used in the assembly of name brands, especially of cars and computers. It implies that the parts are of better quality than might be found on the replacement parts market.

ORIGINAL EQUITY the amount of cash initially invested by the underlying owner. Distinguished from SWEAT EQUITY, capital calls.

ORIGINAL ISSUE DISCOUNT (OID) discount from PAR VALUE at the time a bond is issued. The most extreme version of an original issue discount is a ZERO COUPON BOND, which is originally sold far below par value and pays no interest until it matures. The tax treatment of original issue discount bonds is complex. Generally, OID must be amortized over the life of the debt obligation, which in turn increases the BASIS of the bond.

ORIGINAL MATURITY interval between the issue date and the maturity date of a bond, as distinguished from current maturity, which is the time difference between the present time and the maturity date.

ORIGINAL ORDER first order received from a particular customer. It is important to track the SOURCES of original orders so that efforts to create new first-time buyers can be concentrated on the best sources.

ORIGINATION FEE a lender's charge to a borrower, especially for a mortgage loan to cover the costs of issuing the loan, such as the salesman's commission. It may cover a credit check, appraisal, and title expenses. If the fee is a discount point and is only for the use of money, the fee is considered interest and may be deductible (for purchase of a home) or amortizable (for refinancing of a home). *See also* POINTS.

ORIGINATOR
1. bank, savings and loan, or mortgage banker that initially made the mortgage loan comprising part of a pool of mortgages. *See also* PASS-THROUGH CERTIFICATE.
2. investment banking firm that worked with the issuer of a new securities offering from the early planning stages and that usually is appointed manager of the underwriting SYNDICATE.
3. in banking terminology, initiator of money transfer instructions.

OSHA *see* OCCUPATIONAL SAFETY AND HEALTH ADMINISTRATION.

OTB
1. abbreviation for off-track betting on races.
2. *see* OPEN-TO-BUY.

OTC *see* OVER THE COUNTER.

OTHER INCOME heading on a profit and loss statement for income from activities not in the normal course of business; sometimes called *other revenue.* Examples are interest on customers' notes, dividends and interest from investments, profit from the disposal of assets other than inventory, gain on foreign exchange, and miscellaneous rent income.

OTHER PEOPLE'S MONEY *see* OPM; LEVERAGE.

OUTBID placing a higher bid than a competitor. A person who has been outbid has lost the auction to the highest bidder.

OUTCRY MARKET market in which prices are set by rapid, continuous negotiation among buyers and sellers. Typical outcry markets are those on the floors of COMMODITY EXCHANGES.

OUTLET STORE retail store, operated by a manufacturer, which provides an outlet for selling the manufacturer's irregular, overrun, or end-of-season merchandise. Although it is not always the case, outlet stores are often located close to the manufacturer.

OUT-OF-POCKET EXPENSES expenditures out of a taxpayer's own funds for business or personal use. For example, unreimbursed out-of-pocket expenditures for telephone, uniforms, or equipment incurred in rendering services to a charitable organization may be deductible as a charitable contribution.

OUT OF THE MONEY option whose STRIKE PRICE for a stock is higher than the current market value in the case of a call, or lower in the case of a put. *See also* EXERCISE PRICE.

OUTPLACEMENT job placement assistance and programs administered by organizations implementing DOWNSIZING or other staff reductions. Although actual outplacement activities vary from one organization to another, depending on their needs and capabilities, essential activities usually include résumé preparation instruction, career and personal counseling, and office space with secretarial assistance and use of telephone and fax. Some organizations sponsor job fairs and advertise their available employees. The purpose of *outplacement* activities is to assist separated employees in coping with the pressures of termination while helping them to seek new employers. *See also* REDUCTION IN FORCE.

OUTPUT the amount produced; also, results provided by a computer, as in computer *output.*

OUTSIDE DIRECTOR member of a company's BOARD OF DIRECTORS who is not an employee of the company. Such directors are considered important because they are presumed to bring unbiased opinions to major corporate decisions and they also can contribute diverse experience to the decision-making process.

OUTSIDE THE BOX *see* THINKING OUTSIDE THE BOX.

OUTSOURCING having a service or product supplied or manufactured by another, who could be a manufacturer, merchant wholesaler, agent, or broker.

OUTSTANDING
1. unpaid; ACCOUNTS RECEIVABLE and debt obligations of all types.
2. not yet presented for payment, as a check or draft.
3. stock held by shareholders, shown on corporate balance sheets under the heading of capital stock ISSUED AND OUTSTANDING.

OUTSTANDING BALANCE amount currently owed on a DEBT.

OUTSTANDING CHECK *see* OUTSTANDING.

OUTSTANDING CAPITAL STOCK shares in the hands of stockholders. Outstanding shares are issued shares minus treasury shares. Dividends are based on outstanding shares. *See also* TREASURY STOCK.

OVERAGE
1. too much; opposite of *shortage*.
2. in leases for retail stores, amount to be paid, based on gross sales, over the base rent. *See also* OVERRIDE; PERCENTAGE LEASE.

OVERALL RATE OF RETURN (OAR) percentage relationship of net operating income divided by the purchase price of property. *See also* CAPITALIZATION RATE.

OVER-AND-SHORT difference between recorded sales data and audited statements. Over-and-short is usually the result of errors in making change and the handling of receipts.

OVERBOOKED condition of hotel, airline, or other business that accepts more reservations for a certain date or flight than it can offer accommodations. No-shows (people who have reserved but who do not arrive and do not cancel) are used to justify overbookings.

OVERBOUGHT description of a security or a market that has recently experienced an unexpectedly sharp price rise and is therefore vulnerable to a price drop, called a CORRECTION by technical analysts, because there are few buyers left to drive up the price further. The opposite condition is *oversold*— when there are few sellers left and the price would be expected to rise.

OVERBUILDING a situation in a given area where there has been more real estate construction than the market can economically support.

OVERCHARGE retail price charged that is greater than the actual retail price of an item. Overcharges are usually the result of errors and must be refunded to the customer.

OVERDRAFT extension of credit by a lending institution. An *overdraft* check for which there are not sufficient funds (NSF) available may be rejected (bounced) by the bank. A bounced-check charge will be assessed on the check writer's account. Alternatively, the bank customer may set up an *overdraft* loan account, which will cover NSF checks.

OVERFLOW error condition that arises when the result of a calculation is a number too big to be represented on an electronic computer or calculator.

OVERHANG sizable block of real estate, securities, or commodities contracts that, if released on the market, would put downward pressure on prices. Examples of overhang include shares held in a dealer's inventory, a large institutional holding, a secondary distribution still in registration, and a large commodity position about to be liquidated.

OVERHEAD indirect expenses of running a business not directly associated with a particular item or service sold. For example, wages paid to factory workers and the cost of production materials are direct costs. Electricity, insurance, and benefits paid to workers are overhead expenses. By applying a factor called the *burden rate,* cost accounting attempts to allocate overhead, where possible, to the cost of goods sold.

OVERHEATING term describing an economy that is expanding so rapidly that economists fear a rise in INFLATION. In an overheated economy, too much money is chasing too few goods, leading to price rises, and the productive capacity of a nation is usually nearing its limit.

OVERIMPROVEMENT land use considered too valuable for the land, such as a single-family home worth $500,000 situated on a relatively undesirable lot worth $5,000.

OVERISSUE shares of CAPITAL STOCK used in excess of those authorized. Preventing overissue is the function of a corporation's REGISTRAR (usually a bank acting as agent), which works closely with the TRANSFER AGENT in canceling and reissuing certificates presented for transfer and in issuing new shares.

OVERKILL expensive promotional effort that produces diminishing returns because it repels rather than attracts consumer interest.

OVERPAYMENT money received from a credit buyer that exceeds the amount due. Unless the payment is for a continuous service that can be extended, such as a newspaper subscription, the amount of the overpayment must be refunded or must be credited to the buyer's account to be applied against future purchases.

OVERPRODUCTION excessive production; supply beyond market demand at remunerative prices; glut. *See also* OVERRUN.

OVERRIDE
1. fee paid to someone higher in the organization, or above a certain amount.
2. ESTATE carved out of a working interest in an oil or gas lease.
3. to go beyond an agreement or to ignore part of a contract.
4. in government, legislative body casting enough votes to overturn a veto by the executive branch.

OVERRUN production beyond the production limits. Overruns can occur because of estimating errors, reduction in order size, or attempts to take advantage of excess materials. *See also* OVERPRODUCTION.

OVERSELL continue a sales presentation after the customer has agreed to buy. Once the sale has been made, salespeople who keep talking run the risk that the customer will hear something unfavorable and cancel the order.

OVERSHOOT exceed a target figure, such as an economic goal or an earnings projection.

OVER (SHORT) difference between initially recorded store sales figures and actual cash or audited figure. The discrepancy might be caused by human error in making change or recording sales slips. If a cash register contains more money than expected, it is over; if less, it is short.

OVERSOLD description of a stock or market that has experienced an unexpectedly sharp price decline and is therefore due, according to some proponents of TECHNICAL ANALYSIS, for an imminent price rise.

OVER THE COUNTER (OTC)
1. security that is not listed and traded on an organized exchange.
2. market in which securities transactions are conducted through a telephone and computer network connecting dealers in stocks and bonds, rather than on the floor of an exchange.
3. drugs that are available without a prescription.

OVER-THE-COUNTER MEDICINE nonprescription medications that are legally sold over the counter in a retail store. Over-the-counter medicines can be purchased in any quantity without restrictions at the retail store level.

OVER-THE-COUNTER RETAILING store-based retailing operations where merchandise is sold "over-the-counter" at stated prices.

OVERTIME time worked in excess of an agreed upon time for normal working hours by an employee. Hourly or nonexempt employees must be compensated at the rate of one and one-half their normal hourly rate for overtime work beyond 40 hours in a WORKWEEK. Working on holidays or weekends is sometimes referred to as overtime work.

OVERTRADING
Finance: practice of a firm that expands sales beyond levels that can be financed with normal WORKING CAPITAL.
Securities: (1) practice whereby a member of an underwriting group induces a brokerage client to buy a portion of a new issue by purchasing other securities from the client at a premium; (2) excessive buying and selling by a broker in a *discretionary account. See also* CHURNING.

OVERVALUED description of a stock whose current price does not seem justified. It is therefore expected that the stock will drop in price.

OVERVALUED CURRENCY currency whose value is artificially higher than its market value because of governmental support.

OVERWRITE record computer data in a disk location formerly occupied by other data. If you save a new file under the same name as an older file, the older file will be *overwritten*.

OWNER the person who has legal TITLE to property; the person in whom ownership, dominion, or title of property is vested. *See also* OWNER OF RECORD.

OWNER FINANCING same as SELLER FINANCING.

OWNER OF RECORD the person(s) who, according to the public records, is/are the owner(s) of a particular property.

OWNER-OPERATOR individual who owns as well as operates his own business or the equipment used in business for the purpose of earning income. For example, truckers often are *owner-operators* of their trucks.

OWNERS AND CONTRACTORS PROTECTIVE LIABILITY INSURANCE endorsement to OWNERS, LANDLORDS, AND TENANTS LIABILITY POLICY, MANUFACTURERS AND CONTRACTORS LIABILITY INSURANCE, or other liability policies for business firms that provide liability coverage for an insured who is sued because of negligent acts or omissions of an independent contractor or subcontractor resulting in bodily injury and/or property damage to a third party.

OWNER'S EQUITY portion of a company belonging to the owners, represented by capital investments and accumulated earnings less any dividends or other financial obligation. *See also* STOCKHOLDERS' EQUITY.

OWNERS, LANDLORDS, AND TENANTS LIABILITY POLICY coverage for bodily injury and property damage liability resulting from the ownership, use, and/or maintenance of an insured business's premises as well as operations by the business anywhere in the United States or Canada.

OWNERSHIP exclusive right of possessing, enjoying, and disposing of a thing; often said to include the concepts of POSSESSION and of TITLE, thus being broader than either.

OWNERSHIP FORM method of owning real estate, which affects income tax, estate tax, continuity, liability, survivorship, transferability, disposition at death and at bankruptcy. Ownership forms include: CORPORATION; JOINT TENANCY; LIMITED PARTNERSHIP; PARTNERSHIP; S CORPORATION; LIMITED LIABILITY COMPANY; LIMITED LIABILITY PARTNERSHIP; TENANCY BY THE ENTIRETIES; TENANCY IN COMMON; and TENANCY IN SEVERALTY.

P

PA, P.A. *see* professional association.

PACESETTER something that sets the standard for others to follow. A machine, fashion, or process that is widely copied and imitated is the *pacesetter* for the industry.

PACIFIC STOCK EXCHANGE *see* REGIONAL STOCK EXCHANGE.

PACKAGE
In general: set of items sold as one; also called *package deal.*
Advertising: television or radio programming available for purchase by advertisers either singly or as a discounted package deal.
Direct mail:
1. components constituting a direct-mail promotion piece. Packages usually include the outer envelope, the reply envelope, the order form, and a letter.
2. multiple pieces of mail, usually presorted, batched by destination, and bound together for handling by the U.S. Postal Service.
Merchandising: container or wrapper used to present individual items of merchandise for sale or for shipping to buyers.

PACKAGE BAND advertisements, announcements, or special price offers printed on a strip of paper that forms a band around a package.

PACKAGE CODE identification used by direct marketers to track a particular mailing package. *Package codes* are important when testing a new package against a control package, so that response to each promotion can be compared. '

PACKAGE DESIGN
In general: planning and fashioning the complete form and structure of a product's package. In creating a new design or revamping an existing design, the following aspects of a product's package are usually reviewed: size and shape, color, closure, outside appearance, protection and economy, convenience, labeling, and the packaging material's effect on the environment.
Direct mail: creating and developing the complete assemblage of a direct mail PACKAGE, including the envelope, letter, brochure, premium slip, and reply device.

PACKAGED GOODS consumer products packaged by manufacturers and sold through retail outlets. Food, tobacco, toiletries, health and beauty aids, and household products are typically involved in this product classification.

PACKAGE MORTGAGE MORTGAGE arrangement whereby the principal amount loaned is increased because personalty, such as appliances, as well as realty serve as collateral.

PACKAGING LAWS *see* LABELING LAWS.

PACKET a unit of data sent across a NETWORK. When a large block of data is to be sent over a network, it is broken up into several *packets*, sent, and then reassembled at the other end.

PACKING LIST statement of the contents of a container, usually put into the container so that the quantity of merchandise may be counted by the person who opens the container.

PAC MAN DEFENSE in corporate mergers and acquisitions, transaction in which a target company turns the tables and makes a counteroffer to buy the shares of an unwelcome suitor. The name is derived from the electronic video game.

PADDING adding unnecessary material or expenses for the purpose of increasing the size or volume, as for example, *padding* an expense account to increase the company's reimbursement.

PAGINATION process of dividing a document into pages. Many computer word processors offer a "paginate" command that shows you where page breaks will occur in the printed text.

PAID-IN CAPITAL capital received from investors in exchange for stock, as distinguished from capital generated from earnings or donated. The paid-in capital account includes capital stock and contributions of stockholders credited to accounts other than capital stock, such as an excess over PAR VALUE.

PAID-IN SURPLUS amount that stockholders contributed in excess of the corporation's PAR VALUE.

PAID STATUS customer RECORD status that indicates whether and how the order was paid. Status types include CASH ORDER, paid CREDIT ORDER, credit card order, claims-paid complaint, unpaid credit order, and complimentary subscription.

PAID-UP POLICY life insurance policy in which all premiums have been paid. Some policies require premium payments for a limited number of years, and if all premium payments have been made over those years, the policy is considered paid in full and requires no more premium payments. The policy remains in force until the INSURED dies or cancels the policy.

PAINTING THE TAPE
1. illegal practice by manipulators who buy and sell a particular security among themselves to create artificial trading activity, causing a succession of trades, which will lure unwary investors to the "action." The manipulators hope to sell at a profit.
2. consecutive or frequent trading in a particular security, resulting in its repeated appearances on the ticker tape. Such activity is usually attributable to special investor interest in the security.

PAIRED SHARES COMMON STOCKS of two companies under the same management that are sold as a unit, usually appearing as a single certificate printed front and back. Also called *Siamese shares* or *stapled stock*.

PALM PILOT *see* PDA.

P&I *see* PRINCIPAL AND INTEREST (PAYMENT).

P&L *see* PROFIT AND LOSS STATEMENT.

PANIC BUYING/SELLING flurry of buying or selling accompanied by high volume done in anticipation of sharply rising or falling prices. A sudden news event will trigger panic buying or selling, leaving investors little time to evaluate the fundamentals of individual stocks or bonds.

PAPER credit given, evidenced by a written obligation that is backed by property; slang for debt, as when a seller finances a sale.

PAPER GOLD certificates that can be converted into gold at the offices of the issuer of the paper, private or government. Paper gold often is used in exchange since it is much less cumbersome than the actual metal.

PAPER MONEY certificates issued by government (and, at times, private entities) that are generally accepted within the economy as reliable media of exchange.

PAPER PROFIT (LOSS) unrealized GAIN (LOSS) in an investment or portfolio. Paper profits and losses are calculated by comparing the current market price to the investor's cost.

PAR equal to the established value; face amount or stated value of a negotiable instrument, stock, or bond, and not the actual value it would receive on the open market. Bills of exchange, stocks, and the like are *at par* when they sell for their stated value.

PARADIGM SHIFT change in a model or pattern that has been nearly universally accepted. For example, a change in consumer buying habits from buying airline tickets through travel agents to buying them over the Internet would be a *paradigm shift*.

PARALEGAL one not a member of the BAR who is employed, usually by a law office, to perform a variety of tasks associated with a law practice, any of which may be performed properly and conveniently by one not trained or authorized to practice as a lawyer.

PARALLEL LOAN an arrangement by which two independent firms with separate foreign subsidiaries in their respective countries make offsetting loans to each other's subsidiaries. This procedure makes the companies indifferent to exchange rate changes. *See also* LINK FINANCING.

PARALLEL PORT an output device that lets a computer transmit data to another device using parallel data transmission—that is, several bits sent simultaneously over separate wires. PC parallel ports are usually designated LPT1, LPT2, and so on. *Contrast with* SERIAL PORT.

PARALLEL PRINTER a printer connected to a computer's PARALLEL PORT.

PARALLEL PROCESSING simultaneous performance of two or more tasks by a computer. For example, parallel processing takes place when one instruction is being run while another instruction is being read from memory.

PARAMETER measure used to describe a population, such as the number of rental units in a given city. Parameters are known for certain. If the number is based on a sample rather than actual count, it is called an *estimate*.

PAR BOND bond that is selling at par, the amount equal to its nominal value or face value. A corporate bond redeemable at maturity for $1,000 is a *par bond* when it trades on the market for $1,000. *See also* BOND DISCOUNT.

PARCEL
1. piece of property under one ownership; lot in a SUBDIVISION.
2. package sent through a common carrier.
3. to distribute or separate into parts, as in "to parcel out."

PARCEL POST class of mail service, also known as fourth class, offered by the U.S. Postal Service for mailing merchandise or printed matter weighing more than 16 ounces. The contents are subject to postal inspection. The weight limit is 70 pounds per package; length plus girth cannot exceed 108 inches. Special rules and rates apply to certain items.

PARENT COMPANY company that owns or controls subsidiaries through the ownership of voting stock. A parent company is usually an operating company in its own right. Where it has no business of its own, the term HOLDING COMPANY is often preferred.

PARETO'S LAW theory that the pattern of income distribution is constant, historically and geographically, regardless of taxation or welfare policies; also called *law of the trivial many and the critical few* or *80-20 law.* Thus, if 80% of a nation's income will benefit only 20% of the population, the only way to improve the economic lot of the poor is to increase overall output and income levels. Pareto is also credited with the concept, called *Paretian optimum* or *Pareto optimality,* that resources are optimally distributed when an individual cannot be moved into a better position without putting someone else into a worse position.

PARITY characteristic of a number being odd or even. When groups of bits (1's and 0's) are being transmitted or stored by computer, an extra bit is often added so that the total number of 1's is always odd (or, alternatively, always even). This is called the parity of the data.

PARITY PRICE price for a commodity or service that is pegged to another price or to a composite average of prices based on a selected prior period. As the two sets of prices vary, they are reflected in an index number on a scale where 100 is parity.

PARKING placing assets in a safe investment while other investment alternatives are under consideration. For instance, an investor will *park* the proceeds of a stock or bond sale in an interest-bearing MONEY MARKET FUND while considering what other stocks or bonds to purchase.

PARKINSON'S LAW rule of the paralysis of organizations propounded by C. Northcote Parkinson. Under Parkinson's law organizations become infected with a disease termed *injelitis*, which causes the organization to become moribund, resulting in little constructive activity and accomplishment.

PARLIAMENTARY PROCEDURE formal procedure followed in the conduct of any meeting, usually following Roberts' Rules of Order. Parliamentary procedures are followed to expedite the orderly conduct of a meeting's agenda.

PARTIAL DELIVERY DELIVERY where a broker does not transfer the full amount of a security or commodity called for by a contract. For example, 10,000 shares were to be delivered, but only 7,000 shares are transferred. *See also* GOOD DELIVERY.

PARTIAL-EQUILIBRIUM ANALYSIS approach of economic analysis that focuses only upon the part of the economy that is affected by the factors being studied.

PARTIAL INTEREST ownership of a part of the ownership rights to a parcel of real estate, such as mineral rights, easements on another's property, etc.

PARTIAL LIQUIDATION distributions from a corporation to shareholders, which may receive CAPITAL GAIN treatment. To qualify, distributions to a corporate shareholder must be one of a series of distributions in redemption of all of the stock of a corporation pursuant to a plan.

PARTIAL RELEASE provision in a MORTGAGE that allows some of the property pledged to be freed from serving as COLLATERAL when certain conditions are met.

PARTIAL TAKING acquisition by CONDEMNATION of only part of the property or some property rights. It requires just COMPENSATION.

PARTICIPATING INSURANCE policy that pays a dividend to its owner.

PARTICIPATING POLICY INSURANCE COVERAGE under which the insured receives DIVIDENDS on company earnings, which may be applied to reduce the amount of PREMIUM that must be paid by the insured.

PARTICIPATING PREFERRED STOCK PREFERRED STOCK that, in addition to paying a stipulated dividend, gives the holder the right to participate with the common stockholder in additional distributions of earnings under specified conditions.

PARTICIPATION CERTIFICATE certificate representing an interest in a POOL of funds or in other instruments, such as a mortgage pool. *See also* PASS-THROUGH SECURITY.

PARTICIPATION LOAN
1. loan made by more than one lender and serviced by one of the participants, called the *lead bank* or *lead lender.*
2. mortgage loan, made by a lead lender, in which other lenders own an interest.

PARTICIPATIVE BUDGETING system enabling key employees in a department to provide input into the budgetary process. Thus, the accountant receives useful budgeting information from those affected by the budget.

PARTICIPATIVE LEADERSHIP consultative management method that encourages others to participate. Leadership decisions are achieved as the end result of group participation. *Participative management is* the process of consultative management.

PARTICIPATIVE MANAGEMENT an open form of management where employees have a strong decision-making role. Participative management is developed by managers who actively seek a strong cooperative relationship with their employees. The advantages of participative management include increased productivity, improved quality, and reduced costs. *See also* PARTICIPATIVE LEADERSHIP.

PARTITION
1. judicial separation of interests in land of joint owners or tenants in common, so that each may take possession of, enjoy, and control his separate estate.
2. device to separate space, as used to break a large office area into smaller portions.
3. a portion of a computer's HARD DISK that is treated by the computer as if it were a separate disk drive. A very large drive is more efficient if partitioned because the file clusters are smaller (so that small files do not waste so much space) and because the computer does not have to search as large an area for data. Communication between partitions, however, is more cumbersome.

PARTNER a member of a partnership, which may be a SYNDICATE, association, pool, JOINT VENTURE, or other unincorporated organization. Partners generally include in their personal tax returns their pro rata share of partnership ORDINARY INCOME, CAPITAL GAIN, CHARITABLE CONTRIBUTIONS, etc. *See also* GENERAL PARTNER; LIMITED (SPECIAL) PARTNER.

PARTNER'S DRAWING *see* DRAWING ACCOUNT.

PARTNERSHIP organization of two or more persons who pool some or all of their money, abilities, and skill in a business and divide profit or loss in predetermined proportions. PARTNERS are individually responsible for debts of the partnership. However, in a LIMITED PARTNERSHIP, limited partners generally assume no monetary responsibility beyond the capital originally contributed. Death of a GENERAL PARTNER will normally terminate the partnership.

PARTNERSHIP LIFE AND HEALTH INSURANCE protection to maintain the value of a business in case of death or disability of a partner. Upon the death or long-term disability of a partner, insurance can provide for the transfer of a deceased or disabled partner's interest to the surviving partner according to a predetermined formula.

PARTS PER MILLION (PPM) ratio to determine the molecular presence of a particular substance per million parts in relation to others. Often used in chemical analysis, ppm is a critical measure for determining the significant presence or absence of a particular substance in a medium.

PART-TIME employment that is less than a full-time organizational commitment on the part of the employee. Part-time employees usually do not receive the same health insurance, retirement, and other benefits full-time employees receive. For qualified retirement plan vesting purposes, *part-time* refers to an employee with less than 1,000 hours of service during a 12-month period.

PARTY a person or entity.

PARTY LINE telephone service available at a lower rate than a PRIVATE LINE. It allows multiple users to share the same line, but users are not allowed to interfere with each other.

PAR VALUE stated or FACE VALUE of a stock or bond. It has little significance for common stock. The par value on bonds specifies the payment at maturity.

PASCAL computer programming language developed by Niklaus Wirth, designed to encourage programmers to write modular and well-structured programs. Pascal has become one of the most popular languages for microcomputers, and there are several common versions.

PASSBOOK book issued by a bank to record deposits, withdrawals, and interest earned in a savings account, usually known as a *passbook savings account*. The *passbook* lists the depositor's name and account number as well as all transactions. Passbook savings accounts, though usually offering low yields, are safe because deposits in them are insured up to $100,000 by the FEDERAL DEPOSIT INSURANCE CORPORATION (FDIC).

PASSED DIVIDEND
1. dividend customarily paid on common shares that the board of directors fails to declare, usually because of financial difficulties at the company; also called OMITTED DIVIDEND.

2. omitted dividend on CUMULATIVE PREFERRED STOCK. A passed dividend on these shares accrues until paid.

PASSENGER MILE unit of measure that is a product of average trip length multiplied by number of passengers. Statistics for transportation safety, for example, are cited on the basis of passenger miles.

PASSIVE ACTIVITY LOSS (PAL) any rental activity or other activity in which the investor does not materially participate. With certain exceptions, losses generated by passive activities may not be used to offset ACTIVE INCOME or PORTFOLIO INCOME. Losses from passive activities are suspended until passive income is generated.

PASSIVE INCOME GENERATOR (PIG) investment or activity that generates passive income. The most common example is an income-oriented real estate LIMITED PARTNERSHIP. The income from a PIG may offset, for tax purposes, a PASSIVE ACTIVITY LOSS (PAL).

PASSIVE INVESTMENT INCOME gross receipts of an S CORPORATION derived from ROYALTIES, RENTS, DIVIDENDS, INTEREST, ANNUITIES, and gains from sales and exchanges of STOCKS and SECURITIES.

PASSIVE INVESTOR one who invests money but does not manage the business or property. *See also* LIMITED PARTNER; STOCKHOLDER.

PASSPORT
1. official document issued by a country to a citizen, which identifies that person and allows travel to foreign countries.
2. document that provides its holder entry to a particular place.

PASS-THROUGH CERTIFICATE an investment that receives income from another form. For example, a group of mortgages, called a POOL, may be represented by certificates of equal face amounts. The mortgage receipts are collected and passed through to the certificate owners.

PASS-THROUGH ENTITY nontaxable entity such as a PARTNERSHIP, LIMITED PARTNERSHIP, S CORPORATION, SIMPLE TRUST, ESTATE, REGULATED INVESTMENT COMPANY, or REAL ESTATE INVESTMENT TRUST (REIT) or LIMITED LIABILITY COMPANY. Generally, the income or expense is passed to the underlying owner and retains its character as, for example, ORDINARY INCOME, CAPITAL GAIN, or CHARITABLE CONTRIBUTION.

PASS-THROUGHS
1. operating expenses that can be charged to a TENANT along with the usual RENT, as defined in the LEASE.
2. *same as* PASS-THROUGH CERTIFICATES.

PASS-THROUGH SECURITY security that passes income from debtors through intermediaries to investors. The most common form of pass-through is a mortgage-backed security, in which the principal and interest payments from homeowners are passed from the banks, mortgage bankers, or savings and loan associations that originated the mortgages to investors.

PASSWORD secret character string that is required to log onto a computer system, thus preventing unauthorized persons from obtaining access to the computer. Computer users may password-protect their files in some systems.

PAST SERVICE BENEFIT private pension plan credit given to an employee's past service with an employer prior to establishment of a pension plan. Usually, a lower percentage of compensation is credited for benefits for past service than for future service benefits, since the employee's past compensation is likely to be longer than future compensation after a pension plan has been installed.

PAST SERVICE CREDIT *see* PAST SERVICE BENEFIT.

PAST SERVICE LIABILITY funding of an employee's benefits in a pension plan for his beginning past service of employment. This is a significant cost factor in pension planning and financing of future benefits.

PATCH a small alteration to a computer program, installed as a correction. Although *patches* are most often used as bug fixes or to plug security leaks, they can also add functionality to make an aging program more competitive. Users with Internet access can usually download patches from a software publisher's WEB SITE.

PATENT
1. evident; obvious.
2. *see* PATENT OF INVENTION.
3. CONVEYANCE of title to government land.

PATENT APPEALS COURT *see* CUSTOMS COURT.

PATENT INFRINGEMENT act of trespassing upon the rights secured by a PATENT. The test of infringement is whether the device in question does substantially the same work in substantially the same way and accomplishes the same result as the device that has been patented. COPYRIGHTS and TRADEMARKS can also be the subject of an infringement action.

PATENT MEDICINE *see* OVER-THE-COUNTER MEDICINE.

PATENT MONOPOLY form of temporary MONOPOLY granted by government to inventors and producers of innovative goods. It is a means of encouraging research and innovation by assuring that the producer will be able to collect rewards for producing successful new products.

PATENT OFFICE U.S. agency that provides protection to registered inventions.

PATENT OF INVENTION grant of right to exclude others from the making or selling of an invention during a specified time; often simply called a patent. It gives to its owner a legitimate monopoly. *See also* PATENT INFRINGEMENT.

PATENT PENDING U.S. Patent Office statement that a patent search is being conducted in the United States and other countries. This statement is issued after a patent has been filed while the Patent Office determines whether the invention is in fact new and patentable under the law.

PATENT WARFARE practice of using multiple patents having different expiration dates on slightly different aspects of the same invention. The objective of patent warfare is to prevent others from competing when the original patent expires. It is form versus substance.

PATERNALISM management method assuming ultimate responsibility for employee welfare in such areas as benefit decisions, job assignments, and promotions. The term is also pejorative in the sense that management assumes inferior status for employees.

PATH the hierarchical description of where a computer directory (folder) or file is located on your computer or on a NETWORK.

PATRIOT BOND special designation given the SERIES EE SAVINGS BOND after the September 11, 2001, World Trade Center terrorist attack.

PATRON
In general: one who patronizes a business, customer.
Taxation: one who does business with a COOPERATIVE, but not necessarily a member.

PATTERN BARGAINING individual employee unions and employers reach a negotiated agreement on the basis of a collective bargaining settlement developed elsewhere. Pattern bargaining can be based on a national or regional basis. Strong national pattern bargaining results in very similar agreements, whereas weak national pattern bargaining allows more flexibility in the individual agreement. National pattern bargaining can be developed by either a union or an industry.

PAUPER individual who is destitute and dependent on others for support.

PAWN person or organization at the mercy of another's will. For example, a company may be a pawn in a takeover battle between several larger companies.

PAY
1. compensation to personnel for services performed.
2. to exchange money for goods or services.

PAYABLE amount owing, usually from the purchase of supplies or inventory (accounts payable) but also for other purposes (bank loans payable).

PAYABLES accounts, rates, and mortgages owed by a business or person. The term often refers to current liabilities instead of all debts.

PAY AS YOU GO payments for a good or service as it is used rather than as an outright purchase. For example, college tuition is on a pay-as-you-go basis to obtain the courses necessary for completing college degree requirements.

PAYBACK PERIOD in capital budgeting, length of time needed to recoup the cost of a CAPITAL INVESTMENT. The payback period is the ratio of the initial investment (cash outlay) to the annual cash inflows for the recovery period. The major shortcoming of the payback period method is that it does not take into account cash flows after the payback period and is therefore not a measure of the profitability of an investment project. For this reason, analysts generally prefer the discounted cash flow methods of capital budgeting, namely, the internal rate of return and the net present value methods.

PAYCHECK check paying an employee's wages from an organization. The net wages contained in the paycheck are those after deductions for social security and union dues and other benefit adjustments have been made. Paychecks are made on PAYDAY.

PAYDAY day on which employees receive their PAYCHECKS.

PAYEE one to whom a debt should be paid; one to whose order a bill of exchange, note, or check is made payable.

PAYEE STATEMENT any of a multitude of required tax information statements indicating the amount paid to a payee. Some examples are those that report income from securities brokers, tip income, income tax withheld from employees' wages, and mortgage interest payments.

PAY FOR PERFORMANCE salary scheme of accepting a lower base pay in return for bonuses predicated upon meeting production or other organizational goals.

PAYER person who pays a bill or fees.

PAYING AGENT agent, usually a bank, that receives funds from an issuer of bonds or stock and in turn pays principal and interest to bondholders and dividends to stockholders, usually charging a fee for the service; sometimes called *disbursing agent.*

PAYLOAD
1. cargo or freight producing revenue or income, usually expressed in weight. Any kind of merchandise that a carrier transports and that will be sold for profit is considered a payload.
2. returned merchandise transported by truck to a wholesaler, while en route to another merchandise delivery. Since the truck did not have to make an extra trip to return the unwanted products, its trip was not considered unprofitable.

PAYMENT satisfaction of a claim or DEBT. Delivery of money in fulfillment of an obligation.

PAYMENT DATE
1. date on which a declared stock DIVIDEND or a bond interest payment is scheduled to be paid.
2. date on which a bill is due for payment.

PAYMENT IN DUE COURSE payment of a NEGOTIABLE INSTRUMENT at or after its date of maturity, made to its holder in good faith and without notice of any defect in his title.

PAYMENT IN KIND payment for goods and services made in the form of other goods and services rather than cash or other forms of money. *Payment in kind* is different from BARTER because the payer gets the same goods and services in return, not other goods and services of equivalent value, as is the case in barter.

PAYMENT METHOD means of payment employed by a customer, such as cash, check, money order, or credit card with order or upon invoicing; also called *payment type*. Customer RECORDS usually contain information regarding payment method and may include claims paid as a payment method.

PAYOFF (AMOUNT) the remaining amount of a loan, including any PREPAYMENT PENALTY.

PAYOLA secret or private payment in return for the promotion of a product or service. Term originates from the record industry.

PAYOUT return on investment equal to the original marketing expenditure; also known as *payback*. When a company recovers its investment plus the expected built-in return from launching or reintroducing a new product or service, it has realized a profit from its original capital outlay. A company's payout, therefore, represents the minimum amount of dollar sales that must be generated to offset the cost of an advertising program. *See also* BREAK-EVEN ANALYSIS.

PAYOUT RATIO percentage of a firm's profits that is paid out to shareholders in the form of dividends.

PAY PERIOD time duration, typically a week, half a month, or a month, within which the amount a worker has earned is determined so that the worker can be paid properly.

PAYROLL aggregate periodic amount a business pays its workers; list of employees and their compensation.

PAYROLL DEDUCTION reduction of amounts paid to a worker from the gross amount earned. Reductions are for taxes, voluntary savings or pension contributions, union dues, and insurance premiums. The paycheck reflects gross pay less these payroll deductions. *See also* PAYROLL TAX.

PAYROLL PERIOD period for which a payment of wages is ordinarily made by an employer to an employee. The amount of withholding varies depending on the *payroll period.*

PAYROLL SAVINGS PLAN arrangement between employer and employee whereby a specified amount of money is deducted from the employee's pay and invested for the employee in stocks, bonds, or other investments. The full salary is ordinarily taxable, though deductions are allowed for qualified pension plan contributions.

PAYROLL TAXES taxes levied on wages and salaries, such as for Social Security (FICA) and unemployment insurance.

PAYROLL WITHHOLDING *see* WITHHOLDING.

PBGC GUARANTEED BENEFITS the portion of pension benefits that is guaranteed by the PBGC in the event that the PENSION PLAN sponsor defaults. Non-guaranteed pieces of pensions usually include nonqualified and executive pension plans not covered under ERISA, pension benefits above a fixed-dollar threshold, and pension benefits attributable to plan amendments within five years of the plan termination.

PC, P.C. *see* PERSONAL COMPUTER; PROFESSIONAL CORPORATION.

PC-COMPATIBLE able to run software intended for the IBM PC. Virtually all microcomputers currently available, except some made by Apple Computer, are *PC-compatible.*

PDA *personal digital assistant,* a handheld (or *palmtop*) personal computer with a touch screen (often with handwriting recognition) or limited keyboard that serves as an address book and scheduler, such as the Compaq iPaq or the former Palm Pilot. Some PDAs use the Pocket PC operating system from Microsoft, and some, such as the RIM BLACKBERRY and Palm Treo, are *smartphones,* incorporating cellular technology for wireless connectivity. *See also* PREGNANCY DISCRIMINATION ACT.

PDF *Portable Document Format,* a universal computer file format, developed by ABOBE SYSTEMS, INC., that preserves all the fonts, formatting, colors, and graphics of any source document, regardless of the application and platform used to create it. Adobe ACROBAT software was designed to create PDF documents, but the specification is an open one, and numerous other applications (as well as any application running under the MacOS X operating system) also have this capability. PDF files can be shared, viewed, and printed by anyone with free Adobe Reader software.

PEAK high point of the business cycle of some particular phase of economic activity. For example, summer is the time of peak electrical demand for utilities as people run their air conditioners.

PEAK PERIOD in transportation, period when equipment gets the most use, as for commuting equipment in morning and evening rush hours.

PECKING ORDER hierarchy or rank order in an organization; derived from the behavior of chickens.

PECULATION fraudulent misappropriation to one's own use of money or goods entrusted to one's care. *See also* EMBEZZLEMENT.

PECUNIARY consisting of money, that which can be valued in money. A *pecuniary* loss is a loss of money or one that can be translated in terms of money.

PECUNIARY BEQUEST money given to an HEIR by a DECEDENT.

PEFCO (PRIVATE EXPORT FUNDING CORPORATION) a corporation established by the U.S. government to facilitate unsubsidized funding of U.S. exports.

PEG to stabilize the price of a security, commodity, or currency by intervening in a market. Since 1971, a FLOATING EXCHANGE RATE system has prevailed in which countries use pegging—the buying or selling of their own currencies—simply to offset fluctuations in the EXCHANGE RATE. The U.S. government uses pegging to support the prices of agricultural commodities.

PENALTY money or other cost one will pay for breaking a law or violating part or all of the terms of a contract. Penalties are often imposed for prepaying a loan (PREPAYMENT PENALTY), failing to complete a contract sale, or breaking a lease; penalties are not tax deductible. *See also* SPECIFIC PENALTIES.

PENALTY FOR EARLY WITHDRAWAL OF SAVINGS charge by a bank or savings institution on funds withdrawn from a time deposit before maturity. This penalty is deductible by individuals as an adjustment to GROSS INCOME.

PENCIL OUT estimate in approximate figures whether a proposed investment is expected to be profitable.

PENETRATION PRICING establishing low product pricing as a method of seeking rapid entry into a given market. The low profit potential discourages competitors from matching these prices. After the product has been established in the market, prices can be raised.

PENNY STOCK stock that typically sells for less than $1 a share. Penny stocks are issued by companies with a short or erratic history of revenues and earnings. Such stocks often are more volatile than those of large, well-established firms traded on the New York or American stock exchange.

PENSION BENEFIT GUARANTY CORPORATION (PBGC) a federal corporation created by the EMPLOYEE RETIREMENT INCOME SECURITY ACT (ERISA) of 1974. It currently protects the pensions of 44.1 million American workers and retirees in 30,330 private single-employer and multi-employer DEFINED-BENEFIT PENSION PLANS. PBGC receives no funds from general tax revenues. Operations are financed by insurance premiums set by Congress and paid by sponsors of defined-benefit plans, investment income, assets from pension plans trusteed by PBGC, and recoveries from the companies formerly responsible for the plans.

PENSION EQUITY PLAN (PEP) a type of DEFINED-BENEFIT PENSION PLAN design in which a participant's benefit is stated as a lump sum based on the participant's age, service, and average pay, where the average pay is usually based on only the final few years of employment.

PENSION FREEZE situation that occurs when a pension plan sponsor elects to eliminate future pension accruals for the plan participants, but the pension plan itself continues to exist under the sponsor to pay out the previously accrued pension benefits. Some pension freezes involve freezing only participation in the plan, allowing existing participants to continue to receive benefit accruals, while other pension freezes eliminate future pension accruals for everyone.

PENSION FUND fund set up by a corporation, labor union, governmental entity, or other organization to pay the pension benefits of retired workers. Pension funds invest billions of dollars annually in the stock and bond markets, and are therefore a major factor in the supply-and-demand balance of the markets. Earnings on the investment portfolios of pension funds are tax exempt.

PENSION PLAN *see* DEFINED-BENEFIT PENSION PLAN; DEFINED-CONTRIBUTION PLAN; QUALIFIED PLAN; QUALIFIED TRUST.

PENSION PLAN FUNDING: GROUP DEPOSIT ADMINISTRATION ANNUITY pension plan funding instrument in which contributions paid by an employer are deposited to accumulate at interest. Upon retirement, an *immediate annuity is* purchased for the employee. The benefit is determined by a formula and the investment earnings on funds left to accumulate at interest. Since the annuity is purchased at point of retirement, the deposit administration plan can be used with any benefit formula.

PENSION PLAN LIABILITY RESERVE obligation recognized by the employer for the future liability to make annuity payments to employees. The reserve is typically a liability when it results from charging pension expense. However, in a revocable plan, the reserve is considered an appropriation of retained earnings regardless of whether it affects specific assets.

PENTHOUSE luxury housing unit generally located on a top floor of a high-rise building. It commands a premium rental or sales price.

PEO *see* PROFESSIONAL EMPLOYER ORGANIZATION.

PEON
1. person who works in a servile capacity.
2. in Spanish, laborer or servant.

PEOPLE INTENSIVE process requiring many people to complete; not easily automated. A hospital is an example of a people-intensive organization.

PER ANNUM once each year, annual, annually.

PER CAPITA by or for each individual. Anything figured per capita is calculated by the number of individuals involved and is divided equally among all. For example, if property taxes total $1 million in a town and there are 1,000 inhabitants, the *per-capita property tax is* $1,000.

PER-CAPITA DEBT total bonded debt of a municipality, divided by its population. The result, compared with ratios of prior periods, reveals trends in a municipality's debt burden, which bond analysts evaluate.

PERCENT, PERCENTAGE a statistical term to express a quantity as a portion of the whole, which is assigned a value of 100. Price changes are often reported as percentage increases or declines.

PERCENTAGE DEPLETION METHOD method that permits a taxpayer with an economic interest in a mineral deposit to deduct a specified percentage of the gross income from the deposit instead of COST DEPLETION. Percentage depletion is generally available for most types of solid minerals but is restricted to independent producers, royalty owners, and some other narrow categories of oil and gas owners.

PERCENTAGE LEASE LEASE of property in which the rental is based on a percentage of the volume of sales made upon the leased premises. It usually stipulates a minimum rental and is regularly used for retailers who are TENANTS. *See also* OVERAGE; PERCENTAGE RENT.

PERCENTAGE-OF-COMPLETION METHOD method of reporting income from LONG-TERM CONTRACTS based on the percentage of a contract completed during the tax year. Costs allocated to the contract and incurred before the close of the tax year are compared to total estimated costs of the completed contract. That *percentage of completion* is applied to the GROSS REVENUE from the contract to determine the amount to be included in taxable income for that tax year. Taxpayers using the percentage-of-completion method are also subject to the LOOK-BACK RULE for recomputing prior-year tax liability.

PERCENTAGE-OF-SALES METHOD procedure used to set advertising budgets, based on a predetermined percentage of past sales or a forecast of future sales. This method of budget allocation is popular with advertisers because of its simplicity and its ability to relate advertising expenditures directly to sales. Management usually determines the budget's percentage figure, which is based on the industry average or the company's historical or previous year's advertising spending.

PERCENTAGE RENT rent payable under a PERCENTAGE LEASE. Typically the percentage applies to sales in excess of a preestablished base amount of the dollar sales volume. *Percentage rents* in a shopping center vary typically from less than 1% for a supermarket to more than 7% for a jewelry store. Apparel stores and gift shops typically pay from 3 to 6% of sales.

PERCENTILE statistical ranking designation. The *p*th percentile of a list is the number such that *p* percent of the elements in the list are less than that number. For example, if a student scores in the 85th *percentile* on a standardized test, then 85% of those taking the test had lower scores.

PER DIEM (Latin for "by day") daily allowance, usually for travel, entertainment, employee compensation, or miscellaneous outofpocket expenses while conducting a business transaction. The sum of money is always calculated on a daily basis and may be paid in advance or after the expense is incurred. Employees are sometimes paid on a *per diem* basis. If an employer pays for expenses using a per diem allowance, an employee can use the allowance as proof of the amount of expenses incurred. The IRS publishes yearly per diem rates that businesses may use for the purpose of reimbursing employee travel expenses, and that employees and self-employed individuals may use for substantiating the expenses.

PERFECT COMPETITION market condition wherein no buyer or seller has the power to alter the market price of a good or service. Characteristics of a perfectly competitive market are a large number of buyers and sellers, a homogeneous (similar) good or service, an equal awareness of prices and volume, an absence of discrimination in buying and selling, total mobility of productive resources, and complete freedom of entry. Perfect competition exists only as a theoretical ideal. Also called *pure competition*.

PERFECTED complete beyond practical or theoretical improvement; practical application or technological development that cannot be improved substantially.

PERFECT (PURE) MONOPOLY market dominated by a single producer, where no competition of any kind to that producer can arise.

PERFORMANCE
Law: fulfillment of an obligation or a promise; especially, completion of one's duty under a CONTRACT.
Marketing: high level of capability in a product, such as a *high-performance* car.

PERFORMANCE APPRAISAL (EVALUATION) personnel evaluation method seeking the measurement of employee work effectiveness using objective criteria. *Performance appraisal* systems hope to achieve higher productivity outcomes by delineating how employees meet job specifications. A major challenge for performance appraisal systems is to define performance standards while maintaining objectivity.

PERFORMANCE BOND contractor's bond, guaranteeing that the contractor will perform the contract and providing that, in the event of a default, the SURETY BOND may complete the contract or pay damages up to the bond limit.

PERFORMANCE FEE *see* INCENTIVE FEE.

PERFORMANCE FUND MUTUAL FUND designed for growth of capital. A performance fund invests in high-growth companies that pay small dividends or no dividends at all.

PERFORMANCE STOCK high-growth stock that an investor feels will significantly rise in value. Also known as GROWTH STOCK, such a security tends to pay either a small dividend or no dividend at all.

PERIOD interval of time as long or short as fits the situation.

PERIOD EXPENSE, PERIOD COST amount based on the passage of time and considered to occur in that time interval, such as rent on a building.

PERIODIC INVENTORY METHOD accounting process used to find the cost of inventory sold or put in production. Data on beginning inventory, purchases, and ending inventory are used to find the amount and cost of withdrawals from inventory.

PERISHABLE something liable to perish, decay, or spoil rapidly. Fresh fish, for example, is a very *perishable* commodity requiring great care in handling.

PERJURY criminal offense of making false statements under oath. In COMMON LAW, only a willful and corrupt sworn statement made without sincere belief in its truth, and made in a judicial proceeding regarding a material matter, was perjury. Today, STATUTES have broadened the offense so that in some JURISDICTIONS any false swearing in a legal instrument or legal setting is perjury.

PERK *see* PERQUISITE.

PERMANENT DIFFERENCE difference between book income and taxable income caused by an item that affects one but not the other. The difference will *not* reverse. For example, interest on municipal bonds is included in book income but not in taxable income.

PERMANENT FINANCING or PERMANENT MORTGAGE
    Corporate finance: long-term financing by means of either debt (bonds or long-term notes) or equity (common or preferred stock).
    Real estate: long-term mortgage loan or bond issue, usually with a 15-, 20-, or 30-year term. *Contrast with* CONSTRUCTION LOAN.

PERMANENT INCOME a long-run measurement of average income, in which temporary fluctuations in income do not have much effect upon consumption. Many economists believe that consumers view their incomes in this way, and do not change their consumption patterns much in response to what they believe are temporary income changes.

PERMIT document, issued by a government regulatory authority, that allows the bearer to take some specific action. *See also* BUILDING PERMIT.

PERMIT BOND bond that guarantees that the person who is licensed by a city, county, or state agency will perform activities for which the bond was granted, according to the regulations governing the license.

PERMUTATIONS different subgroups, which can be formed by sampling from a larger group or population a given number of observations, and which depend on the order in which the elements are withdrawn. *See also* COMBINATIONS.

PERPETUAL INVENTORY inventory accounting system whereby book inventory is kept in continuous agreement with stock on hand; also called *continuous inventory.* A daily record is maintained of both the dollar amount and the physical quantity of inventory, and this is reconciled to actual physical counts at short intervals. *See also* PERIODIC INVENTORY METHOD.

PERPETUITY forever; never ending; *see* RULE AGAINST PERPETUITIES.

PERQUISITE (PERK) any of a number of privileges granted to employees in addition to basic wages and salaries. *Perks* may include ordinary employee BENEFITS, FRINGE such as health insurance and pensions, but the term is more often used to apply to executive perks such as automobiles and limos, resort vacations, club memberships, special washroom and dining facilities, reserved parking spaces, and use of corporate aircraft and other equipment.

PERQUISITES OF OFFICE taxable fringe benefit if used for personal or family purposes. For example, even the president of the United States is taxed on using government facilities for purely personal and family affairs.

PER SE by means of itself. The term relates to a circumstance that does not require extraneous evidence or support to establish its existence.

PERSON an individual, trust, estate, partnership, association, company, or corporation having certain legal rights and responsibilities.

PERSONAL ALLOWANCES exemptions from withholding for the taxpayer, spouse, and dependents, used in calculating the amount of income tax to be withheld from periodic wage payments. The employee/ taxpayer completes Form W-4 indicating the number of allowances to be considered for purposes of withholding.

PERSONAL COMPUTER (PC) a computer designed for use by a single user. Although other MICROCOMPUTERS preceded it, the IBM PC was the first to use the name specifically. As a result, the term *PC* now applies to an IBM-compatible computer as contrasted to the Apple Macintosh, these being the two standards that emerged from an abundance of competitors in the early 1980s.

PERSONAL DATA SHEET questionnaire often given by organizations to individuals for the purpose of eliciting specific information relative to the individual.

PERSONAL EXEMPTION in determining taxable income, an individual taxpayer is entitled to a deduction for each allowable *personal exemption.* A separate exemption is allowed for the taxpayer, the taxpayer's spouse, and each dependent of the taxpayer. The deduction allowable for each exemption is indexed for inflation.

PERSONAL EXEMPTION PHASEOUT *see* PHASEOUT OF PERSONAL EXEMPTIONS.

PERSONAL FINANCIAL PLANNING SOFTWARE program assisting users in examining revenue and expenses, comparing actual to budget, monitoring assets and liabilities, goal analysis, investment portfolio analysis, tax planning, and retirement planning. Personal financial planning templates can be used in conjunction with a spreadsheet program. Examples of personal financial planning software are Andrew Tobias' *Managing Your Money* and *Quicken*, published by Intuit.

PERSONAL FINANCIAL STATEMENT document prepared for an individual using the ACCRUAL BASIS of accounting rather than the CASH BASIS. A Statement of Financial Condition shows ASSETS at estimated current values listed by order of liquidity and maturity without classification as current and noncurrent. Business interests that constitute a large part of total assets should be shown separately from other investments. Only the person's interest (amount that the person is entitled to) as beneficial owner should be included when assets are jointly owned. LIABILITIES are shown by order of maturity without classification as current or noncurrent.

PERSONAL HOLDING COMPANY (PHC) a CORPORATION: (1) that derives more than 60% of its gross income, after certain adjustments, from investment sources such as dividends, interests, rents, royalties, and so on, and from certain personal service contracts; and (2) of which more than 50% of the stock is owned by five or fewer individuals. Such a corporation has at times been described as an "incorporated pocketbook." A penalty tax of 15% is applicable in addition to the corporate tax. This penalty tax is applied to the corporate taxable income, less distributions to shareholders, income taxes, and certain other adjustments. Because of its severity, the personal holding company tax operates as a barrier against the use of a closely held corporation for the avoidance of personal taxes on investment and personal service income.

PERSONAL INCOME element in the NATIONAL INCOME accounts. It is national income less retained corporate profits, corporate income taxes, and social insurance contributions; to this sum are added transfer payments, interest paid to consumers, and net government interest payments. Personal income is, hence, the amount of income actually received by households.

PERSONAL INFORMATION MANAGER (PIM) type of computer software that could be likened to an electronic daily planner. It combines the functions of a calendar, appointment book/scheduler, to-do list, address book/phone directory (and sometimes dialer), notebook, and database for keeping track of contacts. *See also* PDA.

PERSONAL INJURY wrongful conduct causing false arrest, invasion of privacy, libel, slander, defamation of character, and bodily injury. The injury is against the person in contrast to property damage or destruction.

PERSONAL INTEREST EXPENSE any interest that is not home mortgage interest, investment interest, or business interest. The tax deduction for personal interest expense was completely eliminated after 1990.

PERSONALITY behavior pattern of an individual, established over time. An individual's personality is a combination of lifetime experiences as well as genetic characteristics. Personality is indelible characteristic and results in a pattern of predictable behavior.

PERSONAL LIABILITY obligation that exposes (or potentially exposes) one's personal assets. Corporate STOCKHOLDERS generally avoid personal liability since they can lose only their investment in the corporation. The same holds true for LIMITED PARTNERS. However, GENERAL PARTNERS incur personal liability.

PERSONAL PROPERTY things movable, as distinguished from REAL PROPERTY, or things attached to the realty; also called *personalty*. Gains on the sale of personal property used in a TRADE OR BUSINESS are generally taxed under SECTION 1231 as though they were CAPITAL GAINS except for DEPRECIATION RECAPTURE ORDINARY INCOME. Section 1231 losses are ORDINARY LOSSES. Personal property used in a trade or business may qualify for INVESTMENT TAX CREDIT or a rapid write-off in the year of purchase. *See also* ADDITIONAL FIRST-YEAR DEPRECIATION.

PERSONAL PROPERTY FLOATER coverage for all personal property, regardless of location of the insured and household residents, including children away at school. Written on an *all-risk* basis, subject to excluded perils such as war, wear and tear, mechanical breakdown, vermin, and nuclear disaster. Personal property includes clothing, televisions, musical instruments, cameras, jewelry, watches, furs, furniture, radios, and appliances. Coverage can be extended to damage of real property as the result of theft of personal property.

PERSONAL RESIDENCE the dwelling unit that one claims as one's primary home. This dwelling establishes one's legal residence for voting, tax, and legal purposes.

PERSONAL SELLING delivery of a specially designed message to a prospect by a seller, usually in the form of face-to-face communication, personal correspondence, or a personal telephone conversation. Unlike advertising, a personal sales message can be more specifically targeted to individual prospects and easily altered if the desired behavior does not occur.

PERSONAL SERVICE CORPORATION CORPORATION whose principal activity is the performance of personal services, which are substantially performed by employee-owners. Such corporations are treated adversely in that all income is taxed at the highest corporate rate.

PERSONALTY *see* PERSONAL PROPERTY.

PERSONNEL people who actually compose an organization's work force; HUMAN RESOURCES of an organization.

PERSONNEL ADMINISTRATION now called *human resources (HR) administration* or *HR management*. Study and practice of managing an organization's human resources. It has the functional areas of recruitment, selection, retention, development, assessment, and adjustment of personnel.

PERSONNEL DEPARTMENT now called *human resources (HR) department*. Organizational unit or department having the functional responsibility of personnel administration. The personnel department must have sufficient power and authority to help ensure that personnel policies are implemented legally and proactively.

PERSONNEL PSYCHOLOGY *see* INDUSTRIAL PSYCHOLOGY.

PERSON-TO-PERSON CALLS long-distance operator-assisted call whereby the caller specifies the name of the person being called. The caller need not pay for the call if the specified person is not available.

PER STIRPES distribution of an estate whereby each beneficiary receives a share in the property, not necessarily equal, but in certain proportions, some receiving a fraction of the fraction to which the person through whom they claim from the ancestor would have been entitled. It is distinguished from a distribution PER CAPITA. For example: Frank dies without a will. His wife has predeceased him, and he is survived by two children. Under a per stirpes distribution, Frank's two children each receive one-third of his estate. The remaining one-third is distributed to the children of the third child who had predeceased Frank.

PERSUASION act of inducing attitude changes and influencing a target market to action, by appealing to reason or emotion. Persuasion is a primary objective of modern advertising and can be achieved by creating advertisements with some combination of the following elements: effective attention-getting devices, a strong appeal to selfinterest, a stimulation of desire for a product or service, and a powerful call-to-action response.

PERSUASIVE ADVERTISING promotional advertising that encourages product sampling and brand switching.

PERT *Program Evaluation and Review Technique*, a method for project planning by analyzing the time required for each step; diagrammed on a *PERT chart*.

PETER PRINCIPLE theory that people rise in their career in every hierarchy to the level of their own incompetence; based on the book *The Peter Principle and Why Things Always Go Wrong* by Lawrence J. Peter. Work in organizations is accomplished by those employees who have not yet reached their level of incompetence.

PETITION
  1. written application addressed to a court or judge, stating facts and circumstances relied upon as a cause for judicial action.
  2. written statement of political desires, with names or signatures of those in agreement.

PETITIONER party requesting action in the court. A taxpayer is quite often the petitioner (plaintiff) in a tax dispute to appeal an IRS position. If the government loses and petitions a higher court, however, the IRS becomes the petitioner (plaintiff or appellant).

PETITION IN BANKRUPTCY the petition by which an insolvent debtor declares bankruptcy and invokes the protection of the bankruptcy court from creditors.

PETRODOLLARS dollars paid to oil-producing countries and deposited in Western banks. When the price of oil skyrocketed in the 1970s, Middle Eastern oil producers built up huge surpluses of *petrodollars* that the banks lent to oil-importing countries around the world. By the mid-1980s and 1990s, these surpluses had shrunk because consumption increased while oil exporters spent a good deal of the money on development projects. The flow of petrodollars, therefore, is very important to understanding the current world economic situation. Also called *petrocurrency* or *oil money*.

PETTY CASH FUND, PETTY CASH VOUCHER small cash fund used to make impromptu cash payments. A voucher or piece of paper is used for each payment. *See also* INTEREST FUND.

PHANTOM INCOME likely to result when leveraged real estate is sold because, during the ownership period, more depreciation was claimed than was paid to amortize the mortgage. The excess of the mortgage relieved in a sale over the ADJUSTED TAX BASIS represents TAXABLE GAIN. In this instance, however, no cash is released, yet tax is still paid. The TAXABLE INCOME is called *phantom income* because the investor receives no cash.

PHANTOM STOCK PLAN deferred-compensation plan that uses the employer's stock as a measuring rod for determining the value of the compensation payment.

PHASEOUT OF PERSONAL EXEMPTIONS reduction in personal exemptions as income rises. Taxpayers whose ADJUSTED GROSS INCOME exceeds a prescribed threshold must reduce or eliminate the deduction for personal exemptions to which they would otherwise be entitled. For 2006, the thresholds were $225,750 for married individuals filing joint returns, $150,500 for heads of households, $188,150 for unmarried individuals, and $112,875 for married individuals filing separate returns. For subsequent years, these threshold amounts will be indexed for inflation. This phaseout is itself being phased out between 2006 and 2009. After 2009, this phaseout will be repealed.

PHILADELPHIA STOCK EXCHANGE *see* REGIONAL STOCK EXCHANGE.

PHILLIPS CURVE economic proposition stating that there is a negative relationship between UNEMPLOYMENT and the level of INFLATION. As inflation increases, unemployment decreases and vice versa.

PHISHING form of Internet fraud that attempts to trick victims into providing sensitive personal information such as bank or credit card account details, SOCIAL SECURITY NUMBERS, PINS, or PASSWORDS. The usual approach is to send an e-mail message purporting to be from a financial institution or online auction site, often an alarming notice that the user's account is threatened in some way. The message contains a link to a Web site that misleadingly appears to be that of the purported sender of the message, where the information can be captured.

PHYSICAL COMMODITY actual COMMODITY that is delivered to the contract buyer at the completion of a commodity CONTRACT in either the spot market or the futures market. Some examples of physical commodities are corn, cotton, gold, oil, soybeans, and wheat.

PHYSICAL DEPRECIATION or PHYSICAL DETERIORATION loss of value from all causes of age and action of the elements. Sources of physical depreciation include breakage, deferred maintenance, effects of age on construction material, and normal WEAR AND TEAR. DEPRECIATION expense for tax purposes is generally based on lives set by law for the given type of property and is not necessarily related to the USEFUL LIFE of the property.

PHYSICAL DISTRIBUTION process of moving finished products from the producer to the consumer.

PHYSICAL EXAMINATION
1. direct physical inspection of an object. It is necessary, for example, to do a physical examination of bridge structures at periodic intervals to ensure that they are structurally sound and not presenting a public hazard.
2. medical examination performed on people, called a *physical*.

PHYSICAL INVENTORY actual count of items in inventory, as contrasted with accepting the values shown on accounting records.

PHYSICAL LIFE the expected period of time for an asset, such as a real estate improvement, to exist physically.

PICKETING practice, used in labor and political disputes, of patrolling, usually with placards, to publicize a dispute or to secure support for a cause. Picketing is a constitutionally protected exercise of free expression when done in accordance with law.

PIECE *see* PACKAGE.

PIECE RATE postage due per individual piece of mail, as distinguished from charges based upon the distance traveled. Mailing a FIRST-CLASS letter costs the same regardless of whether it is mailed across town or across the country. Periodicals mailed SECOND CLASS pay postage based upon a combination of zone charges and piece rates.

PIECE WORK work performed by outside contractors getting paid by the piece. Piece workers are those who agree to perform certain production services on an individual basis; they often do piece work in their homes.

PIE CHART graph where a circle represents the whole amount, and wedge-shaped sectors indicate the fraction in each category.

PIERCING THE CORPORATE VEIL process of imposing liability for corporate activity, in disregard of the corporate entity, on a person or entity other than the offending corporation itself. There are times when the court will ignore the corporate entity and strip the organizers and managers of the corporation of the limited liability that they usually enjoy. In doing so, the court is said to *pierce the corporate veil*. The S CORPORATION provisions *pierce the corporate veil* and allow the income to be taxed to the shareholders. The COLLAPSIBLE CORPORATION rules also pierce the corporate veil.

PIER TO HOUSE shipping from a place where containers are stored to the consignee.

PIGEONHOLED (of people or things) filed in the appropriate category or compartment (like the pigeonholes in a desk), often with the sense of being dealt with and forgotten; shelved.

PIGGYBACK to transport truck trailers and containers designed to ride as rail cargo from terminal to terminal. Piggybacking combines the fuel- and labor-saving advantages of rail cargo with the point-to-point movement of truck cargo.

PIGGYBACK LOAN
1. combination of CONSTRUCTION LOAN with permanent loan commitment.
2. mortgage held by more than one lender, with one lender holding the rights of the others in SUBORDINATION.

PIGOU EFFECT effect of price changes upon the real value of privately held money balances. A decrease in the price level increases the buying power of money that people have, and so increases their consumption, and thus has an expansionary effect upon the economy. The effect was first demonstrated in 1943 by A. C. Pigou of Cambridge University.

PILOT PLANT small facility producing a modest number of units, designed to prove or test methods that may be used in full scale plants. A pilot plant reduces the investment risk in unproven production methods.

PIM *see* PERSONAL INFORMATION MANAGER.

PIN acronym for *p*ersonal *i*dentification *n*umber. Customers use *PIN* numbers to identify themselves when using an ATM or making purchases with a DEBIT CARD.

PINK SHEETS daily publication of Pink Sheets, LLC (formerly the National Quotation Bureau) that details the BID AND ASKED prices of thousands of over-the-counter (OTC) stocks. Brokerage firms subscribe to the pink sheets, named for their color, because they give current prices and list MARKET MAKERS who trade each stock.

PIN MONEY small sum for incidental expenses; a small cash advance with a major contract might be called pin money.

PIPELINE
1. line of supply or channel by which information is transmitted.
2. conduit through which materials are transported, as in an oil pipeline.
3. work in progress.

PIRACY the illegal use, copying, or distribution of computer software.

PITCH the number of characters per inch (cpi) in a particular size and style of type. Accurate only for monospaced (fixed-width) fonts.

PITI abbreviation for *principal, interest, taxes, and insurance,* the primary components of monthly mortgage payments.

PIVOT TABLE a multidimensional table that can be rearranged to allow different views of the data. Recent versions of Excel contain a wizard that automatically creates pivot tables.

PIXEL (*pic*ture *el*ement) one of the individual dots that make up a graphical image, each of which combines red, green, and blue (RGB) phosphors to create a specific color. A VGA screen in high-resolution mode consists of 640×480 or 307,200 pixels.

PLACED IN SERVICE (the date when property is) in a state of readiness and is available for a specific use.

PLACEMENT TEST examination measuring the skills, intelligence, motivation, interests, needs, and goals of applicants for the purpose of selecting those most likely to have the greatest success in particular occupations. Placement test scores are comparable and can be used for finding the best applicants from a group for particular occupations.

PLACE UTILITY adding consumer value by locating products in convenient locations. *See also* FOUR PS.

PLAINTIFF one who initially brings the SUIT. In a personal action, he seeks a remedy in a court of justice for an injury to, or a withholding of, his rights.

PLAN organized sequence of predetermined actions management has chosen to complete future organizational objectives. PLANNING is one of the primary responsibilities of organizational managers.

PLAN B alternative plan if a principal plan of action is unsuccessful; backup plan. For example, if a new product is less than successful, plan B's strategy is to repackage it and advertise it in a different market.

PLANNED ECONOMY economy in which government planning dominates the direction of economic activity, and market forces are not allowed to do so to any considerable degree. Socialist and, especially, communist economies are planned economies, whereas capitalist economies are much less so.

PLANNED UNIT DEVELOPMENT (PUD) zoning classification that allows flexibility in the design of a SUBDIVISION. PUD zones generally set an overall density limit for the entire subdivision, allowing the dwelling units to be clustered to provide for common open space.

PLANNING function of organizing a sequence of predetermined actions to complete future organizational objectives. Planning is one of the primary management functions. *See also* PLAN.

PLANNING COMMISSION group of citizens appointed by local government officials to conduct hearings and recommend amendments to the ZONING ORDINANCE. The planning commission generally oversees the work of a professional planning department, which prepares a comprehensive plan. It may also be called a *planning board, zoning commission,* or *zoning board,* depending on the locality.

PLAN SPONSOR entity that establishes and maintains a pension or insurance plan. This may be a corporation, labor union, government agency, or nonprofit organization. Plan sponsors must follow government guidelines in the establishment and administration of these plans, including informing plan participants about the financial health of the plan and the benefits available.

PLANT assets composed of land, buildings, machinery, natural resources, furniture and fixtures, and all other equipment permanently employed; synonymous with FIXED ASSETS. In a limited sense, the term is used to mean only buildings or only land and buildings: "property, plant, and equipment" or "plant and equipment."

PLAT
1. to draw a description of land.
2. plan or map of a specific land area. *See also* DESCRIPTION; GOVERNMENT RECTANGULAR SURVEY.

PLAT BOOK public record containing maps of land, showing the division of the land into streets, blocks, and lots, and indicating the measurements of the individual PARCELS.

PLATFORM the standards that set the parameters for what a system can and cannot do; generally refers to the microprocessor and/or the operating system. The term *cross-platform* refers to applications, formats, or devices that work on different *platforms.*

PLEADING statement, in logical and legal form, of the facts that constitute plaintiff's CAUSE OF ACTION and defendant's ground of defense. Pleadings are either ALLEGATIONS by the parties affirming or denying certain matters of fact, or other statements in support or derogation of certain principles of law, which are intended to describe to the court or jury the real matter in dispute.

PLEDGE or PLEDGING deposit of PERSONAL PROPERTY as security for a debt; delivery of goods by a debtor to a creditor until the debt is repaid; generally defined as a LIEN or a CONTRACT that calls for the transfer of personal property only as security. *See also* BAILMENT; COLLATERAL.

PL/I (PL/1) (Programming Language) very powerful computer programming language developed by IBM in the early 1960s to accompany its System 360 computer.

PLOT
1. piece of land. *See also* PLOT PLAN.
2. scheme, possibly with sinister motives.
3. preparing charts or graphs of business matters, possibly aided by a computer output device called a *plotter.*

PLOT PLAN diagram showing the proposed or existing use of a specific PARCEL of land.

PLOTTAGE VALUE increment in the value of land resulting from ASSEMBLAGE of smaller plots into one ownership.

PLOTTER computer output device that draws graphs on paper by moving pens according to directions from the computer.

PLOW BACK to reinvest a company's earnings in the business rather than pay out those profits as dividends. Smaller, fast-growing companies usually *plow back* most or all earnings into their businesses, whereas more established firms pay out more of their profits as dividends.

PLUG-AND-PLAY (PnP) a standard way of configuring PC-compatible computer hardware automatically, developed by Microsoft and a number of other companies in the mid-1990s. When a *PnP* component is first connected to a computer, the operating system detects it, reads its identifying information, and makes the necessary adjustments to use the device appropriately.

PLUS TICK *see* UPTICK.

PMI abbreviation for PRIVATE MORTGAGE INSURANCE.

POA *see* POWER OF ATTORNEY.

POINT
Bonds: percentage change of the face value of a bond, expressed as points. For example, a change of 1% is a move of one *point*. For a bond with a $1,000 face value, each point is worth $10. *See also* BASIS POINT.

Real estate, commercial lending: upfront fee charged by the lender, designed to increase the overall yield to the lender. A point is 1% of the total principal amount of the loan. For example, on a $100,000 mortgage loan, a charge of three points equals $3,000.

Stocks: change of $1 in the market price of a stock. If a stock has risen five points, it has risen by $5 a share. The movements of stock market averages, such as the Dow Jones industrial average, are also quoted in points, but these are not percentages.

POINTING DEVICE an input device that lets a user manipulate a pointer in a graphical user interface. The most common *pointing device* is a MOUSE; others are the TRACKBALL, graphics tablet, joystick, and various kinds of pen-type devices.

POINT-OF-PURCHASE DISPLAY device promoting consumer purchases by providing consumer information and product advice. These devices are normally located at convenient retail locations and are quite attractive. A *point-of-purchase display* may be a computer-driven device providing textual and graphical descriptions of products and giving specific advice when queried.

POINT-OF-SALE (POS) SYSTEM a computer used in place of a cash register in retail applications. Besides recording transactions, the computer can track inventory, print informative invoices and receipts, and handle credit and debit card payments. The system usually incorporates some form of BAR CODE reader.

POINT-TO-POINT PROTOCOL (PPP) a protocol used by TCP/IP routers and PC computers to send packets over dial-up and leased-line connections.

POISON PILL strategic move by a TAKEOVER target company to make its stock less attractive to an acquirer. For instance, a firm may authorize a new series of PREFERRED STOCK that gives shareholders the right to redeem it at a premium price after a takeover.

POISSON DISTRIBUTION type of probability distribution typically used in studies concerned with the count or number of occurrences of events.

POLICE POWER inherent power of governments to impose upon private rights those restrictions that are reasonably related to promotion and maintenance of the health, safety, morals, and general welfare of the public. It includes restrictions upon the use of one's property, such as ZONING laws, or upon the conduct of one's business.

POLICY
1. **Management:** a company's plan, procedure, course of action.
2. **Insurance:** a written agreement of insurance coverage.

POLICYHOLDER individual or other entity who owns insurance policy. Synonymous with *policyowner.*

POLICY LOAN loan from an insurance company secured by the cash surrender value of a life insurance policy. The amount available for such a loan depends on the number of years the policy has been in effect, the insured's age when the policy was issued, and the size of the death benefit.

POLISH NOTATION way of writing algebraic expressions that does not require parentheses to state which operations are done first; also called *reverse Polish notation*. It is named in honor of its inventor, Jan Lukasiewicz (1878–1956).

POLITICAL ACTION COMMITTEE (PAC) separate and segregated fund established by an organization for making political contributions. These funds were authorized by the Federal Election Campaign Act of 1971 and clarified through subsequent court decisions. PACs allow organizations to contribute money to federal elections, control the disbursement of funds, solicit contributions from an organization's shareholders and employees, and accept contributions from any lawful source. PACs have been extremely important in financing elections.

POLLUTION
1. in industry, disposal of waste products into air, water, and land.
2. crossbreeding that can be regarded as the source of degeneration of a stock. Mixing inferior product components with standard components results in the pollution of a product.

PONZI SCHEME any false investment opportunity where the promoter uses money from new investors to pay interest and principal redemptions of existing investors. The scheme collapses when required redemptions exceed new investment. Named after Charles Ponzi who perpetuated such a scheme in the 1920s under the pretense of his opportunities to make money through international currency transactions.

POOL
Corporate finance: concept that investment projects are financed out of a pool of funds rather than out of bonds, preferred stock, and common stock individually. A weighted average cost of capital is thus used in analyses evaluating the return on investment projects. *See also* COST OF CAPITAL.
Industry: joining of companies to improve profits by reducing competition. Such poolings are generally outlawed in the United States by various ANTITRUST LAWS.
Insurance: association of insurers who share premiums and losses in order to spread risk and give small insurers an opportunity to compete with larger ones.
Investments: (1) combination of resources for a common purpose or benefit; (2) group of investors joined together to use their combined power to manipulate security or commodity prices or to obtain control of a corporation. Such pools are outlawed by regulations governing securities and commodities trading.

Real estate: a group of mortgages that are used as collateral for a PASS-THROUGH SECURITY. *See also* BLIND POOL.

POOLING OF INTERESTS accounting method formerly used in the combining or merging of companies following an acquisition, whereby the balance sheets (assets and liabilities) of the two companies are simply added together, item by item.

POOP AND SCOOP illegal scheme whereby unfavorable information about a stock is circulated, usually on the Internet, to drive down its price so it can be bought cheaply and later converted into a profit. *Contrast* PUMP AND DUMP.

POPULATION *see* UNIVERSE.

POPUP ADVERTISING messages that pop up in a new browser window to advertise products and services. There is strong consumer resentment about this method of advertising, resulting in software to block popups as well as *pop-unders,* new browser windows that open behind the current window (as opposed to in front of it), to be revealed when the current window is closed.

POPUP MENU a secondary MENU that appears above a selected menu item.

PORTABILITY characteristic of employee benefits such as pension and insurance coverage. Benefits are *portable* if employees can retain them when they leave to take a job with another employer.

PORTABLE COMPUTER *see* NOTEBOOK COMPUTER.

PORTABLE DOCUMENT FORMAT *see* PDF.

PORTAL-TO-PORTAL PAY compensation for all expenses incurred while traveling from door to door. Portal-to-portal pay is used in business organizations for business-related purposes, such as business travel where all expenses including transportation are covered.

PORTFOLIO
1. group of SECURITIES held by an individual or institutional investor, which may contain a variety of common and preferred stocks, corporate and municipal bonds, certificates of deposit, and Treasury bills, that is, appropriate selections from the equity, capital, and money markets. The purpose of a portfolio is to reduce risk by diversification.
2. case or folder carried by artists to show their best works.

PORTFOLIO INCOME in taxation, includes interest, dividends, royalties, and gains and losses from investments, but not passive activity investments. The concept distinguishes passive, active, and portfolio income. PASSIVE LOSSES generally may not be offset against active or portfolio income.

PORTFOLIO MANAGER professional responsible for the securities PORTFOLIO of an individual or institutional investor. A portfolio manager may work for a mutual fund, pension fund, profit-sharing plan, bank trust department, or insurance company, as well as for private investors.

PORTFOLIO REINSURANCE coverage in which an insurance company's portfolio is *ceded* to a *reinsurer,* who reinsures a given percentage of a particular line of business.

PORTFOLIO THEORY sophisticated investment decision approach that permits an investor to classify, estimate, and control both the kind and the amount of expected risk and return; also called *portfolio management theory* or *modern portfolio theory*. Essential to portfolio theory are its quantification of the relationship between risk and return and the assumption that investors must be compensated for assuming risk.

PORT OF ENTRY shipping entry into a country where customs may inspect the shipment and assess duties when applicable.

PORTRAIT orientation of a computer screen or sheet of paper (for viewing or printing) in which the vertical dimension is greater than the horizontal.

POS *see* POINT-OF-SALE SYSTEM.

POSITION
In general: to deliberately put oneself, or a company, in a certain place such as a strategic market location.
Banking: bank's net balance in a foreign currency.
Finance: firm's financial condition.
Investments: (1) investor's stake in a particular security or market. A LONG POSITION equals the number of shares *owned;* a SHORT POSITION is the number of shares *owed*. (2) to take on a long or a short position in a stock.

POSITIONING *see* POSITION.

POSITION SCHEDULE BOND *see* FIDELITY BOND.

POSITIVE CARRY situation in which the cost of money borrowed to finance securities is lower than the yield on the securities. For example, if a fixed-income BOND yielding 10% is purchased with a loan bearing 8% interest, the bond has *positive carry*. The opposite situation is *negative carry*.

POSITIVE CASH FLOW *see* BEFORE-TAX CASH FLOW.

POSITIVE CORRELATION direct association between two variables. As one variable becomes large, the other also becomes large, and vice versa. Positive correlation is represented by CORRELATION COEFFICIENTS greater than 0. *See also* NEGATIVE CORRELATION.

POSITIVE LEVERAGE use of borrowed funds that increases the return on an investment. *See also* LEVERAGE; REVERSE LEVERAGE.

POSITIVE YIELD CURVE usual situation in which interest rates are higher on long-term debt securities than on short-term debt securities of the same quality. *See also* INVERTED YIELD CURVE.

POSITIVE YIELD CURVE

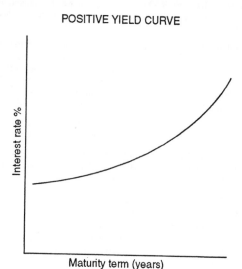

FIGURE 7

POSSESSION having, holding, or detaining PROPERTY in one's control. When compared with mere CUSTODY, possession involves custody plus the assertion of a right to exercise dominion.

POSSESSION UTILITY additional consumer value created by transferring a product's ownership. Various time payment, leasing, and credit purchase strategies can be important in making a product more attractive to a consumer. *See also* FOUR PS.

POST transfer accounting entries from a journal of original entry into a ledger book, in chronological order according to when they were generated. Banks would traditionally *post* checking account deposits and withdrawals in a ledger, then summarize these transactions on the monthly bank statement. Now such operations are computerized.

POSTAGE METER machine used to apply postage in lieu of printed stamps. The owner or renter puts postage in the machine by having post office personnel set it for the amount paid. The postage meter can then issue postage by printing on an envelope or on gummed labels until the amount of money paid is exhausted by postage consumed.

POSTAGE RATE cost of mailing a letter or package that is set by the U.S. Postal Service. The rate depends upon the parcel's weight and destination and the service sought.

POST-CLOSING TRIAL BALANCE TRIAL BALANCE after the CLOSING ENTRIES have been recorded.

POSTDATED CHECK check dated in the future. It is not negotiable until the date becomes current.

POSTING
1. to affix physically in order to display.
2. in bookkeeping, to list on the company's records, such as to list the detail of sales and purchases on the accounts receivable or payable records.
3. in civil procedure, affixing of certain required information as a substitute form of service of process.
4. in commercial law, procedure that a bank follows in deciding to finally pay a negotiable instrument and in recording its payment.
5. exhibition of notices on real property, warning potential trespassers that fishing or hunting is not permitted by the property owner.

POSTMARK cancellation affixed on stamps by the U.S. Postal Service to indicate use of the postage. The date and place of mailing are usually indicated by the postmark and may be offered as evidence in a legal dispute of when and where something was mailed.

POSTSCRIPT a graphical command language for output devices such as laser printers. Many application programs are designed so that they send *PostScript* code to the printer, which directs the printer to print text and graphics—provided that the printer is PostScript-compatible.

POUND SIGN the character 00, used by some applications in number formatting switches or as a wildcard in searches. Also called *number sign* or *hash mark*.

POVERTY
1. relative measure within a society, being the state of having income and/or wealth so low as to be unable to maintain what is considered a minimum STANDARD OF LIVING.
2. in absolute terms, having income and/or wealth too low to maintain life and health at a SUBSISTENCE level.

POWER CENTER a shopping center with few TENANTS, most of them ANCHOR TENANTS. Generally, a *power center's* anchor tenants are "category killers," that is, the dominant retailers in the markets they serve.

POWER OF ATTORNEY (POA) instrument by which one person, as principal, appoints another as his agent and confers upon him the authority to perform certain specified acts or kinds of acts on behalf of the principal. The primary purpose of a *power of attorney* is to evidence the authority of the agent to third parties with whom the agent deals. A person need not be an attorney-at-law to have the power of attorney to act for another. There are several types of POA: general, specific, durable, and springing.

POWER OF SALE clause, sometimes inserted in mortgages or deeds of trust, which grants the lender (or trustee) the right to sell the property upon certain default. The property is to be sold at auction but court authority is unnecessary. *See also* POWER OF ATTORNEY.

POWERS OF APPOINTMENT *see* GENERAL POWER OF APPOINTMENT; SPECIAL POWER OF APPOINTMENT.

POWERPOINT presentation software from Microsoft, included in the OFFICE suite. Used for preparing "slides" to be printed as overhead projector transparencies or projected directly from a computer screen. Coordinated speaker notes and handouts can also be produced.

POWER SURGE sudden increase in voltage that enters a computer or word processor through the power line; potentially damaging to electrical equipment, especially computers.

PPM pages per minute, a measure of the speed of printers.

PPP *see* POINT-TO-POINT PROTOCOL.

PRACTICAL CAPACITY highest activity level at which the factory can operate with an acceptable degree of efficiency, taking into consideration unavoidable losses of productive time (i.e., vacations, holidays, repairs to equipment); also called *maximum practical capacity. See also* CAPACITY.

PRECAUTIONARY MOTIVE cause of an action preventing something else from occurring. For example, a home owner puts the car in the garage at night to prevent it from being stolen.

PRECIOUS METALS gold, silver, platinum, and palladium. These metals are valued for their intrinsic value, backing world currencies, as well as their beauty or industrial applications. Fundamental issues of supply and demand are important factors in their prices, along with political and economic considerations, especially when producing countries are involved. Inflation fears will stimulate gold accumulation and higher prices, as will war and natural disaster, especially in major producing or consuming countries or regions.

PRECLOSING rehearsal of the closing whereby instruments are prepared and signed by some or all parties to the contract; used when closings are expected to be complicated.

PRECLOSING TRIAL BALANCE *see* TRIAL BALANCE.

PREDATORY LENDING a practice attributed to certain mortgage lenders that seeks to take advantage of the ignorance or gullibility of borrowers. Often associated with refinancing, HOME EQUITY LINES OF

CREDIT, or home improvement lending, these practices can take one (or more) of several forms: saddling borrowers with more debt than they can handle, tricking a borrower into a loan with high rates and fees, and overcharging or charging twice for routine services.

PREDATORY PRICING deliberate pricing of merchandise or services for the sole purpose of driving competitors of similar products or services out of the market. Once these competitors are eliminated, the intent is to raise the price. *See also* ANTITRUST ACTS.

PREDICTION foretelling of a future event. Predictions are probabilistic estimates of future occurrences based upon many different estimation methods, including past patterns of occurrence and statistical projections of current data.

PREEMPTIVE RIGHTS right specified in the CHARTER of a corporation, granting to existing shareholders the first opportunity to buy a new issue of stock.

PREEXISTING USE land use that is not in conformance with the current ZONING code, but is allowed to continue because the use was in effect at the time the code was passed; also called NONCONFORMING USE. Continuation of the land use is typically conditioned on certain limitations on improvement and rebuilding of the existing structures.

PREFABRICATED
1. constructed, as building components, in a factory prior to being erected or installed on the construction site.
2. constructed, as a house, of prefabricated components. *See also* MODULAR HOUSING.

PREFERENCE choice of one alternative over another. For example, some people show a preference for certain colors over others because they make them feel happy.

PREFERENCE ITEM *see* TAX PREFERENCE ITEM.

PREFERENCES settings that allow a computer user to customize the working environment; also called *options*. For example, mouse software allows users to set the double-click rate and tracking, whereas other programs allow users to choose the appearance of certain screen elements such as dialog boxes (whether buttons are "sculptured," for example), the extent to which the program provides automated assistance, and whether or not a reminder to save or information about the function of a button is displayed. In many applications, users can choose where files will be stored, whether backups will be made, and the file format to be used as the default.

PREFERENCE SHARES *see* PRIOR-PREFERRED STOCK.

PREFERENTIAL REHIRING provision in Title VII of the 1964 Civil Rights Act according to which companies can be enjoined under Section 203(g) to reinstate or hire employees with back pay, where appropriate, in cases where illegal job discrimination as defined under the law has occurred. The purpose is to "make whole" victims of past discrimination.

PREFERRED DIVIDEND distributions from corporate earnings and profits paid to owners of PREFERRED STOCK. These payments take priority over those to be made to common shareholders.

PREFERRED DIVIDEND COVERAGE net income after interest and taxes, but before common stock dividends, divided by the dollar amount of preferred stock dividends. The result tells how many times over the preferred dividend requirement is covered by current earnings.

PREFERRED-PROVIDER ORGANIZATION (PPO) group health-care provider that gives reduced rates when there is an agreement to provide medical care through the provider's organization.

PREFERRED RISK insured, or an applicant for insurance, with lower expectation of incurring a loss than the *standard applicant*. For example, an applicant for life insurance who does not smoke can usually obtain a reduced premium rate to reflect greater life expectancy.

PREFERRED STOCK part of the CAPITAL STOCK of a corporation that enjoys priority over the remaining stock, or COMMON STOCK, in the distribution of dividends and in the event of dissolution of the corporation, also in the distribution of assets.

PREGNANCY DISCRIMINATION ACT (PDA) an amendment to Title VII of the Civil Rights Act of 1964. Discrimination on the basis of pregnancy, childbirth, or related medical conditions constitutes unlawful sex discrimination. Women who are pregnant must be treated in the same manner as other applicants or employees with similar abilities or limitations.

PRELEASE to obtain LEASE commitments in a building or complex prior to its being available for occupancy. As a requirement for obtaining a permanent mortgage, a developer must often *prelease* 50% of the space in an office building or shopping center.

PRELIMINARY PROSPECTUS first document released by an underwriter of a new issue to prospective investors. The document offers financial details about the issue, but parts of the document may be changed before the final prospectus is issued. Because portions of the cover page of the preliminary prospectus are printed in red ink, it is popularly called the *red herring*. This also applies to the sale of cooperative apartments.

PREMISES
1. land and its appurtenances; land or a portion thereof and the structures thereon.
2. any place where an employee may go in the course of his employment when injuries insured under Workers' Compensation Acts are considered.

PREMIUM amount that an insured is charged, reflecting an expectation of loss or risk. The insurance company will assume the risks of the insured (length of life, state of health, property damage or destruction, or liability exposure) in exchange for a premium payment.

PREMIUM BOND bond with a selling price above face or redemption value. A bond with a face value of $1,000, for instance, is a *premium bond* if it sells for $1,050. For tax purposes, the premium may be amortized on a straight-line basis over the life of the bond.

PREMIUM INCOME income received by an investor who sells a PUT OPTION or a CALL OPTION.

PREMIUM PAY special pay rate given to employees for working weekends, holidays, or late shifts, or for doing hazardous work. Sometimes referred to as penalty pay, it is a premium paid as an incentive to work at either unattractive times or dangerous occupations.

PREMIUM RATE
1. price of a unit of insurance.
2. in finance, premium fee on some stocks when borrowed for trading, as in selling short.

PRENUPTIAL AGREEMENT or PRENUPTIAL CONTRACT agreement between a future husband and wife that details how the couple's financial affairs are to be handled both during the marriage and in the event of divorce. The agreement may cover insurance protection, ownership of housing and securities, and inheritance rights.

PREPAID EXPENSES amounts that are paid prior to the period they cover. Such expenses often include insurance and rent. *Prepaid expenses* are not tax deductible until the appropriate period. Rent paid in advance is not tax deductible even by a cash basis taxpayer. *See also* ECONOMIC PERFORMANCE RULE.

PREPAID INCOME includes rents or interest received in advance and compensation for services to be performed later. *Prepaid income* is generally included in taxable income in the year received.

PREPAID INTEREST interest paid in advance of the time it is earned. *Prepaid interest* is not tax deductible. An exception is for customary points paid by a borrower on the initial mortgage to purchase a principal residence.

PREPAYMENT
In general: paying a debt obligation before it comes due. *See also* RULE OF 78s.
Accounting: expenditure for a future benefit.
Banking: paying a loan before maturity. Some loans, in particular mortgages, have a prepayment clause that allows prepayment at any time without penalty, while others charge a fee if a loan is paid off before being due.

Securities: paying a seller for a security before the settlement date.
Taxes: prepaying taxes, for example, to have the benefit of deducting state and local taxes from one's federal income tax return in the current calendar year rather than in the next year.

PREPAYMENT CLAUSE clause in a bond or mortgage that gives the borrower the privilege of paying the mortgage indebtedness before it becomes due. Sometimes there is a penalty for prepayment, with waiver of the interest that is not yet due. *See also* CALL FEATURE.

PREPAYMENT PENALTY fee paid by a borrower for the privilege of retiring a loan early. A prepayment penalty on a personal loan or home mortgage is not a tax deductible interest expense. *See also* CALL PREMIUM; CLOSED PERIOD.

PREPAYMENT PRIVILEGE right of a borrower to retire a loan before maturity. *See also* prepayment clause; call privilege.

PREQUALIFY estimate the most expensive home a buyer can afford based on the buyer's income and available liquid assets. The exercise does not promise any specific financing or obligate the buyer to accept it; it merely indicates that the buyer may be able to afford a home up to a specific price. Prequalification differs from *pre-approval,* whereby a lender agrees to a loan amount for that borrower.

PREROGATIVE unquestioned right or privilege belonging to an individual.

PRESALE sale of proposed properties, such as condominiums, before construction begins. For example, a developer may presell condominium units at a discount before construction begins. Based on the presales, a developer is able to get a favorable CONSTRUCTION LOAN.

PRESCRIPTION
1. means of acquiring an EASEMENT on the land of another by continued regular use over a specified period of time. ADVERSE POSSESSION bestows complete ownership, whereas *prescription* bestows an easement.
2. remedy to cure a problem.
3. pharmaceutical product that requires a physician's authorization; the written authorization itself.

PRESCRIPTIVE RIGHT *see* PRESCRIPTION.

PRESENTATION setting forth in words and visuals a speech to enlighten an audience and/or persuade them to commit themselves to a course of action. An effective presentation is usually planned, organized, and tailored to a specific audience to help facilitate the behavior change desired by the presenter.

PRESENT FAIRLY term used in the *auditor's report* where there exists sufficient disclosure, reasonable detail, and absence of bias. Adequate disclosure requires all management information necessary to interpret financial statements. *Reasonable detail* requires that certain particulars of broad statement classifications be presented, such as intangible assets that are broken down into types. *Absence of bias* means that the auditor is independent and impartial and does not favor one party over another (i.e., STOCKHOLDER over INVESTOR).

PRESENTMENT online billing. Useful for sending online invoices to customers after their orders have been fulfilled. (*See also* FULFILLMENT.)

PRESENT VALUE (WORTH) today's value of a future payment, or stream of payments, discounted at some appropriate compound interest, or discount, rate; also called *time value of money*. The *present value* method, also called the DISCOUNTED CASH FLOW method, is widely used in corporate finance to evaluate a proposed capital investment project or to measure the expected return. In security investments, the method is used to determine how much money should be invested today to result in a certain sum at a future time. Presentvalue calculations are facilitated by present-value tables, which are compound interest tables in reverse.

PRESENT VALUE (WORTH) OF ANNUITY today's value of a level stream of income to be received each period for a finite number of periods. The formula is

$$\text{present value of annuity} = \frac{1 - \frac{1}{(1+i)^n}}{i}$$

where i is the interest rate and n the number of periods. For example, the present value of an annuity of $1.00 per year for 10 years, discounted at 12%, is $5.65. *See also* ORDINARY ANNUITY.

PRESENT VALUE (WORTH) OF 1 today's value of an amount to be received in the future, based on a COMPOUND INTEREST rate. For example, at a 12% interest rate, the receipt of one dollar one year from now has a present value of $0.89286. One dollar to be received in two years has a present value of $0.79719. Factors are based on the following formula:

$$\text{present value of \$1} = \frac{1}{(1+i)^n}$$

where i is the interest rate and n the number of periods.

PRESIDENT highest ranking officer in a corporation after the CHAIRMAN OF THE BOARD, unless the title CHIEF EXECUTIVE OFFICER (CEO) is used, in which case the president can outrank the chairman. The president is appointed by the BOARD OF DIRECTORS and usually reports directly to the board.

PRESIDENTIAL ELECTION CYCLE THEORY hypothesis of investment advisers that major stock market moves can be predicted based on the four-year presidential election cycle. Stocks should start to rise in anticipation of the economic recovery that the incumbent president wants to be roaring at full steam by election day.

PRESOLD ISSUE issue of municipal bonds or government bonds that is completely sold out before the price or yield is publicly announced.

PRESORT FIRST-CLASS MAIL reduced rate offered by the U.S. Postal Service for first-class mail that is part of a group of 10 or more pieces sorted to the same five-digit ZIP code or 50 pieces to the ZIP code with the same first three digits. The total mailing must exceed 500 pieces and the shipper must pay an annual fee in addition to postage for each piece.

PRESS KIT set of prepared press releases and related materials given to the press for general dissemination. Press kits are prepared by an organization, often by the public relations or press department, to give an official statement or view regarding a particular newsworthy event.

PRESS RELATIONS process of communicating with representatives of the mass media, including reporters, editors, and administrators.

PRESTIGE ADVERTISING advertising designed to enhance the prestige of a company or a company's products or services.

PRESTIGE PRICING pricing reflecting the assumption that consumers will not pay less than a predetermined price floor for merchandise since it is believed that otherwise it will be of inferior quality. Bloomingdale's, for example, does not carry inexpensive retail items since this would be perceived as inferior quality.

PRESUMPTION
1. impertinent or irritating opinion, conduct, or speech.
2. assumption made until proven incorrect; inference made from available information.

PRETAX EARNINGS or PRETAX PROFIT NET INCOME (earnings or profit) before federal income taxes.

PRETAX INCOME the amount earned from a business or investment before deducting income taxes.

PRETAX RATE OF RETURN yield or capital gain on a particular security before taking into account an individual's tax situation. *See also* RATE OF RETURN.

PREVENTIVE HEALTH SERVICES *see* HEALTH MAINTENANCE ORGANIZATION (HMO).

PREVENTIVE MAINTENANCE keeping property and equipment in a good state of repair so as to minimize the need for more costly major repair work or replacement. The life of a system can be prolonged through continual preventive maintenance.

PRICE/BOOK RATIO ratio of a stock's price to its BOOK VALUE per share. This number is used by SECURITIES ANALYSTS and money managers to judge whether a stock is undervalued or overvalued. A stock selling at a high *price/book ratio*, such as 3 or higher, may represent a popular GROWTH STOCK with minimal book value. A stock selling below its book value may attract value-oriented investors.

PRICE DISCRIMINATION the practice of charging different people different prices for the same goods or services. When price discrimination is engaged in for the purpose of reducing competition, as, for instance, through tying the lower prices to the purchase of other goods or services, it constitutes a violation of ANTITRUST ACTS.

PRICE-EARNINGS (P/E) RATIO price of a stock divided by its earnings per share, also known as the *multiple*. The P/E ratio may either use the reported earnings from the latest year (called a *trailing P/E*) or employ an analyst's forecast of next year's earnings (called a *forward P/E*). The trailing P/E is listed along with a stock's price and trading activity in the daily newspapers. For instance, a stock selling for $20 a share that earned $1 last year has a trailing P/E of 20. If the same stock has projected earnings of $2 next year, it will have a forward P/E of 10.

PRICE ELASTICITY relationship between the total amount spent on a good in the market and the price of the good. It is the percentage change in quantity divided by the percentage change in price. If a price decrease results in larger total expenditure (and vice versa), the good is *price elastic*. If a price decrease results in less total expenditure (or vice versa), the good is price inelastic.

PRICE-FIXING under federal ANTITRUST LAWS, combination or conspiracy for the purpose and with the effect of raising, lowering, or stabilizing the price of a commodity in interstate commerce.

PRICE INDEX index that traces the relative changes in the price of an individual good, or a MARKET BASKET of goods, over time. Wellknown price indexes are the CONSUMER PRICE INDEX (CPI) and the PRODUCER PRICE INDEX (PPI).

PRICE INELASTICITY *see* PRICE ELASTICITY.

PRICE LEADER (LEADERSHIP) the firm in an OLIGOPOLISTIC industry whose output pricing decisions are most likely to be matched (up or down) by most other firms. The *price leader* establishes the pricing of products or services that becomes a pattern in the industry. This reduces competition and makes it less difficult for competitors to make pricing decisions.

PRICE LEVEL range of market prices of a good, or prices of goods, usually used in comparison with prices of the same items at different times.

PRICE STABILIZATION collection of government policies designed to halt or slow down rapid changes of price, usually during inflationary episodes or shortages.

PRICE SUPPORT government-set price floor designed to aid farmers or other producers of goods. For instance, the government sets a minimum price for sugar that it guarantees to sugar growers. If the market price drops below that level, the government makes up the difference.

PRICE SYSTEM element of an economic system in which the market-determined price determines the ALLOCATION OF RESOURCES; generally accepted as part of the capitalist system.

PRICE WAR retailers in the same line of business continually trying to underprice each other, sometimes below actual merchandise costs, as a competitive strategy to attract customers. Price wars result in low profits and often in bankruptcy. Since deregulation the major air carriers have frequently waged price wars.

PRICEY
In general: product offered at a price at or near the top of what the market will bear.
Investment: unrealistically low bid price or unrealistically high offer price. If a stock is trading at $15, a pricey bid might be $10 a share, and a pricey offer $20 a share.

PRICING ABOVE (BELOW) THE MARKET retail pricing strategy to attract customers either with a high price image, strong personal service, and merchandise quality or by underbidding the competition in the case of below-the-market pricing. For example, retailers in a highly competitive environment, such as gas stations, may price below the market in order to attract customers.

PRIMA FACIE at first view, on its face. The term relates to a circumstance that does not require further support to establish existence, validity, credibility. For example, Sid is caught with untaxed cigarettes. In the state where he is caught, untaxed cigarettes are designated *prima facie* contraband and are immediately subject to forfeiture to the state.

PRIMARY BENEFICIARY *see* BENEFICIARY.

PRIMARY BOYCOTT union boycott of an employer's products, goods, or services by preventing their use, purchase, or transportation. No effort is made to involve or persuade those not directly involved in the dispute, as in a SECONDARY BOYCOTT.

PRIMARY DATA original data compiled and studied for a specific purpose. For example, a structured survey might be conducted for the purpose of discovering current attitudes on a particular topic; raw survey responses would be *primary data.*

PRIMARY DEMAND market demand by consumers of noncapital goods. *See also* DERIVED DEMAND.

PRIMARY DISTRIBUTION sale of a new issue of stocks or bonds, as distinguished from a SECONDARY DISTRIBUTION, which involves previously issued stock. All issuances of bonds are primary distributions.

Also called *primary offering,* but not to be confused with *initial public offering,* which refers to a corporation's *first* distribution of stock to the public.

PRIMARY EARNINGS PER (COMMON) SHARE earnings available to common stock (which is usually net earnings after taxes and preferred dividends) divided by the number of common shares outstanding. *See also* DILUTION.

PRIMARY LEASE LEASE between the owner and a tenant whose interest, all or in part, has been sublet.

PRIMARY MARKET market for new issues of securities, as distinguished from the SECONDARY MARKET, where previously issued securities are bought and sold. A market is primary if the proceeds of sales go to the issuer of the securities sold.

PRIMARY MARKET AREA
1. newspaper or related publication's major area of editorial and advertising coverage. For example, XYZ newspaper may do a story on the XYZ fire department because it is situated in its primary market area. Similarly, retailers would place an ad in the XYZ newspaper if they were interested in reaching consumers living in XYZ's primary market area.
2. major area of sale and distribution for an advertiser's product or service; also called *heartland.* For example, the primary market area for woolen hats would be northern states or other coldweather regions. Abbreviated PMA.

PRIMARY METROPOLITAN STATISTICAL AREA (PMSA) a geographic entity designated by the federal Office of Management and Budget for use by federal statistical agencies. If an area that qualifies as a METROPOLITAN AREA (MA) has a census population of one million or more, two or more primary metropolitan statistical areas (PMSAs) may be defined within it if they meet official standards and local opinion favors the designation. When PMSAs are established within an MA, that MA is designated a CONSOLIDATED METROPOLITAN STATISTICAL AREA (CMSA).

PRIMARY PACKAGE package in which a unit of the product is sold. For example, a bag of potato chips is the *primary package*, and the carton in which the potato chips are shipped is the *outer package*.

PRIMARY STORAGE DEVICES memory area of computer where current data are stored. This section of the computer is referred to as RANDOM ACCESS MEMORY (RAM) and consists of volatile memory chips. Unless this information is saved to a SECONDARY STORAGE DEVICE, it will be lost when the computer is powered down. *See also* READ-ONLY MEMORY (ROM).

PRIME CONTRACTOR *see* GENERAL CONTRACTOR.

PRIME COST *see* DIRECT COST.

PRIME PAPER highest quality COMMERCIAL PAPER, as rated by Moody's Investor's Service and other rating agencies. Prime paper is considered INVESTMENT GRADE. Moody's has three ratings of prime paper: P-1 (highest quality), P-2 (higher quality), and P-3 (high quality).

PRIME RATE interest rate banks charge to their most creditworthy customers. The rate is determined by the market forces affecting a bank's cost of funds and the rates that borrowers will accept. The prime rate tends to become standard across the banking industry when a major bank moves its prime rate up or down. Banks may offer major customers discounts on the prime rate.

PRIME TENANT in a shopping center or office building, tenant who occupies the most space. Prime tenants are considered creditworthy and attract customers or traffic to the center. *See also* ANCHOR TENANT.

PRINCIPAL
1. one who owns or will use property. For example, the principals to the lease are the landlord and the tenant; principals to a sale are the buyer and the seller.
2. one who contracts for the services of an agent or broker; the broker's or agent's client.
3. amount of money raised by a mortgage or other loan, as distinct from the INTEREST paid on it. *See also* PRINCIPAL AMOUNT.

PRINCIPAL AMOUNT FACE VALUE of an obligation, such as a bond or a loan, that must be repaid at maturity, as separate from the INTEREST. Principal payments are not tax deductible. Principal receipts in repayment of a loan are not taxable income, but principal receipts from a sale may be taxable if the sale was reported as an INSTALLMENT SALE.

PRINCIPAL AND INTEREST PAYMENT (P&I) periodic payment, usually paid monthly, that includes the interest charges for the period plus an amount applied to amortization of the principal balance; commonly used with amortizing loans. *See also* AMORTIZATION; DEBT SERVICE; MORTGAGE CONSTANT.

PRINCIPAL, INTEREST, TAXES, AND INSURANCE PAYMENT (PITI) periodic, typically monthly, payment required by an amortizing loan that includes ESCROW deposits. Each periodic payment includes a principal and interest payment plus a contribution to the escrow account set up by the lender to pay insurance premiums and property taxes on the mortgaged property.

PRINCIPAL PLACE OF BUSINESS test for determining whether a home office is deductible. *See* HOME OFFICE.

PRINCIPAL RESIDENCE place where one lives most of the time.

PRINCIPAL STOCKHOLDER stockholder who owns a significant number of shares in a corporation. Under Securities and Exchange

Commission (SEC) rules, a principal stockholder owns 10% or more of the voting stock of a REGISTERED COMPANY.

PRINCIPAL SUM
Finance: obligation due under a debt instrument exclusive of interest.
Insurance: amount specified as payable to the beneficiary under a policy, such as the death benefit.

PRINCIPLE rule or general standard adhered to in most areas of human conduct. A principle can be an ethical declaration, as in "do unto others as you would have them do unto you."

PRINTER device for putting computer output on paper. Printer types include line printer, daisy-wheel printer, dot-matrix printer, electrostatic printer, ink jet printer, laser printer, and thermal printer.

PRINTOUT HARD COPY (paper) output from a computer, such as selected information from or analyses of computer files or simply a printout of the information currently on the computer screen. Some printouts, such as statistical analyses, require special programs to tell the computer how to produce them. Others, such as a printout of the screen, are produced by the basic operating system programs.

PRIORITY (1) preference; (2) coming before, or coming first, in a bankruptcy proceeding; (3) right to be paid before other creditors out of the assets of the bankrupt party. The term may also be used to signify such a right in connection with a prior lien, prior mortgage, and so on.

PRIORITY MAIL class of mail offered by the U.S. Postal Service for parcels that weigh more than 12 ounces, up to 70 pounds; combined length and girth must not exceed 108 inches. The most expeditious method of shipping is used on Priority Mail; two-day service is generally provided but not guaranteed. Letter mail may also be expedited by being sent Priority Mail; the minimum rate (which covers letters and parcels up to one pound) is currently $4.05.

PRIORITY OF TAX LIEN a federal TAX LIEN for nonpayment of taxes has priority over most other liens. However, a federal tax lien is not valid against any purchaser, holder of a security interest, mechanic's lienor, or judgment lien creditor until the tax lien has been properly recorded. Certain "superpriorities" (e.g., on securities, automobiles) may be superior to a tax lien.

PRIOR PERIOD ADJUSTMENT in accounting, charge that relates to a previous year that should have no effect on the current year, such as the collection or payment of money arising from litigation of an event that occurred in the past. Once made by changing RETAINED EARNINGS, accountants should consult the most recent statement of the Financial Accounting Standards Board for instructions.

PRIOR-PREFERRED STOCK PREFERRED STOCK that ranks ahead of other issues of preferred stock or common stock in terms of payment of dividends and its claim on assets in the event of liquidation; also known as *preference shares.*

PRIOR SERVICE COST amount that needs to be contributed for employee benefits under a pension plan for employment before a given date.

PRIVACY LAWS laws passed by the United States Congress upon the recommendations of the Privacy Protection Study Commission established by the Privacy Act of 1974. The laws require mailing list owners who rent their list to other direct marketers to inform people on the list that the list is being rented and to give each individual "an opportunity to indicate to the organization that he does not wish to have his address . . . made available for such purposes."

PRIVATE ACCOUNTANTS in-house accountants employed by an organization for the purpose of maintaining financial control and supervising the organization's accounting system. A CONTROLLER is an organization's most senior private accountant.

PRIVATE BRANDS product brands owned by a retailer or a wholesaler rather than the manufacturer; also called *house brands.* They normally retail at a less expensive price than a NATIONAL BRAND.

PRIVATE CARRIER company's transportation system designed for its own shipping requirements.

PRIVATE CORPORATIONS corporations whose shares are owned by private individuals or companies. Their shares trade on the major STOCK EXCHANGES, giving them great liquidity. *See also* PUBLIC CORPORATIONS.

PRIVATE FOUNDATION family or corporate foundation engaged in charitable activities. Stricter contribution limitations and various penalty and excise taxes apply to private foundations. *See* PUBLIC CHARITY.

PRIVATE ISSUE *see* PRIVATE PLACEMENT.

PRIVATE LAW law governing relationships between two or more private individuals, companies, or organizations. It has not been passed or ruled upon by a public authority. *See also* PUBLIC LAW.

PRIVATE MORTGAGE INSURANCE DEFAULT insurance on conventional loans, provided by private insurance companies. *See also* MORTGAGE INSURANCE.

PRIVATE OFFERING or PRIVATE PLACEMENT investment or business offered for sale to a small group of investors, generally under exemptions to registration allowed by the Securities and Exchange Commission and state securities registration laws. *See also* REGULATION D.

PRIVATE RULING reply from the Internal Revenue Service regarding the tax treatment of a proposed transaction. At one time, private rulings were unpublished, but they have been made public information and are published by several private companies. Nonetheless, only the party to whom the private ruling was issued may rely on it. *See also* ADVANCE RULING.

PRIVATIZATION
1. process of making private, such as a public corporation repurchasing its outstanding stock or a nationalized company or government service agency reverting to the private sector. Privatization involves removing an organization from public ownership.
2. in international affairs, transferring ownership of housing, businesses, and other property from government or social ownership to individuals or businesses, especially in Eastern Europe in the 1990s.

PRIVILEGE right or prerogative to do something that is unique to the individual or to a group. For example, wealth has its privileges.

PRIVITY relationship between parties out of which arises mutuality of interest. *See also* EASEMENT; RUN WITH THE LAND.

PRIZE BROKER arranger of the exchange of an advertiser's merchandise for free broadcast time or publicity plugs on a radio or television show; also called *barter broker.* A prize broker is employed by a company specializing in the "bartering" of merchandise for broadcast services, and is frequently called upon by game shows for these services.

PROACTIVE having an orientation to the future, anticipating problems and taking affirmative steps to deal positively with them rather than reacting after a situation has already occurred.

PROBABILITY chance or likelihood that something will happen or has happened.

PROBABILITY DENSITY FUNCTION for a discrete random variable, the *probability density function* at a specific value is the probability that the random variable will have that value; for a continuous random variable, the probability density function is represented by a curve such that the area under the curve between two numbers is the probability that the random variable will be between those two numbers.

PROBATE
1. act of proving that an INSTRUMENT purporting to be a WILL was signed and otherwise executed in accordance with the legal requirements for a will, and of determining its validity.
2. combined result of all procedures necessary to establish the validity of a will. *See* AVOIDING PROBATE.

PROBATE ASSETS those assets in an ESTATE that are subject to PROBATE and court disposition and thus become part of public records.

PROBATE ESTATE property passing by WILL or by operation of state INTESTATE succession law from a DECEDENT to his or her HEIRS or other BENEFICIARIES. Probate estate may be quite different from GROSS ESTATE.

PROBATIONARY EMPLOYEE
1. new employee being considered for permanent status. A probationary employee has no seniority privileges or status and may be discharged without cause, except where the discharge violates affirmative action laws.
2. current employee being placed on probation as a disciplinary act before being dismissed.

PROCEEDS
1. funds given to a borrower after all interest costs and fees are deducted.
2. money received by the seller of an asset after commissions are deducted; for example, the amount a stockholder receives from the sale of shares, less broker's commission.

PROCEEDS FROM RESALE *see* RESALE PROCEEDS.

PROCESS CONTROL SYSTEM computerized sensing system that monitors specialized devices and processes within a controlled environment. The system has the capability of automatically making adjustments to maintain preset environmental specifications.

PROCESS DIVISION management method of dividing the productive procedures in a manufacturing organization into organizational segments. For example, in an automobile factory the processes may be divided according to engine block casting, engine assembly, and engine testing.

PROCUREMENT acquisition of goods (materials, parts, supplies, equipment) required to carry on an enterprise. Procurement expenses can be a major cost of doing business.

PROCURING CAUSE legal term that means the cause resulting in accomplishing a goal, used in real estate to determine whether a broker is entitled to a commission.

PRODIGY an ONLINE SERVICE now owned by AT&T (formerly SBC Corporation).

PRODUCE
1. to make, fabricate, or bring forth something. For example, farmers produce wheat and corn. Automobile manufacturers produce cars.
2. fruits and vegetables.

PRODUCER COOPERATIVE organization of producers who cooperate in the areas of buying supplies and equipment and of marketing.

PRODUCER GOODS new machinery and equipment bought for business use; *durable goods* used in business production. *See also* CAPITAL GOODS.

PRODUCER PRICE INDEX (PPI) measure of wholesale prices, formerly called the *wholesale price index,* released on a monthly basis by the U.S. Bureau of Labor Statistics. Prices are calculated as products move through the manufacturing and distribution stages, before they reach the consumer.

PRODUCT output or end result of production process. For example, automobiles are a product of the automobile companies.

PRODUCT ADVERTISING advertising targeted at specific products or services that describes features, benefits, and performance.

PRODUCT DEVELOPMENT PROCESS stages of introducing a new product or service concept and managing its development until it actually comes to market. The stages include analyzing the market, targeting potential buyers, understanding the productive capacity of the organization, developing a product to fit the market needs, distributing it to the marketplace, and analyzing customer feedback.

PRODUCT DIFFERENTIATION *see* DIFFERENTIATION STRATEGY.

PRODUCT IMAGE *see* BRAND IMAGE.

PRODUCTION formal activity that adds value to goods and services, including creation, transport, and warehousing until used. Production is an organized process with specific goals.

PRODUCTION AND OPERATIONS MANAGEMENT (POM) planning, coordination and controlling of an organization's resources to facilitate the production process. POM is an extremely important management area. Issues such as the location of production facilities, labor and transportation costs, and PRODUCTION FORECASTING are extremely important considerations.

PRODUCTION CONTROL planning, routing, scheduling, dispatching, and inspection of operations or given items being manufactured.

PRODUCTION FORECASTING process of judging how much production is required to meet estimated sales in a particular forecasting period. Considerations include previous sales, the general state of the economy, consumer preferences, and competitive products. Production forecasting decisions affect budgetary and scheduling decisions.

PRODUCTION-ORIENTED ORGANIZATION organization whose primary function is production. A production-oriented organization can either perform the production itself or contract for the production. For example, an automobile company is a production-oriented organization.

PRODUCTION-POSSIBILITY CURVE graphic representation of various possible outputs of two goods with a fixed supply of resources that are fully employed; also called *transformation curve*. A production-possibility curve is useful for determining possible product mixes.

PRODUCTION RATE rate at which a production line manufactures a product.

PRODUCTION WORKER workers directly concerned with the manufacturing operation processes of an organization, as opposed to supervisory and clerical employees; also called *production line workers.*

PRODUCTIVE state of being creative. For example, an artist who is very prolific is said to be *productive. See also* PRODUCTIVITY.

PRODUCTIVITY measured relationship of the quantity and quality of units produced and the labor per unit of time. For example, an increase in productivity is achieved through an increase in production per unit of labor over time. *See also* PRODUCTIVE.

PRODUCT LIABILITY in general, a manufacturer's responsibility to market safe products. Under the law of TORTS, a manufacturer is held strictly liable when one of its products, placed on the market with the knowledge that it will be used without inspection for defects, proves to have a defect that causes injury to a human being.

PRODUCT LIFE CYCLE development of a product from introduction or birth, through various growth and development stages, to deletion or death. Names have been given to four stages in the life cycle: introduction, growth, maturity, and decline. It guides marketing managers in developing marketing strategy and decisions.

PRODUCT LINE group of products manufactured by a firm that are closely related in use and in production and marketing requirements. The *depth* of the product line refers to the number of different products offered in a product line.

PRODUCT MANAGER *see* BRAND MANAGER.

PRODUCT MIX the assortment of merchandise made or held for sale.

PRODUCT RESEARCH AND DEVELOPMENT (PR&D) activity performed by a team of professionals working to transform a product idea into a technically sound and promotable product; also called *research & development (R&D).* Corporate research and development (R&D) departments are found in both large and small companies and are generally responsible for product development and testing, researching brand names, and creating an effective packaging concept.

PROFESSION certain activity that requires a high level of education and standard of ethical behavior. Professions include medicine, law, teaching, professional accountancy, and architecture.

PROFESSIONAL ASSOCIATION *see* PROFESSIONAL CORPORATION.

PROFESSIONAL CORPORATION a corporation formed for the purpose of engaging in one of the learned professions, such as law, medicine, or architecture. Traditionally, corporations were prohibited from engaging in such professions because they lacked the human, personal qualifications necessary to pursue them. Within recent years, however, most states have enacted a *professional corporation* or association act that allows professional persons to practice in the corporate form provided that all shareholders are members of the profession.

PROFESSIONAL EMPLOYER ORGANIZATION (PEO) a staffing firm that provides employees to another company through *employee leasing* or *staff leasing*. The PEO is the employer of record and, in exchange for a fee from the client company, may provide many or all of the following services: paying wages and employment taxes of the employee out of its own accounts; reporting, collecting, and depositing employment taxes with state and federal authorities; establishing and maintaining a co-employment relationship with its employees that is intended to be long-term and not temporary; assuming responsibility as an employer for specified purposes of the workers assigned to the client locations; and sharing the responsibility of co-employees' wages and safety with the client. In essence, PEOs assume the burden of HUMAN RESOURCES MANAGEMENT for client companies.

PROFESSIONAL LIABILITY INSURANCE coverage for specialists in various professional fields. Since basic liability policies do not protect against situations arising out of business or professional pursuits, *professional liability insurance* is purchased by individuals who hold themselves out to the general public as having greater than average expertise in particular areas.

PROFIT

Finance: positive difference that results from selling products and services for more than the cost of producing these goods. *See also* NET INCOME.

Investment: difference between selling price and purchase price of commodities or securities when the selling price is higher.

PROFITABILITY, PROFITABILITY RATIO measure of earnings, expressed as a percentage of earnings on sales, total costs, total assets, or equity.

PROFIT AND LOSS STATEMENT (P&L) summary of the revenues, costs, and expenses of a company during an accounting period; also called INCOME STATEMENT, *operating statement, statement of profit and loss, income and expense statement.*

PROFIT CENTER segment of a business organization that is responsible for producing profits on its own. A conglomerate with interests in hotels, food processing, and paper may consider each of these three businesses separate profit centers, for instance.

PROFITEER making excessive profits, often to the detriment of others. One who is profiteering is pursuing the act of making excessive profits.

PROFIT MARGIN *see* MARGIN OF PROFIT.

PROFIT MOTIVE desire to earn a favorable financial return on a business venture. Without a profit motive, tax losses from an activity may be considered a hobby loss, deductible only to the extent of income.

PROFITS AND COMMISSIONS FORM insurance coverage protecting future profits to be earned from a manufacturer's inventory. A manufacturer may lose all or part of an inventory due to a peril such as fire and still be able to operate. But in the event that an inventory and other merchandise is destroyed by an insured peril, the insured is indemnified for the loss of profit or commissions.

PROFIT-SHARING PLAN agreement between a corporation and its employees that allows the employees to share in company profits. Annual contributions are made by the company, when it has profits, to a profit-sharing account for each employee, either in cash or in a deferred plan, which may be invested in stocks, bonds, or cash equivalents. The funds in a profit-sharing account generally accumulate tax deferred until the employee retires or leaves the company. Many plans allow employees to borrow against profit-sharing accounts for major expenditures such as purchasing a home or financing children's education.

PROFIT SQUEEZE expression that indicates more difficulty to maintain the same amount or rate of profit as in the past, due to reduced prices or rising production costs, financing costs, general and administrative expenses, or taxes.

PROFIT SYSTEM element of the capitalist economic system in which profit directs the activities of entrepreneurs and determines the makeup of the production side of markets. *See also* INVISIBLE HAND.

PROFIT TAKING action by short-term securities or commodities traders to cash in on gains earned on a sharp market rise. Profit taking pushes down prices.

PROFIT-TAKING STRATEGY *see* MILKING STRATEGY.

PRO FORMA presentation of data, such as a BALANCE SHEET or INCOME STATEMENT, where certain amounts are hypothetical. For example, a *pro forma* balance sheet might show a debt issue that has been proposed but has not yet been consummated, or a pro forma income statement might reflect a merger that has not yet been completed.

PROGRAM
1. organized event, typically over a set time period, such as a *training program.*
2. set of instructions for a computer to execute. A program can be written in a programming language, such as BASIC or Pascal, or in an assembly language.

PROGRAM BUDGETING method of budgeting expenditures to meet programmatic objectives rather than on a line-item basis. In program budgeting, specific performance objectives are used in formulating systematic costs for all related functions, as opposed to totaling line-item requests.

PROGRAM EVALUATION AND REVIEW TECHNIQUE (PERT) planning and control technique to minimize interruptions and/or delays in a process with interrelated functions. PERT is used to assist in reducing the time required for completion of a project.

PROGRAMMABLE FUNCTION (PF) KEY key on a computer keyboard whose function depends on the software being run. In many cases, PF keys can be defined as equivalent to combinations or sequences of other keys.

PROGRAMMER person who prepares instructions for computers. A programmer receives directions from a *systems analyst.*

PROGRAM TRADE institutional buying (*buy program*) or selling *(sell program)* of all stocks in a program or index on which options and/or futures are traded. Massive program trade activity has been held responsible for large-scale daily stock market fluctuations.

PROGRESSIVE TAX tax whose rate increases as the amount subject to tax increases, thereby taxing the wealthy at a higher rate than the poor or middle class. *See also* REGRESSIVE TAX.

PROGRESS PAYMENTS payments to a contractor as work is performed; in construction, loan payments issued to the builder as building is completed. *See also* DRAW.

PROJECTED BENEFIT OBLIGATION actuarial present value as of a date of all benefits attributed by the pension benefit formula to employee service performed before that date. It is measured using assumptions as to *future* compensation levels if the pension benefit formula is based on those future salary levels (e.g., pay-related, final-pay).

PROJECTED FINANCIAL STATEMENT *see* PRO FORMA.

PROJECTION estimate of future performance made by economists, corporate planners, and credit and securities analysts. Economists use econometric models to project GROSS DOMESTIC PRODUCT (GDP), inflation, unemployment, and many other economic factors. Corporate financial planners project a company's operating results and CASH FLOW, using historical trends and making assumptions where necessary.

PROJECTION PERIOD the time duration for estimating future CASH FLOWS and the RESALE PROCEEDS from a proposed investment. For example, a 10-year *projection period* is typically used in a DISCOUNTED CASH FLOW analysis of income-producing real estate.

PROJECT MANAGEMENT organizational management system that assigns employees to specific projects teams when special projects are contracted and then reassigns them back to the organization when the project is completed. Project management also involves coordinating project activities with organizational divisions and departments in order to complete their objective.

PROMISSORY NOTE NEGOTIABLE INSTRUMENT wherein the maker agrees to pay a specific sum at a definite time; often simply called a *note.*

PROMOTION
1. job advance, with higher level of pay and responsibility.
2. selling techniques, including advertising, printing, and salesperson commissions.

PROMOTIONAL ALLOWANCE reduction of the wholesale price as an incentive to retailers or middlemen. A promotional allowance compensates the retailer for expenditures made promoting the product. *See also* ALLOWANCE.

PROMOTION MIX promotion that supports marketing objectives, including advertising, personal (face-to-face) selling, publicity (non-paid advertising such as news bulletins or magazine articles), and sales promotion (product displays, trade shows and other sales events, dealer allowances, coupons, contests, and a variety of other promotions that don't fit into the other three types).

PROMPT
1. payment on or before the due date.
2. symbol that appears on a computer terminal screen to signal to the user that the computer is ready to receive input. Different programs use different prompts. For example, under CP/M and IBM PC DOS, the prompt looks like A> or B>, depending on whether A or B is the default disk drive.

PROOF OF CLAIM a document filed with a court by a creditor to verify position as a holder of debt.

PROOF OF LOSS documentation of loss required of a policyowner by an insurance company. For example, in the event of an insured's death, a death certificate must be submitted to the company for a life insurance death benefit to be paid to the beneficiary.

PROPERTY
1. every valuable right or interest that is subject to ownership, has an exchangeable value, or adds to one's wealth or estate. *Property* describes one's exclusive right to possess, use, and dispose of a thing, as well as the object, benefit, or prerogative that constitutes the subject matter of that right.
2. real estate.

PROPERTY DAMAGE LIABILITY INSURANCE coverage in the event that the negligent acts or omissions of an insured result in damage or destruction to another's property.

PROPERTY DEPRECIATION INSURANCE coverage that provides for replacement of damaged or destroyed property on a new replacement cost basis without any deduction for depreciation. This is equivalent to *replacement cost* property insurance.

PROPERTY INSURANCE *see* INSURANCE PROPERTY COVERAGE.

PROPERTY LINE recorded boundary of a plot of land.

PROPERTY MANAGEMENT operation of property as a business, including rental, rent collection, maintenance, and so on. For example, the following tasks are often required in the ownership of property: accounting and reporting, leasing, maintenance and repair, paying taxes, provision of utilities and insurance, remodeling, and rent rate setting and collection.

PROPERTY REPORT required by the Interstate Land Sale Act for the sale of SUBDIVISIONS of 50 lots or more, if the subdivisions are not otherwise exempt. It is filed with HUD's OFFICE OF INTERSTATE LAND SALES REGISTRATION.

PROPERTY RIGHTS rights to the ownership and stewardship of, and profits from, land, capital, and other goods. Extensive property rights of private individuals in most goods is a basic element of the capitalist system.

PROPERTY TAX tax imposed by municipalities upon owners of property within their jurisdiction, based upon the assessed value of such property. The property tax on real estate is the principal method of financing for local governments and school districts. *See* AD VALOREM.

PROPORTIONAL TAXATION tax whose burden is applied at the same rate to the poor as to the wealthy. *Contrast* PROGRESSIVE TAX, REGRESSIVE TAXATION.

PROPRIETARY owned by a particular person. In TRADE SECRETS law, proprietary property is information or knowledge in which the person developing it has ownership rights. Such rights are usually protected by contract and have not been the subject of a PATENT application.

PROPRIETARY DRUGS *see* OVER-THE-COUNTER MEDICINE.

PROPRIETARY INTEREST any right in relation to a CHATTEL that enables a person to retain its possession indefinitely or for a period of time.

PROPRIETARY LEASE lease between the resident/stockholder in a cooperative apartment and the cooperative as owner of the building. *See also* CONDOMINIUM.

PROPRIETARY OPERATING SYSTEM computer operating system that functions on only one type of computer. Proprietary operating systems limit the ability of SOFTWARE applications to run on other systems and also limit the market for any APPLICATION SOFTWARE.

PROPRIETOR owner; the person who holds TITLE to property. *See* PROPRIETARY; PROPRIETORSHIP; SOLE PROPRIETORSHIP.

PROPRIETORSHIP unincorporated business owned by a single person. The individual proprietor has the right to all the profits from the business and also responsibility for all the firm's liabilities. The income of a proprietorship is reported on Schedule C of the owner's

Form 1040. If the taxpayer is actively involved in the business, the net income is also subject to SELF-EMPLOYMENT TAX.

PRO RATA proportionate allocation. For example, a *pro rata* property tax rebate might be divided proportionately (*prorated*) among taxpayers based on their original assessments, so that each gets the same percentage. *See also* PRORATE.

PRO RATA CANCELLATION revocation of a policy by an insurance company, which returns to the policyholder the *unearned premium* (the portion of the premium for the remaining period that the policy will not be in force). There is no reduction for expenses already paid by the insurer for that time period.

PRO RATA DISTRIBUTION CLAUSE provision in many property insurance policies that automatically distributes coverage over insured property at various locations in proportion to their value.

PRORATE to allocate between seller and buyer their proportionate share of an obligation paid or due; for example, when a house is sold to prorate real property taxes or insurance; or to refund unused rent or an unexpired subscription.

PROS AND CONS strategic advantages and disadvantages regarding a particular situation. For example, the *pros and cons* of launching a new product at a particular time have to be weighed in terms of competitive and other market factors.

PROSPECT
1. to seek customers.
2. person considered likely to buy; prospective purchaser. *See also* COLD CANVASS.
3. potential employee, particularly in professional sports.
4. *see* QUALIFIED PROSPECT.

PROSPECTUS formal written offer to sell securities that sets forth the plan for a proposed business enterprise or the facts concerning an existing one that an investor needs to make an informed decision. *See also* PRELIMINARY PROSPECTUS.

PROSPERITY situation of ECONOMIC GROWTH, low UNEMPLOYMENT, and general sense of well-being of most of the economy's population.

PROTECT, PROTECTION, PROTECTIONISM, PROTECTIONIST economic policies designed to restrict imports of goods that compete with domestic producers. Protectionists advocate protectionism in order to protect domestic producers from foreign competition.

PROTECTIVE COVENANT *see* COVENANT.

PROTEST
1. stated objection, disapproval, or complaint regarding a particular matter or product.
2. to remonstrate or complain about something.

PROTOCOL
  1. formal diplomatic rules of etiquette.
  2. a series of rules and conventions that allow different kinds of computers and applications to communicate over a NETWORK.

PROVEN PROPERTY the principal value of an oil or gas property, demonstrated by prospecting, exploration, or discovery work. A development well would be *proven property,* but not a wildcat well.

PROVISION *see* ALLOWANCE.

PROVISO condition or stipulation. Its general function is to except something from the basic provision, to qualify or restrain its general scope, or to prevent misinterpretation.

PROXY
  In general: person authorized to act or speak for another.
  Business: (1) written POWER OF ATTORNEY given by shareholders of a corporation, authorizing a specific vote on their behalf at corporate meetings; (2) person authorized to vote on behalf of a stockholder of a corporation.

PROXY FIGHT technique used by an acquiring company to attempt to gain control of a TAKEOVER target. The acquirer tries to persuade the shareholders of the target company that the present management of the firm should be ousted in favor of a slate of directors favorable to the acquirer. If the shareholders agree, they can sign proxy statements allowing the acquiring company the right to vote their shares.

PROXY STATEMENT information that the Securities and Exchange Commission requires to be provided to shareholders before they vote by proxy on company matters. The statement contains proposed members of the board of directors, inside directors' salaries, and pertinent information regarding their bonus and option plans.

PRUDENCE displaying foresight, caution, and discretion in one's actions; not acting carelessly and recklessly. One acts prudently by being careful with one's actions.

PRUDENT-MAN RULE standard adopted by some U.S. states to guide those with responsibility for investing the money of others. Such FIDUCIARIES (executors of wills, trustees, bank trust departments, and administrators of estates) must act as a prudent man or woman would be expected to act, with discretion and intelligence, to seek reasonable income, preserve capital, and, in general, avoid speculative investments.

PSYCHIC INCOME income in a form other than monetary. Psychic income gratifies psychological and emotional needs. Power, prestige, recognition, and fame are all forms of *psychic income.*

PSYCHOGRAPHICS determining market segmentation based on consumer psychological profiles. The two general areas include how the consumer views himself or herself in relation to the rest of the world and income characteristics.

PUBLIC ACCOUNTANT recognized in a few states, accountants who served the public before there was an accountancy law could be grandfathered as public accountants; distinguished from CERTIFIED PUBLIC ACCOUNTANT (CPA).

PUBLIC ACCOUNTING independent CERTIFIED PUBLIC ACCOUNTANT'S function, resulting in an ACCOUNTANT'S OPINION or auditor's report.

PUBLIC ADJUSTER representative of an insurance claimant, as may be needed by an owner in the event of major property damage.

PUBLIC CARRIER *see* COMMON CARRIER.

PUBLIC CHARITY organization that draws its support from a broad base within the community, along with schools, churches, and hospitals. More generous contribution limitations apply to donors. Generally, aggregate income from the four previous years must be received from individual contributions or governmental sources, and not more than one-third may consist of investment income and unrelated business income.

PUBLIC CORPORATIONS corporations formed by federal, state, and local governments for specific public purposes, including education, health and hospitals, waste removal, and transportation. The Port Authority of New York and the Tennessee Valley Authority (TVA) are two examples.

PUBLIC DEBT borrowings by governments to finance expenditures not covered by current tax revenues.

PUBLIC DOMAIN
1. all lands and waters in the possession of the United States, and all lands owned by the several states, as distinguished from lands possessed by private individuals or corporations.
2. information, the source of which is available to anyone and is not subject to COPYRIGHT.

PUBLIC EMPLOYEE person employed in the public sector. Public employees are found at all levels of government, from the federal, state, and local levels to special districts. Public employees are elected, appointed, or chosen for the civil service on the basis of merit examinations.

PUBLIC GOODS products the government is best positioned to utilize as compared to the private marketplace. Police power and military-related hardware are most effectively managed by the government.

PUBLIC HOUSING government-owned housing units made available to low-income individuals and families for nominal rental rates.

PUBLIC HOUSING AUTHORITY BOND obligation of local public housing agencies, secured by an agreement between the Department of Housing and Urban Development and the local housing agency, that provides that the federal government will loan the local authority a sufficient amount of money to pay principal and interest to maturity.

PUBLIC INTEREST values generally thought to be shared by the public at large. However, there is no one public interest. Rather, there are many public interests depending upon individual needs.

PUBLIC INTEREST RESEARCH GROUP (PIRG) *see* U.S. PUBLIC INTEREST RESEARCH GROUP (USPIRG).

PUBLIC LAND acreage held by the government for conservation purposes. Public lands are generally undeveloped, with limited activities such as grazing, wildlife management, recreation, timbering, mineral development, water development, and hunting. Many western states, such as Alaska and Nevada, have large amounts of public lands. A part of this area is held by the federal government and is dedicated to national parks, wilderness, and wildlife refuges. Some oil and mineral exploration is allowed under LEASE to private firms.

PUBLIC LAW constitutional, statutory, or judicial law developed by governments and applied equally to the general public. *Contrast with* PRIVATE LAW.

PUBLICLY HELD CORPORATION a corporation that has a class of common stock registered on a national stock exchange.

PUBLICLY TRADED CORPORATION *see* PUBLICLY HELD CORPORATION.

PUBLICLY TRADED PARTNERSHIP (PTP) a LIMITED PARTNERSHIP formed under state partnership law where limited partnership interests are publicly traded on an established exchange or "over the counter"; also called MASTER LIMITED PARTNERSHIP. Registration of interests in publicly traded partnerships is required under federal securities laws.

PUBLIC OFFERING soliciting the general public for the sale of investment units. It generally requires approval by the Securities and Exchange Commission and/or state securities agencies. *See also* GOING PUBLIC; PRIVATE OFFERING.

PUBLIC OWNERSHIP
Government: government ownership and operation of a productive facility for the purpose of providing some good or service to citizens. Examples of publicly owned enterprises in the United States include the postal service and numerous transportation and public utilities corporations.
Investment: portion of a corporation's stock that is publicly owned and traded in the open market.

PUBLIC RECORD

1. in real estate, land transaction records kept at the county courthouse. Documents that are evidence of real estate transactions should be taken to the county courthouse to be officially entered in the public record. Recording gives CONSTRUCTIVE NOTICE of a document's existence.
2. court documents, such as pleading in a case, consent decrees, divorce, and so on.

PUBLIC RELATIONS (PR) form of communication that is primarily directed to image building and that tends to deal with issues rather than specifically with products or services. Public relations uses publicity that does not necessitate payment in a wide variety of media and is often placed as news or items of public interest.

PUBLIC SALE sale upon notice to the public and in which members of the public may bid.

PUBLIC USE right of the public to use or to benefit from the use of property condemned by the government through the exercise of its power of EMINENT DOMAIN. One of the limitations upon the use of this power is that property so taken must be for a public use.

PUBLIC UTILITY a for-profit company that, because of the nature of its business, has characteristics of a *natural monopoly*. For instance, an electric company will have a natural monopoly over the sale of electric power in a given area, since having a single supplier of electricity for that area is the most efficient method of producing and distributing electricity. Because no free market or competition exists for the services or goods sold by *public utilities*, they are subject to government regulation of the price they may charge and the means by which they may distribute their goods. The concept of natural monopoly is currently being challenged, and deregulation of utilities, permitting competition, is now occurring in certain segments.

PUBLIC WORKS government project created for the public good and paid for from public revenues. Examples are the construction of dams, highways, schools, and government buildings.

PUD *see* PLANNED UNIT DEVELOPMENT.

PUFFING overstating the qualities of a property, often by a salesperson. It could be grounds for a misrepresentation lawsuit.

PULL-DOWN MENU a secondary MENU that appears below a selected menu item.

PULL STRATEGY promotional strategy whereby the seller concentrates marketing efforts on the end user through advertising, direct mail, flyers, and related activities. The concept seeks to educate consumers regarding the target products so they will ask retailers to offer them to the public. Subsequently the retailers request the products from wholesalers or manufacturers.

PUMP PRIMING economic policy of increasing government expenditures and/or reducing taxes in order to stimulate the economy to higher levels of output. Pump priming measures are supposed to be temporary, existing only until the economy spontaneously develops and sustains growth on its own.

PUMP AND DUMP illegal scheme whereby a large stockholder hires a promoter to help publicize, or pump, the stock, often by means of SPAM emails or JUNK FAXES. The shareholder then makes a profit by dumping his investment at an artificially inflated price. *Contrast* POOP AND SCOOP.

PUNCH CARD index card punched with holes representing data. Punch cards were the dominant way of feeding information into computers in the 1960s but became obsolete as interactive terminals became widely used. *See also* KEYPUNCH.

PUNCH LIST enumeration of items that need to be corrected, such as repairs to a machine or building, prior to or after a sale.

PUNCTUALITY quality of being on time and meeting deadlines. A person displaying punctuality is responsible and reliable.

PUNITIVE DAMAGES compensation in excess of actual damages that is a form of punishment to the wrongdoer and reparation to the injured. Punitive damages are awarded only in rare instances of malicious and willful misconduct. They are taxable unless the damages arise from physical injury or sickness; such damages are excludable from income taxes.

PUR AUTRE VIE for the life of another; estate that one person grants to another only for the duration of the life of a third person.

PURCHASE acquisition that is bought, as contrasted with an EXCHANGE, GIFT, or INHERITANCE. Generally the purchase price serves as the ORIGINAL COST BASIS.

PURCHASE CAPITAL the amount of money used to purchase a business or investment, regardless of the source.

PURCHASE CONTRACT *see* CONTRACT OF SALE; PURCHASE AGREEMENT.

PURCHASE DISCOUNT *see* CASH DISCOUNT.

PURCHASE JOURNAL book where purchases on ACCOUNT are first recorded.

PURCHASE MONEY MORTGAGE loan from a seller in lieu of cash for the purchase of property. Such mortgages make it possible to sell property when mortgage money is unavailable or when the only buyers are unqualified to borrow from commercial sources.

PURCHASE ORDER written authorization to a vendor to deliver specified goods or services at a stipulated price. Once accepted by the supplier, the purchase order becomes a legally binding purchase CONTRACT.

PURCHASING POWER value of money as measured by the goods and services it can buy. For example, the PURCHASING POWER OF THE DOLLAR can be determined by comparing an index of consumer prices for a given base year to the present.

PURCHASING POWER OF THE DOLLAR measure of the amount of goods and services that a dollar can buy in a particular market, as compared with prior periods, assuming always an INFLATION or a DEFLATION factor and using an index of consumer prices. It might be reported, for instance, that one dollar in 1982–1984 had 50 cents of purchasing power in 2006 because of the erosion caused by inflation.

PURE CAPITALISM economic system in which the principles of CAPITALISM operate unfettered by any limiting factor such as government control or interference. By inference, government performs little except those functions that cannot be performed by any other entity.

PURE COMPETITION market for a homogeneous product in which there are many producers and consumers, none of which are large enough to have any individual effect upon the market on their own. In theory such a market produces the largest output at the lowest price. There are few, if any, real-world markets of this nature; probably the closest in the United States are markets for farm products.

PURE-MARKET ECONOMY economy in which PURE COMPETITION prevails.

PURE RISK situation where there is a risk of loss with no opportunity for gain. These are conditions, including fires, natural disasters, and liability, where the need for insurance coverage is clearly indicated as there is only the risk of loss with no possibility of beneficial gain. *Contrast with* SPECULATIVE RISK.

PUSH MONEY (PM) money or other incentives given by a manufacturer to retail salespeople for selling its own products. Push money, also called *promotional money* or *prize money,* is additional compensation given to salespeople by the manufacturer. It is controversial with retailers because of possible divided loyalties.

PUT OPTION contract that grants the right to sell at a specified price a specific number of shares by a certain date. A put or call is considered a CAPITAL ASSET when held by a nondealer. *See also* CALL OPTION; WRITER.

PUT TO SELLER phrase used when a PUT OPTION is exercised. The option WRITER is obligated to buy the underlying shares at the agreed-upon price.

P **VALUE** statistic relating whether or not the sample supports the tested hypothesis. *P* values are the probability that a calculated test statistic as large or larger occurred by chance alone. *P* values range from 0 to 1. A zero *P* value would indicate that the probability of sampling a population and obtaining a test statistic with as large or larger a value was nonexistent. Typically, *P* values less than 0.05 are deemed statistically significant, resulting in rejection of the NULL HYPOTHESIS.

PYRAMIDING

1. use of financial leverage or paper profits from an investment to finance purchases of additional investments.
2. building of a business through a dealership network designed primarily to sell dealerships rather than useful products.
3. fraudulent business practice in which the chain of distribution is artificially expanded by an excessive number of distributors selling to other distributors at progressively higher wholesale prices, ultimately resulting in unnecessarily inflated retail prices.
4. *see* PONZI SCHEME.

Q

Q-TIP TRUST *see* QUALIFIED TERMINABLE INTEREST PROPERTY (QTIP) TRUST.

QUALIFIED CHARITY an organization that has applied for and received tax-exempt status.

QUALIFIED ENDORSEMENT ENDORSEMENT that contains wording designed to limit the endorser's liability. "Without recourse" means that if the instrument is not honored, the endorser is not responsible.

QUALIFIED OPINION language in the auditor's opinion accompanying financial statements that calls attention to limitations of the audit or exceptions the auditor takes to items in the statements. Typical reasons for qualified opinions: pending lawsuit that, if lost, would materially affect the financial condition of the company; indeterminable tax liability relating to an unusual transaction; inability to confirm a portion of the inventory because of inaccessible location. *See also* ACCOUNTANT'S OPINION.

QUALIFIED ORGANIZATION an organization to which a deductible charitable contribution may be made.

QUALIFIED PLAN or QUALIFIED TRUST pension or profitsharing plan set up by an employer for the benefit of employees that adheres to the rules set forth by the Internal Revenue Service in 1986. An employer receives an immediate deduction, the trust income is not taxable, and the employee is taxed on the income only upon receipt.

QUALIFIED PROSPECT prospective buyer who has the requisite financial resources, motivation, and authority to make a purchase of a given product or service.

QUALIFIED REPLACEMENT PROPERTY property acquired in a LIKE-KIND EXCHANGE or due to an INVOLUNTARY CONVERSION if it has the same qualified use as that of the replaced property before the exchange.

QUALIFIED RESIDENCE the PRINCIPAL RESIDENCE and one other residence of a taxpayer or spouse. Interest paid on a *qualified residence* may be deductible as an ITEMIZED DEDUCTION; *see* INTEREST DEDUCTION.

QUALIFIED RESIDENCE INTEREST interest on a home mortgage, which may be deductible as an ITEMIZED DEDUCTION. Includes interest on ACQUISITION INDEBTEDNESS and on HOME EQUITY LOANS. *See also* INTEREST DEDUCTION.

QUALIFIED TERMINABLE INTEREST PROPERTY (Q-TIP) TRUST strategy providing that all income from assets in trust be paid at least annually for the life of the surviving spouse. This trust, which prohibits transfer of any assets to anyone else, can provide for the surviving spouse to will the property to one or more individuals among a group previously designated by the deceased spouse.

QUALIFIED TRANSFER any amount paid for an individual (1) to an educational organization for the individual's education or training or (2) to any person for medical care provided to the individual. For gift tax purposes, total gifts for the year do not include qualified transfers.

QUALIFIED TUITION PROGRAM (QTP, 529 PLAN) an investment vehicle created under the Small Business Job Protection Act of 1996 that allows individuals to make tax-deductible contributions to accounts that accumulate tax-free income if used to cover a beneficiary's qualified educational expenses.

QUALIFYING PERSON for purposes of HEAD OF HOUSEHOLD filing status:
1. a child, grandchild, stepchild, or adopted child. *a.* A *single* child does not have to be a dependent, except for a foster child. *b.* A *married* child must be the taxpayer's dependent unless the other parent claims the child as a dependent under the noncustodial rules.
2. any relative living with the taxpayer whom the taxpayer can claim as a dependent. A dependent parent does not have to live with the taxpayer if the taxpayer paid more than half the cost of keeping up a home that was the parent's main home for the entire year.

QUALIFYING STOCK OPTION privilege granted to an employee of a corporation that permits the purchase, for a special price, of shares of its CAPITAL STOCK, under conditions sustained in the Internal Revenue Code.

QUALITATIVE ANALYSIS analysis that evaluates important factors for their presence or absence but does not measure them precisely. *See also* QUANTITATIVE ANALYSIS.

QUALITATIVE RESEARCH research that deals with the quality, type, or components of a group, substance, or mixture, whose methods are applied to advertising audience research in order to determine the quality of audience responses to advertising. Qualitative research is exploratory in nature and uses procedures such as indepth interviews and focus group interviews to gain insights and develop creative advertising tactics.

QUALITY characteristic or standard measure of excellence; basic character of something. Quality is a measure of the degree to which something meets a standard.

QUALITY ASSURANCE management method of guaranteeing high-quality product and service standards are established and achieved. Quality assurance has to be a comprehensive management system that achieves TOTAL QUALITY MANAGEMENT having the ultimate objective of achieving zero defects.

QUALITY CIRCLES small groups of employees meeting on a regular basis within an organization for the purpose of discussing and developing management issues and procedures. Quality circles are established with management approval and can be important in implementing new procedures. While results can be mixed, on the whole, management has accepted quality circles as an important organizational methodology.

QUALITY CONTROL process of assuring that products are made to consistently high standards of quality. Inspection of goods at various points in their manufacture by either a person or a machine is usually an important part of the quality control process.

QUALITY ENGINEERING portion of quality management concerned with prevention planning and the correction of nonconformance with the production or service cycle.

QUALITY MANAGEMENT *see* TOTAL QUALITY MANAGEMENT.

QUALITY OF WORK LIFE (QWL) general employment environment within an organization affecting individual attitudinal and motivational mindset.

QUANT person with mathematical or computer skills who provides numerical and analytical support services.

QUANTITATIVE ANALYSIS analysis dealing with mathematically measurable factors as distinguished from such qualitative considerations as the character of management or the state of employee morale. *See also* QUALITATIVE ANALYSIS.

QUANTITATIVE RESEARCH research that deals with the quantities of things and that involves the measurement of quantity or amount, applied to advertising audience research to develop actual numbers of audience members in order to accurately measure market situations.

QUANTITY DISCOUNT discount in dollars or percent, allowed on the basis that the buyer will purchase a given quantity of merchandise; also called *volume discount.* For example, the unit price of an item may be $10.00. If more than 10 are bought at a time, the unit price drops to $7.50 for a 25% discount.

QUARTERLY
In general: every three months (one quarter of a year); magazine published every three months.
Securities: basis on which earnings reports to shareholders are made; also, usual time frame of dividend payments.

QUARTERLY RETURNS employment tax returns that are due quarterly to report gross wages paid and withholdings of income tax, Social Security tax, and Medicare tax. These include Forms 941, 942, and 943. Some state unemployment tax returns are also due quarterly.

QUARTILE statistical measurement. The first quartile of a list is the number that has three quarters of the numbers in the list below it; the fourth quartile is the number that has three quarters of the numbers above it; the second quartile is the same as the median.

QUASI CONTRACT obligation created by law for reasons of justice and fairness. The doctrine of quasi contract is based upon the principle that a party must pay for a benefit he desired and received under circumstances that render it inequitable for him to retain it without making compensation. For example, a car owner brings his car in for brake repairs. The mechanic fixes the brakes and in doing so he also fixes a separate part of the axle that has a direct relationship to the car's ability to brake correctly. Although the axle repair was not specifically contracted for, a quasi contract is implied for which the owner must pay the mechanic.

QUASI-PUBLIC CORPORATIONS organizations such as utilities or cable television companies with exclusive public charters to operate within a given service area. Quasi-public corporations have essentially been granted by a governmental entity a monopoly to provide a service.

QUEUE
1. line waiting to be served.
2. in computer use, data structure from which items are removed in the same order in which they were entered. Series of items such as PACKETS or print jobs waiting to be processed. For example, a print *queue* holds files waiting to be printed.

QUEUING THEORY (WAITING LINE THEORY) quantitative technique for balancing services available with services required. It evaluates the ability of service facilities to handle capacity and load at different times during the day. It is useful in problems of balancing cost and service level, such as determining the number of toll booths on a highway and the number of tellers in a bank.

QUICK ASSET cash or something that is readily convened into cash, including MARKETABLE SECURITIES and ACCOUNTS RECEIVABLES.

QUICK RATIO cash, marketable securities, and accounts receivable divided by current liabilities. By excluding inventory, this key liquidity ratio focuses on the firm's more LIQUID ASSETS, whose values are relatively certain. It is also called *acid-test ratio, quick asset ratio.*

QUID PRO QUO something for something; in some legal contexts, synonymous with consideration. It is sometimes referred to as the *Quid* and always indicates that which a party receives or is promised in return for something he promises, gives, or does.

QUIET ENJOYMENT right to unimpaired use and enjoyment of property. (1) For leased premises, a guarantee of quiet enjoyment is usually expressed by a COVENANT of quiet enjoyment in a written lease, but such a covenant may be implied today from the landlord-tenant relationship, even where it is not so expressed. (2) The covenant may be and often is included in a deed conveying title to property. If it is present in a deed, the grantor is obligated to protect the estate of his grantee against lawful claims of ownership by others.

QUIET TITLE SUIT to settle a controversy. For example, a lawsuit to *quiet title* to a piece of property can be undertaken when one believes oneself to be owner of a tract of land. If such is proven, one can legally extinguish claims of those who falsely assert ownership. A suit to quiet title enables the rightful owner to transfer clear title to the property. Historically, such lawsuits have been used to extinguish claims of a squatter on property.

QUIT end a session with a computer program by purposely closing the application; exit.

QUITCLAIM DEED DEED that conveys only that right, title, or interest that the grantor has, or may have, and does not warrant that the grantor actually has any particular title or interest in the property. The grantor under a quitclaim deed releases whatever interest he may have to the grantee. *See also* CLOUD TITLE; GENERAL WARRANTY DEED.

QUORUM minimum number of members of any body who must be present in order to transact the business of that body.

QUOTA
1. predetermined goal in a sales program established as a total dollar amount, as a percentage of increase over sales from a previous time, or in quantities of merchandise sold.
2. predetermined goal in a media plan established in terms of money to be spent, gross rating points to be achieved, or number of insertions and spots to be bought.
3. *see* QUOTA SAMPLE.

QUOTA SAMPLE sample group of people used for research purposes who have been selected at the discretion of the interviewer. The interviewer will be instructed to make selections from a minimum number of persons who fulfill the researcher's QUOTA classifications.

QUOTATION
1. in commercial usage, statement of the price of an item.
2. price stated in response to an inquiry.
3. BID AND ASKED price for stock at any moment.

QUO WARRANTO ancient COMMON LAW writ that was issued out of chancery on behalf of the king against one who claimed or usurped any office, FRANCHISE, or liberty, to inquire by what authority he asserted such a right, in order that the legitimacy of the assertion might be determined. Formerly a criminal method of prosecution, it has long since lost its criminal character and is now a civil proceeding, expressly recognized by STATUTE, and usually employed for trying the title to a corporate franchise or to a corporation or public office.

QWL *see* QUALITY OF WORK LIFE.

R

*r*² *see* COEFFICIENT OF DETERMINATION.

RABBI TRUST an irrevocable trust used to fund DEFERRED COMPENSA-TION benefits for key employees in the absence of a QUALIFIED PLAN OR TRUST. The name derives from an IRS letter ruling involving a rabbi whose congregation had made contributions to such a trust for his benefit. It is considered a GRANTOR trust, so income is taxed to the grantor or employer. The employer receives no deduction for payments of compensation to the trust but receives a deduction when the trust pays funds to the employee. The rabbi trust protects the employee's benefits from many company hazards, but not from insolvency or bankruptcy. *See also* SECULAR TRUST.

RACKET activity designed for the purpose of achieving gains, often involving extortion or the sale of illegal substances or services. *Racketeering* is an organized conspiracy to accomplish such activities.

RACKETEER-INFLUENCED AND CORRUPT ORGANIZATIONS ACT (RICO) *see* RACKETEERING.

RACKETEERING originally, an organized conspiracy to commit extortion. Today, punishable offenses legislated by Congress aimed at eradicating organized crime by providing for enhanced sanctions and new remedies to be used in dealing with the illegal activities of persons involved in organized crime.

RACK JOBBERS merchant wholesalers providing merchandise and rack displays at retail locations. *Rack jobbers* own the merchandise and work cooperatively with retailers in terms of sharing profits, thus relieving the retailer of the need to acquire merchandise while allowing him/her to benefit from the sale of the merchandise.

RADIO BUTTON (computers) a circle in a DIALOG BOX that can be clicked with a mouse to turn it on or off, thereby selecting one option or another. *Radio buttons* (named by analogy to the pushbuttons on a car radio) are used for mutually exclusive options. For example, in a Print dialog, the user may elect to print the entire document, selected pages, or just the current page.

RADIOGRAM message sent by radio, often to and from ships while they are at sea.

RAG CONTENT percentage of cotton fiber content of better quality paper. The percentage of rag content shows in print when paper is held up to light.

RAIDER individual or corporate investor who intends either to take control of a company by buying a controlling interest in its stock and installing new management, or to make a quick profit by threatening to take control and selling the stock back, receiving GREENMAIL.

RAILROAD RETIREMENT ACT congressional act that became effective in 1935. It provides retirement benefits to retired railroad workers and families from a special fund, which is separate from the social security fund.

RAIN INSURANCE business interruption insurance in which the insured is indemnified for loss of earnings and payment of expenses resulting from adverse weather conditions. For example, the raining out of a fair, horse race, or boxing match can cause a substantial loss of money for a promoter who may have spent huge sums in advance of the event for rental, advertising, and site conditioning. However, the policy does not cover damage to property because of rain.

RAINMAKER individual who brings significant amounts of new business to a company such as a law or accounting firm.

RAISED CHECK check on which the amount of money and possibly other information is raised above the smooth surface of the paper to prevent alteration. *See also* CHECK PROTECTOR.

RALLY marked rise in the price of a security, commodity future, or market after a period of decline or sideways movement.

RAM *see* RANDOM-ACCESS MEMORY.

RAMP UP increase rapidly. Describes the expected performance of sales and profits of a new business, which increase rapidly until a plateau is reached at maturity.

R&D research and development. *See* PRODUCT RESEARCH AND DEVELOPMENT.

RANDOM-ACCESS MEMORY (RAM) in computer use, device whereby any location in memory can be found, on average, as quickly as any other location. A computer's RAM is its main memory where it can store data, so the size of the RAM, measured in kilobytes or megabytes, is an important indicator of the capacity of the computer. *See also* MEMORY; READ-ONLY MEMORY (ROM).

RANDOM-DIGIT DIALING method of obtaining respondents for telephone interviews whereby the exchange digits are dialed and then the rest of the digits are dialed at random. Random-digit dialing gives accessibility to unlisted as well as listed telephone numbers.

RANDOM-NUMBER GENERATOR program that generates a sequence of numbers that seem to be completely random. For example, the basic statement $N = RND(0)$ causes the computer to generate a random number and assign its value to N. Random numbers provide a way of selecting a sample without human bias.

RANDOM SAMPLE sample selected from a population such that every member of the population had an equal chance of being selected, regardless of other members selected.

RANDOM VARIABLE a statistical term meaning any data.

RANDOM WALK theory about the movement of stock and commodity futures prices hypothesizing that past prices are of no use in forecasting future price movements. According to the theory, stock prices reflect reactions to new information coming to the market. Since new information arrives in random fashion, changes in stock prices are no more predictable than the walking pattern of a drunken person.

RANGE
Investment: high and low end of security, commodity future, or market price fluctuations over a period of time. Daily newspapers publish the 52-week high and low price range of stocks traded on the New York Stock Exchange, American Stock Exchange, and over-the-counter markets.
Statistics: difference between smallest and largest values in a sample.

RANK-AND-FILE ordinary dues-paying union members. Rank-and-file union members are not union officials.

RAPPORT environment of harmony, consonance, agreement, or accord achieved through activities encouraging this result. For example, a manufacturer develops a good *rapport* with his customers through the use of a hotline service.

RATABLE proportional; capable of estimation; taxable. A *ratable estate* is a taxable estate. In bankruptcy, a *ratable distribution* is a PRO RATA share of the bankrupt's assets. Ratable does not mean equal, but rather pro rata according to some measure fixing proportions.

RATE
1. *see* INTEREST RATE.
2. amount of a charge or payment with reference to some basis of calculation.

RATE BASE value established for a utility by a regulatory body, such as a Public Utility Commission, on which a regulated company is allowed to earn a particular rate of return. *See also* FAIR RATE OF RETURN.

RATE CARD document used in advertising to give the advertising cost per advertising unit. The rate card includes the space, time, mechanical requirement data, and other pertinent information.

RATED POLICY statement in which a life insurance applicant is charged a higher-than-standard premium to reflect a unique impairment, occupation, or hobby, such as a history of heart disease, a circus performer, or a sky diver.

RATE OF EXCHANGE *see* EXCHANGE RATE.

RATE OF INFLATION *see* CONSUMER PRICE INDEX (CPI); INFLATION RATE; PRODUCER PRICE INDEX (PPI).

RATE OF INTEREST same as INTEREST RATE.

RATE OF RETURN

    Corporate finance: *see* INTERNAL RATE OF RETURN (IRR); RETURN OF INVESTED CAPITAL.

    Securities: for bonds and preferred stock, CURRENT YIELD, that is, coupon or contractual dividend rate divided by purchase price. *See also* YIELD; YIELD TO CALL; YIELD TO MATURITY.

    Stocks: (1) dividend yield, that is, annual dividend divided by purchase price; (2) total return rate, that is, dividend plus capital appreciation. *See also* PRESENT VALUE.

RATE OF RETURN ON EQUITY a measure of the profitability of an investment, based not on total returns and total investment but on the amounts the equity owner expects to receive and has invested.

RATE SETTING establishment of utility rates by public service utility commissions.

RATIFICATION approval or confirmation by a person of a previous contract or other act that would not otherwise be binding on him in the absence of such approval.

RATING

    In general: process of systematically assigning ranks to goods and services.

    Credit, investment: evaluation of securities investment and credit risk by rating services such as Fitch Investors Service, Moody's Investors Service, Standard & Poor's Corporation, and Value Line Investment Survey. *See also* CREDIT RATING.

    Insurance: using statistics, mortality tables, probability theory, experience, judgment, and mathematical analysis to establish the rates on which insurance premiums are based.

RATIO ANALYSIS method of analysis, used in making credit and investment judgments, utilizes the relationship of figures found in financial statements to determine values and evaluate risks and compares such ratios to those of prior periods and other companies to reveal trends and identify eccentricities.

RATIONING method for limiting the purchase or usage of an item when the quantity demanded of the item exceeds the quantity available at a specific price. For example, during World War II many domestic items in the United States, including gasoline and other commodities, were *rationed*.

RATIO SCALE highest level of measurement in which not only the differences between observations are quantifiable, but the observations can themselves be expressed as a ratio. A 10,000-square-foot warehouse is both 50% smaller and 10,000 square feet less than a 20,000-square-foot warehouse. The ratio scale is the most powerful measurement scale. *See also* INTERVAL SCALE; NOMINAL SCALE; ORDINAL SCALE.

RAW DATA initial data a researcher has before beginning analysis.

RAW LAND acreage with no added improvements such as landscaping, drainage, streets, utilities, and structures.

RAW MATERIAL any product used as a component in the manufacturing process of finished goods. Wool is the raw material for woolen sweaters.

REACH total number of audience members who will receive a message at least once within a specified time period.

READING THE TAPE monitoring changes in stock prices as displayed on the ticker tape in an attempt to gauge immediate stock market conditions of a particular stock, industry group, or the market as a whole.

READJUSTMENT voluntary reorganization by the stockholders themselves of a corporation facing financial difficulties; the voluntary restructuring of a corporation's debt and capital structure.

README FILE a text computer file (usually with the name README. TXT) to be read before proceeding with, for example, installation of a software application. Usually contains information on compatibility issues discovered too late to be included in the printed documentation (if any) or online Help file.

READ-ONLY MEMORY (ROM) in computer use, device containing instructions that do not need to be changed, such as the instructions for calculating arithmetic functions. The computer can read instructions out of ROM, but no data can be stored in ROM.

READY, WILLING, AND ABLE capable of an action and disposed to act. If a real estate broker finds a *ready, willing, and able* person who agrees to buy under the terms of the listing, the broker has earned a commission because he fulfilled the requirements of the listing.

REAGANOMICS general collection of conservative, free-market economic policies favored by President Ronald Reagan and his administration, 1981–1989.

REAL
1. actual, as opposed to nominal.
2. used in economics, refers to measures such as price and income, which are corrected for inflation over time so as to permit a comparison of actual purchasing power.

REAL ACCOUNT balance sheet account that is carried forward into the next year. It is a proprietary account. *See also* NOMINAL ACCOUNT.

REAL EARNINGS wages, salaries, and other earnings, corrected for INFLATION over time so as to produce a measure of actual changes in PURCHASING POWER.

REAL ESTATE or REAL PROPERTY land and everything more or less attached to it; ownership below to the center of the earth (mineral rights) and above to the heavens (air rights); same as *realty*. Real property includes, but is not limited to:

1. a personal residence owned in fee simple.
2. a LIFE ESTATE to a farm.
3. rights to use land under a LEASE.
4. easements and other partial interests.

REAL ESTATE AGENT *see* AGENT.

REAL ESTATE BROKER person who arranges the purchase or sale of property for a buyer or seller in return for a commission. Brokers must be licensed by the state.

REAL ESTATE, DEPRECIABLE realty that is subject to deductions for DEPRECIATION. It generally includes property used in a trade or business, or an investment subject to an allowance for depreciation under Section 167 of the Internal Revenue Code. Land is generally not depreciable, but land with minerals may be subject to DEPLETION.

REAL ESTATE CLOSING *see* CLOSING.

REAL ESTATE COMMISSION state agency that enforces real estate license laws. Nearly all states have one. *See also* LICENSE LAWS.

REAL ESTATE INVESTMENT TRUST (REIT) a real estate mutual fund, allowed by income tax laws to avoid the corporate income tax. It sells shares of ownership and must invest in real estate or mortgages. It must meet certain other requirements, including minimum number of shareholders, widely dispersed ownership, and asset and income tests. If it distributes 95% of its income to shareholders, it is not taxed on that income, but shareholders must include their share of the REIT's income in their personal tax returns. Its unique feature is to allow small investors to participate, without double taxation, in large real estate ventures.

REAL ESTATE LIMITED PARTNERSHIP LIMITED PARTNERSHIP that invests in real estate. The partnership buys properties such as apartment or office buildings, shopping centers, industrial warehouses, and hotels and passes rental income through to the LIMITED PARTNERS. If the properties appreciate in value over time, they can be sold and the profit passed through to the limited partners. A GENERAL PARTNER manages the partnership, deciding which properties to buy and sell and handling administrative duties, such as distributions to limited partners.

REAL ESTATE MARKET potential buyers and sellers of REAL PROPERTY at the current time; also, current transaction activity for real property. This includes markets for various property types, such as housing market, office market, condominium market, land market.

REAL ESTATE MORTGAGE INVESTMENT CONDUIT (REMIC) a pass-through vehicle created under the TAX REFORM ACT OF 1986 to issue multiclass mortgage-backed securities. REMICs may be organized as corporations, partnerships, or trusts, and those meeting qualificaitons are not subject to DOUBLE TAXATION.

REAL ESTATE OWNED (REO) property acquired by a lender through foreclosure and held in inventory; commonly referred to as REO.

REAL ESTATE SETTLEMENT PROCEDURES ACT (RESPA) law that states how MORTGAGE lenders must treat those who apply for federally related real estate loans on property with one to four dwelling units. It is intended to provide borrowers with more knowledge when they comparison shop for mortgage money.

REAL ESTATE TRANSACTION a sale or exchange of reportable real estate for money, indebtedness, or property other than money or services, regardless of whether the transaction is currently taxable.

REAL INCOME income of an individual, group, or country adjusted for changes in PURCHASING POWER caused by inflation. For instance, if the cost of a market basket increases from $100 to $120 in ten years, reflecting a 20% decline in purchasing power, salaries must rise by 20% if real income is to be maintained.

REAL INTEREST RATE current interest rate minus inflation rate. The real interest rate may be calculated by comparing interest rates with present or, more frequently, with predicted inflation rates. With a bond yielding 8% and inflation of 3%, for instance, the real interest rate of 5% beats inflation. If inflation were at 9%, however, the investor would fall behind as prices rise.

REALIZABLE VALUE *see* NET REALIZABLE VALUE.

REALIZED GAIN gain that has occurred financially, but is not necessarily taxed. *See also* BOOT; RECOGNIZED GAIN.

REAL PROPERTY
1. land and whatever is erected or growing on it, or affixed to it.
2. rights issuing out of, annexed to, and exercisable within or about the land.

REAL RATE OF RETURN generally, current RATE OF RETURN minus current rate of inflation. This measure shows the return on investment expressed in actual purchasing power rather than in nominal terms.

REAL-TIME PROCESSING ability of a computer to process information requests in relation to an existing database with as little time delay as possible while simultaneously updating the existing database. This requires rapid computational capabilities and sophisticated APPLICATION SOFTWARE.

REALTIST member of the National Association of Real Estate Brokers, a group comprising mainly minority brokers.

REALTOR professional in real estate who subscribes to a STRICT CODE OF ETHICS as a member of the local and state boards and of the National Association of Realtors.

REALTY *see* REAL ESTATE.

REAL VALUE OF MONEY actual PURCHASING POWER of money, as corrected for INFLATION over time.

REAL WAGES money wages corrected for INFLATION over time so as to provide a measure of actual changes in PURCHASING POWER over time.

REAPPRAISAL LEASE LEASE where the rental level is periodically reviewed by independent appraisers. Often lessor and lessee will each select an appraiser; if they do not agree on a value, they will choose a third appraiser.

REASONABLE CARE the degree of care that under the circumstances would ordinarily or usually be exercised by or might reasonably be expected of an ordinary prudent person (a REASONABLE MAN). The exercise or absence of *reasonable care*, which is a jury question, often determines the verdict in tort cases or cases involving injury to others.

REASONABLE MAN or **REASONABLE PERSON** phrase used to denote a hypothetical person who exercises qualities of attention, knowledge, intelligence, and judgment that society requires of its members for the protection of their own interest and the interests of others. *See also* PRUDENT-MAN RULE.

REASONABLE TIME a subjective standard based on the facts and circumstances within a particular case, with applicability in a variety of contexts. Within commercial law, the term applies to the amount of time in which to accept an OFFER, to inspect goods prior to payment or acceptance, or to await performance by a party who repudiates a contract, or the time in which a seller may substitute conforming goods for goods rejected by a buyer as nonconforming.

REASSESSMENT
In general: reviewing a policy or a decision.
Real estate: process of revising or updating the value estimate of property for AD VALOREM tax purposes. Local property tax assessors are required to periodically conduct a reassessment of all property. Value estimates are revised based on recent sales and other data, and tax assessments are based on the new estimates.

REBATE
1. refund resulting from a purchase or tax.
2. kickback of a charge, often illegal if done without knowledge of all parties.

REBOOT to restart a computer, that is, turn it off and then on again. *See also* BOOT.

RECALL manufacturer ordering that previously sold products be returned to repair or replace a defective part or parts. In some cases, the government orders the manufacturer to issue a recall, particularly in the case of automobiles having possible safety hazards. *See also* RECALL CAMPAIGN; RECALL STUDY.

RECALL CAMPAIGN coordinated advertising effort by a manufacturer to notify all owners of a particular product that it should be returned to the manufacturer. It can include mass-media advertising as well as direct mailings. *See also* RECALL; RECALL STUDY.

RECALL STUDY study done by a manufacturer and/or the government to determine whether a recall order is necessary. An effort is made to determine whether a product defect is an isolated case or serious enough to warrant having the product returned to the manufacturer to be repaired or replaced. A recall order would be issued if the results of the study were positive. *See also* RECALL; RECALL CAMPAIGN.

RECAPITALIZATION alteration of a corporation's capital structure, such as an exchange of bonds for stock, or of preferred stock for common stock, or of one type of bond for another. Bankruptcy frequently gives rise to recapitalization.

RECAPTURE
1. taxing at ordinary rates part of the gain on a sale that represents prior depreciation allowances. *See also* DEPRECIATION RECAPTURE.
2. included in tax liability as a result of a sale that represents prior tax credits (such as the rehabilitation tax credit, investment tax credit, or low-income housing credit).

RECAPTURE CLAUSE in a contract, a clause permitting the party who grants an INTEREST or right to take it back under certain conditions.

RECAPTURE OF DEPRECIATION *see* DEPRECIATION RECAPTURE.

RECAPTURE RATE in appraisal, rate of recovery of an investment in a WASTING ASSET. This rate is added to the DISCOUNT RATE to derive a CAPITALIZATION RATE in appraisal terminology. It may be based on the straight-line, sinking fund, or annuity method.

RECAPTURE RULE covers situations in which tax benefits claimed under certain rules for DEPRECIATION and INVESTMENT TAX CREDIT must be paid back because of something that occurs in a later year, such as early disposition of an asset, or because the 50% business use percentage test for LISTED PROPERTY is no longer being met.

RECASTING A DEBT process of adjusting a loan arrangement, especially under the threat of default. *See also* WORKOUT.

RECEIPT, RECEIPT BOOK paper given to a payer to evidence payment of an invoice. It generally includes the payer's name, amount, date, and purpose and should be retained by anyone who pays in cash to prove payment. A receipt book typically retains a duplicate for the person paid while the original has perforations to be detached and given to the payer.

RECEIVABLES *see* ACCOUNTS RECEIVABLE; NOTES RECEIVABLE.

RECEIVABLES AGING SCHEDULE *see* AGING OF ACCOUNTS RECEIVABLE.

RECEIVABLES TURNOVER number of times average ACCOUNTS RECEIVABLE are collected in a year. If the amount of the average outstanding receivables is collected in two months, the turnover rate would be six times per year.

RECEIVER court-appointed person who takes possession of, but not title to, the assets and affairs of a business or estate that is in a form of bankruptcy called RECEIVERSHIP. The receiver collects rents and other income and generally manages the affairs of the entity until a disposition is made by the court.

RECEIVERSHIP equitable remedy whereby a court orders property placed under the control of a RECEIVER so that it may be preserved for the benefit of affected parties A failing company may be placed in receivership in an action brought by its creditors. The business is often continued but is subject to the receiver's control. *See also* BANKRUPTCY.

RECEIVING CLERK employee in a firm's receiving department. The receiving clerk inspects all incoming goods as to quality and condition, and determines the quantities received by counting, measuring, or weighing. All records are entered into the receiving record. *See also* RECEIVING RECORD.

RECEIVING RECORD (REPORT) serially numbered reports for each shipment received by a company in the receiving department. One copy of the receiving record is sent to the accounting department for verifying the invoice. *See also* RECEIVING CLERK.

RECESSION downturn in economic activity, defined by many economists as at least two consecutive quarters of decline in a country's GROSS DOMESTIC PRODUCT (GDP).

RECIPROCAL BUYING any arrangement under which a seller of one product or service buys another product or service from one of his customers.

RECIPROCITY generally, relationship between persons, corporations, states, or countries whereby privileges granted by one are returned by the other.

RECKONING settling accounts through counting. Reckoning involves computations to achieve a final total or conclusion.

RECOGNITION
1. formal acknowledgment granted by the various publications or broadcast media to an advertising agency after the agency has

proven financially able, competent, ethical, and bona fide. Recognition, which is also known as *agency recognition,* entitles the agency to receive commissions for the time and space it sells and also entitles the agency to make purchases on credit.

2. consumer awareness of having seen or heard an advertising message.

RECOGNIZED GAIN in a TAX-FREE EXCHANGE, portion of gain that is taxable. A REALIZED gain will generally be recognized to the extent of boot received. *See also* SECTION 1031.

RECOMPENSE act of paying or rewarding an individual for services; remuneration for goods or other property.

RECONCILIATION bringing together after a difference; resolution of a difference. It may be an amount or an opinion. In personal finance, it is the process of determining agreement between the bank balance per books with the bank statement. In real estate appraisals, *reconciliation* is the thought process of weighing all the available information from all appraisal approaches used to estimate the value of the subject being appraised.

RECONDITIONING PROPERTY restoring property to its original specifications. Reconditioning property improves its value by repairing it or making changes to enhance it.

RECONSIGN to change destination or consignee of freight while it is being shipped.

RECONVEYANCE transaction when a MORTGAGE debt is RETIRED. The lender conveys the property back to the equity owner, free of the debt.

RECORD in data processing, collection of related data items. A collection of records is called a *file.* For example, a company may store information about each employee in a single record consisting of a field to represent the name, a field to represent the Social Security number, and so on.

RECORD DATE *see* DATE OF RECORD; EX-DIVIDEND DATE; PAYMENT DATE.

RECORDING act of entering a transaction in a book of public records, notably instruments affecting the title to real property. Recording in this manner gives notice to the world of facts recorded. *See also* CONSTRUCTIVE NOTICE.

RECORDS *see* ACCOUNTING RECORDS.

RECORDS MANAGEMENT system used to collect, record, store, and eventually discard information.

RECOUP, RECOUPMENT regaining what was lost.

RECOURSE ability of a lender to claim money from a borrower in default, in addition to the property pledged as collateral. *See also* NONRECOURSE.

RECOURSE LOAN
  1. loan for which an endorser or guarantor is liable for payment in the event the borrower defaults.
  2. loan made to a direct participation program or LIMITED PARTNERSHIP whereby the lender, in addition to being secured by specific assets, has recourse against the general assets of the partnership. *See also* NONRECOURSE.

RECOVERY
  Economics: period in a business cycle when economic activity picks up and the GROSS DOMESTIC PRODUCT grows, leading into the expansion phase of the cycle.
  Finance: (1) absorption of cost through the allocation of depreciation; (2) collection of an ACCOUNT RECEIVABLE that had been written off as a bad debt; (3) residual cost, or salvage value, of a fixed asset after all allowable depreciation.
  Investment: period of rising prices in a securities or commodities market after a period of falling prices.

RECOVERY FUND in real estate, fund that requires licensees to contribute, then reimburses aggrieved persons who are unable to collect from brokers for wrongdoings. A recovery fund is generally administered by a state Real Estate Commission.

RECOVERY OF BASIS process by which a taxpayer receives a return of cost through distributions or payments with respect to a property. A recovery of BASIS is generally nontaxable if it follows a taxable distribution of earnings and profits from a corporate liquidation.

RECOVERY PERIOD the number of years over which the cost of an asset may be depreciated (for example, five years for an automobile).

RECRUITERS individuals, normally associated with a human resource department, who have the responsibility for locating and obtaining new employees. Recruiters can use many different methods for obtaining new employees. In addition to visiting college campuses and employment agencies, they also develop advertising campaigns, attend job fairs, and develop sources through referrals.

RECRUITMENT act of seeking prospective new employees or members for an organization. Recruitment is a vital function for an organization to maintain its personnel.

RECRUITMENT BONUS bonus often given by employers and employment agencies for locating potential employees. A recruitment bonus is usually given for employee categories where a scarcity of qualified candidates exists.

RECYCLING reprocessing used on abandoned materials to create new products. For example, glass can be crushed and then refired to form new glass having perfect quality.

REDACT prepare for publication or presentation by correcting, revising, or adapting. In current parlance, *redaction* usually refers to the blacking out of private, confidential, or sensitive information in a document, especially a public record, so that it cannot be read. Accomplishing this in electronic files can be difficult.

REDEEM
In general: buy back.
Finance: cash in, as a maturing note or bond.
Mortgage: cure a DEFAULT by paying all overdue loan payments and penalties after receiving a notice of default but before the lender can FORECLOSE the mortgage.

REDEEMABLE BOND *see* CALLABLE.

REDEMPTION
1. regaining possession by payment of a stipulated price; especially, process of annulling a defeasible title, such as is created by a mortgage or tax sale, by paying the debt or fulfilling other obligations.
2. for tax purposes, purchase by a corporation of its own stock.
3. in marketing, accepting a coupon for partial payment of goods bought.
4. acquisition by a corporation of its own stock in exchange for property, without regard to whether the redeemed stock is canceled, retired, or held as treasury stock.

REDEMPTION FEE a charge to repurchase an asset or release the asset from creditor claims.

REDEMPTION PERIOD period during which a former owner can reclaim foreclosed property or property posted for FORECLOSURE. *See also* EQUITY REDEMPTION.

REDEMPTION PRICE *see* CALL PRICE.

REDEVELOPMENT process of demolition of the existing improvements and construction of new improvements on a site. The new improvements are often a different type from the old.

RED HERRING *see* PRELIMINARY PROSPECTUS.

RED INK slang for loss.

REDISCOUNT to DISCOUNT short-term negotiable debt instruments, such as bankers' acceptances and commercial paper, that have been discounted with a bank, that is, exchanged for an amount of cash adjusted to reflect the current interest rate.

REDISCOUNT RATE rate of interest charged to member banks when they borrow from the FEDERAL RESERVE SYSTEM; also called DISCOUNT RATE.

REDLINING illegal practice of refusing to originate MORTGAGE loans in certain NEIGHBORHOODS on the basis of race or ethnic composition.

The term derives from the alleged practice of drawing a red line on a map around certain neighborhoods to designate them as off limits for loan approvals.

RED TAPE necessity to complete extensive paperwork to gain approval by several people in order to accomplish a goal. The term is often used with bureaucracy, as in "bureaucratic red tape."

REDUCED RATE
1. *see* DISCOUNT.
2. *see* ALLOWANCE.
3. periodical subscription or newsstand-sold copy sold at a price less than the basic rate. Most new subscriptions are sold at reduced rates as an incentive for new customers. When the subscriptions are renewed, the publisher attempts to get the full price. Subscriptions are usually not profitable until renewed at the full rate.

REDUCTION CERTIFICATE document in which the MORTGAGEE (lender) acknowledges the sum due on the MORTGAGE loan. It is used when mortgaged property is sold and the buyer assumes the debt.

REDUNDANCY intentional or unintentional repetition of computer data. Data files can be compressed by removing *redundancy* and expressing the same data more concisely, whereas reliability of data transmission can be increased by sending the same data twice.

REENGINEERING making major structural changes in a corporation or important business operations.

REFEREE quasijudicial officer appointed by a court for a specific purpose, to whom the court refers power and duty to take testimony, determine issues of fact, and report the findings for the court to use as a basis for judgment.

REFERRAL
1. suggesting the use of a certain professional, company, or broker.
2. suggestion that leads to hiring a certain employee.

REFI abbreviation for "refinanced mortgages." Refers to the volume of mortgage loans originating from the refinancing of existing debt.

REFINANCE refund existing debt. It usually implies selling a new bond issue to provide funds for redemption of a maturing issue, or placing a new mortgage on a house that retires an old mortgage. Refinancing is generally used to raise cash, reduce interest rates, or both.

REFORMATION EQUITABLE remedy consisting of a revision of a contract by the court, in cases where the written terms of the contract do not express what was actually agreed upon. Thus, reformation is generally only decreed upon a clear and convincing showing of mutual mistake (*see* MISTAKE); if only one party was mistaken, reformation is not appropriate unless the mistake of one party resulted from the other party's FRAUD.

REFRESH clear part or all of a computer screen and redraw it. When an Internet site "hangs" in loading, using the *Refresh* button sometimes clears the problem.

REFUND, REFUND CHECK to return cash or a check; check itself. Also, paid to a taxpayer by the IRS when withholding and estimated tax payments exceed tax for the year. A refund of federal taxes paid is not TAXABLE INCOME. A refund of state taxes is taxable if the taxpayer claimed a deduction.

REFUNDABLE CREDIT a credit that is paid to a taxpayer even if the amount of the credit exceeds the tax liability (for example, the earned income credit and taxes withheld on wages).

REFUNDING
Finance: process of selling a new issue of securities to obtain funds needed to retire existing securities. Debt refunding is done to extend maturity and/or to reduce debt service cost. *See also* REFINANCE.
Merchandising: returning money to a customer who is dissatisfied with a product.

REGIONAL BANK bank that specializes in collecting deposits and making loans in one region of the country, as distinguished from a MONEY CENTER BANK, which operates nationally and internationally.

REGIONAL SHOPPING CENTER area containing 300,000 to 900,000 square feet of shopping space and at least one major department store; larger than strip, neighborhood, and community shopping centers; smaller than a super-regional center.

REGISTERED BOND bond that is recorded in the name of the holder on the books of the issuer or the issuer's REGISTRAR and can be transferred to another owner only when endorsed by the registered owner. *Contrast with* COUPON BOND.

REGISTERED CHECK check issued by a bank for a customer who places funds aside in a special register. The customer writes in his name, the name of the payee, and the amount of money to be transferred. The registered check is similar to a money order for someone who does not have a checking account at the bank.

REGISTERED COMPANY company that has filed a REGISTRATION STATEMENT with the Securities and Exchange Commission in connection with a PUBLIC OFFERING of securities and must therefore comply with SEC DISCLOSURE requirements.

REGISTERED INVESTMENT COMPANY investment company, such as an open-end or closed-end MUTUAL FUND, that files a registration statement with the Securities and Exchange Commission and meets all the other requirements of the INVESTMENT COMPANY ACT OF 1940.

REGISTERED MAIL service offered at extra cost for any first-class mail. It is the safest way to send valuables through the U.S. Postal

Service. The fee includes proof of mailing and delivery. Up to $25,000 of insurance and restricted delivery service are available at extra cost.

REGISTERED MAIL AND EXPRESS MAIL INSURANCE coverage for damage or destruction of property with relatively high monetary value, such as stock brokerage house and bank shipments that involve the transfer of securities and monies to different locations and whose loss would result in great expense. Coverage is on ALL-RISK basis, excluding war, nuclear disaster, and illegal trade items.

REGISTERED REPRESENTATIVE (RR) employee of a stock exchange member broker/dealer who acts as an ACCOUNT EXECUTIVE for clients. As such, the registered representative gives advice on which securities to buy and sell, and he collects a percentage of the commission income he generates as compensation. "Registered" means licensed by the Securities and Exchange Commission and the New York Stock Exchange.

REGISTERED SECURITY

1. security whose owner's name is recorded on the books of the issuer or the issuer's agent, called a REGISTRAR; for example, a *registered bond* as opposed to a *bearer bond*.
2. securities issue registered with the Securities and Exchange Commission as a new issue or as a secondary offering. *See also* LETTER STOCK.

REGISTRAR

In general: person who keeps official records, such as of students in a college or holdings of a museum.

Real estate: person who is to maintain accurate official records, such as for deeds, mortgages, and other recorded documents.

Securities: agencies responsible for keeping track of the owners of bonds and the issuance of stock. The registrar also makes sure that no more than the authorized amount of stock is in circulation.

REGISTRATION

In general: enrollment process; for example, selecting classes in a college.

Securities: process set up by the Securities Acts of 1933 and 1934 whereby securities that are to be sold to the public are reviewed by the Securities and Exchange Commission. The REGISTRATION STATEMENT details pertinent financial and operational information about the company.

REGISTRATION STATEMENT document detailing the purpose of a proposed public offering of securities. The statement outlines financial details, a history of the company's operations and management, and other facts of importance to potential buyers.

REGISTRY OF DEEDS officially maintained book that provides a place and mechanism for registering evidences of CONVEYANCES of interests in REAL PROPERTY, so that notice may be available to all third parties that there has been a change in the ownership of property effected by a conveyance of that property.

REGRESSION ANALYSIS statistical technique used to establish the relationship of a dependent variable, such as the sales of a company, and one or more independent variables, such as family formations, gross national product, per capita income, and other ECONOMIC INDICATORS. By measuring exactly how large and significant each independent variable has historically been in its relation to the dependent variable, the future value of the dependent variable can be predicted. Essentially, regression analysis attempts to measure the degree of correlation between dependent and independent variables, thereby establishing the latter's predictive value.

REGRESSION LINE line calculated in regression analysis that is used to estimate the relation between two quantities, the independent variable and the dependent variable. *See also* MULTIPLE REGRESSION.

REGRESSIVE TAX tax that takes a higher percentage of the earnings of a low-income family than of those of a high-income family. A sales tax on food is considered regressive because low-income people pay the same amount of tax on a loaf of bread, for example, as do high-income people.

REGULAR-WAY DELIVERY (AND SETTLEMENT) completion of a securities transaction at the office of the purchasing broker on (but not before) the third full business day following the date of the transaction, as required by the New York Stock Exchange.

REGULATED COMMODITIES commodities under the jurisdiction of the Commodity Futures Trading Commission, which include all commodities traded in organized contract markets. The CFTC polices matters of information and disclosure, fair trading practices, registration of firms and individuals, protection of customer funds, record keeping, and maintenance of orderly FUTURES and OPTIONS markets.

REGULATED FUTURES CONTRACT in tax law, a contract that: (1) provides that amounts must be deposited or withdrawn from a margin account based on daily market conditions (a system of marking to market); and (2) is traded on, or subject to the rules of, a qualified board of exchange. *See also* MARK TO THE MARKET.

REGULATED INDUSTRY industry that is regulated by government to a significant extent. UTILITY industries are excellent examples; their pricing, profits, and, sometimes, production methods are regulated by both federal and state governments.

REGULATED INVESTMENT COMPANY (RIC) MUTUAL FUND or REAL ESTATE INVESTMENT TRUST (REIT) eligible under Regulation M of the Internal Revenue Service to pass capital gains, dividends, and interest earned on fund investments directly to its shareholders to be taxed at the personal level, thus avoiding the double taxation on corporations and stockholders.

REGULATION rules used to carry out a law; act of administering a law. Many government agencies prepare regulations to administer a law.

REGULATION D regulation of the Securities and Exchange Commission that sets forth conditions necessary for a PRIVATE OFFERING (PRIVATE PLACEMENT) exemption.

REGULATIONS (TAX) official interpretations of the Internal Revenue Code by the Treasury Department that have the force and effect of law. *See also* TREASURY REGULATIONS.

REGULATION T regulation of the Federal Reserve Board that governs the maximum amount of credit that securities brokers and dealers may extend to customers for the initial purchase of regulated securities. *See also* MARGIN.

REGULATION U rule of the Securities and Exchange Commission that governs the maximum amount of credit that banks may extend for the purchase of regulated securities.

REGULATION Z body of regulations promulgated by the FEDERAL RESERVE BOARD pursuant to the federal TRUTH IN LENDING ACT that entrusts that administrative agency with supervision of compliance by all banks in the Federal Reserve System with the cost of credit disclosure requirements established under the Act. Under this regulation, lenders must inform borrowers of the ANNUAL PERCENTAGE RATE (APR) and the total cost of credit.

REGULATORY AGENCY government body responsible for control and supervision of a particular activity or area of public interest.

REHABILITATION restoring something, such as a structure, to a good condition.

REHABILITATION TAX CREDIT a 10% tax credit allowed for the costs of rehabilitating certain older buildings or 20% for certified historic structures.

REIMBURSEMENT payment of an employee or another party for incurred expenses or losses. For example, an employer may reimburse an employee for travel and entertainment expenses, which makes such expenses deductions for ADJUSTED GROSS INCOME (AGI). *See also* ACCOUNTABLE PLAN; NONACCOUNTABLE PLAN.

REINDUSTRIALIZATION process of revitalizing a former industrial area through recapitalization and the introduction of new technology. War-torn Germany and Japan were reindustrialized after the end of World War II.

REINSTATEMENT restoration of a policy that has lapsed because of nonpayment of premiums after the grace period has expired. In life insurance, the reinstatement time period is three years from the premium due date. The company usually requires the insured to show evidence of continued insurability (for example, by taking a medical examination); to pay all past premiums plus interest due; and to either reinstate or repay any loans that are still outstanding. Because the insured is now older and a new policy would require a higher premium, it may be to the advantage of an insured to reinstate a policy.

REINSURANCE sharing of RISK among insurance companies. Part of the insurer's risk is assumed by other companies in return for a part of the premium fee paid by the insured. Reinsurance allows an individual company to take on clients whose coverage would be too great a burden for one insurer to carry alone.

REINVESTMENT RATE rate of return resulting from the reinvestment of the interest from a bond or other investment. The reinvestment rate on a ZERO COUPON FUND is predictable and locked in, since no interest payments are ever made, and therefore all imputed interest is reinvested at the same rate. The reinvestment rate on bonds with regular interest payments is less predictable because it rises and falls with market interest rates.

REIT *see* REAL ESTATE INVESTMENT TRUST (REIT).

RELATED-ITEM APPROACH *see* CROSS MERCHANDISING.

RELATED PARTY TRANSACTION interaction between two parties, one of whom can exercise control or significant influence over the operating policies of the other. *A special relationship* may exist, for example, between a business enterprise and its principal owners.

RELATIONSHIP MARKETING marketing strategy designed to achieve long-term relationships with customers, suppliers, and distributors to improve overall profitability and success.

RELATIVE (CELL) REFERENCE in computer spreadsheet programs, a CELL address that indicates the position of a cell relative to another cell. If the reference is copied to another location, the reference will be changed to refer to the cell in the same position relative to the new location. *Contrast with* ABSOLUTE (CELL) REFERENCE.

RELEASE
In general: document one signs to give permission, such as the release of a copyright.
Real estate: to free real estate from a MORTGAGE. *See also* PARTIAL RELEASE.
Computers: a version of software. Integers generally indicate a major upgrade, while fractions are used for minor upgrades and bug fixes. Interim upgrades may also be designated by the addition of a letter (6.0a) or as a "service release" (SR-1); these are usually just bug fixes.

RELEASE CLAUSE clause in a MORTGAGE that gives the owner of the property the privilege of paying off a portion of the mortgage indebtedness, thus freeing a portion of the property from the mortgage.

RELEASE ON RECOGNIZANCE (R.O.R.) method by which an individual is released in lieu of providing bail, upon his promise to appear and answer a criminal charge. The R.O.R. procedure permits release on nonmonetary conditions, generally involving only the promise to appear, but sometimes involving special conditions (e.g., remaining in the custody of another, abiding by travel restrictions).

RELEVANCE item that is capable of making a difference in decision making. The three elements of relevance follow. Information is available in a *timely* fashion before it loses its value in decision making. Data have *predictive value* about outcomes past, present, and future. Information has *feedback value* that provides information about earlier expectations.

RELIABILITY
1. in auditing, confidence that the financial records have been properly prepared and that accounting procedures and internal controls are correctly functioning.
2. in financial accounting theory, term describing information that is reasonably free from error and bias and accurately presents the facts.

RELOCATE to move to another location, such as to move a business or a residence.

RELOCATION CLAUSE a LEASE stipulation that allows the landlord to move the tenant within the building.

RELOCATION SERVICE a company that contracts with other firms to arrange the relocation of employees from one city to another. The service generally handles the sale of the employee's home and purchase of a new home. Furniture-moving services may also be included.

REMAINDER part of an ESTATE in land that is left upon the termination of the immediately preceding estate (often a life estate or estate for a term of years) and that does not amount to a reversion to the original grantor or his heirs.

REMAINDER INTEREST *see* REMAINDER.

REMAINDERPERSON one who has an interest in an estate that becomes possessory after the termination of a present possessory interest. It usually refers to one who holds an interest in a REMAINDER, whether vested or contingent.

REMEDIATION the cleanup of an environmentally contaminated site. *See* CERCLA; SITE ASSESSMENT; STIGMA.

REMEDY relief available from a court by which the violation of a legal right is prevented or a legal wrong is redressed.

REMIC *see* REAL ESTATE MORTGAGE INVESTMENT CONDUIT.

REMINDER ADVERTISING advertising intended to keep product or service availability in the forefront for existing customers.

REMIT pay for purchased goods or services by cash, check, or electronic payment.

REMITTANCE *see* REMIT RATE.

REMITTANCE, REMITTANCE COUPON BOOK, REMITTANCE SLIP payment, which may be accompanied by a preprinted coupon indicating the account number, date, and purpose; or by an individually prepared slip, which indicates the account, invoice paid, trade discount paid, and returns.

REMONETIZATION reinstatement of a commodity or other means of exchange as an acceptable currency. In current usage, remonetization usually refers to reinstating the backing of the currency by gold or other precious metal.

REMOVAL BOND *see* JUDICIAL BOND.

REMUNERATION direct or indirect compensation for services performed. WAGES are a form of direct remuneration, while fringe benefits are a form of indirect remuneration.

RENEGOTIATE to legally revise the TERMS of a CONTRACT.

RENEWABLE NATURAL RESOURCE natural resource that can be replaced over time and so is not used up irrevocably. Petroleum is not renewable; solar energy is (because it is always there) and forest products can be (because they can be regrown).

RENEWAL continuation in force and effect of a previously existing arrangement for a new period, as a LEASE or NOTE, on the same or different terms.

RENEWAL OPTION right, but not obligation, of a TENANT to continue a lease at specified term and rent.

RENT
1. payment for the use of property.
2. in economics, excess amount paid or earned over the minimum amount that would keep the activity in business.

RENTABLE AREA *see* NET LEASABLE AREA.

RENTAL RATE periodic charge per unit for the use of a property. The period may be a month, quarter, or year. The unit may be a dwelling unit, square foot, or other unit of measurement. For example, the rental rate for a two-bedroom apartment might be $1,200 per month. The rental rate for office space could be $28 per square foot per year.

RENT CONTROL laws that govern the maximum rate that may be charged for space. Though popular among tenants, rent control can be economically detrimental to an area because it distorts the forces of supply and demand.

RENT-FREE PERIOD portion of the term of a LEASE when no rent is required; offered by a landlord as a rental CONCESSION to attract tenants.

RENT ROLL a list of TENANTS, generally with the lease rent and expiration date for each.

RENT-UP PERIOD time it takes for newly constructed properties to be fully occupied. *See also* ABSORPTION RATE.

REO *see* REAL ESTATE OWNED.

REOPENER CLAUSE provision providing for the reopening of a COLLECTIVE BARGAINING contract before its expiration upon certain conditions. Generally, a reopener clause is limited to the reconsideration of wages if the CONSUMER PRICE INDEX surpasses a particular point or if other economic factors change rapidly.

REORDER POINT minimum level of INVENTORY at which a new order must be placed. The *reorder point* considers the time delay in receiving new inventory, the typical rate of inventory consumption, and the STOCKOUT COST. *See also* JUST-IN-TIME INVENTORY CONTROL (JIT).

REORGANIZATION
Law: financial restructuring of a firm after it has filed for protection from creditors while it works out a plan to repay its overdue debt. Company reorganizations usually take place under Chapter 11 of the federal BANKRUPTCY code under the supervision of a bankruptcy court. If the plan does not restore the company's health, the company may be liquidated and its assets sold to pay off the claims of creditors and shareholders.
Management: changing lines of authority, organization chart, and so on to improve the management structure of a company.

REORIENTATION changing the market appeal of a property or business.

REP
1. CUSTOMER SERVICE REPRESENTATIVE.
2. short for *sales representative*.

REPAIRS work performed to return property to a former condition without extending its useful life, as distinguished from CAPITAL IMPROVEMENTS. In income property, repairs are an OPERATING EXPENSE for accounting and tax purposes. As examples, patching a hole in the roof (but not replacing the roof) and mending (but not rebuilding) a fence are *repairs*.

REPATRIATION movement of the financial assets or profits of an organization or individual from a foreign country to the home country.

REPETITIVE MANUFACTURING method of manufacturing where the same products are continually and repetitiously manufactured. This is the ideal setting for MASS PRODUCTION where HARD MANUFAC-

TURING can be used with a large fixed cost investment. Numerous products, ranging from appliances to automobiles, are manufactured in this manner.

REPLACEMENT COST cost of erecting a building to serve the functions of a previous structure; cost of replacing lost or stolen personal property. *Compare* REPRODUCTION COST.

REPLACEMENT COST ACCOUNTING accounting method allowing additional DEPRECIATION on part of the difference between the original cost and current replacement cost of a depreciable asset.

REPLACEMENT COST INSURANCE property and casualty insurance that replaces damaged property. *Replacement cost contents insurance* pays the dollar amount needed to replace damaged personal property with items of like kind and quality, without deducting for depreciation. *Replacement cost dwelling insurance* pays the policyholder the cost of replacing the damaged property without deduction for depreciation, but is limited by the maximum dollar amount indicated on the declarations page of the policy. In addition, if the property is deemed not to have been insured to 100% of its replacement cost, coverage of partial damage will be prorated according to the percentage of total coverage.

REPLACEMENT PERIOD these are periods for tax-free gain on the replacement of certain assets under special circumstances:
1. *Inventory interruption*—three tax years following the LIQUIDATION year.
2. *Involuntary conversion*—two years after the close of the first taxable year in which any part of a gain upon conversion is realized (three years for business real estate).
3. *Sale of principal residence*—period beginning two years before the date of such sale and ending two years after such date.
4. See TAX-FREE EXCHANGE; STARKER EXCHANGE.

REPLACEMENT RESERVE amount set aside from net operating income to pay for the eventual wearing out of short-lived assets; sometimes used by a HOMEOWNERS' ASSOCIATION. *See also* RESERVE FUND.

REPLEVIN legal form or action ordinarily employed only to recover possession of specific PERSONAL PROPERTY unlawfully withheld from the plaintiff, plus DAMAGES for its detention. In this primarily possessory action, the issues ordinarily are limited to the plaintiff's TITLE to the goods. For example, Arthur leaves a shipment of goods in a warehouse and prepays storage costs for three months. At the end of that time, he goes to pick up the goods, but the warehouse refuses to release them until he pays for the storage. Arthur sues for *replevin* to obtain the goods.

REPO
1. slang for REPOSSESSED or FORECLOSED property.
2. *see* REPURCHASE AGREEMENT.

REPOSSESSION act by which a seller takes back property for which payments have not been made according to contract. *See also* FORECLOSURE.

REPRESSIVE TAX tax designed to discourage a certain activity rather than to produce revenue. High TARIFFS and high taxes on such COMMODITIES as tobacco and alcohol are repressive in the sense that they discourage consumption of the taxed product by raising its price. Such taxes are sometimes called "sin taxes."

REPRODUCTION COST cost of exact duplication of a property, real or personal, as of a certain date. Reproduction differs from replacement in that replacement requires the same functional utility for a property, whereas reproduction is an exact duplication. *Compare* REPLACEMENT COST.

REPUDIATION refusal by one party to perform a contractual obligation to another party.

REPURCHASE AGREEMENT (REPO; RP) agreement between a seller and a buyer, usually of U.S. government securities, whereby the seller agrees to repurchase the securities at an agreed upon price and, usually, at a stated time. It is widely used as a MONEY MARKET investment vehicle and as an instrument of the Federal Reserve Board's MONETARY POLICY.

REPUTATION esteem, position, character, distinction, or renown someone or something enjoys in society. A reputation is a distinction earned in a society by meeting approved societal standards.

REQUEST FOR PROPOSALS (RFP) announcement, often by a government agency, of a willingness to consider BIDS for the performance of a specified project or program component. Requests for proposals are often issued when seeking bids for a specified research project.

REQUIRED RATE OF RETURN rate of return that must be attained for an investment to be made. *See also* DISCOUNTED CASH FLOW; HURDLE RATE.

REQUISITION
1. form issued by a using department to the supply or materials department requesting the acquisition of material not regularly carried in using department's normal stock; also called *purchase requisition* and *stock requisition.*
2. to request the acquisition of materials.

RES (Latin for "thing") the property underlying a trust.

RESALE PRICE in a projection of investment performance, the assumed selling price a property could fetch at the end of the PROJECTION PERIOD. *See* RESALE PROCEEDS.

RESALE PROCEEDS amount a former owner receives upon a sale after paying TRANSACTION COSTS, remaining debt, and, sometimes, income taxes; same as *proceeds from resale*.

RESCHEDULE to schedule an activity or event for a time different than the time originally scheduled. For example, because of rain the outdoor concert was *rescheduled* for the following evening.

RESCIND cancel a contract agreement. The Truth in Lending Act confers the RIGHT OF RESCISSION, which allows the signer of a contract to nullify it within three business days without penalty and have any deposits refunded. Contracts may also be rescinded in cases of fraud, failure to comply with legal procedures, or misrepresentation.

RESCISSION cancellation of a CONTRACT and the return of the parties to the positions they would have occupied if the contract had not been made. Grounds for rescissions may include original invalidity of the agreement, FRAUD, failure of CONSIDERATION, or material BREACH or DEFAULT. Rescission may be brought about by the mutual consent of the parties, by the conduct of the parties or by a decree by a court of equity.

RESEARCH
1. scientific method of systematically gathering, recording, and analyzing data important to advertisers. Research information is used to plan, create, and execute more effective advertising and marketing campaigns.
2. department within a company whose primary responsibility is conducting these types of investigations.

RESEARCH AND DEVELOPMENT (R&D) scientific and marketing evolution of a new product or service. Once such a product has been created in a laboratory or other research setting, marketing specialists attempt to define the market for the product. Steps are then taken to manufacture the product to meet the needs of the market.

RESEARCH DEPARTMENT division within a corporation, brokerage firm, investment company, bank trust department, insurance company, or other institutional investing organization that analyzes products, markets, or securities. *See also* RESEARCH AND DEVELOPMENT (R&D).

RESEARCH INTENSIVE product, project, or industry requiring many MAN-HOURS of research. Most research-intensive applications involve complex technology.

RESERVATION
1. booking, appointment, or date to perform some activity at a particular time and place.
2. reluctance, doubt, suspicion, or misgiving entertained about something or someone.

RESERVE

1. segregation of retained earnings to provide for such payouts as dividends, contingencies, improvements, or retirement of preferred stock.
2. valuation reserve, also called ALLOWANCE, for depreciation, bad debt losses, shrinkage of receivables because of discounts taken, and other provisions created by charges to the profit and loss statement.
3. hidden reserves, represented by understatements of balance sheet values.
4. cash on hand and deposit maintained by a commercial bank in a Federal Reserve Bank to meet the Fed's RESERVE REQUIREMENT.
5. gold and foreign currency held by governments to pay for imports and foreign debts.

RESERVE FOR DEPRECIATION *see* ACCUMULATED DEPRECIATION.

RESERVE FUND in real estate, account maintained to provide funds for anticipated expenditures required to maintain a building. A reserve may be required by a lender in the form of an escrow to pay upcoming taxes and insurance costs. A *replacement reserve* may be maintained to provide for REPLACEMENT COST of short-lived components, such as carpets, heating equipment, or roofing. Deposit of money into such a fund does not achieve a tax deduction.

RESERVE METHOD (BAD DEBTS) accrual of bad-debt expense based on the projected worthlessness of receivables or prior experience with uncollectible receivables. The use of the reserve method by ACCRUAL BASIS taxpayers is permitted only for some small banks and thrift institutions with assets of $500 million or less. Other accrual taxpayers must use the SPECIFIC CHARGE-OFF METHOD.

RESERVE PRICE *see* UPSET PRICE.

RESERVE REQUIREMENT FEDERAL RESERVE SYSTEM rule mandating the financial assets that member banks must keep in the form of cash and other liquid assets as a percentage of DEMAND DEPOSITS and TIME DEPOSITS. This money must be in the bank's own vaults or on deposit with the nearest regional Federal Reserve Bank. Reserve requirements, set by the Fed's Board of Governors, are one of the key tools in deciding how much banks can lend, thus setting the pace at which the nation's money supply grows. The higher the reserve requirement, the tighter the money.

RESERVE-STOCK CONTROL technique designating appropriate inventory levels for the maintenance of business until new merchandise can be supplied. Reserve-stock control considers the length of time necessary to physically replenish needed inventory.

RESIDENCE *see* PERSONAL RESIDENCE; PRINCIPAL RESIDENCE; QUALIFIED RESIDENCE.

RESIDENT a person who is liable for tax in a county or state because of DOMICILE, residence, citizenship, place of management, place of incorporation, or other similar criteria. A person is not a resident merely by having income derived from a source in a county or state, even though the income is subject to tax.

RESIDENT ALIEN person who has been admitted to permanent resident status but has not been granted citizenship.

RESIDENT BUYER individual with an office in an important merchandise center. A resident buyer is crucial to providing valuable merchandising information and allows a company to keep in close touch with the market. A resident buyer can be inside or outside the organization.

RESIDENT MANAGER one who supervises the care of an apartment complex while living in one of the units in the complex. Duties include showing vacant units to prospective tenants, making sure the building is kept clean, and providing entry to repair persons. Also called *superintendent.*

RESIDENTIAL *see* RESIDENTIAL PROPERTY.

RESIDENTIAL BROKER in real estate, one who lists and sells houses or condominiums. *See also* COMMERCIAL BROKER.

RESIDENTIAL DISTRICT district where people reside, as contrasted with commercial or industrial areas; often found in the zoning law or ZONING MAPS.

RESIDENTIAL MORTGAGE mortgage on a residential property. Interest on such mortgages is deductible for federal and state income tax purposes up to $1 million; for home equity loans, interest up to $100,000 is deductible.

RESIDENTIAL PROPERTY in real estate brokerage terminology, owner-occupied housing.

RESIDENTIAL RENTAL PROPERTY rental units used for dwelling purposes, not of a transient (hotel, motel) nature. To qualify as residential, at least 80% of a building's income should be derived from dwelling units. This type of property is eligible for a 27½-year life for tax depreciation purposes, as compared to a 39-year life for nonresidential property.

RESIDENTIAL SERVICE CONTRACT insurance CONTRACT or home WARRANTY, generally for one year, covering the plumbing, mechanical, and electrical systems of a home. It is available in most areas upon the purchase of an existing home. Either the buyer or the seller can pay for the contract.

RESIDUAL VALUE
1. realizable value of a FIXED ASSET after costs associated with the sale.
2. amount remaining after all allowable DEPRECIATION charges have been subtracted from the original cost of a depreciable asset.
3. scrap value, which is the value to a junk dealer.

    4. in automobile leasing, an estimate of what the car's value will be when the lease expires. This estimate is used to help calculate the approximate monthly lease payment.

RES IPSA LOQUITUR Latin for "the thing speaks for itself." The phrase refers to a rule of evidence whereby NEGLIGENCE of the alleged wrongdoer may be inferred from the mere fact that the accident happened, provided that (1) in the absence of negligence, the accident would not have occurred and (2) the thing that caused the injury is shown to have been under the exclusive control of the alleged wrongdoer. This shifts the burden to the defendant, who is thereby charged with introducing evidence to refute the PRESUMPTION of negligence that has been created.

RES JUDICATA matter adjudged. The phrase reflects a rule by which a final JUDGMENT by a court of competent JURISDICTION is conclusive upon the parties in any subsequent LITIGATION involving the same CAUSE OF ACTION. For example, two parties litigate an issue in one federal district court, and the defendant loses. Under the principle of *res judicata*, the defendant could not then go to another federal district court and litigate the same issue a second time.

RESOLUTION
    1. in general, expression of desire or intent.
    2. formal document representing an action of a corporation's BOARD OF DIRECTORS.
    3. legal order or contract by a government entity, called a *bond* resolution, authorizing a bond issue and spelling out the rights of bondholders and the obligations of the issuer.
    4. a measure of the amount of detail that can be shown in the images produced by a printer or computer screen. Printer resolution is measured in dots per inch (DPI); screen resolution is expressed as the number of PIXELS displayed vertically and horizontally.

RESOURCE money, people, time, and equipment necessary for any organization. Resource allocation is one of the most critical of the manager's decisional roles.

RESPA *see* REAL ESTATE SETTLEMENT PROCEDURES ACT.

RESPONDEAT SUPERIOR in agency law, doctrine that a PRINCIPAL is liable for the acts of an AGENT.

RESPONDENT
    1. the party sued in an action at law (*see* DEFENDANT).
    2. one who responds to a survey.

RESPONSE replies and reactions to stimuli, such as those responses in a research study that account for the findings of the study.

RESPONSE PROJECTION forecast of total expected response to a PROMOTION based on the number of responses received to date or based upon previous experience with this promotion, LIST, or product. A marketer might use the response projection to decide whether an additional promotion is necessary or to plan FULFILLMENT work volumes.

RESPONSIBILITY commitments and duties associated with a position in an organization. The manner in which responsibilities are fulfilled determines overall organizational effectiveness and productivity.

RESTATEMENT correction of a previously issued financial statement because of an accounting irregularity or misrepresentation. Although restatement can result from honest error, the practice became notorious during the wave of corporate scandals in the early 2000s.

RESTITUTION act of making good or of giving the equivalent for loss, damage, or injury.

RESTRAINING ORDER an order granted without notice or hearing, demanding the preservation of the status quo until a hearing can be held to determine the propriety of injunctive relief, temporary or permanent. A *restraining order* is always temporary, since it is granted pending a hearing; hence it is often called a TRO or temporary restraining order.

RESTRAINT OF TRADE in common law and as used in antitrust laws, illegal restraints interfering with free competition in commercial transactions that tend to restrict production, affect prices, or otherwise control the market to the detriment of consumers of goods and services.

RESTRAINT ON ALIENATION restriction on the ability to convey real property interests, any attempt at which is in derogation of the COMMON LAW policy in favor of free alienability. Such restrictions often are void or voidable as unlawful restraints on ALIENATION.

RESTRICTED SECURITIES SECURITIES acquired from an issuer in a nonpublic transfer, that is, on terms and at a price not offered to the general public through an underwriter. Because the securities were not part of a public offering and thus not subject to the safeguards of the Securities Act of 1933, such as the registration of the securities and the issuing of a prospectus, their sale to the public is restricted. *See* LETTER STOCK.

RESTRICTED STOCK *see* RESTRICTED SECURITIES.

RESTRICTED SURPLUS portion of RETAINED EARNINGS not legally available for the payment of dividends; also called *restricted retained earnings*.

RESTRICTION
In general: any limitation.
Real estate: limitation placed upon the use of property, for example, as contained in the deed or other written INSTRUMENT in the chain of title or in local ordinances pertaining to land use.

RESTRICTIVE COVENANT a covenant or deed restriction that limits the property rights of the owner.

RESTRUCTURING process of reorganizing where the composition and operations of an organization can be completely changed. Restructuring frequently results in the elimination or replacement of departments and divisions, causing temporary and permanent LAY-OFFS. *See also* DOWNSIZING.

RÉSUMÉ statement of one's background, education, and work experiences. A *résumé* can be structured chronologically or free form. The basic purpose of a résumé is to market the individual to obtain an interview for employment.

RETAIL business of selling products and services to the public as the ultimate consumer. Retailing involves selling many different products and services, either from a store location or in direct selling through vending machines and in-home presentations, mail order, and so on.

RETAIL CREDIT credit given to a customer by a retailer for the payment of purchases. Retail credit can be granted either through outside credit cards such as Visa, MasterCard, and American Express or through retailer-generated credit cards. In-house credit cards encourage store loyalty.

RETAIL CREDIT BUREAU *see* CREDIT BUREAU.

RETAIL DISPLAY ALLOWANCE decrease in the amount paid by a retailer to a manufacturer in exchange for a more prominent display of the product in the store or on the shelf.

RETAILER'S SERVICE PROGRAM advertising, promotion, or similar sales enhancement services designed specifically to help independent retailers be more competitive. As part of retailer's service program, a producer or wholesaler may provide cooperative advertising, display material and/or advertising layouts in order to help the retailer reduce the cost of selling the product.

RETAIL INVENTORY METHOD inventory technique using the cost method of accounting. Similar types of merchandise are pooled for purposes of estimating an average percentage of cost to retail price. That percentage is applied to the inventory to estimate cost of inventory. The retail inventory method, also called *cost method,* can use either the physical inventory of counting merchandise on hand or the book inventory system (perpetual inventory system). *See also* COST ACCOUNTING.

RETAIL OUTLET store selling merchandise and/or services directly to the public in unlimited quantities.

RETAIL RATE media advertising rate offered to local retailers.

RETAIL TRADE SALES AND FOOD SERVICE SALES monthly data that track U.S. sales, changes from previous periods, and where sales rose and/or fell. The data measures personal consumption across retail industries (except for autos) and tracks consumer spending.

RETAINAGE in a construction CONTRACT, money earned by a CONTRACTOR but not paid to the contractor until the completion of construction or some other agreed-upon date. The amount is held back as assurance for the quality of the work.

RETAINED EARNINGS net profits kept to accumulate in a business after dividends are paid; also called *undistributed profits* or *earned surplus. Retained earnings* are distinguished from contributed capital. *Compare with* EARNINGS AND PROFITS; PAID-IN CAPITAL. *See also* ACCUMULATED EARNINGS TAX; ACCUMULATED EARNINGS AND PROFITS.

RETAINED EARNINGS, APPROPRIATED account used to indicate that a portion of RETAINED EARNINGS is not available for DIVIDENDS. It is earmarked for some other special purposes.

RETAINED EARNINGS STATEMENT reconciliation of the beginning and ending balances in the RETAINED EARNINGS account on a company's BALANCE SHEET. It breaks down changes affecting the account, such as profits or losses from operations, dividends declared, and any other items charged or credited to retained earnings.

RETAINER a payment in advance to cover services expected to be performed. Frequently used by attorneys and consultants.

RETALIATORY EVICTION requirement that a tenant vacate a unit in response to a complaint from the tenant concerning the condition of the building. Landlord-tenant laws in many states forbid such EVICTIONS if proper channels are taken to lodge the complaint.

RETIRE to withdraw, leave, or depart from a particular activity or situation.

RETIREMENT leaving active employment permanently, for the remaining years of life, with income being provided through Social Security, pensions, and savings.

RETIREMENT AGE point at which retirement benefits are payable; there are several variations:
1. NORMAL RETIREMENT AGE is the earliest age at which one may retire and receive full benefits.
2. an employee may elect EARLY RETIREMENT, provided minimum age and service requirements are met, but there is a proportionate reduction in benefits.
3. an employee may opt for DEFERRED RETIREMENT, working beyond the normal retirement age, usually with no increase in benefits.
4. some organizations have an *automatic retirement age,* at which retirement is automatically effective.

RETIREMENT AGE, FULL *see* FULL RETIREMENT AGE.

RETIREMENT FUND monies specifically reserved by an organization for retiring employees. The investment of retirement funds has become a major factor in the stock market. They are regulated by the federal EMPLOYEE RETIREMENT INCOME SECURITY ACT (ERISA) of 1974.

RETIREMENT INCOME amount a retired employee receives. It may include Social Security benefits or a pension.

RETIREMENT PLAN plan provided by an employer or a selfemployed individual for an employee's or self-employed individual's retirement. Because of the tax advantages, most retirement plans are designed to insure a present deduction to the employer while the employee is permitted to avoid recognizing the income until he has actually or constructively received it. *See also* INDIVIDUAL RETIREMENT ACCOUNT (IRA); KEOGH PLAN; SECTION 401(K) PLAN; QUALIFIED PLAN; SEP-IRA.

RETIREMENT SYSTEM *see* GENERAL RETIREMENT SYSTEM.

RETROACTIVE any policy going back to an earlier date. Retroactive pay may be provided under the terms of a new COLLECTIVE BARGAINING agreement for work completed before or at the beginning of the new contract's implementation.

RETROACTIVE ADJUSTMENT
1. restatement of prior years' financial statements to show financial data on a comparable basis.
2. PRIOR PERIOD ADJUSTMENT.

RETURN
Finance, investment: profit on a securities or capital investment, usually expressed as an annual percentage rate.
Retailing: exchange of previously sold merchandise for refund or credit against future sales.
Taxes: form on which taxpayers submit information required by the government when they file with the Internal Revenue Service. For example, Form 1040 is a tax *return* used by individual taxpayers.
Trade: physical return of merchandise for credit against an invoice.

RETURN OF CAPITAL a DISTRIBUTION from a corporation that is not paid out of earnings and profits. It is a return of the shareholder's investment in the stock of the company. A return of capital is first applied to reduce the BASIS of the shareholder's stock to zero. Any distribution in excess of that amount is taxed as a capital gain. If a corporation has CURRENT EARNINGS AND PROFITS or ACCUMULATED EARNINGS AND PROFITS, distributions are treated as taxable DIVIDENDS to such extent, not as a return of capital.

RETURN ON EQUITY amount, expressed as a percentage, earned on a company's common stock investment for a given period. It is calculated by dividing common stock equity (net worth) at the beginning of the accounting period into NET INCOME for the point in time after preferred stock dividends but before common stock dividends. Return on equity tells common shareholders how effectually their money is being employed.

RETURN ON INVESTED CAPITAL amount, expressed as a percentage, earned on a company's total capital—its common and preferred stock EQUITY plus its long-term FUNDED DEBT—calculated by dividing total capital into earnings before interest, taxes, and dividends.

RETURN ON INVESTMENT (ROI) *see* RATE OF RETURN; RETURN ON INVESTED CAPITAL.

RETURN ON SALES net pretax profits as a percentage of NET SALES—a useful measure of overall operational efficiency when compared with prior periods or with other companies in the same line of business. It is important to recognize, however, that return on sales varies widely from industry to industry.

RETURNS
1. responses to a direct-mail promotion.
2. merchandise returned to a supplier for credit.

REUTERS London-based business and investment news broadcaster. Reuters is larger than Bridge Information System (which acquired Dow Jones Telerate) and Bloomberg LP in terms of screens installed worldwide that carry its data.

REVALUATION change in the value of a country's fixed exchange rate, which is based on the decision of authorities rather than on fluctuations in the market. *Revaluation* refers to an increase in the currency's value; DEVALUATION refers to a decrease.

REVALUATION CLAUSE *see* REAPPRAISAL LEASE.

REVENUE amount received. It generally denotes a GROSS figure, such as sales from a business, taxes collected by a government, or an amount received for performing a service.

REVENUE AND EXPENSE ACCOUNTS *see* INCOME ACCOUNTS.

REVENUE ANTICIPATION NOTE (RAN) short-term debt issue of a municipal entity that is to be repaid out of anticipated revenues such as sales taxes. When the taxes are collected, the RAN is paid off. Interest from the note is usually tax-free to RAN holders.

REVENUE BOND MUNICIPAL BOND issue paid off with revenues from the project built with the proceeds, such as a toll bridge, highway, educational facility, hospital, sewer system, stadium, or other structure that serves a public need and generates revenue. Unlike GENERAL OBLIGATION BONDS, revenue bonds are usually not backed by the taxing power of the municipality.

REVENUE NEUTRAL changes in the tax laws that result in no change in the amount of revenue coming into the government's coffers. For example, a provision may require individuals to pay less tax, but corporations will pay correspondingly more taxes.

REVENUE PROCEDURE official published statement of the IRS about procedural and administration matters of the tax laws, first published in the *Internal Revenue Bulletin* and later transferred to the *Cumulative Bulletin.*

REVENUE RECONCILIATION ACT OF 1993 *see* OMNIBUS BUDGET RECONCILIATION ACT OF 1993.

REVENUE RULING an official interpretation by the IRS of the internal revenue laws, related statutes, tax treaties, and regulations, published in the *Cumulative Bulletin.* Revenue rulings are issued only by the National Office of the IRS and are published for the information and guidance of taxpayers, IRS officials, and others concerned. Their purposes are to promote uniform application of the tax laws by IRS employees and to assist taxpayers in attaining maximum voluntary compliance by informing IRS personnel and the public of National Office interpretations of the internal revenue laws, related statutes, tax treaties, and regulations, as well as statements of IRS procedures affecting the rights and duties of taxpayers.

REVERSAL
1. change in direction in the stock or commodity futures markets, as charted by technical analysts.
2. accounting entry that offsets a previous entry.
3. business events with negative impact, such as the failure of a new product, resignation of a key employee, or declining sales.
4. action by which an appeals court reverses a trial court's decision.

REVERSE ANNUITY MORTGAGE (RAM) MORTGAGE instrument that allows an elderly person to live off the equity in a fully-paid-for house. Such a homeowner would enter into a *reverse annuity mortgage* agreement with a financial institution such as a bank, which would guarantee a lifelong fixed monthly income or a large cash advance in return for gradually giving up ownership of the house. The longer the payments continue, the less equity the elderly owner would retain.

REVERSE CHANNELS marketing CHANNEL OF DISTRIBUTION where products are moved from the consumer back to the producer. The two most frequent examples of this are RECYCLING and product RECALLS.

REVERSED indication that a decision of one court has been reversed by a higher court.

REVERSE DISCRIMINATION condition occurring when an employer illegally favors the hiring and promotion of protected groups of minorities and women while excluding other candidates from consideration. Reverse discrimination can result when hiring quotas are imposed without the sanction of an AFFIRMATIVE ACTION plan.

REVERSE ENGINEERING process whereby a competitor's product is completely dismantled to learn everything about it, usually for the purpose of replication.

REVERSE IMPORTS products made by a multinational corporation's overseas units for exportation to the home country.

REVERSE LEVERAGE situation in which financial benefits from ownership accrue at a lower rate than the interest rate paid for money; also called *negative leverage*. See also LEVERAGE.

REVERSE SPLIT procedure whereby a corporation reduces the number of shares outstanding. The total number of shares will have the same market value immediately after the reverse split as before it, but each share will be worth more. See also SPLIT.

REVERSING ENTRY JOURNAL ENTRY that exactly offsets a different journal entry; for instance, a debit equal to a previous entry's credit, and vice versa.

REVERSION giving the grantor some right or interest in a property to arise in the future.

REVERSIONARY FACTOR mathematical factor that indicates the present worth of one dollar to be received in the future; same as PRESENT VALUE OF 1. The formula is

$$\text{reversionary factor} = 1/(1 + i)^n$$

where i is the interest rate and n the number of years (or periods). See also DISCOUNTED CASH FLOW; PRESENT VALUE.

REVERSIONARY INTEREST interest a person has in property upon the termination of the preceding estate. See REMAINDER; REMAINDER-PERSON.

REVERSIONARY VALUE estimated value of property at the expiration of a certain time period.

REVIEW accounting service providing some assurance to the Board of Directors and interested parties as to the reliability of financial data without the CPA conducting an examination in accordance with generally accepted auditing standards. The AICPA Auditing Standards Board formulates review standards for public companies while the AICPA Accounting and Review Services Committee provides review standards for nonpublic businesses. A limited review consists primarily of inquiry and ANALYTICAL REVIEW.

REVOCABLE BENEFICIARY see BENEFICIARY.

REVOCABLE TRANSFERS term used for property transferred where the transfer may be rescinded (or revoked). Because of this possibility, the property will be included in the transferor's GROSS ESTATE upon death.

REVOCABLE TRUST agreement whereby income-producing property is deeded to heirs. The provisions of such a TRUST may be altered as many times as the grantor pleases, or the entire trust agreement can be canceled, unlike *irrevocable trusts*. Differs from an irrevocable trust, which permanently transfers assets from the estate during the grantor's lifetime and therefore escapes estate taxes.

REVOCATION

1. recall of authority conferred.
2. cancellation of an INSTRUMENT previously made.
3. cancellation of an OFFER by the offeror, which, if effective, terminates the offeree's power of ACCEPTANCE.

REVOLUTION

1. any total and complete change. For example, the introduction of an automated assembly line into an organization formerly relying on manual production techniques would be a technological *revolution* in its production system.
2. complete movement on an axis, as in revolutions per minute (rpm).

REVOLVING CHARGE ACCOUNT account that does not have to be paid to a zero balance. Although there is a credit limit, a payment on the account will allow further borrowing.

REVOLVING CREDIT

1. in commercial banking, contractual agreement between a bank and its customer, whereby the bank agrees to make loans up to a specified maximum for a specified period. As the borrower repays a portion of the loan, an amount equal to the repayment can be borrowed again under the terms of the agreement.
2. in consumer banking, loan account requiring monthly payments of less than the full amount due. The balance carried forward is subject to a financial charge.

REVOLVING FUND account or sum of money that, if used or borrowed, is intended to be replenished to its original balance, so it may be spent or loaned repeatedly.

REVOLVING LINE OF CREDIT *see* REVOLVING CREDIT.

REV. PROC. *see* REVENUE PROCEDURE.

REV. RUL. *see* REVENUE RULING.

REZONING action to change the designation of a subject PARCEL or group of parcels on the ZONING MAP. The effect of a rezoning is to change the permitted uses for the affected parcels. *See also* DOWNZONING.

RGB (red-green-*b*lue) technology used to produce color images on a display by combining red, green, and blue phosphor dots. Computer monitors have three separate wires for the three colors, as contrasted with the single-wire *composite video* used on TV screens.

RIC *see* REGULATED INVESTMENT COMPANY.

RICH

1. security whose price seems too high in light of its price history. For bonds, the term may also imply that the yield is too low.

    2. rate of interest that seems too high in relation to the borrower's risk.

    3. synonym for *wealthy*.

RICH TEXT FORMAT (RTF) a computer format for text documents that includes formatting attributes, such as different FONTS and TYPEFACES.

RICO *see* RACKETEER-INFLUENCED AND CORRUPT ORGANIZATIONS ACT.

RIDER endorsement to an insurance policy that modifies clauses and provisions of the policy, adding or excluding coverage.

RIGHT

    1. correct, true.

    2. a moral or legal claim. *see* SUBSCRIPTION RIGHT.

RIGHT-CLICK click the right or secondary button of a computer MOUSE.

RIGHT OF FIRST REFUSAL opportunity of a party to match the TERMS of a proposed contract before the contract is executed. In some states, a tenant whose apartment is converted to a CONDOMINIUM is given a right of first refusal for the unit when it is sold. This means the tenant may purchase the unit at the same price and terms as any outside purchaser.

RIGHT OF REDEMPTION right to recover property transferred by a MORTGAGE or other LIEN by paying off the debt either before or after foreclosure; also called *equity of redemption.*

RIGHT OF RESCISSION right granted by the federal CONSUMER CREDIT PROTECTION ACT OF 1968 to void a credit contract within three business days with full refund of any downpayment and without penalty. The right is designed to protect consumers from high-pressure door-to-door sales tactics and hastily made credit commitments.

RIGHT OF RETURN option of purchaser to give goods back to the seller for full credit.

RIGHT OF SURVIVORSHIP right of a surviving joint tenant to acquire the interest of a deceased joint owner; distinguishing feature of both JOINT TENANCY and TENANCY BY THE ENTIRETY.

RIGHT-OF-WAY right to use a particular path for access or passage; type of EASEMENT.

RIGHT-TO-WORK LAW outlawing a UNION SHOP in states that have adopted it, according to Section 14(b) of the TAFT-HARTLEY ACT. It prohibits agreements requiring membership in a union as a condition of continued employment of a person who was not a member when hired.

RIPARIAN RIGHTS rights that accrue to owners of land on the banks of bodies of water, such as the use of such water and ownership of soil under the water. The lands to which these natural rights are attached are called in law *riparian lands.*

RISK measurable possibility of losing or not gaining value. Risk is differentiated from *uncertainty*, which is not measurable. Among the commonly encountered types of risk are these:

Actuarial risk: risk an insurance underwriter covers in exchange for premiums, such as the risk of premature death.

Exchange risk: chance of loss on foreign currency exchange.

Inflation risk: chance that the value of assets or income will be eroded as inflation shrinks the value of a country's currency.

Interest rate risk: possibility that a fixed-rate debt instrument will decline in value as a result of a rise in interest rates.

Inventory risk: possibility that price changes, obsolescence, or other factors will shrink the value of inventory.

Liquidity risk: possibility that an investor will not be able to buy or sell a commodity or security quickly enough or in sufficient quantities because buying or selling opportunities are limited.

Political risk: possibility of nationalization or other unfavorable government action.

Repayment (credit) risk: chance that a borrower or trade debtor will not repay an obligation as promised.

Risk of principal: chance that invested capital will drop in value.

Systematic risk: risk affecting an entire business or industry, not just one company.

Underwriting risk: risk taken by an investment banker that a new issue of securities purchased outright will not be bought by the public and/or that the market price will drop during the offering period.

Unsystematic risk: one-time occurrence that may affect a single property of business, such as a fire.

See also AMOUNT AT RISK; AT-RISK RULES; ASSUMPTION OF RISK.

RISK-ADJUSTED DISCOUNT RATE in PORTFOLIO THEORY and CAPITAL BUDGET analysis, rate necessary to determine the present value of an uncertain or risky stream of income. It is the risk-free rate (generally the return on short-term U.S. Treasury securities) plus a risk premium for the particular investment.

RISK ARBITRAGE ARBITRAGE involving risk, as in the simultaneous purchase of stock in a company being acquired and sale of stock in its proposed acquirer; also called *takeover arbitrage.*

RISK AVERSE investors who seek the security offering the least risk. Put another way, the higher the degree of risk, the greater the return that a risk-averse investor will demand.

RISK AVOIDANCE management methods utilized to avoid as much situational risk as possible. While the elimination of all risk is rarely possible, in many situations it is prudent to develop methods where risk can at least be avoided.

RISK CAPITAL *see* VENTURE CAPITAL.

RISK-CONTROL TECHNIQUES methods used to reduce the amount of inherent risk. The four basic *risk control techniques* are RISK AVOIDANCE, RISK-CONTROL TRANSFER, loss prevention, and loss reduction.

RISK-FINANCING TECHNIQUES reduction of financial risk by using RISK RETENTION or RISK-FINANCING TRANSFER.

RISK-FINANCING TRANSFER paying an insurance premium to an insurance firm for insurance covering certain risk hazards. *See also* CATASTROPHE HAZARD.

RISK-FREE RATE (OR RETURN) the INTEREST RATE on the safest investments, such as federal government obligations.

RISKLESS TRANSACTION trade guaranteeing a profit to the trader who initiates it. *See* ARBITRAGE.

RISK MANAGEMENT procedure to minimize the adverse effect of a possible financial loss by: (1) identifying potential sources of loss; (2) measuring the financial consequences of a loss occurring; and (3) using controls to minimize actual losses or their financial consequences.

RISK PREMIUM in PORTFOLIO THEORY, the difference between the RISK-FREE RETURN and the TOTAL RETURN from a risky investment. In the CAPITAL ASSET PRICING MODEL (CAPM), the *risk premium* reflects market-related risk (SYSTEMATIC RISK).

RISK RETENTION method of SELF-INSURANCE whereby the organization retains a reserve fund for the purpose of offsetting unexpected financial claims. *See also* CONTINGENCY FUND.

RISK-RETURN TRADE-OFF concept, basic in investment management, that RISK equals (varies with) RETURN; in other words, the higher the return, the greater the risk, and vice versa. In practice, this means that a speculative investment, such as stock in a newly formed company, can be expected to provide a higher potential return than a more conservative investment.

RISK VS. REWARD a financial concept that attempts to compare the potential fluctuations (especially the downside) with potential benefits to determine whether the proposed investment (or cost) is worthwhile.

ROBBERY use of the threat of violence, or of actual violence, in taking property from someone else's possession. This peril is covered on a personal basis through the purchase of a *homeowner's insurance policy* or *renter's insurance* or on a business basis through a SPECIAL MULTIPERIL POLICY (SMP). Specialty items such as art works, jewelry, and coin and stamp collections must be specifically scheduled on a property policy in order for the insured to receive full value for a loss.

ROBERT'S RULES the parliamentary procedures often followed when conducting a meeting, codified in *Robert's Rules of Order.*

ROBINSON-PATMAN ACT *see* ANTITRUST ACTS.

ROBOT computerized machine that can be programmed to perform certain tasks. Robots are useful in doing work that is extremely monotonous, repetitive, and even dangerous. *See also* ROBOTICS.

ROBOTICS science and study of robots; developing applications for robots. *See also* ROBOT.

ROCKET SCIENTIST individual with high intelligence who may develop new techniques or products. Often used negatively, as in the phrase "It doesn't take a rocket scientist . . . ," meaning that individuals of normal intelligence can understand the subject in question. *See also* NO-BRAINER; QUANT.

ROCK THE BOAT to upset the status quo. Someone who is rocking the boat is challenging the customary sequence of procedures or events.

ROD linear unit of measurement equal to 16½ feet.

ROLE PLAYING simulation exercise where the participants act out specified roles in a dramatization of an event or situation. The purpose of role playing is to achieve better understanding of a situation by experiencing a realistic simulation. Role playing is useful as a training exercise.

ROLLING STOCK transportation equipment that moves on wheels. Examples include railroad cars and locomotives, tractor-trailers, and trucks.

ROLLOVER
1. to replace a loan or debt with another.
2. to change the institution that invests one's pension plan, without recognition of taxable income.
3. *see* INDIVIDUAL RETIREMENT ACCOUNT (IRA) ROLLOVER.

ROLLOVER LOAN type of MORTGAGE loan, commonly used in Canada, in which the AMORTIZATION of principal is based on a long term but the interest rate is established for a much shorter term. The loan may be extended, or rolled over, at the end of the shorter term at the current market interest rate.

ROM *see* READ-ONLY MEMORY.

ROOT DIRECTORY the top level in a hierarchical computer file system. For example, on a PC, the root directory of the C: drive contains all the second-level SUBDIRECTORIES on that drive.

RO-RO (ROLL ON-ROLL OFF) specially designed cargo ship allowing any cargo with wheels to be rolled on and then rolled off at the destination. This allows rapid turnaround, fewer man hours, and greater ship utilization.

ROTATING SHIFT work shift that changes its hours of work at stated intervals. Rotating shifts work around the clock.

ROTH IRA INDIVIDUAL RETIREMENT ACCOUNT created by the TAXPAYER RELIEF ACT OF 1997 permitting account holders to allow their capital to accumulate tax free under certain conditions. The Roth IRA is named for Delaware Senator William V. Roth, Jr., who championed the idea of expanded IRAs. Individuals can invest up to $4,000 per year in 2006, plus CATCH-UP CONTRIBUTIONS of up to $1,000 for those eligible. They can withdraw the principal and earnings totally tax free after age 59½, as long as the assets have remained in the IRA for at least five years after making the first contribution. If the account holder dies before beginning to withdraw from a Roth, the proceeds go to his or her beneficiaries tax free. Unlike with regular IRAs, participants do not have to take any distributions from a Roth IRA starting at age 70½; in fact, they can continue to contribute after reaching age 70½ and need not take any distributions at all during their lifetime. On the other hand, participants in Roth IRAs do not receive deductions for contributing to the account.

ROUND FILE wastebasket; also called *circular file; file 13*.

ROUNDHOUSE building used for the maintenance and repair of railroad equipment.

ROUND LOT generally accepted unit of trading on a securities exchange. On the New York Stock Exchange, for example, a round lot is 100 shares for stock and $1,000 or $5,000 par value for bonds. *Contrast* ODD LOT.

ROUTING production method of determining the sequence of manufacturing steps necessary to complete a product. Routing is determined by the type of product and its associated production process.

ROYALTY share of the product, or of the proceeds therefrom, reserved by an owner for permitting another to exploit and use his PROPERTY; rental paid to the original owner of property, based on a percentage of profit or production. It is used for mining leases, conveyances, as well as literary works, inventions, and other intellectual productions.

ROYALTY TRUST oil or gas company SPIN-OFF of an oil-producing property to shareholders. As long as the trust distributes most of its income directly to shareholders, it is not taxed at the corporate level. In addition, shareholders get the tax benefits from DEPLETION allowances.

RSS *R*eally *S*imple *S*yndication (or *R*ich *S*ite *S*ummary or *R*DF *S*ite *S*ummary), a family of XML file formats used by news Web sites and BLOGS to notify subscribers of updated content. Software called a *news aggregator* checks subscribed sites at specified intervals and provides a list of headlines and/or short descriptions of the content, together with a link to the full version. This is called an *RSS feed, webfeed, RSS stream,* or *RSS channel*. RSS allows users to stay up to date on topics of interest without having to check Web sites frequently for updates.

RS-232 standard American format for serial data transmission by cable, such as from computer terminal to modem. RS-232 transmission utilizes a distinctive 25-pin connector, but under most circumstances only a few of the 25 conductors are used.

RTF *see* RICH TEXT FORMAT.

RUBBER CHECK check for which insufficient funds are available (OVERDRAFT). It is called a *rubber check* because it bounces.

RULE AGAINST PERPETUITIES rule that no *contingent interest* is good unless it vests not later than 21 years after the death of a person living at the time the interest is created. It prevents a person from keeping property in his family for multiple generations.

RULE OF 72s approximation of the time it takes for money to double when earning COMPOUND INTEREST. The percentage rate is divided into 72 to derive the number of years to double the principal.

RULE OF 78s method for computing unearned interest used on installment loans with ADD-ON INTEREST. The number 78 is based on the sum of the digits from 1 to 12. For example, a 12-month loan is made for $1,000 with 8% add-on interest. The loan payments are based on a total of $1,080, payable at the rate of $90 per month for 12 months. If the borrower prepays the loan at the end of one month, 12/78 of the $80 interest is charged; the balance of interest is refunded. If the borrower prepays at the end of the second month, $(12 + 11)/78 = 23/78$ is charged. Prepayment at the end of the eleventh month results in a 1/78 refund.

RULING
1. ADVANCE RULING from the IRS.
2. court decision.

RUN
Banking: demand for their money by many depositors all at once. If large enough, a run on a bank can cause it to fail, as hundreds of banks did in the Great Depression of the 1930s. Such a run is caused by a breach of confidence in the bank, perhaps as a result of large loan losses or fraud.
Computers: to perform a routine or use a computer program.

RUNAWAY out of control; usually used in reference to INFLATION or other undesirable economic phenomena.

RUNDOWN status report or summary.

RUN OF PAPER (ROP) in publishing, logistical position of a newspaper advertisement determined at the publisher's discretion. Rates are constructed to take this into account.

RUN OF SCHEDULE (ROS) advertising time allocated wherever in the schedule the radio or television station sees fit. Rates are constructed to reflect this.

RUN WITH THE LAND right or RESTRICTION that affects all current and future owners of a property. It is contrasted to an agreement, between a current owner and other parties, that is not passed on to future owners in a deed. *See also* RESTRICTIVE COVENANT.

RURAL pertaining to the area outside larger and moderate-sized cities and surrounding population concentrations, generally characterized by farms, ranches, small towns, and unpopulated regions. *See also* SUBURB; URBAN.

RURBAN areas, on the fringe of URBAN development, that are in the process of being developed for urban uses.

RUST BELT geographical area of the United States, mainly in Pennsylvania, West Virginia, and the industrial Midwest, where iron and steel are produced and where there is a concentration of industries that manufacture products using iron and steel. Used broadly to mean traditional American manufacturing with largely unmodernized plants and facilities.

S

S.A. (SOCIEDAD ANONIMA OR SOCIÉTÉ ANONYME) the respective Spanish and French designations for a corporation.

SABOTAGE direct interference with or destruction of productive capabilities in a plant or factory by those opposed to a company's management or to the country in time of warfare. Saboteurs perform such acts. Disgruntled employees can often be industrial saboteurs.

SACK discharge, terminate, fire (an employee); the employee "gets the sack," originally meaning that he picked up his sack of tools and moved on.

SAFE HARBOR RULE in taxation, guidelines provided by the IRS for certain transactions, indicating specific parameters a taxpayer can observe to ensure favorable tax treatment or to avoid an unfavorable one. An example is a list of parameters that, if followed, will assure SALE AND LEASEBACK treatment to certain transactions.

SAFE HAVEN politically secure currency. The American dollar, the euro, and gold are typically considered safe havens.

SAFEKEEPING storage and protection of assets, valuables, or documents. Some individuals use a bank safe deposit box; others might rely on a bank or a brokerage firm to hold stock certificates or bonds, keep track of trades, and provide periodic statements of changes in position.

SAFE RATE an INTEREST RATE provided by relatively low-risk investments such as high-grade BONDS or well secured FIRST MORTGAGES. *See also* FINANCIAL MANAGEMENT RATE OF RETURN (FMRR).

SAFETY COMMISSION governmental organization having as its prime function the review and encouragement of safety practices within an organization. In the private sector, usually referred to as a Safety Committee, it plays an important safety supervision role in labor and management relations.

SAFETY MARGIN excess of actual sales over break-even sales. For example, if the break-even point is 3,000 units and actual sales volume is 3,400 units, a *safety margin* of 400 units exists. Thus, sales can decrease by 400 units before the company would incur a loss. *See also* BREAK-EVEN POINT.

SAGACITY characteristics of intelligence, shrewdness, or wisdom; soundness of judgment.

SALARIAT working class; those who work.

SALARY regular compensation received by an employee as a condition of employment. Salaries are composed of basic wage and performance-based pay and indirect fringe benefit compensation, usually computed on an annual basis.

SALARY CONTINUATION PLAN arrangement, often funded by LIFE INSURANCE, to continue an employee's salary in the form of payments to a BENEFICIARY for a certain period after the employee's death. The employer may be the beneficiary, collecting the death benefit and making payments to the employee's beneficiary.

SALARY REDUCTION PLAN plan that allows employees the opportunity to have a certain percentage of their gross salary withheld and invested in the employee's choice of a stock, bond, or money market fund. *See also* SECTION 401(K) PLAN; SIMPLE IRA; SIMPLIFIED EMPLOYEE PENSION (SEP) PLAN.

SALE

In general: any exchange of goods or services for money. *See also* BARTER.

Finance: income received in exchange for goods and services recorded for a given accounting period, either on a CASH BASIS (as received) or on an ACCRUAL BASIS (as earned).

Law: *see* SALE OR EXCHANGE.

Marketing: price reduction for certain merchandise.

Securities: in trading, transaction when a buyer and a seller have agreed on a price for the security.

SALE AND LEASEBACK form of LEASE ARRANGEMENT in which a company sells an asset to another party—usually an insurance or finance company, a leasing company, a limited partnership, or an institutional investor—in exchange for cash, then contracts to lease the asset for a specified term. Generally, any gain or loss on sale is recognized, except when the risks and rewards of ownership are not transferred; in that case the transaction is treated as though the "seller" merely arranged a loan.

SALE AND LEASEBACK

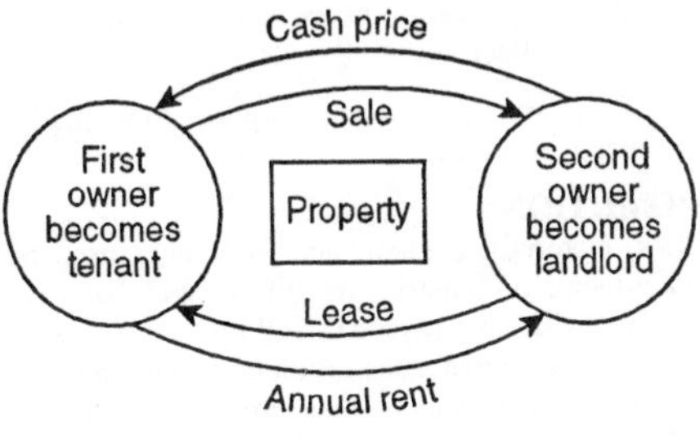

FIGURE 8

SALE OR EXCHANGE disposition of property in a value-for-value exchange, as opposed to a disposition by gift, contribution, or the like.

SALES ANALYST person in an accounting department with the job of tracking sales by region, product, or account to assure proper accounting and make recommendations to enhance profitability.

SALES BUDGET estimated amount of anticipated sales allocated by product, territory, or person; prepared weekly, monthly, or annually.

SALES CHARGE fee paid on purchasing an investment or product. For example, the sales charge for some mutual funds starts at 81/2% of the capital invested and decreases as the size of the investment increases. *See also* FRONT-END LOAD; LOAD FUND; NO-LOAD FUND.

SALES CONTRACT CONTRACT by which buyer and seller agree to the terms of sale. *See also* AGREEMENT OF SALE; EARNEST MONEY contract.

SALES EFFECTIVENESS TEST testing designed to judge the ability of an advertising campaign, promotion, or communications medium to sell a product.

SALES INCENTIVE remuneration offered to a salesperson for exceeding some predetermined sales goal. Sales incentives are offered by manufacturers as part of a promotion for the sale of their goods. The incentive may be in cash, or it may take the form of a special prize, such as a trip to an exotic or exciting vacation place.

SALES JOURNAL JOURNAL where credit sales are first posted to ACCOUNTING RECORDS.

SALES LITERATURE written material designed to help sell a product or service.

SALES LOAD *see* SALES CHARGE.

SALES OFFICE manufacturer-owned office having no inventory, primarily intended to increase customer sales.

SALESPERSON one whose main activity is selling a product, service, or investment. Salespersons in many industries (real estate, insurance, securities) must be licensed.

SALES PRICE the amount of money required to be paid or previously paid for property or product.

SALES PROMOTION
1. activities, materials, devices, and techniques used to supplement the advertising and marketing efforts and help coordinate the advertising with the personal selling effort. SWEEPSTAKES are among the best-known sales promotion tools, but other examples include special displays, coupons, promotional discounts, contests, and gift offers.
2. casually, combined activities employed to sell a product or service.

SALES RETURNS AND ALLOWANCES account to accumulate price reductions given to customers because of goods returned and defective merchandise not suited to the customers' needs.

SALES REVENUE amount received or to be received from selling a service or product.

SALES TAX percentage tax imposed on the retail sale of certain items. Sales taxes, which are based on the value of the item sold, are a form of REGRESSIVE TAX. They are a major source of revenue for most states.

SALES TYPE LEASE accounting by LESSOR in which one or more of the four criteria required for a capital lease are met and both of the following criteria are satisfied: (1) collectibility of minimum lease payments is predictable and (2) no important uncertainties surround the amount of unreimbursable costs yet to be incurred.

SALLIE MAE *see* SLM CORPORATION.

SALVAGE VALUE estimated value of a property when the taxpayer completes his use of the property. In determining the amount of depreciation allowable, salvage value must be subtracted from BASIS. Salvage value is ignored by the MACRS and ACRS rules.

SAMI *see* SALES AREA MARKETING, INC.

SAMPLE group of items chosen from a population. In statistics, it is used to estimate the properties of a population.

SAMPLE BUYER individual who purchases at a special introductory rate or obtains at no cost a sample of a product, such as a travel-size bottle of shampoo or a box of detergent big enough for one washload. *See also* TRIAL SIZE.

SAMPLING
1. **Marketing research:** studying a small group of people who are representative of a larger group. If the research is correctly conducted, conclusions drawn from the sample can be applied to the larger group without incurring exorbitant costs.
2. **Sales promotion:** offering a product or a small portion of it to consumers at little or no cost in order to stimulate regular usage.

S&L *see* SAVINGS AND LOAN ASSOCIATION.

S&P 500 *see* STANDARD & POOR'S INDEX.

SANDWICH LEASE LEASE held by a lessee who becomes a lessor by subletting. Typically, the sandwich leaseholder is neither the owner nor the user of the property. *See also* SUBLEASE.

SARBANES-OXLEY ACT OF 2002 (SARBOX) legislation introduced on the heels of a series of corporate financial scandals, especially those affecting Enron, Tyco International, and WorldCom. Sponsored by Senator Paul Sarbanes (D-Md.) and Representative Michael G. Oxley

(R-Oh.), the Act was approved by the House by a vote of 423–3 and by the Senate 97–0. Major provisions include
- Requirement for certification of financial reports by CEO and CFO.
- Ban on personal loans to any executive officer or director.
- Accelerated reporting of INSIDER TRADING.
- Prohibition on insider trades during pension fund blackout periods.
- Public reporting of CEO and CFO compensation.
- Auditor independence, including bans on certain work and precertification by the company's Audit Committee of all non-audit work.
- Criminal and civil penalties for violations of securities law.
- Longer jail sentences and larger fines for corporate executives who knowingly and willfully misstate financial statements.
- Prohibition on audit firms providing extra *value-added* services to their clients, including actuarial services and consulting unrelated to their audit work.
- A requirement that publicly traded companies furnish independent annual audit reports on internal controls related to financial reporting.

SARL (SOCIETÀ A RESPONSIBILITÀ LIMITADA) the Italian designation for a firm with limited liability.

SATELLITE COMMUNICATION use of orbital satellites to send voice, data, video, and graphics from one location to another.

SATISFACTION OF A DEBT release and discharge of an obligation in reference to which performance is executed.

SATISFACTION PIECE instrument for recording and acknowledging final payment of a mortgage loan. The lender acknowledges that the debt has been satisfied.

SATURATION greater than normal presence in the market, achieved by, for example, providing a store outlet in every neighborhood or advertising so frequently that everyone has heard the message numerous times.

SAVE write computer data to a semipermanent storage medium, such as a FLOPPY DISK, HARD DISK, TAPE backup, or CD-ROM. Until *saved*, data exist only in the computer's volatile RAM.

SAVINGS ACCOUNT deposit account at a COMMERCIAL BANK, SAVINGS BANK, or SAVINGS AND LOAN ASSOCIATION that pays interest, usually from day of deposit to day of withdrawal. Savings deposits are insured up to $100,000 per account if they are on deposit at a bank insured by the FEDERAL DEPOSIT INSURANCE CORPORATION (FDIC) or a savings and loan insured by the SAVINGS ASSOCIATION INSURANCE FUND (SAIF). SAIF is administered by the FDIC.

SAVINGS AND LOAN ASSOCIATION (S&L) institution similar to a savings bank in history and operation, except that the savings and loan association's primary purpose has been to provide loans for purchasing and building homes; also called *building and loan association*.

Insurance for depositors may be provided by the Federal Deposit Insurance Company (FDIC).

SAVINGS BANK type of bank, prevalent on the East Coast and in the Midwest, whose major service traditionally has been the timesavings account. The bank is usually owned by its depositors as creditors whose dividends are paid as interest on their accounts. Functions are similar to those of SAVINGS AND LOAN ASSOCIATIONS (S&LS).

SAVINGS BOND U.S. government bond issued in FACE VALUE denominations ranging from $50 to $10,000. Issued at a discount, these bonds are redeemed at face value at maturity. From 1941 to 1979, the government issued SERIES E BONDS. Since 1980, SERIES EE and SERIES HH BONDS have been issued. *See also* QUALIFIED SAVINGS BOND.

SAVINGS ELEMENT cash value of life insurance that accumulates according to a table in a policy. It reflects premiums in the early years that exceed the *pure cost of protection* during that period. If a policy is surrendered the policyowner receives the cash value and the insurance ends. This is why a cash value policy can be considered a savings or investment vehicle.

SAVINGS RATE rate at which savings occur out of income. *See also* MARGINAL PROPENSITY TO SAVE.

SAY'S LAW proposition, in 19th-century (classical) economics, that supply creates its own demand, that whatever quantity is supplied will also be demanded. It is named for the 19th-century French economist J. B. Say.

SBA *see* SMALL BUSINESS ADMINISTRATION.

SCABS individuals who work for an employer while a strike condition exists. The term, used by union members, is applied to nonunion and union members who cross a union picket line to perform work for an employer. *See also* STRIKEBREAKERS.

SCALABLE FONT a font that can be printed at any size. The shapes of the characters in a *scalable font* are stored as vector graphics (that is, as a series of mathematical expressions that define the curves and lie of the letters) rather than as bitmaps. Also called *vector* or *outline font*.

SCALAGE percentage deduction granted in business dealings with goods that are likely to shrink, leak, or otherwise vary in the amount or weight originally stated.

SCALE
  Economics: amount of production, as in *economy* or *diseconomy of scale*. *See also* MARGINAL COST.
  Labor: wage rate for specific types of employees. For example, the union *scale* for carpenters is $30.00 per hour.

Modeling: proportional relationship between the dimensions of a drawing, plan, or model and the dimensions of the physical object it represents.

SCALE ORDER order for a specified number of shares that is to be executed in stages in order to average the price. Such an order might provide for the purchase of a total of 5,000 shares to be executed in lots of 500 shares at each quarter-point interval as the market declines.

SCALE RELATIONSHIP
1. comparison by use of a given scale, such as wage scale, social scale, scale of a thermometer.
2. relationship between a representative dimension and the object it represents, such as a scale of one inch to a mile.

SCALPER speculator who enters into quasi-legal or illegal transactions to turn a quick and sometimes unreasonable profit. For example, a ticket scalper buys tickets for a major theatrical or athletic event at regular prices; then, when the event is sold out, the scalper resells the tickets at the highest price possible.

SCANNER device that can read or scan typed characters from paper (hard) copy and automatically transfer this information onto something else. *See also* MACHINE READABLE.

SCARCITY, SCARCITY VALUE relative abundance of a commodity or good. The *scarcity value* of a commodity is that element of its value that is due to its scarcity. Scarcity is only one element of value; smallpox is very scarce, but has no value because nobody wants it.

SCATTER DIAGRAM diagram showing relation between two quantities. One quantity is measured on the vertical axis, the other on the horizontal axis, and each observation is represented by a dot.

SCATTER PLAN broadcast media plan that schedules advertising announcements to run during a variety of radio and/or television programs. This schedule gives an advertiser a wider audience for the advertising dollar than being a SPONSOR of a single program would achieve.

SCENIC EASEMENT ENCUMBRANCE on the TITLE to a property to preserve it in a more or less natural or undeveloped state. *See also* EASEMENT.

SCHEDULE
1. written or printed statement of details.
2. timetable of events. *See also* SCHEDULING.
3. IRS income tax form.

SCHEDULE C the tax form schedule an individual uses for each business (or self-employed activity). A taxpayer lists income less expenses on this schedule.

SCHEDULED PRODUCTION timetable for the production of a product or products; when a production sequence is to occur.

SCHEDULE K-1 tax form used to report to each partner or beneficiary his or her share of income, losses, capital gains, and other tax information passed through from a partnership or trust.

SCHEDULING devising a timetable of events; deciding when and possibly where certain events shall occur. *See also* SCHEDULE.

SCHOLARSHIP *see* QUALIFIED SCHOLARSHIP; TAXABLE SCHOLARSHIP AND FELLOWSHIP GRANTS.

SCIENTER previous knowledge of operative facts, frequently signifying guilty knowledge. As used in PLEADINGS, the term signifies that the alleged crime or TORT was done designedly or with guilty knowledge. The term is usually employed in relation to FRAUD, and means a person's knowledge that he was making false representations, with intent to deceive.

SCOOP news story published before one by a rival news organization.

SCOPE OF AUTHORITY in the law of agency, those acts proper for the accomplishment of the goal of the agency, including not only the actual authorization conferred upon the agent by his or her principal but also that which has apparently or implicitly been delegated to the agent.

SCOPE OF EMPLOYMENT acts done while performing one's job duties. The phrase was adopted by the courts for the purpose of determining an employer's liability for the acts of employees. The employer is said to be vicariously liable only for those torts of the employee that are committed within the range of his job activities.

SCORCHED-EARTH DEFENSE disposal by the target of a corporate acquisition of its CROWN JEWELS for the purpose of thwarting a hostile TAKEOVER. Such a strategy often results in a permanent impairment of its earning power and value.

SCORE Counselors to America's Small Business, formerly SERVICE CORPS OF RETIRED EXECUTIVES. Volunteer organization founded in 1964 with 10,500 members. SCORE's main office is in Washington, D.C.; it has 10 regional groups and 389 chapters. SCORE is sponsored by the U.S. Small Business Association and consists of active and retired businesspersons who provide free management advice to small businesspeople.

S CORPORATION CORPORATION with a limited number of stockholders (100 or fewer) that elects not to be taxed as a regular (C) corporation and meets certain other requirements. Family members may elect to be treated as one shareholder. Shareholders include in their personal tax returns their PRO RATA share of capital gains, ordinary income, tax preference items, and so on. This form avoids corporate DOUBLE TAXATION while providing limited liability protection to shareholders of a corporation.

SCRAP, SCRAP VALUE *see* SALVAGE VALUE.

SCREEN
1. a computer display; a MONITOR.
2. a screenful of information.
3. process a grayscale image for printing by breaking down the various shades of gray into very small dots. *See* HALFTONE.

SCRIP
In general: receipt, certificate, or other representation of value recognized by both payer and payee. Scrip is not currency but may be convertible into currency.
Securities: temporary document issued by a corporation to represent a fractional share of stock resulting from a STOCK SPLIT, exchange of stock, or SPIN-OFF.

SCROLL to move up and down (or from side to side) in a computer file, bringing different information into view, as if the computer screen were the visible portion of a scroll being unrolled at one end and rolled up at the other.

SCROLL BAR the bar on the side (vertical) or bottom (horizontal) of a computer screen window that allows users to navigate up and down (or from side to side) through the window's contents. Scroll bars have arrows at either end that can be clicked with a mouse and a scroll box that can be dragged with a mouse for faster scrolling. The MACINTOSH equivalent is the *elevator bar*.

SDR *see* SPECIAL DRAWING RIGHTS.

SEAL in COMMON LAW, impression on wax or other substance capable of being impressed. The purpose of a seal is to attest to the execution of an INSTRUMENT. The word seal and the letters L.S. *(locus sigilli,* place of the seal) have the same significance and today are commonly used for the same purpose.

SEALED BID cost estimate presented to potential customer. Sealed bids are held secret from competitors.

SEAL OF APPROVAL documentation offered by such organizations as Good Housekeeping Institute or Underwriter's Laboratories that a product has been tested by these organizations and has been found to meet the standards set by the organization in order to gain the seal of approval.

SEARCH ENGINE a program or WEB SITE that permits users to search for keywords on WEB PAGES throughout the WORLD WIDE WEB.

SEASONAL ADJUSTMENT statistical procedure for time series data to remove seasonal variations, allowing a clearer view of nonseasonal changes in the data.

SEASONALITY variations in business or economic activity that recur with regularity as the result of changes in climate, holidays, and vacations. It is often necessary to make allowances for seasonality when

interpreting or projecting financial or economic data, a process economists call *seasonal adjustment.*

SEASONAL UNEMPLOYMENT unemployment expected at a given
time of year. Resort areas, for example, can expect to experience *seasonal unemployment* during the off-season. Unemployment statistics
provided by the government are seasonally adjusted.

SEASONED ISSUE securities (usually from established companies)
that have gained a reputation for quality with the investing public and
enjoy liquidity in the SECONDARY MARKET.

SEASONED LOAN BOND OR MORTGAGE on which several payments
have been collected. It is easier to sell a seasoned mortgage.

SEAT figurative term for membership on a securities or commodities
exchange. Seats are usually bought and sold at prices set by supply
and demand. *See also* MEMBER FIRM.

SEC *see* SECURITIES AND EXCHANGE COMMISSION.

SECA *see* SELF-EMPLOYMENT CONTRIBUTIONS ACT.

SECONDARY BENEFICIARY *see* BENEFICIARY.

SECONDARY BOYCOTT union boycott of products, goods, or services indirectly related to a primary employer by preventing their use,
purchase, or transportation. In a secondary boycott it is a union's
objective to force an employer to stop doing business with another
person or company undergoing a union job action. The TAFT-HARTLEY
ACT limits the use of secondary boycotts by unions.

SECONDARY DATA data initially gathered for a different objective.

SECONDARY DISTRIBUTION public sale of previously issued securities held by large investors, usually corporations, institutions, or
other affiliated persons, as distinguished from a new issue or PRIMARY
DISTRIBUTION, where the seller is the issuing corporation.

SECONDARY FINANCING *see* JUNIOR MORTGAGE; SECOND MORTGAGE.

SECONDARY MARKET
1. exchanges and over-the-counter markets where securities are
   bought and sold subsequent to original issuance, which took place
   in the PRIMARY MARKET.
2. market in which money market instruments are traded among
   investors.

SECONDARY MORTGAGE MARKET market for buying and selling
mortgages that have already been issued or originated. *See also* FED-
ERAL HOME LOAN MORTGAGE CORPORATION (FHLMC); FEDERAL NATIONAL
MORTGAGE ASSOCIATION (FNMA).

SECONDARY OFFERING *see* SECONDARY DISTRIBUTION.

SECONDARY STORAGE DEVICE computer storage location for data not currently being accessed. The principal forms of secondary storage are HARD DISK drives, FLOPPY DISKS, and TAPE storage. Secondary storage provides readily accessible file retrieval as well as security against loss. *See also* PRIMARY STORAGE DEVICE.

SECOND-CLASS MAIL class of mail offered by the U.S. Postal Service for newspapers and other periodicals. Periodicals must be sent at least quarterly and must not be primarily for advertising. The rate depends on the advertising content, distance shipped, and whether the paper is sent within the county in which it is published.

SECOND HOME a residence that is not one's PRINCIPAL RESIDENCE. A taxpayer may deduct interest on two personal residences provided certain occupancy requirements are met.

SECOND LIEN or SECOND MORTGAGE subordinated LIEN, created by a mortgage loan, over the amount of a FIRST MORTGAGE. Second mortgages are used at purchase to reduce the amount of a cash downpayment or in refinancing to raise cash for any purpose. *See also* JUNIOR MORTGAGE; WRAPAROUND MORTGAGE.

SECTION (OF LAND) one square mile in the GOVERNMENT RECTANGULAR SURVEY. There are 36 sections in a 6-mile-square township.

SECTION 167 section of the INTERNAL REVENUE CODE dealing with depreciation. *See also* DEPRECIATION; MACRS.

SECTION 179 *see* ADDITIONAL FIRST-YEAR DEPRECIATION.

SECTION 401(K) PLAN plan that allows an employee to contribute pretax earnings to an individual account, which is invested in stocks, bonds, or money market instruments; also known as a SALARY REDUCTION PLAN. The contributions as well as earnings on them are taxed only when withdrawn.

SECTION 501(c)(3) ORGANIZATION an organization that is specifically exempted from income tax. It must meet certain criteria including:
1. Purpose: religious, charitable, scientific, testing for public safety, literary, educational purposes.
2. Earnings: Does not inure to the benefit of any private shareholder or individual.
3. Not lobbying: no substantial activity to influence legislation.
4. Not political: does not participate on behalf of any candidate for public office.

SECTION 8 HOUSING privately owned rental DWELLING units participating in the low-income rental assistance program created by 1974 amendments to Section 8 of the 1937 Housing Act. Under the program, landlords receive rent subsidies on behalf of qualified low-income tenants, allowing the tenants to pay a limited proportion of their incomes toward the rent.

SECTION 1031 section of the INTERNAL REVENUE CODE that deals with tax-free exchanges of certain property. General rules for a tax-free exchange of real estate are that the properties must be: (1) exchanged; (2) LIKE-KIND PROPERTY (real estate for real estate, for example); and (3) held for use in a trade or business or held as an investment. Delayed exchanges within certain limits are allowed. *See also* BOOT; TAX-FREE EXCHANGE.

SECTION 1231 section of the INTERNAL REVENUE CODE that deals with ASSETS used in a trade or business. Generally, gains on Section 1231 assets are taxed at CAPITAL GAINS rates (except for depreciation recapture), and losses are tax deductible as ORDINARY LOSSES. Section 1231 assets include:
1. vehicles used in business.
2. machinery used in business.
3. hotels, office buildings, warehouses, apartments.

SECTOR
1. particular group of stocks, usually found in one industry. SECURITIES ANALYSTS often follow a particular *sector* of the stock market, such as airline or chemical stocks.
2. part of the economy, as in *private sector* or *public sector.*
3. division of a computer FLOPPY DISK.

SECULAR TRUST a variation of the irrevocable Rabbi trust arrangement used with a nonqualified DEFERRED COMPENSATION PLAN. Because the assets in a *secular trust* are not subject to the claims of creditors, it offers an executive more security than a Rabbi trust.

SECURED BOND bond backed by the pledge of collateral, a mortgage, or other lien. The exact nature of the security is spelled out in the INDENTURE. Secured bonds are distinguished from unsecured bonds, called DEBENTURES.

SECURED DEBT debt obligation, including bonds, that is guaranteed by the pledge of assets or other collateral. *See also* ASSIGN; HYPOTHECATE.

SECURED TRANSACTION transaction based on a security agreement that concerns a security interest, whereby personal or real property is pledged as collateral for performance or for a debt.

SECURITIES
1. STOCK CERTIFICATES, BONDS, or other evidence of a secured indebtedness or of a right created in the holder to participate in the profits or assets distribution of a profit-making enterprise.
2. written assurances for the return or payment of money.
3. INSTRUMENTS giving to their legal holders right to money or other property.

SECURITIES ACT OF 1933 first law enacted by Congress to regulate the SECURITIES MARKETS, approved May 26, 1933, as the Truth in Securities Act. It requires REGISTRATION of securities prior to public sale and adequate DISCLOSURE of pertinent financial and other data in a PROSPECTUS to permit informed analysis by potential investors. It also contains antifraud provisions prohibiting false representations and disclosures.

SECURITIES ANALYST individual, usually employed by a stock brokerage house, bank, or investment institution, who performs investment research and examines the financial condition of a company or group of companies in an industry and in the context of the securities markets.

SECURITIES AND COMMODITIES EXCHANGES organized, national exchanges where securities, options, and commodities futures contracts are traded by members for their own accounts and for the accounts of customers. The stock exchanges are registered with and regulated by the SECURITIES AND EXCHANGE COMMISSION; the commodities exchanges are registered with and regulated by the Commodity Futures Trading Commission (*see* REGULATED COMMODITIES). Where options are also traded on an exchange, such activity is regulated by the SEC.

SECURITIES AND EXCHANGE COMMISSION (SEC) federal agency empowered to regulate and supervise the selling of SECURITIES, to prevent unfair practices on security exchanges and over-the-counter markets, and to maintain a fair and orderly market for the investor.

SECURITIES EXCHANGE ACT OF 1934 law governing the SECURITIES MARKETS, enacted June 6, 1934. The act outlaws misrepresentation, MANIPULATION, and other abusive practices in the issuance of securities. It created the SECURITIES AND EXCHANGE COMMISSION (SEC) to enforce both the SECURITIES ACT OF 1933 and the Securities Exchange Act of 1934.

SECURITIES INVESTOR PROTECTION CORPORATION (SIPC) nonprofit corporation supported by its membership of securities brokers and dealers, developed to protect their customers and to promote confidence in the securities markets. In principle, SIPC provides certain amounts of insurance on cash and securities left on deposit in a brokerage account. This insures investors against failure of the brokerage firm but not against a decline in the value of securities.

SECURITIES LOAN
1. loan of securities by one broker to another, usually to cover a customer's short sale. The lending broker is secured by the cash proceeds of the sale.
2. in a more general sense, loan collateralized by MARKETABLE SECURITIES.

SECURITIES MARKETS general term for markets in which SECURITIES are traded, including both organized securities exchanges and OVER-THE-COUNTER (OTC) markets.

SECURITIZATION process of distributing RISK by aggregating DEBT INSTRUMENTS in a pool, then issuing new SECURITIES backed by the pool. *See also* ASSET-BACKED SECURITIES.

SECURITY
Finance: collateral offered by a debtor to a lender to secure a loan, called *collateral security.*
Investment: INSTRUMENT that signifies an ownership position in a corporation (a STOCK), a creditor relationship with a corporation or governmental body (a BOND), or other ownership rights.

SECURITY DEPOSIT nontaxable cash payment received by a LANDLORD to be held during the term of the LEASE to offset damages incurred due to actions of a tenant. If the tenant violates the lease, the landlord may apply the amount as RENT, and the deposit becomes TAXABLE income.

SECURITY INTEREST interest in real property or personal property that secures the payment of an obligation. In common law, security interests are either consensual (by agreement) or arise by operation of law, as in the case of judgment liens and statutory liens.

SECURITY RATING evaluation of the credit and investment risk of a securities issue by commercial rating agencies, such as Moody's, Fitch's, and Standard & Poor's.

SEED MONEY venture capitalist's first contribution toward the financing or capital requirements of a start-up business. It frequently takes the form of a loan, often SUBORDINATED, or an investment in convertible bonds or preferred stock.

SEGMENTATION STRATEGY
  1. *see* DIFFERENTIATION STRATEGY.
  2. marketing plan where all marketing efforts are directed at one particular market segment. For example, all advertising efforts on behalf of Piaget watches position the watch as a luxury item, and the advertising is targeted toward an upscale audience.

SEGMENT MARGIN profitability measure used to evaluate the financial performance of a business segment (i.e., division, territory, product line). It equals segmental revenue less related product costs and traceable operating expenses attributable to that segment.

SEGMENT REPORTING presentation required in the ANNUAL REPORT when a reportable segment meets one or more of the following tests: (1) revenue is 10% or more of combined revenue; (2) operating profit is 10% or more of combined operating profit (operating profit excludes unallocable general corporate revenue and expenses, interest expense, and income taxes); or (3) identifiable assets are 10% or more of the combined identifiable assets; also called *line of business reporting.* FASB Statement No. 14 requires that financial statements include information about operations in different industries, foreign operations, export sales, major customers, and government contracts.

SEGREGATION OF DUTIES internal control concept in which individuals do not have responsibility for incompatible activities. For example, the recordkeeping or authorization function should be divorced from the physical custody of the asset to guard against misuse.

SEISIN POSSESSION of realty by one who claims to own a FEE SIMPLE estate or a LIFE ESTATE or other salable interest. *See also* TITLE.

SELECTIVE CREDIT CONTROLS ability of the FEDERAL RESERVE BOARD (FRB) to establish selective terms for various credit instruments. MARGIN requirements can be altered by the FRB to affect the trading of securities in the STOCK MARKET.

SELECTIVE DISTRIBUTION DISTRIBUTION of products only to those wholesalers or retailers who: (1) agree to sell the product for no less than a certain price; (2) patronize the distributor on a regular basis or for at least a certain dollar amount annually; or (3) meet specific requirements established by the distributor as outlined by the manufacturer.

SELF-AMORTIZING MORTGAGE MORTGAGE that will retire itself through regular principal and interest payments. *See also* BALLOON; DIRECT-REDUCTION MORTGAGE; INTEREST-ONLY LOAN.

SELF-DIRECTED IRA INDIVIDUAL RETIREMENT ACCOUNT that can be actively managed by the account holder, who designates a CUSTODIAN to carry out investment instructions. The account is subject to the same conditions and early withdrawal limitations as a regular IRA.

SELF-EMPLOYED individuals who work for themselves and are not employed by another. The owner-operator of a SOLE PROPRIETORSHIP or a partner in a PARTNERSHIP is considered *self-employed*. Those who are self-employed assume all the risks and responsibilities of a business enterprise and are subject to SELF-EMPLOYMENT TAX, in addition to INCOME TAX, on net income from self-employment activities. The self-employment tax is paid in lieu of the Social Security payments.

SELF-EMPLOYMENT CONTRIBUTIONS ACT the federal law that provides for the imposition of the SELF-EMPLOYMENT TAX. Also referred to as SECA.

SELF-EMPLOYMENT INCOME the income of self-employed persons, which is covered by Social Security if net profit from the trade or business is at least $400 for the year. The self-employed person pays taxes on earnings in excess of the $400. In some instances, a person's self-employment income may count for Social Security even if actual net earnings are less than $400.

SELF-EMPLOYMENT RETIREMENT PLAN *see* KEOGH PLAN.

SELF-EMPLOYMENT TAX provision for Social Security (old-age, survivor's, and disability insurance) and Medicare (hospital insurance) for self-employed individuals. In 2006, the Social Security portion of self-employment tax is 12.4% on net earnings from self-employment up to $94,200, and the Medicare portion is 2.9% on net earnings from self-employment. Estimated self-employment tax must be paid quarterly with estimated income tax.

SELF-FULFILLING PROPHECY causing something to happen by believing it will occur. For example, forecasting the election of a particular political candidate may have the effect of convincing enough people to cast favorable votes, thereby creating an electoral victory as a self-fulfilling prophecy.

SELF-HELP efforts of a landlord to cure a DEFAULT on the LEASE without aid of legal proceedings. In most states, self-help remedies are not considered a legitimate substitute for a legal eviction.

SELF-IMAGE conceptualization, idea, or mental image one has of oneself; concept of ego.

SELF INSURANCE protecting against loss by setting aside one's own money. This can be done on a mathematical basis by establishing a separate fund into which funds are deposited on a periodic basis. Through self insurance it is possible to protect against highfrequency, low-severity losses.

SELF-TENDER OFFER offer by a company to buy a portion of its own stock from its shareholders in an effort to prevent an unfriendly takeover. *See also* TENDER OFFER.

SELLER FINANCING a debt instrument taken back by the seller as part of the purchase price for a property. Such financing is used as an inducement to a sale when normal third-party financing is expensive or unavailable and in situations where the existing, first lien may be assumed by the buyer but the difference between the existing debt and sales price exceeds the cash resources of the buyer. Seller financing may be in the form of a SENIOR or JUNIOR MORTGAGE.

SELLER'S MARKET situation in which there is more demand for a security or product than there is available supply. As a result, the prices tend to be rising, and the sellers can set both the prices and the terms of sale. It contrasts with a BUYER'S MARKET, characterized by excess supply, low prices, and terms suited to the buyer's desires.

SELLING AGENT or **SELLING BROKER** licensed real estate agent (broker) who brings forth the buyer. *See also* LISTING AGENT; LISTING BROKER.

SELLING CLIMAX sudden plunge in security prices when those who hold stocks or bonds panic and decide to dump their holdings all at once. Sometimes a selling climax can signal the bottom of a BEAR MARKET, meaning that after the climax the market will start to rise.

SELLING, GENERAL, AND ADMINISTRATIVE (SG&A) EXPENSES grouping of expenses reported on a company's profit and loss statement between cost of goods sold and income deductions. Included are salespersons' salaries and commissions, advertising and promotion, travel and entertainment, office payroll and expenses, and executives' salaries. SG&A expenses do not include financing costs or income taxes.

SELLING SHORT selling securities, commodities, or foreign currency not actually owned by the seller. In making the short sale, the seller hopes to cover—that is, buy back—sold items at a lower price and thus earn a profit.

SELLING SHORT AGAINST THE BOX SELLING SHORT stock actually owned by the seller but held in safekeeping at a brokerage firm, called *the box* in Wall Street jargon, which postpones recognition of the gain until the following year. The seller delivers borrowed stock and later repays the lender with the stock held in the box.

SELL-OFF selling securities under pressure to avoid further declines in prices. *See also* DUMPING.

SEMIANNUAL twice a year; same as BIANNUAL.

SEMICONDUCTOR material, such as silicon, that is neither a good conductor nor a good insulator. Semiconductor devices, such as diodes, transistors, and integrated circuits, are the essential parts that make it possible to build computers and other small, inexpensive electronic machines.

SEMIMONTHLY occurring twice each month; for example, some payrolls are prepared semimonthly.

SEMIVARIABLE COSTS costs that change in response to changes in volume, but by less than a proportionate amount.

SENIOR CITIZEN generally someone age 65 or over. Discounts on goods and services are often offered to *senior citizens,* with privileges often extended to those as young as 55. A number of special tax rules favor senior citizens:
1. higher filing thresholds for those 65 and over.
2. elderly tax credit for those 65 and over.
3. higher STANDARD DEDUCTION for those age 65 or over.

SENIOR DEBT loans or debt securities that have claim prior to junior obligations and equity on a corporation's assets in the event of liquidation.

SENIORITY SYSTEM system based upon length of service for determining employment advantages. A seniority system is instrumental in determining who receives promotions and layoffs. Unions are strongly in favor of using seniority as the only criterion for making distinctions among employees.

SENIOR MORTGAGE same as FIRST MORTGAGE.

SENIOR REFUNDING replacement of securities maturing in 5 to 12 years with issues having original maturities of 15 years or longer. The objectives may be to reduce the bond issuer's interest costs, to consolidate several issues into one, or to extend the maturity date.

SENIOR SECURITY security that has claim prior to a junior obligation and equity on a corporation's assets and earnings. Senior securities are repaid before junior securities in the event of liquidation. Debt, including notes, bonds, and debentures, is senior to stock; first mortgage bonds are senior to second mortgage bonds; and all mortgage bonds are senior to debentures, which are unsecured.

SENSITIVE MARKET market easily swayed by the announcement of positive or negative news. Such a market's fluctuations will be wider than those of a market in which investors are more confident of the outlook for prices.

SENSITIVITY ANALYSIS consideration of various possible outcomes on the rate of return or other measure of profitability. For example, an analyst may prepare a forecast of expected profitability based on the most likely situation, then prepare others based on more and less optimistic scenarios. SPREADSHEET programs such as Excel facilitate sensitivity analysis by automatic recalculations for a change in any variable.

SENSITIVITY TRAINING method of laboratory training where an unstructured group of individuals exchange thoughts and feelings on a face-to-face basis. Sensitivity training helps give insight into how and why others feel the way they do on issues of mutual concern.

SENTIMENT INDICATORS measures of the bullish or bearish mood of investors. Many technical analysts look at these indicators as contrary indicators; that is, when most investors are bullish, the market is about to drop, and when most are bearish, the market is about to rise.

SEP *see* SIMPLIFIED EMPLOYEE PENSION PLAN.

SEPARATELY MANAGED ACCOUNT (SMA) professionally managed portfolio of securities that uses pooled money to buy investments owned directly by the account holder. SMAs, also called *separate accounts, individually managed accounts,* or *managed accounts,* are usually marketed by broker-dealers, who select money managers, called *subadvisors,* for clients from a selected list.

SEPARATE PROPERTY in community property states, property acquired by either spouse before marriage or by gift or devise after marriage, as distinct from COMMUNITY PROPERTY. Income from separate property is taxed to its owner.

SEPARATE (TAX) RETURN *see* MARRIED FILING SEPARATELY.

SEPARATION OF SERVICE action of an employee in severing his or her connection with an employer.

SEP-IRA *see* SIMPLIFIED EMPLOYEE PENSION PLAN.

SEQUENCE order of occurrence; process or fact of following in order. For example, a production-line sequence requires that bottles of soda be filled before the caps are secured.

SEQUENTIAL ACCESS electronic storing of records based upon some sequence determination, such as alphabetic or numeric order. Direct access file processing requires a direct access device such as a magnetic disk unit, where retrieval time can be in milliseconds as compared to several seconds or even minutes in a sequential file utilizing a tape unit. A majority of today's computerized information systems that use the direct access method also use sequential processing for some portion of the processing activities in the same information system.

SERIAL BOND bond issue, usually of a municipality, with various MATURITY dates scheduled at regular intervals until the entire issue is retired. Each bond certificate in the series has an indicated REDEMPTION date.

SERIAL CORRELATION a problem that arises in regression analysis involving time series data when successive values of the random error term are not independent. This implies that an important variable has not been identified. Same as *autocorrelation*.

SERIAL PORT a connection by which a computer can transmit data to another device using SERIAL TRANSMISSION. Serial ports on a PC are commonly designated as COM1 and COM2; one is usually used for a modem. *Contrast with* PARALLEL PORT.

SERIAL PRINTER a printer that connects to a computer's SERIAL PORT.

SERIAL TRANSMISSION sending data one bit at a time over a single wire. It is the normal way of linking computers to terminals and is often used to link microcomputers to printers, especially relatively slow ones.

SERIES BONDS group of bonds issued at different times with different maturities but under the same INDENTURE.

SERIES E BOND savings bond issued by the U.S. government from 1941 to 1979. Generally issued at 75 cents per dollar face value, maturing at par in a specified number of years that fluctuated with the rate of interest. A taxpayer may report the interest income each year or report the entire amount when the bond is cashed.

SERIES EE BOND *see* EDUCATION SAVINGS BOND.

SERIES HH BOND U.S. government bond formerly available in denominations of $500 to $10,000 in exchange for Series E or EE bonds. August 31, 2004, was the last issue date for HH/H bonds. After that date, the government discontinued the exchange of bonds for HH/H bonds. This action does not affect current holders of HH/H bonds.

SERIES I BOND an accrual-type security designed for investors seeking to protect the purchasing power of their investment and earn a guaranteed real rate of return. I Bonds are sold at face value and grow in value with inflation-indexed earnings for up to 30 years; interest is added to the bond monthly and paid when the bond is cashed. The earnings rate is a combination of a fixed rate of return, which remains the same throughout the life of the bond, and a variable semiannual inflation rate. The fixed rate is announced by the Treasury Department each May and November and remains the same for the life of bonds purchased within the next six months. Purchases may be made through banks or in Treasury Direct accounts.

SERVER a computer that provides information to client machines. For example, there are WEB SERVERS that send out WEB PAGES, mail servers that deliver E-MAIL, list servers that administer mailing lists, FTP servers that hold FTP sites and deliver files to users who request them, and name servers that provide information about Internet host names. The central computer on a LOCAL AREA NETWORK (LAN) is also a *server*.

SERVICE
1. work done by one person that benefits another.
2. type of business that sells assistance and expertise rather than a tangible product. For example, the field of management consulting is a *service* industry.
3. after-purchase assistance that is offered by the manufacturer to maintain the quality of the product during its use. Service is often the main selling point for big-ticket items such as cars, washing machines, and television sets.

SERVICE BUREAU service business that makes its resources (computers, people) available to others for a fee—for example, a merge/purge, list maintenance, or FULFILLMENT service. In practice most service bureaus offer a variety of related services at a lower cost than individual users could achieve, because the service bureau has the advantage of economies of scale.

SERVICE BUSINESS form of business providing various types of labor services in a wide variety of business sectors. For example, a lawn service and maid service provide consumers with lawn mowing and housekeeping services. *See also* SERVICE SECTOR.

SERVICE CLUB any of a number of service organizations dedicated to providing member or community services. The Kiwanis Club, Rotary Club, and Masons are examples.

SERVICE CORPS OF RETIRED EXECUTIVES (SCORE) former name of SCORE, Counselors to America's Small Business.

SERVICE DEPARTMENT section or department of retail store giving ancillary services to customers. Service departments accept merchandise returns and credit applications, approve checks, wrap merchandise, make service appointments, and so on.

SERVICE ECONOMY economy in which activity is dominated by the service sector, as opposed to manufacturing, agriculture, or extraction. The United States is said to be a service economy inasmuch as over 50% of the labor force is in the SERVICE SECTOR.

SERVICE FEE money paid to an advertising agency by an advertiser. In most cases, the agency is paid a retainer for general services. Any services beyond those are compensated at special rates.

SERVICE SECTOR sector of the economy where service businesses provide employment and contributions to the GROSS DOMESTIC PRODUCT (GDP). The service sector employs over 80% of the American work force. *See also* SERVICE BUSINESS.

SERVICE WORKER employee who works in the SERVICE SECTOR of the economy. As manufacturing employment declines in the United states, the service sector and its workers have grown very rapidly. The service worker is the least represented by unions.

SERVICING
In general: regular maintenance and routine repairs to equipment.
Finance: act of billing, collecting payment, and filing reports on a LOAN. For example, *servicing* for a mortgage loan includes loan analysis, default follow-up, and management of tax and insurance escrow accounts. It is often performed for a fee by mortgage bankers after loans are sold to investors.

SET-ASIDE percentage of a job set aside for bidding from minority contractors. Government and corporate contracts for products and services stipulate that a certain percentage of the business must be handled by minority firms. *Set-aside* programs are designed to help minority firms become established more quickly than they might if they had to compete on an equal footing with entrenched competitors.

SETBACK
1. distance from the curb or other established line within which no buildings may be erected. *See also* BUILDING LINE.
2. problems, often in business or manufacturing, that result in lower profits or a delay in realizing a certain event.

SETOFF
In general: counterclaim by DEFENDANT against PLAINTIFF that grows from an independent CAUSE OF ACTION and diminishes the plaintiff's potential recovery; a counterdemand arising out of a transaction different from that on which the plaintiff's cause of action is based. It does not deny the justice of the plaintiff's claim but seeks to balance it in whole or in part by a counterobligation alleged to be due by the plaintiff to the defendant in another transaction.
Tax law: the amount of refund that a taxpayer could claim to be offset against the amount of deficiency that could be properly assessed; conversely, the amount of deficiency the government could assess can

be offset by the amount the taxpayer could properly claim as a refund for the same taxable year.

SETTLE
In general: to pay an obligation.

Law: (1) to resolve a legal dispute short of adjudication; (2) to arrange for disposition of property, such as between spouses or between parents and children, if there has been a dispute such as a divorce.

Securities: to complete a securities trade between brokers acting as AGENTS or between broker and customer.

SETTLEMENT
Estates: distribution of an estate's assets by an executor to beneficiaries after all legal procedures have been completed.

Law: agreement reached through negotiation.

Real estate: *see* CLOSING.

SETTLEMENT COST *see* CLOSING COST.

SETTLEMENT DATE
Real estate: date when property is purchased (or sold) and the deed is transferred. *See also* CLOSING DATE.

Securities: date by which an executed order must be settled, either by a buyer paying for the securities with cash or by a seller delivering the securities and receiving the proceeds of sale for them. In a REGULAR-WAY DELIVERY of stocks and bonds, the SETTLEMENT DATE is three business days. For taxpayers, the TRADE DATE rather than the settlement date affects the HOLDING PERIOD.

SETTLEMENT STATEMENT *see* CLOSING STATEMENT.

SETTLOR person in the TRUST relationship who creates or intentionally causes the trust to come into existence. Other terms used to designate this person are *donor, trustor,* and *grantor.*

SETUP COST costs associated with establishing a new manufacturing procedure. *Setup costs* include design costs, acquisition and location of machinery, and employee hiring and training.

SEVERALTY ownership of real property by an individual as an individual. *See also* TENANCY IN COMMON; TENANCY IN SEVERALTY.

SEVERANCE BENEFIT *see* SEVERANCE PAY.

SEVERANCE DAMAGES element of value arising out of a condemnation of which a tract was a part. Suppose the state highway department needed a strip of land 100 feet wide from the middle of a farm. They award $1,000 per acre for the land taken, plus $15,000 *severance damages* for the owner's inconvenience in getting from one side of the highway to the other.

SEVERANCE PAY income bridge provided by some employers for employees going from employment to unemployment. Amount is negotiable. Severance pay is taxable in the year received.

SEWER system of pipes, containments, and treatment facilities for the disposal of waste and containment of rainwater.

SEX STEREOTYPING inferred traits and expected behavior based upon sex. Sex stereotyping is a form of prejudice that can be applied to employment opportunities, credit ratings, consumer behavior, and so on.

SEXUAL HARASSMENT unwelcome and often intimidating verbal or physical sexual advances. Sexual harassment often carries with it threats of employment reprisals if such advances are refused. Sexual harassment has been defined by the federal government and courts as illegal employment discrimination.

SHAKEDOWN trial run before putting a procedure or application into production; attempt to locate all the problems or "bugs" before actual utilization. For example, a new ship is taken on a shakedown cruise without paying passengers before it is placed into service.

SHAKEOUT change in market conditions that results in the elimination of the weaker or marginally financed participants in an industry. In the securities market, a shakeout occurs when speculators are forced by market events to sell their positions, usually at a loss.

SHAKEUP rapid change in the management and structure of an organization. An organization undergoing a shakeup often experiences a period of trauma and uncertainty while the changes occur. The purpose of a shakeup is to change the direction and policies of an organization undergoing some form of stress.

SHAM TRANSACTION a transaction without substance, which will be ignored for tax purposes.

SHARE portion of something; INTEREST in a corporation. *See also* STOCK; STOCK CERTIFICATE.

SHARE BROKER *see* ACCOUNT EXECUTIVE.

SHARECROPPER tenant farmer who works the land for the owner of the property. Sharecroppers traditionally receive seed, tools, and other necessities, often including housing, from the landlord. Sharecroppers are usually paid a portion of the proceeds from the harvested crop.

SHARED-APPRECIATION MORTGAGE (SAM) residential loan with a FIXED INTEREST RATE set below market rates, with the lender entitled to a specified share of APPRECIATION in property value over a specified time interval.

SHARED-EQUITY MORTGAGE (SEM) home loan in which the lender is granted a share of the equity, thereby allowing the lender to participate in the proceeds from resale.

SHAREHOLDER owner of one or more shares of a CORPORATION, REAL ESTATE INVESTMENT TRUST (REIT), or MUTUAL FUND. A shareholder possesses the evidence, usually in the form of certificates, of real ownership of a portion of the property in actual or potential existence, held by the company in its name for the common benefit of all the owners of the entire company.

SHAREHOLDERS' EQUITY total ASSETS minus total LIABILITIES of a corporation, also called *stockholders' equity and net worth.*

SHARE OF MARKET *see* BRAND SHARE.

SHARE OF MIND *see* BRAND ASSOCIATION.

SHARES AUTHORIZED number of shares of stock provided for in the ARTICLES OF INCORPORATION of a company. This figure is ordinarily indicated in the capital accounts section of a company's balance sheet and is usually well in excess of the shares ISSUED and OUTSTANDING.

SHARES OUTSTANDING *see* ISSUED AND OUTSTANDING.

SHARE/STOCK REPURCHASE PLAN program by which a corporation buys back its own shares in the open market. It is usually used when shares are UNDERVALUED. Because it reduces the number of shares outstanding and thus increases EARNINGS PER SHARE, it tends to elevate the market value of the remaining shares held by stockholders.

SHAREWARE software that you can download from a NETWORK and "try before you buy." If you like the software and decide to use it, you must register with the author and pay a registration fee.

SHARK REPELLENT measure undertaken by a corporation to discourage unwanted TAKEOVER attempts. *See also* POISON PILL; SCORCHED-EARTH DEFENSE.

SHARK WATCHER firm specializing in the early detection of TAKEOVER activity. Such a firm, whose primary business is usually the solicitation of proxies for client corporations, monitors trading patterns in a client's stock and attempts to determine the identity of parties accumulating shares.

SHEKELS money; first form of money noted in the Bible; monetary unit of Israel.

SHELL CORPORATION
1. company that is incorporated but has no significant assets or operations. Such a corporation may be formed to obtain financing prior to starting operations.
2. corporation set up by fraudulent operators as a front to conceal tax evasion schemes.

SHERMAN ANTI-TRUST ACT OF 1890 *see* ANTITRUST ACTS.

SHIFT time at which an employee is assigned to work. Most work shifts are eight hours long plus a 45-minute to 1-hour lunch period.

SHIFT DIFFERENTIAL extra compensation paid as an inducement to accept shift work. Those employees willing to work evening and midnight hours usually receive a *shift differential.*

SHIFTING AND INCIDENCE OF TAXATION determination of the economic entity that actually ends up paying a particular tax. Some taxes are added to the price of the good(s) produced so that the incidence of the tax is clearly upon the consumer of the good. Generally, the corporate income tax is absorbed by the corporation (not passed to consumers), whereas the sales tax is passed on.

SHOP
1. area of a business location where production takes place, as distinguished from office or warehouse areas.
2. factory work force of an employer, as in *union* shop.
3. office of a broker-dealer in securities.
4. small retail establishment.
5. to canvass for the most favorable price.

SHOPPER locally distributed newspaper, usually free-of-charge, that advertises local stores, restaurants, and shopping centers; also called *shopping newspaper. Shoppers* usually include sale announcements and discount coupons for local stores.

SHOPPING CENTER collection of retail stores with a common parking area and generally one or more large department, discount, or food stores; sometimes including an *enclosed mall* or *walkway.* The smallest of these are strip shopping centers; somewhat larger are neighborhood and community centers. The largest are regional or super-regional malls. *See also* ANCHOR TENANT.

SHOPPING PRODUCTS consumer products requiring concentration and research to make an informed judgment about their relative merits and price. Shopping products can take a considerable amount of a consumer's time and concentration before an informed purchase decision is reached.

SHOPPING SERVICE
1. service provided by independent businesses who send representatives to stores to comparison shop for specific products. A shopping service is hired by contract and will compare competitive prices or prices for the same item in competitive stores, depending on the requests and needs of the client.
2. service offered to cable television subscribers where consumers can buy products (usually at discounts) that are displayed on a special shopping service channel.

SHOP STEWARD union member elected by other union members to represent them to management with grievances and other requests.

SHORT BOND
1. bond with a short maturity; generally meaning one year or less.
2. bond repayable in one year or less and thus classified as a current liability in accordance with the accounting definition of SHORT-TERM DEBT.
3. short coupon bond.

SHORT COVERING actual purchase of securities by a short seller to replace those borrowed at the time of a short sale. *See also* SELLING SHORT.

SHORTFALL smaller amount than planned or budgeted, as in a revenue shortfall caused by low sales or reduced contributions received.

SHORT FORM
   Law: instrument, seldom longer than two pages, that refers to another document. The short form is often recorded in lieu of a cumbersome longer document.
   Taxation: certain federal income tax forms, such as the 1040A and 1040EZ.

SHORT INTEREST total number of shares of stock that have been sold short and have not yet been repurchased to close out SHORT POSITIONS. The short interest figure for securities on the New York Stock Exchange is published monthly.

SHORT POSITION
   Commodities: contract in which a trader has agreed to sell a commodity at a future date for a specific price.
   Securities: stock shares that an individual has sold short (by delivery of borrowed certificates) and has not covered as of a particular date. *See also* SELLING SHORT.

SHORT RUN a period of time long enough for existing firms in an industry to increase production in reaction to changing economic conditions, but not long enough to allow them to increase capacity or for new firms to enter the industry.

SHORT SALE sale of a security without ownership in the hopes of a price decline that will allow repurchase at a lower price. The broker typically borrows the stock from another customer to deliver for the short sale. Those who maintain SHORT POSITIONS are responsible for dividends and face constant threats of a price rise; they face the risk that the security can no longer be borrowed, especially for thinly traded securities.

SHORT-SALE RULE Securities and Exchange Commission rule requiring that short sales be made only in a rising market; also called *plus-tick rule.* A short sale can be transacted only on an UPTICK or zero plus tick.

SHORT SELLING *see* SHORT INTEREST; SHORT POSITION; SHORT SALE.

SHORT SQUEEZE situation when many traders with SHORT POSITIONS are forced to buy stocks or commodities in order to COVER their positions and prevent losses. This sudden surge of buying leads to even higher prices, further aggravating the losses of short sellers who have not covered their positions. *See also* SELLING SHORT.

SHORT TERM

Accounting: assets expected to be converted into cash within the normal operating cycle (usually one year), or liabilities coming due in one year or less. *See also* CURRENT ASSETS; CURRENT LIABILITY.

Investment: investment with a maturity of one year or less.

Taxation: stock, bonds, or other property held less than one year, the capital gains on which were once taxed as ordinary income, in contrast to long-term gains, which were once taxed at a more favorable rate.

SHORT-TERM CAPITAL GAIN (LOSS) for tax purposes, profit (loss) realized from the sale of securities or other capital assets not held long enough for a LONG-TERM CAPITAL GAIN (LOSS). *See also* CAPITAL GAIN (LOSS).

SHORT-TERM DEBT or **SHORT-TERM LIABILITY** debt obligation coming due within one year; shown on a balance sheet as part of CURRENT LIABILITIES.

SHORT YEAR a tax year of a taxpayer that is less than 12 months. *See also* ANNUALIZING; SHORT PERIOD.

SHRINKAGE

1. difference between actual physical inventory and the amount that should be on hand by the book inventory.
2. the difference between the weight of natural grain and its weight after proper drying.
3. weight loss of a commodity that normally results during processing into a finished product.

SHRINKWRAP the clear plastic coating that covers the boxes in which commercial software is sold. The integrity of the shrinkwrap is viewed as a guarantee that the software is genuine and has not been tampered with, but many retail outlets have the ability to rewrap returned software that may already have been installed and possibly tainted.

SHUTDOWN production stoppage. A shutdown occurs due to the installation or breakdown of equipment, shortage of work orders, lack of materials or skilled labor, and so on.

SHYSTER unscrupulous professional person, often used in connection with the law profession.

SICK PAY payment to an employee to replace wages during the period when the employee is absent from work because of illness or personal injury. Sick pay is taxable income to the employee and includes payments made by any of the following:

1. employer.
2. welfare fund.
3. state sickness or disability fund.
4. association of employers or employees.

5. an insurance company, if the employee paid for the plan. Benefits received under an accident or health insurance policy on which the employer paid the premiums are not taxable.

SIGHT DRAFT DRAFT payable on demand; BILL OF EXCHANGE for immediate collection.

SIGNATURE GUARANTEE written confirmation from a financial institution such as a bank or brokerage firm that a customer's signature is valid. The institution will compare a new signature from a customer with the signature on file. TRANSFER AGENTS require signature guarantees when transferring STOCKS, BONDS, MUTUAL FUNDS, or other SECURITIES from one party to another to ensure that the transactions are legitimate.

SIGNING BONUS an inseverable part of the cost of obtaining a new employee's service.

SILENT PARTNER LIMITED PARTNER. Such partners are called silent because, unlike GENERAL PARTNERS, they have no direct role in management and no liability beyond their individual investments.

SILICON VALLEY area in California where a significant amount of high-tech research is conducted. Silicon is a component in advanced computer chips.

SILVER STANDARD backing of a currency by guaranteeing its exchangeability for silver. U.S. silver certificates had been backed by silver.

SIMPLE INTEREST method of calculating the future value of a sum assuming that INTEREST paid is not compounded, that is, interest is paid only on the principal. *See also* COMPOUND INTEREST.

SIMPLE IRA form of SALARY REDUCTION PLAN that qualifying small employers may offer to their employees. Employers with no more than 100 employees earning $5,000 or more in a year who do not offer any other retirement plan can offer simple IRAs. Selfemployed workers are also eligible to establish such accounts.

    Workers offered a simple IRA were able to contribute up to $10,000 per year to the account in 2006. Employees who are at least age 50 could contribute a catch-up contribution of $2,500 in 2006, and annually thereafter. Employee contributions are excluded from taxable income on Form W-2 and are not subject to income tax withholding, although Social Security taxes are paid on those earnings.

SIMPLE LINEAR REGRESSION method for analyzing the relation between one independent variable and one dependent variable.

SIMPLE RATE OF RETURN rate of return that results from dividing the income and capital gains from an investment by the amount of capital invested. For example, if a $1,000 investment produced $50 in income and $50 in capital appreciation in one year, the investment would have a 10% simple rate of return. This method of calculation does not factor in the effects of compounding.

SIMPLE TRUST TRUST that is required, by the terms of its creation or under state law, to distribute all of its income currently. A simple trust is allowed a $300 standard deduction.

SIMPLE YIELD return equal to the nominal dollar interest divided by the MARKET VALUE (price) of the bond. It is an approximate, simplified rate reflecting the cost to the debtor and the return to the holder of a debt instrument. *See also* YIELD TO MATURITX.

SIMPLIFIED EMPLOYEE PENSION PLAN (SEP-IRA) retirement plan specifically designed for self-employed people and small business owners. The owner and any eligible employees establish their own separate SEP-IRAs; employer contributions are then made into each eligible employee's SEP-IRA. The plan is available to sole proprietors, partners in a partnership, or owners of businesses (either unincorporated or incorporated, including S CORPORATIONS) and to self-employed persons who earn income by providing a service, either full time or part time, even those already covered by a retirement plan at their full-time job. Those eligible may contribute up to 25% of compensation (as much as $44,000 for 2006), and any investment earnings are tax-deferred until withdrawn.

SIMULATION or SIMULATE
1. process of representing one system by another.
2. in computer science, representation of the real world by a mathematical model operated by a computer. A mathematical model of population growth can simulate a real population. A *deterministic simulation* occurs when the future path of the system is exactly determined by the parameters of the system. A *Monte Carlo simulation* occurs when probabilities are known and a selection of random numbers is used to guide the system.

SINGLE-ENTRY BOOKKEEPING accounting system that does not use balancing debits and credits. Transactions are recorded in just one account.

SINGLE-FAMILY HOUSING type of residential structure designed to include one DWELLING. Adjacent units may share walls and other structural components, but generally have separate access to the outside and do not share plumbing and heating equipment. Single-family housing includes detached housing units; TOWN HOUSES; and ZERO-LOT-LINE homes.

SINGLE LIFE DISTRIBUTIONS monthly ANNUITY payments made to a retired employee for life from a retirement plan; they are taxed when received.

SINGLE PREMIUM LIFE INSURANCE coverage in which one premium payment is made and the policy is fully paid up with no further premiums required. *See also* LIMITED PAYMENT LIFE INSURANCE.

SINGLE TAXPAYER one who is not married on the last day of the tax year. A taxpayer who is legally separated from his spouse under a decree of divorce or separate maintenance is deemed to be single for tax purposes unless the sole purpose of the divorce is tax-motivated. Rate schedules and tax tables are provided for single taxpayers, and many tax provisions apply specifically to a single taxpayer.

SINKING FUND money accumulated on a regular basis in a separate custodial account that is used to redeem debt securities or preferred stock issues. A bond indenture or preferred stock charter may specify that payments be made to a sinking fund, thus assuring investors that the issues are safer than bonds or preferred stocks, for which the issuer must make payment all at once, without the benefit of a sinking fund.

SIN TAX *see* REPRESSIVE TAX.

SIT-DOWN STRIKE form of protest involving stop-work tactics. It was first used by the CIO in 1936, when workers seized several General Motors plants in Flint, Michigan, beginning a 44-day sit-down strike. Sit-down strikes were determined to be illegal by the Supreme Court in 1939 and have since been largely abandoned as an organized labor tactic.

SITE plot of land prepared for or underlying a structure or development; location of a property.

SITE ASSESSMENT (ENVIRONMENTAL) an evaluation of a site, prior to acquisition of title to the property, for the existence of hazardous waste. Under the Comprehensive Environmental Response, Compensation, and Liability Act of 1980 (CERCLA), as amended by the Superfund Amendments and Reauthorization Act of 1986 (SARA), anyone acquiring title to a site is responsible for environmental damages resulting from hazardous wastes on the site. However, there are legal defenses for landowners who conduct proper site assessments prior to acquisition.

A CERCLA *site assessment* may be conducted in two phases. A phase I assessment involves research into previous uses of the site and whether a hazardous waste condition is likely to exist. If evidence from this phase suggests a problem, a phase II assessment is conducted to discover the extent of the problem. Either assessment requires the use of an environmental consultant and special legal counsel.

SITUATIONAL MANAGEMENT management method whereby the current state of the organization determines what operational procedures will be implemented to achieve desired outcomes. *Situational management* emphasizes a very adaptive management style.

SKILL INTENSIVE occupation or job requiring a highly skilled work force. Examples of *skill-intensive* work include machinists, computer programmers, tool and die makers, and cooks.

SKILL OBSOLESCENCE trade, occupation, or skill that has been replaced by technology. Examples include ditch diggers, production-line workers, and typesetters.

SKIMMING
1. illegal practice of failing to account for some sales, frequently with the intent of tax evasion or cheating a partner.
2. marketing strategy where a high initial price is charged for a newly introduced product in order to expedite the development cost recovery. At a later point the price is reduced to offset competitive products and slowing demand.

SKU *see* STOCKKEEPING UNIT.

SLACK
Business: dull or inactive business period, slack season.
Manufacturing: time in which a minor operation can be completed in advance of the next major operation that depends on it.

SLAMMING widespread illegal practice of changing a customer's long distance telephone service provider without the customer's permission. Happens to more than a million telephone customers each year.

SLANDER to engage in defamation orally; spoken words that tend to damage another's reputation. If defamatory meaning is apparent on the face of the statement, it is said to be slanderous *per se*. If the defamatory meaning is not self-evident, but arises only from extrinsic facts, the statement is slanderous *per quod*. *See also* LIBEL.

SLASH the character / , also called *forward slash*.

SLEEPER stock in which there is little investor interest but that has significant potential to gain in price once its attractions are recognized. Sleepers are most easily recognized in retrospect, after they have already moved up in price.

SLEEPING BEAUTY potential TAKEOVER target that has not yet been approached by an acquirer. Such a company usually has particularly attractive features, such as a large amount of cash or undervalued real estate or other assets.

SLM CORPORATION publicly traded stock corporation that guarantees student loans traded on the SECONDARY MARKET. Formerly the Student Loan Marketing Association (SLMA), and known as *Sallie Mae,* it purchases student loans from originating financial institutions and provides financing to state student loan agencies.

SLOWDOWN deliberate reduction of output by employees. Slowdowns usually are a work protest designed to bring economic pressure upon an employer without incurring the costs of a strike.

SLUMP drop in economic or productive activity. In popular usage, a slump is not as severe as a RECESSION or depression.

SLUSH FUND an account with excess money, formerly used to provide small treats for employees; now generally has the connotation of a fund used for paying bribes.

SMALL BUSINESS according to the U.S. Department of Commerce, a business employing less than 100 people. Small businesses play a disproportionately important role in innovation as well as in the economic and employment growth in the United States.

SMALL BUSINESS ADMINISTRATION (SBA) federal government agency in Washington, D.C., that encourages small business. The SBA offers low-interest-rate loans to qualified businesspersons.

SMALL BUSINESS CORPORATION STOCK (SECTION 1244 STOCK) ordinary deduction treatment is available to certain individuals and partnerships on the sale of stock or bankruptcy of a company. This ordinary deduction (rather than a CAPITAL LOSS) is available on disposition or worthlessness of Section 1244 stock as an ORDINARY LOSS, to the extent of $50,000 in any one taxable year for a single individual, or to $100,000 in any one taxable year in the case of a married couple filing a joint return.

SMALL BUSINESS INVESTMENT COMPANY (SBIC) a company operating under the Small Business Investment Act of 1958. A loss on the sale of small business investment company stock is treated as an ordinary trade or business loss.

SMALL-CAP shorthand for *small-capitalization* STOCKS or MUTUAL FUNDS holding such stocks. *Small-cap* stocks usually have a MARKET CAPITALIZATION of $500 million or less. Those under $50 million in market cap are known as *microcap issues*. Small-cap stocks represent companies that are less well established, but in many cases faster-growing, than MID-CAP or LARGE-CAP stocks. Since they are less established, small-cap stocks are usually more volatile than BLUE CHIPS.

SMALL CLAIMS COURT court of limited jurisdiction, where a claim for a relatively small amount can be settled on an informal basis.

SMALL CLAIMS DIVISION a Tax Court division in which taxpayers whose disputed tax liability does not exceed $10,000 can try their case on a less formal basis than otherwise.

SMALL INVESTOR individual investor who buys small amounts of stock or bonds, often in odd-lot quantities; also called *retail investor.*

SMALL OFFICE/HOME OFFICE (SOHO) used to describe a work environment. Especially with faxes, modems, and personal computers, many individuals find themselves capable of competing from their homes to deliver a product that once required the facilities of large corporations. Manufacturers of business equipment are targeting many products to those with small and home offices.

SMART CARD card resembling a CREDIT CARD in size and shape but containing an embedded MICROPROCESSOR retaining security information. Smart cards may have up to 8 kilobytes of RAM, 346 KB of ROM, 256 KB of programmable ROM, and a 16-bit microprocessor.

SMITHSONIAN AGREEMENT December 1971 agreement that ended the FIXED EXCHANGE RATES established at the Bretton Woods Conference of 1944 and substituted a FLOATING EXCHANGE RATE. In the Agreement, the GROUP OF TEN countries, meeting at the Smithsonian Institution, agreed to appreciate their currencies against the United States dollar. This became necessary when the United States removed the gold backing of the dollar in August 1971.

SMOKE CLAUSE provision in the EXTENDED COVERAGE ENDORSEMENT, stating that smoke damage is covered when it results from the sudden, unusual, and faulty operation of an on-premises cooking or heating unit, provided that it has been connected to the chimney by means of a vent.

SMOKESTACK INDUSTRY heavy industry, typified by the steel and auto industries. The term originates in the fact that these industries usually have large smokestacks for their operations. U.S. smokestack industries are facing intense international competition.

SNA *see* SYSTEMS NETWORK ARCHITECTURE.

SNAIL MAIL (*slang*) mail sent by conventional methods (including express services), as contrasted with ELECTRONIC MAIL (E-MAIL).

SNOWBALLING business activity that rapidly increases, building momentum.

SOCIAL AUDIT method of measuring a company's level of social responsibility.

SOCIAL CLUB tax-exempt club organized for pleasure, recreation, and other nonprofitable purposes, substantially all of the activities of which are for such purposes, and no part of the net earnings of which inures to the benefit of any private shareholder.

SOCIALISM economic system in which government owns or controls major critical industries, but may allow collective ownership and some private ownership in agriculture, services, and less critical industries.

SOCIALLY CONSCIOUS INVESTMENTS investing in securities of companies that do not conflict with certain social priorities. A product of the social consciousness movement of the 1960s and 1970s, these would exclude companies that derive significant profits from defense contracts or whose activities cause environmental pollution or companies with significant interests in countries with repressive or racist governments.

SOCIAL RESPONSIBILITY ethical and societally moral behavior. Socially responsible conduct supports acceptable societal standards and laws.

SOCIAL SECURITY ACT the federal retirement plan enacted by Congress in 1935. The original purpose (unchanged today) of the Act was to adopt a system that required the current working generation to contribute to the support of older, retired workers. The Act was passed in response to old-age dependency resulting from Depression-generated phenomena.

SOCIAL SECURITY ADMINISTRATION, REPORT TO requirement of an employer to report annually to the U.S. Treasury Department the names of employees who terminated employment with vested benefits, and the amount of the benefits. The Treasury sends the Social Security Administration a copy, which is available to an employee on request. A statement of vested benefits is given by the Social Security Administration to an applicant for Social Security benefits.

SOCIAL SECURITY BENEFITS, TAXATION OF a portion of Social Security benefits is included in taxable income. The percentage included is 50% or 85%, depending on the FILING STATUS and the amount of income.

When income is above the BASE AMOUNT (the tier 1 threshold) up to the tier 2 amount, 50% of Social Security benefits is included. When income is above the tier 2 amount, up to 85% of Social Security benefits is included in TAXABLE INCOME. Income for this purpose is MODIFIED ADJUSTED GROSS INCOME, which includes TAX-EXEMPT income such as municipal bond interest and half of Social Security benefits.

Tier 1 amounts (base amounts) are $32,000 for married joint returns; $25,000 for singles and heads of households. Tier 2 amounts are $44,000 for married joint returns and $34,000 for singles and heads of households. For marrieds who lived together during any part of the year but filed separately, the threshold amount is $0.

SOCIAL SECURITY CREDITS under Social Security, they determine one's eligibility for Social Security programs. A person earns credits by working in a job covered by Social Security and by paying Social Security taxes. In 2006, one credit was earned for each $970 in Social Security earnings. A maximum of four credits can be earned in a year. A minimum of 40 credits must be earned to qualify for retirement benefits. *See also* TAX CREDITS.

SOCIAL SECURITY DISABILITY INCOME INSURANCE insurance, financed by the SOCIAL SECURITY TAX, that replaces lost income to qualifying employees whose disabilities are expected to last at least one year. Benefits are payable until death.

SOCIAL SECURITY NUMBER an identifying number for individuals that is furnished by the Social Security Administration rather than the IRS. Social Security numbers are required for all individual taxpayers and dependents. It is the counterpart of the Employer Identification Number (EIN) that is used for non-individual entities such as businesses, trusts, and partnerships.

SOCIAL SECURITY TAX the old-age, survivor's, and disability (OASDI) portion of the tax assessed on compensation and self-employment earnings under the Federal Insurance Contributions Act (FICA). The OASDI tax is 12.4% of earnings up to $94,200 (in 2006). An employer is required to withhold one-half of the tax (6.2%) from employee wages and to make a matching contribution of the remaining half. Employer-withheld and matching taxes are deposited at regular intervals with the IRS. Self-employed individuals pay the entire 12.4% tax, which they include with their quarterly estimated income tax payments. *See* MEDICARE TAX.

SOCIETY OF ACTUARIES organization that is committed to advancing the actuarial profession and to expanding relationships with members, volunteers, and other actuarial organizations to enhance the role and overall impact of actuaries. Offers the highly coveted FSA (Fellow, Society of Actuaries) designation.

SOFT CURRENCY funds of a country that are not acceptable in exchange for the hard currencies of other countries. Soft currencies, such as the Russian ruble, are fixed at unrealistic exchange rates and are not backed by gold, so that countries with hard currencies, like U.S. dollars or British pounds, are reluctant to buy them.

SOFT DOLLARS often refers to a situation where an investor need not take money from his or her own funds (which would be *hard dollars*), or where the cost is tax deductible, thus costing less than the face amount.

SOFT GOODS merchandise that is soft to the touch, such as clothing and other textile goods; considered in the merchandising industry to be nondurable goods. *See also* HARD GOODS.

SOFT LANDING used to describe a rate of growth sufficient to avoid recession but slow enough to prevent high inflation and interest rates. When the economy is growing very strongly, the Federal Reserve typically tries to engineer a *soft landing* by raising interest rates to head off inflation.

SOFT MARKET a market in which demand has shrunk, or supply has grown faster than demand, and in which sales at reasonable prices have become more difficult; a buyers' market.

SOFT MONEY
1. in a proposed development or an investment, money contributed that is tax deductible.
2. sometimes used to describe costs that do not physically go into construction, such as interest during construction, architect's fees, and legal fees.

SOFT SPOT small weakness, such as a weakness in selected stocks or stock groups, in the face of a generally strong and advancing market.

SOFTWARE in a computer system, set of programs that tell the computer what to do. By contrast, the HARDWARE is the actual physical machines that make up a computer system.

SOFTWARE ENGINEERING the programming and production that go into the software development process.

SOHO *see* SMALL OFFICE/HOME OFFICE.

SOILBANK land held out of agricultural production in an effort to stabilize commodity prices and promote soil conservation. Subsidies to farmers participating in the soil bank program are provided by the U.S. Department of Agriculture.

SOL statute of limitations.

SOLE PROPRIETOR LIFE AND HEALTH INSURANCE coverage for the owner of a business. When a proprietor dies, debts of the business become the debts of the estate since in this circumstance the law recognizes business and personal assets as one. The executor is required to dispose of the business.

SOLE PROPRIETORSHIP business or financial venture that is carried on by a single person and is not a TRUST or CORPORATION. A sole proprietor (sole owner) has unlimited liability. Schedule C of Form 1040 is used to report income and expenses of a *sole proprietorship.*

SOLVENCY or SOLVENT
  1. ability to pay all debts and just claims as they come due.
  2. adequacy of property to satisfy one's obligations when sold under execution.
  3. in certain contexts, excess of assets over liabilities.

SORT to arrange a group of items in numerical or alphabetical order. Many computer operating systems include built-in sorting programs.

SOURCE channel of sale that generated an order or customer. SOURCE EVALUATION is an essential part of DIRECT MARKETING that enables marketers to concentrate their promotion expenditures on the best sources.

SOURCE PROGRAM computer program written in a programming language (such as BASIC; FORTRAN, or Pascal) and fed into a computer. The computer translates the program into a MACHINE LANGUAGE object program that it is capable of analyzing.

SOURCES AND APPLICATIONS (USES) OF FUNDS STATEMENT analysis of changes in the FINANCIAL POSITION of a firm from one accounting period to another; also called *sources and uses of funds statement.* It consists of two parts: (1) *sources of funds* summarizes the transactions that increased working capital, such as net income, depreciation, issue of bonds, sale of stock, or an increase in deferred taxes; (2) *application of funds* summarizes the way funds were used, such as purchase or improvement of plant and equipment, payment of dividends, repayment of long-term debt, redemption or repurchase of shares, or payment of taxes.

SOURCES OF FUNDS section within the statement of changes in financial position showing the increase in funds for the accounting period. Funds are typically defined as WORKING CAPITAL or cash. Sources of working capital include: (1) working capital provided from operations (net income plus nonworking capital expenses less non-working capital revenue); (2) decrease in NONCURRENT ASSETS; (3) increase in noncurrent liabilities; and (4) increase in stockholders' equity. If funds are defined as cash rather than working capital, the following two additional sources of funds are used: (1) decrease in current assets other than cash; and (2) increase in current liabilities.

SOVEREIGN RISK risk that a foreign government will default on its loan or fail to honor other business commitments because of a change in national policy. Throughout periods of worldwide economic volatility, the United States has been able to attract foreign investment because of its perceived lack of sovereign risk; also called *country risk* or *political risk.*

SPA (SOCIETÀ PER AZIONI) the Italian designation for a corporation.

SPAM junk E-MAIL. Unsolicited messages (often of a commercial nature) sent indiscriminately (and sometimes more than once) to a large group of users or posted to multiple NEWSGROUPS.

SPAN OF CONTROL principle of management stating the number of people a manager can supervise effectively. The ability to supervise people depends on the job in question, whether the employees are professionals, and on their location.

SPDR abbreviation for *Standard & Poor's Depositary Receipt*, traded on the American Stock Exchange under the ticker symbol "SPY." Called "spiders," they are securities that represent ownership in a long-term unit investment trust that holds a portfolio of common stocks designed to track the performance of the S&P 500 INDEX.

SPEC HOUSE single-family dwelling constructed by a builder or developer in anticipation of finding a buyer, that is, speculatively.

SPECIAL AGENT
1. one who is engaged to act for another with limited authority. For example, a real estate broker, engaged by an owner to find a buyer, is considered a *special agent* of the owner.
2. Internal Revenue Service employee who is called upon to investigate possible fraud.

SPECIAL ASSESSMENT ASSESSMENT made against a property to pay for a public improvement by which the assessed property is supposed to be especially benefited, such as sewers, curbs, or sidewalks.

SPECIAL DELIVERY service of the U.S. Postal Service, available at extra cost. Special delivery receives preferential handling in processing and rapid delivery at the destination, including Sundays and holidays. Available for all classes except Express Mail, which gets more rapid treatment.

SPECIAL DRAWING RIGHTS (SDR) part of a nation's reserve assets in the international monetary system; known informally as *paper gold.* First issued by the INTERNATIONAL MONETARY FUND (IMF) in 1970, SDRs are designed to supplement the reserves of gold and convertible currencies, or hard currencies, used to maintain stability in the foreign exchange market.

SPECIAL FOURTH-CLASS MAIL reduced mailing rates offered for certain books, movies, and other educational products that contain no advertising. Packages must be marked *special fourth-class mail.*

SPECIAL HANDLING service available at extra cost to accelerate the movement of third- and fourth-class packages sent through the U.S. Postal Service. It does not provide special delivery. Such packages should be clearly identified *Special Handling.*

SPECIALIST
In general: anyone with extensive knowledge of a small area.
Securities: member of a stock exchange who maintains a fair and orderly market in one or more securities.

SPECIAL MASTER person recognized for expertise, appointed by a court to help understand and possibly resolve a complex matter.

SPECIAL MULTIPERIL POLICY (SMP) insurance coverage usually provided for large businesses in four areas:
1. *Section I (Property)*—The building(s) and contents are either covered against any peril (*all-risk* basis), or only perils listed in Section I. It is to the advantage of the business to have coverage written on an all-risk basis.
2. *Section II (Liability)*—The insured is covered for actions or nonactions that result in liability exposure arising out of ownership, use, possession, and/or maintenance of the covered locations and structures. Also covered are the business's activities conducted by the insured whether at or from the covered locations and structures.
3. *Section III (Crime)*—Coverage for employee dishonesty, premises loss both inside and outside of the structure, forgery by depositions, paper currency that proves to be counterfeit, and money orders.
4. *Section IV (Boiler and Machinery)*—Coverage for explosion of a boiler, engine, turbines, and/or pipes owned or under the control of the insured.

SPECIAL PURCHASE expression often used by retailers to satisfy federal controls when advertising special sales. The advertising usually accents the low prices available, and the customer makes mental comparisons with prices on the retailer's regular line of merchandise. It usually indicates a lower-cost, lower-quality line of merchandise being sold at the full price for that product.

SPECIAL-PURPOSE ENTITY (SPE) finite-life entities created by corporations, usually as subsidiaries but sometimes as partnerships, trusts, or other forms of unincorporated structures, for a single, well-defined, and narrow purpose, such as those (sometimes also called *derivative products companies*) established to issue *income-preferred securities.* Also known as *special-purpose vehicles* or *variable-interest entities,* SPEs got a bad name when they were used by Enron to conduct improper OFF-BALANCE-SHEET FINANCING activities.

SPECIAL-PURPOSE TEAMS temporary organizational teams created to resolve a specific issue.

SPECIAL SITUATION
1. undervalued stock that should soon rise in value because of an imminent favorable turn of events.
2. stock that fluctuates wildly in daily trading, often influencing market averages, because of a particular news development such as the announcement of a takeover bid.

SPECIALTY ADVERTISING form of advertising that uses advertising novelties as medium for the message. Examples include buttons, bumper stickers, and balloons with writing.

SPECIALTY RETAILER retailer concentrating on selling one merchandise line of goods for a particular and usually selective clientele. Examples are stores selling video tapes, bagels, leather goods, and imported china. Specialty retailers have a narrow but deep selection in their specialty. *See also* SPECIALTY SHOP.

SPECIALTY SELLING direct retailing of items or services not generally carried in a retail store. Examples are encyclopedias and life insurance.

SPECIALTY SHOP retail store specializing in a narrow range of items for a particular clientele. Examples are shops specializing in pipe tobacco, wedding gowns, lawn mowers, and bicycles. *See also* SPECIALTY RETAILER.

SPECIAL-USE PERMIT right granted by a local ZONING authority to conduct certain activities within a zoning district. Such activities are considered conditional uses, which are permitted within the zone only upon special approval of the zoning authority; also termed *conditional use* permit.

SPECIAL WARRANTY DEED DEED in which the grantor limits the TITLE warranty given to the grantee to anyone claiming by, from, through, or under him, the grantor. The grantor does not warrant against title defects arising from conditions that existed before he owned the property. *See also* WARRANTY DEED.

SPECIE money with intrinsic value, such as gold and silver coins.

SPECIFICATION description or detailed instruction provided in conjunction with product plans or a purchase order. Specifications may stipulate the type of materials to be used, special construction techniques, dimensions, colors, or a list of the qualities and characteristics of a product.

SPECIFIC CHARGE-OFF METHOD (BAD DEBTS) deduction of BAD DEBT for an uncollectible receivable at the time the specific receivable becomes worthless, after all possible methods of collection have been pursued. ACCRUAL BASIS taxpayers must use this method, as they are no longer allowed to accrue reserves for bad debts; *see* RESERVE METHOD (BAD DEBTS).

SPECIFIC IDENTIFICATION inventory method that considers the sale and cost of each item specifically. An investor's securities can be identified in this manner, which gives the investor flexibility in reporting taxable income when the securities were acquired at different costs, since it is possible to sell specific securities.

SPECIFIC LIEN charge against a certain piece of property making it a security for the payment of a debt.

SPECIFIC PERFORMANCE requires the party guilty of BREACH OF CONTRACT to complete performance of his obligations under the contract on pain of punishment for contempt. Specific performance is available only where the subject matter of the contract is unique, such as a particular parcel of real property or a rare painting.

SPECULATION purchase of any property or security with the expectation of obtaining a quick profit as a result of price change, possibly without adequate research. *Compare with* gambling, which is based on random chance; *contrast with* INVESTMENT.

SPECULATIVE BUILDING land development or construction with no formal commitment from the end users of the finished product. *Contrast with* CUSTOM BUILDING, where the builder is under contract to produce a specific structure. The speculative builder anticipates that a demand exists or will form for the product when it is put on the market.

SPECULATIVE RISK uncertainty of the chance of a financial loss or a financial gain. For example, betting on a horse presents a chance for financial gain or financial loss. Insurance is not intended to cover speculative risks.

SPECULATOR market participant who tries to profit from buying and selling. *Speculators* assume market price risk and add liquidity and capital to the futures markets. Speculators may purchase volatile assets and hold them for a short time in order to reap a profit. They may also sell stocks short and hope to cash in when the stock price drops quickly.

SPEECH RECOGNITION SOFTWARE program in which verbal commands activate the microcomputer to perform functions such as WORD PROCESSING, SPREADSHEET, or DATABASE MANAGEMENT.

SPEEDUP efforts by employers to obtain increased productivity without a corresponding increase in wages. *See also* STRETCHOUT.

SPELLING CHECKER software available on some word processing programs that "reads" through a document looking for misspelled words, stopping at words "recognized" as misspelled, and allowing the operator to make corrections.

SPENDABLE INCOME *see* AFTER-TAX CASH FLOW.

SPENDING MONEY money used for the purpose of small current expenses; also called *pocket money*.

SPENDTHRIFT TRUST trust fund created to provide financial maintenance for another while securing it with restrictions to guard against its unwise use. Spendthrift trusts are often created by parents for their children.

SPIDER *see* SPDR.

SPILLOVER effects of economic activity or process upon those who are not directly involved in it. Odors from a rendering plant are negative spillover effects upon its neighbors; the beauty of a homeowner's flower garden is a positive spillover effect upon neighbors.

SPIN-OFF similar to a tax-free SPLIT-OFF except that the shares of the new corporation (or the subsidiary corporation) are distributed to the original shareholders (or the parent's shareholders) without their surrendering any of their stock in the original (or parent) corporation.

SPLINTERED AUTHORITY division of authority between many managers. A manager with splintered authority will have to deal with many other managers before decisions can be finalized.

SPLIT increase in a corporation's number of outstanding shares of stock, to make the stock more marketable, without any change in the shareholders' equity or the aggregate market value at the time of the split. In a split, also called a *split up*, the share price declines. If a stock at $100 per share splits 2 for 1, the number of authorized shares doubles (for example, from 10 million to 20 million) and the price per share drops by half, to $50. A holder of 50 shares before the split now has 100 shares at the lower price. Dividends per share will also fall proportionately.

SPLIT COMMISSION COMMISSION divided between the securities broker who executes a trade and another person who brought the trade to the broker, such as an investment counselor or financial planner. Split commissions between brokers are also common in real estate transactions.

SPLIT DOLLAR LIFE INSURANCE policy in which premiums and ownership rights and death proceeds are split between an employer and an employee, or a parent and a child. The employer pays at least the part of each year's premium that equals the increase in the cash value, and in some cases the employer pays the entire premium. A beneficiary chosen by the employee splits the death payment with the employer.

SPLIT-OFF either of two types of tax-free reorganizations. Under a Type No. 1 exchange, a corporation transfers part of its assets to a new corporation in exchange for stock of the new corporation. The original corporation then distributes the same stock to its shareholders, who in turn surrender part of their stock in the original corporation.

A Type No. 2 contraction occurs when a parent company transfers stock of a controlled corporation to its stockholders in redemption of a similar portion of their stock. "Control" refers to the ownership of 80% or more of the corporation whose shares are being distributed.

SPLIT SHIFT work shift interrupted with an unpaid time-off period. For example, a school bus driver may be requested to work early in the morning and later in the afternoon while having the middle of the day off.

SPLIT-UP form of reorganization by which a corporation splits into two or more smaller corporations and the stock of the new corporations is distributed tax free to the shareholders of the old corporation, who in turn surrender the stock of the old corporation. *See also* DIVISIVE REORGANIZATION.

SPOKESPERSON individual who speaks on behalf of a product or service and whose name becomes associated with the product or service. A spokesperson may be a celebrity or someone who begins as an unknown and gains a measure of celebrity through association with the product. *See also* PERSONALITY; TESTIMONIAL.

SPONSOR
1. in a limited partnership, GENERAL PARTNER who organizes and sells a limited partnership.
2. investment company, such as a mutual fund, that offers shares in its funds; also called the UNDERWRITER.
3. in securities trading, important investor, typically, an institution, mutual fund, or other big trader, whose favorable opinion of a particular security influences other investors and creates additional demand for the security.
4. advertiser who pays for part or all of a television or radio program by running one or more advertisements during the program.

SPOOL a QUEUE of computer files waiting to be printed.

SPOT CHECK supervisory check on work performance or product quality done at random intervals. Spot checks are unannounced and can occur at any time. The purpose is to ensure a continually high performance level on the part of employees.

SPOT COMMODITY COMMODITY traded with the expectation that it will actually be delivered to the buyer, as contrasted to a FUTURES CONTRACT, which will usually expire without any physical delivery taking place. Spot commodities are traded in the SPOT MARKET.

SPOT DELIVERY MONTH nearest month of those currently being traded in which a commodity could be delivered. In late January, therefore, the spot delivery month would be February for commodities with a February contract trade.

SPOT MARKET commodities market in which goods are sold for cash and delivered immediately. Trades that take place in FUTURES CONTRACTS expiring in the current month are also called spotmarket *trades.* See CASH MARKET.

SPOT PRICE current delivery price of a commodity traded in the SPOT MARKET; also called *cash* price.

SPOT RATE the price at which a currency can be purchased or sold and then delivered within two business days.

SPOT ZONING rezoning a PARCEL of land where all surrounding parcels are zoned for a different use, in particular where the rezoning creates a use that is incompatible with surrounding land uses. Spot zoning is generally disallowed in the courts.

SPOUSAL IRA INDIVIDUAL RETIREMENT ACCOUNT created in the name of a nonworking spouse. The maximum contribution to any IRA in 2006 is $4,000 for each spouse ($5,000 when a CATCH-UP CONTRIBUTION is allowed). If one spouse has little or no compensation, however, that spouse may *borrow* his or her spouse's compensation to permit the maximum contribution.

SPREAD
Banking: difference between cost of funds and lending rate.
Bonds: difference between yields on securities of the same quality but different maturities; also difference between yields on securities of the same maturity but different qualities.
Stocks: difference between bid and offer prices; also, difference between high and low prices of a particular security over a given period.
Underwriting: difference between the proceeds an issuer of a new security receives and the price paid by the public for the issue.

SPREADING AGREEMENT agreement that extends the COLLATERAL of a loan to include several properties.

SPREADSHEET table of numbers arranged in rows and columns, related by formulas. Spreadsheet calculations can be very tedious. Changing a single number can affect the results in many different rows and columns. Therefore, it helps greatly to have a computer perform spreadsheet calculations. Microsoft EXCEL is a commonly used spreadsheet program.

SPRINGING POWER OF ATTORNEY a special type of POWER OF ATTORNEY that has no effect until a certain event occurs, such as disability of the principal. At that point, it springs into effect.

SPUR rail line extending from a regularly serviced line; for example, a spur might run from a main rail line to a manufacturing plant for the convenience of loading and unloading cargo at the plant's door.

SPYWARE any software that covertly gathers user information or monitors user activity without the user's knowledge. Spyware applications are typically bundled as a hidden component of freeware or shareware applications; once installed, the spyware uses the user's Internet connection to transmit information to someone else, usually for advertising purposes, but *keystroke-logging* software can be used to extract passwords and other private information.

SQUARE FOOTAGE area, measured in square feet, of something for sale or rent. What is included in square footage can vary considerably; for instance, the square footage of an office in an office building may or may not include a common area adjacent to elevators.

SQUATTER'S RIGHTS legal allowance to use the property of another in absence of an attempt by the owner to force EVICTION. This right may eventually be converted to title to the property over time by ADVERSE POSSESSION, if recognized by state law.

SQUEEZE
1. tight money period, when loan money is scarce and interest rates are high, making borrowing difficult and expensive; also called a *credit crunch*.
2. any situation where increased costs cannot be passed on to customers in the form of higher prices.
3. *See also* SHORT SQUEEZE.

SSI *see* SUPPLEMENTAL SECURITY INCOME.

STABILIZATION
Currency: buying and selling of a country's own currency to protect its exchange value; also called *pegging*.
Economics: leveling out of the business cycle, unemployment, and prices using fiscal and monetary policies.
Securities: intervention in the market by a managing underwriter in order to keep the market price from falling below the public offering price during the offering period of a new issue.

STACHYBOTRYS CHARTARUM a type of mold that can grow in parts of a structure exposed to constant moisture. Many claim adverse health effects from exposure to this hazard. Called *stachy* for short; also known as *black mold*.

STAFF
1. in general, personnel in an organization. For example, a firm has a *staff* of 250 people.
2. in the concepts of line and staff, management functions of planning, organizing, budgeting, directing, and coordinating an organization. *See also* STAFF AUTHORITY.

STAFF AUTHORITY authority to advise, but not to direct, other managers. For example, a personnel department has staff authority to advise functional managers in an organization.

STAGFLATION term coined by economists in the 1970s to describe the previously unprecedented combination of slow economic growth and high unemployment (*stag*nation) with rising prices (in*flation*).

STAGGERED ELECTION system of electing a percentage of the board of directors of a public corporation, usually one third, each year for a period of from one to three years. The purpose of staggering the elections is to slow any attempts to take over the corporation.

STAGGERING MATURITIES technique used by a bond investor to lower risk. Since long-term bonds are more volatile than short-term ones, an investor can hedge against interest rate movements by buying short-, medium-, and long-term bonds.

STAGNATION period of no or slow economic growth or of economic decline in real (inflation-adjusted) terms. Economic growth of about 1% or less per year is generally taken to constitute stagnation.

STAKE ownership in an enterprise. For example, an individual has a stake in the company. The term originated in the colonial era when one would mark one's property by putting stakes in the ground, thus acquiring a stake in the community.

STAND-ALONE SYSTEM workstation made up of a single unit used by one person at a time and not connected to other systems or a computer. Examples are personal computer and automatic typewriter.

STANDARD established and fixed measure used in assessing quality or performance. For example, a company has a particular quality *standard* for a product, which is used to measure the productivity of its workers.

STANDARD ADVERTISING REGISTER two companion directories, the *Standard Directory of Advertising Agencies* and the *Standard Directory of Advertisers,* which have become an invaluable tool of the advertising industry. The books are referred to in the advertising trade as the Red Books because of their red covers.

STANDARD & POOR'S CORPORATION subsidiary of McGraw-Hill, Inc., providing a broad range of investment services, including rating securities, compiling the Standard & Poor's composite indexes of stocks, and publishing a wide variety of statistical materials, investment advisory reports, and other financial information.

STANDARD & POOR'S INDEX broad-based measurement of changes in stock-market conditions based on the average performance of 500 widely held common stocks; commonly known as the *Standard & Poor's 500* (or *S&P 500).*

STANDARD & POOR'S RATING classification of stocks and bonds according to risk issued by Standard & Poor's Corporation. S&P's top four grades, called INVESTMENT GRADE AAA, AA, A, and BBB, indicate a minimal risk that a corporate or municipal bond issue will default in its timely payment of interest and principal. Bonds or stocks rated BB or below by Standard & Poor's are considered speculative, and fiduciaries are not allowed to invest in them.

STANDARD COST estimate, based on engineering and accounting studies, of what the costs of production should be, assuming normal operating conditions.

STANDARD DEDUCTION provision allowing a taxpayer to deduct, in lieu of itemized deductions, a certain amount of income from his or her GROSS INCOME. These amounts are indexed for inflation each year and were as follows for 2006:

Married couples filing jointly	$10,300
Heads of households	7,550
Single individuals	5,150
Married couples filing separately	5,150

There are more restrictive limits on the standard deduction allowed to those fro whom a dependency deduction is allowable to another taxpayer. An additional (above the amounts in the table above) is allowed for taxpayers age 65 or above or who are blind.

STANDARD DEVIATION statistical measure of the degree to which an individual value in a probability distribution tends to vary from the mean of the distribution. From a normal distribution, one standard deviation includes about 66% of the population; two standard deviations include about 95%.

STANDARD ERROR *see* STANDARD DEVIATION.

STANDARD FIRE POLICY *see* FIRE INSURANCE—STANDARD FIRE POLICY.

STANDARD INDUSTRIAL CLASSIFICATION (SIC) SYSTEM federally designed standard numbering system identifying companies by industry and providing other information. It has been used by market researchers, securities analysts, and others, but is being replaced by the NORTH AMERICAN INDUSTRY CLASSIFICATION SYSTEM.

STANDARD MILEAGE METHOD method that permits an automobile business expense deduction based on a standard mileage rate, which was 48.5 cents per mile after September 1, 2005. The rate will increase in the future. Parking and tolls are allowed in addition to this standard deduction. As an alternative to the *standard mileage method,* a taxpayer may keep detailed records of the various expenditures of a business automobile.

STANDARD OF CARE a statement of duties expressing the conduct expected of a professional.

STANDARD OF LIVING sum total of amenities, quality, and quantity of goods and services consumed by consuming units within an economy.

STANDARD TERMINATION *see* TERMINATION OF A PLAN.

STANDARD TIME
1. time for any given time zone as established by the Standard Time Act (1918). There are five time zones in the United States—Eastern, Central, Mountain, Pacific, and Alaska.
2. *see* ALLOWED TIME.

STANDARD WAGE RATE normal or base salary of an employee before any overtime or premium pay is computed. *See also* PREMIUM PAY.

STANDBY FEE sum required by a lender to provide a standby commitment. The fee is forfeited should the loan not be closed within a specified time. *See also* STANDBY LOAN.

STANDBY LOAN commitment by a lender to make available a sum of money at specified terms for a specified period. This is generally not a desirable loan. It is intended to be replaced by another commitment.

STANDING ORDER order for repeated shipments of goods to be sent without specific reorders. Standing orders must comply with certain quantity and time limitations.

STAPLE STOCK goods that have fairly constant demand over a period of years. There is very little seasonality to them. Retailers continually carry these goods in stock.

STARE DECISIS (Latin for "to stand by [previously] decided [cases]") rule by which courts rely upon judicial precedent as a compelling guide to decision of cases raising issues similar to those in previous cases.

START MENU the computer menu that is called up by the Start button on the *taskbar* at the bottom of the screen in WINDOWS. It provides access to Windows Help and several utilities, as well as to all the applications installed on the computer.

START-UP new business venture. In VENTURE CAPITAL parlance, start-up is the earliest stage at which a venture capital investor or investment pool will provide funds to an enterprise, usually on the basis of a business plan detailing the background of the management group along with market and financial projections. *See also* SEED MONEY.

START-UP COSTS expenditures incurred after the decision has been made to establish a particular business but before business operations begin. A taxpayer who subsequently enters a trade or business can elect to amortize these expenses over a period of not less than 60 months, starting with the month in which the business begins.

START-UP DISK a diskette or CD used to initialize a computer's start-up process. It contains enough of the computer's OPERATING SYSTEM to BOOT the computer in an emergency. Also called a *boot disk*.

STAT medical term meaning *immediately,* which has come into common usage.

STATE BANK bank organized under a charter granted by a regulatory authority in one of the 50 U.S. states, as distinguished from a NATIONAL BANK, which is federally chartered. The powers of a state-chartered commercial bank are generally consistent with those of national banks since state laws tend to conform to federal initiatives and vice versa.

STATE DISTRIBUTION CENTER (SDC) main post office(s) in a state that receives and distributes all mail for that state to and from the various other post offices within the state. *See also* SECOND CLASS; THIRD CLASS.

STATED VALUE assigned value given to a corporation's stock for accounting purposes in lieu of *par value*. For example, the stated value may be set at $1 a share, so that if a company issued 10 million shares, the stated value of its stock would be $10 million. The stated value of the stock has no relation to its market price.

STATEMENT
1. summary for customers of the transactions that occurred over the preceding month (or other period). For example, a bank statement lists all deposits and withdrawals, as well as the running account balances.
2. document drawn up by businesses to show the status of their assets and liabilities and the results of their operations as of a certain date. *See also* FINANCIAL STATEMENT.
3. in a computer program, instructions that make up one unit of the program. Each line of the program is a *statement*.

STATEMENT OF AFFAIRS financial report showing assets and liabilities at expected liquidation values, and stockholders' equity. The statement is prepared primarily when an actual or pending BANKRUPTCY exists.

STATEMENT OF CASH FLOW *see* CASH FLOW.

STATEMENT OF CHANGE IN FINANCIAL POSITION *see* SOURCES AND APPLICATIONS (USES) OF FUNDS STATEMENT.

STATEMENT OF CONDITION
Banking: sworn accounting of a bank's resources, liabilities, and capital accounts as of a certain date.
Finance: summary of the status of assets, liabilities, and equity of a person or a business organization as of a certain date. *See also* BALANCE SHEET.

STATEMENT OF INCOME *see* PROFIT AND LOSS STATEMENT.

STATEMENT OF PARTNERS' CAPITAL on balance sheet, showing NET WORTH of each partner's interest in the business.

STATIC ANALYSIS economic model that does not consider or allow for changes over time, and within which all variables are simultaneously solved. Economists use static analysis in supply and demand models for goods and services.

STATIC BUDGET fixed budget that does not allow for changes. *See also* FLEXIBLE BUDGET.

STATIC RISK choices that offer a constant level of uncertainty regarding the outcome or payoff. Players of slot machines with constant payout ratios face *static risk*.

STATISTIC descriptive measure calculated from data sampled from a population. *See also* TEST STATISTIC.

STATISTICAL INFERENCE process of using observations of a sample to estimate the properties of the population. *See also* INFERENTIAL STATISTICS.

STATISTICALLY SIGNIFICANT test statistic that is as large as or larger than a predetermined requirement, resulting in rejection of the NULL HYPOTHESIS.

STATISTICAL MODELING *see* SIMULATION.

STATISTICAL PROCESS CONTROL (SPC) method of using statistical charts to monitor product quality and quantity in the product process. The attempt is to maintain high QUALITY ASSURANCE by insuring that the job is performed correctly the first time. *See also* TOTAL QUALITY MANAGEMENT.

STATISTICAL QUALITY CONTROL (SQC) monitoring statistically representative production samples for the purpose of determining quality. Careful sample monitoring helps to improve overall quality by locating defect sources. Dr. W. Edwards Deming has been instrumental in assisting companies to implement SQC.

STATISTICAL SAMPLING the process of selecting elements of a population for either descriptive or inferential purposes. Assume, for example, that an auditor was estimating the value of accounts receivables. To determine whether or not every receivable was valid would require a great effort. Alternatively, an adequate number could be randomly selected. These would make up the sample selected. The values determined for the sample would be descriptive statistically of the sample. Based on the sample, an estimate (inference) could be made as to the value of the population of receivables.

STATISTICAL SOFTWARE computer programs that perform functions helpful to accountants, particularly managerial accountants. A model base management system produces mathematical models, and can change and store components. Examples of statistical programs are *SPSS/PC* and *Systat*.

STATISTICS study of ways to analyze data. It consists of DESCRIPTIVE STATISTICS and STATISTICAL INFERENCE.

STATUS position, class, standing, or rank achieved in a society by virtue of achievement or financial wealth.

STATUS SYMBOL tangible mark or sign of an individual's social status within a society or organization. Expensive cars, homes, and boats are often seen as status symbols.

STATUTE written law; act of a legislature, under constitutional authority, that becomes law, governing conduct within its scope. Statutes are enacted to prescribe conduct, define crimes, create inferior government bodies, appropriate public monies, and in general promote the public welfare.

STATUTE OF FRAUDS statutory requirement that certain kinds of CONTRACTS must be in writing to be enforceable. Contracts to answer to a creditor for the debt of another, contracts made in consideration of marriage, contracts for the sale of real estate or affecting any interest in real estate, and contracts not to be performed within one year of their making normally must be in writing and signed by the party sought to be bound by the contract.

STATUTE OF LIMITATIONS law that fixes the time within which parties must take judicial action to enforce rights or else be thereafter barred from enforcing them. The *statute of limitations* during which the IRS may assess an additional tax or collect a tax or the taxpayer can file an amended return is generally three years from the due date of the return or its filing or, if later, two years from the date the taxes were paid. The period can be extended by agreement between the taxpayer and the IRS. It is also extended for material omissions, and the statute does not apply if a required return is not filed or is fraudulent.

STATUTORY AUDIT AUDIT required by law. A municipality may be required by its own law to have an annual audit of financial records.

STATUTORY FORECLOSURE any foreclosure proceeding not conducted under court supervision. *Contrast with* JUDICIAL FORECLOSURE.

STATUTORY MERGER legal combination of two or more corporations in which only one survives as a LEGAL ENTITY. It differs from *statutory consolidation,* in which all the companies in a combination cease to exist as legal entities and a new corporate entity is created. *See also* MERGER.

STATUTORY NOTICE period of time required by law to give notice of the date that something will occur.

STATUTORY VOTING one-share, one-vote rule that governs voting procedures in most corporations. Shareholders may cast one vote per share either for or against each nominee for the board of directors, but may not give more than one vote to one nominee. *See also* CUMULATIVE VOTING.

STAYING POWER ability of an investor to stay with (not sell) an investment that has fallen in value. For example, a commodity trader with *staying power* is able to meet margin calls as the commodities futures contracts he has bought fall in price. In real estate, an investor with staying power is able to meet mortgage and maintenance payments on his properties and is therefore not forced to sell as occupancy rates rise or fall or as the properties become temporarily difficult to sell. A slang term for staying power is *deep pockets*.

STEADY-GROWTH METHOD subscription SOURCE EVALUATION technique that estimates the cost and impact on profitability of building the RATE BASE over time via various sources of business. The cost of acquiring, billing, and renewing subscriptions is taken into account, as well as expected PAY-UP, cancellation, and RENEWAL rates. *See also* CHANNEL OF SALES; MAINTENANCE METHOD.

STEAMER, STEAMSHIP ship that gets its power from steam. Steamships may take various forms (tanker, freighter, luxury liner) and haul cargo or passengers.

STEEL-COLLAR WORKER use of robots as employees on a production line. It symbolizes the replacement of the blue-collar worker.

STEEL INTENSIVE products or production technologies based on high amounts of steel content.

STEERING illegal practice of limiting the housing shown to a certain ethnic group.

STEPPED-UP BASIS process by which a person's TAX BASE is increased to a certain level (usually FAIR MARKET VALUE) as of a certain date. A stepped-up basis generally applies to property received by an heir from a decedent.

STEP-UP LEASE *see* GRADUATED LEASE.

STEREOTYPING classifying people because of one unique characteristic. Stereotyping is a form of prejudice that can form damaging images of people because of a particular characteristic without having any knowledge of the person.

STET proofreader's or editor's direction to the printer or typesetter indicating that material marked for correction should remain as it was before the correction. The work to remain is underscored with a series of dots, and the word *stet* is written in the margin. The term is Latin for "let it stand."

STEVEDORE company or person who unloads cargo, especially from a ship.

STEWARD
1. union representative who handles day-to-day matters affecting workers in a unionized workplace. A steward is also an employee in the same BARGAINING UNIT. *See also* SHOP STEWARD; STEWARDSHIP.
2. male flight attendant.

STEWARDSHIP exercising the responsibilities of a steward; representing day-to-day matters affecting workers in a unionized workplace. *See also* STEWARD.

STIFF failure to pay for services rendered; for example, stiffing a waiter by not leaving a tip.

STIPEND, STIPENDIARY payment of salaries or wages for services; person who receives such payment.

STIPULATED FACTS facts agreed to by the parties ahead of time in a tax or legal dispute.

STIPULATION term within a written contract; also, any set of conditions.

STOCHASTIC statistical term describing a variable with values determined by chance (a random variable). In REGRESSION ANALYSIS, the DEPENDENT VARIABLE is *stochastic* if the model does not perfectly explain all observations. *Stochastics* is also an important branch of technical securities analysis.

STOCK
1. ownership of a corporation represented by shares that are a claim on the corporation's earnings and assets. *See also* COMMON STOCK; PREFERRED STOCK.
2. inventories of accumulated goods in manufacturing and retailing businesses.

STOCKBROKER *see* REGISTERED REPRESENTATIVE.

STOCK BUYBACK *see* SHARE/STOCK REPURCHASE PLAN.

STOCK CERTIFICATE written INSTRUMENT evidencing a share in the ownership of a corporation.

STOCK DIVIDEND payment of a corporate DIVIDEND in the form of stock rather than cash.

STOCK EXCHANGE organized marketplace in which stocks, common stock equivalents, and bonds are traded by members of the exchange, acting both as agents (brokers) and as principals (dealers or traders). Such exchanges have a physical location where brokers and dealers meet to execute orders from institutional and individual investors to buy and sell securities. *See also* AMERICAN STOCK EXCHANGE; NEW YORK STOCK EXCHANGE; OVER THE COUNTER; NASDAQ.

STOCK-FOR-ASSET REORGANIZATION form of reorganization in which an acquiring corporation obtains solely for all or part of its voting stock (or its parent's voting stock) substantially all of the assets of a second corporation.

STOCK-FOR-STOCK REORGANIZATION form of reorganization in which one corporation acquires at least 80% of another corporation's stock in exchange solely for all or part of its own (or its parent's) voting stock, and the acquired corporation becomes a subsidiary.

STOCKHOLDER individual or organization with an ownership position in a corporation; also called a SHAREHOLDER or *share owner.* Stockholders must own at least one share, and their ownership is confirmed by either a stock certificate or a record by their broker if shares are in the broker's custody.

STOCKHOLDER OF RECORD common or preferred stockholder whose name is registered on the books of a corporation as owning shares as of a particular date. Dividends and other distributions are made only to shareholders of record.

STOCKHOLDERS' DERIVATIVE ACTION suit by a corporation in which the grievance has been suffered primarily by the corporation, conducted by the shareholders as the corporation's representative. Such suits are the only civil remedy a stockholder has for breach of a fiduciary duty by those entrusted with the management of their corporation.

STOCKHOLDERS' EQUITY balance sheet item that includes the book value of ownership in the corporation. It includes CAPITAL STOCK, PAID-IN SURPLUS, and RETAINED EARNINGS.

STOCK INDEX FUTURE security that combines features of traditional commodity futures trading with securities trading using composite stock indexes. Investors can speculate on general market performance or can buy an index future contract to hedge a long position or a short position against a decline in value.

STOCK INSURANCE COMPANY group owned by STOCKHOLDERS to whom company earnings are paid in the form of shareholder dividends. Under state laws, however, the interest of POLICYHOLDERS takes precedence over stockholder interests.

STOCKKEEPING UNIT (SKU) department or unit having supervisory responsibility for stock inventory in a mercantile house. Bar code assigned to product.

STOCK LEDGER record of a corporation's stock ownership. It is kept current by recording all purchases and sales of stock.

STOCK MARKET organized market, such as a STOCK EXCHANGE or an OVER-THE-COUNTER market, where stocks and bonds are actively traded.

STOCK OPTION
1. right to purchase or sell a stock at a specified price within a stated period. Options are a popular investment medium, offering an opportunity to hedge positions in other securities, to speculate in stocks with relatively little investment, and to capitalize on changes in the market value of options contracts themselves through a variety of options strategies. *See also* CALL OPTION; PUT OPTION.
2. widely used form of employee incentive and compensation, usually for the executives of a corporation. The employee is given an option to purchase the corporation's shares at a certain price (at or

below the market price at the time the option is granted) for a specified period of years.

STOCKOUT COST cost incurred to a firm when current inventory is exhausted for one or more items. Lost sales revenue costs are incurred when the firm is unable to meet current orders because of a stockout condition.

STOCKPILE
1. reserve supply of raw materials or goods; total available materials not yet being used.
2. to accumulate a stockpile or stockpiles.

STOCK POWER POWER OF ATTORNEY form transferring ownership of a REGISTERED SECURITY from the owner to another party. A separate piece of paper from the CERTIFICATE, it is attached to the latter when the security is sold or pledged to a brokerage firm, bank, or other lender as loan COLLATERAL.

STOCK PURCHASE PLAN organized program permitting employees of a company to buy shares of its stock, sometimes at a discount. Could constitute an employee benefit if the employer matches employee stock purchases. *See* EMPLOYEE STOCK OWNERSHIP PLAN.

STOCK RECORD control, usually in the form of a ledger card or computer report, used by brokerage firms to keep track of securities held in inventory and their physical location within the firm. Securities are recorded by name and owner.

STOCK RIGHTS rights to subscribe to additional shares of stock at a set price, which may be offered to some or all shareholders.

STOCKROOM area or room where stock of goods and materials and other supplies are maintained.

STOCKS, BONDS, BILLS & INFLATION annual publication by IBBOTSON & ASSOCIATES that provides long-term historical data on various financial instruments.

STOCK SPLIT *see* SPLIT.

STOCK SYMBOL abbreviations (mostly one to four letters) used to identify companies on the securities exchanges on which they trade; also called *trading symbols.*

STOCK-TRANSFER AGENT *see* TRANSFER AGENT.

STOCK TURNOVER index of speed with which inventory moves in and out of a business location. Stock turnover is an indicator of sales volume.

STONEWALLING refusing to acknowledge that a condition exists despite overwhelming evidence; refusing to cooperate.

STOOL PIGEON spy or police informant. A stool pigeon betrays another and their confidences to the authorities.

STOP CLAUSE in a lease, amount of operating expense above which the tenant must assume payment. Often the base amount that the lessor pays is the amount of expense for the first full year of operation under the lease. *See also* ESCALATOR CLAUSE.

STOP ORDER order to a securities broker to buy or sell at the market price once the security has traded at a specified price called the *stop price;* intended to protect a profit or limit a loss.

STOP PAYMENT revocation of payment on a check after the check has been sent or delivered to the payee. So long as the check has not been cashed, the writer has up to six months in which to request a stop payment. The stop payment right does not carry over to electronic funds transfers.

STOPWATCH STUDIES time and motion studies performed on work procedures by management; result of Frederick W. Taylor's *Scientific Management* study where he advocated using a stopwatch to accurately time all the procedures in performing a job. *See also* TIME-AND-MOTION STUDY.

STORE establishment used for the purpose of selling merchandise and services, usually at the retail level. Stores range in size from small shops to large modern shopping malls and supermarkets.

STORE BRAND product such as coffee, rice, canned vegetables, that carries the store's name (Kroger, Safeway) in contrast to the manufacturer's brand or NATIONAL BRAND.

STOREKEEPERS BURGLARY AND ROBBERY INSURANCE coverage for small mercantile establishments on a package basis. Combines six layers of protection: burglary of a safe; damage caused by robbery and burglary, whether actual or attempted; robbery of a guard and burglary of the business's merchandise; robbery inside or outside the premises of the business; kidnapping to force a business owner or a representative to open the premises of the business from the outside; and theft of securities and monies either from the home of a messenger of the business or from a night depository of a bank.

STOREKEEPERS LIABILITY INSURANCE coverage for bodily injury and property damage liability resulting from ownership, use, and/or maintenance of the insured business's premises, completed operations, and products. Covers medical payment expenses associated with bodily injury to another party when an accident causes hazardous conditions on the business's premises or within the business's operation. Also covers costs in defending the insured against liability suits, even if the suits are without foundation.

STOWAGE manner in which freight is arranged in a ship's storage area so as to minimize the risk to ship and cargo.

STRADDLE position consisting of an equal number of PUT OPTIONS and CALL OPTIONS on the same underlying stock, stock index, or commodity future at the same exercise price and maturity date. Profits occur on volatile prices, no matter which direction.

STRAIGHT BILL OF LADING nonnegotiable bill of lading, merely stating that the carrier is to deliver the goods to a specified person at a specified place.

STRAIGHT DEBT debt that
1. is evidenced by a written unconditional promise to pay a fixed amount on demand, or on a specific date,
2. provides for an interest rate and an interest payment date that is not contingent on the borrower's profits or discretion or similar factors, or on the payment of dividends,
3. is not convertible into stock or any other equity interest, and
4. is owed to a creditor who is eligible to own stock in an S corporation, such as an individual, estate, or qualified subchapter S trust.

STRAIGHT-LINE (METHOD OF) DEPRECIATION DEPRECIATION method whereby an equal amount of the asset's cost is considered an expense for each year of the asset's USEFUL LIFE.

STRAIGHT-LINE PRODUCTION traditional production-line method of production where all the parts to the process are done on a straight-line production belt; sequential assembling of pieces on a production line.

STRAIGHT TIME standard time or number of work hours established for a particular work period. An employee working straight time is not being paid overtime.

STRAPHANGER bus or rail commuter, especially one who stands up while traveling. Early subways had leather straps that standees could grasp—since replaced by metal bars or handles.

STRATEGIC ALLIANCE long-term association between two or more organizations to share initiatives and resources for the purpose of gaining a mutual COMPETITIVE ADVANTAGE.

STRATEGIC PLANNING
1. management act of determining a firm's future environment and response to organizational challenges; crucial decisions determining the direction of a firm.
2. in a business firm, deciding what principal products and services to produce for what major markets.
See CORPORATE STRATEGIC PLANNING.

STRATEGY management plan or method for completing objectives; plan of procedures to be implemented, to do something.

STRATIFIED RANDOM SAMPLING process of dividing a population into segments (*strata*) and sampling each stratum independently of the others. If elements within each stratum are similar (homogeneous), greater accuracy in estimates of the parameters may be obtained. For example, market research firms often divide product users into age groups, such as under 5, 5 to 15, 16 to 20, 21 to 30, and so on, and sample each age group.

STRAW BOSS underforeman or group leader having delegated authority to supervise others. Straw bosses often have no formal title or permanent status. Their supervisory activities are incidental to their production performance.

STRAW MAN one who purchases property that is, in turn, conveyed to another for the purpose of concealing the identity of the eventual purchaser. *See also* NOMINEE.

STREET short for Wall Street, referring to the financial community in New York City and elsewhere.

STREET NAME phrase describing securities held in the name of a broker or another nominee instead of a customer. Since the securities are in the broker's custody, transfer of the shares at the time of sale is easier than if the stock were registered in the customer's name and physical certificates had to be transferred.

STREET PRICE the average or usual (or sometimes the lowest available) price charged for a product, especially one that is rarely sold at the MANUFACTURER'S SUGGESTED RETAIL PRICE, if any. The *street price* is commonly cited in magazine reviews of personal computers and their peripherals, whose price varies widely depending on the retail outlet.

STREET SMARTS intuitive intelligence or reasoning power not gained by formal education.

STRETCHOUT
1. accelerating the work pace without additional compensation for the workers, requiring workers to do more with little or no additional compensation. *See also* SPEEDUP.
2. stretching the time needed to pay for a purchase.

STRICT PRODUCT LIABILITY liability of all parties associated with the manufacture, distribution, and sale of any product for damage caused by that product.

STRIKE organized work stoppage by labor for the purpose of exerting pressure on management with regard to agreeing on better contract terms or working conditions, correcting an unsettled grievance, or recognizing a union as a BARGAINING AGENT. Strike is the ultimate labor weapon. Public sector strikes are usually illegal.

STRIKE BENEFITS union benefits, including strike pay, to striking members, usually in the form of flat payments or graduated payments according to family needs. Strike benefits may also include welfare payments in those states allowing benefits for strikers. *See also* STRIKE PAY.

STRIKEBREAKERS management-hired replacements for striking employees. Strikebreakers must cross a picket line and are bitterly resented by striking employees. *See also* SCABS.

STRIKE NOTICE formal notice to an employer, the Federal Mediation and Conciliation Service, or a state labor-management relations agency that a union has rejected the company's latest offer and that a strike is imminent. It is an indication that the employees will not work until their demands are met.

STRIKE PAY monies paid by the union to striking members to help compensate for lost income as a result of the strike. Strike pay is derived from a strike fund that is generated during those periods when a contract is in force and the union members are working. *See also* STRIKE BENEFITS.

STRIKE PRICE dollar price per share at which, during the life of an option, a call option buyer can purchase the underlying stock or a put option buyer can sell the stock. An XYZ May 50 call has a strike price of $50 a share; also called *exercise price*. *See also* OUT OF THE MONEY.

STRIKE VOTE vote by the members of a union to go on strike against an organization. A strike vote requires a clear majority to be effective. A strike vote authorizes a strike by a union, but the union leadership chooses when or if to call a strike vote.

STRIP DEVELOPMENT form of commercial land use in which each establishment is afforded direct access to a major thoroughfare; generally associated with intensive use of signs to attract passersby.

STRIPPED COUPON *see* STRIPS.

STRIPS
Bonds: brokerage-house practice of separating a bond into its CORPUS and coupons, which are then sold separately as zero coupon securities. A variation known by the acronym strips (*S*eparate *T*rading of *R*egistered *I*nterest and *P*rincipal of *S*ecurities) is a prestripped zero coupon bond that is a direct obligation of the U.S. Treasury.
Options: option contract consisting of two put options and one call option on the same underlying stock or stock index with the same strike and expiration date.

STRUCTURAL UNEMPLOYMENT unemployment that is part of the "system" and exists even during periods of FULL EMPLOYMENT. Those who are unemployed are in the wrong area for their job skills, are illiterate or uneducated, are school dropouts, or belong to minority groups.

STRUCTURE any constructed improvement to a site. Structures include buildings; fencing and enclosures; garages; gazebos, greenhouses, and kiosks; and sheds and utility buildings. *See also* FINANCIAL STRUCTURE.

STUDENT for purposes of determining whether a person is DEPENDENT for tax purposes, the term *student* means an individual who during each of five calendar months during a tax year is a full-time student at a qualified educational institution or is pursuing a full-time course of institutional on-farm training.

SUBCHAPTER C the portion of the Internal Revenue Code that covers corporate taxation.

SUBCHAPTER J portion of the Internal Revenue Code that concerns ESTATES, TRUSTS, BENEFICIARIES, and DECEDENTS.

SUBCHAPTER S CORPORATION former name for S CORPORATION.

SUBCONTRACTOR one to whom a GENERAL CONTRACTOR or other subcontractor sublets part or all of a contract.

SUBDIRECTORY (SUBFOLDER) a lower level of a DIRECTORY or FOLDER, which may itself also contain one or more subdirectories or subfolders. The whole hierarchy of directories and subdirectories is known as the *directory tree*.

SUBDIVIDER one who partitions a tract of land for the purpose of selling the individual plots. If a structure is built, the *subdivider* becomes a *developer*.

SUBDIVIDING dividing a TRACT of land into smaller tracts. *See also* SUBDIVIDER.

SUBDIVISION tract of land divided into lots suitable for homebuilding purposes. Most states and localities require that a subdivision PLAT be recorded.

SUBJECT TO MORTGAGE condition of sale whereby the purchaser takes land encumbered by a preexisting mortgage. The purchaser's obligation to the mortgagee is limited to the property subject to the mortgage, unless the purchaser becomes personally liable on the debt by assuming the mortgage.

SUBLEASE lease from one lessee to another lessee. The new lessee is the sublessee or subtenant. *See also* SANDWICH LEASE.

SUBLET to lease from under a lease. A tenant who leases property to another has sublet. *See also* ASSIGNMENT OF LEASE.

SUBLIMINAL ADVERTISING advertising messages presented below the level of consciousness, such as words flashed across a television or movie screen at intervals of no more than 10 seconds in length, during the presentation of regular programming or a feature film. Some amount of subliminal advertising was done in the 1950s, but it has since been declared illegal.

SUBMARGINAL less than marginal. In economics and business, submarginal entities are unable to maintain the minimum profit, production level, and so on to remain permanently in existence.

SUBOPTIMIZE to use to less than the maximum degree of output; not to the fullest potential.

SUBORDINATED DEBT debt that is junior in claim on assets to other debt, repayable only after other debts with a higher claim have been satisfied. Some subordinated debts may have a lower claim on assets than other subordinated debt; a *junior subordinated debenture* ranks below a subordinated DEBENTURE, for example.

SUBORDINATION
1. establishment of priority of one claim or debt over another. A subordination agreement is one in which a creditor agrees in a contract that claims of other creditors must be fully paid before there is any payment to the subordinated creditor.
2. in real estate law, establishment of priority between different existing interests, claims, liens, and encumbrances on the same parcel of land.

SUBPOENA (Latin for "under penalty") a writ issued under the authority of a court to compel the appearance of a witness or documents for a judicial proceeding.

SUBROGATION substitution of another person, the *subrogee*, in the place of the creditor, to whose rights to the debt the other person succeeds; one's payment or assumption of an obligation for which another is primarily liable. Subrogation typically arises when an insurance company pays its insured under the provisions of an insurance policy; in that event the company is subrogated to the cause of action of its insured against the one responsible for the damage for which the insurance company has paid.

SUBROUTINE in a computer program, set of instructions, given a particular name, that will be executed when the main program calls for it. In BASIC, a subroutine is labeled by the number of its first line and is executed when a GOSUB command is reached. The command RETURN marks the end of the subroutine and tells the computer to return to the main program.

SUBSCRIPT number or letter used to identify a particular element in an array. In mathematics, subscripts are written below the line, as in x_1, or a_{23}. In most computer languages, however, subscripts are enclosed in parentheses, as in X(l) or A(J).

SUBSCRIPTED VARIABLE another name for *array,* since it is necessary to use subscripts to identify a particular element.

SUBSCRIPTION
1. agreement of intent to buy newly issued securities.
2. agreement to give money for a specific purpose, such as a contribution to a charity or to purchase a periodical publication.

SUBSCRIPTION PRICE price at which existing shareholders of a corporation are entitled to purchase common shares in a rights offering or at which subscription warrants are exercisable.

SUBSCRIPTION PRIVILEGE right of existing shareholders of a corporation, or their transferees, to buy shares of a new issue of common stock before it is offered to the public. *See also* PREEMPTIVE RIGHT; SUBSCRIPTION RIGHT.

SUBSCRIPTION RIGHT contractual right of an existing shareholder to purchase additional shares of a new issue of common stock before it is offered to the public.

SUBSEQUENT EVENT material happening occurring after the date of the financial statements but before the audit report is issued. Footnote disclosure is required so that financial statement users are properly informed. The subsequent event typically has a significant impact on financial position or earning capacity. Examples of subsequent events requiring disclosure are lawsuits, impairment of assets, and permanent decline in price of securities.

SUBSET all or portion of a set. Set *A* is a subset of set *B* if all elements in *A* are also in *B*. However, all elements in *B* need not be in *A*.

SUBSIDIARY company whose voting stock is more than 50% owned by another firm. For tax purposes, a PARENT COMPANY must own at least 80% of a subsidiary to file a CONSOLIDATED TAX RETURN.

SUBSIDIARY LEDGER details of an account that support the amount in the general ledger. *See also* ACCOUNTS PAYABLE LEDGER; ACCOUNTS RECEIVABLE LEDGER.

SUBSIDY payment or other favorable economic stimulus (such as remission of taxation) given by government to certain individuals or groups of economic entities, usually to encourage their continued existence, growth, development, and profitability. In the United States, subsidies are given to the agricultural industry, the very poor, and many other groups.

SUBSISTENCE maintenance without growth; usually used with reference to the STANDARD OF LIVING. A subsistence standard is sufficient to keep the economic unit alive and reasonably healthy, but provides nothing more.

SUBSISTENCE THEORY OF WAGES economic proposition that wages cannot fall below the SUBSISTENCE level for very long because such a level cannot maintain the labor force.

SUBSTANCE VS. FORM CONCEPT *substance* is the material or essential part of something, as distinguished from *form,* which is the observance of a legal or technical manner or order. In some tax situations, the courts and the IRS look past the *form* to determine the *substance* of a transaction in order to find out what was done in fact rather than what the taxpayer contends occurred. In other situations, the form controls, even though the substance of the transaction could have resulted from a different form.

SUBSTITUTED BASIS in taxation, property that has either an exchanged basis or a transferred basis. *Exchanged basis* is an amount determined by the BASIS of other property held by the owner. *Transferred basis* is an amount determined by the basis of property in the hands of the DONOR, GRANTOR, or other TRANSFEROR. Transferred basis and exchanged basis are sometimes referred to as CARRYOVER BASIS.

SUBSTITUTION
Banking: replacement of collateral by other collateral.
Contract law: replacement of one party to a contract by another.
Economics: principle that, if one product or service can be replaced by another, their prices will reflect the substitutability. **Law:** replacement of one attorney by another in the exercise of stock powers relating to the purchase and sale of securities.
Securities: exchange or swap of one security for another in a client's portfolio.

SUBSTITUTION EFFECT in economics, the effect of a change in the price of a commodity, which encourages consumers to substitute one good for another. If a good's price falls, consumers will tend to buy it in preference to other goods; if its price rises, consumers will buy other goods instead.

SUBSTITUTION LAW economic proposition that no good is absolutely irreplaceable, that at some set of prices, consumers will substitute other goods for it.

SUBSTITUTION SLOPE in a graphic diagram illustrating relative consumption, at different prices, of two or more goods out of a given income, relationship of the substitution of any pair of goods with respect to one another.

SUBSURFACE RIGHTS *see* MINERAL RIGHTS.

SUBTENANT one who leases all or part of rented premises from the original lessee for a term equal to or less than that held by the original lessee. The original lessee becomes the sublessor. *See also* SUBLEASE; SUBLET.

SUBTOTAL preliminary sum intended to be added to other amounts.

SUBURB town or unincorporated developed area close to a city. Suburbs, since they are largely residential, are usually dependent on a city for employment and support services and are generally characterized by low-density development relative to the city. However, considerable industrial development has occurred in many suburbs so that their dependency on a city has been reduced. *See also* URBAN; RURAL.

SUGGESTED RETAIL PRICE selling price suggested by the manufacturer of merchandise. The suggested retail price is not mandatory, although manufacturers may hope that retail outlets maintain a price within the range of the suggested retail price.

SUGGESTION BOX method of eliciting worker suggestions for management by having a box or receptacle where employees can place anonymous or signed comments; method of obtaining employee feedback. *See also* SUGGESTION SYSTEM.

SUGGESTION SYSTEM method of eliciting worker suggestions for management; method of obtaining employee feedback. Some suggestion systems have bonuses awarded for the most valuable or costeffective suggestion. *See also* SUGGESTION BOX.

SUICIDE CLAUSE limitation in all life insurance policies to the effect that no death payment will be made if an insured commits suicide within the first two years that the policy is in force. This clause protects the company against *adverse selection*— that is, purchase of a policy in contemplation of planned death in order for a beneficiary to collect the proceeds.

SUIT a legal proceeding to pursue a remedy that could be allowed by a court.

SUMMARY POSSESSION *see* EVICTION.

SUMMONS mandate requiring the appearance of the defendant under penalty of having JUDGMENT entered against him for failure to appear. The object of the summons is to notify the defendant that he has been sued. *See also* SUBPOENA.

SUM-OF-THE-YEARS'-DIGITS (SYD) DEPRECIATION method of allocating the cost of an ASSET over its USEFUL LIFE. It requires a fraction to be computed each year, which is applied against the depreciable amount. The numerator is the number of years left to be depreciated. The denominator is the sum of the years' digits of the depreciable life. The formula for the denominator is

$$\frac{N \times (N+1)}{2}$$

where N is the depreciable life. *See also* ACCELERATED DEPRECIATION. For example, an automobile used in business costs $10,000 and has a four-year depreciable life. Sum-of-the-years'-digits depreciation results in the deductions shown below:

Year	Fraction	Asset	Depreciation Deduction
1	4/10	$10,000	$ 4,000
2	3/10	10,000	3,000
3	2/10	10,000	2,000
4	1/10	10,000	1,000

SUNK COSTS costs that have already been expended and therefore have little or no relevance in considering whether to continue with a business operation. The term originated in the oil industry, where the decision to abandon an oil well depends on expected future benefits, not the past costs of drilling.

SUNSET INDUSTRY mature industry at the end of the product life cycle. For example, the buggy whip industry was a *sunset industry*.

SUNSET PROVISION condition in a law or regulation that includes its own expiration date unless specifically reinstated by legislation.

SUNSHINE LAW state or federal law, also called *government in the sunshine law,* that requires most meetings of regulatory bodies to be held in public and most of their decisions and records to be disclosed.

SUPERCOMPUTERS extremely powerful and technologically advanced computers used for solving complex and computationally intensive scientific or engineering problems. These computers are extremely expensive.

SUPERFUND account established by the federal government to be spent on cleaning up areas polluted with hazardous waste when no other source is available for payment.

SUPERINTENDENT person who has oversight and charge of a department in an organization; senior manager.

SUPERMARKET large self-service food store selling groceries, meats, household goods, and so on, usually on a cash-and-carry basis. To be classified as a supermarket, it is necessary to have sales of at least $2 million.

SUPERSTORE self-service store having a large selling area and carrying a large diversified assortment of food and nonfood items. Superstores carry everything from lawn items, to automotive accessories, electronic consumer goods, clothing, and groceries.

SUPPLEMENTAL AGREEMENT agreement that amends a previous agreement and contains additional conditions.

SUPPLEMENTAL SECURITY INCOME also called SSI, one of five programs in the Social Security system, under which monthly payments are made to people with both low income and few assets. Disability payments may also be made under the SSI program.

SUPPLEMENTAL UNEMPLOYMENT BENEFITS payments received by terminated employees from an employer-financed fund, which are not UNEMPLOYMENT COMPENSATION. These payments are taxable as wages and subject to income tax withholding but not subject to Social Security, Medicare, or federal unemployment taxes.

SUPPLEMENTAL WAGES include bonuses, commissions, overtime pay, and certain SICK PAY. An employer can withhold income tax at a flat 25% rate or use the same method as for regular wages.

SUPPLEMENTAL YOUNG CHILD (SYC) CREDIT *see* EARNED INCOME TAX CREDIT.

SUPPLIER one who supplies materials, products, or services to others; firm in either the wholesale or the retail supply business.

SUPPLY
1. amount of a commodity offered at a given price or available for meeting a demand.
2. to give or furnish (something needed or desirable) to others.

SUPPLY AND DEMAND CURVES, SUPPLY AND DEMAND EQUI-LIBRIUM graphic representation of supply and demand schedules of a particular market. The point at which the supply and demand curves intersect demonstrates the EQUILIBRIUM point of the market; equilibrium price and equilibrium quantity supplied.

SUPPLY AND DEMAND CURVES

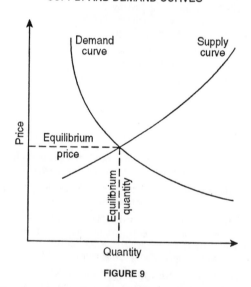

FIGURE 9

SUPPLY CHAIN MANAGEMENT (SCM) tracking the movement of and demand for components used to manufacture a product across a variety of potential and actual suppliers, known as the *supply chain,* to provide insight and the ability to respond instantly to shortages, surpluses, and changes in market conditions. It seeks to optimize production, decrease manufacturing time, minimize inventory, streamline order fulfillment, and reduce cost.

SUPPLY PRICE price, according to a supply schedule or supply curve, that is necessary to get producers to produce a given quantity of a good or service.

SUPPLY-SIDE ECONOMICS theory of economics contending that drastic reductions in tax rates will stimulate productive investment by corporations and wealthy individuals, to the benefit of the entire society; championed in the late 1970s by Professor Arthur Laffer. *See also* LAFFER CURVE.

SUPPORT LEVEL price level at which a security tends to stop falling because there is more demand than supply.

SUPPORT TEST one of five tests for claiming a person as a DEPENDENT. The taxpayer must provide more than half of a person's total support during a calendar year to meet the support test. Support includes amounts spent to provide food, lodging, clothing, education, medical and dental care, recreation, transportation, and similar necessities.

SUPREME COURT highest appellate court or court of last resort in the federal court system and in most states. The constitutionality of a tax law and a small number of tax decisions by Courts of Appeal are reviewed by the U.S. Supreme Court under its *certiorari* procedure.

SURCHARGE charge added to a charge, cost added to a cost, or tax added to a tax. *See also* SURTAX.

SURETY BOND contract by which one party agrees to make good the default or debt of another. Actually, three parties are involved: the *principal,* who has primary responsibility to perform the obligation (after which the bond becomes void), the *surety,* the individual with the secondary responsibility of performing the obligation if the principal fails to perform; and the *obligee,* to whom the right of performance *(obligation) is* owed.

SURFING *(slang)* browsing or exploring a NETWORK or the WORLD WIDE WEB to find places of interest, usually without a specific goal in mind. Analogous to "channel surfing" with a TV remote control.

SURPLUS
  In general: any excess amount.
  Finance: remainder of a fund appropriated for a particular purpose. In corporations, *surplus* denotes assets left after liabilities and debts, including capital stock, have been deducted. *See also* EARNED SURPLUS.

SURRENDER cancellation of a LEASE by mutual consent of the lessor and the lessee.

SURVEY
  1. process by which a parcel of land is measured and its area ascertained.
  2. plan showing the measurements, boundaries, area, and contours.

SURVEY AREA
1. geographic location represented by a sample group in a study.
2. geographic area in a radio market.

SURVEYOR one who prepares SURVEYS.

SURVIVING SPOUSE a widow or widower. A surviving spouse may file a JOINT RETURN with the deceased spouse in the year of death and may use joint return tax rates for two years following the death of the deceased spouse if the survivor remains unmarried and maintains a home for a child, adopted child, stepchild, or foster child for whom he or she is entitled to a DEPENDENCY EXEMPTION.

SURVIVORSHIP the right of a joint tenant or tenants to maintain ownership rights following the death of another joint tenant. Survivorship prevents HEIRS of the deceased from making claims against the property.

SURVIVORS PROGRAM a program in the Social Security System, under which a lump-sum payment and monthly payments are made to a qualifying worker's survivors.

SUSPENDED TRADING temporary halt in trading in a particular security, in advance of a major news announcement or to correct an imbalance of orders to buy and sell.

SUSPENSE ACCOUNT in accounting, account used temporarily to carry receipts, disbursements, or discrepancies, pending their analysis and permanent classification.

SUSPENSION disciplinary action for a stated period of time against an employee. A suspension is less critical than a discharge or dismissal. An employee can resume employment after the suspension period has elapsed.

SUSTAINABLE BUSINESS business environment that does not overwhelm the ecosystem, allowing sufficient environmental resources to remain for future generations. *See also* ECOLOGY.

SWAP to exchange one investment for another. A swap may be executed to change the maturities of a bond portfolio or the quality of the issues in a stock or bond portfolio, or because investment objectives have shifted. *See also* INTEREST RATE SWAP.

SWEAT EQUITY value added to a property by improvements resulting from work performed personally by the owner. *See also* UNEARNED INCREMENT.

SWEATSHOP place of employment having unacceptable working conditions. Sweatshops are commonly characterized by low pay, poor working conditions, safety violations, and generally inhumane treatment of employees.

SWEEPSTAKES popular type of SALES PROMOTIONS where lavish prizes are offered to entrants who have only to submit entries with their name and address by return mail or at a location determined by the sweepstakes sponsor, usually in a retail outlet where the sponsor's products are sold.

SWEETENER feature added to a securities offering to make it more attractive to purchasers. A bond may have the *sweetener* of convertibility into common stock added, for instance. *See also* KICKER.

SWIFT (SOCIETY FOR WORLDWIDE INTERBANK FINANCIAL TELECOMMUNICATIONS) an interbank telecommunications network for confirming international funds transfers.

SWING SHIFT work shift in industry from midafternoon until midnight or until the midnight shift.

SWITCHING moving assets from one MUTUAL FUND to another, either within a family of funds or between different fund families.

SWOT ANALYSIS evaluation of a company's Strengths, Weaknesses, Opportunities, and Threats; often a component of STRATEGIC PLANNING or a BUSINESS PLAN.

SYD SUM-OF-THE-YEARS'-DIGITS (method of depreciation).

SYMPATHETIC STRIKE strike by workers with no direct dispute against management to display solidarity with another striking union. Sympathy strikes give added power to labor by presenting a united front.

SYNDICATE group of individuals or companies who have formed a joint venture to undertake a project that the individuals would be unable or unwilling to pursue alone. A syndicate may be treated as a partnership or corporation for tax purposes.

SYNDICATION method of selling property whereby a sponsor, or syndicator, sells interests to investors. It may take the form of a partnership, limited partnership, tenancy in common, corporation, limited liability company, or S Corporation. For example, a syndication was formed whereby limited partnership interests were sold to investors. The partnership bought land with the equity raised.

SYNDICATION COSTS expenditures incurred for promoting and marketing interests, which are capitalized as an intangible asset (and not deductible or amortizable).

SYNDICATOR person in business who sells an investment in shares or units. *See also* SYNDICATE.

SYNERGY action of a combined enterprise to produce results greater than the sum of the separate enterprises. For example, a merger of two oil companies, one with a superior distribution network and the other with more reserves, would have synergy and would be expected to result in higher earnings per share than before.

SYNTAX in a computer programming language, set of rules that specify how the language symbols can be put together to form meaningful statements. If a program violates the language syntax rules, a *syntax error* is noted.

SYNTHETIC LEASE rental agreement that shifts all obligations, risks, and costs of the property to the tenant. The owner receives an absolute fixed rent. Also called *credit-tenant lease.*

SYNTHETIC SYSTEM production process that combines two or more materials or parts to complete a finished product.

SYSTEM organization of functionally interactive units for the achievement of a common goal. All systems have inputs, outputs, and feedback, and maintain a basic level of equilibrium. For example, in the human body the heart functions to support the circulatory system, which is vital to the survival of the entire body.

SYSTEMATIC RISK that part of a security's risk that is common to all securities of the same general class (stocks and bonds) and thus cannot be eliminated by DIVERSIFICATION; also known as *market* risk. The measure of systematic risk in stocks is the BETA COEFFICIENT.

SYSTEMATIC SAMPLING sampling procedure beginning with one randomly selected observation, and then sampling each nth observation within the population. Door-to-door surveys are often completed on a systematic basis. If 10% of 100 residences require sampling, a random number from 1 to 10 would be selected. If 5 was drawn, residences to be surveyed would be 5, 15, 25, 35, 45, 55, 65, 75, 85, and 95.

SYSTEM PROGRAM product of the computer manufacturer to aid the user in easily and productively operating the system. *See also* OPERATING SYSTEM.

SYSTEMS PROGRAMMER person who writes the programs needed for a computer system to function, such as operating systems, language processors and compilers, and data file management programs. Systems programming, which is usually done in an assembly language, requires considerable knowledge of the particular computer system being used.

T

TABLE coherent and systematic presentation of data and data calculations combined with textual descriptions for the purpose of conveying understanding of particular findings and information. A SPREADSHEET is a typical example.

TABLET PC a notebook computer with a sensitive screen, running under a special version of the WINDOWS operating system. Using a special pen instead of a keyboard or mouse, a user can write directly on the screen, much as one would write on a tablet or slate. Built-in handwriting recognition technology converts the handwritten input to editable text; text can also be entered on an onscreen keyboard display, and some Tablet PCs, similar to NOTEBOOK COMPUTERS, have attached keyboards. Unlike a touch screen, the Tablet PC screen receives information only from the complementary pen, not a stylus, finger, or any other pressure.

TABLOID newspaper with a page size smaller than that of the standard newspaper. Approximate page dimensions are 14″ deep by 10″ to 12″ wide, with five or six columns each 2″ wide. A tabloid typically contains news in condensed form, with a great many photographs—for example, the *New York Post*. A tabloid has the appearance of an unbound magazine and is sold flat, rather than folded in half, as is the standard-size newspaper.

T-ACCOUNT in accounting, using two perpendicular lines that look like the capital letter T to represent an account of any title. The account name is put above the horizontal line, DEBITS are on the left side below the line and CREDITS on the right.

TACTIC short-term method for resolving a particular problem. For example, a *tactic* for quickly increasing a product market share may be a television advertising blitz.

TACTICAL OBJECTIVES performance targets established by middle management for achieving specific organizational outcomes. Also called *tactical plans.*

TAFT-HARTLEY ACT popular name for the Labor-Management Relations Act of 1947, whose stated purpose is to protect employers' rights to resist unionization and restrict union activities. It imposes on unions many of the conditions for good faith bargaining that were imposed on management by earlier laws.

TAG SALE garage sale where individuals mark used household items with tags displaying the price. Tag sales are commonly held on weekends at the vendor's home, often having the merchandise displayed in the driveway. Tag sales are an American tradition.

TAKE

In general: (1) profit realized from a transaction; (2) gross receipts of a lottery or gambling enterprise; (3) open to bribery, as in *being on the take.*

Law: to seize possession of property. When a debtor defaults on a debt backed by COLLATERAL, that property is taken back by the creditor.

Securities: act of accepting an OFFER price in a transaction between brokers or dealers.

TAKE A BATH, TAKE A BEATING to suffer a large loss on a product, SPECULATION, or investment, as in "I took a bath on my XYZ stock when the market dropped last week."

TAKE A FLIER to speculate, that is, to buy securities with the knowledge that the investment is highly risky.

TAKE A POSITION

1. to buy stock in a company with the intent of holding for the long term or, possibly, of taking control of the company. An acquirer who *takes a position* of 5% or more of a company's outstanding stock must file information with the Securities and Exchange Commission, with the exchange on which the target company is listed, and with the target company itself.
2. to hold stocks or bonds in inventory. A position may be either long or short. *See also* LONG POSITION; SHORT POSITION.

TAKE-HOME PAY amount of wages a worker actually receives after all deductions, including taxes, have been made.

TAKEOFF point in the development and growth of a producer, an industry, or an economy at which it becomes economically viable.

TAKE-OR-PAY an arrangement whereby a customer agrees to buy a certain quantity over a period of time, often at a predetermined price. If the customer does not buy as contracted, he must pay the seller. This protects the buyer against price rises and the seller against price drops.

TAKEOUT

Real estate: long-term mortgage loan made to refinance a short-term CONSTRUCTION LOAN (interim loan).

Securities: withdrawal of cash from a brokerage account, usually after a sale and purchase have resulted in a net credit balance.

TAKE-OUT LOAN, TAKE-OUT FINANCING COMMITMENT to provide permanent financing following construction of a planned project. The take-out commitment is generally predicated upon specific conditions, such as a certain percentage of unit sales or leases, for the permanent loan to take out the construction loan. Most construction lenders require take-out financing.

TAKEOVER change in the controlling interest of a corporation. A takeover may be in the form of a friendly acquisition and merger or an unfriendly bid that the management of the TARGET COMPANY might fight with SHARK REPELLENT techniques.

TAKING
1. acquisition of a parcel of land through CONDEMNATION.
2. in land use law, application of POLICE POWER restrictions to a parcel of land that are so restrictive as to preclude any reasonable use.

TAKING DELIVERY
In general: accepting receipt of goods from a COMMON CARRIER or other shipper, usually documented by signing a BILL OF LADING or other form of receipt.
Commodities: accepting physical delivery of a commodity under a FUTURES CONTRACT or SPOT MARKET contract.
Securities: accepting receipt of stock or bond certificates that have been recently purchased or transferred from another account.

TAKING INVENTORY physical counting and valuation of stock in trade; typically performed annually at year-end, but may be performed more frequently or at other times. *See also* PHYSICAL INVENTORY.

TALL ORGANIZATION traditional hierarchical organization having many supervisory levels and a narrow SPAN OF CONTROL.

TALLY count of some specific items; usually associated with keeping a vote tally. *See also* TALLYMAN.

TALLYMAN
1. person who carries on a tally trade or supplies goods on credit to be paid for by installments.
2. person who tallies or keeps the count of anything, for example, votes; clerk who tallies or checks a cargo in loading or discharging. *See also* TALLY.

TANGIBLE ASSET any ASSET having physical existence, like real estate, gold, or machinery.

TANGIBLE PERSONAL PROPERTY property that may be seen or touched, but is not real estate. The method by which a fixture is attached is considered when determining whether the fixture becomes real estate or remains tangible personal property.

TANK CAR in transportation equipment, vehicle that carries liquids, such as a railroad car that carries milk.

TAPE
1. service that reports prices and size of transactions on major exchanges; also called *ticker tape* because of the sound made by the machine that printed the tape before the process was computerized.
2. service of Dow Jones and other news wires.
3. magnetic computer storage medium. It is much the same as ordinary tape-recorder tape, and some personal computers can store

information on ordinary cassette tapes. Tape is cheaper than DISKS but slower to record and access.

TAPE DRIVE device that converts information stored on magnetic TAPE into signals that can be sent to a computer.

TARE WEIGHT weight of any empty container, such as an empty truck or packing material.

TARGET AUDIENCE audience to whom the advertising is directed. The target audience is defined in terms of DEMOGRAPHIC (and sometimes psychographic) characteristics, such as age, sex, education, income, buying habits, and the like.

TARGET COMPANY firm that has been chosen as attractive for TAKEOVER by a potential acquirer.

TARGET MARKET group of persons for whom a firm creates and maintains a PRODUCT MIX that specifically fits the needs and preferences of that group.

TARGET PRICE
Finance: price at which an acquirer aims to buy a company in a TAKEOVER.
Manufacturing: maximum wholesale or retail price for a product being developed.
Options: price of the underlying security after which a certain option will become profitable to its buyer.

TARIFF
1. federal tax (usually AD VALOREM) on imports or exports usually imposed either to raise revenue (called a *revenue tariff*) or to protect domestic firms from import competition (called a *protective tariff*).
2. schedule of rates or charges, usually for freight.

TARIFF WAR international trade war featuring the counterbalancing of national tariff rates in retaliation for another nation's tariff rates. The ultimate objective is to gain a trade advantage over other nations, but it is almost always self-defeating.

TASK FORCE temporary team of people assembled to achieve a specific objective, usually involving investigative activities. Often used in private and public organizations, a task force actively pursues the achievement of its mission, after which it is disbanded.

TASK GROUP similar to a work group, but operating within a larger organizational context. A task group is charged with the responsibility for making a specific contribution to the goals of the parent organization. Some task groups may pursue ongoing responsibilities, such as a pension review board, while others are oriented to a short-term task, such as preparing a new product proposal.

TASK MANAGEMENT management procedure for coordinating the sequence of procedures and materials for the completion of various tasks.

TAX rate or sum of money assessed on a citizen's person, property, or activity for the support of government, levied upon assets or real property, upon income, or upon the sale or purchase of goods. Examples include AD VALOREM TAX, EXCISE TAX, INCOME TAX, PROPERTY TAX, SALES TAX, ESTATE TAX, school tax, and USE TAX.

TAX ABATEMENT reprieve from a tax obligation. Tax abatements vary from partial to complete, according to how much of the tax is forgiven. Tax abatements are often given by governments as an incentive for real estate or industrial development.

TAXABLE ESTATE result of subtracting any marital deduction and charitable contributions from the ADJUSTED GROSS ESTATE.

TAXABLE INCOME
1. *Individuals:* GROSS INCOME reduced by deductions allowable in obtaining ADJUSTED GROSS INCOME and further reduced by the STANDARD DEDUCTION or ITEMIZED DEDUCTIONS and allowed PERSONAL EXEMPTIONS.
2. *Corporations:* total income reduced by total deductions, NET OPERATING LOSS deduction, and special dividend deductions.
3. *Trusts and estates:* total income reduced by allowable expenses, income distribution deduction, and specific exemption.
4. *Other:* any amount of income subject to income tax, such as excess net PASSIVE INCOME and BUILT-IN GAINS for an S CORPORATION, and undistributed personal holding company income for a PERSONAL HOLDING COMPANY.

TAXABLE VALUE *see* ASSESSED VALUATION.

TAXABLE YEAR period (usually 12 months) during which the tax liability of an individual or entity is calculated; in the case of certain nontaxable entities, period for which tax information is provided. *See also* SHORT YEAR.

TAX ACCOUNTING accounting specialization focusing on tax preparation and planning.

TAX AND LOAN ACCOUNT account in a private-sector depository institution, held in the name of the district Federal Reserve Bank as fiscal agent of the United States, that serves as a repository for operating cash available to the U.S. Treasury. Withheld income taxes, employers' contributions to the Social Security fund, and payments for U.S. government securities routinely go into a tax and loan account.

TAX ANTICIPATION BILL (TAB) short-term obligation issued by the U.S. Treasury in competitive bidding at maturities ranging from 23 to 273 days. TABs typically come due within five to seven days after the quarterly due dates for corporate tax payments, but corporations can tender them at PAR VALUE on those tax deadlines in payment of taxes without forfeiting interest income.

TAX ANTICIPATION NOTE (TAN) short-term obligation of a state or municipal government to finance current expenditures pending receipt of expected tax payments. TAN debt evens out the cash flow and is retired once corporate and individual tax revenues are received.

TAX ASSESSOR *see* ASSESSOR.

TAXATION, INTEREST ON DIVIDENDS interest earned on dividends from a *participating life insurance policy* left on deposit with the insurance company and subject to taxation.

TAX AUDIT *see* AUDIT.

TAX AVOIDANCE tax reduction methods permitted by law, such as the deferral of income into the following year. *See also* AVOIDANCE OF TAX; *contrast with* TAX EVASION.

TAX BASE collective value of property, income and other taxable activity or assets subject to a tax. Tax revenues are computed at the tax base times the tax rate. For property taxation, the tax base is the total assessed value of all taxable property less exemptions.

TAX BASIS *see* BASIS.

TAX BENEFIT RULE states that:
1. if a taxpayer recovers an amount that was deducted or credited against tax in a previous year, the recovery must be included in income to the extent that the deduction or credit reduced the tax liability in the earlier year. If no tax benefit was derived from a prior-year deduction or credit, the recovery does not have to be included in income.
2. if a taxpayer repays an amount that was previously included in taxable income, the repayment can be deducted in the year in which it is repaid.

TAX BRACKET point on the income tax rate schedules where an individual's taxable income—that is, income subject to tax after exemptions and deductions—lands. Also called the *marginal tax bracket,* it is expressed as a percentage to be applied to each additional dollar earned over the base amount for that bracket. *See also* AVERAGE TAX BRACKET; MARGINAL TAX BRACKET.

TAX COURT independent 19-judge federal administrative agency that functions as a court to hear appeals by taxpayers from adverse administrative decisions by the INTERNAL REVENUE SERVICE. The Tax Court does not require the taxpayer to pay the alleged deficiency prior to suit. An adverse decision may be appealed as of right to the Court of Appeals and in rare cases to the U.S. Supreme Court.

TAX CREDIT dollar-for-dollar reduction in the amount of tax that a taxpayer owes. Unlike DEDUCTIONS or EXEMPTIONS, which reduce the amount of income subject to tax, a *credit* reduces the actual amount of tax owed; *see* specific credits, such as CHILD CARE CREDIT, EARNED INCOME CREDIT, REHABILITATION TAX CREDIT, TUITION TAX CREDIT, and ELDERLY OR DISABLED TAX CREDIT.

TAX CREDIT FOR ELDERLY AND DISABLED TAXPAYERS *see* ELDERLY OR DISABLED TAX CREDIT.

TAX DEDUCTIBLE applies to an expense that can be used to reduce TAXABLE INCOME. Interest on housing and AD VALOREM taxes are generally tax deductible. DEPRECIATION, repairs, maintenance, utilities, and other ORDINARY and NECESSARY EXPENSES are tax deductible for businesses. *See also* DEDUCTION; TAX DEDUCTION.

TAX DEDUCTION reduction of TAXABLE income. *See also* TAX CREDIT; TAX DEDUCTIBLE; and specific deductions, such as INTEREST DEDUCTIONS and MEDICAL EXPENSE DEDUCTION.

TAX DEED INSTRUMENT given to a GRANTEE by a government that has claimed the property for unpaid taxes.

TAX-DEFERRED refers to an investment whose accumulated earnings are free from taxation until the investor takes possession of the assets. *See also* TAX-DEFERRED ANNUITY; TAX-DEFERRED EXCHANGE.

TAX-DEFERRED ANNUITY (TDA) retirement vehicle permitted under Section 403(b) of the U.S. Internal Revenue Code for employees of a public school system or a qualified charitable organization. Under such an agreement, the maximum annual contribution in 2006 is $15,000 plus up to $4,000 of CATCH-UP CONTRIBUTIONS for those over age 50 who are eligible. Cash value and dividends accrue but are not taxed until the ANNUITANT actually receives benefits. At that time, the ANNUITANT is taxed only on the amount that exceeds the investment in the annuity.

TAX-DEFERRED (TAX-FREE) EXCHANGE exchange of one piece of property for another, often both real estate, under SECTION 1031 of the INTERNAL REVENUE CODE. *See also* LIKE-KIND PROPERTY, TAX-FREE EXCHANGE, DELAYED.

TAX DEPOSIT payment of federal tax liability through a Federal Reserve Bank or a commercial bank that has been designated as a U.S. depository. The types of taxes deposited, rather than paid directly to the IRS, include corporate income taxes, excise taxes, withheld income and employment taxes, and income tax withheld from payments to foreign taxpayers.

TAX DISTRICT *see* CENTRAL ASSESSMENT DISTRICT.

TAX-EQUIVALENT YIELD pretax yield that a taxable BOND would have to pay to equal the tax-free yield of a MUNICIPAL BOND in an investor's tax bracket. To calculate the *tax-equivalent yield*, an investor must subtract his or her MARGINAL TAX BRACKET from 100, which results in the *tax bracket reciprocal*. This figure must then be divided by the yield of the tax-free municipal bond. The result is the yield that a taxable bond would have to pay to give the investor the same after-tax return.

TAX EVASION any method of reducing taxes not permitted by law. It carries heavy penalties. Involves deceit, subterfuge, camouflage, concealment, or an attempt to color or obscure events. *Tax evasion* is to be distinguished from TAX AVOIDANCE, which denotes the legal interpretation of relevant tax laws to minimize tax liability.

TAX-EXEMPT INCOME includes certain Social Security benefits, welfare benefits, nontaxable life insurance proceeds, armed forces family allotments, nontaxable pensions, and tax-exempt interest. For purposes of the SUPPORT TEST for the dependency exemption, tax-exempt income is included in total support.

TAX EXEMPTION *see* EXEMPTION.

TAX-EXEMPT ORGANIZATION *see* NOT FOR PROFIT.

TAX-EXEMPT PROPERTY real property that is not subject to AD VALOREM property taxes. In many local communities, churches, HOMESTEADS, and government land and buildings are tax exempt.

TAX-EXEMPT SECURITY obligation whose interest is exempt from taxation by federal, state, and/or local authorities. It is frequently called a MUNICIPAL BOND, even though it may have been issued by a state government or agency, or by a county or other political district or subdivision rather than a city or town.

TAX FORECLOSURE process of enforcing a LIEN against property for nonpayment of delinquent property taxes. Taxing authorities hold a superior lien against all taxable property to enforce the payment of their taxes.

TAX-FREE EXCHANGE exchange of one piece of property for another, often both real estate, under SECTION 1031 of the INTERNAL REVENUE CODE.

TAX-FREE EXCHANGE, DELAYED a transaction in which a property is traded for the promise to provide a replacement LIKE-KIND PROPERTY in the near future. Investment property or productive property used in a trade or business can be sold with the tax on the gain deferred, provided replacement property is identified within 45 days and closed within 180 days. The taxpayer may not receive cash and then use the cash to purchase the replacement property. Other strict requirements must be observed. *See also* LIKE-KIND EXCHANGE; SECTION 1031; TAX-FREE EXCHANGE.

TAX IMPACT effect of a tax upon production and consumption of the good being taxed; also effect of a tax upon an economic process, such as consumption or production.

TAX INCENTIVE feature of the taxation system that encourages or discourages certain economic activities. Common *tax incentives* are DEPRECIATION allowances and TAX CREDITS.

TAX INCIDENCE *see* INCIDENCE OF TAX.

TAX LIEN an encumbrance placed upon property as a claim for payment of a TAX LIABILITY. Gives constructive notice to other creditors of a tax liability. It can attach to any property owned by the taxpayer or acquired after the lien is placed. A tax lien may be imposed for failure to pay city, county, estate, income, payroll, property, sales, or school taxes. The lien continues until the tax liability is satisfied or becomes unenforceable; *see* STATUTE OF LIMITATIONS.

TAX LOOPHOLE *see* LOOPHOLE.

TAX LOSS CARRYBACK or **CARRYOVER** tax benefit that allows a taxpayer to use losses from one year to reduce tax liability in another year. A TAXPAYER may carry a NET OPERATING LOSS back to the two immediately preceding years for the purpose of obtaining a refund of taxes previously paid. After applying the carryback, a net operating loss may be carried forward up to 20 years.

A CORPORATION may carry a net CAPITAL LOSS back for three years, then carry over any remaining losses for five years. The capital losses may offset CAPITAL GAINS only and not operating income. The carryover is treated as a short-term capital loss and may not increase a net operating loss in the carryback year.

An individual may not carry back a capital loss but may carry it over to offset future capital gains and to reduce ordinary income by up to $3,000 annually until the loss is exhausted.

TAX MAP document showing the location, dimensions, and other information pertaining to a PARCEL of land subject to PROPERTY TAXES. Maps are generally bound into books and kept as public records at the local tax office.

TAXPAYER any person who is determined to bear the liability for a tax. In connection with the IRS and tax law, the term *person* includes an individual, a CORPORATION, a PARTNERSHIP, a TRUST or ESTATE, a joint-stock company, an association, or a SYNDICATE, group, POOL, JOINT VENTURE, or other unincorporated organization or group.

TAXPAYER IDENTIFICATION NUMBER (TIN) identifying number assigned to a taxpayer. The TIN for an individual is the individual's Social Security number. An EMPLOYER IDENTIFICATION NUMBER (EIN) is used for corporations, partnerships, estates and trusts.

TAX PLANNING systematic analysis of differing tax options aimed at the minimization of tax liability in current and future tax periods. Whether to file jointly or separately, the timing of a sale of an asset, ascertaining over how many years to withdraw retirement funds, when to receive income, when to pay expenditures, the timing and amounts of gifts to be made, and ESTATE PLANNING are examples of tax planning. TAX SOFTWARE can be used for tax planning purposes.

TAX PREFERENCE ITEM item of income, tax deduction, or tax credit deemed to be an extra benefit according to the federal tax law. Such items are thought to result in preferential treatment that may lead to excessively low tax liability for certain taxpayers. Therefore, an ALTERNATIVE MINIMUM TAX is imposed on the aggregate of a taxpayer's tax preference items and adjustments in an attempt to insure a minimum tax liability.

TAX RATE percentage rate of TAX imposed. Tax liability is computed by applying the applicable tax rate to the tax base. *See also* EFFECTIVE TAX RATE; MARGINAL TAX RATE.

TAX RATE SCHEDULES must be used by taxpayers with TAXABLE INCOME of $100,000 or more. Most other taxpayers use the more detailed *tax tables*.

TAX REFORM ACT OF 1986 most sweeping tax legislation since the beginning of World War II, having the objective of requiring people with the same amount of income to pay the same amount of taxes. It reduced the importance of tax incentives to cure social and economic problems and instead relied on taxes as a means to collect revenues.

TAX REFUND refund of overpaid taxes from the government to the taxpayer. Refunds are due when the taxpayer has been overwithholding or has overestimated income or underestimated deductions, exemptions, and credits.

TAX RETURN form used for providing information concerning TAXABLE INCOME. To report income to the Internal Revenue Service, individuals use Form 1040, 1040A, or 1040EZ; corporations use Form 1120 or 1120A; S corporations use Form 1120S; and partnerships use Form 1065. There may also be forms for state or other income tax. Supporting schedules may also be filed. Forms may be downloaded from the IRS web site *http://www.irs.gov*.

TAX RETURN PREPARER anyone who is paid to prepare, assist in preparing, or review a tax return. Paid preparers must sign the tax returns they have prepared, assisted in preparing, or reviewed. A paid preparer is not required to have any special education or certification.

TAX ROLL listing and description of all taxable property within a tax jurisdiction. It includes assessed value and assessed amounts. *See also* TAX BASE.

TAX SALE sale of property after a period of nonpayment of taxes. The grantee receives a TAX DEED. In most states, the defaulting party has a redemption period during which he may pay the unpaid taxes, interest, court costs, and the purchase price to redeem the property.

TAX SELLING selling of securities, usually at year end, to realize losses in a PORTFOLIO, which can be used to offset capital gains and thereby lower an investor's tax liability.

TAX SHELTER prior to October 23, 2004, defined by the IRS (in brief) as any investment with a greater than 2:1 ratio of deductions plus 350% of the credits to the amount invested or any investment whose purpose was primarily the avoidance or evasion of income taxes. Such investments were required to be registered with the IRS. These rules have since been repealed. After October 22, 2004, each *material advisor* must file an information return with the IRS that includes information on every *reportable transaction* required by the IRS, to be described at a later date.

TAX SHIELD deductions that reduce tax liabilities. For example, mortgage interest, charitable contributions, unreimbursed business expenses, and property tax expenses can be considered *tax shields* if a taxpayer qualifies for the deduction. The higher the marginal tax rate, the more the deduction is worth.

TAX SOFTWARE software that helps taxpayers plan for and prepare their tax returns. Programs such as Turbo Tax and TaxCut help taxpayers analyze their tax situation and take actions to minimize tax liability. Different versions of tax software are appropriate for large and small businesses, partnerships, individuals, and estates.

TAX STATUS ELECTION selection of filing status for state and federal income taxes. Individuals may choose single, married filing jointly, married filing separately, or head of household. Businesses may elect C corporation, S corporation, limited partnership, or sole proprietorship status, among others. Taxpayers may choose to calculate their tax returns under two filing status categories to find out which status is more advantageous.

TAX STOP clause in a LEASE that stops a lessor from paying property taxes above a certain amount. *See also* ESCALATOR CLAUSE; STOP CLAUSE.

TAX STRADDLE technique formerly used to postpone liability for a year. An investor with a short-term capital gain would take a position in a commodities future or option so as to show a short-term "artificial" loss in the current tax year and realize a long-term gain the next tax year. Tax reform sharply curtailed this practice by requiring gains and losses on commodity transactions to be reported based on values at year end, even when the positions are not closed out. *See also* MARK TO THE MARKET.

TAX TREATIES treaties negotiated between the United States and other countries to avoid double taxation and to prevent tax evasion.

TAX WAIVER a document issued by the state specifically stating that the tax department consents to the transfer of the stock being presented for transfer. A *tax waiver* is often needed to settle an estate or to transfer ownership of real estate.

TAX WEDGE in economics, the effect of taxes that may inhibit a certain result. For example, if a tax on luxury cars results in selling 10%

fewer cars, the tax caused a wedge between the economic desires of producers and consumers.

TAX YEAR *see* CALENDAR TAX YEAR; FISCAL TAX YEAR.

TCP/IP *see* TRANSMISSION CONTROL PROTOCOL/INTERNET PROTOCOL.

T.D. Treasury Decision.

TEAM BUILDING ORGANIZATION DEVELOPMENT technique for improving a work group's performance and attitudes by clarifying its goals and its members' expectations of each other.

TEAM MANAGEMENT management of a prescribed set of activities by an organized work group in an organization. Team management includes setting goals and priorities, analyzing the group's work methods, and examining the team's decision-making processes.

TEASER AD brief advertisement designed to tease the public by offering only bits of information without revealing either the sponsor of the ad or the product being advertised. Teaser ads are the frontrunners of an advertising campaign, and their purpose is to arouse curiosity and get attention for the campaign that follows.

TEASER RATE INTEREST RATE, applied to a mortgage loan for a limited period of time, that is lower initially than the rate justified by the current value of the index that determines the interest rate charged on the loan. It is commonly offered on ADJUSTABLE-RATE MORTGAGES during the first year as a marketing technique.

TECHNICAL ANALYSIS research into the demand and supply for securities and commodities based on trading volume and price studies. Technical analysts use charts or computer programs to identify price trends in a market, security, or commodity future, which they think will foretell price movements. *Contrast with* FUNDAMENTAL ANALYSIS.

TECHNICAL RALLY short rise in securities or commodities futures prices within a general declining trend. Such a rally may result because investors are bargain-hunting or because analysts have noticed a particular SUPPORT LEVEL at which securities usually bounce up.

TECHNICAL SKILLS operational capabilities necessary to perform certain job specifications. WORD PROCESSING is a very widely used technical skill in many organizations.

TECHNOLOGICAL OBSOLESCENCE technology becoming outdated due to technological advances; technology that has been surpassed by newer technology. For example, word processing software has made traditional typewriters virtually obsolete.

TECHNOLOGICAL UNEMPLOYMENT UNEMPLOYMENT resulting from the application of new technology, either by eliminating jobs or by changing the nature of work so that those who had performed the work no longer have applicable skills to do so.

TECHNOLOGY developed applications for industry and the industrial arts; use of applied science for the development of technical applications. For example, desktop computers represent advanced electronic technology.

TELECOMMUNICATIONS transmission of messages by computers, telephone, telegram, or television.

TELECOMMUTING performing job-related requirements using TELECOMMUNICATIONS to transmit data and textual messages to the central organizational office without being physically present. Many of the job requirements of today's organizations involve information processing, which is the primary capability of telecommunications. *Telecommuting* utilizes telecommunications to accomplish these job requirements while avoiding all of the inconvenience and expense of physically commuting to work as well as requiring less organizational OVERHEAD.

TELEFACSIMILE *see* FACSIMILE TRANSMISSION (FAX).

TELEGRAM message sent by telegraphic equipment, which involves using coded signals over electronic wires. The message is phoned or delivered to the receiver within hours. Still used for money transfers; information transfers are now usually made by FAX; *see* FACSIMILE TRANSMISSION.

TELEGRAPH MONEY ORDER method of sending money to someone in urgent need of cash. The sender places cash with a telegraph office, which then wires the telegraph office at the city of destination to disburse the cash or acceptable equivalent (money order).

TELEMARKETING use of the telephone as an interactive medium for promotion or promotion response; also known as *teleselling*. Telemarketing as a response vehicle includes receiving orders, inquiries, and donation pledges in response to print and broadcast advertisements, catalogs, and direct-mail promotions, and also receiving customer inquiries and complaints.

TELEPHONE SWITCHING process of shifting assets from one MUTUAL FUND to another by telephone. Such a switch may be among the stock, bond, or money market funds of a single FAMILY OF FUNDS, or it may be from a fund in one family to a fund in another.

TELESELLING *see* TELEMARKETING.

TELEVISION SUPPORT advertisement broadcast on television to serve as a secondary part of a MULTIMEDIA campaign. For example, the television medium is sometimes used to announce a newspaper insert and/or to remind the viewer to read the insert. The insert will contain detailed information on the product or promotion not provided in the television broadcast and may include a reply form.

TELEX system of national and international telecommunication whereby messages can be sent from one typewriter to another, provided both users subscribe to the electronic service. The FAX machine has generally replaced the telex.

TEMPLATE

1. any sort of pattern, especially one cut from plastic or thin metal, similar to a stencil. Templates with flowcharting symbols facilitate the drafting of flowcharts.
2. in computer use, particular pattern for a frequently used spreadsheet or data-base program. Storing the template saves the user from having to retype the specifications each time the program is used.

TENANCY

1. right of possession of real property.
2. right to possess an ESTATE, whether by LEASE or by TITLE.
3. holding in subordination to another's title, as in the landlordtenant relationship. *See also* JOINT TENANCY; TENANCY IN COMMON.

TENANCY AT SUFFERANCE TENANCY established when a person who had been a lawful tenant wrongfully remains in possession of property after expiration of a LEASE. A tenant at sufferance may be ejected from the property any time the landlord decides to do so.

TENANCY AT WILL LICENSE to use or occupy lands and buildings at the will of the owner. The tenant may decide to leave the property at any time or must leave at the landlord's will. Agreement may be oral or written. *See also* EMBLEMENT.

TENANCY BY THE ENTIRETY ESTATE that exists only between husband and wife with equal right of possession and enjoyment during their joint lives and with the right of survivorship; that is, when one dies, the property goes to the surviving tenant. It is recognized in some states.

TENANCY FOR YEARS LEASE for a fixed term, such as two months, three years, ten years, and so on.

TENANCY IN COMMON ownership of realty by two or more persons, each of whom has an UNDIVIDED INTEREST, without the RIGHT OF SURVIVORSHIP. Upon the death of one of the owners, the ownership share of the decedent is inherited by the party or parties designated in the decedent's will. *See also* JOINT TENANCY; PARTITION; SYNDICATION; TENANCY BY THE ENTIRETY.

TENANCY IN SEVERALTY ownership of property by one person or one legal entity (corporate ownership).

TENANT

1. one who leases PREMISES from the owner (landlord) or from a tenant as a subtenant.
2. one who holds land by any kind of TITLE or right, whether permanently or temporarily.
3. one who purchases an ESTATE and is entitled to possession, whether exclusive or to be shared with others.

TENANT FINISH-OUT ALLOWANCE monetary allowance given to a prospective retail or office tenant in recognition of the tenant's individual needs to acquire, build or move walls, partitions, and light fixtures; usually expressed in dollars per square foot.

TENANT FIXTURES fixtures added to leased real estate by lessees, which, by contract or by law, may be removed by the lessee upon expiration of the lease.

TENANT IMPROVEMENTS (TIs) those changes, typically to office, retail, or industrial property, to accommodate specific needs of a tenant. TIs include installation or relocation of interior walls or partitions, carpeting or other floor covering, shelves, windows, toilets, etc. The cost of these is negotiated in the lease.

TENANT REIMBURSEMENTS especially in shopping centers and office buildings, amounts paid by a tenant to a landlord for the tenant's share of expenses. Frequently encountered in NET LEASES and leases with STOP CLAUSES.

TENANT REPRESENTATIVE broker who represents tenants, trying to find the best property to lease and negotiating the most favorable transaction terms.

TENDER unconditional offer to pay or perform in full an obligation to another, together with actual presentation of the thing or sum owed, or some clear manifestation of ability to pay or perform. *See also* LEGAL TENDER.

TENDER OF DELIVERY seller's placement at the buyer's disposal of goods sold to him. A seller's failure to tender delivery according to contract may constitute a BREACH unless he has a lawful excuse; a buyer's refusal to take delivery may constitute a breach on his part.

TENDER OFFER public offer made to shareholders of a particular corporation to purchase from them a specific number of shares of stock at a specific price. The price quoted in such an offer may be payable only if the offerer is able to obtain the total amount of stock specified in the offer.

TENEMENT permanent and fixed property, including both corporeal and incorporeal real property. In modern usage, tenement applies to any structure attached to land and also to any kind of dwelling inhabited by a tenant. *Tenement* is frequently used to mean dilapidated apartment dwellings.

10-K REPORT *see* FORM 10-K.

10-Q *see* FORM 10-Q.

TENURE
  1. nature of an occupant's ownership rights; indication of whether one is an owner or a tenant.

2. length of time one has been employed by a certain company, with important implications in cases of layoffs.
3. academic privilege granted to associate and full professors, allowing freedom of speech (academic freedom) and conveying implications of continued employment except in extraordinary circumstances.

TENURE IN LAND mode in which a person holds an ESTATE in land.

TEN-YEAR AVERAGING a method of calculating income tax on a lump-sum distribution from a QUALIFIED BENEFIT PLAN that reduces a beneficiary's tax liability on the distribution. It is available only to a participant who was 50 years of age or older before January 1, 1986, and had been a participant in the plan for at least five years before the year of distribution.

TERM
1. period of time during which the conditions of a CONTRACT will be carried out. This may refer to the time in which loan payments must be made, or the time when interest payments will be made on a certificate of deposit or a bond. It also may refer to the length of time a life insurance policy is in force. *See also* TERM LIFE INSURANCE.
2. provision specifying the nature of an agreement or contract, as in *terms and conditions.*

TERM, AMORTIZATION period of time during which PRINCIPAL and INTEREST payments for a loan must be made. It is generally the time needed to amortize the loan fully. *See also* AMORTIZATION.

TERM BOND all the bonds of an issue mature at the same date. If a term bond has a CALL FEATURE, it may be redeemed at an earlier date. *Contrast with* SERIAL BOND.

TERM CERTIFICATE CERTIFICATE OF DEPOSIT with a long maturity date. Such CDs can range in length from one year to ten years, though the most popular term certificates are those for one or two years.

TERMINAL device that allows a user to communicate directly with a computer. A terminal must have a keyboard so that the user can type in instructions and input data, and a means of displaying output, such as a MONITOR or a printer. When a terminal cannot be used by itself as a computer, it is called a *dumb terminal.*

TERMINAL VALUE the remaining value or expected remaining value of a property at the end of a certain period, such as income projection period. *See also* REVERSIONARY VALUE.

TERMINATION BENEFITS amounts due employees who cease to work for the employer. The amount of the termination benefit may be in the form of an ANNUITY or LUMP-SUM payment.

TERM LIFE INSURANCE coverage that stays in effect for only a specified, limited period. If an insured dies within that period, the BEN-

EFICIARY receives the death payments. If the insured survives, the policy ends and the beneficiary receives nothing.

TERMINATION OF A PLAN either of two ways in which a pension plan can be terminated: standard and distress. A *standard termination* can occur only if the plan has enough money to fully fund the benefits or the plan sponsor agrees to pay the unfunded amount. The sponsor can choose to purchase annuities from an insurance company to cover the remaining benefits or pay lump sums to the participants. A *distress termination* can occur only for reasons of business necessity and is usually associated with bankruptcy.

TERM LOAN intermediate to long-term (typically two to ten years) secured CREDIT granted to a company by a commercial bank, insurance company, or commercial finance company, usually to finance capital equipment or provide working capital.

TERMS conditions and arrangements specified in a CONTRACT. A sales contract will generally include terms relating to the price, financing available to the buyer, contingencies based on the condition of the property, how to prorate closing costs, and items of personal property included in the sale.

TERRORISM nonconventional warfare strategy where many types of violent acts, including bombings, kidnapping, murder, and torture, are employed.

TEST
1. examination or final determination of a grade or score for measuring achievement.
2. proving, assaying, or trying a particular concept; for example, performing a marketing *test* on the consumer reaction to a product.

TESTAMENT will, generally used to dispose of personal property after death. Common usage employs the words *will, testament,* and *last will and testament* as synonyms.

TESTAMENTARY POWERS OF APPOINTMENT *see* POWERS OF APPOINTMENT.

TESTAMENTARY TRUST trust created by a WILL, as distinguished from an INTER VIVOS TRUST created during the lifetime of the grantor.

TESTATE having made a valid WILL. *Contrast with* INTESTATE.

TESTATOR (TESTATRIX) a person who makes a WILL. If one leaves no will, the property passes to one's HEIRS according to state law or reverts (escheats) to the state.

TESTCHECK substantiation of certain items in an account of financial record so the auditor can form an opinion as to the accuracy of the entire account or financial record. The items examined can be based on a representative sample. An example is testchecking every fifth entertainment expense voucher for supporting documentation and approval.

TESTIMONIAL statement of worth or value by a respected source. Testimonials are often used to certify the value of a particular product in its advertising. Testimonials provide credibility.

TESTIMONIUM clause that cites the act and date in a DEED or other CONVEYANCE. Before signing a deed, the grantor should make sure that everything is in order, such as the spelling of names and legal descriptions. A sample testimonium clause is "In witness whereof, the parties to these presents have hereunto set their hands and seals this day and year written above."

TEST MARKET geographic location selected for the introduction of a new product, new advertising campaign, or both. The use of a test market allows the advertiser or manufacturer to evaluate the product performance on a small scale, and to evaluate the MARKETING PLAN for the product before embarking on a national introduction of the product.

TEST MARKETING form of marketing occurring in the product-testing step of the overall product development process. Selected areas of the country are chosen during *test marketing* for the actual introduction of the product. Sales and consumer reactions are monitored for an overall evaluation of the product. Test marketing is very expensive and gives the competition lead time to study new products.

TEST STATISTIC measure calculated from data sampled from a population, used to either reject or fail to reject the NULL HYPOTHESIS. Rejection of the null hypothesis will take place if either the P value is small enough or the test statistic is larger than a predetermined requirement. *See also* HYPOTHESIS; P VALUE; STATISTIC; STATISTICALLY SIGNIFICANT.

TEXT-EDITING MACHINE *see* TYPEWRITER.

THEORETICAL CAPACITY *see* CAPACITY.

THEORY X management theory developed by Douglas McGregor, stating that managers must coerce, cajole, threaten, and closely supervise subordinates in order to motivate them. Theory X is an authoritarian supervisory approach to management. *See also* THEORY.

THEORY Y beliefs, in contrast to THEORY X, held by some managers that *given the right conditions and rewards,* the average employee finds work to be a source of satisfaction, will exercise self-direction toward goals he is committed to, seeks responsibility, and is creative. *See also* ORGANIZATION DEVELOPMENT.

THEORY Z management theory developed by William Ouchi, describing the Japanese system of management characterized by the workers' deep involvement in management, higher productivity than the U.S. management model, and a highly developed system of organizational and sociological rewards. Ouchi contends that this management system can be used anywhere with equal success.

THIN CAPITALIZATION (THIN CORPORATION) a CORPORATION whose capital is supplied primarily by loans from shareholders rather than stock investment. The main tax advantage attempted is that the distributions of interest on the debts may be deducted by the corporation as INTEREST, whereas distributions on stock are nondeductible DIVIDENDS. If the debt-to-stock ratio becomes excessive, the IRS may contend that the capital structure is unrealistic and the debt is not BONA FIDE. The acceptable debt-to-stock ratio varies according to industry norms. If the corporation's debt is recast as stock, the corporation loses its deductible interest expense.

THINKING OUTSIDE THE BOX breaking away from traditional or conventional thought to develop a unique, superior solution to a difficult problem.

THINKING PROGRAMS computer software used by accountants preparing written reports for clients, including management letters and specialized analyses of operations. Writing skills can be greatly enhanced through the use of thinking software.

THIN MARKET stock market situation where there are few bids to buy and few offers to sell. A thin market may apply to an entire class of securities or commodities futures—such as small over-the-counter stocks or the platinum market—or it may refer to a particular stock, whether exchange listed or over the counter. Prices in thin markets generally are more volatile than in markets with great liquidity.

THIRD-CLASS MAIL service offered by the U.S. Postal Service for mailing greeting cards, small parcels, farm products, printed matter, booklets and catalogs, newsletters, shoppers' guides, and advertising circulars. The maximum weight for each piece is 16 ounces.

THIRD-GENERATION COMPUTER computer made with INTEGRATED CIRCUITS. Computers made with circuits that have largescale integration are often called *fourth-generation computers.*

THIRD MARKET nonexchange-member broker-dealers and institutional investors trading OVER THE COUNTER in exchange-listed securities.

THIRD PARTY someone other than the parties directly involved in the action or transaction; outsider with no legal interest in the matter.

THIRD-PARTY CHECK
1. check negotiated through a bank, except one payable to the writer of the check, that is, a check written for cash. The *primary party* to a transaction is the bank on which a check is drawn. The *secondary party* is the drawer of the check against funds on deposit in the bank. The *third party* is the payee who endorses the check.
2. double-endorsed check. The payee endorses the check by signing the back, then passes the check to a subsequent holder, who

endorses it prior to cashing it. Recipients of checks with multiple endorsements are reluctant to accept them unless they can verify each endorser's signature.

THIRD-PARTY SALE sale made by an agency acting as an intermediary between a buyer and a seller. *See also* LISTING BROKER.

30-DAY LETTER a formal notice from the IRS giving the taxpayer 30 days to appeal the proposed finding of the REVENUE AGENT.

THOMSON FINANCIAL source of integrated information and technology applications in the financial services industry. Thomson ONE helps clients act upon investment, business, and trading opportunities.

THREAD a series of bulletin board or NEWSGROUP postings on a particular topic. For example, one user may post a question, and all replies (which repeat the original header prefixed by Re:) will be displayed appended to the original question.

THREE-MARTINI LUNCH derisive term for lavish lunches characterized by having three martinis and claimed as tax-deductible business expenses. A *three-martini lunch* became a symbol for business extravagance and resulted in 1993 tax act provisions making only 50% of the cost of business meals deductible for tax purposes.

THRESHOLD-POINT ORDERING minimum ordering of inventory to meet expected user demand; predetermined point of inventory reordering based upon anticipated usage. Threshold-point ordering represents very precise inventory management techniques.

THRIFT INSTITUTION generic name for savings banks and savings and loan associations.

THRIFT SHOP retail store selling second-hand goods at reduced prices. Thrift shops are often associated with churches and charitable service organizations such as the Salvation Army.

THRIFTY person or purchase characterized as frugal, economical, or sparing. A *thrifty* buy or product is one where the consumer gets good value for the price.

THROUGH RATE total cost of shipping goods when two or more carriers are used, derived by either a joint rate or the sum of the rates charged by each carrier.

TICK upward or downward price movement in a security's trades. Technical analysts watch the tick of a stock's successive up or down moves to get a feel of the stock's trend.

TICKER system that produces a running report of trading activity on the stock exchanges, called *ticker tape*. Today's ticker tape is a computer screen, and the term is used to refer both to the consolidated tape, which shows the stock symbol, latest price, and volume of trades on the exchanges, and to news ticker services.

TICKER SYMBOL *see* STOCK SYMBOL.

TICKER TAPE *see* TICKER.

TICK MARKS (accounting) symbols used by auditors to indicate that they have performed a certain operation, such as agreeing a number on a trial balance to the source document or checking the addition of a column of numbers. A legend should appear on the work papers to indicate the meaning of each *tick mark*.

TICs refers to TENANCY IN COMMON ownership. Some TICs have been used to facilitate tax-free exchanges of real estate under SECTION 1031.

TIGHT MARKET market in general or market for a particular security marked by active trading and narrow bid-offer price spreads. In contrast, inactive trading and wide spreads characterize a *slack market.*

TIGHT MONEY economic condition in which credit is difficult to secure, usually as the result of Federal Reserve Board action to restrict the MONEY SUPPLY. *See also* MONETARY POLICY.

TIGHT SHIP indication that organizational management procedures are followed very closely. When an organization is run like a *tight ship*, few allowances are permitted for unorthodox procedures.

TILL cash register, drawer, or any location where money is kept or stored for business purposes.

TIME-AND-A-HALF payment of one and a half times the worker's regular hourly wage for work beyond 40 hours per week to certain categories of workers. Time-and-a-half payments are required by the Federal Fair Labor Standards Act.

TIME AND BILLING SOFTWARE computer program that tracks hours spent by function and chargeable expenses of staff accountants for a given client. Sources are hourly rates, time sheets, practice and time management reports, and accounting reports. At the end of a period, a bill based on expenses, time spent, and hourly rates is sent. When billing on a flat-fee basis, hourly information is useful to the practitioner in evaluating staff accountants' proficiency.

TIME-AND-MOTION STUDY measuring the time and motions necessary for the completion of specific job tasks. Time-and-motion studies were first advocated by Frederick W. Taylor in his book *Scientific Management* in order to create a management standard for evaluating individual employee productivity. *See also* STOPWATCH STUDIES.

TIME CARD/card recording actual employee hours of work. Many time cards are designed to be inserted into a time-recording device, which stamps the current time on the card, indicating check-in and check-out times.

TIME DEPOSIT savings account or CERTIFICATE OF DEPOSIT held in a financial institution for a fixed term or with the understanding that the depositor can withdraw only by giving notice. Certificates of deposit are issued for a specified term of 30 days or more and carry penalties for early withdrawal.

TIME DRAFT DRAFT payable at a specified or determinable time in the future, as distinguished from a *sight* draft, which is payable on presentation and delivery.

TIME IS OF THE ESSENCE phrase that, when inserted in a contract, requires that all references to specific dates and times of day noted in the contract be interpreted exactly. In its absence, extreme delays might be legally acceptable.

TIMEKEEPER person who keeps time records; traditional clerical function in an organization where the working hours of employees are recorded and monitored.

TIME MANAGEMENT managing the use of daily schedules for the purpose of achieving maximum productivity; maximum time utilization; not wasting time.

TIME SERIES ANALYSIS use of historical data and mathematical techniques to model the historical path of a price, demand for a good, or consumption. Time series analysis is based on the premise that by knowing the past, the future can be forecast.

TIMES FIXED CHARGE *see* FIXED-CHARGE COVERAGE.

TIME-SHARING
Computers: method of running more than one program on the same computer at the same time, so that the computer serves many users at different terminals simultaneously. A dumb terminal and a MODEM from a remote location provide access to a mainframe computer set up for time-sharing.
Real estate: form of property ownership under which a property is held by a number of people, each with the right of possession for a specified time interval. Time-sharing is most commonly applied to resort and vacation properties, but may be used for other properties.

TIMES INTEREST EARNED *see* FIXED-CHARGE COVERAGE.

TIMETABLE tabular statement of the times at which certain things will occur; commonly used in the arrivals and departures of trains, airlines, and high and low tides.

TIME UTILITY enhancing a product's marketability by making it available at a convenient time.

TIME VALUE
In general: price put on the time an investor has to wait until an investment matures, as determined by calculating the PRESENT VALUE of the investment at maturity. *See also* YIELD TO MATURITY (YTM).

Options: that part of a STOCK OPTION premium that reflects the time remaining on an option contract before expiration.

TIME VALUE OF MONEY a concept that money available now is worth more than the same amount in the future because of its potential earning capacity. Used for computations involving IMPUTED INTEREST and ORIGINAL ISSUE DISCOUNT. *See also* PRESENT VALUE.

TIN acronym for TAXPAYER IDENTIFICATION NUMBER.

TIP

In general: payment over and above a formal cost or charge, ostensibly given in appreciation for extra service, to a waiter, bellhop, cabdriver, or other person engaged in service; also called a *gratuity*. Tip is popularly believed to be an abbreviation for "*t*o *i*nsure *p*romptness."

Investments: information passed by one person to another as a basis for buy and sell action in a security. Such information is presumed to be of material value and not available to the general public.

TIPS *see* TREASURY INFLATION-PROTECTED SECURITIES.

TITLE

1. ownership.
2. in property law, composite of facts that will permit one to recover or to retain possession of a thing. *See also* CLEAR TITLE; MARKETABLE TITLE.

TITLE ABSTRACT *see* ABSTRACT OF TITLE.

TITLE BAR the bar at the top of a computer screen window that displays information about the item, usually the file or folder name.

TITLE COMPANY firm examining TITLE to real estate and/or issuing TITLE INSURANCE.

TITLE DEFECT unresolved claim against the ownership of property that prevents presentation of a MARKETABLE TITLE. Such claims may arise from failure of the owner's spouse, or former part owner, to sign a deed, current liens against the property, or an interruption in the title records of a property.

TITLE GUARANTY *see* TITLE INSURANCE.

TITLE GUARANTY COMPANY *see* TITLE COMPANY; TITLE INSURANCE.

TITLE INSURANCE insurance policy that protects the holder from loss sustained through defects in the TITLE. Mortgage lenders virtually always require borrowers to buy a mortgagee's policy of title insurance. The premiums paid on a business title insurance policy are normally deductible.

TITLE REPORT document indicating the current state of the TITLE, such as EASEMENTS, COVENANTS, LIENS, and any other defects. The title report does not describe the chain of title. *See also* ABSTRACT OF TITLE.

TITLE SEARCH investigation of documents in the public record office to determine the state of a TITLE, including all LIENS, ENCUMBRANCES, MORTGAGES, future interests, and so on, affecting the property; means by which a chain of title is ascertained.

TITLE THEORY modern version of the COMMON LAW mortgage under which the creditor has the legal right to possession although in fact the debtor remains in possession of the property.

TITLE-THEORY STATE state in which the law splits the title to mortgaged property into *legal title,* held by the lender, and *equitable title,* held by the borrower. The borrower gains full title to the property upon retiring the mortgage debt. In a title-theory state, mortgage lenders may possess the property upon default of the borrower. In a LIEN-THEORY STATE, lenders must go through the process of foreclosure.

TOGGLE (computers) switch between two alternate settings, defined as On and Off. *Toggle* switches are used to turn on and off formatting attributes, such as italics and boldface; window components, such as toolbars and rulers; display features, such as field codes, nonprinting characters, or text boundaries; and a variety of other software options. Keyboard *toggles* include the Caps Lock and Insert keys.

TOKENISM formalistic compliance with affirmative action legislation by hiring a small (token) number of people to comply with requirements for having representatives of impacted groups. Tokenism is a formalistic affirmative action compliance policy.

TOKYO STOCK EXCHANGE (TSE) largest of eight stock exchanges in Japan and one of the largest, most important, and most active stock markets in the world. Formerly a continuous auction market (similar to OPEN OUTCRY), the TSE is now completely computerized; there is no trading floor.

TOLL
1. to bar, defeat. To *toll* the STATUTE OF LIMITATIONS is to suspend the limitation.
2. charge for the use of another's property.
3. CONSIDERATION for the use of roads, bridges, ferries, or other public facilities.

TOMBSTONE AD advertisement placed in newspapers by INVESTMENT BANKERS in a PUBLIC OFFERING of securities. It gives basic details about the issue and lists the underwriting group members involved in the offering in alphabetically organized groupings according to the size of their participation. The name is derived from the similarity in appearance of the ad to a tombstone.

TON
1. bond traders' jargon for $100 million.
2. measure of weight. 2,000 avoirdupois pounds is a *short ton,* 2,240 pounds is a *long ton,* and 2,204.6 pounds is a *metric ton.*

TOOLBAR area of a computer screen, often across the top, containing BUTTONS and MENUS. In some applications a toolbar can be *docked* at any edge of the screen or *torn off* to become a *floating palette*. Toolbars can also be *turned off* (caused not to appear). Also called a *button bar*.

TOP-DOWN PORTFOLIO or **APPROACH TO INVESTING** method in which an investor first looks at trends in the general economy, and next selects industries and then companies that should benefit from those trends. *Contrast with* BOTTOM-UP APPROACH TO INVESTING.

TOPOGRAPHY state of the surface of the land, such as rolling, rough, or flat.

TOPPING OUT market or security that is at the end of a period of rising prices and can now be expected to stay on a plateau or to decline.

TORONTO STOCK EXCHANGE (TSE) largest stock exchange in Canada, listing some 1,200 company stocks and 33 options. The exchange uses both OPEN OUTCRY and the Computer Assisted Trading System (CATS).

TORRENS REGISTRATION SYSTEM title registration system used in some states. The condition of the title can easily be discovered without resorting to a TITLE SEARCH. *See also* MUNIMENTS OF TITLE.

TORT wrongful act that is neither a crime nor a breach of contract, but that renders the perpetrator liable to the victim for damages, such as nuisance, trespassing, or negligence. An example of negligence is a landlord's failure to fix reported defective wiring. The law provides remedy for damages from resulting fire.

TOTAL CAPITALIZATION CAPITAL STRUCTURE of a company, including LONG-TERM DEBT and all forms of EQUITY.

TOTAL DISABILITY injury or illness that is so serious that it prevents a worker from performing any functions for which he or she is educated and trained. Workers with *total disability* may qualify for DISABILITY INCOME INSURANCE, either through a private employer's plan or through the SOCIAL SECURITY DISABILITY INCOME INSURANCE PROGRAM.

TOTAL LOSS damage so extensive that repair is not economical.

TOTAL PAID paid circulation of an issue of a periodical, including paid subscription copies, newsstand and other single-copy sales, graced copies (*see* GRACE PERIOD), and other copies considered to be paid according to audit bureau of circulations or business publications audit of circulations regulations governing paid-copy reporting; also called *total net paid*.

TOTAL QUALITY MANAGEMENT (TQM) concept developed by W. Edwards Deming, encompassing 14 points. It is an all-embracing philosophy in which the central focus is continual quality improvement achieved through organizationwide cooperation and ongoing employee training. Deming rejects inspection, performance reviews, work quotas, and sloganeering to get the job done. He believes strongly in reinstituting individual employee pride of workmanship.

TOUR OF DUTY
1. in the military, duration of a specific military assignment.
2. hours an employee is scheduled to work. Tours of duty are contiguous blocks of time. For example, a daytime tour of duty may be from 8 A.M. to 4 P.M.

TOUT aggressive promoting of a particular item by a corporate spokesperson, public relations firm, broker, or analyst. *Touting* a stock is unethical if it misleads investors.

TOWN HOUSE DWELLING unit, generally having two or more floors and attached to other similar units via party walls. Town houses are often used in planned unit developments and condominium developments, which provide for clustered or attached housing and common open space.

TRACE, TRACER attempt to locate a delayed or lost shipment. A tracer is an inquiry that attempts to find the lost parcel or to determine where it was sent. It is often used for REGISTERED, CERTIFIED, or INSURED MAIL.

TRACING MAIL *see* TRACER.

TRACKAGE charge imposed by a railroad for use of its rails by another line.

TRACKBALL a computer POINTING DEVICE that resembles an upside-down MOUSE. Instead of rolling the mouse around the desktop, the user rotates the ball on the trackball with a thumb or finger. *Trackballs* are frequently used with NOTEBOOK COMPUTERS, which are often used where there is not enough desktop space to operate a mouse.

TRACKING *see* TRACE.

TRACK RECORD a businessman's reputation for producing on a timely and economical basis. A good *track record* can be helpful in arranging financing or attracting investors for a new venture.

TRACT PARCEL of land, generally held for subdividing; SUBDIVISION.

TRACT HOUSE DWELLING that has a similar style and floor plan to those of all other houses in a development. *See also* CUSTOM BUILDER.

TRADE business, profession, or occupation. A trade often implies a skilled handicraft, which is pursued on a continuing basis, such as the carpenter *trade*. Trade or business expenses are tax deductible. *See* EXCHANGE TRANSACTION; SECTION 1031.

TRADE ACCEPTANCE a time draft that is guaranteed by a nonbank firm and sold in the secondary money market. It is similar to a BANKER'S ACCEPTANCE but more risky.

TRADE ADVERTISING consumer-product advertising designed to stimulate wholesalers or retailers to purchase products for resale to their customers.

TRADE AGREEMENT agreement, usually between or among governments, that encourages, regulates, and/or restricts elements of trade among the respective countries.

TRADE ALLOWANCE producer discount given to distributors or retailers as a promotional effort. Retailers pass along the discount to the consumer, which encourages sales. Although trade allowances reduce producer profits, the practice is widely followed in many industries.

TRADE AREA same as MARKET AREA.

TRADE BALANCE *see* BALANCE OF TRADE.

TRADE BARRIER any form of governmental or operational activity or restriction that renders importation of some goods into a country difficult or impossible. TARIFFS are an example; so is the plethora of regulations and inspections that hamper importation of automobiles into Japan.

TRADE BOOK *see* TRADE MAGAZINE.

TRADE CREDIT open-account arrangements with suppliers of goods and services, and a firm's record of payment with the suppliers. Trade liabilities constitute a company's accounts payable. Trade credit is an important external source of working capital for a company, although such credit can be highly expensive. Terms of 2% 10 days, net 30 days (2% discount if paid in 10 days, the net [full] amount due in 30 days) translate into a 36% annual interest rate.

TRADE DATE day on which a SECURITY or a COMMODITY future trade actually takes place. The SETTLEMENT DATE usually follows the *trade date* by three business days, but this varies depending on the transaction and method of delivery used. *See also* DELAYED DELIVERY; DELIVERY DATE; REGULAR-WAY DELIVERY (AND SETTLEMENT); SELLER'S OPTION.

TRADE DEFICIT (SURPLUS) excess of imports over exports (deficit) or of exports over imports (surplus), resulting in a negative or positive BALANCE OF TRADE.

TRADE DISCOUNT producer discount given to retail trade members to help increase sales. *See* CASH DISCOUNT.

TRADE FIXTURE property placed on or annexed to rented real estate by a tenant for the purpose of the conduct of a trade or business. The law makes provision for, and leases often expressly permit (or require), the tenant's removal of such fixtures at the end of his tenancy. Examples are light fixtures, bar stools, and neon signs.

TRADE MAGAZINE magazine with editorial content of interest only to persons engaged in a particular industry, occupation, or profession; also called *business publication. A* trade magazine may be as wide in scope as manufacturing management or sales, or as narrow in scope as patio-furniture manufacturing or used-car sales.

TRADEMARK [superscript] ® ™ insignia or logo that distinguishes one maker's goods from all others; any mark, word, letter, number, design, picture, or combination thereof in any form that is adopted and used by a person to denominate goods that he makes, is affixed to the goods, and is neither a common nor generic name for the goods nor a picture of them, nor is merely descriptive of the goods. Protection from INFRINGEMENT upon a trademark is afforded by the common-law action for unfair competition.

TRADE NAME business name that may or may not be trademarked.

TRADE-OFF giving up one advantage in order to gain another. For example, a trade-off may be realized by taking a financial loss in order to gain a tax deduction that will lower total tax liability.

TRADE or **BUSINESS** regular and continuous activity undertaken for a profit, other than that of an investor trading in securities.

TRADE PROMOTION *see* TRADE ALLOWANCE.

TRADER
In general: anyone who buys and sells goods or services for profit; dealer or merchant. *See also* BARTER; TRADE.
Investment: individual who buys and sells securities—for example stocks, bonds, options, or commodities such as wheat, gold, or foreign exchange—for his or her own account, that is, as a dealer or principal, rather than as a broker or agent.

TRADE RATE special price offered to retailers by wholesalers, manufacturers, or distributors or by a seller to individuals or organizations in a related industry. For example, an over-the-counter drug might be sold at a special trade rate to physicians who will dispense it to their patients.

TRADE SECRET any formula, pattern, machine, or process of manufacturing used in a business that may give the user a competitive advantage; plan or process, tool, mechanism, or compound known only to its owner and those of its employees to whom it is necessary to disclose it.

TRADE SHOW exhibit of goods and services for the benefit of individuals or companies involved in a particular TRADE. Generally, a trade show is held in an exhibition hall, and each exhibitor is allowed to rent space to display goods and services.

TRADE UNION association of workers to promote and protect the welfare, interests, and rights of its members; also called *labor union.*

TRADE WAR a conflict involving two or more countries as part of an effort by each to improve its own import/export position.

TRADING AUTHORIZATION document giving a brokerage firm employee acting as AGENT (BROKER) the POWER OF ATTORNEY in buy-sell transactions for a customer.

TRADING BLOCS nations belonging to a mutual trade pact agreeing to give each other reduced trade tariffs and other accommodations while imposing trade barriers and restrictions to nonmember nations.

TRADING HALT *see* SUSPENDED TRADING.

TRADING LIMIT *see* FLUCTUATION LIMIT.

TRADING POST physical location on a stock exchange floor where particular securities are bought and sold.

TRADING RANGE
Commodities: trading limit set by a commodities futures exchange for a particular commodity. The price of a commodity future contract may not go higher or lower than that limit during one day's trading. *See also* LIMIT UP; LIMIT DOWN.
Securities: range between the highest and lowest prices at which a security or a market has traded.

TRADING UNIT number of shares, bonds, or other securities that is generally accepted for ordinary trading purposes on the exchanges. *See also* ODD LOT; ROUND LOT.

TRADITIONAL ECONOMY economy dominated by methods and techniques that have strong social support even though they may be old-fashioned or out of date.

TRAFFIC
Communications: flow of data over telephone lines or other communications networks.
Retailing: activity of potential customers, such as *pedestrian traffic.*

TRAMP ship or boat that travels wherever freight shipments take it. It has no regular schedule or itinerary.

TRANCHE in a COLLATERALIZED MORTGAGE OBLIGATION or a REMIC, a separately priced and marketed ownership interest that entitles the investor to income from a mortgage pool with an expected maturity within specified limits. This is done by assigning each tranche a priority from loan principal repayments. The higher the priority, the shorter the maturity of the tranche. For example, the typical CMO has A, B, C, and Z *tranches*, representing fast-pay, medium-pay, and slow-pay mortgages.

TRANSACTION any sale, assignment, lease, license, loan, advance, contribution, or other transfer of any interest in or right to use any property (whether tangible or intangible) or money, however such transaction is effected, and whether or not the terms of such transaction are formally documented.

TRANSACTION COST costs associated with buying and selling investments. Examples of real estate transaction costs are appraisal fees, brokerage commission, legal fees, mortgage discount points, mortgage origination fees, recording fees, state transfer taxes, survey fees, and title search. Transaction costs in securities are mainly brokerage commissions.

TRANSFER AGENT individual or firm that keeps a record of the shareholders of a corporation by name, address, and number of shares owned. When stock is sold, the new owner through his agent presents the shares purchased to the transfer agent, who cancels the old certificates and issues new certificates registered in the name of the owner.

TRANSFER DEVELOPMENT RIGHTS (TDR) type of ZONING ORDINANCE that allows owners of property zoned for low-density development or conservation use to sell development rights to other property owners. For example, suppose two adjacent landowners, A and B, are each allowed to build a ten-story office building on their own property. Using TDRs, landowner A could sell his development rights to landowner B, allowing B to build twenty stories high provided that A leaves his land undeveloped.

TRANSFER PAYMENT payment by government to persons, which is neither for wages nor for goods and/or other services supplied. Social Security payments are *transfer payments*.

TRANSFER PRICE price charged by individual entities in a multientity corporation on transactions among themselves; also termed *transfer cost*. This concept is used where each entity is managed as a PROFIT CENTER and must therefore deal with the other internal parts of the corporation on an arm's length (or market) basis.

TRANSFER TAX tax paid upon the passing of TITLE to property or to a valuable interest.

TRANSFORMATIONAL LEADERSHIP motivational management method whereby employees are encouraged to achieve greater performance through inspirational leadership, which develops employee self-confidence and higher achievement goals.

TRANSIENT temporary, fleeting, or passing phenomenon. A transient condition is of brief duration.

TRANSIENT WORKER one who moves from job to job, maintains no fixed home, and is not associated with any particular business locality. Each place he or she works becomes the main place of business and tax home. A transient worker cannot deduct expenses for meals and lodging.

TRANSLATE
1. express in another language; to interpret into a form others can understand.
2. to transform.

TRANSLATION RISK monetary value risk that occurs in international trade when two or more currencies are used in a transaction. The longer the period before the transaction ends, the greater the *translation risk.*

TRANSMISSION CONTROL PROTOCOL/INTERNET PROTOCOL (TCP/IP) a standard format for transmitting data in PACKETS from one computer to another on the INTERNET. Developed by the U.S. Department of Defense, TCP/IP is two separate protocols. TCP deals with the construction of data packets (including checking for errors); IP routes them from machine to machine.

TRANSMITTAL LETTER letter sent with a document, security, or shipment describing the contents and the purpose of the transaction.

TRANSNATIONAL going beyond the borders of a country. A transnational shipment involves more than one country.

TRANSPARENCY in financial reporting, ease of understanding, made possible by the full, clear, and timely disclosure of relevant information. In securities transactions, *price transparency* means access to such information concerning *depth of the market* as to permit detection of fraud or manipulation.

TRANSPORTATION FRINGE *see* QUALIFIED TRANSPORTATION FRINGE.

TRANSPORTATION INSURANCE *see* MARINE INSURANCE, INLAND.

TRAVEL AND ENTERTAINMENT (T&E) EXPENSES ORDINARY AND NECESSARY EXPENSES paid while traveling AWAY FROM HOME for a business, profession, or job. An *ordinary expense* is one that is common and accepted in a given field of business, trade, or profession. A *necessary expense* is one that is helpful and appropriate to the business. LAVISH OR EXTRAVAGANT EXPENSES are not tax deductible. *See also* COMMUTING EXPENSE. Entertainment expenses are incurred for a client, customer, or employee. Entertainment includes any activity generally considered to provide entertainment, amusement, or recreation. Examples include taking a guest to a night club; a social, athletic, or sporting club; theater or sporting event. As a result of the 1993 tax act, only 50% of entertainment expenses and business meals is deductible.

TREASURER company officer responsible for the receipt, custody, investment, and disbursement of funds, for borrowings, and, if it is a public company, for the maintenance of a market for its securities. Depending on the size of the organization, the treasurer may also function as the CONTROLLER, with accounting and audit responsibilities.

TREASURIES negotiable debt obligations of the U.S. government, secured by its FULL FAITH AND CREDIT and issued at various schedules and maturities. The income from U.S. Treasury securities is exempt from state and local, but not federal, taxes. *See also* TREASURY BILL; TREASURY BOND; TREASURY NOTE.

TREASURY BILL (T-BILL) U.S. government promissory note issued by the U.S. Treasury, having a maturity period of up to one year. Notes having longer maturities are called Treasury *notes,* and those with very long maturities are called Treasury *bonds.* Treasury bills are sold at a DISCOUNT to face value, which is paid at maturity. The difference is the interest income to the owner.

TREASURY BOND

1. long-term (more than 10 years) DEBT INSTRUMENT issued by the U.S. government. Issues of the U.S. government have the highest rating among so-called fixed income or debt securities and, therefore, offer the lowest taxable yield of any bonds.

2. BOND that has been bought back by the issuing corporation. Such *Treasury bonds* are usually retired as part of SINKING FUND requirements or held in the corporate treasury, which reduces interest expense. *See also* TREASURY STOCK.

TREASURY DEPARTMENT an executive department of the U.S. government that is responsible for money and budgetary matters. The INTERNAL REVENUE SERVICE is an agency of the *Treasury Department.*

TREASURY DIRECT system through which an individual investor can make a NONCOMPETITIVE BID on U.S. Treasury securities (TREASURIES), thus bypassing middlemen like banks or broker-dealers and avoiding their fees. The system works through FEDERAL RESERVE BANKS and branches, and the minimum purchase is $1,000.

TREASURY INFLATION-PROTECTED SECURITIES (TIPS) inflation-indexed TREASURY BONDS. The principal is adjusted to the CONSUMER PRICE INDEX. TIPS pay a small rate of interest; principal is increased with inflation as measured by the CPI. TIPS are currently offered in 5-, 10-, and 20-year maturities. May be purchased from TREASURY DIRECT accounts.

TREASURY INVESTORS GROWTH RECEIPT (TIGER; TIGR) form of zero coupon security. TIGERs are U.S. government backed bonds that have been stripped of their coupons. Both the CORPUS (principal) of the bonds and the individual coupons are sold separately at a deep discount from their face values. Investors receive face value for the TIGERs when the bonds mature, but do not receive periodic interest payments.

TREASURY NOTE intermediate-term (one to 10 years) obligation of the U.S. government that bears interest paid by coupon. Like all direct U.S. government obligations, Treasury notes carry the highest domestic credit standing and thus have the lowest taxable yield available at equivalent maturity.

TREASURY STOCK common or preferred stock that had been issued by a company and later reacquired. The stock may be used for a variety of corporate purposes, such as a stock bonus plan for management and employees or to acquire another company.

TREE DIAGRAM graphic expression of a sequence of events where subsequent decisions depend on the results of previous decisions. Tree diagrams are used to map the possible alternatives and to develop strategies for decision making. *Also called* DECISION TREE.

TREND
In general: any general direction of movement; for example, a *trend* toward increased computerization.
Securities: long-term price or trading volume movements, either up, down, or sideways, that characterize a particular market, commodity, or security; also applies to interest rates and yields.

TREND ANALYSIS a study of a company's financial performance over an extended period of time. Trend analysis helps to understand overall financial performance over a period of time.

TREND LINE line used by technical analysts to chart the past direction of a security or commodity future in order to help predict future price movements.

TREO *see* PDA.

TRESPASS unlawful entry or possession of property.

TRIAL AND ERROR empirical method to test a hypothesis or procedure by repeating an experiment until the chance of error or outcome is known to some degree of reliability. Trial and error is generally used when no theory is known. Optimum advertising strategies are often obtained by trial and error across several test markets.

TRIAL BALANCE in accounting, one of the first steps in closing the books at year-end. All accounts are listed; debits and credits are totaled and should balance.

TRIAL BUYER *see* TRIAL OFFER; TRIAL SUBSCRIBER.

TRIAL COURT a court of original jurisdiction of a tax dispute.

TRIAL OFFER soft-offer technique that allows a first-time buyer to examine, use, or test a product for a short period of time before deciding to purchase or return it; also called *free trial offer, free examination offer.* A trial offer may also be a special reduced rate for firsttime buyers and/or may be in a special reduced quantity or TERM.

TRIAL SIZE a small quantity of a product offered at no charge (or a low promotional price) to induce the customer to try the product, often used in a product promotion.

TRICKLE DOWN theory that economic growth can best be achieved by letting investors and businesses flourish, since their prosperity will ultimately *trickle down* to middle and lower income people, who will benefit by increased economic activity. *See also* SUPPLY-SIDE ECONOMICS.

TRIGGER POINT, TRIGGER PRICE price of an imported commodity that is well below that charged in the country of origin. When the imported good's price reaches or falls below the trigger point, it results in swift trade restrictions against that particular imported commodity or product.

TRIP CARGO INSURANCE *see* CARGO INSURANCE.

TRIPLE-A TENANT tenant with an excellent credit record.

TRIPLE-NET LEASE LEASE under which the tenant pays all operating expenses of the property. The landlord receives a net rent.

TROJAN (HORSE) a type of MALWARE disguised as an innocuous, useful, and desirable program, such as a screensaver or game. Unlike VIRUSES and WORMS, Trojans usually gain access through software intentionally installed by the user.

TROUBLESHOOTER person specializing in finding problems and solving them. Troubleshooters are often used in organizations to clear up difficulties.

TROUGH bottom of a RECESSION or depression; point at which recovery begins.

TROY WEIGHT system of weights in which 12 ounces make a pound (the ounces, at 480 grains, are about 10% heavier than the 437.5-grain avoirdupois ounce); used to measure precious metals, including gold, silver, and platinum.

TRUCKLOAD (TL) quantity of cargo that fills a truck.

TRUE LEASE LEASE where risk and rewards of ownership are retained by the LESSOR. *See also* FINANCIAL LEASE.

TRUNCATION
Banking: eliminating the service of returning canceled checks to customers.
Computers: dropping the digits of a number to the right of the decimal point. For example, the truncation of 6.45 is 6, and the truncation of 737.984 is 737; contrast *rounding off.*

TRUST fiduciary relationship in which a person, called a *trustee,* holds title to property for the benefit of another person, called a *beneficiary.* The person creating the trust is the *creator, settlor, grantor,* or *donor.* The property itself is called the *corpus, trust res, trust fund,* or *trust estate,* which is distinguished from any income earned by it. If the trust is created while the donor is living, it is called a LIVING TRUST or INTER VIVOS TRUST. A trust created by a will is called a TESTAMENTARY TRUST. The trustee is usually charged with investing trust property productively. *See also* TRUST COMPANY; TRUSTEE IN BANKRUPTCY.

TRUST ACCOUNT separate bank account, segregated from a broker's own funds, in which the broker is required by state law to deposit all monies collected for clients; in some states called an *escrow* account.

TRUST AGREEMENT *see* TRUST INSTRUMENT.

TRUST CERTIFICATE INSTRUMENT issued to finance the purchase of railroad equipment, under which the trustees hold title to the equipment as security for the loan.

TRUST COMPANY organization, usually combined with a commercial bank, that is engaged as a TRUSTEE, FIDUCIARY, or AGENT for individuals or businesses in the administration of trust funds, estates, custodial arrangements, stock transfer and registration, and related services. Trust companies also engage in fiduciary investment management functions and estate planning. They are regulated by state law.

TRUST DEED CONVEYANCE of real estate to a THIRD PARTY to be held for the benefit of another. It is commonly used in some states in place of mortgages that conditionally convey title to the lender.

TRUST, DISCRETIONARY agreement that allows the TRUSTEE to administer the TRUST according to his own judgment; also called *general management trust.* The trust must be administered, however, with a reasonable amount of prudence and common sense.

TRUSTEE
  1. one who holds legal TITLE to property in trust for the benefit of another person, and who is required to carry out specific duties with regard to the property, or who has been given power affecting the disposition of property for another's benefit.
  2. loosely, anyone who acts as a GUARDIAN or FIDUCIARY in relationship to another, such as a public officer toward his constituents, a state toward its citizens, or a partner to his copartner.

TRUSTEE IN BANKRUPTCY officer, elected and approved by the REFEREE or judge of a bankruptcy proceeding, who takes legal title to the property or money of the bankrupt and holds it in trust for equitable distribution among the bankrupt's creditors.

TRUSTEE'S SALE a FORECLOSURE SALE conducted by a trustee under the stipulations of a DEED OF TRUST. When a deed of trust is exercised, a specific trustee is designated. Upon default, the trustee is authorized to foreclose the mortgage and put the property up for a *trustee's sale.* The proceeds of the sale are distributed by the trustee according to the priorities listed in the deed of trust.

TRUST FUND real property or personal property held in trust for the benefit of another person; the CORPUS of a trust.

TRUST, GENERAL MANAGEMENT *see* TRUST, DISCRETIONARY.

TRUST INSTRUMENT legal document that creates a TRUST and stipulates its terms, TRUSTEE, BENEFICIARIES, income, and CORPUS disposition.

TRUSTOR one who creates a TRUST, often called the *settlor.*

TRUST SHARE partial participation and ownership in a corporation's management. A trust share entitles the holder to a portion of the profits.

TRUTH IN LENDING ACT federal law, the provisions of which assure individuals applying for commercial credit information relating to the cost of credit, enabling them to decide which credit source offers them the most favorable credit terms. Under this law, the commercial lender must inform the borrower of the dollar amount of the interest charges and the interest rate, computed on an annual basis according to a specified formula, and must afford borrowers who pledge real property as security for the loan a three-day period in which to rescind the transaction. *See also* REGULATION Z.

T **STATISTIC** statistical procedure that can test the NULL HYPOTHESIS: (1) regression coefficients are equal to 0. (2) Two population means are equal. (3) A population mean is equal to, less than, or greater than some specified value.

TUITION amounts paid to an educational organization that normally maintains a regular faculty and curriculum and has a regularly enrolled body of pupils in attendance at the place where its educational activities are carried on. Tuition is not tax deductible unless it is incurred for maintenance of job skills required for employment; *see* EDUCATIONAL EXPENSE.

TUITION REDUCTION a benefit often provided to employees of educational institutions and their dependents, which is excludable from GROSS INCOME. Tax-free educational assistance up to $5,250 is available to employees under certain employer plans.

TUITION TAX CREDIT *see* HOPE TAX CREDIT; LIFETIME LEARNING CREDIT.

TULIPOMANIA speculative bubble in Holland in the early 1620s, when incredibly high prices were paid for tulip bulbs. Frequently used to describe investment price rises that are unjustified by the underlying fundamentals.

TURKEY disappointing investment. The term may be used with reference to a business deal that went awry, or to the purchase of a stock or bond that dropped in value sharply, or to a new securities issue that did not sell well or had to be sold at a loss.

TURKEY, TALK get serious; get down to the real business at hand.

TURNAROUND favorable reversal in the fortunes of a company, a market, or the economy at large. Stock market investors speculating that a poorly performing company is about to show a marked improvement in earnings might profit handsomely from its *turnaround*.

TURNAROUND TIME time it takes to get a job done and deliver the output, once the job is submitted for processing. Turnaround may be as simple as unloading and reloading a delivery truck before sending it out again, or as complex as completing a merge/purge of several rented lists, getting a product into the buyer's hands once it is ordered, or receiving approval on a proof that has been submitted to the print buyer. In most cases, a short turnaround time is economically advantageous, making the most efficient use of time and materials.

TURNKEY any project constructed or manufactured by a company where the company ultimately turns it over in finished form to the client that will use it, so that all the user has to do is turn the key, so to speak, and the project is underway. The term is used of housing projects, computer systems, utility plants, and other projects.

TURNOVER

Finance: (1) number of times a given asset is replaced during an accounting period, usually a year. *See also* ACCOUNTS RECEIVABLE TURNOVER; INVENTORY TURNOVER; (2) ratio of annual sales of a company to its net worth, measuring the extent to which a company can grow without additional capital investment when compared over a period. *See also* CAPITAL TURNOVER.

Labor: total employment divided by the number of employees replaced during a given period.

Securities: volume of shares traded as a percentage of total shares listed on an exchange during a period, usually either a day or a year. The same ratio is applied to individual securities and the portfolios of individual or institutional investors, especially mutual funds.

TURN THE CORNER turning point in a series of events. When the corner is turned, there is hope for improvement.

12-b-1 FEE promotional fee charged by a mutual fund, usually a noload fund. The charge, generally 1%, must be disclosed.

24/7 24 hours a day, seven days a week. Used to indicate round-the-clock availability or activity.

TWIN PLANTS *see* MAQUILADORA.

TWO-TAILED TEST two-sided or nondirectional test of a HYPOTHESIS. The hypothesis examines whether or not two estimates of PARAMETERS are equal or not, without caring which one is smaller or larger. The tested hypothesis is rejected if the test statistic has an extremely small or large value.

TWO-TIER WAGE PLANS union wage concessions permitting new employees to be paid a lower rate than veteran employees, in an effort to allow companies to compete more effectively.

TWO-WAY ANALYSIS OF VARIANCE test procedure that can be applied to a table of numbers in order to test two HYPOTHESES: (1) there is no significant difference between rows; (2) there is no significant difference between columns.

TYCOON industrialist, magnate, or corporate captain. A *tycoon* is a leader in business who has achieved great wealth, power, and influence.

TYPEFACE a particular design of lettering, in a consistent weight and style. Though *typeface* and FONT are frequently confused, a font is a particular size (10-point, 12-point, etc.) and style (bold, italic, bold italic, etc.) of a given typeface.

TYPE 1 ERROR in statistical testing, rejecting the NULL HYPOTHESIS when it is true. *See also* TYPE 2 ERROR.

TYPE 2 ERROR in statistical testing, failure to reject the NULL HYPOTHESIS when it is false. *See also* TYPE 1 ERROR.

TYPEWRITER
1. manual or electric device with no memory storage, used to print on paper, one character at a time.
2. word processing keyboard (typing) equipment designed for composing, repeating, and revising or editing work and having memory storage; for example, *automatic typewriter, electronic typewriter,* and *memory typewriter.*
3. dedicated word processing machine, used for word processing only, not for games or keeping accounting records; also called *text-editing machine.*

TYING CONTRACTS contractual agreements whereby sellers give buyers access to a product only if the buyers agree to purchase other products as well. This is forbidden under Section 3 of the CLAYTON ANTI-TRUST ACT. *See also* ANTITRUST LAWS.

U

UBI *see* UNRELATED BUSINESS INCOME.

UCC *see* UNIFORM COMMERCIAL CODE.

UDDI *U*niversal *D*escription, *D*iscovery, and *I*ntegration; a standard established for building online registries of companies and the goods and services they provide. Such registries, which are an electronic directory for businesses desiring to locate customers and suppliers through the Internet, should include product data and contact information as well as the technical details necessary to connect to a given supplier's own E-COMMERCE system.

UGMA *see* UNIFORM GIFTS TO MINORS ACT.

ULTRA VIRES ACTIVITIES actions of a corporation that are not authorized by its charter and that may therefore lead to shareholder or third-party suits.

UMBRELLA LIABILITY INSURANCE excess liability coverage above the limits of a basic business liability insurance policy such as the OWNERS, LANDLORDS, AND TENANTS LIABILITY POLICY.

UMBRELLA POLICY insurance policy providing additional liability coverage over a basic insurance liability policy.

UNAFFILIATED UNION union not affiliated with the AFL/CIO. The United Mine Workers and the Teamsters are two of the largest unaffiliated unions. *See also* INDEPENDENT UNION.

UNAMORTIZED BOND DISCOUNT difference between the face value (par value) of a bond and the proceeds received from the sale of the bond by the issuing company, less whatever portion has been amortized, that is, written off to expense, as recorded periodically on the profit and loss statement.

UNAMORTIZED PREMIUMS ON INVESTMENTS unexpensed portion of the amount by which the price paid for a security exceeded its PAR VALUE (bond or preferred stock) or MARKET VALUE (common stock).

UNAPPROPRIATED PROFIT *see* RETAINED EARNINGS.

UNAPPROPRIATED RETAINED EARNINGS same as RETAINED EARNINGS, unless part of the retained earnings has been appropriated for a special purpose. Such an appropriation would be specified.

UNAUTHORIZED STRIKE *see* WILDCAT STRIKE.

UNBALANCED GROWTH economic growth in which certain sectors of the economy grow faster than others, thus causing economic dislocations or economically risky overreliance of the economy upon certain sectors.

UNBIASED ESTIMATOR if the average estimate of several RANDOM SAMPLES equals the population parameter, the estimate is unbiased. For example, if credit card holders in a city were repetitively random sampled and questioned what their account balances were as of a specific date, the average of the results across all samples would equal the population parameter. If however, only credit card holders in one neighborhood were sampled, the average of the sample estimates would be a biased estimator of all account balances for the city and would not equal the population parameter.

UNCOLLECTED FUNDS portion of bank deposit made up of checks that have not yet been collected by the depository bank; that is, payment has not yet been acknowledged by the bank on which a check was drawn. A bank will usually not let a depositor draw on uncollected funds.

UNCOLLECTIBLE *see* DEADBEAT.

UNCOLLECTIBLE ACCOUNT customer account that cannot be collected because of the customer's unwillingness or inability to pay. A business normally writes off such a RECEIVABLE as worthless after several attempts at collecting the funds.

UNCONSOLIDATED SUBSIDIARY subsidiary showing individual financial statements that are not presented in the CONSOLIDATED FINANCIAL STATEMENTS. The EQUITY METHOD of accounting is used for unconsolidated subsidiaries.

UNCOVERED OPTION *see* NAKED OPTION.

UNDERAPPLIED OVERHEAD in cost accounting, situation where an insufficient amount of factory overhead was charged to the products manufactured.

UNDERCAPITALIZATION situation in which a business does not have enough capital to carry out its normal business functions.

UNDERCLASS economically disadvantaged people in a society. The underclass are economically deprived for a wide variety of sociological reasons.

UNDEREMPLOYED people who are not fully employed according to their education, abilities and experience. Underemployed people are not utilizing their full capabilities and talents, which often leads to frustration and anger.

UNDERGROUND ECONOMY portion of the economy that goes largely undetected by taxing authorities. Transactions usually are BARTER or in cash and include both illegal activities and activities that would be legal except for their unrecorded nature.

UNDERHAND sly, deceitful; perhaps derived from card cheats who deal from the bottom of the deck.

UNDERINSURED person who does not have sufficient insurance coverage to compensate in the event of loss of life or property.

UNDERLYING COMPANY *see* SUBSIDIARY COMPANY.

UNDERLYING DEBT Real estate: senior debt. *See also* WRAPAROUND MORTGAGE. **Securities:** municipal bond term referring to the debt of government entities within the jurisdiction of larger government entities for which the larger entity has partial credit responsibility.

UNDERLYING FUTURES CONTRACT FUTURES CONTRACT that underlies an OPTION on that future. For example, the Chicago Board of Trade offers a U.S. Treasury bond futures option. The underlying future is the Treasury bond futures contract traded on the Board of Trade.

UNDERLYING MORTGAGE FIRST MORTGAGE when there is a WRAP-AROUND MORTGAGE. A wraparound mortgage for $100,000 might include a $60,000 underlying first mortgage in its balance, so the additional money provided by the wrap is $40,000.

UNDERLYING SECURITY

Options: security that must be delivered if a PUT OPTION or CALL OPTION contract is exercised.

Securities: common stock that underlies certain types of securities issued by corporations. This stock must be delivered if a subscription warrant or subscription right is exercised, if a convertible bond or preferred stock is converted into common shares, or if an incentive stock option is exercised.

UNDERPAY inadequate wages. An underpay situation occurs when individuals are being paid less than a job or procedure is worth in market or perceived terms.

UNDERPAYMENT PENALTY (TAX) penalty for inadequate tax withholding or estimated tax payments. A penalty can generally be avoided by paying at least 90% of current-year actual tax liability (through withholding or estimated tax payments) before the tax return filing deadline.

UNDERREPORTING the improper failure to report an adequate amount of income on a tax return.

UNDER THE COUNTER illegal payments made for merchandise or services, usually in excess of the stated price. Under-the-counter payments are a form of bribery and extortion.

UNDERTONE
1. subdued voice or whisper.
2. subtle suggestion or indication.

UNDERVALUED security selling below its LIQUIDATION value or the MARKET VALUE analysts believe it deserves. A company's stock may be undervalued because the industry is out of favor, because the company is not well known or has an erratic history of earnings, or for many other reasons. Undervalued companies are frequently targets of TAKEOVER attempts, since acquirers can buy assets cheaply this way.

UNDERWITHHOLDING situation in which taxpayers have too little federal, state, or local income tax withheld from their salaries. Because they have underwithheld, these taxpayers may owe income taxes when they file their tax returns. If the underwithholding is large enough, penalties and interest may also be due.

UNDERWRITE

Insurance: assume risk in exchange for a premium.

Investments: assume the risk of buying a new issue of securities from the issuing corporation or government entity and reselling it to the public, either directly or through dealers. The *underwriting group* (*underwriter*) makes a profit on the difference between the price paid to the issuer and the public offering price, called the UNDERWRITING SPREAD. *See also* INVESTMENT BANKER.

UNDERWRITERS LABORATORIES, INC. private organization that performs a wide range of product safety tests on fire-protective equipment, electric and heating appliances, wiring, and building materials. Their certification label appears on thousands of products that have been tested successfully for their fire, shock, and casualty hazards.

UNDERWRITING SPREAD difference between the amount paid to an *issuer* of securities in a PRIMARY DISTRIBUTION and the PUBLIC OFFERING PRICE. The amount of spread varies widely, depending on the size of the issue, the financial strength of the issuer, the type of security involved (stock, bonds, rights), the status of the security (senior, junior, secured, unsecured), and the type of commitment made by the investment bankers.

UNDISCOUNTED goods or services sold at the full established price without ALLOWANCES or DISCOUNTS. Undiscounted pricing protects catalog houses and other direct marketers from the cost of reprinting price sheets and promotions each time a price is changed. It also reduces the possibility that a customer will be annoyed to discover someone else paid less for the same thing. Undiscounted pricing works best for goods and services with stable demand and little price elasticity.

UNDISTRIBUTED PROFITS (EARNINGS, NET INCOME) *see* RETAINED EARNINGS.

UNDIVIDED INTEREST an ownership right to use and possession of a property that is shared among co-owners, with no one co-owner having exclusive rights to any portion of the property. For example, ten investors form a TENANCY IN COMMON and purchase a 100-acre tract of land. Each cotenant obtains an *undivided interest* in the property. All decisions as to the use and disposition of the land are made collectively by all cotenants. No one cotenant may unilaterally mortgage, develop, or sell a portion of the tract. A partnership tax return is filed. Each co-owner also includes a share of the income, loss, gain, etc., in his/her own personal income tax return.

UNDIVIDED PROFIT account shown on a bank's BALANCE SHEET representing profits that have neither been paid out as dividends nor transferred to the bank's SURPLUS account.

UNDOCUMENTED not described or explained in the printed manual (documentation) or online Help file of a computer software application.

UNDUE INFLUENCE influence of another that destroys the requisite free will of a TESTATOR or DONOR and creates a ground for nullifying a WILL or invalidating an improvident GIFT. The exercise of *undue influence* is suggested by excessive insistence, superiority of will or mind, the relationship of the parties or pressure on the donor or testator by any other means to do what he is unable, practically, to refuse.

UNEARNED DISCOUNT account on the books of a lending institution recognizing interest deducted in advance, which will be taken into income as earned over the life of the loan.

UNEARNED INCOME (REVENUE)
Accounting: income received but not yet earned, such as rent received in advance or other advances from customers. Unearned income is usually classified as a CURRENT LIABILITY on a company's BALANCE SHEET.
Taxes: income from sources other than wages, salaries, tips, and other employee compensation, such as dividends, interest, and rent.

UNEARNED INCREMENT increase in the value of real estate unrelated to effort on the part of the owner, often due to an increase in population. *See also* SWEAT EQUITY.

UNEARNED INTEREST interest that has already been collected on a loan but that cannot yet be counted as book earnings. PREPAID INTEREST received falls into this category; prepaid interest is taxable when received by CASH or ACCRUAL BASIS taxpayers.

UNEARNED PREMIUM insurance premium that is paid beyond the current period, so it is not yet earned by the insurer. If the policy is canceled, the insured should receive a refund of the unearned amount.

UNEMPLOYABLE those who are not employable because of their lack of skills, education, and experience. The unemployable are chronically unemployed. *See also* HARD-CORE UNEMPLOYED.

UNEMPLOYED LABOR FORCE portion of population that is not employed but is willing and able to work and is actively seeking work.

UNEMPLOYMENT state of being without paid work, though willing and able to work and actively seeking work; also, proportion of labor force that is without paid work.

UNEMPLOYMENT COMPENSATION unemployment compensation is taxable to the recipient. It includes:

1. benefits paid by a state from the Federal Unemployment Trust Fund.
2. unemployment insurance benefits.
3. railroad unemployment compensation benefits.
4. disability payments from a government program paid as a substitute for unemployment compensation.
5. trade readjustment allowances under the Trade Act of 1974.
6. benefits under the Airline Deregulation Act of 1978.
7. unemployment assistance under the Disaster Relief Act Amendments of 1974.

UNEMPLOYMENT INSURANCE TAX deductible as a business expense of an employer. *See also* FEDERAL UNEMPLOYMENT TAX ACT (FUTA).

UNEMPLOYMENT RATE percentage of the CIVILIAN LABOR FORCE actively looking for work but unable to find jobs. The rate is compiled by the U.S. Department of Labor, in cooperation with the labor departments in all the states, and released to the public on the first Friday of every month.

UNEMPLOYMENT, SEASONAL *see* SEASONAL UNEMPLOYMENT.

UNEMPLOYMENT, STRUCTURAL *see* STRUCTURAL UNEMPLOYMENT.

UNENCUMBERED PROPERTY real estate with free and clear title; property owned in FEE SIMPLE, that is, there are no mortgage, vendor, mechanic's, or tax liens on the property, no restrictive covenants exist, and no easements have been granted.

UNETHICAL not ethical; not in accordance with the standards followed in a business or profession.

UNEXPIRED COST cost left until an item has paid for itself; difference between the price paid for an item and the amount of money it has generated. The unexpired or unused portion of the economic benefits from an expenditure represents an asset for future usage.

UNFAIR COMPETITION

1. unfair, untrue, or misleading advertising likely to lead the public to believe that certain goods are associated with another manufacturer.
2. imitating a competitor's product, package, or trademark in circumstances where the consumer might be misled.
3. representations or conduct that deceive the public into believing that the business name, reputation, or goodwill of one person is that of another.
4. pirating a product, such as reproducing computer software illegally.
5. selling in a foreign country for less than the cost of manufacture. *See also* DUMPING.

UNFAIR LABOR PRACTICE illegal union or management labor practices. The National Labor Relations Board determines whether a particular labor practice is an unfair labor practice subject to court appeal. The WAGNER ACT and the TAFT-HARTLEY ACT define unfair labor practices.

UNFAIR LABOR PRACTICE (BY UNIONS) certain practices identified by the TAFT-HARTLEY ACT in 1947 to protect workers and employers from UNIONS. This act made it illegal to coerce workers into joining unions, to restrain employers from recognizing unions, to cause an employer to discriminate against any worker, or to charge excessive membership fees.

UNFAVORABLE BALANCE OF TRADE value of a country's imports exceeding the value of its exports. The United States has had an unfavorable balance of trade since the mid-1970s.

UNFREEZE to remove economic restrictions, usually upon price increases or imports.

UNFUNDED with reference to a PENSION or PROFIT-SHARING PLAN, failing to meet or have a minimum funding standard. *See also* FUNDED.

UNICAP RULES *see* UNIFORM CAPITALIZATION RULES.

UNIFORM CAPITALIZATION RULES a method of valuing INVENTORY for tax purposes that requires CAPITALIZATION of DIRECT COSTS (such as material and labor costs) and an allocable portion of INDIRECT COSTS that benefit or are incurred because of production or resale activities. Certain expenses must be included in the BASIS of property produced or in inventory costs rather than currently de- ducted. These costs are then recoverable through DEPRECIATION or AMORTIZATION or as COST OF GOODS SOLD.

UNIFORM COMMERCIAL CODE (UCC) code of laws governing various commercial transactions, including the sale of goods, banking transactions, secured transactions in personal property, and other matters, that was designed to bring uniformity in these areas to the laws of the various states, and that has been adopted, with some modifications, in all states (except Louisiana) as well as in the District of Columbia and in the Virgin Islands.

UNIFORM GIFTS TO MINORS ACT (UGMA) law adopted by most states that sets up rules for the distribution and administration of assets in the name of a child. The Act provides for a CUSTODIAN of the assets, often the parents, but sometimes an independent TRUSTEE.

UNIFORM RESOURCE LOCATOR *see* URL.

UNIFORM SETTLEMENT STATEMENT the form prescribed by RESPA for federally related loans, which must be prepared by the person who handles a closing, must contain certain relevant closing information, and must be given to buyer and seller.

UNIFORM STANDARDS OF PROFESSIONAL APPRAISAL PRACTICE (USPAP) a code of professional standards, promulgated by the Appraisal Foundation, that appraisers belonging to certain appraisal organizations are expected to follow in preparing appraisal reports.

UNILATERAL CONTRACT agreement whereby one makes a promise to do, or refrain from doing, something in return for an actual performance by the other, rather than a mere promise of performance. *See also* BILATERAL CONTRACT.

UNIMPROVED PROPERTY land that has received no development, construction, or site preparation so that it qualifies for capital gain or loss treatment (that is, *raw land*). Improvements to property cause the property to receive ORDINARY INCOME treatment as INVENTORY of a DEALER.

UNINCORPORATED ASSOCIATION organization formed by a group of people. If the organization has too many characteristics of a corporation, it may be treated like one for income tax purposes. Unique corporate characteristics are:
1. perpetual life.
2. limited liability.
3. free transferability of interests.
4. centralized management.

UNINSURABLE RISK risk that is so great or so difficult to calculate that no insurance company wants to insure.

UNINSURABLE TITLE *see* INSURABLE TITLE.

UNINSURED MOTORIST INSURANCE form of insurance that covers the policyholder and family members if injured by a hit-and-run driver or a motorist who carries no liability insurance, assuming the driver is at fault.

UNION employee association designed to promote employee rights and work-related welfare. Union organizations are formally recognized under the Railway Labor Act and WAGNER ACT as well as by related legislation. *See also* LABOR UNION.

UNION CONTRACT *see* LABOR AGREEMENT.

UNION LABEL identifying mark placed on goods to show that they were produced by a LABOR UNION or in a shop that deals with organized labor. It encourages patronage of these goods by other union members and supporters.

UNION RATE hourly wage rate, usually single rate for an occupation or trade, established by collective bargaining. Usually it is the minimum rate that can be paid to qualified people in the job.

UNION RECOGNITION recognition achieved after a secret-ballot election, supervised by the NATIONAL LABOR RELATIONS BOARD, has been conducted, in which a successful BARGAINING AGENT achieves at least 50 percent of the vote; also called *union certification*. After winning the election, a union is certified by the NLRB as the official bargaining agent for the bargaining unit.

UNION SALTING union organizing method of having one or more union members join a nonunionized organization as an employee for the purpose of organizing its membership.

UNION SHOP workplace where all the employees must be members of a union. Nonunion members may work in such shops provided they agree to join the union. *See also* CLOSED SHOP; OPEN SHOP.

UNION SHOP, MODIFIED labor agreement providing that existing employees may continue as union or nonunion members, but new employees must join the union.

UNIQUE IMPAIRMENT phrase used in underwriting risks, denoting factors that set an applicant apart from the standard applicant. For example, an applicant with untreated epilepsy has a *unique impairment* not common to the general population. This impairment may adversely affect the life expectancy of the applicant, who might have to pay a higher-than-standard premium.

UNISSUED STOCK shares of a corporation's stock authorized in its charter but not issued. They are shown on the balance sheet along with shares ISSUED AND OUTSTANDING. Unissued shares cannot pay dividends and cannot be voted. They are not to be confused with TREASURY STOCK, which is issued but not outstanding.

UNIT
1. any division of quantity accepted as a standard of measurement or of exchange. For example, in the commodities market, a unit of wheat is a bushel, a unit of coffee a pound, and a unit of shell eggs a dozen. The unit of U.S. currency is the dollar.
2. part of a larger business entity. For example, a division or subsidiary might be called a *unit* of the business.

UNITARY ELASTICITY situation where a change in the market price of a good results in no change in the total amount spent for the good within the market. *See also* PRICE ELASTICITY.

UNITED PARCEL SERVICE (UPS) freight company that transports letters and packages.

UNITED STATES GOVERNMENT SECURITIES direct government obligations, that is, debt issues of the U.S. government, such as Treasury bills, notes, and bonds and Series EE, Series HH, and Series I savings bonds as distinguished from government-sponsored AGENCY issues. *See also* GOVERNMENT SECURITIES.

UNITED STATES PERSON for income tax purposes, a citizen or resident of the United States, a DOMESTIC PARTNERSHIP, a DOMESTIC COR-

PORATION, or any ESTATE or TRUST (except certain foreign estates and trusts).

UNIT INVESTMENT TRUST (UIT) investment vehicle, registered with the SEC under the INVESTMENT COMPANY ACT OF 1940, that purchases a fixed PORTFOLIO OF SECURITIES, such as corporate, municipal, or government BONDS, MORTGAGE-BACKED SECURITIES, COMMON STOCK, or PREFERRED STOCK.

UNIT-LABOR COST cost of labor needed for one unit of some good. It is calculated so that the price of the unit reflects the cost of the labor necessary to produce it.

UNIT OF TRADING normal number of shares, bonds, or commodities constituting the minimum unit of trading on an exchange. For stocks, this is usually 100 shares. For corporate bonds on the New York Stock Exchange, the unit for exchange trading is $1,000 or $5,000 par value.

UNITS-OF-PRODUCTION METHOD accounting method where a provision for depreciation is computed at a fixed rate per unit of product, based on an estimate of the total number of units the property will produce during its service life. This method is useful only when the total number of units of production can be accurately estimated.

UNITY OF COMMAND principle of management stating that each subordinate should report to only one superior.

UNIVERSAL LIFE INSURANCE ADJUSTABLE LIFE INSURANCE under which: (1) premiums are flexible, not fixed; (2) protection is adjustable, not fixed; and (3) insurance company expenses and other charges are specifically disclosed to a purchaser.

UNIVERSAL PRODUCT CODE (UPC) number used to identify a product. Translated into BAR CODES consisting of a series of vertical parallel bars, the UPC can be used for scan entry, by an electronic cash register, of information for product sales and inventory TRACKING.

UNIVERSAL RESOURCE LOCATOR *see* URL.

UNIVERSAL VARIABLE LIFE INSURANCE policy containing features of UNIVERSAL LIFE INSURANCE and VARIABLE LIFE INSURANCE in that excess interest credited to the cash value account depends on investment results of separate accounts (equities, bonds, real estate, etc.). The policyowner selects the accounts into which the premium payments are to be made.

UNIVERSE statistical term representing all possible elements in a set. The universe of shoppers in the United States would consist of all shoppers in the United States. Because the large number makes a total analysis impossible, a representative sample (statistical sample) is selected for study to determine shopping habits of all shoppers.

UNIX powerful operating system, developed by AT&T Bell Laboratories in 1969, that can be used on many PLATFORMS and can run a wider variety of hardware than other operating systems. More popular for workstation computers on networks rather than individual PCs; used primarily by universities and mid-sized businesses.

UNJUST ENRICHMENT gain or benefit that is the result of another's efforts or acts but for which that other has received no compensation, and for which the one receiving the benefit has not paid. A person who is deemed by law to have been unjustly enriched at the expense of another is required to make *restitution* to the other.

UNLIMITED LIABILITY risk associated with the PROPRIETORSHIP form of business or a general partner, where there is no distinction between business and personal liability. For example, a business liability could force the businessowner to use personal assets to retire the debt.

UNLISTED SECURITY stock or bond not listed on a stock exchange and therefore traded only in the over-the-counter market.

UNLOADING
Finance: selling off large quantities of merchandise inventory at below-market prices, either to raise cash quickly or to depress the market in a particular product.
Investment: selling securities or commodities when prices are declining to preclude further loss.

UNMAILABLE MATTER materials that cannot be accepted by the U.S. Postal Service because of size, weight, or contents.

UNMARRIED TAXPAYER a taxpayer who is single or who has obtained a final decree of divorce or separate maintenance or a decree of annulment by the last day of the tax year; considered unmarried for the entire year.

UNOCCUPANCY absence of people from a given property for at least 60 consecutive days. Many property insurance policies suspend coverage after a structure has been unoccupied for 60 consecutive days because the probability of loss from such perils as vandalism and malicious mischief increases dramatically. Unoccupancy results in an increase in hazards within the control of an insured, which gives the insurance company the right to suspend the policy. *See also* VACANCY.

UNOCCUPIED *see* VACANT.

UNPAID DIVIDEND dividend that has been declared by the board of directors of a corporation but has not reached its PAYMENT DATE. Once a board acts to DECLARE a dividend, it is then recognized as a corporate LIABILITY until paid.

UNQUALIFIED OPINION independent auditor's opinion that a company's financial statements are fairly presented, in all material respects, in conformity with GENERALLY ACCEPTED ACCOUNTING PRINCIPLES. The justification for the expression of the auditor's opinion rests on the conformity of his or her audit with generally accepted auditing standards and on his or her opinion. *See also* ACCOUNTANT'S OPINION; ADVERSE OPINION; QUALIFIED OPINION.

UNREALIZED APPRECIATION the excess of an asset's FAIR MARKET VALUE over its ADJUSTED BASIS, for determining gains on sale or other disposition of the asset. No income tax is due until a sale occurs. *Contrast with* UNREALIZED DEPRECIATION.

UNREALIZED DEPRECIATION the excess of the ADJUSTED BASIS of an asset over its FAIR MARKET VALUE, for determining losses on sale or other disposition of the asset. *Contrast with* UNREALIZED APPRECIATION.

UNREALIZED PROFIT (LOSS) profit (loss) that has not become actual. It is realized when a security or commodity futures contract in which there is a gain (loss) is actually sold. *See also* PAPER PROFIT (LOSS).

UNRECORDED DEED instrument that transfers title from one party (grantor) to another party (grantee) without providing public notice of change in ownership. Recording is essential to protect one's interest in real estate.

UNRECOVERED COST unexpired BOOK VALUE of an asset; ORIGINAL COST less ACCUMULATED DEPRECIATION.

UNREGISTERED STOCK *see* LETTER STOCK.

UNRELATED BUSINESS INCOME (UBI) income from a trade or business that is not substantially related to a not-for-profit organization's tax-exempt function and that is regularly carried on by the organization. Annuities, interest, dividends, royalties, and rent from certain real and certain personal property are specifically excluded from the definition of unrelated business income. A corporate tax is imposed on UBI in excess of $1,000 in order to place the tax-exempt organization on an equal footing with taxable organizations with respect to their business operations.

UNRELATED PERSON person who does not fit into any of the categories under RELATED PARTIES.

UNREPORTED INCOME the improper failure to include certain income on a tax return.

UNSECURED DEBT obligation not backed by the pledge of specific COLLATERAL.

UNSKILLED describing an individual having no formal skills, training, or education. Unskilled workers are the least employable and most easily replaced through automation.

UNSTATED INTEREST when no interest or low interest is provided in an INSTALLMENT SALE agreement, part of each payment will be treated as interest. The amount treated as interest is referred to as *unstated* or *imputed interest.* Imputed interest reduces the selling price and increases the seller's interest income and the buyer's interest expense.

UNWIND A TRADE to reverse a securities transaction through an off-setting transaction.

UPDATE
1. computerized file maintenance process in an OFF-LINE system that applies all necessary TRANSACTIONS against the old file, producing a new file reflecting all adds, deletes, and CHANGES that have become necessary since the last update.
2. provide current information to an individual or group of persons, or revise printed information according to the most current information available.

UP FRONT
1. money given immediately upon the completion of a financial agreement.
2. to be frank and candid by giving full factual disclosure.

UPGRADING improving the quality or performance of something by making changes. For example, a computer's storage capability can be upgraded by adding a larger data storage disk.

UPKEEP necessary care and management of equipment and operations. All mechanical equipment and organizations need continual maintenance to forestall a total system breakdown. *See also* MAINTENANCE.

UPLOAD process of providing data from a microcomputer to a MAIN-FRAME or MINICOMPUTER or another MICROCOMPUTER. For example, an accountant can upload information from his or her computer to the client's computer system. *See also* DOWNLOAD.

UPSET PRICE term used in AUCTIONS that represents the minimum price at which a seller of property will entertain bids; also called *reserve price.*

UPSIDE POTENTIAL amount of upward price movement an investor or an analyst expects of a particular stock, bond, or commodity. This opinion may result from either FUNDAMENTAL ANALYSIS or TECHNICAL ANALYSIS.

UPSWING change to or acceleration of ECONOMIC GROWTH.

UP TICK indicates that the latest trade in a stock is at a higher price than the previous trade. A zero-plus tick is a trade at the last price with the preceding different price registered as an up tick. A SHORT SALE can be transacted only on an up tick or zero-plus tick.

UPTIME time in which a machine is actually operational and a worker is occupied. For example, the computer is *up*. This is the opposite of DOWNTIME, when the machine is no longer operational, usually because of the need for repairs or maintenance.

UPTREND upward direction in the price of a stock, bond, or commodity futures contract or overall market.

UPWARDLY MOBILE description of a segment of the population that is attempting to move up on the socioeconomic class scale. *Upwardly mobile* describes a trend toward higher status in terms of income, material goods, and lifestyles. The YUPPIES are an example of this upwardly mobile trend.

URBAN relating to cities or intensively developed areas. *Contrast with* rural, which refers to sparsely developed areas, or SUBURB, which is a moderately developed area.

URBAN RENEWAL process of redeveloping deteriorated section of a city, often through demolition and new construction. Although urban renewal may be privately funded, it is most often associated with government renewal programs. The typical program attempts to demolish concentrations of dilapidated housing and attract developers of middle-income or mixed housing. Often, however, urban renewal areas become sites for new public buildings, such as civic auditoriums, sports arenas, and universities.

URBAN SPRAWL pejorative term for low-density development in suburban and the fringe of urban areas. Characteristics include distance from employment and commercial centers, dependence on automobile travel, and extended public INFRASTRUCTURE.

URL uniform resource locator or universal resource locator; an addressing scheme used by WORLD WIDE WEB browsers to locate resources on the Internet.

USB *U*niversal *S*erial *B*us, a type of serial interface for computer peripherals and other electronic devices, now largely supplanting PARALLEL PORTS. Most USB devices are PLUG-AND-PLAY: they can be connected and disconnected without powering down the system. Also, most computers now come with several USB ports (as compared to a single parallel port), and several devices can be *daisy-chained* (connected in series) or connected separately to a USB hub plugged into one of the USB ports.

USB DRIVE portable PLUG-AND-PLAY computer storage device, small enough to be attached to a keychain, that can be plugged into any USB port and is immediately recognized by the computer as an external drive. Also called *flash drive, jump drive, memory stick, thumb drive,* etc. Capacities currently range from 8MB to 2GB.

U.S. CITIZEN every person born or naturalized in the United States who is subject to its jurisdiction.

USEFUL LIFE period of time over which a depreciable asset is expected to provide a competitive return. The MODIFIED ACCELERATED COST RECOVERY SYSTEM allows depreciable lives for tax deduction purposes that are not necessarily related to the useful life of the property.

USENET NEWSGROUPS *see* NEWSGROUPS.

USER FEE charge usually by a municipality to users of a service. Municipal parks, swimming pools, and toll roads, for example, are paid for by those who benefit rather than by broad-based taxes.

USER-FRIENDLY computer hardware or software designed to be easy for people, especially novices, to use. When computers were operated only by specialists, little attention was paid to making programs user-friendly. However, when computers became more popular, it became very important to write programs that could be easily understood by the people who use them.

USER ID the name by which a user is identified on a particular computer NETWORK. In order to log onto a system, the user must supply both an ID and a password.

USPAP *see* UNIFORM STANDARDS OF PROFESSIONAL APPRAISAL PRACTICE.

U.S. SAVINGS BOND *see* SAVINGS BOND.

USUFRUCTUARY RIGHT right that allows the use of property that belongs to another. The owner of land that bounds or contains a natural water channel has a usufructuary right to use of the water. The water itself is considered to be held by the public with all adjacent property owners holding rights to its use. Restrictions on that use vary under state law.

USURY charging a rate of interest greater than that permitted by state law. In most states, usury limits vary according to the type of lender and the type of loan. Federal laws have been passed to preempt certain usury limits under certain conditions.

UTILITARIANISM field of the teleological theory of ethics stating that decisions should be made on the basis of achieving the greatest good for the greatest number without making an intrinsic value judgment about the decision itself. *Utilitarianism* is sometimes called a consequentialist theory in that the primary consideration is the consequence of the decision.

UTILITY
1. service, such as water, sewerage, gas, electricity, and telephones, that is generally required to operate a building.
2. computer program that provides a specific function to assist in the operation of the computer, such as checking for viruses, defragmenting the hard disk, or compressing data. *Contrast with* APPLICATION SOFTWARE.

UTILITY EASEMENT use of another's property for the purpose of laying gas, electric, water, and sewer lines. A property owner grants a utility easement to the electric power company to extend power lines to the owner's home.

V

VACANCY, VACANT unoccupied. An empty structure.

VACANCY RATE percentage of all units or space that is unoccupied or not rented. On a pro-forma income statement, a projected vacancy rate is used to estimate the *vacancy allowance*, which is deducted from potential gross income to derive effective gross income. *See also* ABSORPTION RATE; BREAK-EVEN POINT; OCCUPANCY LEVEL.

VACANT LAND land not currently being used. It may have utilities and off-site improvements. *See also* RAW LAND.

VACATE
Real estate: to move out. For example, a tenant *vacates* an apartment by terminating occupancy and removing all possessions. The tenant is responsible for rent to the end of the lease term.
Law: to avoid or annul, as to *vacate* an order.

VACATION HOME a dwelling used by the owner occasionally for recreational or resort purposes. It may be rented to others for a portion of the year. Income tax deductions pertaining to vacation homes depend on the frequency of use by the owner. Generally, a business loss cannot be claimed on a vacation home.

VACATION PAY any amount paid to employees while they are on vacation. It includes amounts paid even if the employee chooses not to take a vacation.

VALID having legally binding force; legally sufficient and authorized by law. *See also* NULL AND VOID; VOIDABLE.

VALLEY *see* TROUGH.

VA LOAN home loan guaranteed by the U.S. Department of Veterans Affairs (VA) under the Servicemen's Readjustment Act of 1944 and later. The VA guarantees restitution to the lender in the event of default. The amount of guarantee available has been raised on a regular basis. The home must be the borrower's principal residence.

VALUABLE CONSIDERATION type of promised payment upon which a promisee can enforce a claim against an unwilling promisor. It includes money, extension of time, and other equivalents for the grant, and is distinguished from *good consideration*, which may be love and affection toward a relative, generosity, and the like.

VALUATION
1. estimated worth or price.
2. act of estimating the worth of a thing. *See also* APPRAISAL.

VALUE worth of all the rights arising from ownership; quantity of one thing that will be given in exchange for another. Of course, a piece of property may have a certain value to its owner (*value in use*) equal to the amount of other property (typically cash) that the owner would be willing to accept in exchange for the property without loss in wealth or well-being. The same property may have a different FAIR MARKET VALUE (*value in exchange*) equal to the amount of other property exchanged for the property when many typically motivated buyers and sellers are allowed to interact.

VALUE-ADDED TAX (VAT) tax imposed at each step in the production process, levied upon the difference between the purchase cost of the asset to the taxpayer and the price at which it may be sold—the *value added* to it. The VAT is a primary source of tax revenue in certain European countries but has not been extensively used in the United States, although certain presidents have studied the matter.

VALUE DATE
1. In banking, official date when money is transferred, that is, becomes good funds to the depositor. The *value date* differs from the *entry date* when items are received from the depositor, since the items must then be forwarded to the paying bank or otherwise collected.
2. In Eurodollar and foreign currency transactions, synonymous with SETTLEMENT DATE or DELIVERY DATE.

VALUE IN EXCHANGE amount of other goods and services for which a unit of a specific good can be exchanged in a market. The money price often is one measure of value in an exchange.

VALUE IN USE *see* VALUE.

VALUE INVESTING investment philosophy that focuses on buying stocks that are trading at bargain prices based on FUNDAMENTAL ANALYSIS, then holding them until they become fully valued. Stocks with low PRICE/EARNING RATIOS, low PRICE/BOOK RATIOS, or high DIVIDEND YIELD are likely to attract value investors.

VALUE JUDGMENT judgment reflecting values and opinions. A value judgment is a biased opinion.

VALUE LINE INVESTMENT SURVEY investment advisory service that ranks hundreds of stock for "timeliness" and safety. Using a computerized model based on a company's earnings momentum, value Line projects which stocks will have the best or worst relative price performance over the next 12 months.

VA MORTGAGE *see* VETERANS ADMINISTRATION (VA).

VARIABLE data item that can change its value; also called a *factor* or an *element*.

VARIABLE ANNUITY life insurance ANNUITY whose value fluctuates with that of an underlying securities portfolio or other index of performance. The variable annuity contrasts with a *conventional* or *fixed annuity*, whose rate of return is constant.

VARIABLE COST cost that changes directly with the amount of production, such as direct material or direct labor needed to complete a product. *See also* FIXED COST.

VARIABLE COSTING *see* DIRECT COSTING.

VARIABLE COSTS or **EXPENSES** business costs that increase with production or sales. *Contrast with* FIXED COSTS.

VARIABLE INTEREST RATE amount of compensation to a lender that is allowed to vary over the maturity of a loan. The amount of variation is generally governed by an appropriate index. *See also* ADJUSTABLE-RATE MORTGAGE; FLOATING-RATE NOTE.

VARIABLE LIFE INSURANCE policy under which the face value (death benefit) can fluctuate. It increases or decreases in value, but never below a guaranteed minimum, based on the investment performance of a separate account in which the premiums are placed by the policyowner. For example, one account might be composed of equities, another of bonds. As with conventional whole life insurance, premiums are level and the policy has loan and surrender values.

VARIABLE PRICING marketing strategy that allows a different price to be charged to different customers or at different times. This type of pricing is common among street vendors, antique dealers, and other small, independently owned businesses but is not practical for direct marketers, who rely upon preprinted promotion forms.

VARIABLES SAMPLING sampling designed to predict the value of a given variable for a population. The variables under AUDIT are typically the total population or the arithmetic mean. An example is the CPA's estimation of the cost of a group of inventory components.

VARIANCE
Accounting: difference between actual cost and standard cost in the categories of direct material, direct labor, and direct overhead.
Finance: (1) difference between corresponding items on a comparative balance sheet and profit and loss statement; (2) difference between actual experience and budgeted or projected experience in any financial category.
Statistics: measure of the dispersion of a distribution. It is the sum of the squares of the deviations from the mean. *See also* STANDARD DEVIATION.
Zoning: exemption from the application of a zoning ordinance or regulation, permitting a use that varies from that otherwise permitted. The exception is granted by the appropriate authority in special circumstances to protect against undue hardship wrought by strict enforcement. *See also* NONCONFORMING USE.

VARIETY STORE retail store carrying a variety of items in the low and popular price ranges, targeted for the family market. Variety stores carry items such as apparel, women's accessories, gift items, and stationery.

VAT *see* VALUE-ADDED TAX.

VEEP *see* VICE-PRESIDENT.

VELOCITY turnover of money, that is, the number of times a dollar is spent in a given period of time. The GROSS DOMESTIC PRODUCT is the product of total MONEY SUPPLY and velocity.

VENDEE buyer, especially in a CONTRACT for the SALE of REAL ESTATE.

VENDOR seller, especially a person who sells real property; also supplier, retailer, or street peddler.

VENDOR'S LIEN collateral granted to the seller of property as security for a PROMISSORY NOTE taken by the seller as part of the selling price.

VENTURE business undertaking entailing a degree of risk. A business venture is an entrepreneurial activity in which capital is exposed to the risk of loss for the possibility of reaping a profit reward.

VENTURE CAPITAL important source of financing for START-UP companies or others embarking on new or TURNAROUND ventures that entail some investment risk but offer the potential for aboveaverage future profits; also called *risk* capital. Prominent among firms seeking venture capital are those classified as emerginggrowth or high technology companies.

VENTURE TEAM management team assembled for the purpose of a new business operation. A venture team supervises and manages a start-up business, attending to all the details from raising VENTURE CAPITAL to managing the initial operations.

VERBATIMS research reports that are word-for-word duplications of interviews, without editorial comment.

VERTICAL ANALYSIS financial statement item that is used as a base value. All other accounts on the financial statement are compared to it. In the balance sheet, for example, total assets equal 100%. Each asset is stated as a percentage of total assets. Similarly, total liabilities and stockholders' equity are assigned 100% with a given liability or equity account stated as a percentage of the total liabilities and stockholders' equity. *See also* HORIZONTAL ANALYSIS.

VERTICAL CONFLICT conflict occurring between two or more different hierarchical members of a CHANNEL OF DISTRIBUTION. For example, a retail distributor may refuse to carry a manufacturer's product because of low sales, further decreasing the manufacturer's total sales. *Contrast with* HORIZONTAL CONFLICT.

VERTICAL DISCOUNT special reduced rate for the purchase of several radio or television time slots to be broadcast at intervals within a set period of time such as a day. It is called a *vertical* discount because the time slots on a media schedule are listed with hours vertically and days horizontally.

VERTICAL INTEGRATION a company's domination of a market by controlling all steps in the production process, from the extraction of raw materials through the manufacture and sale of the final product. *Contrast with* HORIZONTAL INTEGRATION.

VERTICAL MANAGEMENT STRUCTURE hierarchical structure and functioning of an organization in terms of the layers of management delegation of authority. A vertical management structure has divisions of authority with various levels of responsibility. For example, a vice-president of marketing might have an assistant vicepresident who is in charge of a departmental director, and so on.

VERTICAL MARKETING SYSTEMS systems whereby hierarchical CHANNEL OF DISTRIBUTION members coordinate marketing efforts to reduce conflicts.

VERTICAL MERGER BUSINESS COMBINATION in which members of a vertical CHANNEL OF DISTRIBUTION merge. Essentially this eliminates the middleman, lowering costs and causing it to be more competitive if the savings are passed on to the consumer.

VERTICAL MOBILITY societal opportunity for one to advance one's economic and social status.

VERTICAL ORGANIZATION hierarchically structured organization where all management activities are controlled by a centralized management staff. This traditional type of organization often develops strong bureaucratic control over all organizational activities.

VERTICAL PROMOTION advancement or upgrading of management or supervisory responsibilities in an organization with an accompanying increase in compensation. For example, an individual receives a vertical promotion from a department manager to the position of vice-president, including an increase in responsibilities and compensation.

VERTICAL SPECIALIZATION delegation of responsibilities and duties to others within the same line of authority. Vertical specialization occurs as an organization grows, becoming more complex and requiring additional personnel to cope with the additional workload.

VERTICAL UNION labor union consisting of many crafts and unskilled occupations within the same industry. The CIO under the leadership of John L. Lewis was instrumental in creating industrial unions causing vertical unionization in industries, as opposed to the horizontal craft union policy of the AFL.

VEST to become owned, as when an employee has worked for the company long enough to be entitled to a pension; at that time, even if the employee then resigns, the pension is *vested*.

VESTED INTEREST one in which there is a present fixed right of present or future enjoyment. For example, a person is immediately vested in any amount in his/her INDIVIDUAL RETIREMENT ACCOUNT. However, another employee may have to work for five years for the company before the right to a pension will vest.

VESTING entitlement of a pension plan participant (employee) to receive full benefits at NORMAL RETIREMENT AGE, or a reduced benefit upon EARLY RETIREMENT, whether or not the participant still works for the same employer. Vesting rules as of January 1, 1989, are as follows:
1. full vesting (100%) after a participant completes five years of service with an employer; or
2. vesting of 20% after completion of three years of service with an employer, increasing by 20% for each year of service thereafter, until 100% vesting is achieved at the end of seven years of service.

VETERANS ADMINISTRATION (VA) agency of the federal government that provides services for eligible veterans. Generally, a veteran who has served (beyond basic training) more than 120 days in active duty in the armed forces is eligible for a home loan with no DOWNPAYMENT, as well as educational and other benefits.

VICARIOUS LIABILITY LIABILITY imputed to one person for the actions of another, where the law contemplates that the other should be held responsible for a wrong in fact committed by someone else. Sometimes this doctrine is called *imputed* liability.

VICE-PRESIDENT corporate officer, subordinate to the president, often having responsibility over a functional department, such as the vice-president of marketing or of production.

VIDEOTEXT information that passes via telephone lines between a computer and a home TV screen. It is an interactive system. Data may be entered on the keyboard to the computer system. Giving a supplier an order or making a bank transaction are examples.

VIETNAM-ERA VETERAN a veteran who served in the U.S. armed forces during the Vietnam War (August 5, 1964 to May 7, 1975) and who must be given employment preference in work on federal government contracts under the Vietnam-Era Veterans Readjustment Assistance Act.

VIGORISH usurious rates of interest.

VIOLATION act or condition contrary to law or to permissible use of real property. *See also* FINE.

VIRTUAL COOPERATION group of companies that form a temporary alliance using a computer network for the purpose of accomplishing some shared objective.

VIRUS an insidious piece of computer code written to damage systems. Viruses can be hidden in executable program files posted online; micro viruses can infect documents created in Microsoft Word and Excel, both of which support executable MACROS written in VBA code.

VISIBILITY the immediate insights into a business operation that managers gain from SUPPLY CHAIN MANAGEMENT.

VISION view of the future that can shape current management strategies.

VITA *Volunteer Income Tax Assistance.* An organization of unpaid individuals who help others prepare their tax returns. Principally assisted are elderly, disabled, and non-English-speaking taxpayers.

VOCATIONAL GUIDANCE counseling in seeking a career. The person who performs vocational guidance is a *career counselor.*

VOCATIONAL REHABILITATION equipping an individual with updated job skills to return to the workplace. For example, a returning homemaker may need to learn word processing in order to return to a job as a secretary/typist.

VOICE ACTIVATED machines that can recognize and respond to spoken words.

VOICE RECOGNITION A computer's ability to recognize spoken commands and act on them as if they were keyboard or mouse commands and to "take dictation." Voice recognition software is still in its relative infancy; even after being "trained" to recognize a user's accent and speech patterns, programs still generate a significant number of errors.

VOID empty; having no legal force; incapable of being ratified.

VOIDABLE capable of being later annulled. A voidable act remains valid unless or until the defect in the transaction has been effectively asserted or judicially ascertained and declared.

VoIP *Voice over IP (Internet Protocol),* the technology used to transmit voice communications over a data network such as the Internet or a corporate INTRANET; in the simplest terms, Internet telephony. Skype and Vonage are currently the best-known providers of VoIP service, but many local cable and telephone utilities are adding VoIP options as quality improves.

VOLATILE tending to rapid and extreme fluctuations. The term is used to describe the size and frequency of the fluctuations in the price of a particular stock, bond, or commodity. Market-related volatility in stocks is measured by the BETA COEFFICIENT.

VOLTAGE REGULATOR protective device that maintains electric line voltage within a prescribed range; used to prevent damage to computers or other electronic devices from a POWER SURGE.

VOLUME
1. total number of stock shares, bonds, or commodities futures contracts traded in a particular period.
2. set of issues, usually one year, of a periodical.
3. amount of space occupied in three dimensions.

VOLUME DISCOUNT *see* QUANTITY DISCOUNT.

VOLUME MERCHANDISE ALLOWANCE manufacturer's discount offered to a retailer or wholesaler for buying large volumes of merchandise.

VOLUNTARY ACCUMULATION PLAN plan subscribed to by a MUTUAL FUND shareholder to accumulate shares in that fund on a regular basis over time. The amount of money to be put into the fund and the intervals at which it is to be invested are at the discretion of the shareholder.

VOLUNTARY BANKRUPTCY legal proceeding that follows a petition of bankruptcy filed by a debtor in the appropriate U.S. district court under the Bankruptcy Act. Voluntary bankruptcy contrasts with *involuntary* bankruptcy, in which the creditors petition the court to have the debtor judged insolvent. *See also* CHAPTER 11 OF THE 1978 BANKRUPTCY ACT; INSOLVENCY.

VOLUNTARY CONVEYANCE SALE or transfer of property without being forced to do so. Contrast with involuntary acts, such as CONDEMNATION or threat of condemnation.

VOLUNTARY EMPLOYEES' BENEFICIARY ASSOCIATION (VEBA) group that provides for the payment of life, sickness, or accident benefits to individuals with an employment-related bond.

VOLUNTARY LIEN debt that the property owner agrees to have recorded, typically a mortgage. *See also* INVOLUNTARY LIEN.

VOLUNTARY PLAN short for *voluntary deductible employee contribution plan*, a type of pension plan where the employee elects to have contributions (which, depending on the plan, may be beforeor after-tax) deducted from each paycheck.

VOTING RIGHT right of a common shareholder to vote in person or by PROXY on the affairs of a company.

VOTING STOCK shares in a corporation that entitle the shareholder to voting and PROXY rights.

VOTING TRUST CERTIFICATE transferable certificate of BENEFICIAL INTEREST in a voting trust, a limited-life trust set up to center control of a corporation in the hands of a few individuals, called *voting trustees.* The usual purpose for such an arrangement is to facilitate reorganization of a corporation in financial difficulty by preventing interference with management.

VOUCHER document that acknowledges a liability and provides authorization to pay the debt.

VOUCHER REGISTER book where VOUCHERS are listed, generally chronologically and numerically.

VULTURE FUND type of LIMITED PARTNERSHIP that invests in depressed property, usually REAL ESTATE, aiming to profit when prices rebound.

W

WACC *see* WEIGHTED AVERAGE COST OF CAPITAL.

WAGE actual remuneration paid to an employee for services rendered. Minimum wages are established by the federal FAIR LABOR STANDARDS ACT.

WAGE AND SALARY ADMINISTRATION administrative procedure of establishing and supervising wage levels and operations in an organization. In most organizations, wage and salary administration is performed in the personnel department, although larger organizations often have a payroll or wage and salary administration department.

WAGE AND SALARY SURVEY survey conducted with other employers in the same labor market to determine pay levels for specific job categories. Generally wage and salary surveys are conducted in the surrounding community or metropolitan area for the purposes of comparability.

WAGE ASSIGNMENT voluntary transfer of earned wages to a third party to pay debts, buy savings bonds, pay union dues, or contribute to a pension fund.

WAGE BRACKET range of salaries for a particular occupation. Wage brackets are often set by seniority and experience levels. For example, grade 1 may be for those having less than one year's experience, while grade 13 may be for those having 20 years' experience or more. *See also* WAGE SCALE.

WAGE CEILING highest pay possible within a particular wage bracket. A wage ceiling is agreed upon as the upper range of a wage bracket.

WAGE CONTROL control establishing the extent to which wages can be increased, usually in percentage terms. Wage controls usually occur during a period of governmental wage and price restraints. Wage controls are established to achieve a particular national priority, often the restraining of inflation.

WAGE FLOOR minimum wage established either by law or by an agreed-upon wage bracket.

WAGE INCENTIVE method of motivating the worker to increase his productivity by paying increased wages for the higher output. *See also* PIECE RATE.

WAGE-PRICE SPIRAL a macroeconomic situation in which rising prices push wages higher; the rising wages then increase production costs that lead to further price increases, etc.

WAGE PROTECTION LAWS *see* JUDGMENT PROOF.

WAGE-PUSH INFLATION inflationary situation in which increasing wages are not offset by increasing productivity. Thus costs rise and the result is higher prices for goods produced.

WAGE RATE established pay rate for a particular job during a given period of time, usually on an hourly basis. Minimum wage rates are established by the federal FAIR LABOR STANDARDS ACT.

WAGE SCALE wage rate structure for all employees in a department, division, or company. Wage scales are determined by the type of job, its duties and responsibilities, and the general labor market, and are distributed within the range of wage brackets. *See also* WAGE BRACKET.

WAGE STABILIZATION when wages cease to change rapidly; also a collection of policies intended to bring about an end to inflationary wage increases.

WAGNER ACT legislation of 1935 that significantly strengthened labor's bargaining power; also called NATIONAL LABOR RELATIONS ACT. The act created the NATIONAL LABOR RELATIONS BOARD (NLRB), and prohibited antilabor practices by management. In 1937, the Supreme Court declared the Wagner Act constitutional.

WAITING FOR THE OTHER SHOE TO DROP waiting for a related announcement or event to occur after an initial announcement or situation. When waiting for the other shoe to drop, one expects a pending situation to occur that is dependent upon an initial event; for example, waiting for a presidential nominee to indicate his vice-presidential preference.

WAIVER intentional and voluntary surrender of some known right, which generally may either result from an express agreement or be inferred from circumstances.

WAIVER OF PREMIUM clause in an insurance policy providing that all policy premiums will be waived if the policyholder becomes seriously ill or disabled, either permanently or temporarily, and therefore is unable to pay the premiums. Some policies include a *waiver-of-premium* clause automatically, whereas in other cases it is an optional feature that requires a higher premium.

WALKOUT sudden work stoppage by employees for the purpose of obtaining an improvement in working conditions. *See also* WILDCAT STRIKE.

WALLFLOWER stock that has fallen out of favor with investors. Such stocks tend to have a low PRICE-EARNINGS RATIO.

WALLPAPER worthless SECURITIES. The implication of the term is that certificates of STOCKS and BONDS that have gone bankrupt or defaulted have no other use than as wallpaper. However, there may be some slight value in the worthless certificates themselves for collectors who prize rare or historically significant certificates. Also, in computers, a picture or other graphic design used as background for the DESKTOP instead of a solid color.

WALL STREET
1. common name for the financial district at the lower end of Manhattan in New York City, where the New York and American stock exchanges and numerous brokerage firms are headquartered; also referred to as *the Street.*
2. investment community, such as in "Wall Street really likes the prospects for that company" or "Wall Street law firm," meaning a firm specializing in securities law and mergers.

WAREHOUSE a structure designed for storage of commercial inventory.

WAREHOUSE CLUBS low-price retail outlets selling annual memberships to consumers and businesses. These stores are normally established in warehouse-type buildings where merchandise is displayed without any frills. Perhaps the best known is SAM's Club, a division of Wal-Mart Stores, Inc.

WAREHOUSE RECEIPT document listing goods or commodities kept for SAFEKEEPING in a warehouse. The receipt can be used to transfer ownership of that commodity, instead of having to deliver the physical commodity.

WARES goods, merchandise; manufactured goods of the same kind used in combination, such as glassware.

WARRANT *see* SUBSCRIPTION RIGHT.

WARRANTY guarantee given by a seller to a buyer that the goods or services purchased will perform as promised, or a refund will be given, an exchange made, or a repair done at no charge. Warranties usually become effective when the manufacturer receives a warranty application from the buyer (not at the date of purchase) and are effective for a limited period of time. Warranties usually include limitations that exclude defects not caused by the manufacturer.

WARRANTY DEED DEED that warrants that the grantor has the title he claims he has. It purports to convey property free and clear of all ENCUMBRANCES. As a guarantee of title, the warranty deed creates liability in the grantor if the title transferred is defective. *Contrast with* QUITCLAIM DEED.

WARRANTY OF HABITABILITY implied assurance given by a LANDLORD that an apartment offered for rent is free from safety and health hazards.

WARRANTY OF MERCHANTABILITY WARRANTY that the goods are reasonably fit for the general purposes for which they are sold.

WASH SALE a sale or other disposition of stock or securities at a loss accompanied by a purchase of substantially identical stock or securities during a period beginning 30 days before the date of sale or other disposition and ending 30 days after that date—a total of 61 days. The taxpayer is denied a tax deduction for any loss incurred on a wash sale. If the disposition during the 61-day period is at a gain, it is not a wash sale, and the gain will be taxable.

WASTE

In general: unwanted result of a process, further called *hazardous* waste, *nuclear* waste, or *solid* waste.

Real estate: unauthorized use or neglect of property by a party with the right to possession when another party owns an interest in the property. The party may be a tenant, a mortgagor, or a life tenant.

WASTING ASSET

1. fixed asset, other than land, that has a limited useful life and is therefore subject to DEPRECIATION.
2. natural resource that diminishes in value because of extractions of oil, ores, or gas, the removal of timber, or similar DEPLETION.

WATCH LIST list of securities singled out for special surveillance by a brokerage firm or an exchange or other self-regulatory organization to spot irregularities. Firms on the watch list may be TAKEOVER candidates, companies about to issue new securities, or others that seem to have attracted an unusually heavy volume of trading activity.

WATER DAMAGE INSURANCE protection in the event of accidental discharge, leakage, or overflow of water from plumbing systems, heating, air conditioning, and refrigerating systems, and rain or snow through broken doors, open doors, windows, and skylights resulting in damage or destruction of the property scheduled in the policy.

WATERED STOCK stock issue offered to public investors by founders and promoters of a company at a greatly inflated price compared to book value or cost; stock a company issues for property that is worth less than the stock. The term was possibly derived from the cattle industry, where the animals were encouraged to drink water before being weighed for sale.

WATS, WATS LINE *see* WIDE AREA TELEPHONE SERVICE.

WAYBILL paper prepared by a common carrier at the start of a shipment that details the route the goods will follow to their final destination and states the transportation cost. The waybill typically accompanies the shipment to its destination.

WEAK DOLLAR dollar that has fallen in value against foreign currencies. This means that those holding dollars will get fewer pounds, yen, marks, francs, or other currencies in exchange for their dollars. A *weak dollar* makes it easier for U.S. companies to export their goods to other countries because it enhances foreigners' buying power.

WEAKEST LINK THEORY sequence of events or objects dependent on the support of the whole. The whole is only as reliable as the weakest member or link.

WEAK MARKET market characterized by a preponderance of sellers over buyers and a general declining trend in prices.

WEALTH EFFECT an increase in spending that accompanies an increase in wealth, whether real or perceived.

WEAR AND TEAR physical deterioration of property as the result of use, weathering, and age.

WEAROUT FACTOR condition that may apply to the point at which an advertisement or advertising campaign is no longer effective. The wearout factor depends on the frequency of communications, the target market, the quality of the advertising copy, the novelty of the campaign, and the variety of messages used. Some ads or campaigns wear out in a relatively short time, whereas others last for years.

WEB *see* WORLD WIDE WEB.

WEB ADDRESS *see* URL.

WEB BROWSER computer software that allows the user to read HTML in files or on the WORLD WIDE WEB. The two most popular *Web browsers* are Microsoft Internet Explorer and Netscape Navigator.

WEBMASTER the person in charge of administrating a WEB SITE. By convention, the Webmaster of Internet DOMAIN *www.foo.com* can be reached at the E-MAIL ADDRESS *webmaster@foo.com.*

WEB PAGE an HTML document made available for viewing on the WORLD WIDE WEB and seen by the user as a page on the screen.

WEB SERVER a computer that is connected to the Internet and contains WEB PAGES (HTML files) than can be viewed using a WEB BROWSER.

WEB SITE a virtual location managed by a single entity that provides information such as text, graphics, and audio files to users, as well as connections (hypertext links, hyperlinks, links) to other Web sites. Every Web site has a HOME PAGE, the initial document seen by users, which acts as a table of contents to other offerings available at the site.

WEIGHT
Advertising:
1. number of exposures of an advertising message.
2. number of GROSS RATING POINTS an advertiser wants to place in a market (ADI [*area of dominant influence*] or DMA [*designated market area*]).
3. *see* MEDIA WEIGHT.

Paper stock: method by which a grade of paper is determined. The weight of paper stock is calculated by the ream (500 sheets) in terms of any one of three standard sizes: bond (writing) paper—17″ × 22″;

book paper—25″ × 38″; and cover stock—20″ × 26″. Hence, 20-pound paper means that a ream of bond paper measuring 17″ × 22″ weighs 20 pounds.

Physical: Although most of the rest of the world has converted to metric weights and measures, the United States continues to use the English system, under which the weight of most objects is given in ounces, pounds, and tons *avoirdupois*. For gold, silver, and other precious metals, TROY WEIGHT is used.

Print advertising: size as well as color, shape, and degree of blackness of an element in an ad.

WEIGHTED AVERAGE COST OF CAPITAL (WACC) method of deriving the average cost of a corporation's capital by weighting each component:

Source of Capital	Rate		Percentage of Total		Weighted Rate
Common Stock	.15	×	.50	=	.075
Preferred Stock	.12	×	.10	=	.012
Debt	.08	×	.40	=	.032
Less: $t = .33 × .08$		×	.40	=	−0.156
Total					.1034

The WACC rate is 10.34%.

t = income tax savings from interest expense deduction.

WELFARE STATE country in which government provides many services to its population, particularly in the areas of medical care, minimum income guarantees, and retirement pensions.

WELL-HEELED having plenty of money.

WELLNESS PROGRAMS employee-centered programs featuring proactive personal fitness programs, including physical examinations, substance abuse and group counseling, and individualized diet and exercise programs. Wellness programs have been very effective in improving employee productivity while reducing absenteeism and health care costs.

WESTERN UNION company that dominates telegraph services in the United States.

WETLANDS land, such as swamps, marshes, and bogs, normally saturated with water. Development may be prohibited because it could disturb the environment. The U.S. Army Corps of Engineers (COE) and the U.S. Environmental Protection Agency (EPA) have adopted a regulatory definition for administering the Section 404 permit program of the Clean Water Act (CWA) as follows: "those areas that are inundated or saturated by surface or groundwater at a frequency and duration sufficient to support, and that under normal circumstances do support, a prevalence of vegetation typically adapted for life in saturated soil conditions."

W-4 FORM EMPLOYEES WITHHOLDING ALLOWANCE CER-TIFICATE certificate used by new employees and existing employees who wish to change the number of personal exemptions claimed for tax withholding purposes.

WHAT IF *see* SENSITIVITY ANALYSIS.

WHEEL OF RETAILING retail marketing process whereby original low-price discounters upgrade their services and gradually increase prices. As they evolve into full-line department stores, a competitive opportunity develops for new low-price discounters to develop, and the process continues with the next generation.

WHEN ISSUED short form of "when, as, and if issued," a term referring to a transaction made conditionally because a security, although authorized, has not yet been issued. New issues of stocks and bonds, stocks that have split, and U.S. Treasury securities are all traded on a when-issued basis. In a newspaper listing, WI next to the price indicates such a security.

WHIPSAWED caught in volatile price movements and therefore making losing trades as prices rise and fall. A trader is *whipsawed* if he buys just before prices fall and sells just before they rise.

WHISTLE BLOWER an employee who reports his/her employer's violation of a law.

WHITE-COLLAR CRIME catch-all phrase for a variety of frauds, schemes, and commercial offenses by businesspersons, confidence men, and public officials. It includes a broad range of nonviolent offenses that have cheating as their central element. Consumer fraud, bribery, and stock manipulation are examples.

WHITE-COLLAR WORKER classification for employees performing nonmanual work, which includes the majority of employees in the United States today. White-collar workers are those employees who work in clerical, administrative, and professional nonmanual occupations.

WHITE ELEPHANT a useless and troublesome possession that one cannot easily get rid of. Legend has it that rare albino elephants in ancient Siam automatically became the property of the king. At least one such monarch gave a white elephant to any courtier who fell out of favor; the subject was soon ruined by the cost of maintaining this precious gift.

WHITE GOODS in retailing, all those heavy household appliances that were originally manufactured with a white enamel finish, such as refrigerators, freezers, washers and dryers, or stoves. Today the term applies to all such goods, even though they are available in a variety of decorator colors and finishes.

WHITE KNIGHT acquirer sought by the target of an unfriendly TAKEOVER to rescue it from the unwanted bidder's control. The white knight strategy is an alternative to SHARK REPELLENT tactics and is used to avert an extended or bitter fight for control.

WHITE PAPER report of an investigation into a subject intended to provide an unbiased position. A white paper indicates the official government position on a particular public issue.

WHITE-SHOE FIRM anachronistic characterization of certain broker-dealers as venerable, "upper crust," and "above" such practices as participating in HOSTILE TAKEOVERS. Derives from the 1950s culture of Ivy League schools, where white buck shoes were *de rigueur* in elite fraternities and clubs.

WHOLE LIFE INSURANCE form of life insurance policy that offers protection in case the insured dies and also builds up cash surrender value at a guaranteed rate, which can be borrowed against. The policy stays in force for the lifetime of the insured, unless it is canceled or lapses. The policyholder usually pays a set annual premium for whole life, which does not rise as the person grows older (as is the case with *term insurance*). The term is synonymous with *ordinary* or *straight* life insurance.

WHOLE LOAN secondary mortgage market term that distinguishes an investment representing an original residential mortgage loan (*whole loan*) from a loan representing a participation with one or more lenders or a PASS-THROUGH SECURITY representing a pool of mortgages.

WHOLESALE PRICE INDEX (WPI) *see* PRODUCER PRICE INDEX (PPI).

WHOLESALER middleman; person who buys large quantities of goods and resells to other distributors rather than to ultimate consumers.

WIDE AREA NETWORK (WAN) system linking an organization's individual computer workstations throughout a state, a country, or the world using telecommunications for the purpose of simultaneously sharing files and organizational information. *See also* LOCAL AREA NETWORK (LAN).

WIDE AREA TELEPHONE SERVICE (WATS) access to long-distance telephone lines for commercial use at reduced rates. Callers to an incoming WATS line dial 800 instead of a specific area code and are not charged for the service. Organizations who hold the WATS line are charged for incoming calls; costs of outgoing calls using a WATS line are generally less expensive per call than ordinary long-distance service.

WIDGET symbolic gadget, used wherever a hypothetical product is needed to illustrate a manufacturing or selling concept.

WIDOW-AND-ORPHAN STOCK stock that pays high dividends and is very safe. It usually has a low BETA COEFFICIENT and is involved in a noncyclical business.

WI-FI *wireless fi*delity, a set of product compatibility standards for wireless local area networks (WLANs); also called wireless ETHERNET. Wi Fi-enabled computers near a Wi-Fi *hotspot* can gain access to the network and, through it, to the Internet. The active range for a Wi-Fi connection varies with the specification and frequency; for IEEE 802.11b or 802.11g, it is typically 150 indoors and 300 feet outside. Transmission speed also varies.

WILDCAT DRILLING exploring for oil or gas in an unproven area. A wildcat OIL AND GAS LIMITED PARTNERSHIP is structured so that investors take high risks but can reap substantial rewards if oil or gas is found in commercial quantities.

WILDCAT STRIKE sudden and unannounced work stoppage while a labor contract is still in effect. Wildcat strikes are not authorized by union management and are illegal strikes. Wildcat strikes result from disputes regarding wages and working conditions.

WILL legal document that serves as a key vehicle of transfer at death. Within the document are specific instructions as to the disposition of the estate and the designated EXECUTOR (EXECUTRIX). If one does not prepare a will, state law will govern the disposition of one's property after death. *See also* INTESTATE.

WILSHIRE 5000 a stock index of 5,000 common stocks that is the most broadly based barometer of American stock performance.

WINDFALL PROFIT profit that occurs suddenly as a result of an event not controlled by the person or company profiting from it.

WINDING UP process of liquidating a corporation. It consists of collecting the assets, paying the expenses, satisfying creditors' claims, and distributing the net assets, usually in cash but possibly in kind, to shareholders according to their liquidation preferences and rights. *See also* LIQUIDATION.

WINDOW

1. limited time during which an opportunity should be seized, or it will be lost. For example, a period when new stock issues are welcomed by the public may last only a few months or possibly a year; that time is called the *window of opportunity*.
2. discount window of a Federal Reserve Bank.
3. cashier department of a brokerage firm, where delivery and settlement of securities transactions take place.
4. portion of a computer display screen. Some programs allow the user to divide the screen into two or more windows, making it possible to work on two different tasks at once.

WINDOW DRESSING

1. trading activity near the end of a quarter or fiscal year that is designed to dress up a PORTFOLIO to be presented to clients or shareholders.

2. accounting gimmickry designed to make a FINANCIAL STATEMENT show a more favorable condition than actually exists.

WINDOWS the GRAPHICAL USER INTERFACE (GUI) introduced by Microsoft in the 1980s.

WIPEOUT to erase, remove completely. A wipeout can occur inadvertently on a computer or disk.

WIRE HOUSE national or international brokerage firm whose branch offices are linked by a communications system that permits the rapid dissemination of prices, information, and research relating to financial markets and individual securities.

WITHDRAWAL removal of money or the like from the place where it is kept, such as a bank or mutual fund.

WITHDRAWAL PLAN program available through most open-end MUTUAL FUND companies in which shareholders can receive fixed payments of income or CAPITAL GAINS, or both, on a regular basis, usually monthly or quarterly.

WITHHOLDING portion of an employee's wages retained by the employer for the purpose of paying for various taxes, insurance plans, pension plans, union dues, and other deductions.

WITHHOLDING TAX amount of income taxes that an employer is required to withhold from an employee's salary when the salary is paid. The amount withheld is a credit against the amount of income taxes the employee must pay on his income earned for the taxable year.

WITHOUT RECOURSE words used in factoring receivables or endorsing a note or bill to denote that the holder is not to look to the debtor personally in the event of nonpayment. The creditor has recourse only to the property. This is a form of exculpation, synonymous with *nonrecourse*. *See also* ENDORSEMENT; EXCULPATORY.

W-9 FORM IRS form that requires a taxpayer to supply his or her Social Security number, employer identification number, or other identifier to a payor so that interest, dividends, royalties, or other payment made to the taxpayer may be reported to the IRS. If this information is not provided, the payor must withhold some of the payment.

WORD a popular word processing application sold both separately and as part of Microsoft's popular OFFICE suite.

WORDPERFECT a widely used word processing program produced by Corel.

WORD PROCESSING using a computer to prepare a letter, manuscript, or other document. Word processing software makes it easy to revise part of a manuscript and then have the computer print out the entire final document. The user retypes only the changes.

WORD PROCESSING CENTER headquarters of word processing operation for a company serving several on-site and/or off-site stations.

WORD PROCESSOR computer program used to compose, format, sort, and rearrange text upon command. Most current word processing APPLICATIONS have editing, formatting, and layout capabilities that rival those of DESKTOP PUBLISHING software. Microsoft Office Word is currently the most popular word processor.

WORD WRAP feature of most WORD PROCESSING programs that causes the CURSOR to proceed automatically from one line to the next when the end of the line is reached, taking the last word with it if necessary. In contrast to typing, the typist does not have to watch the screen and hit the return key at the end of each line.

WORK CLOTHES, SPECIAL clothing required for the performance of one's job and not suitable for wear when not working. The cost is a miscellaneous itemized deduction, subject to the 2% ADJUSTED GROSS INCOME floor. Examples of workers requiring *special work clothes* are baseball players, bus drivers, and firefighters.

WORKER BUYOUT process of reducing staff by offering financial incentives to employees having seniority. While this can be expensive for a company, it has the advantage of not damaging the morale of current employees as well as motivating them to remain loyal to the company.

WORKERS' COMPENSATION ACTS STATUTES that in general establish LIABILITY of an employer for injuries or sicknesses that arise out of and in the course of employment. The liability is created without regard to the fault or NEGLIGENCE of the employer. Benefits generally include hospital and other medical payments and compensation for loss of income. If the injury is covered by the statute, compensation thereunder will be the employee's only remedy against his employer.

WORKERS' COMPENSATION, COVERAGE A agreement under which an insurance company promises to pay all compensation and all benefits required of an insured employer under the workers' compensation laws of the state or states listed in the policy.

WORKERS' COMPENSATION, COVERAGE B coverage under a commercial *Workers' Compensation Policy* for situations not covered under workers' compensation laws in which an employee could sue for injuries suffered under common-law liability.

WORKERS' COMPENSATION INCOME *see* DISABILITY BENEFIT.

WORK EXPERIENCE experience gained while employed in a particular occupation. Work experience is valuable in building a successful career and fosters the ability to assume greater responsibilities.

WORK FORCE *see* LABOR FORCE.

WORKING CAPITAL funds invested in a company's cash, accounts receivable, inventory, and other current assets (*gross working capital*). It usually refers to *net working capital*, that is, current assets minus current liabilities. Working capital finances the cash conversion cycle of a business—the length of time required to convert raw materials into finished goods, finished goods into sales, and accounts receivable into cash. *See also* CURRENT LIABILITY; CURRENT RATIO; NET CURRENT ASSETS.

WORKING INTEREST customary seven-eighths interest in oil business that bears the cost of development and operation of an oil or gas property.

WORKING PAPERS certificate of age for the state labor department, demonstrating that a minor is older than the age considered to be the child-labor age for a particular occupation.

WORKING POOR people who are economically disadvantaged despite the fact that they are fully employed. The working poor do not have sufficient income to improve their overall lifestyle.

WORK IN PROCESS work or task currently being processed; also called *work in progress*. The task is currently being performed. A *work in process* sign usually is notice to stay away until the job is done.

WORKLOAD measure of the amount and types of work performed by an individual within a given period of time. It is both a quantitative measure of the total work performed and a qualitative measure of the person's perception of his ability to perform the work.

WORK OPPORTUNITY CREDIT tax credit available for wages paid by employers who hire individuals from certain target groups. The list of targeted groups has been extended to include victims of the World Trade Center disaster and Hurricane Katrina.

WORK ORDER form issued by a using department requesting the completion of specified work not normally performed; request for work to be completed by an issuing department.

WORKOUT mutual effort by a property owner and lender to avoid foreclosure or bankruptcy following a default. It generally involves substantial reduction in the DEBT SERVICE burden during an economic downturn. *See also* DISTRESSED PROPERTY.

WORK PERMIT provisional status given by the government to aliens, allowing them to work legally in this country. It certifies that they have gained entry to the country legally and are allowed to work for a stated period of time.

WORK SHARING *see* JOB SHARING.

WORKSHEET paper used for intermediate calculations, writing thoughts, and so on; not included in a final report. *See also* SPREADSHEET.

WORK STATION

1. area reserved or otherwise specially designated for allowing an employee to perform assigned responsibilities; area where a single employee can perform assigned responsibilities without interference from or infringing on others.
2. stand-alone microcomputer work area designed for use by one individual at a time.

WORK STOPPAGE any interruption of work by employees for the purpose of improving working conditions. Work stoppages are usually unexpected and unannounced. *See also* STRIKE; WALKOUT; WILDCAT STRIKE.

WORKWEEK normal number of days and hours in an organization's weekly work schedule. Most organizations work eight hours per day, five days per week; however, other organizations work ten hours per day, four days a week. Organizations design their workweek to accommodate their needs.

WORLD BANK *see* INTERNATIONAL BANK FOR RECONSTRUCTION AND DEVELOPMENT.

WORLD TRADE ORGANIZATION (WTO) global international organization whose goal is to expedite trade between nations. Headquartered in Geneva, Switzerland, this organization, with approximately 150 member countries, encourages international trade, sets the rules, and resolves disputes between its members concerning international trade. Negotiates trade agreements that are signed by the bulk of the world's trading nations and ratified in their parliaments. The WTO replaced the General Agreement on Tariffs and Trade (GATT), though WTO embraces GATT's principles.

WORLD WIDE WEB (WWW) a distributed hypertext system invented by Tim Berners-Lee on a NeXT computer. Currently one of the most popular services offered on the Internet.

WORM

1. Write Once, Read Many, as applied to computer storage media, such as CD-R and DVD-R, that can be written to once but read from multiple times.
2. A type of MALWARE, similar to a computer VIRUS. Instead of infecting other programs, however, a worm makes copies of itself and infects additional computers, typically through network connections or by attaching itself to e-mails. Through self-replication, it may consume enough computer memory and disk space to crash the computer.

WORTH inherent value of a commodity, good, service, or other economic factor. Often worth is measured in nonprice terms, as in COMPARABLE WORTH programs designed to pay equivalent wages for work of equivalent worth, even though the market prices of the services ordinarily would differ.

WORTHLESS SECURITIES SECURITIES that have no value. Ownership of *worthless securities* generally results in a CAPITAL LOSS.

WPM words per minute; measure of speed at which one can type or a machine can print.

WRAPAROUND MORTGAGE a loan arrangement in which an existing loan is retained and an additional loan, larger than the existing one, is made. The new lender accepts the obligation to make payments on the old loan. The existing loan generally carries an interest rate below the rate available on new loans. Consequently, the yield to the wraparound lender is higher than the rate charged on the new loan. Sellers are the most common wraparound lenders. In an INSTALLMENT SALE with a wraparound mortgage, the seller does not reduce the CONTRACT PRICE by the amount of the underlying wrapped mortgage.

WRIT legal order issued by the authority and in the name of the state to compel a person to do something therein mentioned. It is issued by a court or other competent *tribunal,* and is directed to the sheriff or other officer authorized to execute it. In every case the writ itself contains directions for doing what is required.

WRITE-DOWN the reduction in an asset value on the financial statements, often following a drop in market price. *See also* LOWER OF COST OR MARKET.

WRITE-PROTECT to cover a notch in the side of a floppy diskette as a signal to the computer not to write any data on it. Valuable data can thus be read from the disk but not accidentally written over.

WRITER
1. person who sells PUT OPTION and CALL OPTION contracts.
2. insurance UNDERWRITER.

WRITE-UP increase in the value of an asset; seldom allowed under GENERALLY ACCEPTED ACCOUNTING PRINCIPLES.

WRITING NAKED strategy used by an OPTION seller in which the trader does not own the UNDERLYING SECURITY. *See also* NAKED OPTION.

WRIT OF ERROR in some states, procedural method by which appeals in civil matters are brought before an appellate court for review for possible reversal.

WRITTEN-DOWN VALUE BOOK VALUE of an asset after DEPRECIATION or other amortization; also called *net* book value. For example, if the original cost of a piece of equipment was $1,000 and accumulated depreciation charges totaled $400, the written-down value would be $600.

WRONGFUL TERMINATION/DISCHARGE an employee's legal action that asserts that the former employer's dismissal was in violation of federal or state anti-discrimination laws, public policy, an implied or actual employment contract, or an implied covenant of fair dealing and good faith.

WT abbreviation for warrant. *See also* SUBSCRIPTION RIGHT.

WTO *see* WORLD TRADE ORGANIZATION.

W-2 FORM WAGE AND TAX STATEMENT tax form that each employer sends annually to each employee and to the IRS. Shows gross earnings and deductions for federal, state, local income taxes and FICA. Employees must attach a copy to their tax returns.

WWW *see* WORLD WIDE WEB.

WYSIWYG *What You See Is What You Get*. Describes programs (especially page layout and word processing applications) in which a document as displayed on the screen accurately represents printed output.

WYSIWYP *What You See Is What You Print*. Describes graphics applications that use a color management system to calibrate printers and monitors so that printout will reproduce the colors and resolution of the image displayed on the screen.

X Y Z

X or XD symbol used in newspapers to signify that a stock is trading *ex-dividend*, that is, without dividend. The symbol X is also used in bond tables to signify without interest.

YAHOO a popular SEARCH ENGINE for the WORLD WIDE WEB, accessible at *http://www.yahoo.com*. Yahoo also offers other Internet services, such as E-MAIL.

YANKEE BOND MARKET dollar-denominated bonds issued in the United States by foreign banks and corporations. The bonds are issued in the United States when market conditions there are more favorable than on the EURODOLLAR BOND market or in domestic markets overseas.

YARD
1. enclosed area that can be used for storing materials (storage yard) or repairing equipment (repair yard).
2. dimension of 36 inches. A yard (actually a cubic yard) is a unit for the sale of coal, concrete, and some other products.

YEAR *see* CALENDAR TAX YEAR; FISCAL TAX YEAR.

YEAR-END end of an ACCOUNTING PERIOD; often a calendar year, but may be a fiscal year. Books are closed at year-end.

YEAR-END DIVIDEND payment to stockholders from RETAINED EARNINGS, declared at or near the end of the business year.

YEAR-TO-DATE (YTD) accumulation of accounts from the start of the fiscal year to the latest available period. Sales, purchases, and profits for any current week or month may be displayed *year-to-date*.

YELLOW DOG CONTRACT employment CONTRACT expressly prohibiting the named employee from joining LABOR UNIONS under pain of dismissal. Most state constitutions guarantee the right to union affiliation and to collective bargaining. Federal and state statutes now generally declare that such contracts will not form the basis for legal or EQUITABLE remedies.

YELLOW SHEETS daily publication of the National Quotation Bureau that details the bid and asked prices and firms that make a market in corporate bonds traded in the over-the-counter market. Yellow sheets are to bonds what PINK SHEETS are to unlisted stocks.

YIELD
In general: return on an investor's capital investment. A piece of real estate may *yield* a certain return or a business deal may offer a particular *yield*.
Agriculture: agricultural output in terms of quantity of a crop per acre.

Bonds: (1) coupon rate of interest divided by the purchase price, called *current* yield; (2) rate of return on a bond, taking into account the total of annual interest payments, the purchase price, the redemption value, and the amount of time remaining until maturity; called *maturity yield* or *yield to maturity. See also* YIELD TO AVERAGE LIFE.

Lending: total money earned on a loan, that is, the annual percentage rate of interest multiplied by the term of the loan.

Stocks: percentage rate of return on a common or preferred stock in dividends. For example, a stock that sells for $20 and pays an annual dividend of $2 per share has a yield, also called a *dividend* yield, of 10%.

Taxes: amount of revenue received by a governmental entity as a result of a tax.

YIELD CURVE graph showing the term structure of interest rates by plotting the yields of all bonds of the same quality with maturities ranging from the shortest to the longest available. *See also* INVERTED YIELD CURVE; POSITIVE YIELD CURVE.

YIELD EQUIVALENCE rate of interest at which a tax-exempt bond and a taxable security of similar quality provide the same after-tax return. To convert a taxable YIELD to a tax-exempt yield, reduce the taxable yield by the investor's marginal tax bracket. For example, a taxable yield of 7.5% is equivalent to a tax-free yield of 5% for an investor in the 33% marginal tax bracket.

YIELD SPREAD difference in YIELD between various issues of securities. In comparing bonds, it usually refers to issues of different credit qualities since issues of the same maturity and quality would normally have the same yields, as with U.S. Treasury securities, for example.

YIELD TO AVERAGE LIFE YIELD calculation used, in lieu of YIELD TO MATURITY or YIELD TO CALL, where bonds are retired systematically during the life of the issue, as in the case of a SINKING FUND with contractual requirements.

YIELD TO CALL yield on a bond assuming the bond will be redeemed by the issuer at the first call date specified in the INDENTURE agreement.

YIELD TO MATURITY (YTM) calculation of YIELD on a bond, from the current date until it is scheduled to be retired, that takes into account the CAPITAL GAIN on a discount bond or capital loss on a premium bond. In the case of a discount bond, YTM is higher than the current yield or the coupon yield. The reverse is true for a premium bond with YTM lower than both current yield and coupon yield.

Y.K. (YUGEN-KAISHA) Japanese designation for a corporation.

YO-YO STOCK stock that fluctuates in a VOLATILE manner, rising and falling quickly like a yo-yo.

YUPPIE acronym for young urban professional. The term was popularized during the 1980s to describe young career people having relatively high incomes and education, seeking instant success and gratification, often beyond their financial means.

ZERO-BASE BUDGETING (ZBB) method of setting budgets for corporations and government agencies that requires a justification of all expenditures, not only those that exceed the prior year's allocations. Thus all budget lines are said to begin at a zero base and are funded according to merit.

ZERO COUPON BOND security that makes no periodic interest payments but instead is sold at a deep discount from its FACE VALUE. The buyer of such a bond receives the rate of return by the gradual APPRECIATION of the security, which is redeemable at face value on a specified maturity date. *See also* CERTIFICATE OF ACCRUAL ON TREASURY SECURITIES (CATS); COUPON BOND; DEEP DISCOUNT BOND; ORIGINAL ISSUE DISCOUNT.

ZERO ECONOMIC GROWTH when NATIONAL INCOME neither grows nor falls. A few groups advocate zero economic growth as a solution to problems of pollution, resource depletion, and so on.

ZERO INVENTORY a term used to describe a JUST-IN-TIME INVENTORY CONTROL system where emphasis is placed on reducing inventory to minimal levels to reduce costs and promote organizational effectiveness. This can result in sizable profit increases.

ZERO POPULATION GROWTH (ZPG) forecast of no further increase in the population of the United States. Demographers study fertility rates to determine whether the United States will incur ZPG; economic and business implications are significant.

ZERO-SUM GAME sum of the amounts won and lost by all parties, when tallied, is zero. Whatever is gained in a zero-sum game is always achieved at the expense of the other participants.

ZIP CODE five-digit numerical code defined by the U.S. Postal Service to simplify and expedite mail distribution. The United States is divided into 10 large geographical areas, with the first ZIP code digit 0 in the northeast and 9 in the west. The second and third digits are used to divide states; the fourth and fifth digits represent local delivery areas.

ZIP + 4 four additional digits added to the five-digit ZIP codes to improve efficiency for business mailers. The first two numbers represent a sector such as a certain group of streets, the last two are a smaller unit such as one floor in an office building. The use of ZIP + 4 is voluntary.

ZONE OF EMPLOYMENT physical area within which injuries to an employee are compensable by workers' compensation laws. It denotes the place of employment and surrounding areas, including the means of entrance and exit, that are under control of the employer.

ZONING legislative action, usually on the municipal level, that divides municipalities into districts for the purpose of regulating the use of private property and the construction of buildings within the established zones. Zoning is part of the state POLICE POWER, and therefore must be for the furthering of the health, morals, safety, or general welfare of the community.

ZONING MAP map of the local jurisdiction that indicates current ZONING designations.

ZONING ORDINANCE act of city or county or other authorities specifying the type of use to which property may be put in specific areas. A typical zoning ordinance defines: (1) the purpose for which the ordinance is adopted; (2) the various zoning classifications and permitted uses within each; (3) restrictions, such as height limitations; (4) the procedure for handling nonconforming uses; (5) the procedure for granting amendments, variances, and hearing appeals; (6) penalties for violation of the ordinance. *See also* ZONING.

Z SCORE

1. in STATISTICS, the standard normal variate that standardizes a normal distribution by converting an x-scale to the z-scale.
2. score produced by Altman's bankruptcy prediction model, which is as follows:

$$Z = 1.2*X_1 + 1.4*X_2 + 3.3*X_3 + 0.6*X_4 + 0.999*X_5$$

where X_1 = working capital/total assets, X_2 = retained earnings/ total assets, X_3 = earnings before interest and taxes/total assets, X_4 = market value of equity/book value of debt, and X_5 = sales/total assets. The Z score is known to be about 90 percent accurate in forecasting business failure one year in the future and about 80 percent accurate in forecasting it two years in the future.

Appendix

ABBREVIATIONS AND ACRONYMS

A

AAA American Automobile Association

AAII American Association of Individual Investors

ABA American Bankers Association; American Bar Association

ABO accumulated benefit obligation

ABV Accredited in Business Valuation

ACE Active Corps of Executives

ACFE Association of Certified Fraud Examiners

ACI Advertising Council, Inc., The

ACRS accelerated cost recovery system

ADA Americans with Disabilities Act

ADEA Age Discrimination in Employment Act of 1967

ADP automated data processing

ADR alternate dispute resolution; American Depositary Receipt; asset depreciation range

AEA American Economics Association

AFL-CIO American Federation of Labor-Congress of Industrial Organizations

AFY additional first-year depreciation

AGI adjusted gross income

AI artificial intelligence

AICPA American Institute of Certified Public Accountants

ALGOL algorithmic language

AMA American Management Association

AMEX American Stock Exchange

AMI alternative mortgage instrument

AML adjustable mortgage loan

AMVI Amex Market Value Index

AMW average monthly wage

ANOVA analysis of variance

ANSI American National Standards Institute

AOL America Online

APB Accounting Principles Board

APBO accumulated postretirement benefit obligation

APL a programming language

APR annual percentage rate

ARM adjustable-rate mortgage

ASA American Society of Appraisers

ASAP as soon as possible

ASCII American standard code for information interchange

ASO administrative services only

ASP application service provider

ATM automated teller machine

AVM automated valuation model

B

BASIC Beginner's All-Purpose Symbolic Instruction Code

BBA Bachelor of Business Administration

BBB Better Business Bureau

BBS bulletin board system

bc blind copy

bcc blind carbon copy

BFOQ bona fide occupational qualification

BFP bona fide purchaser

BMIR below-market interest rate

BOP businessowners policy

BOV broker's opinion of value

BOY beginning of year
BPPCF business and personal property coverage form
bps bits per second
B2B business to business
B2C business to consumer

C

CAD computer-assisted design
C&F cost and freight
CAE computer-assisted education; computer-assisted engineering
CAFR Comprehensive Annual Financial Report
CAI computer-assisted instruction
CAM certified administrative manager; computer-aided manufacturing
CAPM capital asset pricing model
CAR computer-assisted retrieval
CAT computer-assisted transcription
CATS certificate of accrual on Treasury securities; Computer Assisted Trading System
CATV community antenna television (cable TV)
CBD central business district
CBSA Core Based Statistical Area
cc carbon copy
CCH Commerce Clearing House
CCR conditions, covenants, and restrictions
CD certificate of deposit; compact disc
CD-ROM compact disk read-only memory
CEA Council of Economic Advisers
CEBS certified employee benefit specialists
CED Committee for Economic Development
CEO chief executive officer

CERCLA Comprehensive Environmental Response, Compensation, and Liability Act
CES Current Employment Statistics
CETA Comprehensive Employment and Training Act of 1975
CFA Chartered Financial Analyst
CFC chartered financial consultant
CFE Certified Fraud Examiner
CFO chief financial officer
CFP certified financial planner
CFTC Commodities Futures Trading Commission
CGL comprehensive general liability (insurance)
ChFC Chartered Financial Consultant
CIF cost, insurance, and freight
CIM computer-integrated manufacturing
CLO computerized loan origination
CLU Chartered Life Underwriter
CME Chicago Mercantile Exchange
CMO collateralized mortgage obligation
CMSA consolidated metropolitan statistical area
COBOL common businessoriented language
COBRA Consolidated Omnibus Budget Reconciliation Act
COD cash on delivery; cancellation of debt
CODA cash or deferred arrangement
COLA cost-of-living adjustment
COMECON Council for Mutual Economic Assistance
COMEX securities and commodities exchanges
CONUS contiguous United States

COO chief operating officer
CP/M control program for microcomputer
CPA certified public accountant
CPCU chartered property and casualty underwriter
CPI consumer price index
cps characters per second
CPS certified professional secretary
CPSC Consumer Products Safety Commission
CPU central processing unit
CRC camera-ready copy
CR credit
CRM customer relationship management
CSI Commissioners Standard Industrial Mortality Table
CSO Commissioners Standard Ordinary Mortality Table
CST Central Standard Time
CUSIP Committee on Uniform Securities Identification Procedures

D

D&B Dun & Bradstreet
DBA doing business as
DCF discounted cash flow
DCR debt (service) coverage ratio
DES Data Encryption Standard
DFOR deductions for adjusted gross income
DFROM deductions from adjusted gross income
DIF data interchange format
DINKS dual-income, no kids
DISC domestic international sales corporation
DJIA Dow Jones Industrial Average
DK don't know
DMA Direct Marketing Association
DOC drive other car insurance
DOS disk-operating system

dpi dots per inch
DR debit
DSL digital subscriber line
DSS decision support system
DST Daylight Saving Time
DTC depository trust company
DTP desktop publishing
DUS dollar unit sampling

E

EA enrolled actuary, enrolled agent; environmental assessment
EAI enterprise application integration
EAP employee assistance program
EBIT Earnings Before Interest and Taxes
EBITDA Earnings Before Interest, Taxes, Depreciation, and Amortization
ECB European Central Bank
E-COM electronic computeroriginated mail
ECI Employment Cost Index
ECN electronic communication network
ECPA Electronic Communications Privacy Act
ECU European currency unit
EDGAR Electronic Data Gathering, Analysis, and Retrieval
EDP electronic data processing
EEC European Economic Community
EEOC Equal Employment Opportunity Commission
EFT electronic fund transfer
EIS environmental impact statement; executive information service
EITC earned income tax credit
EMS European monetary system
EOM end of month
EOQ economic order quantity
EOY end of year

EPA Environmental Protection Agency
EPS earnings per share
ERA Equal Rights Amendment
ERISA Employee Retirement Income Security Act
ERO electronic return originator
ERP enterprise resource planning
ERTA Economic Recovery Tax Act of 1981
ESA Education Savings Account
ESOP employee stock ownership plan
Esq. Esquire
EST Eastern Standard Time
EU European Union
EXIMBANK export-import bank
EZ Empowerment Zone

F

FAA Federal Aviation Administration
FAIR fair access to insurance requirements
FAQ frequently asked question(s)
FAS free alongside ship
FASB Financial Accounting Standards Board
FAVR fixed and variable rate allowances
FCBA Fair Credit Billing Act
FCC Federal Communications Commission
FDA Food and Drug Administration
FDIC Federal Deposit Insurance Corporation
Fed Federal Reserve System
FERC Federal Energy Regulatory Commission
FF&E furniture, fixtures, and equipment
FFO funds from operation
FHA Federal Housing Administration
FHLMC Federal Home Loan Mortgage Corporation

FICA Federal Insurance Contributions Act
FIFO first in, first out
FIRPTA Foreign Investment in Real Property Tax Act of 1980
FIRREA Financial Institutions Reform, Recovery and Enforcement Act
FLSA Fair Labor Standards Act
FmHA Farmer's Home Administration
FMLA Family and Medical Leave Act
FMRR financial management rate of return
FNMA Federal National Mortgage Association
FOB free on board
FOIA Freedom of Information Act
FOK fill-or-kill order
FOMC Federal Open Market Committee
4GLs fourth-generation languages
FPC Federal Power Commission
FPM flexible-payment mortgage
FRB Federal Reserve Board
FSA Fellow, Society of Actuaries
FSC foreign sales corporation
FSLIC Federal Savings and Loan Insurance Corporation
FTC Federal Trade Commission
FTP File Transfer Protocol
FTS Federal Telecommunication System
FUTA Federal Unemployment Tax Act
FYI for your information

G

GAAP generally accepted accounting principles
GAO General Accounting Office
GATT General Agreement on Tariffs and Trade
GAW guaranteed annual wage
GDP gross domestic product

GDS general depreciation system
GEM growing-equity mortgage
GIC guaranteed income contract
GIF Graphics Interchange Format
GIGO garbage in, garbage out
GIM gross income multiplier
GIS geographic information systems
GNMA Government National Mortgage Association
GNP gross national product
GOB going-out-of-business sale
GPM graduated-payment mortgage
GPO Government Printing Office
GPR guaranteed premium reduction insurance
GRAT grantor-retained annuity trust
GRIT grantor-retained interest trust
GRM gross rent multiplier
GRUT grantor-retained unitrust
GSE government-sponsored enterprise
GTC good-till-canceled order
GUI graphical user interface

H

HCFA Health Care Financing Administration
HD hard disk
HDD hard disk drive
HMO health maintenance organization
HOW Homeowner Warranty Plan
HSA health savings account
HTML Hypertext Markup Language
http Hypertext Transfer Protocol
HUD Housing and Urban Development (Department of)

I

I/O input/output
IBM-PC IBM personal computer
IBNR incurred but not reported

IBRD International Bank for Reconstruction and Development
ICC Interstate Commerce Commission
IDA International Development Association
IDB industrial development bond
IDC intangible drilling and development costs
IFPS integrated financial planning system
IMF International Monetary Fund
IMM International Monetary Market
IPO initial public offering
IRA individual retirement account
IRR internal rate of return
IRS Internal Revenue Service
ISDN Integrated Services Digital Network
ISO Insurance Service Office; incentive stock option
ISP Internet service provider

J

JEC Joint Economic Committee of Congress
JIT just-in-time inventory control
JPEG Joint Photographic Experts Group
JTPA Job Training Partnership Act

L

L/C letter of credit
LAN local area network
LASH Lighter Aboard Ship
LBO leveraged buyout
LCD liquid crystal display
LCL less than carload
LDC less developed country
LEXIS Legal Exchange Information Service
LIBOR London interbank offered rate
LIC Life Insurers Conference

LIFFE London International Financial Futures Exchange
LIFO last in, first out
LLC limited liability company
LIMRA Life Insurance Marketing and Research Association
LOMA Life Office Management Association
LP linear programming
LTC long-term care
LTL less than truckload
LTV loan-to-value ratio
LUPAC Life Underwriter Political Action Committee
LUTC Life Underwriting Training Council

M

MACRS modified accelerated cost recovery system
MAGI modified adjusted gross income
M&IE meals and incidental expense
MBA Master of Business Administration degree
MBO management by objectives
MBWA management by walking around
MFD multifunction device
MFP multifunction product
MGIC Mortgage Guarantee Insurance Company
MIME Multipurpose Internet Mail Extensions
MIS management information system
MLM multilevel marketing
MLP master limited partnership
MLS multiple listing service
MNC multinational corporation
MO modus operandi
M.O. money order
MPC marginal propensity to consume
MPS marginal propensity to save
MPT modern portfolio theory

MRP material requirements planning
MS-DOS Microsoft disk operating system
MSA Metropolitan Statistical Area
MST Mountain Standard Time; Multistate Tax Commission
MTM methods-time measurement
MUD municipal utility district

N

NAA National Apartment Association
NAARS national automated accounting research system
NACVA National Association of Certified Valuation Analysts
NAFTA North American Free Trade Agreement
NAHB National Association of Homebuilders
NAIC National Association of Insurance Commissioners
NAICS North American Industry Classification System
NAR National Association of Realtors
NASD National Association of Securities Dealers
NASDAQ National Association of Securities Dealers Automated Quotations
NAV net asset value
NDA nondisclosure agreement
NDP net domestic product
NLA net leasable area
NLQ near letter quality
NLRA National Labor Relations Association
NLRB National Labor Relations Board
NOI net operating income
NOL net operating loss
NOW negotiable order of withdrawal
NPV net present value

NR not rated
NSF not sufficient funds
NYSE New York Stock Exchange

O

OAG Official Airline Guide
OAR overall rate of return
OASI old-age and survivors insurance
OBRA Omnibus Budget Reconciliation Act
OCONUS outside contiguous United States
OCR optical character recognition
OECD Organization for Economic Cooperation and Development
OEM original equipment manufacturer
OID original issue discount
OILSR Office of Interstate Land Sales Registration
OJT on-the-job training
OLE object linking and embedding
OMB Office of Management and Budget
OPEC Organization of Petroleum Exporting Countries
OPIC Overseas Private Investment Corporation
OR operations research
ORE, OREO other real estate, other real estate owned
OSHA Occupational Safety and Health Administration
OTB open-to-buy
OTC over the counter
OTS Office of Thrift Supervision

P

PAC political action committee
PAL passive activity loss
PAP personal automobile policy
P&I principal and interest payment
P&L profit and loss statement

PBGC Pension Benefit Guaranty Corporation
PBX private branch exchange
PC personal computer; politically correct; professional corporation
PC-DOS personal computer disk operating system
PDA personal digital assistant (computer); Pregnancy Discrimination Act
PDF Portable Document Format
PE price-earnings ratio
PEFCO Private Export Funding Corporation
PEO Professional Employer Organization
PEP pension equity plan
PERT program evaluation and review technique
PF programmable function key
PFS Personal Financial Specialist
PHC personal holding company
PIA primary insurance amount
PIG passive income generator
PIK payment in kind
PIM personal information manager (software)
PIN personal identification number
PIRG public interest research group
PITI principal, interest, taxes, and insurance payment
PMI private mortgage insurance
PMSA primary metropolitan statistical area
PnP Plug and Play
POA power of attorney
POM production and operations management
POS point-of-sale (system)
PPI producer price index
ppm pages per minute
PPO preferred-provider organization
PPP Point-to-Point Protocol
PS postscript

PSA public-service announcement
PST Pacific Standard Time
PUD planned unit development
PV present value

Q

Q-TIP qualified terminable interest trust
QTP Qualified Tuition Program
QWL quality of work life

R

R&D research and development
RAM random-access memory; reverse annuity mortgage
RAN revenue anticipation note
REIT real estate investment trust
REMIC real estate mortgage investment conduit
REO real estate owned
REPO; RP repurchase agreement
RESPA Real Estate Settlement Procedures Act
RFP request for proposals
RGB red-green-blue
RIC regulated investment company
RICO Racketeer-Influenced and Corrupt Organizations Act
ROG receipt of goods
ROI return on investment
ROM read-only memory
ROR release on recognizance
RR registered representative
RTC Resolution Trust Corporation
RTF Rich Text Format

S

S&L savings and loan association
S&P Standard & Poor's
SAM shared-appreciation mortgage
SarbOx Sarbanes-Oxley Act of 2002
SARSEP salary reduction SEP
SBA Small Business Administration

SBIC small business investment company
SCLP simplified commercial lines portfolio (insurance policy)
SCM supply chain management
SCORE Service Corps of Retired Executives
SDR special drawing rights
SEC Securities and Exchange Commission
SECA Self-Employment Contributions Act
SEM shared-equity mortgage
SEP simplified employee pension
SG&A selling, general; and administrative expenses
SIBOR Singapore Interbank Offered Rate
SIC standard industrial classification
SIMEX Singapore International Monetary Exchange
SIPC Securities Investor Protection Corporation
SKU stockkeeping unit
SLIP specialized lines of industry practice
SLMA Student Loan Marketing Association
SMA separately managed account
SMP special multiperil policy
SMSA standard metropolitan statistical area
SNA Systems Network Architecture
SOHO small office/home office
SOP standard operating procedure
SPC statistical process control
SPDR Standard & Poor's Depositary Receipt
SPE special-purpose entity
SQC statistical quality control
SWIFT Society for Worldwide Interbank Financial Telecommunications

SWOT strengths, weaknesses, opportunities, threats
SYD sum-of-the-years' digits

T

T&E travel and entertainment
TAB tax anticipation bill
TAN tax anticipation note
TAO Taxpayer Assistance Order
TCE Tax Counseling for the Elderly
TCP/IP Transmission Control Protocol/Internet Protocol
TCMP Taxpayer Compliance Measurement Program
T.D. Treasury Decision
TDR transfer development rights
TEFRA Tax Equity and Fiscal Responsibility Act of 1982
TIC tenancy in common
TIN taxpayer identification number
TIPS Treasury inflation-protected securities
TIs tenant improvements
TL truckload
TQM total quality management
TSE Tokyo Stock Exchange; Toronto Stock Exchange

U

UBI unrelated business income
UBIT unrelated business income tax
UDDI Universal Description, Discovery, and Integration
UDITPA Uniform Division of Income for Tax Purposes Act
UCC Uniform Commercial Code
UGMA Uniform Gifts to Minors Act
UIT unit investment trust
UMLER Universal Machine Language Equipment Register
UPS United Parcel Service
URAR Uniform Residential Appraisal Report

URL uniform resource locator; universal resource locator
USB Universal Serial Bus
USITC U.S. International Trade Commission
USPAP Uniform Standards of Professional Appraisal Practice
USPIRG U.S. Public Interest Research Group

V

VA Veterans Administration
VAT value-added tax
VITA Volunteer Income Tax Assistance
VoIP Voice over Internet Protocol
VP vice-president
VRM variable-rate mortgage

W

WACC weighted average cost of capital
WAN wide area network
WARN Worker Adjustment and Retraining Notification Act
WATS wide area telephone service
WCB will call back
WPI wholesale price index
WTO World Trade Organization
WWW World Wide Web
WYSIWYG What You See Is What You Get
WYSIWYP What You See Is What You Print

X

XC Xerox copy

Y

YTD year-to-date
YTM yield to maturity
Y2K Year 2000

Z

ZBB zero-base budgeting
ZPG zero population growth